Monetary Policy and Macroprudential Regulation with Financial Frictions

Monetary Policy and Macroprudential Regulation with Financial Frictions

Pierre-Richard Agénor

The MIT Press
Cambridge, Massachusetts
London, England

This book was set in Times New Roman by Westchester Publishing Services. Printed and bound in the United States of America

Library of Congress Cataloging-in-Publication Data

Names: Agénor, Pierre-Richard, author.
Title: Monetary policy and macroprudential regulation with financial frictions / Pierre-Richard Agénor, School of Social Sciences, University of Manchester.
Description: Cambridge, Massachusetts : MIT Press, [2020] | Includes bibliographical references and index.
Identifiers: LCCN 2019053992 | ISBN 9780262044226 (hardcover)
Subjects: LCSH: Monetary policy—Econometric models. | Macroeconomics.
Classification: LCC HG230.3 .A389 2020 | DDC 339.5/3—dc23
LC record available at https://lccn.loc.gov/2019053992

10 9 8 7 6 5 4 3 2 1

To my daughter Laurence,
for showing me the meaning of
perseverance and dedication

Contents

Introduction and Overview

The 2007–2008 global financial crisis triggered by the collapse of the subprime mortgage market in the United States led to a vigorous debate in academia and policy circles regarding the nature and effectiveness of financial regulation and whether central banks should account more explicitly for financial stability considerations in the conduct of monetary policy. Among the many lessons that have emerged from this debate, two of them stand out. First, financial regulation and supervision must adopt a system-wide, or *macroprudential,* perspective to identify weaknesses in the financial sector and mitigate risks to its overall stability. Second, low and stable inflation does not, by itself, guarantee financial stability; central banks may need to play a more active role in diagnosing, preventing, and reacting to the buildup of financial imbalances. More generally, there is now a better appreciation that macroeconomic stability and financial stability are fundamentally linked and that pursuing one objective without sufficient regard for the other risks achieving neither.

At the analytical level, the crisis also highlighted the need to make financial frictions, and credit market imperfections in particular, front and center in designing macroeconomic models for monetary and macroprudential policy evaluation. Indeed, the crisis demonstrated once more that not only can the financial system significantly amplify and propagate shocks originating elsewhere, it can also be *itself* a source of shocks that can severely impact the real and financial sides of the economy. These amplification and propagation effects imply, in particular, that financial stability considerations cannot be ignored when assessing how monetary policy should respond to developments in the real economy and, conversely, that macroeconomic stability considerations should be accounted for when evaluating how macroprudential policy should respond to financial imbalances.[1]

1. The debate on whether monetary policy should internalize potential risks to financial stability and act preemptively actually predates the global financial crisis. It initially focused on the extent to

Naturally, the recognition that macroeconomic and financial stability are closely linked has led some observers to wonder whether monetary and macroprudential policies should be used jointly to ensure that both objectives are achieved—a logical implication of the so-called *Tinbergen's principle*, according to which the number of policy instruments must be the same as the number of targets. As a result, it has also become increasingly clear that there is a need to better understand how these policies interact, what trade-offs they give rise to and under which circumstances, and how best to design and evaluate an appropriate policy mix to achieve economic stability.

In the past decade or so, various approaches have been developed, or further developed, to address these issues. Among these approaches, much interest has focused on extending models in the tradition of Bernanke et al. (1999), where agency costs, which arise endogenously, are the main source of financial frictions and operate through the cost of investment in physical capital. A key result of these models is that fluctuations in borrowers' net worth (or, more generally, collateral values) tend to magnify the impact of monetary shocks on prices and output through a *financial accelerator* effect. Extensions have taken the form of introducing banking systems explicitly, alternative sources of financial frictions (including strategic complementarities between banks' balance sheet choices), real and financial sector interactions (through asset prices and balance sheets of households and firms), and capital regulation, in closed- and open-economy dynamic stochastic general equilibrium (DSGE) models.[2] Much recent emphasis has also been on the integration of countercyclical regulatory rules in these models and how they interact with monetary policy. From that perspective, macroprudential regulation has been viewed as playing a more active role than simply increasing the structural buffers that banks can rely on (such as, for instance, capital requirements and loan loss provisions) to improve their resilience to adverse shocks.

DSGE models have played a prominent role in macroeconomics, and central bank thinking in general, for the past two decades—in fact, well before the global financial crisis—largely because they were viewed early on as a response to the so-called *Lucas critique* of policy evaluation (Lucas 1976). For many, they provide a rationale for basing macroeconomic analysis on the explicit intertemporal optimization problems of individual agents. Moreover, by allowing a benevolent policymaker to base an intertemporal measure of

---

which monetary policy should respond to (or lean against) perceived misalignments in asset prices, such as real estate and equity prices, as opposed to cleaning up after. See Cecchetti et al. (2000) and Chadha et al. (2004), for instance, and Wadhwani (2008) for a review of the relevant literature.

2. This literature is discussed in more detail in subsequent chapters.

social welfare on individual utility, this approach provides a natural framework for analyzing the welfare effects of government intervention and for studying optimal policy.

However, the core DSGE model, which treats money as a veil and abstracts from financial intermediation, has been, and continues to be, criticized from a variety of perspectives. Caballero (2010) and Muellbauer (2010), for instance, argued that many of these models suffer from unrealistic microfoundations for household behavior and from assuming that aggregate behavior mimics a fully informed "representative agent." Instead, the focus should be on heterogeneity among agents, including differences in individuals' endowments. With heterogeneous preferences, for instance, propensities to save out of wealth will differ across consumers. As a result, the distribution of wealth will affect macroeconomic outcomes. Thus, the common practice of imposing identical homothetic preferences in economies populated by a large number of consumers with time-additive preferences to avoid distributional effects may be unwarranted.[3] More generally, models based on optimizing behavior with representative agents are not entirely immune from the criticism of *ad hockery*; their implications are also dependent on features of the optimization process—in particular, the type of constraints that agents are faced with—which are, to some degree, arbitrary. At the same time, it must be recognized that recent advances have addressed (if only in part) some of these criticisms. Indeed, the models that academics and practitioners in central banks use today are very far removed from the core DSGE model used before the global financial crisis.

The purpose of this book is to provide an integrated analysis of how, from my own perspective, financial frictions can be accounted for in macroeconomic models and how they affect the performance of monetary and macroprudential policies. It combines some of the key elements of the approach initially developed by Bernanke et al. (1999), which emphasizes the role of agency costs as the main source of financial frictions and balance sheets as a key determinant of the cost of external finance, with a range of contributions to the micro-banking,

3. However, while a high degree of homogeneity among individuals is *sufficient* to guarantee the existence of a representative agent, it is not *necessary*. Constantinides (1982) showed that even if individuals have heterogeneous preferences and differ in their level of wealth, a utility function can still be derived for the "representative" agent if asset markets are complete—that is, if individuals have available for trade a sufficiently large set of assets to allow them to diversify any idiosyncratic risk in consumption. Under such conditions, it is possible to construct a "representative" agent because, after trading in complete markets, individuals become *marginally* homogeneous even though they are initially heterogeneous. In addition, there are several examples in the recent literature where the introduction of some form of agent heterogeneity does not seem to affect (qualitatively or quantitatively) the results obtained in a representative agent framework. See Galí (2018) for a discussion.

international finance, and open-economy macroeconomics literature. The result is a consistent and tractable set of closed- and open-economy macroeconomic models, ranging from simple static models to full-blown DSGE and endogenous growth models, where bank credit is central to the financial intermediation process and macroprudential regulatory regimes interact with the monetary transmission mechanism. These models are not stand-alone abstractions; they are *integrated* in the sense that the larger and more complex models incorporate the core intuition and key insights provided by the more parsimonious analytical representations. Interactions between monetary and macroprudential policies, and their implications for macroeconomic and financial stability as well as social welfare, are also systematically examined.

By using an integrated and incremental approach, the book should prove useful to macroeconomists in academia, central banks, and research institutions interested in understanding the analytical and policy insights that can be gleaned from studying the performance of monetary policy and macroprudential regulation in the presence of financial frictions. It should also prove valuable as background material for a graduate course in macroeconomics or as a reference for specialized training in macroeconomic modeling and applications.

Despite these broad objectives, the book is by no means an exhaustive survey. First, a fairly large number of approaches to financial frictions have been developed in recent years and a comprehensive review is beyond its scope.[4] Rather, its goal is to provide a gradual development of a class of models that I have found to be useful for thinking about the issues mentioned earlier. This is a sensible approach because there is no consensus yet, among economists, as to the best way to account for financial market imperfections and capture interactions between the financial system and the real economy. In part, this is due to the fact that the literature aimed at discriminating empirically among the different types of financial frictions has so far provided only mixed evidence. Moreover, as vividly illustrated by Wieland et al. (2016) and Binder et al. (2018), for instance, propagation mechanisms of the same shock can differ markedly among DSGE models with different types of financial market imperfections. As a result, they may lead to conflicting policy prescriptions. I would therefore argue that anyone seeking an entry point to the literature would be better served by starting with a consistent set of closed- and open-economy models that help to address issues of interest subject to a particular type of financial frictions,

4. For overviews of the literature, see Gertler and Kiyotaki (2010), Brunnermeier et al. (2013), Dou et al. (2017), and Galati and Moessner (2018). However, none of these contributions is exhaustive in nature.

instead of trying to digest, at the outset, the key features and implications of a range of alternative approaches. Nevertheless, appropriate (and, at times, copious) references are provided where relevant, and most chapters end with some notes on the literature, which identify possible extensions as well as issues that either need to be explored further or have been addressed differently in other contributions. Although these notes are not as detailed as one would expect in a comprehensive literature survey, they provide a useful roadmap to readers interested in going beyond the material covered in this book or in pursuing an entirely different line of inquiry.

Second, to a very significant extent the book focuses on upper middle-income countries (MICs). By contrast, much of the recent literature has focused on high-income countries.[5] Of course, both groups of countries face a number of common issues associated with macroeconomic policy evaluation, and this militates in favor of using similar analytical *methods* to address them. At the same time, and critical for the focus of this book, there are significant structural differences between their financial systems and their degree of vulnerability to external shocks, both real and financial. Some constraints (such as the reliance on bank credit for financing working capital needs, for instance) are present in both groups of countries but with a greater degree of acuity in lower-income economies, while others (imperfect capital mobility or the inability to borrow abroad in domestic currency, for instance) are largely specific to them. As I have argued elsewhere (Agénor and Montiel 2015), taking these structural characteristics into account in the design of macroeconomic models is in general essential to conduct policy analysis. In addition, there are differences in the nature and significance of policy issues (such as the macroeconomic effects of abrupt shifts in capital flows, for instance) and the ability of policymakers to address them. Naturally enough, given the focus on MICs, unconventional monetary and credit policies of the type implemented in advanced economies in the aftermath of the global financial crisis (including direct lending to the private sector, discount window lending, and equity injections) are not addressed in this book, except in passing.[6] Nevertheless, I believe that much of the analysis, and the broad policy lessons that can be drawn from it, are equally relevant

5. "Middle income countries" and "high income countries" are generally defined in accordance with the World Bank's classification by income groups; see chapter 1.

6. A discussion and quantitative assessment of the performance of unconventional monetary and credit policies, including quantitative easing (the creation of money to purchase assets), can be found in a number of contributions. See, in particular, Gertler and Kiyotaki (2010), Cúrdia and Woodford (2011), Gertler and Karadi (2011), Schabert (2014), Correia et al. (2016), Woodford (2016), and Dell'Ariccia et al. (2018). These papers are all based on models with various types of financial frictions.

for advanced economies. In particular, the simple static and dynamic models of chapters 2, 3, and 7 provide, in my view, useful teaching tools for graduate courses in macroeconomics and banking. Because, by design, they account explicitly for banks and financial frictions at the outset, they provide viable alternatives to standard AA-DD and AA-DD-XX models, or IS-LM and IS-LM-BP models. In that sense, this book is also a response to what Reis (2018, p. 153) referred to as "too little investment in graduate-level textbooks" in macroeconomics by the profession.

The book consists of eleven chapters. Chapter 1 sets the stage by providing a background on financial systems and financial frictions in MICs, how they affect the transmission mechanisms of monetary and macroprudential policies, as well as the implications of these frictions for the design of macroeconomic models. A brief review of the core and more recent DSGE models with financial frictions is also provided, and their role as *exploratory platforms* is emphasized. The discussion makes clear that in specifying the microfoundations of these models, a good deal of arbitrariness persists. The nature of the objective function, the range of decision variables, the specification of the constraints that households, firms, and financial intermediaries are subject to—all typically remain subject to the modeler's prior beliefs. Moreover, the natural tendency to specify models that illustrate basic factors or particular processes involved in the issue at hand, rather than models with more general assumptions and implications, may lead to conclusions that are specific and not generally warranted.[7] Nevertheless, the fact that many of these limitations are progressively being addressed is also noted.

The definition of financial stability and the rationale for macroprudential regulation are also discussed in chapter 1. It is argued that this rationale rests crucially on the presence of externalities—related, in particular, to amplification due to procyclical risk-taking by lenders and borrowers, asymmetric information and agency problems, and contagion among financial institutions. As such, macroprudential policies are indeed more suited to respond to common shocks to the financial system rather than to idiosyncratic (and uncorrelated) shocks faced by individual institutions—except to the extent that the latter propagate through contagion in a destabilizing fashion.

The chapter concludes with a description of the modeling approach adopted in this book. It highlights the fact that although the models presented in

7. As noted by Caballero (2010), replacing empirically based but *ad hoc* behavioral relationships with optimization-based first-order conditions for which knowledge is incomplete or limited does not eliminate the problem. Both approaches may end up making unwarranted assumptions about agents' response to a change in the policy environment.

the subsequent chapters are for the most part in line with contributions that have emphasized the impact of collateral values and balance sheet conditions on the cost of borrowing, it differs from them by emphasizing the existence of endogenous, noncontingent monitoring costs associated with financial intermediation. The resulting banking structure is (at least in my view) simpler, while preserving the same fundamental insights that are obtained from more complex specifications. In addition, the DSGE models presented in this book are parameterized rather than estimated or rigorously calibrated on the basis of (conditional or unconditional) moment-matching exercises. The underlying perspective, consistent with the view of Turnovsky (2011), is that parameterization is essentially a way of conducting comparative statics or comparative dynamics in situations where the complexity of the model is such that doing so analytically with any insight is precluded. At the same time, parameterization is not an exercise devoid of any empirical content; many of the selected parameters are taken from properly calibrated or estimated models, and core simulation results are broadly consistent, *qualitatively*, with available stylized facts regarding policy and exogenous shocks. Sensitivity analysis with respect to some key parameters is also reported, although space and computational constraints prevented an investigation over broad ranges of values.

Chapters 2 to 6 focus on the closed economy. Chapter 2 presents a simple, core static model to conduct monetary and macroprudential analysis with financial frictions. The model is then extended in chapter 3 to a dynamic setting with endogenous capital accumulation. In both chapters, financial frictions take the form of credit market imperfections, and behavioral equations for consumption and investment are postulated rather than derived from underlying microeconomic principles. The lack of explicit microfoundations for the aggregate demand side makes these simple models (as well as the open-economy model presented in chapter 7) vulnerable to the Lucas critique. In fact, as noted earlier, it is precisely this issue that provided the initial impetus for basing macroeconomic analysis on the explicit intertemporal optimization problems of individual agents in a way that ensures consistency between the economy's short- and long-run equilibrium outcomes and individual and aggregate resource constraints.

Nevertheless, the behavioral equations that are specified in chapters 2 and 3 are supported by empirical evidence, as is the case for consumption where the effect of current income can be related to the presence of liquidity constraints. In addition, these simple, semistructural models are useful in the sense that they provide basic intuition that may help to identify fundamental economic forces and transmission mechanisms, which help to interpret the results of more elaborate models with stronger microfoundations.[8] In particular, they help to illustrate the fact that when credit market frictions (in the form of asymmetric information between borrowers and lenders) are introduced, interest rate changes can also affect the supply of loans. And, in line with the financial accelerator effect alluded to earlier, the size of the premium that lenders impose on borrowers depends on the balance sheet conditions of borrowers: When interest rates are low and asset values rise, higher net worth associated with higher collateral values eases borrowing constraints and leads to an expansion in credit. The same mechanism operates in the more rigorous models considered in subsequent chapters. The macroeconomic effects of macroprudential policy, in the form of changes in the required reserve ratio and a generic tax on bank loans, are also examined in both chapters.

Chapter 4 describes a core DSGE model with financial frictions. These frictions take the form not only of asymmetric information between borrowers and lenders but also borrowing to finance working capital needs and monopolistic competition in banking. In the model, as in Iacoviello (2005), which itself builds on Kiyotaki and Moore (1997), housing plays a dual role—as a consumption (rather than investment) good and a collateralizable asset. The model is used to study the macroeconomic effects of a variety of real and financial shocks, including monetary policy.

Using the same model, in chapter 5 the performance of simple countercyclical macroprudential rules, based either on minimizing postulated loss functions for policymakers (themselves motivated by explicit institutional mandates) or maximizing social welfare, is discussed. A key focus of the analysis is the performance of reserve requirements, which have been used extensively in MICs over the years, including in the immediate aftermath of the global financial crisis.[9] The stabilizing effects of a countercyclical tax on bank loans are also examined. The performance of both instruments is contrasted with the case where monetary policy alone is used to address financial stability concerns by responding to changes in credit. As noted earlier, since the global financial crisis there has been an active debate about whether, and how, central banks should incorporate risks to financial stability in setting monetary policy. This debate has moved beyond the precrisis focus on policymakers' ability to identify asset price bubbles and whether monetary policy alone can prick them

8. See Krugman (2000) and Turnovsky (2011) for a more general discussion of the benefits of small analytical models.

9. In recent years, there has also been renewed consideration of required reserves, or interest on these reserves, as a macroprudential instrument in advanced economies. See Stein (2012) and Kashyap and Stein (2012) for a discussion.

through preemptive changes in interest rates (in effect, *leaning against the wind*) to the design of *integrated* rules aimed at preventing financial imbalances from developing in the first place. Three alternative approaches to policy evaluation in DSGE models are discussed, including the use of simple, operational rules to either minimize a policy loss function or maximize welfare, and the determination of the Ramsey policy, under which the objective of a social planner is to maximize social welfare, subject to the constraints imposed by the equilibrium solution. The extent to which coordination between policymakers, the central bank and the regulator, can improve outcomes is also addressed. In the process, the analysis highlights the role of adjustment costs associated with changes in policy instruments. How closely simple macroprudential rules, used independently or in coordination with monetary policy, approximate the Ramsey policy is studied as well.

The model is then extended in chapter 6 to introduce bank capital regulation and study once again the performance of macroprudential and monetary policy rules independently, as well as interactions between these policies. Specifically, the performance of a credit-augmented interest rate rule (as in chapter 5), a countercyclical capital regulatory rule (along the lines recommended by the Basel III arrangement), and the optimal combination of these rules is analyzed. In addition, strategic interactions between policymakers are also considered: The solution under cooperation is compared to the solution obtained under the Nash equilibrium, which assumes that each policymaker pursues its policies independently while being aware of the policy that the other policymaker chooses to follow. This analysis helps to assess the extent to which coordination improves outcomes in terms of social welfare and with respect to specific macroeconomic policy objectives.

Chapters 7, 8, and 9 broaden the analysis to a small open-economy setting. Imperfect capital mobility—viewed as synonymous to imperfect substitutability between interest-bearing, domestic- and foreign-currency denominated assets—is assumed throughout; as a result, domestic interest rates are determined domestically rather than being tied directly to world interest rates through an (uncovered) interest parity condition. Chapter 7 first extends the core static model with credit market imperfections presented in chapter 2 to account for open-economy considerations (namely, trade in goods and assets), with a distinction between fixed and flexible exchange rates. Similarly, chapter 8 extends the core DSGE model with financial frictions discussed in chapters 4 and 5 to an open-economy setting. The model features, in particular, a managed float regime—a common feature of MICs, even among those who adopted inflation targeting as their monetary policy framework—and a two-level financial intermediation structure.

The core model is then extended in chapter 9 to account for simple countercyclical macroprudential rules involving changes in a tax on loans and the required reserve ratio (as in chapter 5), as well as capital controls in the form of a tax on bank foreign borrowing. To the extent that their goal is to mitigate the negative externality or social cost associated with excessive borrowing, in the form of increased financial risks, both taxes are essentially Pigouvian in nature: The intent is to correct an undesirable or inefficient market outcome, and they are set (implicitly) so as to reflect the social cost of these negative externalities. Optimal policies are derived once again and the optimal combination of macroprudential policies is also addressed. The focus is on how these policies (possibly combined with sterilized intervention) should respond to shifts in capital flows induced by exogenous shocks to world interest rates—a key source of macroeconomic fluctuations in MICs, as discussed in chapter 1—in a context where an interest rate defense by the central bank may be unfeasible. The performance of the simple rules is also compared with the Ramsey policy.

Chapter 10 focuses on macroprudential policy coordination in a two-region world, involving major advanced economies (the core) and a group of large or systemically important MICs (the periphery). Research on this issue has proceeded at a rapid pace in recent years, in large part because of greater international financial integration and the greater magnitude of cross-border financial spillovers—operating not only from developed to developing economies but also, and increasingly, from a group of large developing economies to advanced economies (Agénor and Pereira da Silva 2018*a*, 2018*b*). The adoption of Basel III's principle of jurisdictional reciprocity by the international community has also played a role in setting the stage for greater cooperation between national regulators. The framework presented in chapter 10 extends the model presented in chapter 8 to account for financial frictions at two levels: between firms and banks in each region, and also between periphery banks and a global bank located in the core region. As in chapters 5 and 9, macroprudential regulation takes the generic form of a countercyclical tax on bank loans. The analysis shows that the welfare gains from macroprudential policy coordination are positive, albeit not large, for the world economy. In addition, these gains tend to increase with the degree of international financial integration. However, depending on the origin of financial shocks, they can also be highly asymmetric across regions. This asymmetry therefore raises the issue of how to maintain cooperative agreements in practice without side payments. As in previous chapters, the performance of the simple rules is compared with the Ramsey policy.

Chapter 11 moves the discussion to a growth context, in a setting where bank monitoring helps to alleviate incentive problems on the side of borrowers. It builds on the double moral hazard model of Holmström and Tirole (1997), in which financial frictions originate from both an asymmetric information problem between borrowers and lenders and an incentive for banks to shirk when monitoring is costly. In the model, borrowers are tempted to divert resources toward privately beneficial activities. To mitigate the deadweight loss imposed by this agency problem, banks monitor borrowers' actions. However, monitoring involves a non-contingent pecuniary cost. Thus, although it mitigates the moral hazard problem associated with the behavior of borrowers, the fact that monitoring uses up resources creates also an incentive for banks to shirk when they must pay interest on the liabilities that they incur to fund their loans. The growth and welfare effects of macroprudential regulation in this setting are discussed. The modeling of financial frictions in that chapter 11 is limited to bank monitoring only and does not consider the collateral and balance sheet effects that are front and center elsewhere in the book.[10] However, systemic risk is introduced in the analysis in the form of a negative externality that relates the leverage ratio of borrowers to the probability of success of good projects. Balance sheets therefore do matter once again from the perspective of financial stability, albeit in a different way. More generally, the goal is also to highlight the importance of further research on the trade-offs between financial stability and longer-run growth—an issue that has been largely absent from the post-crisis debate on the benefits and costs of financial regulation, whose focus has been mainly on the short-term gains associated with mitigating volatility.

Finally, the epilogue identifies some potentially fruitful directions for future research—beyond those discussed in individual chapters, which relate to the link between monetary policy and risk-taking, the gain from coordinating macroprudential policy instruments among themselves, the analysis of cross-border leakages associated with capital controls, and the distributional effects of prudential regulation in a growth context. These other directions include the treatment of expectations, including recent developments associated with bounded rationality and behavioral macroeconomics, the estimation and solution of DSGE models with financial frictions, and the impact of labor market rigidities on output, prices, and unemployment.

As noted earlier, in the DSGE-based chapters policymakers (the monetary policy authority and the financial regulator) are assumed to achieve either specific objectives, namely, macroeconomic stability or financial stability, or to maximize welfare of the representative household. In both cases, the analysis

10. As discussed in chapter 1, some recent contributions to the DSGE literature have also used the Holmström-Tirole approach to model financial intermediation and financial frictions. Note also that, in line with Chen (2001), collateral and asset prices could be accounted for in that approach.

is generally based on simple rules—that is, rules whereby policy instruments are set on the basis of a few number of observable, aggregate variables. The reason for focusing on policy loss functions is the view that central bankers and regulators are unelected technocrats who are not generally instructed to maximize social welfare; their mandate is whatever is delegated to them by elected politicians. In particular, as discussed in chapter 1, one of the key objectives of financial regulation is to reduce the incidence of credit and asset price booms that lead to excessive borrowing by the nonfinancial private sector and distort the allocation of resources. From that perspective, the fundamental institutional mandate of macroprudential regulators is to manage the credit cycle and its interactions with the business cycle. At the same time, it must be recognized that because some volatility may actually be efficient, setting policies so as to minimize volatility-based measures of economic stability may be a source of distortions and welfare losses. As a result, it is also important to consider welfare maximization as the policy criterion. Chapter 5 provides a discussion of the relationships (or lack thereof) between minimizing simple policy loss functions and maximizing social welfare, in a context where the cost of instrument volatility also matters.

Moreover, as noted earlier, a comparison of the performance of simple rules with the Ramsey policy is conducted in several chapters in order to assess how good of an approximation these rules provide, given the practical difficulties of implementing the Ramsey policy. This is important because the set of policy rules that can be deemed to be "simple" and "implementable" may be fairly large—even when it is guided by empirical regularities or evidence on the revealed preferences of policymakers. For instance, as discussed in chapter 1, there is evidence of a robust correlation between excessive credit expansion and financial crises. This suggests that a regulator concerned with financial stability as an ultimate target would be wise to set its instrument directly as a function of that variable, viewed as an operational target. But how should "excessive credit expansion" be identified? Should it be credit growth, or deviations in the credit-to-GDP ratio from a reference value, as in some empirical studies? The credit-to-bank deposits ratio? The credit-to-bank capital ratio, or leverage? Credit spreads? Should it be total credit or only *uncollateralized* credit, which could arguably be viewed, from a conceptual perspective, as a more relevant indicator of financial fragility, even though seizing collateral in case of default can be difficult in practice? As intuition would suggest, the performance of any particular instrument rule could vary substantially, depending on which of these indicators is used—even when the focus is solely on credit. This uncertainty means that a proper evaluation may require a thorough investigation, both across instruments and variables that trigger their activation. At the same time, as discussed in chapter 5, the Ramsey policy provides a natural benchmark for assessing the performance of alternative specifications of instrument rules.

At first sight, a general limitation of the models presented in this book could be that they focus on the conduct of monetary and macroprudential policies in "normal" times rather than during periods of severe financial stress. As a result, many important aspects that are typical ingredients of boom-bust cycles in asset markets, such as sudden and cumulative shifts in borrowers' credit risk perception and the possibility of banks' default, are not accounted for. Moreover, the numerical experiments reported in the various chapters are often based on the typical techniques used for solving DSGE models (based on first- or second-order approximation techniques, as discussed in chapter 4), which do not allow for the higher-order nonlinear dynamics that typically characterize episodes of severe financial instability. However, understanding how the economy functions in normal times is an essential step for building more complex models, where nonlinearities take center stage, and for understanding how policies should be designed, in the first place, to prevent periods of large financial imbalances from turning into full-blown crises. In that sense, for the ambitious researcher this book is hardly more than a starting point.

It is also worth stressing that the book was designed as a set of lecture notes. This means that most chapters have been written to be as self-contained as possible. The implication is that, inevitably, there is some degree of repetition in presenting parts of their contents—namely, with respect to the simple models described in chapters 2 and 7, as well as the DSGE models presented in chapters 4, 6, 8, and 10. The judgment that was made ultimately is that, from a pedagogical perspective, avoiding the need for readers to go back and forth across chapters and to figure out by themselves how to reconnect material pertaining to different model components is a benefit that largely outweighs the cost of repetition.

Finally, as much as possible, uniform notations have been used throughout the book. Tables of common names for variables and parameters are presented next, with exceptions noted later on where appropriate.

This book is the product of the research that I have conducted for the past several years at the University of Manchester. The university has provided me with unique conditions for developing the agenda on which the book dwells, and for that I am most grateful. I am also thankful to the Financial Stability and Development Group—the research and knowledge-sharing network formed by the major central banks of Latin America and administered by the Inter-American Development Bank—for its support.

In conducting this work, I have benefited from collaborative projects and interactions with several colleagues and former students at the University of Manchester, as well as coauthors in a number of other institutions, including the Bank for International Settlements, the Central Bank of Brazil, the Central Bank of Morocco, the Central Bank of Turkey, and the World Bank. I must mention Joshua Aizenman, Koray Alper, Alessandro Flamini, Leonardo Gambacorta, Gianni Lombardo, Peter Montiel, and Luiz Pereira da Silva. Participants to the various workshops and training courses on macroeconomic models with financial frictions that I have given in central banks all around the world in the past few years—not only in Latin America, in the context of my advisory role with the Financial Stability and Development Group, but also in Egypt, France, Malaysia, Morocco, Tunisia, and the United States—provided valuable feedback and comments on the material presented in several chapters. Keyra Primus and Nestor Romero provided many useful comments as well on a preliminary draft of the book. In addition, I owe a particular debt of gratitude to Timothy Jackson, for contributing in major ways to all the quantitative results reported in this book and for constructive discussions on a number of technical matters. I am thankful to all for their contributions, although I retain sole responsibility for the opinions expressed herein.

In preparing this book, I have used material from several of my papers published in professional journals. I thank the *International Journal of Central Banking*, the *Journal of Banking and Finance*, the *Journal of Financial Stability*, the *Journal of Development Economics*, the *Journal of Economic Dynamics and Control*, the *Journal of Macroeconomics*, the *Journal of International Money and Finance*, the *Journal of Money, Credit, and Banking*, and *Macroeconomic Dynamics* for allowing me to dwell on these contributions.

Common Notations for Variables

a	Household wealth
b	Stock of public debt
C	Household consumption
D, d	Bank deposits
E	Nominal exchange rate
$\mathbb{E}$	Expectation operator
G	Government spending
H	Stock of housing
I	Investment
i^B	Government bond rate
i^D	Bank deposit rate
i^L	Bank loan rate
i^R	Central bank refinance rate
i^T	Central bank base policy rate
J^B	Profits, commercial banks
J^I	Profits, intermediate good producers
J^K	Profits, capital good producers
K	Capital stock
λ, λ^I	Lagrange multipliers
L, l	Total bank loans
L^B, l^B	Borrowing by commercial banks from central bank
L^K, l^K	Investment loans
l^W	Loans for working capital needs
M, m	Household cash balances
mc	Real marginal cost, intermediate good producers
N	Employment, intermediate good producers
P	Price of final goods
π	Inflation rate, in terms of final good prices

P^H, p^H	House prices
π^H	Inflation rate, in terms of real house prices
q	Repayment probability
r^K	Rental rate of capital
T	Lump-sum transfers to households
τ^L	Tax rate on loans by commercial banks
U	Household utility
V^E	Excess bank capital
V^R	Required bank capital
V	Total bank capital
ω	Real wage
x	Composite monetary asset
Y_j	Output of intermediate good j
Y	Output of final goods
z	Real exchange rate

Common Notations for Parameters

α	Share of capital, production of intermediate goods
β	Compensating variation
γ	Relative weight in composite loss function or utility function
δ_K	Capital depreciation rate
ε_1	Response of base policy rate to inflation deviations from target
ε_2	Response of base policy rate to cyclical output
ζ^L	Elasticity of substitution, loans to capital good producers
η	Elasticity of substitution, domestic and imported intermediate goods
η_N	Preference parameter, disutility of labor
η_H	Preference parameter, housing services
η_x	Preference parameter, composite money holdings
θ	Substitution elasticity, intermediate goods
Θ_K	Adjustment cost parameter, investment
κ	Effective collateral-loan ratio
κ^F	Degree of foreign exchange sterilization
μ	Required reserve ratio
μ^F	Degree of exchange rate pass-through
ν	Deposit share parameter, composite money holdings
Λ	Household discount factor
ρ	Capital adequacy (Cooke) ratio
σ	Risk weight, investment loans
ς	Intertemporal elasticity of substitution
τ^L	Tax rate on loans
ϕ_I	Adjustment cost parameter, intermediate good prices
φ_1	Elasticity of repayment probability, collateral-loan ratio
φ_2	Elasticity of repayment probability, cyclical output
φ_3	Elasticity of repayment probability, loan rate
φ^{CB}	Sensitivity of central bank penalty rate to borrowing-deposits ratio
φ_1^R	Degree of exchange rate smoothing, foreign reserves

χ	Degree of interest rate smoothing, central bank base policy rate
χ_1	Persistence parameter, macroprudential policy rules
χ_2^L, χ_2^R	Response parameters, macroprudential policy rules
ψ_G	Share of government spending in final output
ψ_N	Inverse of Frisch elasticity of labor supply
ψ_W	Share of wage bill that must be paid in advance
$\varkappa_X$	Price elasticity of exports

1 Financial Systems, Financial Frictions, and Macroeconomic Models

It is now well recognized that financial markets matter in both originating and propagating macroeconomic shocks, and that bank lending is a key transmission channel of these shocks to the rest of the economy. This chapter begins with a broad discussion of the main features of financial systems, the nature of financial frictions, the state of supervision and financial regulation, and the sources of financial fragility in middle-income countries (MICs).[1] This discussion helps to show that there are important structural differences in financial sector characteristics between middle- and high-income countries, differences in the ability to conduct financial oversight, and differences in the nature of the policy challenges that MICs are confronted with. As argued next, some of these differences provide a rationale for specifying macroeconomic models with analytical and policy features that are specific for that group of countries.

Section 1 begins by highlighting the role of banks in the financial systems of MICs. Section 2 explores the role of credit market imperfections, especially the implications of asymmetric information and guarantees.[2] The link between financial cycles and business cycles is examined in section 3. Weaknesses in the supervisory capacity and the regulatory framework are discussed in section 4, and sources of financial risks and fragility are reviewed in section 5. The nature of systemic risk is discussed first, and sources of financial fragility

1. The most common classification of income categories for countries is by the World Bank, which ranks countries based on their absolute level of gross national income (GNI) per capita. As of September 2019, the World Bank defines low-income countries as those with GNI per capita of $1,025 or less in 2018; lower middle-income those with GNI per capita above $1,025 but less than $3,995; upper middle-income those with GNI per capita above $3,995 but less than $12,375; and high-income those with GNI per capita of $12,376 or more. See http://data.worldbank.org/about/country-and-lending-groups.

2. The discussion in section 2 is based on Agénor and Pereira da Silva (2014, 2019). See also Tornell and Westermann (2004) and Inter-American Development Bank (2005) for a discussion and early review of the evidence.

second. The role of macroprudential regulation in promoting financial stability is also examined in section 6. The next two sections focus on the implications of the preceding discussion for the formulation and design of macroeconomic models aimed at studying the impact of monetary policy and macroprudential regulation in MICs, with a particular focus on dynamic stochastic general equilibrium (DSGE) models. Finally, the last section outlines the modeling approach followed in the remainder of the book.

1.1 Banks and the Financial System

In most MICs, commercial banks continue to dominate the financial system. Equity issues remain limited, despite recent progress in the deepening of local capital markets and greater diversification (or reduced concentration) in the ownership structure of firms. Capital markets remain thin; local currency bond markets are still in their early stages in many economies and do not represent significant alternatives to bank lending. Although privatization and cross-border acquisitions have been accompanied by a significant improvement in the degree of banking sophistication in some countries, their financial systems remain less diversified than those in advanced economies. In particular, and despite some exceptions, the expansion of nonbank financial intermediaries, the shift toward the *originate and distribute* model of banking, and the development of opaque, off-balance sheet instruments have not reached the same importance as they have in richer countries.[3] Indeed, data compiled by Ghosh et al. (2012) on the importance of shadow banking in MICs show that the nonbank financial intermediation sector is large only in a few countries, such as the Philippines and Thailand. A more recent report by the Financial Stability Board (2018) provides a similar picture.

The lack of financial diversification implies that there are limited alternatives (such as corporate bonds and commercial paper) to bank credit in most MICs. As a result, bank finance is the major source of external funding for firms of all sizes in these countries. Indeed, as documented by Ayyagari et al.

3. In some advanced economies, nonbanks—including hedge funds, commodities funds, private equity groups, and money market funds—have become essential sources of credit (Pozsar et al. 2013). Alternatives to conventional bank finance include invoice factoring or discounting (where a business borrows money against its invoices), asset-based financing (where money is borrowed against assets such as a plant or machinery), and peer-to-peer and consumer-to-business lending (in which individuals agree to lend money to each other or to businesses through an online money exchange). New lending models also involve providing cash advances to businesses that derive much of their income from credit card sales. However, some of these new lending models do have high default risks, so the cost of borrowing is not necessarily lower than in conventional banking.

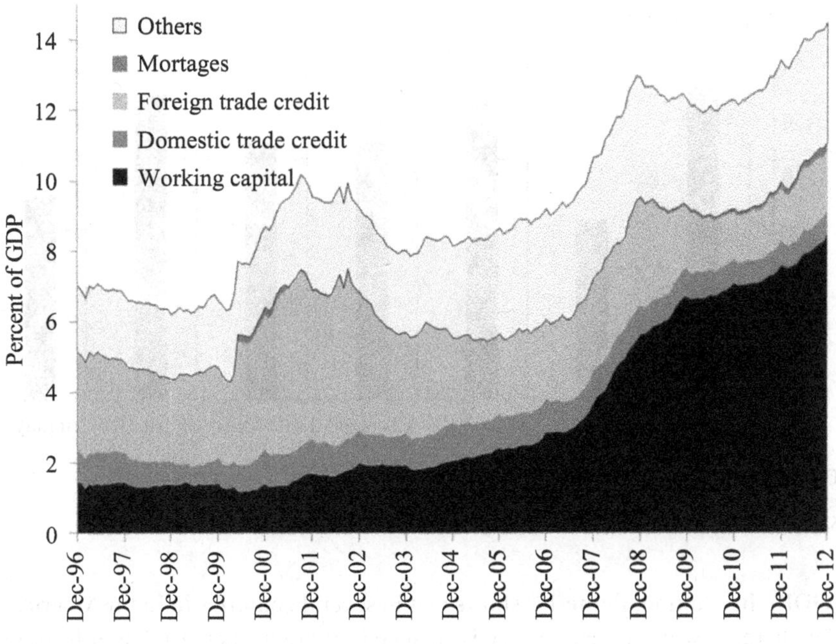

Figure 1.1
Brazil: composition of lending to firms, 1996–2012 (percent of GDP)
Source: Cabezon (2014).

(2012, fig. 1), over the period 2006–2010 the share of bank financing of fixed asset investment by large firms amounted to about 74 percent.[4] By way of comparison, Ajello (2016) found that in the United States, 35 percent of firms' investment in physical capital is funded through financial markets.

Moreover, bank credit serves to finance not only longer-term investment projects but also short-term working capital needs—that is, the acquisition of labor inputs, raw materials, and so on, prior to the sale of output.[5] Figure 1.1 shows the large increase in credit allocated to working capital needs in Brazil since 2006; in 2012, it amounted to almost 7 percent of gross domestic product

4. The corresponding ratios for medium and small firms amounted to 59 and 44 percent, respectively. However, as discussed later, these firms are also more likely to face borrowing constraints on the credit market due to their inability to pledge adequate collateral. Thus, these lower ratios may simply reflect the lack of access to external finance.

5. In some countries, firms depend not on financing from banks but rather on credit from their suppliers (buying now and paying later) with no interest charged as long as they pay on time. Data compiled by Shapiro et al. (2018, table 1), for instance, showed that firms (especially the larger ones) in Mexico finance their working capital needs by up to two-thirds (in proportion of total external finance) with trade credit. In Malaysia, however, that share is ony about 35 percent and in Turkey only 28 percent.

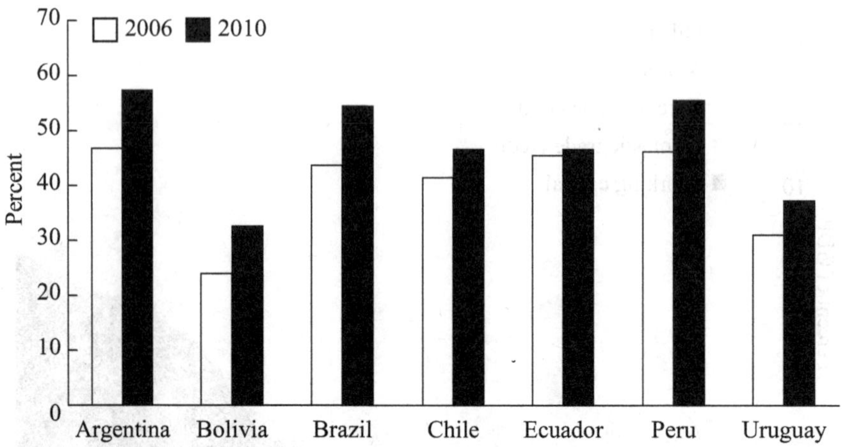

Figure 1.2
Latin America: share of working capital needs financed with bank credit, 2006 and 2010
Source: Cabezon (2014).

(GDP). In addition, figure 1.2 shows that in several countries in Latin America, the share of working capital needs financed by credit increased significantly between 2006 and 2010. Fluctuations in borrowing costs may therefore have a large and direct impact on the supply side of the economy. But while an increase in the cost of loans for consumption or investment (induced by a contractionary monetary policy, for instance) tends to reduce both aggregate demand and inflationary pressures, an increase in the cost of working capital loans affects output and inflation in opposite directions. As discussed in subsequent chapters, this *cost channel* may alter significantly the transmission mechanism of monetary policy.[6]

Household credit has increased at a rapid pace in several MICs during the past decade. However, it remains relatively small compared to lending to firms. For the group of (mostly middle-income) countries considered by Bahadir and Gumus (2016), for instance, it represents about 35 percent of total credit. Overall, total credit to the private sector, scaled by GDP, remains well below the levels observed in high-income economies (see figure 1.3). As discussed next, factors that may have hampered the expansion of credit in MICs include distortions in credit markets, weaknesses in disclosure and transparency requirements for corporate firms, high inflation (which promotes disintermediation), and macroeconomic volatility.

6. There is evidence that the cost channel may be significant in some advanced economies as well. See Chowdhury et al. (2006), Gaiotti and Secchi (2006), Ravenna and Walsh (2006), Fernandez-Corugedo et al. (2011), and Lagoa (2014).

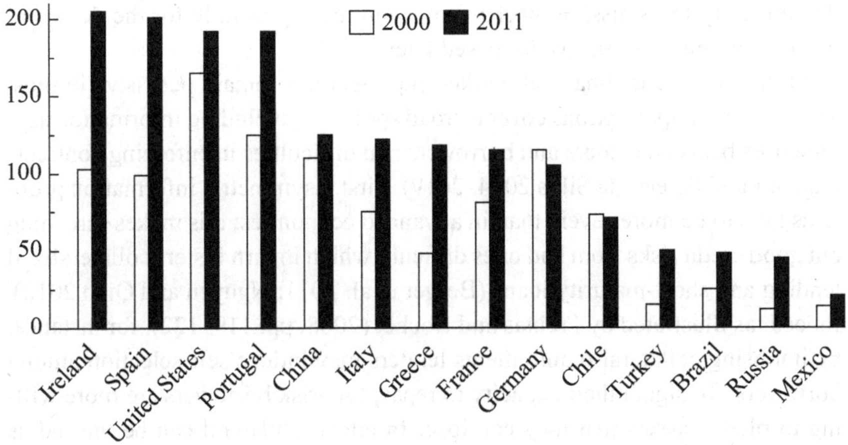

Figure 1.3
Domestic credit to private sector, selected countries, 2000 and 2011 (percent of GDP)
Source: Bank for International Settlements staff.

1.2 Credit Market Imperfections

Credit markets in MICs are often characterized by limited competition among banks. This has led to monopolistic or oligopolistic pricing practices, segmentation of credit markets, outright rationing, and efficiency losses. In the past two decades the degree of competition has increased in many countries, to a significant extent because of large-scale privatization, bank restructuring, and foreign bank penetration. However, from the perspective of this book, it is worth noting that increased competition may have conflicting effects on financial stability. On the one hand, as can be inferred from the results in Kara (2016*b*), countries with less concentrated banking sectors appear to have stronger bank capital regulation. This tends to strengthen the resilience of the financial system. On the other, as documented by Valencia and Bolaños (2018), more competition may lead to lower bank capital buffers, which may increase financial fragility.[7] In addition, greater competition may also reduce profit margins, as documented by Ariss (2010), for instance, while increasing incentives to weaken lending standards and to take greater risks, as argued by Hellmann et al. (2000). This would also make financial institutions more fragile. Nevertheless, lack of competition continues to prevail in many countries and this has important implications for

7. Note also that, in principle, causality could go in both directions. Schargrodsky and Sturzenegger (2000), for instance, presented a model in which tighter capital requirements induce banks to choose a lower degree of product differentiation, which tends to promote competition.

the monetary transmission mechanism—and more generally for the design of macroeconomic models, as discussed later.

At the same time, financial market imperfections remain pervasive in most MICs. These imperfections cover a broad spectrum, including information asymmetries between lenders and borrowers and difficulties in enforcing contracts (Agénor and Pereira da Silva 2014, 2019). First, asymmetric information problems tend to be more severe than in advanced economies; this makes screening out good credit risks from bad ones difficult, which in turn fosters collateralized lending and short-maturity loans (Berger et al. 2011; Nguyen and Qian 2012). Indeed, as illustrated by Freixas and Rochet (2008, pp. 119–122), for instance, by imposing collateral requirements lenders may induce self-selection among borrowers: To signal their capacity to repay, low-risk borrowers are more willing to pledge assets that they can lose. In effect, collateral can be viewed as a screening device, or more generally, a mechanism for commitment against agency risk (Coco 2000; Liberti and Sturgess 2013).[8] Collateral and guarantees may also serve as an incentive device to prevent moral hazard by discouraging borrowers from switching to riskier investment projects, by encouraging borrowers to choose a higher level of effort, and by deterring strategic default.

Second, despite recent trends toward privatization (noted earlier), governments in many MICs continue to play a significant role in banking, directly or indirectly. In Brazil, for instance, state banks continue to account for a large share of total assets held by the financial system. Implicit guarantees to these banks (particularly with respect to the financial safety net) are widespread in these countries, thereby exacerbating moral hazard problems and contributing to distortions in credit markets.

Third, disclosure and transparency requirements on corporate firms are largely inadequate.[9] With poor regulation of corporate governance and weak financial accounting transparency, firms have limited incentives to consider equity issuance as an alternative source of funding—preferring instead either to rely on internal funds or to borrow from banks with which they have established close links. By encouraging *evergreening* in banking (that is, the systematic rolling over of nonperforming loans), these close relationships may contribute to financial fragility.

8. In practice, the use of collateral may depend on a range of other factors, such as the degree of specialization of lenders, the degree of competition in the credit market, the nature and duration of the borrower-lender relationship, the size of the loans, and the state of the business cycle. See Jiménez et al. (2006), Menkhoff et al. (2006), and Steijvers and Voordeckers (2009) for a discussion.

9. See, for instance, Black et al. (2010) for Brazil.

Fourth, in many MICs, and developing countries in general, property rights are not well established and the legal system is highly inefficient; as a result, contract enforcement is difficult (Ranasinghe and Restuccia 2018). In particular, procedures for liquidating the assets of firms in default are cumbersome and highly ineffective in many of these countries.[10] Bankruptcy law typically provides little creditor protection. This, in turn, results in weak intermediation and credit rationing (by discouraging lending in the first place), high rates of collateralized lending, a high cost of borrowing (to account for the cost of seizing collateral in case of default), and low recovery rates for creditors.[11] From that perspective, collateral and guarantees provide now a hedge, or insurance, against default risk—in effect, mitigating incentives to monitor by reducing expected losses upon default.

All these distortions are magnified in a volatile economic environment. Increased exposure to adverse shocks exacerbates the risk of bankruptcy, which in turn also tends to promote collateralized lending. Moreover, the type of credit market imperfections described earlier often lead to a large majority of small and medium-size firms being simply squeezed out of the credit market. Their ability to pledge collateral is often weak to begin with, as documented by Nguyen and Qian (2012), and they often operate in the informal economy—a sector that accounts for about a third of GDP and 70 percent of employment in developing countries, according to estimates by Medina and Schneider (2018) and the World Bank (2019, chap. 3)—with little legal protection. At the same time, firms that do have access to the credit market, such as those with close connections with specific banks, face an elastic supply of loans and borrow at terms that depend on their ability to pledge collateral. In that sense, credit rationing—which can be viewed as resulting from the fact that inadequate collateral would have led to prohibitive rates—is largely exogenous in normal times. However, even with connected lending, actual collateral ratios may be quite high. Indeed, in some countries average collateral values exceed loan values—reflecting to a significant extent a weak judiciary environment and high recovery costs in case of default, as noted earlier. According to the World Bank's enterprise survey data, for instance, the average ratio of collateral value to loan value in developing countries is 206 percent, with estimates ranging

10. See Araujo and Funchal (2005) for the case of Latin America and Djankov et al. (2008) for a general review of bankruptcy and debt insolvency procedures in developing countries.

11. In 2005 Brazil initiated a major reform of its bankruptcy law. The reform increased creditors' protection by facilitating the sale of insolvent firms and by giving higher priority to creditors' claims in case of liquidation. See Ponticelli and Alencar (2016) for a discussion and an analysis of the reform's impact on firms' access to finance and investment.

from 95 percent for Brazil to 158 percent for Egypt, 183 percent for Malaysia, 199 percent for Turkey, and 320 percent for Thailand.[12]

1.3 Business Cycles and Financial Cycles

The evidence on business cycles in MICs suggests that credit often precedes output at turning points (Agénor and Montiel 2015, chap. 1). In addition, as documented by Amador et al. (2014), Calderón and Fuentes (2014), and Gonzalez et al. (2015), the business cycle and the financial cycle—as measured, in the first case, by movements in real GDP, and, in the second, by movements in credit or asset prices—tend to be more closely synchronized in MICs than in advanced economies. Amador et al. (2014), for instance, found that even though, on average, credit cycles are longer in duration and larger in amplitude than output cycles, the largest MICs in Latin America (namely, Brazil, Chile, Colombia, Mexico, and Peru) tend to have cycles that are shorter (albeit deeper) than those exhibited by advanced economies. For Brazil alone, Gonzalez et al. (2015) estimated the periodicity of the financial cycle at about six years, close to the mean frequency of the business cycle. Moreover, credit and house price cycles tend to be positively and highly correlated in MICs, due to the widespread use of housing as collateral.[13]

There is also evidence of strong linkages between different phases of the business and financial cycles. As documented by Claessens et al. (2011, 2012), recessions associated with financial disruption episodes (most notably a collapse in house prices), tend to be longer and deeper than other recessions, whereas recoveries associated with rapid growth in credit and increases in house prices tend to be stronger. The correlation between the business and financial cycles stems from the fact that risks to the financial system are typically built in the upswing of the financial cycle, when credit, asset prices, leverage, and maturity mismatches all rise in a mutually reinforcing manner. In an upturn, credit expansion puts upward pressure on asset prices. This tends to strengthen balance sheets and collateral values, which in turn magnifies the expansion in credit. At the same time, financial institutions tend to weaken lending standards and screening intensity in good times, which also contributes to credit

12. See http://www.enterprisesurveys.org/data.

13. As documented by Calomiris et al. (2017), creditors in developing countries are often reluctant to accept movable assets such as machinery, accounts receivable, or inventory as collateral and favor instead immovable assets, which consist predominantly of real estate. In advanced economies, real estate can also be an important source of collateral to finance investment; see Chaney et al. (2012) and Norden and van Kampen (2013), for instance.

growth.[14] To the extent that decisions of individual financial institutions ignore these self-reinforcing effects, good times will tend to be characterized by excessive increases in credit and leverage. The opposite will happen in bad times, during which a downward spiral may relate asset sales, drops in asset prices, a deterioration in the quality of loan portfolios, and rapid reductions in leverage.

1.4 Financial Supervision and Regulation

In developing countries, the ability to supervise financial institutions and enforce prudential regulations is often weak (see Barth et al. 2013; Klomp and de Haan 2014). As documented by the Inter-American Development Bank (2005) and Demirguc-Kunt et al. (2008), for instance, the quality of bank supervision—as measured by the overall compliance index with the so-called Basel Core Principles for Effective Bank Supervision, which include a number of recommendations on prudential regulation and requirements—tends to be much lower in Latin America, compared to advanced economies. In turn, a weak regulatory environment may lead to regulatory capture and create perverse incentives for banks to engage in risky activities. It also implies, quite importantly, that prudential instruments, especially those that are designed to be manipulated in countercyclical fashion, should not be overly difficult to implement in order for them to be used in a timely and effective manner. The fact that reserve requirements, for instance, are so widely used in MICs (see chapter 5) can be seen at least in part as a reflection of these considerations.

Moreover, in many MICs, bank supervisors lack the ability to assess the effectiveness of banks' risk management practices, especially the adequacy of capital in relation to the risks that they undertake. The lack of expertise in supervisory agencies is especially problematic for those countries that have chosen to use the advanced approaches in the Basel II and Basel III regimes, which allow banks to rely on their own historical data and internal models for the determination of credit risk estimates and regulatory capital requirements (see chapter 6). Lack of supervisory capacity affects the ability to assess other risks as well, such as market and interest rate risks. In some cases, inadequate supervision and porous regulations are the legacy of heavy public sector involvement in the banking system, which weakens enforcement incentives, and an inadequate pay structure, which makes it difficult to lure well-qualified individuals away from more lucrative private activities.

14. Dell'Ariccia and Marquez (2006) discuss the various channels through which credit booms may lead to a weakening of lending standards. See also Gersbach and Rochet (2012) for an alternative set of factors underlying excessive fluctuations in credit, output, and asset prices.

1.5 Systemic Risk and Financial Fragility

Financial fragility is generally associated with systemic risk. This section begins by defining systemic risk and then considers two main sources of financial fragility in MICs: volatile short-term capital flows and excessive credit booms.

1.5.1 Systemic Risk

As defined by Freixas et al. (2015, p. 13) and the IMF-BIS-FSB (2016, p. 4), systemic risk is the risk of threats to financial stability that impair the functioning of a large segment of the financial system, with potentially serious adverse consequences for the broader economy. These threats often result from *negative externalities* related, for instance, to the fact that when they borrow and invest, individuals do not take into account the possibility that their actions could affect asset prices and increase the likelihood of collective asset sales in bad times (Korinek 2011; De Nicolò et al. 2012; Giese et al. 2013). In turn, these sales would tend to depress collateral values and induce a tightening of borrowing constraints across all segments of the financial system (Lorenzoni 2008; Bianchi 2011).[15] The fact that the source of concern is the potential consequences associated with a severe disruption or failure in a financial institution, or market segment, implies that systemic risk is not the same as financial instability but rather the result of an unusual, often largely unexpected, adverse financial shock that has the potential to reverberate throughout the economy.

There are two distinct dimensions of systemic risk. The first is *time-varying* risk, which relates to the procyclicality of the financial system and depends on the amount of risk that it takes at a given point in time relative to its capacity to absorb shocks, itself measured by the capital, provisions, and liquidity that banks have access to. The second is *structural* (or *cross-sectional*) risk, which depends on the connections between entities within the system and the distribution of risk across these entities at a point in time, as well as their common exposure to risk factors. In practice, defining and measuring these two components (which involves assessing the importance of alternative sources of financial externalities) is difficult. But the very fact that systemic risk has a dual nature suggests that regulators may need to employ a combination of different tools in order to make the financial system more resilient and less prone to procyclicality.[16]

15. Alternatively, as noted by Aikman et al. (2015*b*), banks may have incentives to engage in excessive lending due to strategic complementarities (for instance, reputational concerns) when other banks are profitable and are expanding their own lending activities.

16. Given its focus on the performance of simple macroprudential policy rules and interactions between countercyclical monetary and macroprudential policies, only time-varying systemic risk

1.5.2 Sources of Financial Fragility

Volatile short-term capital flows Over the past three decades, and despite a temporary reversal coinciding with the global financial crisis, the degree of integration of international financial markets has increased significantly. For many MICs, greater integration has been accompanied by a substantial rise in gross capital flows (including cross-border bank claims), gross foreign assets and liabilities, and net international asset positions.

Although there are significant potential benefits associated with financial integration and capital flows (especially foreign direct investment, as documented in a number of studies), the risk of volatility and abrupt reversals in short-term capital movements create many challenges for policymakers. These challenges were heightened in the aftermath of the global financial crisis as a result of the massive increase in global liquidity that followed the adoption of quantitative easing and other unconventional policies in advanced economies (see Dell'Ariccia et al. 2018).

Reversals in capital flows have been referred to as *sudden floods* (massive inflows) and *sudden stops* (massive outflows).[17] Sudden floods have been associated with a greater probability of a banking crisis (see Furceri et al. 2011; Caballero 2016). Even if they do not lead to full-blown crises, abrupt changes in capital flows can create or exacerbate systemic risk and financial vulnerabilities. As argued by Korinek (2018), for instance, when external financing constraints are binding, capital outflows associated with repayment needs or profit repatriation tend to be accompanied by a depreciation, which is needed to generate a current account surplus. In turn, this may trigger a self-reinforcing cycle of depreciating exchange rates, deteriorating balance sheets, a further tightening of financing constraints, and declining aggregate demand.[18]

From the perspective of financial stability, the main source of concern is *gross*, rather than *net*, capital flows—purchases of domestic assets by foreign agents, or purchases of foreign assets by domestic agents, rather than the difference between the two. Indeed, although gross inflows and outflows can be close to balance out in terms of size, whether they are each equivalent to 1 percent

is addressed in this book. It should be noted, however, that building resilience through structural buffers and mitigating procyclicality are not in general independent objectives.

17. The term *sudden stops* was coined by Calvo (1998) whereas the term *sudden floods* was used by Agénor et al. (2014*a*). Mendoza (2010) and Korinek and Mendoza (2014) provided a formal interpretation of sudden stops in terms of amplification and asymmetric effects associated with an occasionally binding borrowing constraint on world capital markets. See also Bianchi (2011) and Benigno et al. (2013) for related contributions.

18. See Morandé (1992) for some early evidence on these self-reinforcing cycles, and Mimir and Sunel (2019) for an empirical analysis focusing on the aftermath of the global financial crisis.

or 10 percent of GDP may have significant implications for financial stability. A key reason is that gross flows, intermediated directly or indirectly through the banking system, may lead to credit-fueled bubbles. From that perspective, Forbes and Warnock (2012) found that over the period 1980–2009, although net capital flows were relatively stable, the size and volatility of gross flows increased in many countries. Broner et al. (2013) also found that gross capital flows are very large and volatile relative to net capital flows. In addition, although it has been well documented that abrupt reductions in net capital inflows are often associated with financial crises, it is important to understand whether these reductions are due to sales of domestic assets by foreign agents, purchases of foreign assets by domestic agents, or both. Broner et al. (2013) found that during crises, total gross flows collapse and there is a retrenchment in both inflows by foreigners and outflows by residents. By contrast, during expansions, foreigners tend to invest more domestically and domestic agents invest more abroad.

Among gross flows, bank-related flows are especially important because of their potential direct impact on credit expansion (as noted earlier) and their role in transmitting international financial shocks. For instance, deteriorations in the balance sheet of domestic banks can push them to sell external assets or recall external loans to comply with internal rules or with prudential regulations such as capital requirements or maximum leverage ratios. Global banks may also respond to changes in regulation at home by adjusting their international lending practices. More generally, banks can play a critical role in cross-border financial contagion through the *international finance multiplier*—that is, the possibility that changes in asset prices in one country or region are transmitted internationally through their balance sheets (Krugman 2008). Concerns with bank-related flows have increased in recent years, in light of the rapid pace at which the globalization of banking has proceeded (Claessens 2017; World Bank 2018) and the greater incentives for global banks to engage in cross-border regulatory arbitrage (Buch and Goldberg 2017; Forbes et al. 2017).

The volatility associated with short-term capital flows is a major concern because the evidence shows that financial systems in MICs are often highly vulnerable to domestic or external disturbances—and even more so now to global financial cycles, as a result of increased international financial integration (see Ahmed and Zlate 2014; Agénor and Pereira da Silva 2018*a*; Ouyang and Guo 2019). Ahmed and Zlate (2014), for instance, provided evidence that interest rate differentials and global risk aversion are important determinants of net private capital inflows to MICs, especially (for portfolio flows) since the global financial crisis. More generally, there is growing evidence that short-term gross capital flows across regions are driven by a global financial cycle, which is significantly (albeit not exclusively) influenced by US monetary policy.[19]

Abrupt reversals in short-term capital movements tend to exacerbate financial volatility, particularly in countries with relatively fragile financial systems, weak regulatory and supervision structures (as discussed earlier), and policy regimes that lack flexibility. Indeed, a number of studies have documented a positive relationship between increasing international capital flows due to greater integration with world financial markets and vulnerability to sudden reversals in capital flows (see Agénor and Pereira da Silva 2019 and the references therein). Moreover, the probability of a sudden stop appears to increase the longer the preceding capital boom is. Thus, as noted by Agosin and Huaita (2012), sudden stops may not be the result of a (current or expected) deterioration in domestic macroeconomic fundamentals, but rather could represent *downward overreactions* to previous periods of *positive overreactions* in capital flows.

By and large, the evidence shows that the volatility associated with short-term capital inflows is the consequence of the rapid increases in liquidity, aggregate demand pressures, real exchange rate appreciation, and the deterioration of external accounts that these flows generate. It also suggests that the more open and integrated a country is to global financial markets, the deeper are the channels through which reversals in capital flows will impact both the real economy and the financial system—and the more critical the policy response becomes to ensure macroeconomic and financial stability. In addition, cross-border banking capital flows can be a potential source of instability, not because of their size *per se* but rather because they may amplify cyclical movements in domestic financial conditions and exacerbate domestic imbalances—especially in countries where, to begin with, financial vulnerabilities exist and the capacity of regulators to address them is weak. Increased exposure to adverse shocks magnifies the possibility of default and the risk of bankruptcy by borrowers and lenders alike, raising in the process the likelihood of a full-blown financial crisis.

Excessive credit booms

MICs, and developing countries in general, have suffered many costly crises over the past three decades, characterized by large contractions in activity, persistent credit crunches, and sharp increases in unemployment and poverty rates. Less extreme events also tend to be costly in terms of activity and employment, especially when they are associated with financial disruptions. Indeed, studies

19. See Cerutti et al. (2019), Habib and Venditti (2019), and Lodge and Manu (2019) for empirical evidence and a more detailed discussion.

have shown that slowdowns or recessions preceded or accompanied by banking-related stress tend to involve two to three times greater cumulative output losses and endure two to four times as long. Specifically, Claessens et al. (2011, 2012) found that, on average, the decline in output in a recession rises from 5 percent if there is no concomitant credit crunch to 8.5 percent if there is one.

More generally, there is strong evidence to suggest that rapid credit growth—often associated with episodes of large capital inflows in MICs, as documented earlier—is a robust warning sign of financial instability or financial crisis.[20] This evidence relates not only to developing countries (Demirguc-Kunt and Detragiache 2005; Agénor and Montiel 2015, chap. 15; Gertler and Hofmann 2016) but also to advanced economies (Schularick and Taylor 2012; Claessens and Kose 2014; Aikman et al. 2015*a*, 2016; Taylor 2015; Gertler and Hofmann 2016). In addition, several contributions (including Anundsen et al. 2014; Aldasoro et al. 2018) found that booms in house or property prices are a cause of financial fragility and financial crises—especially in an environment where borrowers are able to concomitantly lever up the collateral value of their assets. By contrast, there is no strong evidence that equity prices are good out-of-sample predictors of financial instability (International Monetary Fund 2009).

The key point that can be drawn from the foregoing discussion is that although the exact trigger of financial crises in MICs can be almost any event (including political turmoil, a real estate crash, a sharp decline in the terms of trade, or contagion from a foreign country), making it hard to predict their exact timing, such crises are often preceded by sustained imbalances—often in the form of abnormally high rates of credit growth. Even though not all episodes of credit booms end up in crises, almost invariably financial crises are preceded by episodes of excessive credit growth. Thus, measures that can help prevent excessive credit growth from emerging or developing in the first place may be essential to promote financial stability. In turn, this suggests a key role for countercyclical macroprudential regulation. The same fundamental point holds also for advanced economies.

1.6 Role of Macroprudential Regulation

The fundamental role of macroprudential regulation is to contain systemic risk, in both of its dimensions as defined earlier, and mitigate the potential adverse economic effects of financial instability (Freixas et al. 2015). To do so requires enhancing the resilience of the financial system *as a whole* to aggregate shocks—in contrast to *micro*prudential regulation, whose aim is to promote

20. In addition, although credit and asset price cycles often reinforce each other (as noted earlier), some studies found that credit booms are also a useful leading indicator of asset price busts.

the safety and soundness of *individual* financial institutions. In turn, enhancing resilience means addressing the vulnerabilities that arise through interlinkages and common exposures among financial institutions (in line with the *structural* dimension of systemic risk) and containing the build up of vulnerabilities over time by mitigating credit booms, reducing procyclical interactions between asset prices and credit, and preventing unsustainable increases in leverage and debt (in line with the *time* dimension of systemic risk).[21]

To contain the build up of financial vulnerabilities over time, macroprudential policy must rely on a range of policy instruments, which can be classified in several ways (see Bank of England 2011; Galati and Moessner 2013, 2018; Claessens 2015). One approach consists of distinguishing between policies targeting borrowers (namely, their leverage and financial positions) and those targeting financial institutions (namely, their assets or liabilities). The former includes caps on debt-to-income (DTI) ratios, loan-to-income (LTI) ratios, and loan-to-value (LTV) ratios, whereas the latter includes limits on the leverage ratio for banks, reserve or liquidity requirement ratios, loan-to-deposit ratios, loan loss provisions, and capital buffers (see, for instance, Claessens et al. 2013; Cerutti et al. 2017*a*, 2017*b*). Another approach is based on the frequency of adjustment, which mirrors the distinction alluded to earlier between the time-varying and structural dimensions of systemic risk. From the perspective of the time-varying dimension, as illustrated in figure 1.4, a common functional classification is in terms of *capital requirements* (such as bank equity, capital buffers, sectoral capital requirements, systemic risk buffers, and leverage ratios), *liquidity requirements* (such as required reserves), *provisioning requirements* (such as cyclically adjusted provisions), and *lending restrictions* (such as limits on DTI, LTI, and LTV ratios).[22] These instruments must in principle be adjusted dynamically to counter the build up of risks during upswings and prevent a credit crunch and abrupt shifts in risk perceptions in downturns.[23] In the next chapters the focus will be on the first three categories of

21. See Athanasoglou et al. (2014) for an overview of the literature on procyclicality in banking. As noted earlier, this book deals mainly with the time dimension of systemic risk.

22. In addition to these instruments, Basel III introduced a *net stable funding ratio*, which requires banks to use a minimum share of long-term wholesale funding and deposits to fund their assets. See Basel Committee on Banking Supervision (2011) for a discussion and Jacob and Munro (2018) for a formal analysis focusing on New Zealand, where a similar regulation has been in place since 2010. Another instrument introduced by Basel III is the *liquidity coverage ratio*; see Basel Committee on Banking Supervision (2013) for a description and Bech and Keister (2017) for an analysis of its implications for monetary policy implementation.

23. Note that the direction of adjustment also matters. Indeed, there is evidence of asymmetry in the effects of macroprudential tools. Claessens et al. (2013) and Cerutti et al. (2017*a*) found that while several of these tools can be quite effective to manage the expansionary phase of financial cycles, they don't work as well in busts.

instruments, which have been used extensively in MICs—as well as in some advanced economies—to mitigate credit booms.

A more general point is that countercyclical macroprudential policy must be linked to other policies aimed at moderating cyclical fluctuations—most importantly monetary policy, which also affects, as illustrated in figure 1.4, the behavior of credit and asset prices, two variables that play a critical role in the transmission mechanisms of both policies.[24] In particular, monetary and macroprudential policies are complementary if healthier financial institutions contribute to a smoother transmission of changes in policy interest rates to lending. Conversely, financial stability may benefit from a change in policy interest rates implemented in response to financial sector developments, which may create risks to price stability in the medium term. Interactions between monetary and macroprudential policies may therefore benefit both macroeconomic and financial stability. In the long term, the risk of conflict between the two objectives is limited: Price stability is generally necessary (although not sufficient, as demonstrated by the global financial crisis) for financial stability, and vice versa. Consequently, monetary and macroprudential policies are *complementary* in terms of ensuring economic stability. However, in the short term, trade-offs, or *negative spillovers*, cannot be ruled out. For instance, as discussed in chapter 6, long periods of low policy interest rates, resulting from low inflation, may create incentives on the part of lenders and borrowers to take on greater risks (as a result of a *search for yield* effect), which in turn may exacerbate financial vulnerabilities.

Moreover, these trade-offs depend also on the origin of shocks affecting the economy. Following a shock to aggregate demand, for instance, monetary and macroprudential policies operate in the same direction. If, for instance, the shock is negative, both policies must be eased to stimulate output and credit in order to prevent deflation. Policies are thus complementary, and there is no conflict between price and financial stability. By contrast, matters are different when the economy is subject to a supply shock. A positive supply shock, for instance, raises output and stimulates lending while reducing inflation. The central bank would normally respond to lower inflation by cutting its policy interest rate. This tends also to raise credit and investment, and to stimulate output further. At the same time, to mitigate the increase in lending, the macroprudential regulator may respond by raising temporarily capital requirements,

24. The figure also shows the different channels through which financial frictions may affect the transmission mechanism of both types of policies, under the assumption (discussed further in the next chapters) that the deposit market is competitive and banks set the loan rate.

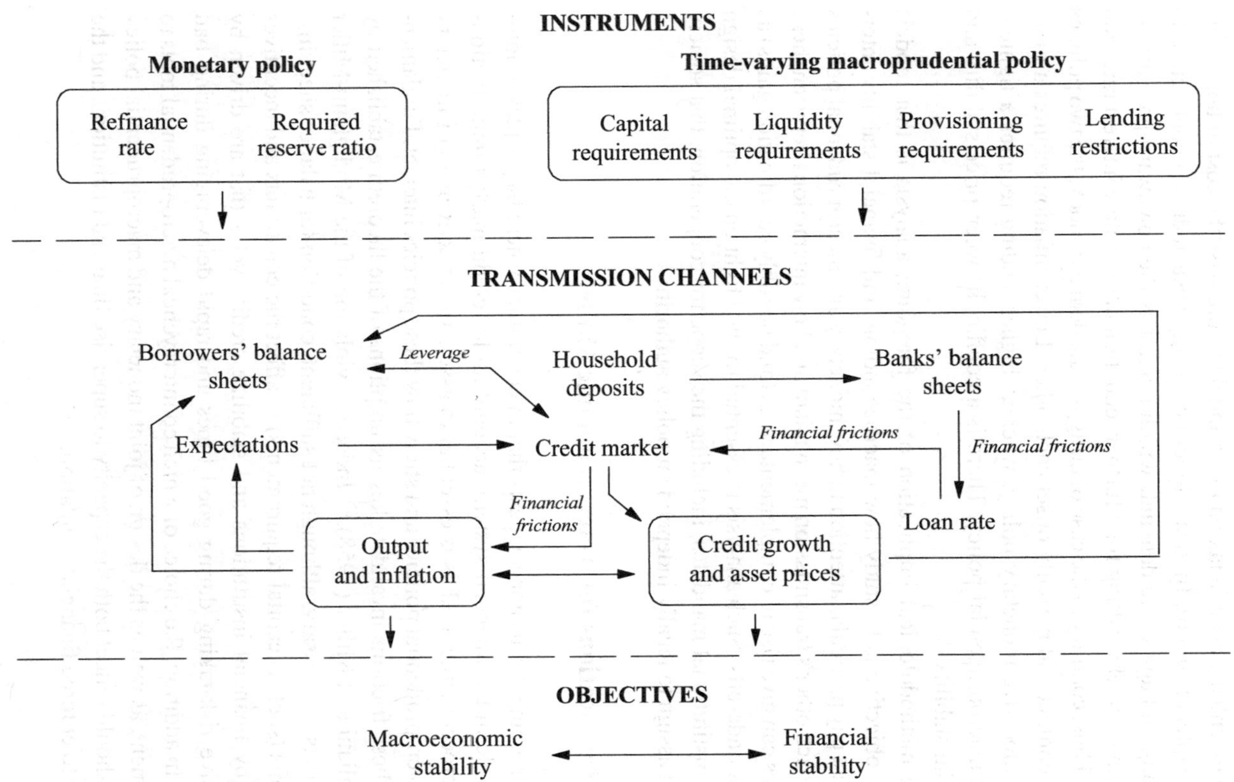

Figure 1.4 Monetary and time-varying macroprudential policies: objectives, instruments, and transmission channels

which essentially act as a tax on loans and therefore raise the cost of borrowing (see chapters 5 and 6). In turn, higher borrowing costs induce a contraction in spending and aggregate demand, which magnifies the downward pressure on inflation—thereby calling for a further reduction in the policy interest rate, and so on. Thus, contrary to the case of an aggregate demand shock, the two policies are in conflict and partially offset each other: Lower inflation requires a more accommodative monetary policy, whereas higher lending requires a tightening of macroprudential policy. There is a conflict between price stability and financial stability.

The methodological implication of the foregoing analysis is that models whose objective is to study how macroeconomic and financial stability interact must pay particular attention to how monetary and macroprudential policies affect each other's transmission mechanism and how interactions between these policies can give rise to complementarities (and possibly coordination gains) as well as trade-offs. Such analysis is essential to shed light on the optimal design of the institutional mandates, including the scope for cooperation, that society should assign to legally independent policy authorities.

1.7 Implications for Macroeconomic Models

The foregoing discussion suggests that in economies where banks play a dominant role in the financial system, accounting for credit market imperfections in macroeconomic models is essential to assess the effectiveness of monetary and macroprudential policies and study how these policies interact. Fundamentally, these frictions invalidate key assumptions of the theorem established by Modigliani and Miller (1958).[25] Indeed, a violation of the Modigliani-Miller theorem is a necessary, although not sufficient, condition for balance sheet instruments (such as capital requirements) to affect the constraints and incentives faced by financial institutions and stabilize credit cycles that are driven by excessive risk-taking during good times and rapid deleveraging during bad times. In addition, the choice of which countercyclical macroprudential tools to implement, as well as the design of joint monetary and macroprudential policy rules, should reflect both the capacity to supervise financial institutions and the ability to enforce financial regulation.

25. The Modigliani-Miller theorem states that the value of a firm is unaffected by how it is financed—that is, by the mix of debt and equity. The theorem holds only in the absence of taxes, bankruptcy costs, agency costs, and asymmetric information, and if markets are efficient. See Villamil (2008) for a discussion.

With asymmetric information between lenders and borrowers, accounting for the role of banks and the *credit channel* in macroeconomic models is essential to analyze the transmission mechanism of monetary policy. As is now well established, the credit channel consists of two sub-channels (Walsh 2010, chap. 10): the balance sheet (or broad credit) channel and the bank lending channel. In the credit channel, information-related financial frictions create a gap between the cost of internal and external financing for borrowers. A contractionary monetary policy can alter this gap for high-information-cost borrowers in two ways. First, policy can weaken the balance sheets of borrowers (by increasing their debt service and decreasing the collateral value of their assets), which therefore affects their ability to borrow. This defines the balance sheet channel. Second, a contractionary monetary policy in the form of an increase in reserve requirements can decrease the core deposit funding of banks. If some banks are unable to raise nonreservable or uninsured funds to support lending, the supply of loans will decline. This is the bank lending channel. In both of these sub-channels, decreases in either loan supply or loan demand lead to reduced investment and consumption. Shifts in the supply of loans associated with the bank lending channel require, first, the existence of some borrowers with high information costs and, second, that monetary policy can affect the capacity of banks to offer credit.

To address these and related issues, a variety of analytical models have been used—even though, at the time of this writing, few of them account explicitly for systemic risk. As illustrated in the next chapters, these models cover simple static and dynamic models of both closed and open economies, most prominently DSGE models. These models have indeed dominated academic research in macroeconomics and central bank thinking for the past two decades. It is thus particularly important to examine their potential role as *exploratory analytical platforms* in the context of a discussion focusing on monetary policy and financial regulation.[26]

1.8 DSGE Models as Exploratory Platforms

To set the stage for the subsequent analysis, this section begins by providing a brief discussion of the structure of the precrisis core DSGE model with nominal rigidities and its limitations. It then discusses some of the main approaches

26. To my knowledge, Olivier J. Blanchard was the first to use, in a blog essay, the expression "analytical platforms" to characterize the purpose of DSGE models. See https://piie.com/blogs/realtime-economic-issues-watch/further-thoughts-dsge-models.

that have been followed to account for financial frictions, which essentially stem either from information asymmetries (between lenders and borrowers, or depositors and banks), and from difficulties in enforcing contracts. These frictions create a channel for procyclical interactions between asset prices, the balance sheet positions of borrowers and lenders, and real economic activity, through changes in leverage.

1.8.1 Structure of the Precrisis Core DSGE Model

The core DSGE model (at least the one prevailing prior to the global financial crisis) is based on eight principles.[27] First, the model is stochastic in nature; every period, random exogenous events perturb the model's equilibrium conditions, which creates uncertainty in the evolution of the economy. The fact that current choices are dependent on future uncertain outcomes makes these models inherently dynamic and assigns a central role to agents' expectations in the determination of current outcomes. The stochastic nature of the model, as well as its general equilibrium structure, make it possible to study the effects of various shocks on the economy, interactions between nominal and real variables, the transmission process of monetary policy, and the implications of alternative policy rules for macroeconomic stability.

Second, households and firms are forward-looking agents whose objective is to solve (micro-based) intertemporal optimization problems. A representative household maximizes its utility subject to a household budget constraint, and a representative firm maximizes profits subject to its production technology. Heterogeneity among agents is thus ignored.[28] Moreover, private agents form rational or *model-consistent* expectations of future conditions. Explicit microfoundations and model-consistent expectations make it possible to study short-run dynamics and the long-run equilibrium in a unified framework. Third, a stable long-run equilibrium path exists for the economy, and deviations from it are limited. This enhances tractability by allowing (as discussed in chapter 4) the use of local approximation techniques for numerical analysis.

Fourth, the core DSGE model introduces a number of distortions, including nominal rigidities, in the form of sluggish price adjustment and

27. See Clarida et al. (1999), Galí and Gertler (2007), Walsh (2010, chap. 8), Christiano et al. (2010b, 2018), Wickens (2012, chapter 16), and especially Galí (2015) for a thorough discussion of this model, also referred to as the canonical New Keynesian framework because of its emphasis on imperfect competition and nominal rigidities. Galí (2015) provided a historical perspective on its development, most notably its links with the general equilibrium real business cycle (RBC) models that preceded them.

28. In some extensions of the core DSGE model, a category of households is assumed to be subject to liquidity constraints and/or myopic horizons, which implies that their consumption is closely tied to their current income. This issue is discussed further in chapter 4.

monopolistic competition in the product market.[29] Price-setting frictions help to accommodate the evidence of inertia in inflation. For these frictions to exist, firms must have the ability to set prices, and this in turn requires the presence of monopoly power. In turn, to create an environment in which there is monopoly power, without contradicting the fact that actual economies have a very large number of firms, DSGE models usually build on the production framework proposed by Dixit and Stiglitz (1977), in which imperfect competition in markets for differentiated goods leads to a markup distortion and results in a less efficient level of output. Asynchronous price adjustment leads to relative price distortions and short-run non-neutrality of money. Indeed, as a consequence of nominal rigidities, changes in nominal interest rates in the short run are not matched by one-to-one changes in expected inflation, and this leads to variations in real interest rates. These nominal-real interactions create a role for monetary policy. In some extensions of the core model, both wage rigidity and monopolistic competition in the labor market are introduced.[30]

Fifth, while some contributions based on the core DSGE model use calibrated values of the parameters (designed to match well-established stylized facts or particular moments of some key variables), in others parameters are estimated with Bayesian system-wide estimation techniques (see Fernández-Villaverde et al. 2016; Herbst and Schorfheide 2016). In doing so, a number of prior constraints deemed reasonable are typically imposed on parameter values. Sixth, money is often introduced through the utility function, a cash-in-advance constraint, or—less frequently—a shopping time or transaction costs restriction.[31] At the same time, the core model abstracts from the financial system and the behavior of financial intermediaries; money is simply a veil and a single interest rate (the policy rate) prevails in the economy. Seventh, the government collects taxes and spends on goods and services, subject to its intertemporal budget constraint. In the most basic model, public debt is constant and the government balances its budget through changes in lump-sum taxes. Eighth, the

29. Alternative models of price adjustment under monopolistic competition are also discussed in chapter 4.

30. Extensions of the core DSGE model have also incorporated an array of other real rigidities, such as habit formation in consumption and hours worked, adjustment costs in capital or labor input, fixed costs in production, labor hoarding, and variable capacity utilization.

31. With complete markets or with a riskless bond yielding positive nominal returns, constraining agents to hold money (which carries no interest) is a source of inefficiency. This issue does not arise in models where money provides liquidity services, which increase utility directly. At the same time, as discussed in chapter 5, there is a functional equivalence between these alternative ways of introducing money in macroeconomic models, and this may have implications for welfare analysis.

central bank sets monetary policy by following an interest rate rule (or so-called Taylor rule), which relates the policy interest rate to deviations in output from its potential value and inflation from its target. The central bank raises (lowers) the nominal interest rate when output is above (below) its potential value or when inflation rises (falls) above target. In turn, changes in the interest rate affect activity and, through it, inflation. To ensure macroeconomic stability and a determinate equilibrium, the interest rate rule must satisfy the so-called *Taylor principle*, which implies that the nominal interest rate should be raised more than one-for-one when inflation increases.

At a more operational level, the precrisis core DSGE model is built around three interrelated blocks: a *demand block* (which determines current activity as a function of the *ex ante* real interest rate and expectations about future real activity), a *supply block* (which determines inflation as a function of current activity and expectations of future inflation), and a *monetary policy reaction function* (with deviations in output and inflation as the key determinants of the policy rate). Consistent with the principle highlighted earlier, the equations that define the first two blocks are derived from micro-foundations—that is, explicit assumptions about the behavior of the main economic agents in the economy (households, firms, and the government). These agents interact in markets that clear every period, consistent with the general equilibrium nature of the model. This feature is key to capturing the interaction between policy decisions and agents' behavior. A fall in the policy rate, for instance, creates an incentive for households to consume more today because it reduces the incentives to save. For production and employment to rise, firms must increase wages to induce employees to work longer hours. In turn, higher wages increase marginal costs, putting pressure on current prices and raising inflation. Moreover, the higher inflation is expected to be in the future, the higher is the increase in current prices, thereby contributing to a rise in inflation today. If the Taylor principle alluded to above holds, when inflation rises (falls), the real interest rate also rises (falls); higher (lower) inflation means therefore lower (higher) output.[32] Finally, at the prevailing policy rate, the supply of liquidity by the central bank is perfectly elastic. Thus, as noted earlier, the model features no explicit analysis of financial market equilibrium. Put differently, monetary policy is studied in a framework where money, or credit for that matter, plays no direct role.

32. However, in more complex models, the Taylor principle may not be sufficient to guarantee uniqueness and determinacy. See Woodford (2003, chap. 2 and 4) and Sveen and Weinke (2013) for a discussion.

1.8.2 Limitations of the Precrisis Core DSGE Model

Several of the principles identified earlier remain at the core of the postcrisis generation of DSGE models. Although progress has been achieved in many areas (including the treatment of financial frictions, as discussed next), they remain subject to a number of criticisms. A scathing attack on these models is the *pretense of knowledge* highlighted by Caballero (2010), who argues that the identifying assumptions and the assumed knowledge in both Bayesian estimation and the calibration of parameters in DSGE models are "incredible." A further symptom of the pretense of knowledge is the belief that these parameters are constant over time. In fact, supposedly structural parameters may exhibit drift over time (see Hurtado 2014).

As argued by Muellbauer (2016), an even deeper problem lies in the unrealistic microfoundations for the behavior of households embodied in the standard rational expectations-permanent income approach to consumption behavior that underlies the core DSGE model and many of its extensions. Indeed, at the core of representative agent DSGE models is the Euler equation for consumption, which connects the present with the future and is essential to the iterative forward solutions of these models. The equation is based on the assumptions of intertemporal optimization by consumers and that every consumer faces the same linear period-to-period budget constraint, linking income, wealth, and consumption. Maximizing expected lifetime utility subject to the constraint results in the optimality condition that links expected marginal utility in the different periods. Under (approximate) certainty equivalence, this translates into a simple relationship between consumption at time t and planned consumption at $t+1$ and in periods further into the future.

This approach faces a number of problems. For instance, evidence on financial illiteracy raises questions about the assumption that all consumers optimize (see Lusardi 2019). In reality, consumers face idiosyncratic (household-specific) and uninsurable income uncertainty, and uncertainty interacts with credit or liquidity constraints. Some models with heterogeneous agents imply that household horizons then tend to differ from each other and to be shorter—contradicting the rational expectations-permanent income model described earlier. In addition, aggregate behavior does not follow that of a representative agent.[33] The combination of uninsurable idiosyncratic shocks and binding borrowing constraints implies that, at any point in time, different households may have very different marginal propensities to consume. Consequently, as

33. With multiple agent types, DSGE models become quickly intractable analytically. Some researchers have turned instead to agent-based modeling; see Tesfatsion (2006) for a discussion of this approach.

noted by Galí (2018), the macroeconomic effects of any aggregate shock will tend to be amplified or mitigated depending on the way the shock (and the variables that are impacted) alters the distribution of income and wealth across households. Kaplan et al. (2018), for instance, showed that with heterogeneous agents monetary policy operates very differently than in the core, representative-agent DSGE model. Finally, despite improvements, the current generation of DSGE models often does not account for household debt (or, more generally, household balance sheets) which may be important for understanding consumption and macroeconomic fluctuations in countries where such borrowing is large.[34]

Despite these weaknesses, DSGE models—with or without forward-looking behavior—currently have few contenders to replace them as core models for policy analysis (Lindé 2018). In addition, DSGE models are flexible enough to be used for a variety of purposes. As discussed next, accounting for financial frictions is particularly important to understand the challenges that monetary policy and macroprudential regulation face in promoting macroeconomic and financial stability.

1.8.3 DSGE Models with Financial Frictions

As noted in the introduction of this book, the recent global financial crisis made it clear that financial factors can be an important source of aggregate fluctuations and a critical propagation channel of a variety of macroeconomic shocks. To understand the role of these factors, a new generation of postcrisis DSGE models, conveniently referred to as DSGE-FF models in this book, has been developed in a number of directions. While welcome in many ways, this diversity of approaches has also created an *embarras de richesses*—at least for now, there is no unique, commonly accepted, core DSGE-FF model that can play the role of a workhorse in the same manner that the precrisis core DGSE model did.

A detailed discussion of the various approaches that have been proposed in the literature to account for financial frictions is beyond the scope of this book.[35] However, it is possible to identify four main approaches that have been widely used by macroeconomists.[36] The first is the model of collateral

34. Blanchard (2017) pointed to a number of other failings of DSGE models and recommended greater openness to more eclectic approaches.

35. See Gertler and Kiyotaki (2010), Quadrini (2011), Brunnermeier et al. (2013), and Dou et al. (2017). However, in several respects, these papers remain partial reviews.

36. A fifth approach to modeling financial market imperfections, which does not rely directly on informational asymmetries or moral hazard, is based on *search and matching frictions*. In these models, studied by Wasmer and Weil (2004), Munakata et al. (2013), Hoyle et al. (2018), and Li (2018), for instance, banks make loans to firms in credit markets characterized by search and

constraints of Kiyotaki and Moore (1997), hereafter KM, which restricts borrowing to a fraction of durable assets and emphasizes the role of collateral constraints in amplifying business cycle fluctuations. The second is the financial accelerator model of Bernanke et al. (1999), hereafter BGG, which is itself based on the costly state verification model of Townsend (1979) and Williamson (1986), the overlapping generations model with agency costs of Bernanke and Gertler (1989), and the numerical implementation of the Bernanke-Gertler model by Carlstrom and Fuerst (1997) under flexible prices. The third is the model with moral hazard between banks and depositors developed by Gertler and Kiyotaki (2010) and Gertler and Karadi (2011), hereafter GKK. The fourth approach, somewhat less popular in the DSGE literature, is the double moral hazard model of Holmström and Tirole (1997), which will be discussed further in a growth context in chapter 11.[37]

Collateral constraints

In the KM model, durable assets (such as land) are used as collateral against borrowing, as well as to either provide consumption services or facilitate production. A credit constraint limits the amount that can be borrowed (at a constant rate) to the value of the underlying collateral. This constraint can be rationalized in terms of limited enforcement; although borrowers could in principle default on their debt obligations, the possibility of losing the asset pledged acts as a deterrent. Borrowing constraints are always binding, so default never occurs in equilibrium.[38] An increase in asset prices raises the collateral value of these assets, which relaxes the borrowing constraint and amplifies the original effects of the shock. In contrast to the agency cost that characterizes the BGG model (discussed next), the KM model does not feature an endogenous lending spread, but the tightness with which the borrowing constraint binds provides a *shadow cost* between the cost of borrowing and the risk-free interest rate. The cost of external financing is constant up to the point where the constraint begins to bind and becomes infinite beyond that point.

The KM model has been extended in a number of directions, in both closed- and open-economy settings. Kiyotaki (1998) considered logarithmic (rather

---

matching (or entry) frictions, and interest rates on loans are set in bilateral bargaining between banks (lenders) and firms (borrowers). However, use of that approach remains limited in the current macro-modeling literature.

37. DSGE models dwelling on the Holmström-Tirole approach include Aikman and Paustian (2006), Kato (2006), Meh and Moran (2010), Cakici (2011), Christensen et al. (2011), Faia (2011), and Silvo (2019).

38. Models in which borrowing capacity is linked to market-determined collateral values via *occasionally* binding credit constraints are reviewed by Korinek and Mendoza (2014) and Mendoza (2016).

than linear) preferences, heterogeneous productivity across agents, and switching of agent types, whereas Krishnamurthy (2003) focused on the role of hedging markets. For their part, Caballero and Krishnamurthy (2001) considered in an open-economy context an amplification mechanism similar to that used in the KM model, in the sense that a fall in asset prices is reinforced by a tightening financial constraint. In the KM model the financial constraint is on the *demand* side—constrained demand reduces the productivity of assets, causing a fall in asset prices and further constraining demand. However, in the Caballero-Krishnamurthy model, as in Krishnamurthy (2003), the constraint is on the *supply* side—constrained supply leads to higher interest rates, causing a drop in capital and further constraining supply. Other applications of the KM model include Leblebicioglu (2009), who focused on international borrowing constraints and the benefits of risk-sharing, and Devereux and Yu (2019), who studied interactions between monetary policy and capital controls in responding to sudden stops in capital flows.

Initial quantitative experiments with the KM model by Kocherlakota (2000) and Cordoba and Ripoll (2004) found that under standard assumptions it does not generate quantitatively significant amplification. In addition, Bacchetta and Caminal (2000) found that, depending on whether shocks are anticipated or unanticipated, the response of output may be dampened rather than amplified. By contrast, subsequent work by Khan and Thomas (2013) found that an unanticipated tightening in borrowing conditions can generate a large recession on its own, with more persistence than the initial financial shock. A strong amplification effect is also obtained by Vlieghe (2010), in a model with plausible values for the capital share in output and the intertemporal elasticity of substitution, and by Mendicino (2012), in a framework that focuses on costly debt enforcement procedures.

In some contributions that have followed in the tradition of the KM model, housing is taken to be the binding collateral constraint. This is the case, for instance, in Aoki et al. (2004), Iacoviello (2005, 2015), Monacelli (2007), Gerali et al. (2010), Andrés and Arce (2012), Liu et al. (2013), Angelini et al. (2014), and Walentin (2014) in a closed economy, and Vitola and Ajevskis (2011) in an open economy. Some of these contributions include several categories of households as well as imperfect competition in banking. In a contribution that was subsequently used in a number of applications, Iacoviello (2005) considered two types of households, patient and impatient, who differ in terms of their discount rate. Each type is grouped in a distinct representative dynasty that provides risk-sharing benefits to its members. In equilibrium, patient households are savers who buy houses outright, while impatient households borrow from banks, using their housing assets as collateral. Mortgage debt is provided to the individual members of the dynasty against their individual housing units.[39] Iacoviello's treatment of household heterogeneity has also been used in other types of models with financial frictions.

Agency costs and the financial accelerator

The BGG model, just like the KM model, focuses on the demand side of the credit market. At its core is the existence of an agency problem between borrowers and lenders, which is solved through an appropriate loan contract with a role for leverage.[40] The key mechanism in the model relies on the interaction between the production technology and asymmetric information. The acquisition of capital is financed through both entrepreneurial net worth (broadly defined as liquid assets, plus the collateral value of illiquid assets, less outstanding liabilities) and external funds. Using the costly state verification approach of Townsend (1979) and Williamson (1986), the BGG model assumes that firms can easily observe the returns to their individual investment projects but lenders must incur a cost to do so. This agency problem is solved with an optimal contract that entails a trade-off between verification costs (which are akin to bankruptcy or liquidation costs) and the likelihood of default.[41] It involves an *external finance premium*—the wedge between the cost of funds raised externally (the bank lending rate for most firms in MICs) and the opportunity cost of internal funds (the bank deposit rate or the government bond rate)—which depends inversely on borrowers' net worth. Thus, in contrast to the KM model, in the BGG model the cost of external financing is increasing in the amount borrowed for a given net worth of the borrower, because higher leverage requires higher agency costs. Because profits and asset prices are procyclical, borrowers' net worth is also procyclical. By implication, the external finance premium is countercyclical, thereby propagating shocks to

39. In Iacoviello's model, mortgage loans are not subject to risk. By contrast, Clerc et al. (2015) and Mendicino et al. (2018) account for the possibility of default on mortgage debt at the individual level, with the borrower losing the housing asset on which the mortgage is secured. In case of default, the repossession of collateral by lenders involves verification costs similar to those considered in the BGG model discussed next.

40. An agency problem describes a situation where one party (the agent) acts on behalf of another (the principal); for instance, a banker acting on behalf of depositors as a *delegated monitor*. In such situations, conflicts of interests can arise if incentives between the agent and the principal are not adequately aligned.

41. See Niepelt (2019, chap. 8) for an exposition. In the BGG model, lenders issue state-contingent contracts with borrowers and returns on their loan portfolio are independent of aggregate shocks. However, although lenders can diversify away idiosyncratic shocks by holding a large loan portfolio, they are vulnerable to aggregate shocks, which create systemic risk. Zhang (2009) extended the BGG model to consider loan contracts where borrowers and lenders share this type of risk. In that setting, aggregate shocks affect not only firms' balance sheets but also lenders' net worth.

the real economy and amplifying swings in borrowing (and hence investment), aggregate demand, and prices. But in both the KM and the BGG frameworks, variations in asset prices are key in determining borrowing behavior, as they affect either the price (via the finance premium) or the quantity (via collateral values) of funds available to borrowers. DSGE models developed in recent years have often built on both channels. Applications of the BGG model, or variants thereof, that have focused on MICs specifically, in both closed and open-economy settings, include Aghion et al. (2004), Cook (2004), Choi and Cook (2004, 2012), Devereux et al. (2006), Gertler et al. (2007), Aysun and Honig (2011), Fernández and Gulan (2015), among others.

What is the empirical evidence with respect to the core assumption of the BGG model (the link between firms' borrowing costs and their net worth) and its overall performance? Brzoza-Brzezina et al. (2013) calibrated and compared the KM model of collateral constraints with the BGG model of external finance premia. They found that in general the business cycle properties of the BGG model are more in line with the empirical evidence for advanced economies. In the same vein, Christiano et al. (2010*a*) found that, quantitatively, financial frictions à la BGG are an important driving force of business cycle fluctuations in both the Euro area and the United States. Evidence supporting a significant role for the financial accelerator mechanism in transmitting shocks from financial markets to the real economy is also documented by Meier and Müller (2006), De Graeve (2008), Nolan and Thoenissen (2009), Aliaga-Díaz and Olivero (2010*a*), Del Negro et al. (2015), Merola (2015), and Lindé et al. (2016) for the United States. However, there are also mixed results, especially during the period surrounding the global financial crisis (see Suh and Walker 2016). In addition, studies such as Rannenberg (2016) and Yépez (2017) found that a *combination* of financial frictions matches the US data better than a single friction, whereas Gertler and Gilchrist (2018) emphasized the importance of balance sheet effects at the level of highly leveraged households and banks, as opposed to nonfinancial firms only, for understanding how the financial crisis of 2007–2008 unfolded in the United States. Although similar evidence is not available for MICs, there is widespread belief among macroeconomists that collateral and balance sheet effects are particularly relevant empirically for these countries. Nevertheless, it is possible that a combination of financial frictions may be better able to explain aggregate fluctuations in these countries as well.

More generally, from a theoretical standpoint the core BGG model suffers from several limitations. First, the model assumes that investors lend directly to borrowers, with no explicit role attributed to financial intermediaries. But as noted earlier, a sizable fraction of financial flows (in MICs as well as in a number of advanced economies) are channeled by banks, and uncovering how the banking sector affects economic fluctuations in a general equilibrium environment, and what role a broader range of financial frictions may play, is critical for policy design. In that regard, one strand of the literature considers perfectly competitive banking sectors in which issuing loans and managing deposits is costly and interest rates are determined by zero-profit conditions. Prominent examples along these lines are Goodfriend and McCallum (2007) and Christiano et al. (2010*a*). Goodfriend and McCallum (2007) considered banks that produce loans using monitoring and collateral. In turn, monitoring requires labor, which is supplied by households. Monitoring costs are thus measured directly in terms of real wages. In this setting, the external finance premium is identified with the real marginal cost of loan production, which includes not only the cost of external finance (as emphasized by BGG) but also labor costs. The presence of collateral—which enables a bank to enforce the repayment of loans with less monitoring and management effort—in the production function generates a *banking accelerator*, similar in some respects to the financial accelerator: Monetary expansions that increase the value of collateralizable assets reduce the external finance premium for a given level of bank deposits. But it also generates a *banking attenuator*, by which the increase in spending raises the demand for bank deposits and the premium for a given value of collateral. Which effect dominates depends on the specific calibration of the model and the origin of the shocks affecting the economy.[42]

Second, the BGG model considers financial frictions only on the borrowers' side of credit markets; credit-supply effects stemming from the behavior of financial intermediaries are ignored. Yet, the global financial crisis showed that shifts in credit supply can play a crucial role in macroeconomic fluctuations. In particular, intermediaries may incur costs for originating and servicing loans (as noted earlier), with marginal costs increasing with the volume of lending. There is therefore a need to consider models that combine financial frictions on both the borrowers' and the lenders' side—that is, the simultaneous presence of a borrower balance sheet channel and a bank credit-supply channel. Such models help to highlight how loan spreads may depend endogenously on banks' leverage, as measured by loan-capital ratios.

In parallel, a number of contributions have analyzed the implications of imperfect competition in the banking sector on economic fluctuations. In some studies, banks have market power because of the switching costs that their customers may incur. As a result, when setting interest rates, they face a trade-off between higher current profits and lower future market share. This generates countercyclical spreads, which amplify the effects of productivity shocks on the economy. For instance, Andrés and Arce (2012) considered a monetary

42. Applications of the Goodfriend-McCallum model to middle-income economies include Hwang (2012) and Chadha and Kang (2016).

economy where spatial monopolistic competition in the banking sector interacts with collateral constraints on borrowers. Stronger banking competition influences cyclical fluctuations through two channels: higher leverage ratios (which increase the volatility of asset prices, consumption, and output in the short run) and lower lending margins (which weaken the transmission mechanism). Following a monetary policy shock the effect on leverage dominates the effect on lending margins, whereas the reverse holds after a credit crunch shock. Gerali et al. (2010) analyzed the effects of sluggish adjustment in nominal loan and deposit rates on cyclical fluctuations. In their model a continuum of banks compete à la Dixit-Stiglitz (as do intermediate good producers in the core DSGE model, discussed earlier) and are subject to costly adjustment of nominal loan rates.

Finally, Christiano et al. (2010*a*) argued that, in addition to the BGG financial accelerator effect, there is a second, complementary channel through which changes in net worth can be propagated: the *Fisher deflation effect* (see Fisher 1933). This effect presupposes that debt contracts are formulated in *nominal* terms. As a result, unexpected changes in the price level can alter *ex post* the real burden of the debt that the borrower will have to bear when the contract eventually matures. Indeed, in their framework, debt contracts embody an important nominal rigidity: Although loans to entrepreneurs are state contingent, banks' obligations to households are expressed in nominal terms. As a result, the opportunity cost perceived by the bank when lending to entrepreneurs at time t is not contingent on time $t+1$ shocks. Fluctuations in the cost of borrowing reflect therefore two general equilibrium effects. The first is the BGG-type financial accelerator effect identified earlier, which makes the contractual loan rate dependent on the net worth that borrowers can pledge to secure loans. The second is due to the fact that, with nominal contracts and state-contingent loans to entrepreneurs, unexpected movements in the price level can alter *ex post* the real burden of entrepreneurial debt. Christiano et al. (2010*a*) showed that the pure accelerator mechanism and the Fisher deflation effect reinforce each other in the case of shocks (such as demand disturbances) that move the price level and output in the same direction, but they tend to cancel each other out in the case of shocks (such as technology shocks) that move these variables in opposite directions.

Moral hazard between banks and depositors

In the GKK model, banks are engaged in maturity transformation; they hold long-term assets financed by short-term deposits. There are no financial frictions between them and nonfinancial firms. Instead, the financial friction is based on a moral hazard problem (or lack of commitment) between banks and depositors: Banks may default on their obligations and walk away with a share of intermediated assets. At the same time, due to limited liability, banks effectively earn rents on their capital, charging more to borrowers than they pay to savers. As a result, banks' liabilities are constrained by their equity capital, and there is an endogenous limit on the extent of funding that households are willing to extend to financial intermediaries. Shocks to bank balance sheets spread to the rest of the economy and amplify business cycles.

The GKK model has been used and extended in a number of contributions, including Gertler et al. (2012), Takamura (2013), Correia et al. (2016), Rannenberg (2016), Gertler et al. (2016), Yépez (2017), and Zhang (2019) in a closed economy; Aoki et al. (2018) and Mimir and Sunel (2019) in a small open economy; and Agénor et al. (2018*c*) and Cuadra and Nuguer (2018) in two-region models of the world economy. In particular, Rannenberg (2016) extended the GKK model by combining the moral hazard problem between banks and depositors with a costly state verification problem between entrepreneurs and banks in the BGG tradition.

The key motivation for the model's specification and some of its extensions was to explain the events surrounding the subprime crisis in the United States. However, there has been some debate regarding its inner structure, the extent to which it is able to reproduce all the relevant facts, and its usefulness for studying the effects of the unconventional monetary policy measures implemented in the aftermath of the crisis in advanced economies (see, for instance, Cole 2011; Villa and Yang 2012).

1.9 Modeling Approach

In this book, as noted in the Introduction, the core methodology is to formulate an integrated set of macroeconomic models with banks and financial frictions and to study systematically the performance of monetary and macroprudential policies in each of these models. Rather than emphasize (continuously or occasionally) binding borrowing constraints based on pledgeable guarantees to lenders, the models presented in this book are for the most part in line with some of the key elements of the BGG approach. They emphasize the impact of collateral values—based on housing assets, rather than physical capital—and balance sheet conditions on the external premium and the cost of borrowing. As such, this view seems more in line with the way credit markets operate in *normal* times in MICs, with binding constraints taking the form of complete exclusion of some potential borrowers from access to loans (small entrepreneurs with limited or no collateral) and others subject to a premium, embedded in the loan rate, which varies as a function of their net worth. In this setting collateral serves as both an insurance mechanism (because borrowers face idiosyncratic risks and may be *forced* to default) and an incentive-mitigating device (because borrowers cannot commit to future actions and may *choose* to default). The existence of collateral is therefore motivated, as noted in some of the banking literature on credit market imperfections, by limited contract enforceability and moral hazard concerns.

In addition, as is made clear in the next chapters, in terms of its microfoundations the approach followed in this book emphasizes *noncontingent* monitoring costs and is more in line with traditional microeconomic approaches to banking.[43] Indeed, in the models developed in this book, the fundamental reason that banks exist is because they provide monitoring services to depositors, avoiding duplication costs. Banks are endowed with technology or specialized skills that allow them to inspect borrowers' cash flows and balance sheets, observe their activities, and ensure that borrowers conform to the covenants specified in the loan contract. Households do not possess this technology, or even if they do, are too disparate to effectively use it. Thus, in the terminology proposed by Diamond (1984), banks act as *delegated monitors*. But although banks are efficient at evaluating borrowers and at ensuring that they comply with their contractual obligations, the cost of performing these activities is not trivial and may vary with the state of the business cycle. At the same time, these monitoring activities differ from the *ex post* monitoring activity emphasized in the costly state verification literature (including the BGG model discussed earlier), where lenders monitor when the project outcome is realized and only when the borrower defaults on repayments. The cost of monitoring in that literature is an expected default or *state-contingent* verification cost, more akin to a bankruptcy cost associated with auditing, accounting, and legal expenses due to liquidation. Finally, by introducing banks, and accounting explicitly for their pricing decisions under monopolistically competition, the analysis in this book accounts not only for the demand side of the credit market (as in the KM and BGG approaches) but also for the supply side. This allows a more thorough description of the channels through which monetary policy and macroprudential regulation operate, making it possible to study the extent to which shocks originating in the financial sector have significant spillover effects on the real economy. The book also dwells on a range of contributions

43. Research based on integrating traditional micro-banking modeling in macroeconomic models has covered a wide variety of topics. Contributions such as Kopecky and VanHoose (2012) and Abo-Zaid (2015), for instance, extended dynamic banking models to consider issues such as bank retail interest rate dynamics and the optimal conduct of monetary policy. See also Gersbach and Rochet (2012, 2017), who provided a microfounded rationale for macroprudential regulation, and Dell'Ariccia et al. (2014), who focused on the impact of monetary policy on bank risk-taking.

to the literature on international finance and open-economy macroeconomics, especially with respect to the effects of exchange rate fluctuations and the role of capital mobility.

More specifically, in the following chapters two types of macroeconomic models are presented. The first type consists of small theoretical models, which are aimed at clarifying the analytical issues associated with monetary policy and macroprudential regulation in the presence of financial frictions. These core models, both static and dynamic, are kept deliberately simple to highlight (at least from my perspective) the main issues at stake. The second type consists of richer, policy-relevant DSGE models, which are more articulate in terms of underlying behavioral assumptions and more explicit about the sources of financial frictions, the sources of price dynamics and asset accumulation, and their description of policy rules. Although more elaborate, these models are built to address well-specified policy issues; as such, they are often deliberately simplified in some dimensions rather than being all-encompassing. For instance, in line with the foregoing discussion on the role of monitoring costs, all the models used in this book rely on a common simplifying assumption in micro-based banking models—the existence of a one-to-one relationship between bank monitoring intensity and the probability that borrowers repay their loans.[44] This assumption translates into a direct link between the probability of default and interest rate spreads. The resulting banking structure is simpler, while preserving fundamentally the same insights as more complex, microfounded specifications—especially with respect to the role of financial accelerator effects, which operate through endogenous changes in the repayment probability.

Moreover, to explore the quantitative properties of these models and the performance of alternative policy rules, they are parameterized rather than estimated or rigorously calibrated. The key problem—beyond the relatively simple task of matching historical averages for some key variables—is that estimated values for a wide range of *structural* parameters remain limited for MICs and, when available, often vary significantly in magnitude across countries. Reasons for this include lack of relevant data, measurement errors, and large structural differences among economies. In addition, as discussed earlier, these countries have often faced a highly volatile environment, which has translated into frequent structural breaks in the data. In turn, these breaks have made it difficult to construct sufficiently long time-series data for reliable statistical inference

44. This one-to-one relationship shares some similarity with a key feature of the banking framework developed in Christiano and Ikeda (2014), for instance, in which costly bank effort is positively related with the probability of identifying good investment projects.

and perform standard model validation exercises, such as historical decompositions. Thus, in contrast to the situation for advanced economies, there is no broad consensus among development macroeconomists on what some key parameter values should be in conducting quantitative exercises. Instead, what is available is a *range* of values to experiment with and a set of stylized facts that are mainly *qualitative* in nature—regarding, for instance, the effects of a contractionary monetary policy on inflation, the impact of excessive credit growth, or the macroeconomic effects of large capital inflows, as discussed earlier—but that one would expect a reasonable model, nevertheless, to replicate in a benchmark scenario. The consequence is that the DSGE models developed in this book cannot by any means be construed as *applied* policy models, in the sense that they are not aimed at fitting the reality of a particular country or providing country-specific policy advice. Rather, they should be viewed as complementary exploratory platforms to further advance the theoretical and policy-oriented discussions initiated with the simpler analytical models.

Also important to note is that the macroeconomic models used in this book do not incorporate an explicit, microfounded definition of systemic risk, which could serve as a rationale for macroprudential policy intervention. As noted earlier, such a definition is fairly broad and hard to operationalize. The nondiversifiable nature of systemic risk, incentives for risk-taking, or the role of interconnections across financial institutions, firms, and markets, for instance, are difficult to integrate in quantitative macroeconomic models. In fact, full-fledged attempts at modeling systemic risk in a DSGE-FF setting remain rare, and the extent to which they have proved successful remains a matter of debate. In addition, macroprudential policy includes a diverse set of tools; translating the goal of financial stability to specific targets and matching it to specific instruments is not an easy task, either. Instead, the approach followed in this book, in line with its emphasis on countercyclical regulation, is to focus on an *intermediate target* for financial stability—credit developments. As noted earlier, the empirical literature suggests that even though episodes of rapid credit growth do not always lead to financial distress, for a variety of reasons financial distress is almost invariably preceded by periods of excessive credit growth.[45] Thus, the role of *countercyclical* macroprudential policy is to mitigate excessive credit expansion, viewed as the manifestation of an underlying

45. Of course, other indicators, such as asset prices (especially house prices) or credit spreads could, and have been, used as intermediate targets for financial stability, although the evidence is not as robust with respect to their predictive capacity. In chapters 5 and 9, composite indicators will also be considered.

distortion that can be addressed only by *structural* regulatory policies. This focus also provides a rationale for the type of macroprudential instruments that are discussed in this book. At the same time, because credit fluctuations can be efficient, from a social welfare perspective it is important to examine whether narrowly defined countercyclical rules perform well relative to fully optimal policies.

Finally, the modeling approach and numerical solution techniques adopted in this book are not well suited to study episodes of excessive volatility, occasionally binding constraints, or full-blown financial crises. An extensive literature has made it abundantly clear that during distress events, the behavior of agents, and their effects on macroeconomic and financial variables (especially risk premiums), tend to differ markedly from conditions that prevail during normal times. For instance, as a result of fire sales, vicious interactions can develop between asset prices, the balance sheets of lenders and borrowers, credit market conditions, and the real economy. These interactions can lead to sudden jumps in lending spreads and an abrupt contraction in credit, which in turn may act as further amplification mechanisms. Nonlinearities are therefore critical to understand episodes of excessive volatility and crises.[46] By construction, discontinuous effects of this type cannot be captured in the type of linearized DSGE-FF models, solved by local approximation methods, used in this book and elsewhere in the literature. Nevertheless, it is precisely because of the need to avoid excessive volatility and crises, and the potentially large costs associated with them, that it is important to understand how economies behave in *normal* times and how monetary and macroprudential policies can be conducted *preemptively* in that environment.

46. In Brunnermeier and Sannikov (2014), for instance, nonlinear amplification effects are front and center in explaining sudden changes in systemic risk and spikes in volatility. Christiano et al. (2004), Cúrdia (2009), Mendoza (2010), He and Krishnamurthy (2012), Adrian and Boyarchenko (2015), Fornaro (2015), and Boissay et al. (2016) also emphasized the role of nonlinearities—in the form, for instance, of a sudden imposition of borrowing constraints—during episodes of financial distress.

2 A Simple Closed-Economy Model with Financial Frictions

As documented in chapter 1, financial market imperfections cover a broad spectrum in middle-income countries (MICs): underdeveloped capital markets, which imply limited alternatives (such as corporate bonds and commercial paper) to bank credit; limited competition among banks; more severe asymmetric information problems, which make screening out good risks from bad credit risks difficult and fosters collateralized lending; a pervasive role of government in banking, both directly or indirectly, which promotes moral hazard; uncertain public guarantees; inadequate disclosure and transparency, coupled with weak supervision and a limited ability to enforce prudential regulations; weak property rights and an inefficient legal system, which makes contract enforcement difficult and also fosters the use of collateral requirements; and a volatile economic environment, which increases exposure to adverse shocks and magnifies both the possibility of default by borrowers and the risk of bankruptcy of financial institutions. One implication of these imperfections, as also noted in chapter 1, is that a large majority of small and medium-size firms are often squeezed out of the credit market. At the same time, those who do have access to it—well-established firms, often directly connected with financial institutions—face an elastic supply of loans and borrow at terms that depend on their ability to pledge collateral. Credit rationing, which results fundamentally from the fact that inadequate collateral or the inability to seize it in case of default would have led to prohibitive rates, is therefore largely exogenous in normal times. A second implication is the importance of the cost channel, which becomes a key part of the monetary transmission mechanism.[1] At the same time, in countries lacking well-functioning securities markets, the credit channel provides an important mechanism of monetary transmission. By

1. As noted in chapter 1, the direct effect of lending rates on firms' marginal production costs is a common feature of MICs, and there is evidence that it may be important also in advanced economies.

affecting directly bank deposit and lending rates, monetary policy determines the spending capacity of households and firms. These effects depend also on the nature of financial frictions, the prudential regulations that banks are subject to, and the extent to which the regulatory regime affects the monetary transmission mechanism.

This chapter provides a simple static model of a closed economy with exogenous expectations in which the impact of monetary policy and financial regulation can be explored and some core intuition established.[2] Its objective is to examine how monetary policy works in countries where the financial system is dominated by banks. In addition, banks lend only to firms, whose investment is financed entirely through bank loans. This is consistent with the evidence, discussed in chapter 1, which shows that household debt in MICs remains relatively low compared to corporate debt, and corporate firms still predominantly rely on bank borrowing (in addition to retained earnings) to finance investment. The analysis focuses on how monetary and regulatory policy decisions are transmitted to the components of aggregate demand, output, and prices in this context.

A key feature of the model is that it accounts explicitly for an important source of imperfection in credit markets—namely, the fact that exposure to idiosyncratic shocks makes borrowers' ability to repay uncertain. In addition, because weak insolvency laws and inefficient judicial systems hamper the ability of financial intermediaries to enforce the terms of loan contracts in case of default (a common feature of MICs, as noted in chapter 1), lending tends to be highly collateralized, and borrowers' net worth has a large impact on the terms of credit. Specifically, because changes in collateralizable wealth have a direct impact on bank pricing behavior, balance sheet effects play a key role in the transmission mechanism of monetary policy. However, in contrast to models in the tradition of Kiyotaki and Moore (1997) and its variants, collateralizable wealth does not act as a strict quantity constraint on bank borrowing; rather, in the tradition of Bernanke et al. (1999), it affects the premium that banks impose on loans for investment purposes. At the (premium-inclusive) loan rate, banks provide all the liquidity that borrowers need. But because the premium varies inversely with the price of pledgeable assets, the model allows monetary policy to generate a financial accelerator effect, to the extent that its impact is amplified by movements in collateral values.

To keep the focus on the financial sector, a minimalist approach to modeling the real sector is adopted. Specifically, behavioral functions related to

2. A counterpart open-economy model is presented in chapter 7.

private spending are postulated, thereby leaving for later chapters a full-blown analysis of microfoundations. Moreover, for the sake of clarity, extensions to the model are presented one at a time, rather than simultaneously. The fact that the model is static, that expectations are exogenous, and that some of the behavioral equations are not explicitly derived from well-defined optimization problems, with fully specified budget constraints, are obvious limitations; nevertheless, the analysis helps to provide some basic insights that will be useful to understand the properties of the more complex models presented later on in the book.

To begin, section 1 describes the core framework with exogenous output. The macroeconomic equilibrium is derived and monetary policy is analyzed. Section 2 endogenizes the supply side and introduces the cost channel by relating the working capital needs of firms to bank credit. The possibility of default and monopolistic competition are explicitly introduced in section 3. The regulatory regime is then accounted for in section 4 and the effects of three instruments of macroprudential policy are analyzed: reserve requirements, taxes on loans, and capital requirements. The model is modified in section 5 to account for land as a portfolio asset for households and collateral for loans to firms—an extension that brings explicitly asset prices into the analysis. The chapter concludes with some brief notes on the literature.

2.1 Exogenous Output

The core model developed here dwells in significant part on the static framework with credit market imperfections developed by Agénor and Montiel (2006, 2007, 2008). As noted earlier, because borrowers' ability to repay is uncertain, lending is collateralized, and effective collateral affects the terms of credit through a premium that banks incorporate in setting the loan rate. Moreover, at the prevailing loan rate, the supply of credit is perfectly elastic. There is therefore no endogenous credit rationing of the Stiglitz-Weiss variety (see Stiglitz and Weiss 1981, 1992). The central bank's supply of liquidity is also perfectly elastic at a target interest rate, which is referred to as the refinance rate.

After presenting the structure of the model, its solution and a graphical illustration are presented. The impact of monetary policy is then analyzed.

2.1.1 Model Structure

Consider a closed economy that produces a single homogenous good, used either for consumption or investment. For the moment, output is exogenous at

$Y = \bar{Y}$. Five types of agents populate the economy: households, firms, banks, a central bank, and a financial regulator. For the time being, the regulator plays no substantive role; in what follows the behavior of each of the first four categories of agents is described.

Households

In the economy, households consume the homogenous good and hold two imperfectly substitutable assets: currency (which bears no interest) in nominal amount M, and bank deposits in nominal amount D. The representative household's wealth, F^H, is thus defined as

$$F^H = M + D. \tag{2.1}$$

The ratio of bank deposits to cash holdings depends positively on the deposit rate, i^D:

$$\frac{D}{M} = \nu(i^D), \tag{2.2}$$

where $\nu' > 0$.[3] Using (2.1), this equation can be written as

$$D = (F^H - D)\nu(i^D),$$

or, equivalently,

$$\frac{D}{F^H} = \frac{\nu(i^D)}{1+\nu(i^D)} = d(i^D), \tag{2.3}$$

where $d' = \nu'/(1+\nu)^2 > 0$. From (2.2), $M = D/\nu(i^D)$; substituting (2.3) in this result yields

$$\frac{M}{F^H} = \frac{1}{1+\nu(i^D)} = m(i^D), \tag{2.4}$$

where $m' = -\nu'/(1+\nu)^2 < 0$. A higher deposit rate therefore raises the demand for deposits and lowers the demand for cash. Note also that at the initial level of financial wealth $d' + m' = 0$, given that households hold only two assets: following a change in the deposit rate, any movement in D must be exactly offset by an opposite movement in M.

Interest on deposits is paid at the end of each period. Real consumption expenditure, C, depends positively on factor income, $\bar{Y}$; negatively on the expected real deposit rate; and positively on the real value of financial wealth

3. Note that (expected) inflation has no effect on the deposit-cash ratio. This is because it is assumed implicitly to affect the (absolute) demand for each asset in the same manner.

at the beginning of the period, F_0^H:

$$C = \alpha_1 \bar{Y} - \alpha_2 (i^D - \pi^e) + \alpha_3 \left(\frac{F_0^H}{P} \right), \tag{2.5}$$

where P is the price level, π^e the expected inflation rate (assumed constant throughout this chapter), $\alpha_1 \in (0, 1)$ the marginal propensity to consume out of available income, and $\alpha_2, \alpha_3 > 0$. The positive effect of income on private spending is consistent with the evidence regarding the pervasiveness of liquidity constraints on households in developing countries.[4] As is well known, life-cycle models predict a relationship between consumption and (present value) *wealth*, rather than income. However, liquidity-constrained households cannot borrow from the financial system to smooth consumption and therefore tend to adjust spending on the basis of changes in current income only. The negative effect of the real deposit rate captures an *intertemporal substitution effect*, even though the model is not explicitly intertemporal: When the real return on deposits increases, households have an incentive to save more and to reduce current consumption.[5] The positive wealth effect is also well documented. The empirical estimates of Peltonen et al. (2012), for instance, based on panel data for 14 countries (most of them MICs) suggest that a 10 percent increase in monetary assets, proxied by the broad money stock, raises consumption by about 0.4 to 0.5 percent.

Firms

As noted earlier, output is exogenous for the moment. Real investment of the representative firm, I, is negatively related to the real loan rate:

$$I = I(i^L - \pi^e), \tag{2.6}$$

where i^L is the nominal loan rate and $I' < 0$. This inverse relationship is well documented in the literature; Krznar and Matheson (2017, fig. 1), for instance, showed such a relationship for Brazil over the period 2000–2016.

Firms borrow all the funds they need to finance investment. The nominal value of investment loans at the end of the period, L^K, is thus

4. See Agénor and Montiel (2015). There is evidence that the proportion of constrained households is also quite significant in advanced economies. For instance, Coenen and Straub (2005) found that the proportion of constrained households in the Euro area varies between 0.25 and 0.37. Similarly, Fève and Sahuc (2017) found a share varying between 0.22 and 0.35.

5. In principle, the real deposit rate is $(1+i^D)/(1+\pi^e)$. Assuming that i^D is small and using the approximation $\ln(1+x) \simeq x$ yields the expression used in equation (2.5). A similar approximation is used in (2.6).

$$L^K = L_0^K + P \cdot I, \tag{2.7}$$

where L_0^K is the stock of investment loans at the beginning of the period.[6]

Commercial banks

There is a continuum of commercial banks, indexed by $i \in (0, 1)$. Assets of each bank consist of credit extended to firms for investment only, $L^i = L^{K,i}$, and mandatory reserves held at the central bank, RR^i. Bank i's liabilities consist of household deposits, D^i, and borrowing from the central bank, $L^{B,i}$. The balance sheet of each commercial bank can therefore be written as

$$L^i + RR^i = D^i + L^{B,i}, \tag{2.8}$$

where all variables are measured in nominal terms. Because the loan-pricing condition used in this section and the next is not explicitly derived from a monopolistic competition framework, in what follows the index i is omitted to economize on notation.

Reserves held at the central bank pay no interest and are set in proportion to deposits:

$$RR = \mu D, \tag{2.9}$$

where $\mu \in (0, 1)$ is the required reserve ratio.

The market for deposits is competitive. Household deposits and loans from the central bank are viewed by banks as perfect substitutes at the margin; thus, the interest rate on deposits must be equal to the cost of central bank liquidity, adjusted for the implicit cost that banks incur for holding reserve requirements on deposits:[7]

$$i^D = (1 - \mu) i^R, \tag{2.10}$$

where i^R is the rate at which banks borrow from the central bank—that is, the refinance rate.

By contrast, the market for loans is monopolistically competitive. A full-blown analysis is provided later on; for the moment, the contractual interest rate on investment loans, or loan rate for short, i^L, is simply assumed to be set by each bank as a premium over the central bank refinance rate, which represents the marginal cost of funds:

6. Internal finance could be added to the model by assuming that retained earnings are a constant fraction $\chi > 0$ of total output $\bar{Y}$; new borrowing by firms would thus be $P(I - \chi \bar{Y})$. This, however, would not affect the results, given that output is exogenous at this stage.

7. In gross terms, this equation can be written as $1 + i^D = (1 - \mu)(1 + i^R)$. However, it is easy to see that if $\mu > i^R(1 + i^R)$, then the net deposit rate would be negative.

$$i^L = i^R + \theta, \tag{2.11}$$

where θ is the premium, which reflects the possibility of default and is taken to vary inversely with the ratio of the *effective* value of collateral pledged by the borrower, divided by its beginning-of-period liabilities, L_0^K. In turn, the effective value of collateral consists of a fraction $\kappa \in (0, 1)$ of the current value of the physical capital stock, measured in terms of the price of the final good:

$$\theta = \theta\left(\frac{\kappa P K_0}{L_0^K}\right), \tag{2.12}$$

where $\theta' < 0$ and K_0 is the beginning-of-period capital stock of the borrower. This specification is consistent with the view (alluded to in chapter 1 and discussed in more detail in chapters 3 and 4) that collateral, by increasing borrowers' effort and reducing their incentives to gamble, reduces moral hazard and raises the likelihood of repayment—thereby inducing lenders to lower the premium on their loans. For simplicity, the capital stock is valued at the price of investment, which corresponds to the price of the final good. Thus, an increase in prices tends to raise the firm's effective asset-to-liability ratio and to reduce the premium demanded by lenders. As discussed later on, the fact that the premium depends endogenously on prices is crucial in allowing monetary policy to generate a financial accelerator effect. Coefficient κ can be viewed as a measure of efficiency of enforcement of debt contracts (see Djankov et al. 2008) or an inverse measure of anticreditor bias in the judicial system (see Cavalcanti 2010).[8]

Note also that in a developing economy it is possible to have $PK_0 > L_0^K$, in which case the value of collateral may exceed the value of outstanding loans. As discussed in chapter 1, this could be because lenders expect the recovery value of collateral to be significantly lower than its face value, implying therefore a fairly low value of κ. Nevertheless, to avoid a corner solution, where banks have no incentives to monitor borrowers, the condition $\kappa PK_0 \leq L_0^K$ is assumed to hold.

Given that firms' demand for credit determines the actual supply of loans, and that the required reserve ratio is set by the monetary authority, the balance sheet constraint (2.8) can be solved using (2.9) residually for borrowing from the central bank, L^B:

$$L^B = \max[L - (1 - \mu)D, 0]. \tag{2.13}$$

8. Although κ is assumed constant throughout, it is worth noting that it could be made an inverse function of the value of collateral to reflect the fact that (as discussed in chapter 1) banks are prone to excessive lending during booms, when asset prices are high.

To ensure that $L^B > 0$ and avoid the case where overly liquid banks may choose not to respond to changes in the cost of central bank borrowing, the condition $L > (1 - \mu)D$ is also assumed to hold at all times.[9]

Central bank

The balance sheet of the central bank consists, on the asset side, of loans to commercial banks, L^B. On the liability side, it consists of the monetary base, given as the sum of total cash in circulation, M^s, and required reserves:

$$L^B = M^s + RR. \tag{2.14}$$

Monetary policy is operated by setting the refinance rate at the constant value i^R and providing liquidity, as determined residually through banks' balance sheets, through a standing facility. In general, standing facilities are used to create—in MICs and advanced economies alike—narrow corridors to limit departures of short-term money market interest rates from target, with open-market operations used for the secondary objective of smoothing liquidity and moderating interest rate fluctuations. These facilities make central bank liquidity endogenous by providing unlimited access—subject, in practice, to collateral requirements and institutional rules on who is eligible to maintain current balances with the central bank—to extra cash at the posted interest rate. For simplicity, abstraction is made of collateral requirements (typically low-risk and low-yield assets such as government securities) and open-market operations; a zero-width band around the target rate is imposed as well. For the time being, the central bank is also assumed to set the required reserve ratio, μ.

Substituting (2.9) in (2.14), the supply of currency by the central bank is given by

$$M^s = L^B - \mu D. \tag{2.15}$$

Market-clearing conditions

There are five market equilibrium conditions to consider: four related to financial markets (for cash, deposits, bank loans to firms, and central bank loans to commercial banks) and one for the goods market. At the going deposit rate set through the no-arbitrage condition (2.10) and a loan rate set by commercial banks as a markup over the refinance rate through (2.11), the markets for deposits and loans adjust through quantities. The supply of central bank credit

9. Note that in the present setting bank profits, given by $i^L L^F - (i^D D + i^R L^B)$, are not necessarily nil. For simplicity, these profits are assumed to be distributed to households only at the end of the period and therefore do not affect spending during the period. In the dynamic models considered in chapter 4 and beyond, a more explicit treatment is provided.

is perfectly elastic at the official refinance rate, and the market also equilibrates through quantity adjustment.

The equilibrium condition of the goods market, which determines the price level P, requires equality between output and aggregate demand, defined as the sum of consumption and investment:

$$\bar{Y} = C + I. \tag{2.16}$$

The last equilibrium condition relates to the market for cash. Suppose that the counterpart to bank loans consists of cash, but that cash is used instantaneously to buy goods for investment. Thus, equilibrium between demand and supply of cash requires equating (2.4) and (2.15). However, there is no need to study that condition explicitly, given that by Walras' law it can be eliminated.[10]

2.1.2 Macroeconomic Equilibrium

To solve for the equilibrium of the economy, note first that from (2.11) and (2.12),

$$i^L = i^R + \theta\left(\frac{\kappa P K_0}{L_0^K}\right).$$

Totally differentiating this expression gives

$$di^L = di^R + \left(\frac{\kappa K_0}{L_0^K}\right)\theta' dP,$$

10. Recall that the model uses an end-of-period specification, where by convention the savings-investment equilibrium refers to flows within the period, whereas the equilibrium of the asset markets refers to stocks at the end of the period (see Buiter 1980). Thus, the outstanding stock of X at the end of the period, after taking account of changes (accumulation or decumulation) within the period, can be written as $X = X_0 + \Delta X$, where X_0 is the beginning-of-period stock; it must equal stock demand. Formally, Walras' law takes the following form for the five markets (deposits, credit to firms, borrowing by commercial banks, cash holdings by households, and goods): $(D^d - D_0 - \Delta D) + (L^d - L_0 - \Delta L) + (L^{B,d} - L_0^B - \Delta L^B) + (M^d - M_0 - \Delta M) + (C + I - \bar{Y}) = 0$, where D^d is the demand for deposits from (2.3), M^d the demand for cash from (2.4), L^d credit demanded by firms, and $L^{B,d}$ the demand for central bank liquidity from (2.13). With markets in deposits, credit to firms, borrowing by commercial banks, and goods always in equilibrium (through a perfectly elastic supply or demand curve in the first three markets, and flexible prices in the last), using the definition of X above gives $\Delta D = D^d - D_0$, $\Delta L = L^d - L_0$, $\Delta L^B = L^{B,d} - L_0^B$; in addition, $\bar{Y} = C + I$. Walras' law yields therefore $M^d - M_0 - \Delta M = 0$. Moreover, from (2.8), (2.9), and (2.14), or equivalently from (2.8) and (2.15), $\Delta M = \Delta L^B - \mu\Delta D = \Delta L - (1-\mu)\Delta D - \mu\Delta D = \Delta L - \Delta D$. Combining the preceding two equations yields $M^d = M_0 + \Delta L - \Delta D$. Intuitively, any expansion in credit that is not funded by a change in deposits translates into a change in central bank borrowing and an increase in the money supply, which must be matched by a change in the demand for cash.

so that

$$i^L = FF(P; i^R, \mu), \tag{2.17}$$

where

$$FF_P = \left(\frac{\kappa K_0}{L_0^K}\right)\theta' < 0,$$

$$FF_{i^R} = 1,$$

$$FF_\mu = 0.$$

Equation (2.17) defines the *financial sector equilibrium* condition, in terms of a relationship between the loan rate and the price level, for given values of the policy instruments. An increase in prices raises the nominal value of firms' collateralizable assets relative to their stock of outstanding loans, which are fixed in nominal terms. Banks therefore demand a lower premium, thereby reducing the loan rate ($FF_P < 0$). An increase in the refinance rate raises the marginal cost of funds for banks, and the loan rate reflects this increase one to one ($FF_{i^R} = 1$). By contrast, an increase in the required reserve ratio has no effect on the loan rate; because the marginal cost of funds is the refinance rate, its only direct effect is to lower the deposit rate. Although this change in the deposit rate affects asset allocation through (2.3) and (2.4), the economy is not directly affected given that consumption depends on the stock of assets at the beginning of the period, which is predetermined. Indeed, the only effect of the deposit rate on the loan rate is an indirect one, through its impact on consumption and the price level, as discussed later.

Substituting the behavioral equations for consumption and investment, (2.5) and (2.6), and the no-arbitrage condition (2.10) in the goods market equilibrium condition (2.16) yields

$$\bar{Y} = \alpha_1 \bar{Y} - \alpha_2[(1-\mu)i^R - \pi^e] + \alpha_3\left(\frac{F_0^H}{P}\right) + I(i^L - \pi^e).$$

With an exogenous expected inflation rate, totally differentiating this expression gives

$$0 = -\alpha_2(1-\mu)di^R + \alpha_2 i^R d\mu - \alpha_3\left(\frac{F_0^H}{P^2}\right)dP + I' di^L,$$

so that

$$i^L = GG(P; i^R, \mu), \tag{2.18}$$

where

$$GG_P = \frac{\alpha_3}{I'}\left(\frac{F_0^H}{P^2}\right) < 0,$$

$$GG_{i^R} = \frac{\alpha_2(1-\mu)}{I'} < 0,$$

$$GG_\mu = -\frac{\alpha_2 i^R}{I'} > 0.$$

Equation (2.18) defines the *goods market equilibrium* condition, again in terms of a relationship between the loan rate and the price level, for given values of the policy instruments. A rise in prices tends to lower aggregate demand through a negative wealth effect on consumption. Thus, with production constant at $\bar{Y}$, an increase in prices creates excess supply. The loan rate must fall to stimulate investment and restore equilibrium in the goods market. A rise in the refinance rate i^R raises the deposit rate, thereby reducing consumption through the intertemporal substitution effect. As a result, there is excess supply on the goods market. Again, with exogenous output, restoring equilibrium at the initial level of prices necessitates an increase in investment and this in turn requires a drop in the loan rate. An increase in μ has the opposite effect, lowering the deposit rate and raising consumption. For a given level of output, the loan rate must now increase to reduce investment.

Equations (2.17) and (2.18) can be solved together for the equilibrium values of the loan rate and the price level. The solution is depicted graphically in figure 2.1 in i^L-P space. The financial sector equilibrium condition (2.17) is represented by the curve labeled *FF*, whose slope is given by F_P. The goods market equilibrium condition (2.18) is shown as the curve labeled *GG*, whose slope is given by G_P. Both *FF* and *GG* have a negative slope, reflecting the earlier discussion of the signs of F_P and G_P. The question then is how steep is *GG* relative to *FF*? The answer to this question, which is crucial for understanding the comparative statics properties of the model and the adjustment process to shocks, can be provided by relying on *Samuelson's correspondence principle*, which essentially involves analyzing the local stability of the dynamic system associated with (2.17) and (2.18).[11]

11. Samuelson's correspondence principle, as discussed in Samuelson (1941), establishes a link between comparative statics properties and (local) dynamic stability analysis. The principle has been criticized because the dynamic adjustment process can often be specified in several alternative ways (see Quirk and Saposnik 1968). In the present case, the adaptive processes that are postulated are both simple and plausible.

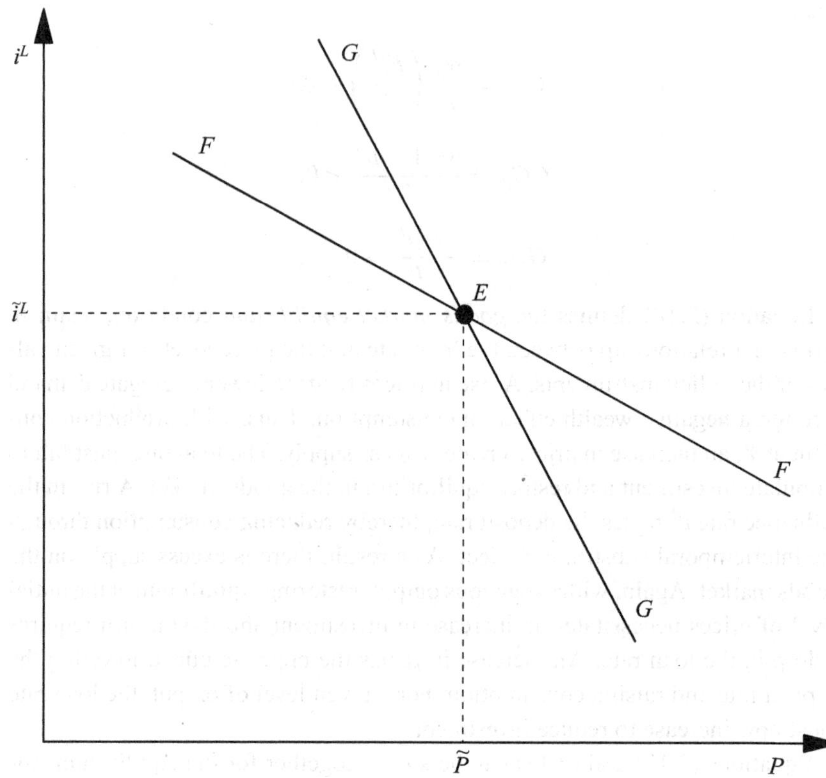

Figure 2.1
Macroeconomic equilibrium with exogenous output

Formally, consider the following dynamic adjustment process for the loan rate and prices: Changes in the loan rate are related to the difference between its equilibrium and current values, and changes in prices are related (in standard Walrasian fashion) to excess demand for goods. Assuming continuous time for simplicity and using (2.17), the first dynamic equation is

$$\frac{di^L}{dt} = \lambda_F[FF(P; i^R, \mu) - i^L], \tag{2.19}$$

where $\lambda_F > 0$ is the speed of adjustment. The second dynamic equation is

$$\frac{dP}{dt} = \lambda_G(C + I - \bar{Y}),$$

or, using (2.18),

$$\frac{dP}{dt} = \lambda_G \left\{ \alpha_1 \bar{Y} - \alpha_2[(1-\mu)i^R - \pi^e] + \alpha_3 \left(\frac{F_0^H}{P} \right) + I(i^L - \pi^e) - \bar{Y} \right\}, \tag{2.20}$$

where again $\lambda_G > 0$ is the speed of adjustment. Thus, at any moment in time, if the current loan rate is lower (higher) than its equilibrium value, it will increase (fall) subsequently, whereas if there is excess demand (supply) for goods, prices will increase (fall) subsequently. Instantaneous adjustment occurs when $\lambda_F, \lambda_G \to \infty$ whereas the steady state corresponds to $di^L/dt = dP/dt = 0$.

Linearizing equations (2.19) and (2.20) in the vicinity of the steady state yields, with a "~" denoting a steady-state value,[12]

$$\begin{bmatrix} di^L/dt \\ dP/dt \end{bmatrix} = \begin{bmatrix} \lambda_F a_{11} & \lambda_F a_{12} \\ \lambda_G a_{21} & \lambda_G a_{22} \end{bmatrix} \begin{bmatrix} i^L - \tilde{\imath}^L \\ P - \tilde{P} \end{bmatrix}, \tag{2.21}$$

and

$$a_{11} = -1,$$

$$a_{12} = FF_P < 0,$$

$$a_{21} = I' < 0,$$

$$a_{22} = -\alpha_3 \left(\frac{F_0^H}{P^2} \right) - -I'GG_P < 0.$$

Because the loan rate and the price level are both predetermined (state) variables, stability of the dynamic system (2.21) requires two negative eigenvalues (see Beavis and Dobbs 1990, p. 153). Necessary and sufficient conditions for that to occur are that the matrix of coefficients (or Jacobian), **A**, has a positive determinant (to guarantee either two positive or two negative eigenvalues) and that its trace be negative (to ensure two negative eigenvalues):[13]

$$\det \mathbf{A} = \lambda_F \lambda_G (a_{11}a_{22} - a_{12}a_{21}) > 0,$$

$$\text{tr}\mathbf{A} = \lambda_F a_{11} + \lambda_G a_{22} < 0.$$

12. Let $dx_t/dt = f(x_t, z_t)$, where x_t and z_t are two variables. A first-order Taylor series expansion in the neighborhood of $(\tilde{x}, \tilde{z})$ yields $dx_t/dt \simeq f(\tilde{x}, \tilde{z}) + f_x(x_t - \tilde{x}) + f_z(z_t - \tilde{z})$. Because in the steady state both x_t and z_t are constant, $f(\tilde{x}, \tilde{z}) = 0$. The same reasoning applies to $dz_t/dt = g(x_t, z_t)$.

13. These conditions are related to the fact that the determinant of the Jacobian is the *product* of the eigenvalues, whereas its trace is equal to the *sum* of the eigenvalues.

The condition on tr**A** is always satisfied, given that $a_{11}, a_{22} < 0$ and $\lambda_F, \lambda_G > 0$. However, given that $a_{12}, a_{21} < 0$, the condition on det **A** does not always hold; for that to occur requires

$$\frac{a_{22}}{a_{21}} > \frac{a_{12}}{a_{11}}.$$

From the definitions of the a_{ij} coefficients provided earlier, $a_{12}/a_{11} = -FF_P > 0$ and $a_{22}/a_{21} = -\alpha_3(P^{-2}F_0^H)/I' = -GG_P > 0$. Thus, the above condition is

$$-GG_P > -FF_P,$$

which implies that the slope of GG must be steeper, in absolute terms, than the slope of FF, as shown in figure 2.1. Intuitively, given that GG_P captures the strength of the wealth effect on consumption, and FF_P the strength of the collateral effect on the loan rate, stability requires the wealth effect of an increase in prices to be stronger than its collateral effect. The equilibrium values of i^L and P are determined at the point of intersection of these two curves—that is, at point E.

Figure 2.2 shows the determination of macroeconomic equilibrium in a more general, four-quadrant diagram. Curves FF and GG are shown again in the northeast quadrant, which corresponds to figure 2.1. The northwest quadrant shows the inverse relationship between the loan rate and investment, as implied by (2.6). The equilibrium level of investment is reported in the southwest quadrant; the difference between that value and the fixed level of output $\bar{Y}$ shown in the southeast quadrant gives the equilibrium level of consumption. Macroeconomic equilibrium obtains at points E, D, H, and J.

2.1.3 Monetary Policy

The central bank can control directly the refinance rate and (for the moment) the required reserve ratio, which both affect market-determined interest rates. The effects of these policies are considered in turn.

Increase in refinance rate

To determine the general equilibrium effects of an increase, di^R, in the refinance rate, equations (2.17) and (2.18) can be totally differentiated and solved simultaneously for di^L and dP, changes in the loan rate and prices. In matrix form, this amounts to solving the system

$$\begin{bmatrix} 1 & -FF_P \\ 1 & -GG_P \end{bmatrix} \begin{bmatrix} di^L \\ dP \end{bmatrix} = \begin{bmatrix} FF_{i^R} \\ GG_{i^R} \end{bmatrix} di^R.$$

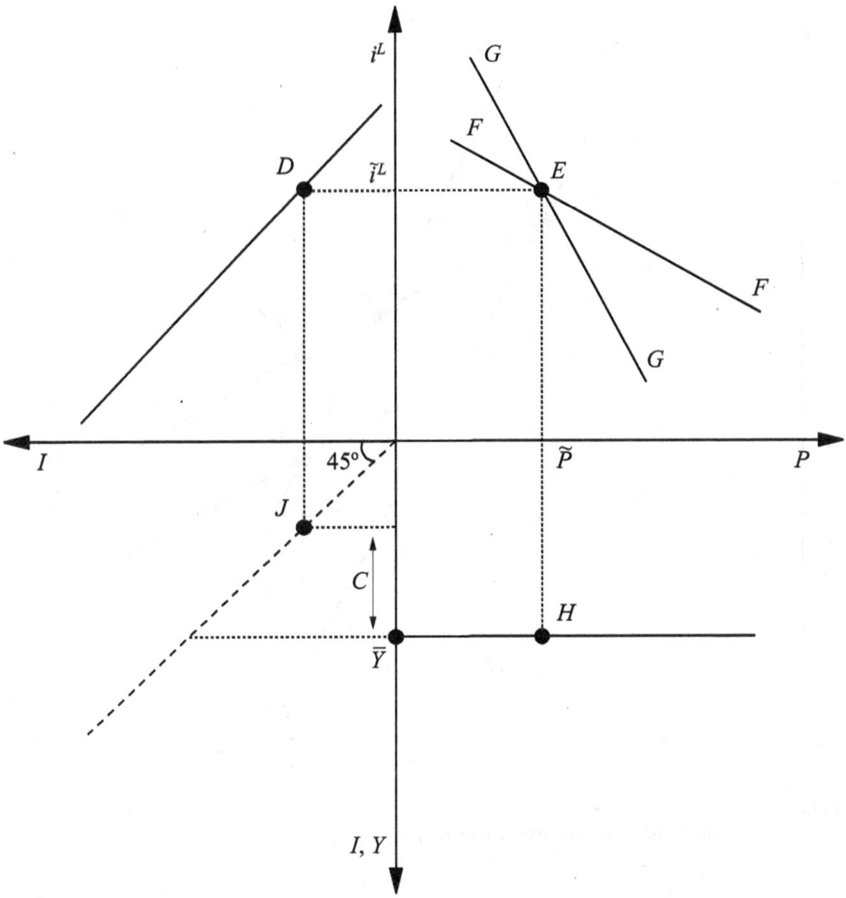

Figure 2.2
Macroeconomic equilibrium with exogenous output: Full diagram

Using Cramer's rule gives

$$\frac{di^L}{di^R} = \frac{\overset{(-)}{GG_{i^R}}\overset{(-)}{FF_P} - \overset{(+)}{FF_{i^R}}\overset{(-)}{GG_P}}{\underset{(-)}{FF_P} - \underset{(-)}{GG_P}}, \quad \frac{dP}{di^R} = \frac{\overset{(-)}{GG_{i^R}} - \overset{(+)}{FF_{i^R}}}{\underset{(-)}{FF_P} - \underset{(-)}{GG_P}}. \tag{2.22}$$

As noted earlier, the condition $-GG_P > -FF_P$, or equivalently $FF_P - GG_P > 0$, is required for dynamic stability. In addition, from the definitions of the partial derivatives provided earlier, $GG_{i^R}FF_P - FF_{i^R}GG_P > 0$ and $GG_{i^R} - FF_{i^R} < 0$. Thus, $di^L/di^R > 0$ and $dP/di^R < 0$. By implication, from (2.6) and (2.16), and given that output is constant,

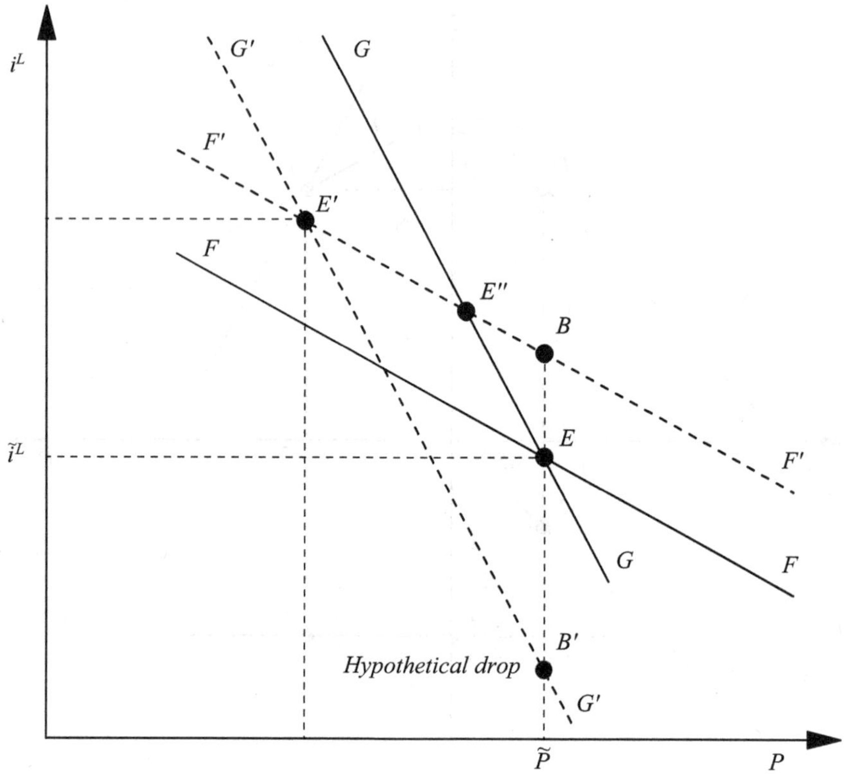

Figure 2.3
Increase in the refinance rate with exogenous output

$$\frac{dI}{di^R} = I'\left(\frac{di^L}{di^R}\right) < 0, \quad \frac{dC}{di^R} = -\frac{dI}{di^R} > 0.$$

These macroeconomic effects are illustrated in figures 2.3 and 2.4. The immediate impact of a higher refinance rate is an increase in the lending rate. Because an increase in the refinance rate raises the marginal cost of funds for lenders, it is "passed on" directly, and fully, to borrowers. Curve *FF* shifts upward or to the right, to $F'F'$.

On the goods market, there are two effects at play at the initial level of prices. First, the higher refinance rate raises directly the deposit rate, thereby lowering consumption as a result of intertemporal substitution. By itself, this reduces aggregate demand; for constant supply and given prices, restoring equilibrium requires a *fall* in the loan rate to stimulate investment. Graphically, curve *GG* shifts downward or to the left, to $G'G'$, and the loan rate would need to fall

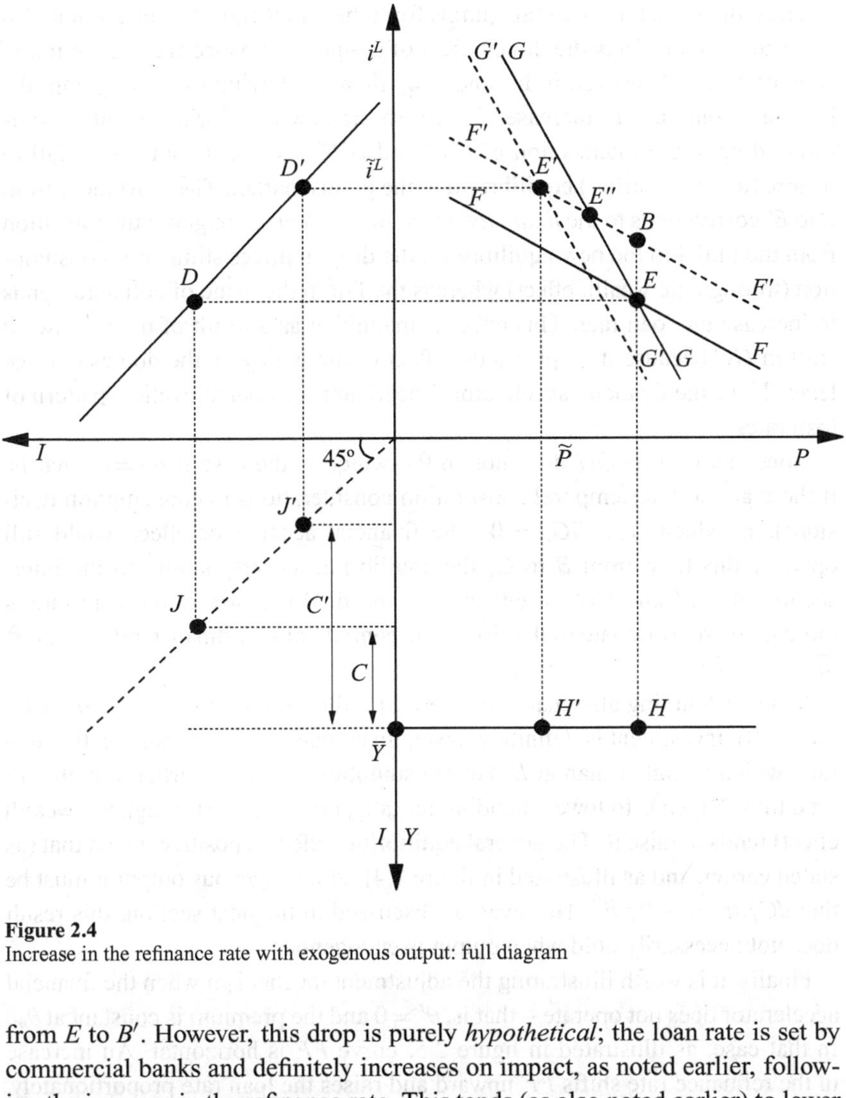

Figure 2.4
Increase in the refinance rate with exogenous output: full diagram

from E to B'. However, this drop is purely *hypothetical*; the loan rate is set by commercial banks and definitely increases on impact, as noted earlier, following the increase in the refinance rate. This tends (as also noted earlier) to lower investment immediately. The net effect on aggregate demand, at the initial level of prices, is thus unambiguously negative.

Because output is constant and nominal wealth predetermined, the fall in aggregate demand requires a drop in prices (which raises real wealth and consumption) to bring total demand back to its initial level and eventually restore equilibrium in the goods market. During that process, the continuous reduction in the price level lowers the value of collateralizable real assets and increases the premium, thereby inducing banks to further increase the loan rate.

Thus, on impact the loan rate jumps from the initial equilibrium at point E to point B, which reflects the direct effect of a higher refinance rate, at the initial level of prices. However, it does not stop there; following its initial jump, the loan rate continues to increase, from B to the new equilibrium point E', corresponding to the intersection of $F'F'$ and $G'G'$, as prices continue to fall to restore (as noted earlier) equilibrium in the goods market. The movement from B to E' corresponds to the *financial accelerator effect*; throughout the transition from the initial to the new equilibrium, the drop in prices stimulates consumption (through the wealth effect) whereas the fall in the value of collateral tends to increase the loan rate. This effect is magnified as a result of the downward shift in GG because it amplifies the effect of the policy on the domestic price level. Thus, the financial accelerator exacerbates the countercyclical pattern of loan rates.

Note that even if GG does not shift—which is the case if $\alpha_2 = 0$ (that is, if there are no intertemporal substitution considerations in consumption decisions), in which case $GG_{i^R} = 0$—the financial accelerator effect would still operate, this time from B to C, the equilibrium corresponding to the intersection of $F'F'$ and GG. In either case, the final increase in the loan rate is more than proportionate to the rise in the central bank's refinance rate—that is, $di^L/di^R > 1$.[14]

It is worth noting also that at the new equilibrium (point E' if $\alpha_2 > 0$, or E'' if $\alpha_2 = 0$), investment is definitely lower, given that it depends only on the loan rate, which is higher than at E. For consumption, as noted earlier, a higher i^R (and thus i^D) tends to lower spending initially, but lower P (through the wealth effect) tends to raise it. The general equilibrium effect is positive, given that (as stated earlier, and as illustrated in figure 2.4) with exogenous output it must be that $dC/di^R = -dI/di^R$. However, as discussed in the next section, this result does not necessarily hold when output is endogenous.

Finally, it is worth illustrating the adjustment mechanism when the financial accelerator does not operate—that is, $\theta' = 0$ and the premium is constant at θ_m. In that case, as illustrated in figure 2.5, curve FF is horizontal. An increase in the refinance rate shifts FF upward and raises the loan rate proportionately, so that $di^L/di^R = 1$. The loan rate jumps to point B and remains at that value while prices fall gradually from point B to point E'. Thus, without the financial accelerator effect, the contraction in investment is smaller, and so is the drop in prices and the increase in consumption.

14. From (2.22), in order for $di^L/di^R > 1$, it must be that $GG_{i^R}FF_P - FF_{i^R}GG_P > FF_P - GG_P$. Given that $FF_{i^R} = 1$, this expression boils down to $FF_P(1 - GG_{i^R}) < 0$, which always holds given that $GG_{i^R} \leq 0$ when $\alpha_2 \geq 0$ and $FF_P < 0$.

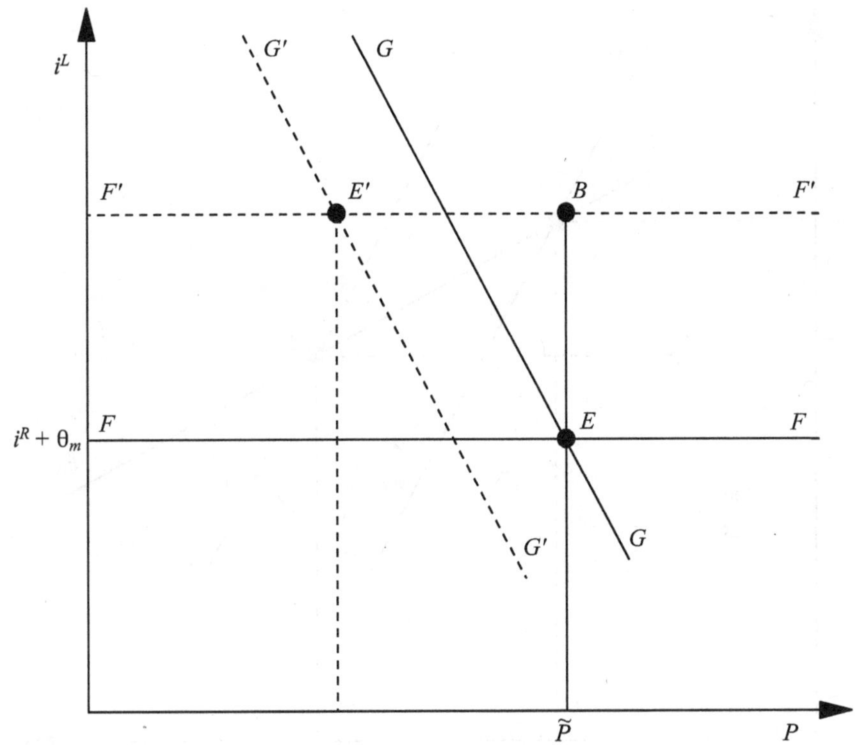

Figure 2.5
Increase in the refinance rate with exogenous output and constant premium

Increase in required reserve ratio

Consider now an increase in the required reserve ratio, μ. As before, equilibrium changes in the loan rate and the price level can be established by totally differentiating and solving (2.17) and (2.18) simultaneously for di^L and dP:

$$\begin{bmatrix} 1 & -FF_P \\ 1 & -GG_P \end{bmatrix} \begin{bmatrix} di^L \\ dP \end{bmatrix} = \begin{bmatrix} 0 \\ GG_\mu \end{bmatrix} d\mu,$$

which gives

$$\frac{di^L}{d\mu} = \frac{\overset{(+)}{GG_\mu}\overset{(-)}{FF_P}}{\underset{(-)}{FF_P} - \underset{(-)}{GG_P}}, \quad \frac{dP}{d\mu} = \frac{\overset{(+)}{GG_\mu}}{\underset{(-)}{FF_P} - \underset{(-)}{GG_P}}. \tag{2.23}$$

With dynamic stability requiring again $-GG_P > -FF_P$, these expressions yield $di^L/d\mu < 0$ and $dP/d\mu > 0$.

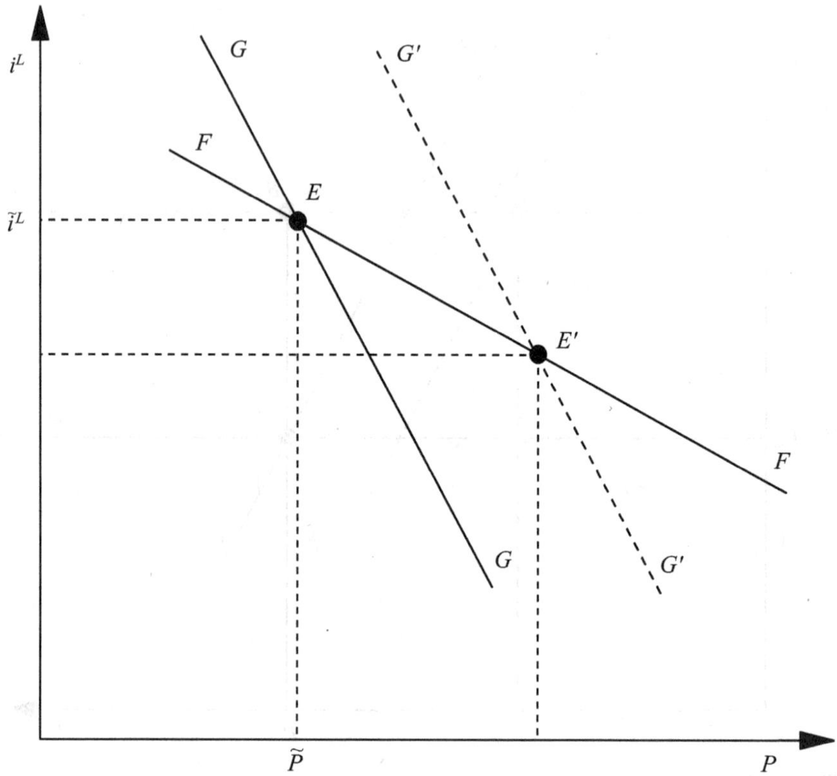

Figure 2.6
Increase in the required reserve ratio with exogenous output

These results are depicted in figure 2.6.[15] The immediate effect of the policy is to lower the deposit rate, which reduces the incentive to save and stimulates current consumption.[16] At the initial level of prices the increase in aggregate demand requires a higher loan rate to clear the goods market; thus *GG* shifts upward or to the left, to $G'G'$. The increase in the deposit rate has no effect on banks' marginal funding cost, which remains constant and equal to the refinance rate; thus, *FF* does not shift (reflecting $FF_{\mu} = 0$). The transition takes the economy from the initial equilibrium at point *E* to the new equilibrium at point E', where $G'G'$ and *FF* intersect. The new equilibrium is characterized

15. The four-quadrant diagram corresponding to figure 2.4 is omitted to save space.

16. Recall that it is beginning-of-period financial wealth that affects current consumption. Thus, the portfolio effect associated with the change in the deposit rate has no direct effect on macroeconomic equilibrium.

by a lower loan rate, higher investment, and higher prices. Thus, the policy is inflationary. There is some evidence to that effect; in their study of Brazil, Glocker and Towbin (2015) found that positive shocks to reserve requirements tend to increase inflation. However, as discussed later and in subsequent chapters, this result does not hold in the presence of imperfect substitutability (from the perspective of the monetary authority) between deposits and central bank liquidity.[17]

2.2 Endogenous Output and the Cost Channel

The core model presented earlier is now extended to account for the supply side, with endogenous output and employment. An important new assumption is that to finance their working capital needs, which consist solely of labor costs, firms must borrow a fraction of their wage bill from the banking system. As documented in chapter 1, in MICs it is indeed common for firms in the formal economy to borrow from banks to finance the purchase of inputs at the start of the production process.

2.2.1 Supply Side

As before, firms produce a single homogeneous good, but output is now endogenous. In addition, firms cannot issue debt or claims on their capital stock. All wages must be paid in advance (at the beginning of the period)—that is, before production and sales take place. However, firms have limited cash flow; therefore, they must also borrow from banks to pay a fraction of their wage bill. Total production costs faced by the representative firm are thus equal to the wage bill plus the interest payments made on bank loans. For simplicity, loans contracted for the purpose of financing working capital are not subject to default and are therefore made at a rate that reflects only the refinance rate, i^R.[18] Firms repay working capital loans, with interest, at the end of the period, after goods have been produced and sold. Profits, if any, are transferred at the end of each period to the firms' owners, households.

17. Alternatively, suppose that interest on deposits is paid *during* the period (rather than at the end, as assumed in the text), based on the beginning-of-period value D_0. The consumption function would now take the form $C = \alpha_1(\bar{Y} + i^D D_0) - \alpha_2 i^D + \alpha_3 P^{-1} F_0^H$, with again $i^D = (1-\mu)i^R$. If $\alpha_2 < \alpha_1$, an increase in μ would now *reduce* consumption and the policy would be deflationary. In that case a higher refinance rate would also *increase* consumption on impact, at the initial level of prices. But because now both *FF* and *GG* shift upward, or to the right, the previous results regarding the equilibrium effects of an increase in i^R would not necessarily hold. A graphical analysis of this particular case is left to the interested reader.

18. Assuming that banks add a fixed profit margin over and above the refinance rate would not affect the results qualitatively.

Let W denote the nominal wage, N the quantity of labor employed, and $\psi_W \in (0, 1)$ the fraction of the wage bill, WN, which is financed by bank borrowing. Total production costs, inclusive of borrowing costs, are thus $(1+i^R)\psi_W WN + (1-\psi_W)WN$, or $(1+\psi_W i^R)WN$. The maximization problem faced by the representative firm can be written as

$$N = \arg\max[PY - (1+\psi_W i^R)WN], \tag{2.24}$$

where Y and P are as defined earlier.

The production function takes a standard Cobb-Douglas form,

$$Y = N^\alpha K_0^{1-\alpha}, \tag{2.25}$$

where $\alpha \in (0, 1)$.

Substituting (2.25) in (2.24), and taking K_0, i^R, P, and W as given, the first-order condition of the firm's maximization problem is

$$\alpha P N^{\alpha-1} K_0^{1-\alpha} - (1+\psi_W i^R)W = 0.$$

Defining the real wage as $\omega = W/P$, this condition yields the demand for labor as

$$N^d = \left[\frac{\alpha}{(1+\psi_W i^R)\omega}\right]^{1/(1-\alpha)} K_0, \tag{2.26}$$

which can be substituted in (2.25) to give

$$Y^s = \left[\frac{\alpha}{(1+\psi_W i^R)\omega}\right]^{\alpha/(1-\alpha)} K_0. \tag{2.27}$$

These equations show that labor demand and goods supply are inversely related to the *effective* cost of labor, $(1+\psi_W i^R)\omega$.

Given the short-run nature of the model, the nominal wage is assumed fixed at $\bar{W}$.[19] Because this implies that $d\omega = -(\bar{W}/P^2)dP$, (2.26) and (2.27) yield

$$N^d = N^d(P; i^R), \quad Y^s = Y^s(P; i^R), \tag{2.28}$$

with

$$N_P^d = \left(\frac{1}{1-\alpha}\right)\frac{N^d}{\omega}\left(\frac{\bar{W}}{P^2}\right) = \left(\frac{1}{1-\alpha}\right)\frac{N^d}{P} > 0, \quad Y_P^s = \left(\frac{\alpha}{1-\alpha}\right)\frac{Y^s}{P} > 0,$$

$$N_{i^R}^d = -\left(\frac{\psi_W}{1-\alpha}\right)\frac{N^d}{1+\psi_W i^R} < 0, \quad Y_{i^R}^s = -\left(\frac{\alpha\psi_W}{1-\alpha}\right)\frac{Y^s}{1+\psi_W i^R} < 0.$$

19. Assuming that the nominal wage is indexed to the price level would not alter qualitatively the results, as long as indexation is less than perfect.

A reduction in prices (which raises the real wage) or an increase in the cost of borrowing (as long as $\psi_W > 0$) exert a contractionary effect on employment and output. If firms do not borrow in advance, $\psi_W = 0$ and $N^d_{i^R} = Y^s_{i^R} = 0$.

Investment is again given by (2.6). Combined with (2.7), the stock of bank loans at the end of the period is now the sum of loans allocated to finance both labor costs and capital accumulation:

$$L = \psi_W \bar{W} N^d(P; i^R) + L^K_0 + P \cdot I(i^R - \pi^e). \tag{2.29}$$

Given that profits from production (if any) are distributed only at the end of the period, consumption depends positively now only on labor income, in addition to (as before) the real deposit rate and real wealth:[20]

$$C = \alpha_0 + \alpha_1 \frac{\bar{W} N^d(P; i^R)}{P} - \alpha_2(i^D - \pi^e) + \alpha_3 \left(\frac{F^H_0}{P}\right). \tag{2.30}$$

Other equations of the model remain the same. Those needed to solve the model are (2.6), (2.10), (2.11), (2.12), and (2.16), which are combined and repeated here for convenience:

$$i^D = (1 - \mu) i^R, \tag{2.31}$$

$$i^L = i^R + \theta \left(\frac{\kappa P K_0}{L^K_0}\right), \tag{2.32}$$

$$Y^s = C + I(i^L - \pi^e). \tag{2.33}$$

Finally, household labor supply is assumed to be perfectly elastic at the going wage. Employment is therefore determined by the demand side of the labor market. This assumption (which implies that effort provides no disutility) helps to simplify the analysis by avoiding the case where, given that the nominal wage is exogenous, unemployment emerges in equilibrium.

2.2.2 Macroeconomic Equilibrium

To solve the model, the first step once again is to solve for the financial sector equilibrium condition. Combining (2.11) and (2.12), or using directly (2.32), yields as before (2.17), which is also repeated here for convenience:

$$i^L = FF(P; i^R, \mu). \tag{2.34}$$

20. The appendix discusses an alternative specification to (2.30) in which consumption depends on total income, rather than wage income only. Although not strictly consistent with the underlying timing of transactions, as described earlier, adopting it could be useful for expositional purposes.

As shown earlier, $FF_P < 0$, $FF_{i^R} = 1$, and $FF_\mu = 0$. The interpretation of these partial derivatives is the same as before. In particular, a rise in prices lowers the premium because it increases the effective value of firms' collateral, which in turn mitigates the borrower's incentive to default. An increase in the refinance rate raises the marginal cost of funds for banks, and this is passed on *pari passu* to borrowers.

The second step involves again solving the equilibrium condition of the goods market, (2.33), this time with the demand for labor and the supply of goods given in (2.28). Substituting that equation, together with (2.30) and (2.31), in condition (2.33) gives, setting $\bar{W} = 1$ for simplicity,

$$Y^s(P; i^R) = \alpha_1 \frac{N^d(P; i^R)}{P} - \alpha_2[(1-\mu)i^R - \pi^e] + \alpha_3 \left(\frac{F_0^H}{P}\right) + I(i^L - \pi^e). \tag{2.35}$$

Totally differentiating this expression yields

$$Y_P^s dP + Y_{i^R}^s di^R = \alpha_1 \left[\left(\frac{N_P^d}{P}\right) dP - \frac{N^d}{P^2} dP + \left(\frac{N_{i^R}^d}{P}\right) di^R\right]$$
$$- \alpha_2(1-\mu)di^R + \alpha_2 i^R d\mu - \alpha_3 \left(\frac{F_0^H}{P^2}\right) dP + I' di^L,$$

which gives

$$i^L = GG(P; i^R, \mu), \tag{2.36}$$

where

$$GG_P = \frac{1}{I'} \left\{ Y_P^s + \frac{\alpha_1}{P^2}(N^d - PN_P^d) + \alpha_3 \left(\frac{F_0^H}{P^2}\right) \Big] \right\},$$

$$GG_{i^R} = \frac{1}{I'} \left\{ Y_{i^R}^s - \alpha_1 \left(\frac{N_{i^R}^d}{P}\right) + \alpha_2(1-\mu) \right\},$$

$$GG_\mu = -\frac{\alpha_2 i^R}{I'} > 0.$$

The partial derivative with respect to the required reserve ratio, GG_μ, takes the same form as before and its sign remains also the same. However, the other two partial derivatives are now more complex and their sign must be established.

Consider first the effect of an increase in prices on the loan rate. This effect is measured by GG_P and can be decomposed as follows. As before, a rise in prices tends to lower aggregate demand through a negative wealth effect on consumption. However, the increase in prices now also (a) boosts aggregate supply by reducing the real wage and (b) may raise or lower consumption as a result of conflicting effects on labor demand and factor income. Indeed, following a rise in prices, real wages fall whereas labor demand increases; the net effect of wage income, ωN, on consumption depends on the sign of $N_P^d - N^d/P$. From the definition of N_P^d in (2.28), $N_P^d = (1-\alpha)^{-1}P^{-1}N^d$; thus

$$N_P^d - \frac{N^d}{P} = \left(\frac{1}{1-\alpha} - 1\right)\frac{N^d}{P} = \left(\frac{\alpha}{1-\alpha}\right)\frac{N^d}{P} > 0.$$

The net effect on the loan rate depends on how much aggregate supply increases, relative to the change in aggregate demand—which itself depends on the magnitude of the income and wealth effects on consumption. It can readily be established that, even though the wage income effect of higher prices is in general ambiguous (as noted earlier), the supply effect always dominates the wage income effect. Given that the wealth effect tends to lower consumption, an increase in prices always creates excess supply. Therefore, the loan rate must fall to stimulate investment and restore equilibrium in the goods market. By implication, $GG_P < 0$.

To establish this result formally, first it can be shown that $Y_P^s + \alpha_1 P^{-2}(N^d - PN_P^d)$, the sum of the supply and wage income effects associated with higher prices is positive. Indeed, the first result in (2.28) yields again

$$N^d - PN_P^d = N^d - \left(\frac{1}{1-\alpha}\right)N^d = -\left(\frac{\alpha}{1-\alpha}\right)N^d,$$

so that using the second result in (2.28) yields

$$Y_P^s + \alpha_1\left(\frac{N^d - PN_P^d}{P^2}\right) = \left(\frac{\alpha}{1-\alpha}\right)\frac{Y^s}{P} - \alpha_1\left(\frac{\alpha}{1-\alpha}\right)\frac{N^d}{P^2}$$

$$= \left[\frac{\alpha}{(1-\alpha)P}\right]\left(Y^s - \alpha_1\frac{N^d}{P}\right).$$

From (2.26) and (2.27), it can also be established that

$$Y^s - \alpha_1\frac{N^d}{P} = K_0P^{\alpha/(1-\alpha)}\left(\frac{\alpha}{1+\psi_W i^R}\right)^{1/(1-\alpha)}\left[\left(\frac{1+\psi_W i^R}{\alpha}\right) - \alpha_1\right] > 0, \tag{2.37}$$

where the inequality holds because

$$\frac{1+\psi_W i^R}{\alpha} > \frac{1}{\alpha} > 1 > \alpha_1.$$

Now, given that $\alpha_3(F_0^H/P^2) > 0$, the expression in brackets in the definition of GG_P is also positive. And because $I' < 0$, the result is indeed $GG_P < 0$.

Consider next the effect of an increase in the refinance rate on the loan rate. This effect is measured by GG_{i^R} and is ambiguous in sign. By inducing a rise in the deposit rate and the incentive to save, a higher refinance rate lowers consumption and aggregate demand. To maintain equilibrium in the goods market at the initial levels of output and prices, investment must increase, and this in turn requires a fall in the loan rate. This effect is the same as the one discussed earlier. In addition, an increase in the refinance rate reduces now also aggregate supply through its effect on the effective cost of labor (captured through $Y^s_{i^R}$) and aggregate demand through a reduction in labor income. The contractionary effect on output is known as the *Cavallo-Patman effect*, emphasized by New Structuralist economists (see Taylor 1983; van Wijnbergen 1982, and Buffie 1984). The latter effect (captured by the term $\alpha_1 N^d_{i^R}$) compounds the direct negative impact on aggregate demand. But because both aggregate supply and aggregate demand fall, the loan rate should either increase or fall to maintain equilibrium in the goods market. If aggregate supply falls relatively more, the loan rate will need to *increase* to further dampen investment and eliminate excess demand ($GG_{i^R} > 0$). Alternatively, it will have to fall ($GG_{i^R} < 0$).

If ψ_W, the proportion of wage costs financed by bank credit is sufficiently small to ensure that $GG_{i^R} < 0$, then the case considered in the previous section when output is exogenous (excess supply following an increase in the refinance rate) will prevail. By extension, the assumption that $GG_{i^R} < 0$ ($GG_{i^R} > 0$) corresponds to the case where the cost channel of monetary policy is weak (strong).

Formally, given that $I' < 0$, in order for $GG_{i^R} < 0$ it must be that $Y^s_{i^R} - \alpha_1 P^{-1} N^d_{i^R} + \alpha_2(1-\mu) > 0$; at the same time, from (2.28),

$$Y^s_{i^R} - \alpha_1\left(\frac{N^d_{i^R}}{P}\right) = -\left(\frac{\psi_W}{1-\alpha}\right)\left(\frac{1}{1+\psi_W i^R}\right)\left[\alpha Y^s - \alpha_1\left(\frac{N^d}{P}\right)\right], \tag{2.38}$$

whereas, again from (2.26) and (2.27),

$$\alpha Y^s - \alpha_1\left(\frac{N^d}{P}\right) = K_0 P^{\alpha/(1-\alpha)}\left(\frac{\alpha}{1+\psi_W i^R}\right)^{1/(1-\alpha)}(1+\psi_W i^R - \alpha_1) > 0, \tag{2.39}$$

where the inequality holds because $\alpha_1 < 1$. Combining the last two results yields

$$Y^s_{i^R} - \alpha_1 \left(\frac{N^d_{i^R}}{P} \right) < 0, \tag{2.40}$$

which implies that the supply-side effect of i^R dominates (in absolute terms) the demand-side income effect.

For $GG_{i^R} < 0$ it must therefore be that, given (2.40),

$$\alpha_2(1-\mu) > \alpha_1 \left(\frac{N^d_{i^R}}{P} \right) - Y^s_{i^R} > 0,$$

which can be combined with (2.38) and (2.39) to give an implicit restriction on ψ_W.[21] Of course, if $\psi_W = 0$, the condition for $GG_{i^R} < 0$ boils down to

$$\alpha_2(1-\mu) > 0,$$

which always holds for $\alpha_2 > 0$.

The equilibrium is shown in figure 2.7. The financial and goods market equilibrium curves, *FF* and *GG*, are shown in the northeast quadrant of the figure. Because $GG_P < 0$ and $FF_P < 0$, once again the two curves have a negative slope. Moreover, with $a_{12} = FF_P$ and $a_{22} = -I'GG_P$ in the dynamic system (2.21) keeping the same sign, local stability requires as before that the slope of *GG* be steeper than the slope of *FF*. As in figure 2.2 also, the northwest quadrant shows the negative relationship between the lending rate and investment; this value is then reported in the southwest quadrant. The difference is that the aggregate supply curve in the southeast quadrant, denoted *YY*, is no longer a flat line but is instead increasing with prices, as implied by (2.28). The difference between output and investment gives once again the equilibrium level of consumption. The economy's equilibrium corresponds to points *E*, *D*, *H*, and *J*.

2.2.3 Monetary Policy

As before, consider the macroeconomic effects of increases in the refinance rate and the required reserve ratio.

Increase in refinance rate

As before, to determine the general equilibrium effects of shocks on the core variables, the loan rate, and the price level, equations (2.34) and (2.36) must be solved simultaneously for i^L and P. The equilibrium response to a shock to the

21. Of course, this restriction must be such that ψ_W is less than unity.

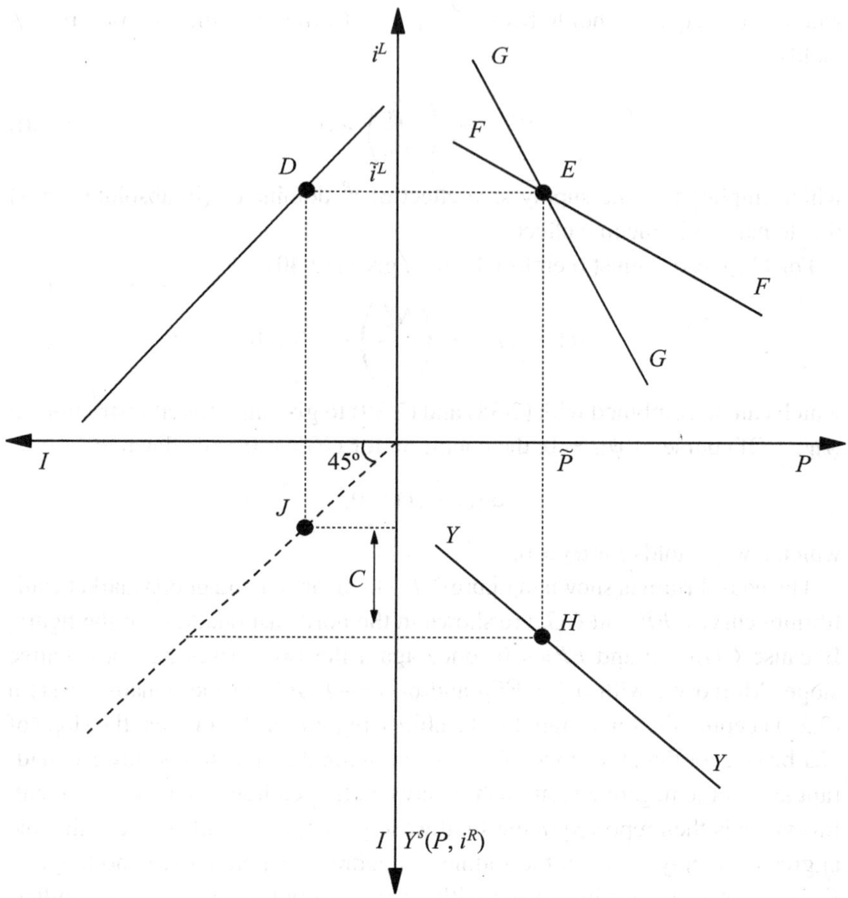

Figure 2.7
Macroeconomic equilibrium with endogenous output

refinance rate can be evaluated by solving once again the system

$$\begin{bmatrix} 1 & -FF_P \\ 1 & -GG_P \end{bmatrix} \begin{bmatrix} di^L \\ dP \end{bmatrix} = \begin{bmatrix} FF_{i^R} \\ GG_{i^R} \end{bmatrix} di^R,$$

which gives

$$\frac{di^L}{di^R} = \frac{\overset{(?)}{GG_{i^R}}\overset{(-)}{FF_P} - \overset{(+)}{FF_{i^R}}\overset{(-)}{GG_P}}{\underset{(-)}{FF_P} - \underset{(-)}{GG_P}}, \quad \frac{dP}{di^R} = \frac{\overset{(?)}{GG_{i^R}} - \overset{(+)}{FF_{i^R}}}{\underset{(-)}{FF_P} - \underset{(-)}{GG_P}}. \tag{2.41}$$

As noted earlier, the condition $|GG_P| > |FF_P|$ is required for local stability. Thus, $FF_P - GG_P > 0$. However, the numerator in both expressions is

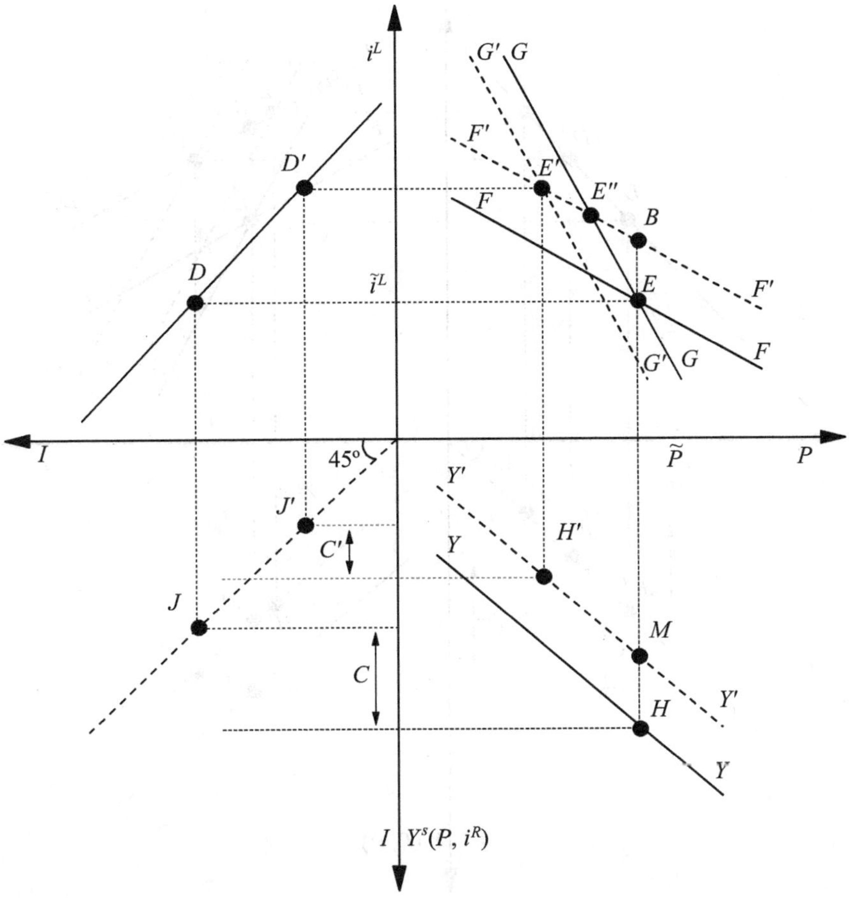

Figure 2.8
Increase in the refinance rate with endogenous output: weak cost channel

now ambiguous in general, so $di^L/di^R \gtrless 0$ and $dP/di^R \gtrless 0$. If, as in the case with exogenous output, $GG_{i^R} < 0$, the results are the same as those established previously: $di^L/di^R > 0$ and $dP/di^R < 0$.

The macroeconomic effects of an increase in the refinance rate are illustrated in figure 2.8 for the case where ψ_W is relatively small (so that the cost channel is weak and $GG_{i^R} < 0$), and in figure 2.9 for the case where the combination of ψ_W and other parameters is such that the cost channel is strong and $GG_{i^R} > 0$.

Consider first figure 2.8. The policy exerts three immediate effects. First, there is a direct impact on the loan rate; because an increase in the refinance rate raises the marginal cost of funds, it is "passed on" directly and fully to borrowers. In the northeast quadrant, curve FF shifts outward to $F'F'$ and the loan

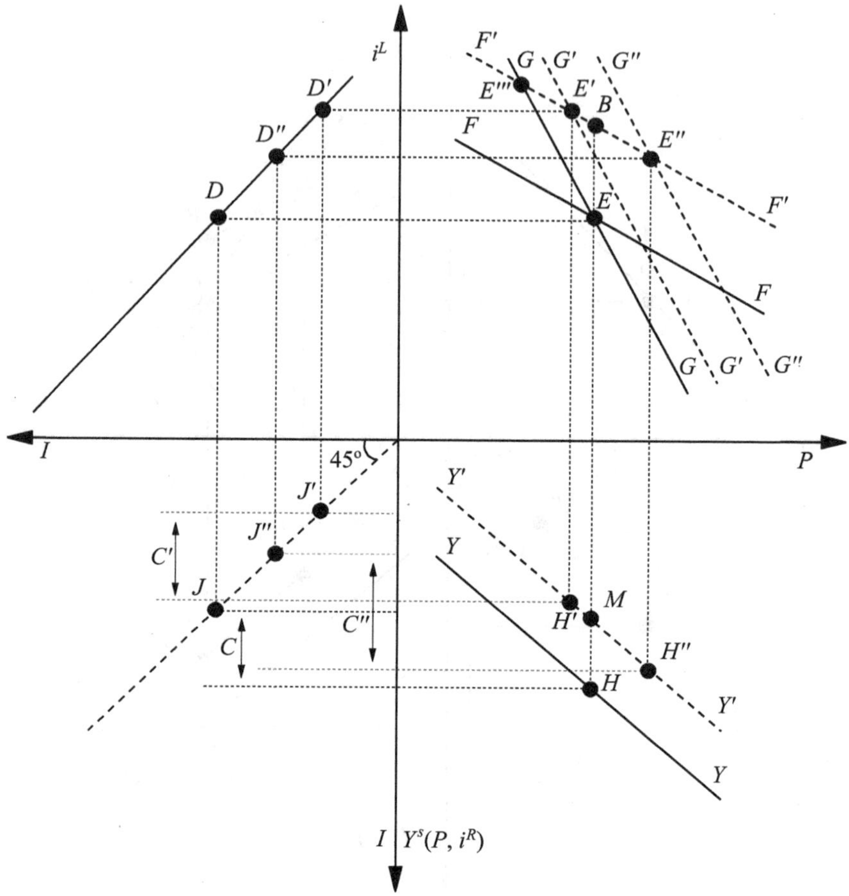

Figure 2.9
Increase in the refinance rate with endogenous output: strong cost channel

rate increases on impact from point E to B. This increase is accompanied by a contraction in investment. Second, because a higher refinance rate also raises the deposit rate, intertemporal substitution leads to a drop in consumption; this leads to an inward shift in GG to $G'G'$. These two effects are the same as those discussed before, with exogenous output; they both operate through aggregate demand. In addition, there is a third effect now—a higher refinance rate also raises production costs and lowers output. Graphically, production drops from point H to M on impact, following an inward shift of the supply curve in the southeast quadrant from YY to $Y'Y'$. At points B and M, both aggregate demand and aggregate supply are lower, but because $GG_{i^R} < 0$, the drop in demand is larger; there is therefore *excess supply* at the initial level of prices.

The transition from the initial equilibrium at E to the new equilibrium at E' proceeds therefore in the same way as before: As prices fall, the loan rate increases from B to E', a movement that corresponds to the accelerator effect. With prices falling, the value of collateral falls also, thereby inducing banks to raise the premium and the loan rate; and through a positive wealth effect, consumption tends to increase. However, in addition, the fall in prices raises the real wage, which reduces supply. After falling from H to M on the new curve $Y'Y'$, output continues to fall from M to H'. This reduction in output and employment translates into lower income for households, which tends to reduce consumption. Thus, while investment unambiguously falls (as before), consumption may now either increase or decrease in the new equilibrium.[22] In the scenario shown in figure 2.8, consumption actually falls (from the distance C to C' in the southwest quadrant) due to a relatively large drop in output.

Consider next the case where $GG_{i^R} > 0$, which is illustrated in figure 2.9. This time, following an increase in the refinance rate curve GG shifts *outward*. But even in that scenario, it is still possible that it does not shift by a large amount; if so, the adjustment process for i^L and P is qualitatively the same as what obtains with $GG_{i^R} < 0$. Formally, from (2.41), given again that the denominator is positive, this occurs if the numerators are such that

$$\overset{(+)}{GG_{i^R}}\overset{(-)}{FF_P} - \overset{(+)}{FF_{i^R}}\overset{(-)}{GG_P} > 0, \quad \overset{(+)}{GG_{i^R}} - \overset{(+)}{FF_{i^R}} < 0,$$

or equivalently, given that (as shown earlier) $FF_{i^R} = 1$,

$$GG_{i^R} > \frac{GG_P}{FF_P} > 0, \quad GG_{i^R} < 1.$$

If these conditions hold, the adjustment process is exactly as before. In particular, the loan rate will follow the path EBE', and aggregate supply will follow the path HMH', just as in figure 2.8. The financial accelerator effect therefore continues to operate. Intuitively, at the initial level of prices, the increase in the refinance rate lowers supply by more than demand, as a result of a strong cost channel. To eliminate excess demand and restore equilibrium of the goods market, the loan rate would need to increase by, say, an amount x to reduce investment. Thus, GG shifts up (or to the right), just like FF. However, the *actual* increase in the loan rate, from point E to point B, resulting from banks passing on the increase in the refinance rate to their borrowers, may be larger than x. If so, the drop in investment is larger than what would be required to restore equilibrium between supply and demand on the goods market, and

22. Also, as before, if there is no intertemporal effect ($\alpha_2 = 0$), the new equilibrium would be at E'' instead of E'.

excess supply prevails as before—implying that prices begin to fall, while the loan rate continues to rise from B to E'.

However, if either one of the conditions stated above, or both, fails to hold, then alternative scenarios may occur. Indeed, figure 2.9 illustrates also the case where the first condition holds but the second does not. This corresponds to a scenario where the cost channel is strong, as noted earlier. In this case, the adjustment process leads to *stagflation*: lower output and higher prices (points E'' and H''). In addition, the transition process is now characterized by a *financial decelerator* effect. On impact, the loan rate jumps again from E to B, but at that point there is *excess demand*, rather than excess supply. As a result, prices during the transition are *increasing*, instead of falling. The value of collateral therefore rises, lowering the premium in the process. The loan rate falls gradually, from B to E''. At the same time, higher prices tend to lower consumption through the wealth effect and to raise output by reducing real wages. After dropping on impact from point H to point M, output begins to expand and increases to the new equilibrium point H''. However, in the case illustrated in the figure, the benefit from a reduction in real labor costs does not allow activity to fully recover; at the new equilibrium production is still lower than it was initially. The combination of higher prices and lower output in the new equilibrium shows indeed that, when the cost channel is strong, a restrictive monetary policy can be stagflationary.[23] In addition, despite output being lower, consumption is higher in the new equilibrium (distance C'' compared to C) due to a relatively larger contraction in investment.

Note also that now the absence of an intertemporal effect ($\alpha_2 = 0$) is no longer sufficient to obtain $GG_{i^R} = 0$ and for GG to remain unchanged, following an increase in the refinance rate. Indeed, in that case

$$GG_{i^R} = \frac{1}{I'}\left\{Y^s_{i^R} - \alpha_1\left(\frac{N^d_{i^R}}{P}\right)\right\} > 0,$$

given that $I' < 0$ and, as shown earlier in equation (2.40), $Y^s_{i^R} - \alpha_1 P^{-1} N^d_{i^R} < 0$. Thus, curve GG always shifts to the right when $\alpha_2 = 0$. Whether the financial accelerator effect (corresponding to the movement from B to E'' in figure 2.8) exists or not depends on the magnitude of the shift in GG, as noted earlier. If there is excess supply (demand) on impact the adjustment process will follow the path EBE' (EBE'') and the new equilibrium will entail a combination of a

23. The positive correlation between policy interest rates and inflation has also been observed in advanced economies, and the cost channel emphasized here has been proposed as an explanation of this *price puzzle* (see Henzel et al. 2009), although parameter identifcation problems may be the culprit (see Estrella 2015).

higher loan rate and lower (higher) prices.[24] For GG not to shift requires not only the absence of an intertemporal effect, $\alpha_2 = 0$, but also no cost channel—or equivalently no borrowing to finance working capital needs, $\psi_W = 0$, in which case $Y^s_{i^R} = N^d_{i^R} = 0$ and thus $GG_{i^R} = 0$. In that case, the new equilibrium would be at E''' and curve YY in the southeast quadrant in figures 2.8 and 2.9 would not shift either in response to an increase in the refinance rate.

Increase in required reserve ratio

The effects of an increase in the required reserve ratio are illustrated in figure 2.10. The results are very similar to those discussed earlier (see figure 2.6): Curve *FF* does not change, whereas curve *GG* shifts outward. In the new equilibrium, the loan rate is lower and both investment and prices are higher. As a result, real wages are lower and aggregate output is also higher. The combination of higher investment and higher output means that consumption may again either rise or fall; in the case shown in the figure, consumption increases, due to a relatively large increase in output. As discussed later, these positive effects on output and prices do not hold under more general assumptions.

2.3 Default Premium and Monopolistic Competition

The foregoing discussion assumed that commercial banks set the lending rate on the basis of the marginal cost of funds and a premium to reflect the possibility of default, and that this premium (or credit spread) varies inversely with the value of collateral. But explicit microfoundations were not provided.

As a step in that direction, suppose that, as before, banks are competitive in the market for deposits, implying that the no-arbitrage condition (2.10) continues to hold. But now they provide differentiated loans to a continuum of firms, defined over the interval (0, 1), in an environment of monopolistic competition. The supply of credit is perfectly elastic at the prevailing loan rate and therefore the total amount of lending provided by banks is given as before by (2.7). The balance sheet of bank $i \in (0, 1)$ is again given by (2.8),

$$L^i + RR^i = D^i + L^{B,i}, \tag{2.42}$$

where $L^i = L^{K,i}$ and RR^i is defined as in (2.9).

The amount borrowed by each firm $j \in (0, 1)$ is a Dixit-Stiglitz basket of differentiated loans, each supplied by a bank i, with a constant elasticity of

24. The case where the shift in *GG* is so large that the new equilibrium is characterized by higher prices and a *lower* loan rate can be ruled out as a curiosity.

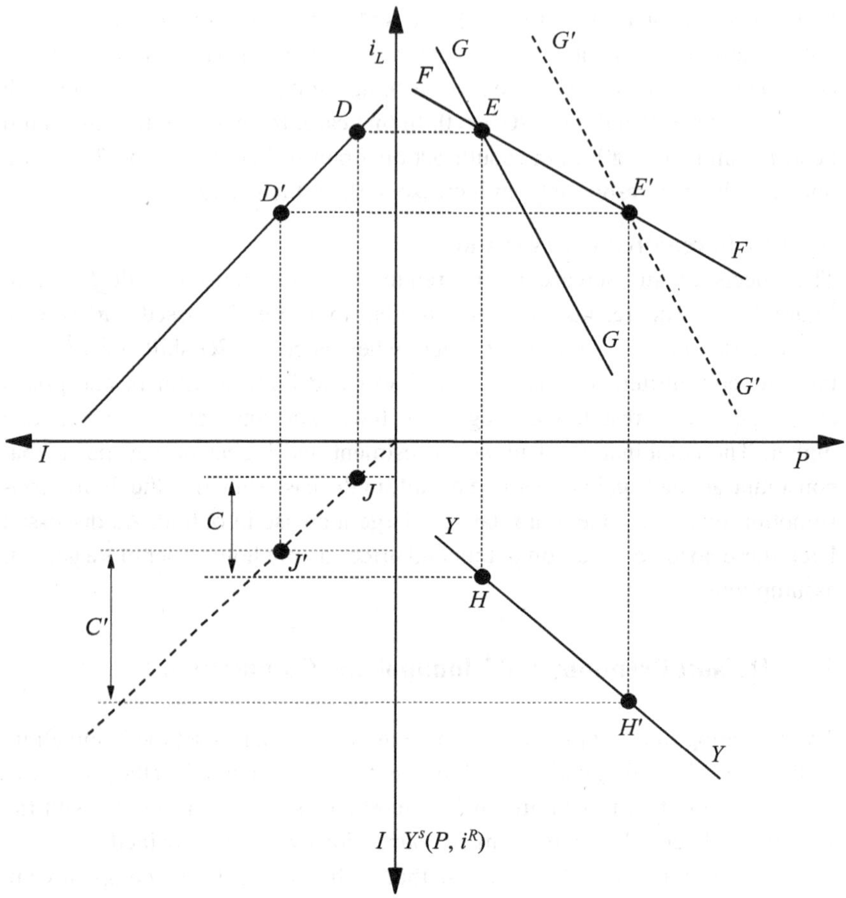

Figure 2.10
Increase in the required reserve ratio with endogenous output and no liability composition effect

substitution $\zeta^L > 1$:[25]

$$L^{K,j} = \left[\int_0^1 (L^{K,j,i})^{(\zeta^L-1)/\zeta^L} di \right]^{\zeta^L/(\zeta^L-1)}. \tag{2.43}$$

Omitting the superscript j for simplicity, the demand for type-i loan, $L^{K,i}$, is thus given by the downward-sloping curve

25. The Dixit-Stiglitz specification used in (2.43) is convenient because it provides a tractable means of introducing monopolistic competition. It is a common feature of dynamic stochastic general equilibrium models and is further discussed in chapter 4.

$$L^{K,i} = \left(\frac{1+i^{L,i}}{1+i^L}\right)^{-\varsigma^L} L^K, \tag{2.44}$$

where $1+i^{L,i}$ is the gross interest rate on the loan extended by bank i and

$$1+i^L = \left[\int_0^1 (1+i^{L,i})^{1-\varsigma^L} di\right]^{1/(1-\varsigma^L)}$$

is the aggregate gross loan rate.

Each bank sets the (gross) loan rate so as to maximize the present value of expected profits, taking the repayment probability on its loans, $q^i \in (0, 1)$, as given.[26] Formally, bank i solves

$$1+i^{L,i} = \arg\max\big[q^i(1+i^{L,i})L^{K,i} + (1-q^i)\kappa^i PK_0^i$$
$$-(1+i^D)D^i - (1+i^R)L^{B,i}\big],$$

where $(1+i^D)D^i$ and $(1+i^R)L^{B,i}$ represent gross interest payments on deposits and central bank borrowing, respectively, and $\kappa^i PK_0^i$ is the value of collateral pledged to bank i, which can be seized in case of default—an event occurring with probability $1-q^i$.

Using (2.42) to substitute out for $L^{B,i} = L^i + RR^i - D^i$, the first-order condition of this problem is

$$q^i L^{K,i} + q^i(1+i^{L,i})\left[\frac{\partial L^{K,i}}{\partial(1+i^{L,i})}\right] - (1+i^R)\left[\frac{\partial L^{K,i}}{\partial(1+i^{L,i})}\right] = 0. \tag{2.45}$$

From (2.44),

$$\frac{\partial L^{K,i}}{\partial(1+i^{L,i})} = -\varsigma^L\left(\frac{1+i^{L,i}}{1+i^L}\right)^{-\varsigma^L-1}\left(\frac{L^K}{1+i^L}\right). \tag{2.46}$$

Substituting (2.44) and (2.46) in (2.45) yields

$$q^i\left(\frac{1+i^{L,i}}{1+i^L}\right)^{-\varsigma^L} L^K - q^i(1+i^{L,i})\varsigma^L\left(\frac{1+i_t^{L,i}}{1+i^L}\right)^{-\varsigma^L-1}\left(\frac{L^K}{1+i^L}\right)$$
$$+(1+i^R)\varsigma^L\left(\frac{1+i^{L,i}}{1+i^L}\right)^{-\varsigma^L-1}\left(\frac{L^K}{1+i^L}\right) = 0.$$

26. In chapter 3, the repayment probability will be treated as a choice variable, by relating it to monitoring intensity.

In a symmetric equilibrium, $i^{L,i} = i^L$ and $q^i = q \; \forall i$, so that

$$qL^K + [-q(1+i^L) + (1+i^R)]\zeta^L \left(\frac{L^K}{1+i^L}\right) = 0.$$

Multiplying this expression by $-(1+i^L)/L^K$ yields

$$-q(1+i^L) + q(1+i^L)\zeta^L - (1+i^R)\zeta^L = 0,$$

so that

$$1+i^L = \frac{\zeta^L}{\zeta^L - 1}\left(\frac{1+i^R}{q}\right). \tag{2.47}$$

Using (2.31), this expression shows that if repayment is certain ($q=1$) and there are no required reserves ($\mu = 0$), the loan rate is a constant mark-up over the deposit rate,

$$1+i^L = \frac{\zeta^L}{\zeta^L - 1}(1+i^D),$$

with the markup rate decreasing in the degree of substitutability between loans, ζ^L. The weaker the degree of competitiveness in banking is (the lower ζ^L is), the higher the markup.

Now, suppose that the repayment probability is increasing in the collateral-loan ratio,

$$q = q\left(\frac{\kappa PK_0}{L_0^K}\right) = \exp\left[g\left(\frac{\kappa PK_0}{L_0^K}\right)\right], \tag{2.48}$$

where $g' > 0$. This positive relationship could be, as discussed in more detail in chapters 3 and 4, the result of a dominant borrower-side moral hazard effect—pledging collateral mitigates incentives for borrowers to take risks.

Taking logarithms of expressions (2.47) and (2.48), using the approximations $\ln(1+x) \simeq x$ and $g(x) = xg'(x)$, in a neighborhood where $g(0) = 0$, and ignoring the constant term $\ln[\zeta^L/(\zeta^L - 1)]$, yields

$$i^L = i^R - \left(\frac{\kappa PK_0}{L_0^K}\right) g'.$$

Setting $-g' = \theta' < 0$ yields an equation very similar to (2.11). Thus, the simpler formulation used earlier can be viewed as a convenient simplification.

2.4 Macroprudential Regulation

As noted in chapter 1, a key lesson of the global financial crisis is that financial regulation must adopt a macroprudential perspective to identify weaknesses and sources of procyclicality in the financial system, strengthen the resilience of financial institutions, and mitigate systemic risk. At the same time, because it operates through credit and market interest rates, it is important to understand the macroeconomic effects of macroprudential policy. The simple model developed earlier provides a convenient starting point in that regard. Indeed, in the context of the model, macroprudential policy can be defined in terms of three instruments: the required reserve ratio, a tax on the provision of loans, and (with some relatively minor changes in specification) capital requirements. These instruments are discussed in turn.[27]

2.4.1 Reserve Requirements and Funding Costs

In the foregoing discussion, the required reserve ratio was presented as an instrument of monetary policy. Indeed, central banks in many developing countries (especially in Latin America) have used changes in required reserves extensively, time and again, as a substitute for monetary policy, especially in response to large capital inflows.[28] At the same time, their potential value as a tool that may help to mitigate systemic risk and promote financial stability has regained importance in recent years—despite the fact that required reserves may distort the financial intermediation process in the long run. One reason for this may be the fact that (as noted in chapter 1) the weak capacity to supervise financial institutions and to enforce financial regulation has led many MICs to rely on prudential instruments that are relatively easy to implement.

To highlight the prudential role of reserve requirements, consider now the case where imperfect substitution between bank deposits and central bank borrowing is introduced. To preserve the simplicity of the model, this is done in an indirect way, by accounting for a *liability composition effect* on the cost of borrowing from the central bank. Suppose that competition prevails in the deposit

27. Another macroprudential tool that could be studied in this setting is an upper limit on banks' leverage ratio. Essentially, this corresponds to the case where the required capital ratio is not sensitive to risk.

28. In recent years reserve requirements were used in a countercyclical fashion to smooth the expansion phase of the cycle and to tighten monetary conditions without attracting capital inflows. By contrast, during the global financial crisis, reserve requirements were lowered in order to inject liquidity rapidly in the financial system and restore market activity affected by sudden reversals in capital flows. See the discussion in chapter 5.

market, so that the no-arbitrage condition (2.10) continues to hold. Thus, from the perspective of commercial banks, bank deposits and central bank borrowing remain perfect substitutes. However, from the perspective of the central bank, this is no longer the case. Specifically, the cost of borrowing from the monetary authority is now defined as the sum of a constant base policy rate, i^T, and a penalty rate, which is increasing in the ratio of central bank borrowing to deposits,

$$i^R = i^T + \upsilon\left(\frac{L_0^B}{D}\right), \tag{2.49}$$

where $\upsilon' \geq 0$. To simplify matters, central bank borrowing is measured at the beginning of the period.[29] By charging a higher refinance rate when the relative share of deposits in banks' liabilities is low, the central bank induces banks to raise their deposit rate, which in turn encourages market funding. The case considered in the previous sections corresponds to $\upsilon' = 0$.

With financial wealth measured at the beginning of the period, (2.3) and (2.10) imply that $D = d(i^D)F_0^H = d[(1-\mu)i^R]F_0^H$. A higher required reserve ratio imposed by the regulator therefore reduces the deposit rate (as before), which lowers deposits and raises the central bank borrowing-deposit ratio. This, in turn, leads to an increase in the penalty and refinance rates, and consequently the loan rate. Thus, in the financial sector equilibrium condition (2.17), $FF_\mu = 0$ no longer holds; instead,

$$FF_\mu = \left(\frac{\partial \upsilon}{\partial D}\right)\left(\frac{\partial D}{\partial \mu}\right) = \left(\frac{L_0^B}{F_0^H}\right)\frac{\upsilon' d' i^R}{d^2} > 0,$$

with the sign of FF_P remaining the same. Because the goods market equilibrium condition does not change, the general equilibrium effect of a rise in μ can now be calculated by solving the system

$$\begin{bmatrix} 1 & -FF_P \\ 1 & -GG_P \end{bmatrix}\begin{bmatrix} di^L \\ dP \end{bmatrix} = \begin{bmatrix} FF_\mu \\ GG_\mu \end{bmatrix} d\mu,$$

which gives, instead of (2.23),

$$\frac{di^L}{d\mu} = \frac{\overset{(+)}{GG_\mu}\overset{(-)}{FF_P} - \overset{(-)}{GG_P}\overset{(+)}{FF_\mu}}{\underset{(-)}{FF_P} - \underset{(-)}{GG_P}}, \quad \frac{dP}{d\mu} = \frac{\overset{(+)}{GG_\mu} - \overset{(+)}{FF_\mu}}{\underset{(-)}{FF_P} - \underset{(-)}{GG_P}}. \tag{2.50}$$

With again $FF_P - GG_P > 0$, as showed earlier, these expressions yield $di^L/d\mu \gtrless 0$ and $dP/d\mu \gtrless 0$. If FF_μ is large enough, which in particular

29. In the more elaborate models presented in subsequent chapters, a more general treatment of the penalty rate is provided.

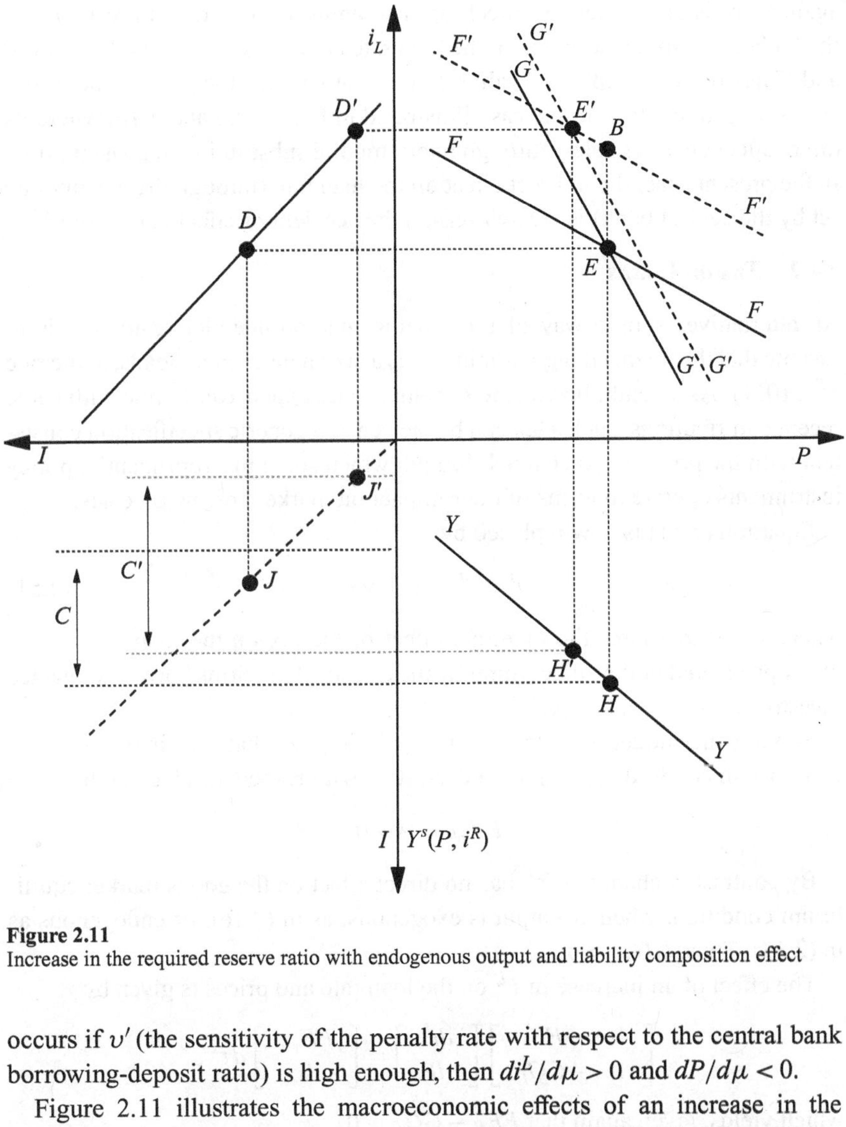

Figure 2.11
Increase in the required reserve ratio with endogenous output and liability composition effect

occurs if υ' (the sensitivity of the penalty rate with respect to the central bank borrowing-deposit ratio) is high enough, then $di^L/d\mu > 0$ and $dP/d\mu < 0$.

Figure 2.11 illustrates the macroeconomic effects of an increase in the required reserve ratio in this setting. Now both *GG* and *FF* shift outward (or to the right) and the net impact on the loan rate and prices is in general ambiguous, as implied by (2.50). The case illustrated in the figure corresponds to the situation where υ' is indeed large enough so that the shift in *FF* is large relative to the shift in *GG*. The supply curve does not shift and the new equilibrium corresponds to points E', D', H', and J', characterized by a higher loan rate, a drop in credit, lower prices, and a contraction in investment and output. Once again there is an accelerator effect; after jumping from E to B in response to the higher required reserve ratio, the loan rate continues to increase between B and E' as prices and collateral values fall. Put differently, the policy is now contractionary, in contrast to the case illustrated in figures 2.6 and 2.10, where its direct effect operates solely through intertemporal substitution in consumption. In the present case, the indirect effect on the loan rate (through the penalty rate set by the central bank) is the key reason the accelerator effect is restored.[30]

2.4.2 Tax on Loans

An alternative, simple way of introducing macroprudential regulation is to assume that the financial regulator imposes a tax on investment loans, at the rate $\tau^L \in (0, 1)$. As a result, borrowing becomes more expensive. In line with some recent contributions, such a tax can be viewed as a generic specification consistent with the price-based channel through which some macroprudential policy instruments operate in terms of their impact on market borrowing costs.[31]

Equation (2.11) is now replaced by

$$i^L = i^R + \theta + \gamma\tau^L, \tag{2.51}$$

where $\gamma > 0$ measures the marginal effect of the tax on the loan rate. Thus, macroprudential policy affects directly the cost at which firms borrow to finance investment.

Solving the model as before with (2.51) implies that the financial sector equilibrium condition (2.17) has a derivative with respect to τ^L given by

$$FF_{\tau^L} = \gamma > 0.$$

By contrast, a change in τ^L has no direct effect on the goods market equilibrium condition, whether output is exogenous, as in (2.16), or endogenous as in (2.33). Thus, $GG_{\tau^L} = 0$.

The effect of an increase in τ^L on the loan rate and prices is given by

$$\begin{bmatrix} 1 & -FF_P \\ 1 & -GG_P \end{bmatrix} \begin{bmatrix} di^L \\ dP \end{bmatrix} = \begin{bmatrix} FF_{\tau^L} \\ 0 \end{bmatrix} d\tau^L,$$

which yields, given again that $FF_P - GG_P > 0$,

$$\frac{di^L}{d\tau^L} = \frac{-\overset{(+)}{FF_{\tau^L}}\overset{(-)}{GG_P}}{\underset{(-)}{FF_P} - \underset{(-)}{GG_P}} > 0, \quad \frac{dP}{d\tau^L} = \frac{-\overset{(+)}{FF_{\tau^L}}}{\underset{(-)}{FF_P} - \underset{(-)}{GG_P}} < 0. \tag{2.52}$$

30. Chapter 5 also shows that similar effects can be obtained by introducing economies of scope in banking.

31. See the discussion in chapters 5 and 6.

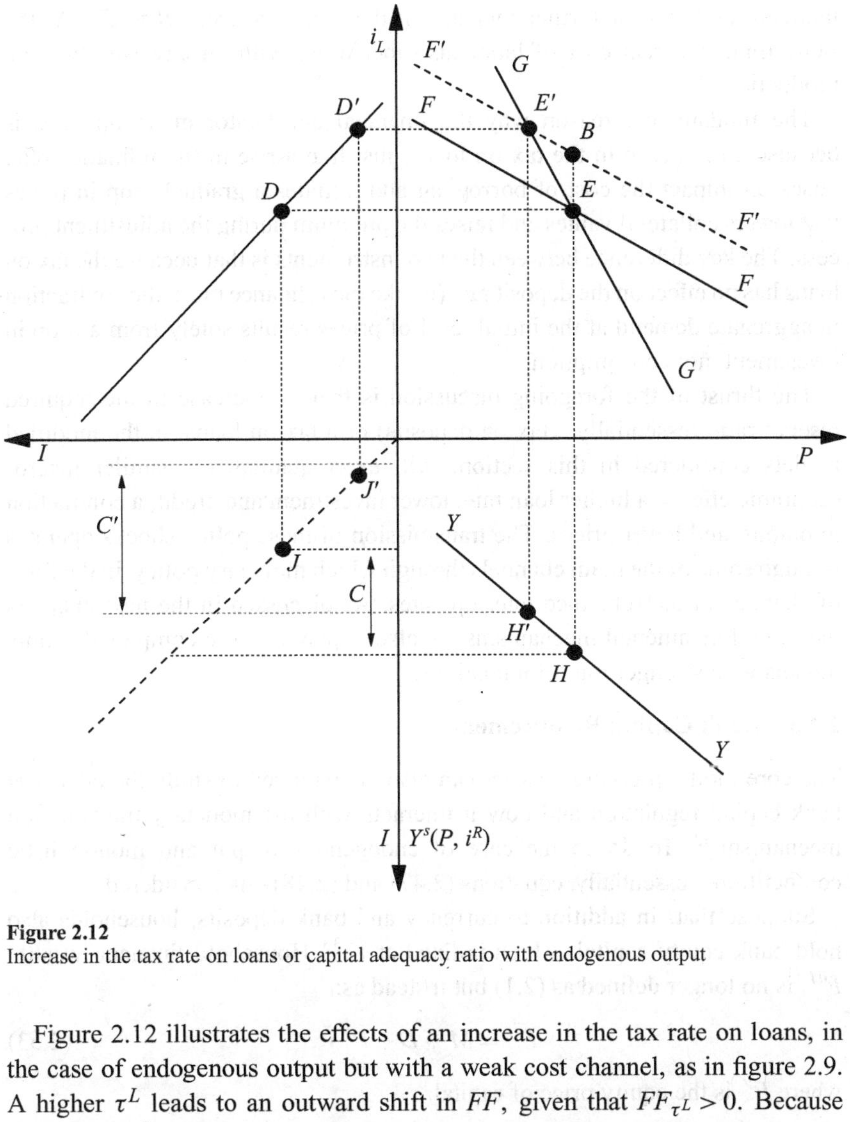

Figure 2.12
Increase in the tax rate on loans or capital adequacy ratio with endogenous output

Figure 2.12 illustrates the effects of an increase in the tax rate on loans, in the case of endogenous output but with a weak cost channel, as in figure 2.9. A higher τ^L leads to an outward shift in *FF*, given that $FF_{\tau^L} > 0$. Because changes in τ^L have no direct effect on aggregate demand, *GG* does not change. The new equilibrium corresponds to *E'*, *D'*, *H'*, and *J'*. The increase in the loan rate is associated with a contraction in credit and investment, as well as a fall in prices; in turn, the fall in prices raises the real wage, which also leads to a contraction in output. A financial accelerator effect is once again at play: After the loan rate jumps from point *E* to point *B*, there is excess supply of goods (at the initial level of prices) due to the contraction in investment. As prices fall and collateral values drop, the premium rises, thereby inducing as before a further increase in the loan rate from B to E'. At the same time, the real cost of labor also increases, with an adverse effect on production.

The fundamental reason why the financial accelerator effect operates is because an increase in the tax on loans, just like a rise in the refinance rate, raises on impact the cost of borrowing and initiates a gradual drop in prices that lowers collateral values and raises the premium during the adjustment process. The key difference between the two instruments is that because the tax on loans has no effect on the deposit rate (unlike the refinance rate), the contraction in aggregate demand at the initial level of prices results solely from a drop in investment, not consumption.

The thrust of the foregoing discussion is that an increase in the required reserve ratio (essentially a tax on deposits) or a tax on loans, in the modified models considered in this section, will exert qualitatively similar macroeconomic effects: a higher loan rate, lower investment and credit, a contraction in output, and lower prices. The transmission of these policy shocks operates through some of the main channels through which monetary policy, in the form of changes in the refinance rate, operates. As discussed in the next chapters the same fundamental mechanisms are also at play in more complex dynamic models with stronger microfoundations.

2.4.3 Bank Capital Requirements

The core model presented earlier can also be extended to study the effects of bank capital regulation and how it interacts with the monetary transmission mechanism.[32] To do so the case of endogenous output and monopolistic competition—essentially, equations (2.47) and (2.48)—is considered.

Suppose that, in addition to currency and bank deposits, households also hold bank equity capital, which is fixed at $\bar{V}$.[33] Household financial wealth, F^H, is no longer defined as (2.1) but instead as:

$$F^H = M + D + P^V \bar{V}, \tag{2.53}$$

where P^V is the equity price of capital.

32. Chapter 6 will consider a more detailed treatment of the interactions between bank capital regulation and monetary policy.

33. It could be assumed, as in Cecchetti and Li (2008), for instance, that bank capital is directly and positively related to aggregate output because an increase in that variable raises the value of bank assets—possibly because borrowers are now more able to repay their debts. However, the assumption that V is fixed is quite reasonable, given the short time frame of the analysis.

Assuming again that the deposit-cash ratio is given by (2.2), and noting from (2.53) that $M = F^H - D - P^V \bar{V}$, the portfolio equation (2.3) becomes

$$D = (F^H - D - P^V \bar{V}) \nu(i^D),$$

or equivalently

$$\frac{D}{F^H - P^V \bar{V}} = \frac{\nu(i^D)}{1 + \nu(i^D)} = d(i^D),$$

with $d' > 0$ as before. The consumption function (2.5) also remains the same.

The balance sheet of the commercial bank is now, instead of (2.8),

$$L + RR = P^V \bar{V} + D + L^B, \tag{2.54}$$

which implies that (2.13) is replaced by

$$L^B = \max[L - (1 - \mu)D - P^V \bar{V}, 0].$$

Regulatory regimes

Banks must now satisfy capital requirements, in quantity V^R. The capital buffer, or excess capital, is thus $\bar{V}/V^R$ in gross terms.

Capital requirements are based on risk-weighted assets. Suppose that the risk weight on safe assets (reserves and loans for working capital needs) is 0, whereas the risk weight on investment loans, which are subject to idiosyncratic risk, is $\sigma \in (0, 1)$. Risk-weighted assets are thus σPI. The capital requirement constraint can therefore be written as

$$P^V V^R = \rho \sigma PI, \tag{2.55}$$

where $\rho \in (0, 1)$ is the capital adequacy ratio (or *Cooke ratio*). If the penalty (pecuniary or reputational) cost of holding capital below the required level is prohibitive, the case where $\bar{V} < V^R$ can be excluded; the issue is therefore whether $\bar{V} = V^R$ or $\bar{V} > V^R$.

Two alternative regimes, discussed further in chapter 6, are considered for the determination of the risk weight σ. Under the first regime, which corresponds to the Basel I regime, the risk weight is exogenous at $\sigma_R \leq 1$; the bank keeps a flat minimum percentage of capital against loans provided for the purpose of investment. If $\sigma_R = 1$, ρ is thus also the inverse of the *leverage ratio*, defined as the ratio of investment loans to bank capital. Under the second regime, which corresponds to the Basel II and III regimes, capital requirements are risk-based; the risk weight is endogenous and inversely related to the probability of default of borrowers. Thus, as allowed under Basel II and III, banks use an *internal ratings-based approach*, or their own default risk assessment, in calculating the appropriate risk weight—and by implication required capital.[34]

Let q denote the repayment probability, as defined earlier. Formally, the two regimes can be defined as[35]

$$\sigma = \begin{cases} \sigma^R & \text{Exogenous risk weight} \\ \sigma(q),\ \sigma' < 0 & \text{Endogenous risk weight} \end{cases}. \tag{2.56}$$

The repayment probability is now related not only to the collateral-loan ratio, as in (2.48), but also positively to the bank capital buffer through a *monitoring incentive effect*, as in Agénor et al. (2012),

$$q = q\left(\frac{\kappa P K_0}{L_0^K}, \frac{\bar{V}}{V^R}\right), \tag{2.57}$$

where as before $q_{\kappa PK_0/L_0^K} > 0$ and now $q_{\bar{V}/V^R} > 0$. As discussed in more detail in chapter 6, microfoundations for this monitoring incentive effect are provided by Allen et al. (2011) and Mehran and Thakor (2011). In Allen et al. (2011), for instance, excess bank capital increases the bank's incentives to screen and monitor borrowers, which raises the borrower's success probability. In turn, a higher repayment probability induces the bank to lower the lending rate while improving its expected payoff.

For ease of exposition, the following analysis considers only the case where existing equity capital is higher than the required value—that is, $\bar{V} > V^R$. This is consistent with the evidence suggesting that, in normal times, banks often hold more capital than the regulatory minimum—possibly as a result of market discipline, as considered in Rochet (2008), or the need to avoid regulatory scrutiny (see chapter 6). However, although bank capital is not a strictly binding constraint on bank behavior, it still plays an indirect role by affecting incentives to monitor.[36] To simplify further, the *real* price of equity, defined as $p^V = P^V/P$,

34. This assumes in turn that the standards embedded in the bank's risk management system have been validated by the regulator, through an Internal Capital Adequacy Assessment Process (ICAAP). The *Standardized Approach* in Basel II and III can be modeled by making the risk weight a function of output, in a manner similar to Zicchino (2006), for instance, under the assumption that ratings are procyclical.

35. If q is procyclical, the negative link between σ and q is also consistent with specifications that relate risk weights to borrowers' probability of default over the business cycle as, for instance, in Tanaka (2002) and Heid (2007).

36. In addition, given (2.55), the condition $\bar{V} > V^R$ sets an upper bound on investment, $I < P^V\bar{V}/P\rho\sigma$. For ease of exposition, it will be assumed that this restriction is not binding. Zilberman (2012) considered the case of binding capital requirements and an exogenous *nominal* price of equity in a related model.

will be assumed to be determined by future expected dividends, which are taken as given.[37]

Macroeconomic equilibrium

Substituting (2.55) in (2.57) and using (2.6) with $\pi^e = 0$, gives

$$q = q\left[\frac{\kappa P K_0}{L_0^K}, \frac{p^V \bar{V}}{\rho\sigma I(i^L)}\right],$$

so that, with an exogenous risk weight,

$$dq = \left(\frac{\kappa K_0}{L_0^K}\right) q_{\kappa P K_0/L_0^K} dP - q_{\bar{V}/V^R}\left(\frac{p^V \bar{V}}{\rho\sigma^R I}\right)\left[\left(\frac{I'}{I}\right) di^L + \frac{d\rho}{\rho}\right], \tag{2.58}$$

whereas with an endogenous risk weight,

$$dq = \left(\frac{\kappa K_0}{L_0^K}\right) q_{\kappa P K_0/L_0^K} dP - q_{\bar{V}/V^R}\left(\frac{p^V \bar{V}}{\rho\sigma I}\right)\left[\left(\frac{I'}{I}\right) di^L + \frac{d\rho}{\rho} + \frac{d\sigma}{\sigma}\right],$$

or again, given that from (2.56) $d\sigma = \sigma' dq$,

$$dq = \frac{1}{\Delta^1}\left\{\left(\frac{\kappa K_0}{L_0^K}\right) q_{\kappa P K_0/L_0^K} dP - q_{\bar{V}/\bar{V}^R}\left(\frac{p^V \bar{V}}{\rho\sigma I}\right)\left[\left(\frac{I'}{I}\right) di^L + \frac{d\rho}{\rho}\right]\right\}, \tag{2.59}$$

where

$$\Delta^1 = 1 + q_{\bar{V}/V^R}\left(\frac{p^V \bar{V}}{\rho\sigma^2 I}\right)\sigma'.$$

Assuming that the signaling effect (as measured by $q_{\bar{V}/V^R}$) is not too strong ensures that $\Delta^1 > 0$. And given that $\sigma' < 0$, it is also the case that $\Delta^1 < 1$.

Similarly, differentiating totally the expression for the equilibrium loan rate (2.47) gives

$$di^L = -\frac{\zeta^L(1+i^R)}{(\zeta^L - 1)q^2} dq + \frac{\zeta^L}{(\zeta^L - 1)q} di^R. \tag{2.60}$$

Substituting (2.58) for dq in (2.60), the financial sector equilibrium condition with an exogenous risk weight is

$$i^L = FF(P; \rho), \tag{2.61}$$

37. As a result, in the consumption function (2.5) the wealth variable is $(M_0 + D_0)P^{-1} + \bar{V}$, which implies that the wealth effect operates in the same manner as before.

where

$$FF_P = -\frac{1}{\Delta^2}\frac{\zeta^L(1+i^R)}{(\zeta^L-1)q^2}\left(\frac{\kappa K_0}{L_0^K}\right)q_{\kappa P K_0/L_0^K} < 0,$$

$$FF_\rho = \frac{1}{\Delta^2}\frac{\zeta^L(1+i^R)}{(\zeta^L-1)q^2}q_{\bar{V}/V^R}p^V\bar{V}\left(\frac{1}{\rho^2\sigma^R I}\right) > 0,$$

$$\Delta^2 = 1 - \frac{\zeta^L(1+i^R)}{(\zeta^L-1)q^2}q_{\bar{V}/V^R}p^V\bar{V}\left(\frac{I'}{\rho\sigma^R I^2}\right) > 0.$$

As before, an increase in prices raises the probability of repayment, which lowers the premium and the loan rate. An increase in the capital adequacy ratio lowers the capital buffer, which reduces monitoring incentives; this tends to reduce the repayment probability and to increase the loan rate.

With an endogenous risk weight, substituting now (2.59) for dq in (2.60), the financial sector equilibrium condition takes the same form as (2.61), but this time with partial derivatives given by

$$FF_P = -\frac{1}{\Delta^3}\frac{\zeta^L(1+i^R)}{(\zeta^L-1)q^2\Delta^1}\left(\frac{\kappa K_0}{L_0^K}\right)q_{\kappa P K_0/L_0^K} < 0,$$

$$FF_\rho = \frac{1}{\Delta^3}\frac{\zeta^L(1+i^R)}{(\zeta^L-1)q^2\Delta^1}q_{\bar{V}/V^R}p^V\bar{V}\frac{1}{\rho^2\sigma I} > 0,$$

where

$$\Delta^3 = 1 - \frac{\zeta^L(1+i^R)}{(\zeta^L-1)q^2\Delta^1}q_{\bar{V}/V^R}p^V\bar{V}\left(\frac{I'}{\rho\sigma I^2}\right) > 0.$$

Comparing the expressions for FF_P under the two regimes it can easily be seen that, because $\Delta^1 < 1$, it must be that $\Delta^3 > \Delta^2$. Thus, the slope of FF with an endogenous risk weight is steeper than with an exogenous weight. Of course, if there is no monitoring incentive effect ($q_{\bar{V}/V^R} = 0$), $\Delta^2 = \Delta^3 = 1$ and the curves have the same slope. In addition, the loan rate becomes independent of the capital adequacy ratio ($FF_\rho = 0$).

Because the regulatory regime has no direct implications for equilibrium in the goods market, condition (2.36) continues to hold with, in particular, $GG_P < 0$. Thus, the graphical illustration in figure 2.7 continues to apply.

Increase in the capital adequacy ratio

Consider now an increase in the capital adequacy ratio. The effects of this policy are illustrated in the same way as in figure 2.12. Curve GG does not change, given that it does not depend directly on that ratio. The increase in ρ raises capital requirements, as implied by (2.55), and lowers the capital buffer. This weakens monitoring incentives and lowers the repayment probability as implied by (2.57), thereby increasing the loan rate from E to B at the initial level of prices. Curve FF therefore shifts outward. The higher loan rate leads to an initial contraction in investment and aggregate demand. To eliminate the excess supply of goods requires a drop in prices. In turn, the fall in prices raises the real wage and leads over time to a contraction in output, from H to H'. Because the fall in prices also lowers the value of collateral, the loan rate continues to rise during the transition period, from B to E', in line with the financial accelerator effect. The new equilibrium point, located at E', is characterized by a higher lending rate, lower credit and investment, lower prices, and lower output.

Thus, tighter capital regulation reduces bank leverage while at the same time it increases the cost of borrowing for firms. The fact that an increase in the capital adequacy ratio leads to a higher equilibrium loan rate and reduced lending is consistent with the prediction of other models based on very different premises (VanHoose 2007). Moreover, as with a direct tax on loans, there is also a financial accelerator effect at play (the movement of the loan rate from B to E'). Because the slope of FF is steeper when the monitoring incentive is present, this effect is more pronounced than when it is not. All else equal, it is also stronger when the risk weight is endogenous, compared to when it is exogenous.

2.5 Land as Portfolio Asset and Collateral

In the foregoing discussion it was assumed that collateral consists only of physical capital. However, as noted in chapter 1, in many countries bank loans are often collateralized by real estate or land. This is particularly so for loans to medium-size firms, whose production technology is often more labor intensive and the only pledgeable asset that they have access to is the owner's house. It is thus important to understand how the transmission mechanism of monetary and macroprudential policies described earlier changes in that case.

Total household wealth is now given by the sum of financial wealth, defined in (2.1), and the value of land,

$$A^H = F^H + P^H \bar{H}, \tag{2.62}$$

where P^H is the price of land and $\bar{H}$ the quantity of land, assumed fixed. Land prices are fully flexible and adjust instantaneously to equilibrate supply and demand. Thus, although financial wealth is again predetermined, total wealth is not.

For simplicity, output is kept exogenous at $\bar{Y}$. The consumption function becomes, instead of (2.5), a function of total wealth,

$$C = \alpha_1 \bar{Y} - \alpha_2 (i^D - \pi^e) + \alpha_3 \left(\frac{F_0^H + P^H \bar{H}}{P} \right), \tag{2.63}$$

which implies that spending now depends also on the capital gains or losses associated with changes in the relative price of land, P^H/P.

The demand function for land can be specified as

$$\frac{P^H \bar{H}}{D} = h(i^D, \pi^{He}), \tag{2.64}$$

where π^{He} is the expected rate of change in land prices (assumed exogenous), $h_{i^D} < 0$, and $h_{\pi^{He}} > 0$. Thus, the demand for land varies inversely with the interest rate on deposits (the rate of return on alternative assets) and positively with the expected rate of increase in house prices.

Because equations (2.1) and (2.2) continue to apply, the demand for deposits is still given by (2.3); writing that expression as $D = d(i^D)F^H$ and substituting for D in (2.64), the demand for land can be written as

$$\frac{P^H \bar{H}}{F^H} = h(i^D, \pi^{He}) d(i^D) = \psi(i^D, \pi^{He}), \tag{2.65}$$

where

$$\psi_{i^D} = hd' + h_{i^D} d, \quad \psi_{\pi^{He}} = h_{\pi^{He}} d > 0,$$

where, to ensure that $\psi_{i^D} < 0$, the restriction $d' i^D / d < -h_{i^D} i^D / h$ is imposed. Essentially, this condition states that the interest elasticity of deposits cannot be too high.

Although households own the land, they make it available to the firms that they own, free of charge, to use as collateral against borrowing. Thus, the premium is now set as, instead of (2.12),

$$\theta = \theta \left(\frac{\kappa P^H \bar{H}}{L_0^K} \right), \tag{2.66}$$

where again $\theta' < 0$.

Because the stock of land is fixed and L_0^K is predetermined, the premium varies only with the nominal price of land, P^H.

To solve the model requires now solving for the equilibrium price of land. From (2.65), using (2.10) to substitute out for i^D and setting $\bar{H} = 1$ for simplicity, this value is given by

$$P^H = \psi[(1-\mu) i^R, \pi^{He}] F_0^H. \tag{2.67}$$

Given that π^{He} is constant and that financial wealth is predetermined, the equilibrium price of land changes only in response to changes in the rate of return on deposits, which under perfect competition in the deposit market depends only on policy variables—the refinance rate and the required reserve ratio.

To assess the implications of endogenous land prices on macroeconomic equilibrium, changes to the derivatives of curves FF and GG must be evaluated. For FF, substituting (2.67) in (2.66) and the result in (2.11) yields now the following partial derivatives in condition (2.17):

$$FF_P = 0,$$

$$FF_{i^R} = 1 + \left(\frac{\kappa \bar{H}}{L_0^K}\right)(1-\mu)F_0^H \theta' \psi_{i^D} > 0,$$

$$FF_\mu = -i^R \theta' \psi_{i^D} < 0.$$

Thus, curve FF is now horizontal, because the equilibrium price of land is independent of goods prices. In addition, although the sign of FF_{i^R} remains the same, now $FF_\mu < 0$ instead of zero. An increase in the refinance rate, by raising the deposit rate, reduces the demand for land and thus its price. As a result of the drop in the value of collateral, the premium increases and the loan rate rises by more than the direct effect. By contrast, an increase in the required reserve ratio lowers the return on deposits and raises the demand for land, which puts upward pressure on land prices—increasing therefore collateral values and reducing the premium.

With respect to curve GG, substituting (2.67) in (2.63) and using (2.10) yields, with $\pi^e = 0$,

$$C = \alpha_1 \bar{Y} - \alpha_2(1-\mu)i^R + \alpha_3 \left(\frac{1+\psi[(1-\mu)i^R, \pi^{He}]}{P}\right) F_0^H.$$

Substituting this equation, together with (2.6), in (2.16), and given that $\psi_{i^D} < 0$, yields now the following partial derivatives in condition (2.18):

$$GG_P = \frac{\alpha_3}{I'}\left(\frac{F_0^H + p^H}{P^2}\right) < 0,$$

$$GG_{i^R} = \frac{1}{I'}\left\{\alpha_2(1-\mu) - \alpha_3(1-\mu)\left(\frac{F_0^H}{P}\right)\psi_{i^D}\right\} < 0,$$

$$GG_\mu = \frac{1}{I'}\left[-\alpha_2 i^R + \alpha_3 i^R \left(\frac{F_0^H}{P}\right)\psi_{i^D}\right] > 0.$$

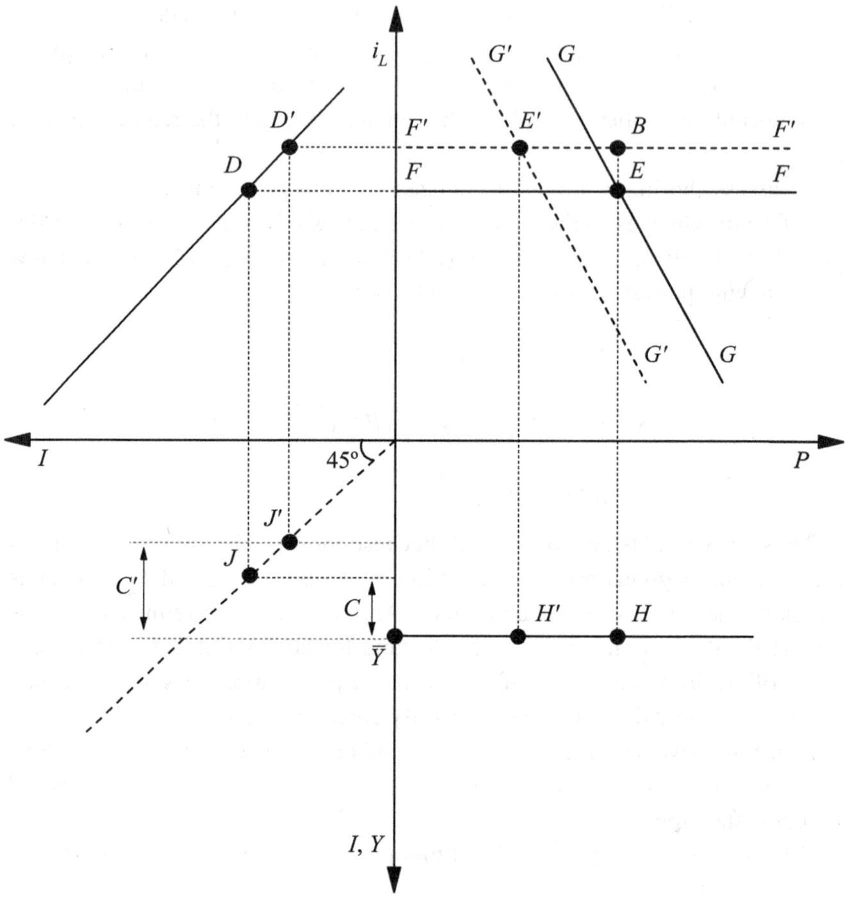

Figure 2.13
Exogenous output and land as collateral: increase in the refinance rate

All three expressions have therefore the same sign as before. By raising the deposit rate an increase in the refinance rate not only reduces consumption through intertemporal substitution but now also reduces the demand for land and its price—thereby exerting a negative wealth effect on private spending. Thus, $GG_{i^R} < 0$. Similarly, by lowering the deposit rate an increase in the required reserve ratio not only reduces incentives to save, as before, but also raises the demand for land—thereby raising its price and inducing an increase in consumption through both intertemporal and wealth effects.

The policy implications are illustrated in figures 2.13 and 2.14. An increase in the refinance rate leads to an upward shift in *FF* and an inward shift in *GG*. As before, the loan rate jumps initially from point *E* to *B* (see figure 2.13). However, now there is no financial accelerator effect because the financial sector

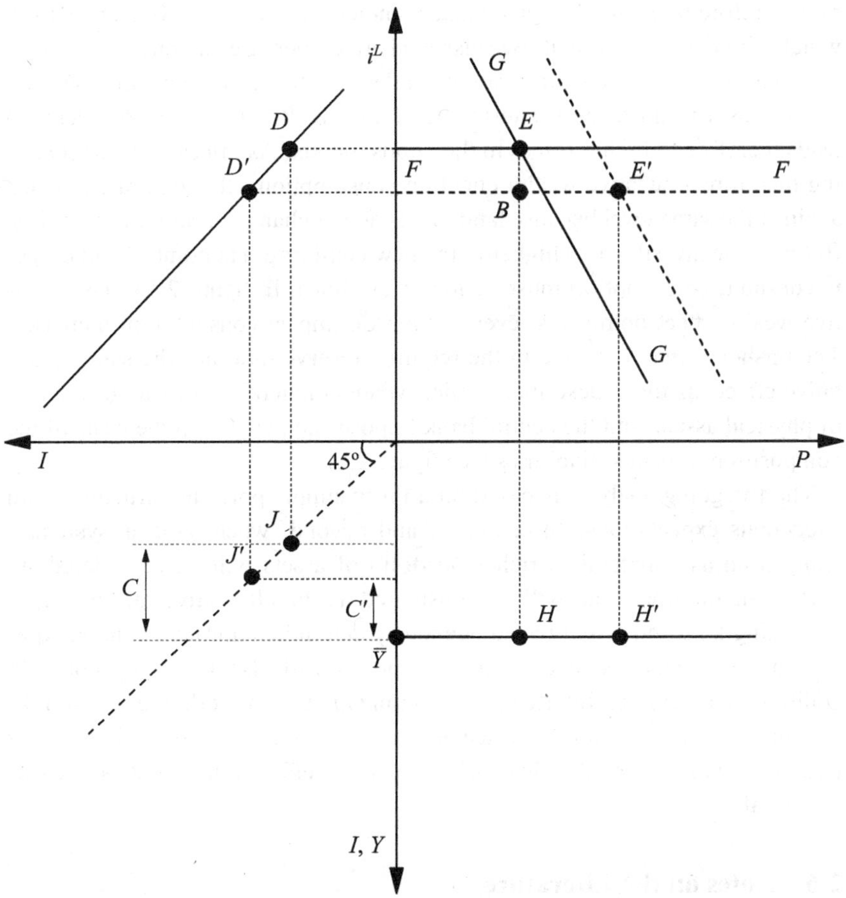

Figure 2.14
Exogenous output and land as collateral: increase in the required reserve ratio

equilibrium condition does not depend on the price of the final good (which is also the price at which physical capital is valued in the model); collateral values depend only on the price of land. After the initial change in land prices associated with the increase in the refinance and deposit rates, these prices remain constant—given that π^{He} remains constant. Although goods prices continue to fall during the transition from *B* to *E'*, the loan rate does not change further.[38]

An increase in the required reserve ratio leads now not only to an outward shift in *GG* but also to a downward shift in *FF* (see figure 2.14). The loan

38. In Agénor and Montiel (2015, chap. 6), land is also introduced as an asset but collateral remains defined in terms of the value of physical capital. As a result, the financial accelerator effect continues to hold.

rate therefore falls initially (given that, as noted earlier, $FF_\mu < 0$) from E to B, which stimulates investment. Because land prices increase on impact (due to the fact that the lower deposit rate raises the demand for land), consumption rises initially as a result of both intertemporal and wealth effects. Excess demand leads therefore to higher prices in the goods market. As prices increase (exerting therefore a negative wealth effect on consumption), the loan rate remains again at the same level because land prices do not change during the transition. But because investment is higher in the new equilibrium at point E' and output is constant, consumption must be lower, as shown in figure 2.14. The negative wealth effect dominates, even though on impact consumption increases. The upshot is that a change in the required reserve ratio has the same qualitative effects as those described earlier, when collateral is measured in terms of physical assets, and the central bank imposes no penalty on the basis of the composition of banks' liabilities (see figure 2.6).

The foregoing analysis is based on a fairly simple portfolio structure, with exogenous expectations. In chapter 4 and beyond, where land is systematically used as collateral, a richer portfolio of assets will be considered. In particular, the bond rate will be considered as the alternative rate of return to holding land and it will be endogenously determined through general equilibrium. The expected change in land prices will also be endogenous. In addition, in an explicit intertemporal optimization framework, the demand for housing can also be shown to depend directly on consumption. This richer treatment will restore the financial accelerator effect when land is used as collateral.

2.6 Notes on the Literature

The literature that studies jointly the transmission mechanism of monetary and macroprudential policies in simple, static macroeconomic models with banks and financial frictions remains scant. Contributions by Blum and Hellwig (1995), Tanaka (2002), Kopecky and VanHoose (2004*a*, 2004*b*, 2006), Zicchino (2006), Heid (2007), and Gersbach and Rochet (2012) have focused mostly on prudential regulation. Blum and Hellwig (1995), for instance, showed that capital regulation may exacerbate macroeconomic fluctuations. If negative shocks to aggregate demand reduce the ability of firms to service their debts, bank profits, and thus the value of bank equity, may fall. In turn, because of capital requirements, banks may be forced to reduce credit, with a negative effect on investment. Zicchino (2006) analyzed the relationship between bank capital, lending, and macroeconomic activity under both Basel I and Basel II regulatory regimes, along the lines discussed earlier, and found that bank lending becomes more responsive to macroeconomic shocks under Basel II, in line with the analysis presented previously. Heid (2007) found that capital buffers tend to mitigate the quantitative effects of Basel II. Kopecky and VanHoose (2004*a*, 2004*b*, 2006) studied the effects of capital requirements on loan rates, the structure of bank liabilities, and aggregate loan quality. However, none of these models accounts for financial frictions.

Tanaka (2002), Kopecky and VanHoose (2004*a*, 2004*b*), and Cecchetti and Li (2008) are some of the few contributions that have studied interactions between monetary policy and regulatory regimes in simple macroeconomic models with banks. Tanaka found that the monetary transmission mechanism is weakened if banks are poorly capitalized or if capital requirements are too stringent. He also found that under Basel II, a rise in credit risk may lead to a sharper loan contraction. Consequently, the effectiveness of monetary policy as a tool for stimulating output during recessions may be weakened. In the same vein, Kopecky and VanHoose (2004*a*) found that risk-based capital requirements mitigate the effect of monetary policy on loan rates and aggregate credit supply. Both studies therefore highlight a potential conflict between the goals of monetary policy and prudential regulation. By contrast, Cecchetti and Li found that by adopting an interest rate rule that accounts for capital requirements, central banks can avoid potential conflicts between ensuring sufficient lending (to promote activity) and excessive lending (which creates financial vulnerabilities). However, once again none of these studies accounts for financial frictions.

Finally, it is worth noting that the model presented in this chapter can be extended to consider, in a closed economy, the existence of excess liquid reserves in the banking system—a common phenomenon in MICs, as considered, for instance, in Deléchat et al. (2012)—and its implications for monetary policy. This issue is formally analyzed in the context of this model by Agénor and El Aynaoui (2010) and is further discussed in chapter 5.

Appendix Alternative Consumption Function

In the model presented in this chapter, it was assumed that loans are repaid, and profits distributed, at the end of the period. Consequently, as specified in (2.30), consumption during the period was assumed to depend only on wages, which are paid at the beginning of the period.

However, to further simplify the exposition of the model when output is endogenous, suppose now that it is total income, Y^s, rather than wage income only, ωN^d, that affects household spending. Thus, instead of (2.30), the consumption function is now specified as,

$$C = \alpha_0 + \alpha_1 Y^s - \alpha_2(i^D - \pi^e) + \alpha_3 \left(\frac{F_0^H}{P}\right). \tag{A2.1}$$

Substituting (2.6), (2.10), and (A2.1) in (2.33), and setting again $\pi^e = 0$, yields

$$Y^s(P; i^R) = \alpha_0 + \alpha_1 Y^s(P; i^R) - \alpha_2(1-\mu)i^R + \alpha_3 \left(\frac{F_0^H}{P}\right) + I(i^L)$$

or equivalently

$$(1-\alpha_1)Y^s(P; i^R) = \alpha_0 - \alpha_2(1-\mu)i^R + \alpha_3 \left(\frac{F_0^H}{P}\right) + I(i^L).$$

Differentiating totally this expression and setting $\Lambda = 1 - \alpha_1 \in (0, 1)$ yields

$$\Lambda Y_P^s dP + \Lambda Y_{iR}^s di^R = -\alpha_2(1-\mu)di^R + \alpha_3 \left(-\frac{F_0^H}{P^2}\right) dP + I' di^L.$$

Rearranging terms gives

$$\left[\Lambda Y_P^s + \alpha_3 \left(\frac{F_0^H}{P^2}\right)\right] dP + \left[\Lambda Y_{iR}^s + \alpha_2(1-\mu)\right] di^R = I' di^L,$$

or again

$$di^L = \left[\Lambda Y_P^s + \alpha_3 \left(\frac{F_0^H}{P^2}\right)\right] \frac{dP}{I'} + \left[\Lambda Y_{iR}^s + \alpha_2(1-\mu)\right] \frac{di^R}{I'}.$$

In functional form, this expression is

$$i^L = GG(P; i^R), \tag{A2.2}$$

where

$$GG_P = \frac{1}{I'}\left[\Lambda Y_P^s + \alpha_3 \left(\frac{F_0^H}{P^2}\right)\right],$$

$$GG_{iR} = \frac{1}{I'}\left[\Lambda Y_{iR}^s + \alpha_2 (1-\mu)\right].$$

From the first expression it is clear that $GG_P < 0$, whereas from the second, given that $Y_{iR}^s < 0$, in general $GG_{iR} \lesseqgtr 0$. Again, with $\psi_W = 0$ (no cost channel), $Y^s_{\tilde{i}R} = 0$ and $GG_{\tilde{i}R} < 0$. The advantage of this simplification, therefore, is that it is easier to show that $GG_P < 0$, whereas the dependence of $GG_{\tilde{i}R}$ on parameter ψ_W can be more easily ascertained. Thus, although not strictly consistent with the timing of financial contracts that underlies the model, using equation (A2.1) instead of (2.30) can be viewed as a useful simplification for expositional purposes.

3 A Simple Dynamic Model with Financial Frictions

The closed-economy model presented in chapter 2 captures some of the key financial frictions that characterize the financial environment in the vast majority of middle-income countries. In particular, the fact that capital markets remain underdeveloped or illiquid implies that firms in these countries have no real alternative but to rely on internal funds or borrow from commercial banks. Such borrowing serves not only to finance investment but also to fund working capital needs, thereby generating a direct link between borrowing costs and the supply side.

This chapter takes a step toward extending that model to a dynamic setting. Again, even though the aggregate demand relationships of this extended framework are not derived from first principles, they are fairly intuitive and consistent with the evidence. In a sense, it can be viewed as an intermediate analytical platform between the static framework presented in chapter 2 and the full-blown, microfounded dynamic models presented in subsequent ones.

The model is used to analyze how monetary and macroprudential policies can mitigate the degree of procyclicality of the financial system. As noted in chapter 1, this issue has received growing attention in the recent literature, but much of it is based on full-blown numerical models, where the intuition regarding the key mechanisms at play is not always clear. By contrast, in this chapter this is done in a fairly transparent setting, and this is important to draw some general lessons. The goal is to highlight, using a dynamic macroeconomic framework, the fact that assessing the performance of monetary policy and macroprudential tools requires improved understanding of how prudential regimes interact with the monetary transmission mechanism, and that this in turn requires models in which financial frictions take center stage. In that sense, the discussion in this chapter largely complements the analysis presented in chapter 2.

Section 1 presents the model, which shares many of the characteristics of the static framework of chapter 2. However, it also has two key sources of dynamics. The first is the assumption that prices adjust gradually to disequilibria between aggregate demand and aggregate supply, in line with the specification proposed by Fuhrer and Moore (1995). The second involves the adjustment process of the capital stock, which determines the evolution of collateral. The model also assumes explicitly that commercial banks engage in costly monitoring to reduce the possibility of default on their loans. In addition, the repayment probability is directly linked to bank monitoring. This leads to an endogenous determination of the premium embedded in loan rates, which varies once again with the ratio of collateral to investment loans. Section 2 presents the model's solution and characterizes its steady-state properties. Section 3 examines the transmission mechanism of monetary and macroprudential policies—namely, autonomous and permanent increases in the central bank refinance rate, the required reserve ratio, and a tax on loans. The case of an endogenous monetary policy rule is considered in section 4. The last section discusses some possible extensions of the analysis.

3.1 The Model

The core features of the model are the same as in chapter 2: A predominant role of banks in financing short-term working capital needs and investment in physical capital; monopolistic credit markets; collateralized lending; a perfectly elastic supply of loans to firms, at the prevailing loan rate; and a central bank that operates a standing facility. In line with the evidence discussed in the previous chapters, households have no access to the credit market and are therefore unable to borrow and lend to smooth consumption.

Also as in the previous chapter, the economy is populated by five types of agents: households, firms, a continuum of commercial banks indexed by $i \in (0, 1)$, the central bank, and a financial regulator. In what follows the behavior of each of these categories of agents is described.

3.1.1 Households

As before, households consume goods and hold two imperfectly substitutable financial assets: currency (which bears no interest) in nominal quantity M_t, and bank deposits in nominal quantity D_t. The ratio of deposits to cash depends again positively on the deposit rate, i_t^D,

$$\frac{D_t}{M_t} = \nu(i_t^D), \tag{3.1}$$

where $\nu' > 0$. In addition, currency holdings are now proportional to consumption spending as a result of a cash-in-advance constraint,

$$M_t = \Lambda P_t C_t, \tag{3.2}$$

where C_t denotes real private expenditure, P_t the price level, and $\Lambda > 0$ a constant parameter.

Combining (3.1) and (3.2) yields

$$\frac{D_t + M_t}{P_t} = [1 + \nu(i_t^D)]\Lambda C_t. \tag{3.3}$$

Real consumption expenditure by households depends positively on income from production and the real stock of financial assets, and negatively on the real deposit rate

$$C_t = A_1(\pi_t)Y_t^s - A_2(i_t^D - \pi_t) + A_3\left(\frac{D_t + M_t}{P_t}\right), \tag{3.4}$$

where Y_t^s is output (or factor income), $\pi_t = \dot{P}_t/P_t$ is the inflation rate, $A_1 \in (0, 1)$ is the marginal propensity to consume out of current income, and $A_2, A_3 > 0$.[1]

The consumption function (3.4) is in line with the specification discussed in chapter 2. The positive effect of current income on private spending is consistent with the evidence regarding the pervasiveness of liquidity constraints in developing countries and the fact that households cannot borrow directly from banks to smooth spending. The real deposit rate captures an intertemporal substitution effect, whereas real monetary balances capture a wealth effect.

In addition, inflation generates a capital loss, or a *wealth erosion effect*, which induces households to cut spending and save more to rebuild their assets; thus, $A_1' < 0$. This is consistent with the buffer stock theory of saving, according to which households adjust their savings to reach or maintain a wealth target (Wen 2009; Carroll 2018).

Substituting (3.3) in (3.4) yields

$$C_t = \alpha_{1,t}(\pi_t)Y_t^s - \alpha_{2,t}(i_t^D - \pi_t), \tag{3.5}$$

where

$$\alpha_{h,t} = \frac{A_h}{1 - A_3[1 + \nu(i_t^D)]\Lambda}, \quad h = 1, 2.$$

For simplicity, it will be assumed in what follows that ν is constant, so that $\nu' = 0$. Given (3.3), this assumption essentially implies that currency and deposits are perfect substitutes as means of transactions. Thus, $\alpha_{1,t}$ depends only on inflation and $\alpha_{2,t}$ is constant. In addition, as long as $A_3(1 + \nu)\Lambda < 1$,

1. Interest payments on deposits are not considered as a source of current income but assumed instead to enter directly into financial wealth accumulation.

and the marginal propensity to consume α_1 remains less than unity, the wealth effect associated with changes in the real value of monetary assets does not affect the analysis. Intuitively, this effect is now "picked up" by changes in α_1 and is related to inflation, rather than changes in the level of prices: Higher inflation lowers consumption, just like higher prices reduced household spending in chapter 2. At the same time, the analysis remains incomplete because the dynamics of household wealth accumulation are not explicitly analyzed.

3.1.2 Firms

As before, firms produce a single, homogeneous good. To finance their working capital needs, which consist solely of labor costs, firms borrow from banks. Total production costs faced by the representative firm are thus equal to the wage bill plus the interest payments made on bank loans. For simplicity, and as in chapter 2, loans contracted for the purpose of financing working capital are not collateralized and are therefore made at a rate that reflects only the cost of borrowing from the central bank, i^R, assumed constant for the moment. Firms repay working capital loans, with interest, after goods have been produced and sold.[2] All profits are transferred to the firms' owners, households.

Let Y_t denote output, N_t the quantity of labor employed, and K_t the capital stock. The production function of the representative firm takes the same Cobb-Douglas form as in chapter 2, which is

$$Y_t = N_t^{\alpha} K_t^{1-\alpha}, \tag{3.6}$$

where $\alpha \in (0, 1)$. Thus, as in models in the Kiyotaki-Moore tradition (discussed in chapter 1), capital is both a variable factor of production and an asset that can be used to pledge collateral.

Again, as in chapter 2, real investment is negatively related to the real lending rate,

$$I_t = I(i_t^L - \pi_t), \tag{3.7}$$

where i_t^L is the nominal loan rate and $I' < 0$. Given this investment demand function, the capital stock evolves according to

$$dK_t/dt = I_t - \delta_K K_t, \tag{3.8}$$

where $\delta_K \in (0, 1)$ is the depreciation rate. Given (3.7) and (3.8), firms choose only the level of employment to maximize profits.

2. This may seem like a rather perplexing statement in a continuous time model where each instant is infinitely short. The assumption is that each instant is the equivalent of a period in a discrete time model.

Let W_t denote the nominal wage, i^R the cost of borrowing from the central bank, and $\psi_W \in (0, 1)$ the share of the wage bill financed by credit. Total production costs are thus once again given by $(1+i^R)\psi_W W_t N_t + (1-\psi_W)W_t N_t = (1+\psi_W i^R)W_t N_t$. The maximization problem faced by the representative firm can be written as

$$N_t = \arg\max[P_t Y_t - (1+\psi_W i^R)W_t N_t]. \tag{3.9}$$

Solving problem (3.9) subject to (3.6), taking i^R, K_t, P_t, and W_t as given, yields

$$\alpha P_t N_t^{\alpha-1} K_t^{1-\alpha} - (1+\psi_W i^R)W_t = 0.$$

This condition yields the demand for labor as

$$N_t^d = \left[\frac{(1+\psi_W i^R)W_t}{\alpha P_t}\right]^{-1/(1-\alpha)} K_t, \tag{3.10}$$

which shows again that labor demand is inversely related to the real effective cost of labor, $(1+\psi_W i^R)W_t/P_t$, which accounts for the cost of bank borrowing.

Suppose now that there is full indexation so that $W_t = P_t$ and the supply of labor is perfectly elastic at the prevailing wage.[3] Equation (3.10) can therefore be written as

$$N_t^d = \left[\left(\frac{\alpha}{1+\psi_W i^R}\right)\right]^{1/(1-\alpha)} K_t = N^d(K_t; i^R), \tag{3.11}$$

where, with a tilde used to denote steady-state values,

$$N_K^d = \left[\left(\frac{\alpha}{1+\psi_W i^R}\right)\right]^{1/(1-\alpha)} > 0, \quad N_{i^R}^d = -\left(\frac{\psi_W}{1-\alpha}\right)\frac{\tilde{N}^d}{1+\psi_W i^R} < 0.$$

Substituting (3.11) in (3.6) gives

$$Y_t^s = \left[\left(\frac{\alpha}{1+\psi_W i^R}\right)\right]^{\alpha/(1-\alpha)} K_t = Y^s(K_t; i^R), \tag{3.12}$$

where

$$Y_K^s = \left[\left(\frac{\alpha}{1+\psi_W i^R}\right)\right]^{\alpha/(1-\alpha)} > 0, \quad Y_{i^R}^s = -\left(\frac{\alpha\psi_W}{1-\alpha}\right)\frac{\tilde{Y}^s}{1+\psi_W i^R} < 0.$$

3. Here again, the assumption that labor supply is perfectly elastic helps to avoid an explicit discussion of the equilibrium condition of the labor market.

Thus, an increase in the capital stock raises the marginal product of labor and stimulates both employment and output, whereas a rise in the refinance rate (as long as $\psi_W > 0$) has a contractionary effect.

The amount of loans demanded to finance labor costs and capital accumulation, L_t, is thus[4]

$$L_t = \psi_W W_t N_t^d + P_t I_t, \tag{3.13}$$

where I_t, the amount borrowed by the representative firm for investment purposes, is a Dixit-Stiglitz basket of differentiated loans, each supplied by a bank $i \in (0, 1)$ with a constant elasticity of substitution $\varsigma^L > 1$:[5]

$$I_t = \left[\int_0^1 (I_t^i)^{(\varsigma^L - 1)/\varsigma} di \right]^{\varsigma^L/(\varsigma^L - 1)}.$$

The demand for type-i loan, I_t^i, is thus given by the downward-sloping curve

$$I_t^i = \left(\frac{1 + i_t^{L,i}}{1 + i_t^L} \right)^{-\varsigma^L} I_t, \tag{3.14}$$

where $1 + i^{L,i}$ is the gross interest rate on the loan extended by bank i and

$$1 + i_t^L = \left[\int_0^1 (1 + i_t^{L,i})^{1 - \varsigma^L} di \right]^{1/(1 - \varsigma^L)}$$

the aggregate loan rate. These equations are similar to those discussed in chapter 2, section 3.

3.1.3 Commercial Banks

Assets of commercial bank i consist of total credit extended to firms, L_t^i, and mandatory reserves held at the central bank, RR_t^i. Bank liabilities consist of household deposits and borrowing from the central bank, $L_t^{B,i}$. The balance

4. Again, given the continuous time nature of the model, the stock specification in equation (3.13) implicitly assumes (somewhat unrealistically) that loan contracts mature instantaneously. In principle, it is the *flow* of credit, dL_t/dt, that should appear in that equation. However, this would increase the order of the dynamic system studied later by one, thereby precluding the use of phase diagrams.

5. The Dixit-Stiglitz specification is attractive because it allow for interest rate-setting by banks even if the heterogeneity among them is expressed via the financial products that they offer, rather than, say, their risk profiles. This would otherwise translate into heterogeneity in loan rates, rather than a unique rate in a symmetric equilibrium. See Stiglitz (2017) for a reflective view of the Dixit-Stiglitz model.

sheet of the representative bank can therefore be written as

$$L_t^i + RR_t^i = D_t^i + L_t^{B,i}. \tag{3.15}$$

Reserves held at the central bank pay no interest and are set in proportion to deposits,

$$RR_t^i = \mu D_t^i, \tag{3.16}$$

where $\mu \in (0, 1)$.

As in chapter 2, the market for deposits is competitive. From the perspective of commercial banks, household deposits and loans from the central bank are perfect substitutes at the margin; thus, the interest rate on deposits is a markup over the refinance rate, adjusted (downward) for the implicit cost of holding reserve requirements:

$$i^D = (1 - \mu)i^R. \tag{3.17}$$

By contrast, the market for loans is monopolistically competitive. Banks are subject to idiosyncratic risk because some borrowers may not repay their loans. They set not only the interest rate on investment loans (as in chapter 2, section 3) but also monitoring effort so as to maximize their expected profits. Specifically, banks can affect directly the repayment probability on their investment loans, $q_t^i \in (0, 1)$, by expending unobservable effort to select (*ex ante*) and—more importantly in this setting—monitor (*ex post*) their borrowers. As in chapter 2, and in line with a number of contributions to the micro-banking literature where lenders are subject to a moral hazard problem—including Allen et al. (2011), De Nicolò and Lucchetta (2012), Dell'Ariccia et al. (2014), and Cordella et al. (2018)—the probability of repayment itself, rather than monitoring effort *per se*, is taken to be the choice variable. Thus, the higher the monitoring effort, the safer the loan. As noted by Allen et al. (2011, pp. 988–989), one way of interpreting this assumption is that banks observe information about borrowers and then use it to help improve the performance of these borrowers. Another is that banks and borrowers have complementary skills: Borrowers have expertise in running the firm, whereas banks provide financial expertise that helps to improve performance. Either way, the important point is that greater monitoring is desirable *also* from the borrower's perspective.[6]

6. Thus, in this setting the borrower does not exert any effort. By contrast, in the model of Holmström and Tirole (1997), discussed in chapter 11, bank monitoring reduces the borrower's private benefit and influences the success probability only indirectly. See also Allen et al. (2011, pp. 1004–1005) for a discussion.

Each bank maximizes its expected profits. Given that $W_t = P_t$, its optimization problem is thus

$$1+i_t^{L,i}, q_t^i = \arg\max \left\{ (1+i^R)\psi_W N_t^d + q_t^i(1+i_t^{L,i})I_t^i + (1-q_t^i)\kappa^i K_t^i \right.$$
$$\left. -\frac{(1+i^D)D_t^i}{P_t} - \frac{(1+i^R)L_t^{B,i}}{P_t} - x_t^{M,i} \right\}. \tag{3.18}$$

The first term on the right-hand side of equation (3.18) is gross income from working capital loans, which are provided at a constant rate. The second term, $q_t^i(1+i_t^{L,i})I_t^i$, represents gross interest payments that the bank receives if there is no default, which occurs with probability q_t^i. The third term represents what banks earn in case of default, which occurs with probability $1-q_t^i$. As in chapter 2, $\kappa^i \in (0, 1)$ is the fraction of the capital stock that can be pledged as collateral to bank i. It is also assumed that $\kappa^i K_t^i \leq I_t^i$, to avoid a corner solution where banks have no incentives to monitor. The fourth and fifth terms are principal and interest payments on deposits and central bank loans. Deposits are guaranteed by the central bank and are therefore not contingent on the borrower's ability, or willingness, to repay.[7] The last term in (3.18), $x_t^{M,i}$, accounts for monitoring costs, which are assumed to be increasing in the amount of (risky) investment loans and the level of effort, or equivalently in this setting, the repayment probability

$$x_t^{M,i} = \phi_t \frac{(q_t^i)^2}{2} I_t^i, \tag{3.19}$$

where $\phi_t > 0$ can be thought of as the unit cost of monitoring.[8]

Banks internalize the fact that the demand for loans depends negatively on the loan rate, and they take prices, the value of collateral, the refinance rate, and ϕ_t as given.

Using (3.15) to substitute $L_t^{B,i}$ out in (3.18), as well as (3.14), (3.16), and (3.19), first-order conditions with respect to q_t^i and $1+i_t^{L,i}$ are given by, respectively,

$$(1+i_t^{L,i})I_t^i - \kappa^i K_t^i - \phi_t q_t^i I_t^i = 0, \tag{3.20}$$

7. For simplicity, the cost of deposit insurance is not explicitly accounted for; it can be thought of as being paid from revenues raised by nondistortionary lump-sum taxes.

8. A similar quadratic cost function is used in Allen et al. (2011), De Nicolò and Lucchetta (2012), and Dell'Ariccia et al. (2014), for instance. However, neither study considers the impact of collateral on monitoring.

$$q_t^i I_t^i + q_t^i (1+i_t^{L,i}) \left[\frac{\partial I_t^i}{\partial (1+i_t^{L,i})} \right] - (1+i^R) \left[\frac{\partial I_t^i}{\partial (1+i_t^{L,i})} \right] = 0. \quad (3.21)$$

Consider first condition (3.21). From (3.14),

$$\frac{\partial I_t^i}{\partial (1+i_t^{L,i})} = -\varsigma^L \left(\frac{1+i_t^{L,i}}{1+i_t^L} \right)^{-\varsigma^L - 1} \left(\frac{I_t}{1+i_t^L} \right). \quad (3.22)$$

Substituting (3.14) and (3.22) in (3.21) yields therefore

$$q_t^i \left(\frac{1+i_t^{L,i}}{1+i_t^L} \right)^{-\varsigma^L} I_t - q_t^i (1+i_t^{L,i}) \varsigma^L \left(\frac{1+i_t^{L,i}}{1+i_t^L} \right)^{-\varsigma^L - 1} \left(\frac{I_t}{1+i_t^L} \right)$$

$$+ (1+i^R) \varsigma^L \left(\frac{1+i_t^{L,i}}{1+i_t^L} \right)^{-\varsigma^L - 1} \left(\frac{I_t}{1+i_t^L} \right) = 0.$$

In a symmetric equilibrium, $i_t^{L,i} = i_t^L$ and $q_t^i = q_t$ $\forall i$, and this expression becomes

$$q_t I_t - q_t (1+i_t^L) \varsigma^L \left(\frac{I_t}{1+i_t^L} \right) + (1+i^R) \varsigma^L \left(\frac{I_t}{1+i_t^L} \right) = 0,$$

or equivalently

$$q_t I_t - [q_t(1+i_t^L) - (1+i^R)] \varsigma^L \left(\frac{I_t}{1+i_t^L} \right) = 0.$$

Multiplying this expression by $-(1+i_t^L)/I_t$ yields

$$-q_t(1+i_t^L) + q_t(1+i_t^L)\varsigma^L - (1+i^R)\varsigma^L = 0,$$

which implies that the equilibrium loan rate is

$$1 + i_t^L = \frac{\varsigma^L}{\varsigma^L - 1} \frac{1+i^R}{q_t}. \quad (3.23)$$

This equation is the same expression as the one derived in chapter 2, under monopolistic competition. The loan rate is proportional to the cost of borrowing from the central bank and inversely related to the repayment probability.

Consider next condition (3.20). In a symmetric equilibrium,

$$(1+i_t^L) I_t - \kappa K_t - \phi_t q_t I_t = 0,$$

which can be rearranged to give

$$q_t = \min\left\{\phi_t^{-1}\left(1+i_t^L-\frac{\kappa K_t}{I_t}\right), 1\right\}. \tag{3.24}$$

Assuming that this solution is such that $q_t < 1$, it implies that the optimal level of monitoring is increasing in the loan rate and decreasing in the collateral-investment loan ratio. Intuitively, a higher loan rate raises the return to lending when borrowers are able to repay, thereby increasing incentives to monitor. This is a standard result in microeconomic models of banking with moral hazard on the lender's side, such as those referred to earlier. By contrast, collateral limits the loss that banks incur in case of default and operates essentially as a hedge, as discussed in chapter 1. Thus, all else equal, a higher collateral value reduces incentives to monitor and screen borrowers—akin to a *lazy bank* effect, as discussed by Manove et al. (2001)—and leads to a *lower* repayment probability.

Suppose now that the unit cost term ϕ_t is also inversely related to the collateral-investment loan ratio,

$$\phi_t = \phi\left(\frac{\kappa K_t}{I_t}\right), \tag{3.25}$$

where $\phi' < 0$. A higher value of collateral (for a given level of loans) mitigates moral hazard on the part of borrowers by mitigating their incentives to take on excessive risk and by inducing them to exert more effort in ensuring that their investments are successful.[9] In turn, improved creditworthiness prompts them to be more compliant with bank monitoring requirements, thereby reducing unit monitoring costs. Thus, $\phi' < 0$ and an increase in the collateral-loan ratio will now tend to *raise* the repayment probability, q_t.

The foregoing discussion suggests therefore that there are conflicting moral hazard effects of the collateral-loan ratio on the level of effort and the repayment probability. In what follows, and consistent with the preponderance of the evidence for middle-income countries (MICs)—which includes Liberti and Sturgess (2013), for instance—the effect on borrowers' incentives will be assumed to dominate the effect on lenders' incentives discussed earlier. Thus, the net impact of an increase in the collateral-loan ratio is to raise the probability of repayment. Combining (3.24) and (3.25) yields therefore

$$q_t = q\left(i_t^L, \frac{\kappa K_t}{I_t}\right), \tag{3.26}$$

where $q_{i^L}, q_{\kappa K/I} > 0$.

9. See, for instance, Boot et al. (1991) and Bester (1994) for a more detailed discussion.

Substituting (3.26) in (3.23) yields

$$1+i_t^L = \frac{\varsigma^L}{\varsigma^L - 1} q\left(i_t^L, \frac{\kappa K_t}{I_t}\right)^{-1} (1+i^R),$$

which can be totally differentiated to give

$$di_t^L = \frac{\varsigma^L}{\varsigma^L - 1}\left\{\tilde{q}^{-1} di^R - \frac{q_{\kappa K/I}(1+i^R)}{\tilde{q}^2} d\left(\frac{\kappa K_t}{I_t}\right) - \frac{q_{i^L}(1+i^R)}{\tilde{q}^2} di_t^L\right\},$$

so that

$$i_t^L = \theta\left(\frac{\kappa K_t}{I_t}; i^R\right), \tag{3.27}$$

where

$$\theta_{\kappa K/I} = -\left[\frac{\varsigma^L - 1}{\varsigma^L} + \frac{q_{i^L}(1+i^R)}{\tilde{q}^2}\right]^{-1} \frac{q_{\kappa K/I}(1+i^R)}{\tilde{q}^2} < 0,$$

$$\theta_{i^R} = \left[\frac{\varsigma^L - 1}{\varsigma^L} + \frac{q_{i^L}(1+i^R)}{\tilde{q}^2}\right]^{-1} \tilde{q}^{-1} > 0,$$

which shows that, all else equal, an increase in the collateral-investment loan ratio, by raising the repayment probability, lowers the loan rate, whereas an increase in the refinance rate (the marginal cost of funding for banks) has the opposite effect. Again, these effects are similar to those obtained in chapter 2. However, in the present setting the increase in the refinance rate also has indirect effects through investment and the capital stock, which is now endogenous. These effects are accounted for later on in the general equilibrium solution of the model.

As in chapter 2, given that L_t and D_t are determined by private agents' behavior, the balance sheet constraint (3.15) together with (3.16) can be used to determine residually bank borrowing from the central bank:

$$L_t^B = \max[L_t - (1-\mu)D_t, 0]. \tag{3.28}$$

3.1.4 Central Bank

The central bank sets the refinance rate i^R and provides all the liquidity demanded by commercial banks through a standing facility. Its balance sheet consists, on the asset side, of loans to the commercial bank, L_t^B; on the liability side is the monetary base, which is itself defined as the sum of total currency in circulation and required reserves:

$$L_t^B = M_t^s + RR_t. \tag{3.29}$$

This equation determines once again the supply of currency. But by construction, neither (3.28) nor (3.29) plays a role in the model's dynamics.

3.1.5 Market Equilibrium and Price Dynamics

As in chapter 2, there are five market equilibrium conditions to consider: four for financial markets (deposits, loans, central bank credit, and cash) and one for the goods market. Markets for deposits and loans adjust through quantities, with prices set either through a no-arbitrage condition (deposit market) or bank optimization behavior (loan market). The supply of central bank credit is perfectly elastic at the official refinance rate and the market also equilibrates through quantity adjustment.

Prices now adjust gradually to disequilibria between aggregate demand and aggregate supply. Using again a simple partial adjustment mechanism yields

$$d\pi_t/dt = \lambda^G(C_t + I_t - Y_t^s), \tag{3.30}$$

where $\lambda^G \geq 0$. The goods market is therefore in continuous equilibrium, and inflation adjusts instantaneously, only when $\lambda^G \to \infty$. This specification is consistent with the backward-looking specification in Fuhrer and Moore (1995) and has been used in a number of contributions.[10]

The last equilibrium condition relates to the market for cash and involves (3.2) and (3.29). Because the goods market is no longer in continuous equilibrium, Walras' law cannot be used to eliminate that condition, as in chapter 2. At the same time, given the portfolio allocation rule (3.1) and the cash-in-advance constraint (3.2), holdings of cash have no direct impact (as noted earlier) on the model's dynamics.

3.2 Solution and Steady State

Substituting equation (3.7) for investment in the equilibrium loan rate equation (3.27) yields

$$i_t^L = \theta\left[\frac{\kappa K_t}{I(i_t^L - \pi_t)}; i^R\right].$$

10. An alternative approach would be to assume a forward-looking specification, as in Calvo (1983) and Calvo and Végh (1995), for instance. However, Calvo pricing (which is discussed in detail in chapter 4) leads to the counterintuitive result that a negative demand shock leads to an *increase* in the change in inflation. Moreover, the evidence provided in Agénor and Bayraktar (2010) suggests that in a number of MICs past inflation is often a more important determinant of current inflation.

Totally differentiating this expression gives

$$di_t^L = -\theta_{\kappa K/I}\left(\frac{\kappa\tilde{K}}{\tilde{I}^2}\right)I'(di_t^L - d\pi_t) + \theta_{\kappa K/I}\left(\frac{\kappa}{\tilde{I}}\right)dK_t + \theta_{i^R}di^R,$$

so that

$$i_t^L = J(K_t, \pi_t; i^R), \tag{3.31}$$

where, recalling that $I' < 0$, $\theta_{\kappa K/I} < 0$, and $\theta_{i^R} > 0$,

$$J_K = \frac{\theta_{\kappa K/I}}{\Omega}\left(\frac{\kappa}{\tilde{I}}\right) < 0,$$

$$J_\pi = \frac{\theta_{\kappa K/I}}{\Omega}\left(\frac{\kappa\tilde{K}}{\tilde{I}^2}\right)I' > 0,$$

$$J_{i^R} = \frac{\theta_{i^R}}{\Omega} > 0,$$

$$\Omega = 1 + \theta_{\kappa K/I}\left(\frac{\kappa\tilde{K}}{\tilde{I}^2}\right)I' > 0.$$

An increase in the capital stock raises the value of collateral, which tends to increase the repayment probability and to reduce the equilibrium loan rate. This reduction is mitigated partially by the fact that the fall in the cost of borrowing stimulates investment and lowers the collateral-loan ratio. A higher inflation rate lowers the real loan rate (at the initial value of the nominal cost of borrowing) and stimulates investment, which reduces the collateral-loan ratio; this raises the premium and the nominal loan rate, which therefore mitigates the initial increase in investment. As in chapter 2, an increase in the refinance rate raises the equilibrium loan rate. However, this effect is not necessarily one-to-one anymore, due to the fact that the loan rate affects both the repayment probability and investment.

Substituting (3.31) in (3.7) and the result in (3.8) yields

$$dK_t/dt = I[J(K_t, \pi_t; i^R) - \pi_t] - \delta_K K_t, \tag{3.32}$$

or equivalently

$$dK_t/dt = KK(K_t, \pi_t; i^R), \tag{3.33}$$

where

$$KK_K = I'J_K - \delta_K = \frac{\theta_{\kappa K/I}}{\Omega}\left(\frac{\kappa}{\tilde{I}}\right)I' - \delta_K \gtrless 0,$$

$$KK_\pi = I'(J_\pi - 1) = I'\left\{\frac{\theta_{\kappa K/I}}{\Omega}\left(\frac{\kappa\tilde{K}}{\tilde{I}^2}\right)I' - 1\right\} \gtrless 0,$$

$$KK_{i^R} = I'J_{i^R} < 0.$$

An increase in the current capital stock lowers the loan rate (both nominal and real, given a constant inflation rate) and raises investment; at the same time, depreciation tends to reduce the rate at which capital is accumulated. The net effect is therefore ambiguous in general. Assuming that the depreciation rate is low enough implies that $KK_K > 0$, given that $I', J_K < 0$. An increase in the inflation rate also has, in general, an ambiguous effect on capital accumulation. On the one hand, it lowers the *real* loan rate, which stimulates capital accumulation; on the other, it raises the *nominal* loan rate, which tends to reduce investment. Because both inflation and the nominal loan rate go up, the net effect on the real interest rate can be either positive or negative. In what follows it is assumed that the direct effect of inflation dominates (so that $J_\pi < 1$), implying that $KK_\pi > 0$. Finally, a higher refinance rate raises the loan rate (both nominal and real) and lowers investment, which reduces the rate of capital accumulation.

The second step is to characterize the dynamics of inflation. Using (3.5), (3.7), (3.12), (3.17), and (3.31) to substitute out for C_t, I_t, Y_t^s, i^D, and i_t^L in (3.30) yields

$$\frac{d\pi_t}{dt} = \lambda^G\left\{-\alpha_2[(1-\mu)i^R - \pi_t] + I[J(K_t, \pi_t; i^R) - \pi_t] - \frac{Y^s(K_t; i^R)}{[1-\alpha_1(\pi_t)]^{-1}}\right\}. \tag{3.34}$$

Solving this expression gives

$$\frac{d\pi_t}{dt} = \lambda^G GG(K_t, \pi_t; i^R, \mu), \tag{3.35}$$

where, recalling that $Y_K^s > 0$, $Y_{i^R}^s < 0$, $I' < 0$, $J_K < 0$, and $J_{i^R} > 0$,

$$GG_K = I'J_K - [1-\alpha_1(\tilde{\pi})]Y_K^s \gtrless 0,$$

$$GG_\pi = \alpha_2 + I'(J_\pi - 1) + \alpha_1'\tilde{Y}^s \gtrless 0,$$

$$GG_{i^R} = -\alpha_2(1-\mu) + I'J_{i^R} - [1-\alpha_1(\tilde{\pi})]Y_{i^R}^s \gtrless 0,$$

$$GG_\mu = \alpha_2 i^R > 0.$$

An increase in the capital stock raises both investment (by lowering the loan rate through its impact on the premium, as discussed earlier) and output; the net effect on excess demand and inflationary pressures is thus ambiguous in general. An increase in the inflation rate exerts three types of effects on excess demand. First, it lowers the real lending rate (given the assumption that $J_\pi < 1$) and stimulates investment. Second, it reduces the real deposit rate, which induces households to increase current consumption. Third, it erodes wealth, which creates incentives to reduce the propensity to spend out of current income. The net effect on excess demand is thus ambiguous. In what follows, the focus is on the case where $GG_K < 0$, which implies that the financial accelerator effect (as measured by $\theta_{\kappa K/I}$) is not too strong, and $GG_\pi < 0$, which implies on the contrary that the wealth erosion effect is relatively powerful.

An increase in the refinance rate has conflicting effects on changes in inflation. On the one hand, it lowers aggregate supply by raising the effective cost of labor; on the other, it lowers aggregate demand by reducing both consumption (through the intertemporal effect) and investment (through a higher loan rate). If the cost channel is weak or inexistent—that is, $\psi_W = 0$, which implies from (3.12) that $Y^s_{i^R} = 0$ also—only the standard aggregate demand effect operates and a tightening of monetary policy lowers unambiguously the inflation rate, so that $GG_{i^R} < 0$. By contrast, if the cost channel is sufficiently strong, this effect is reversed and $GG_{i^R} > 0$. In what follows, as in chapter 2, both cases will be considered. Finally, an increase in the reserve requirement rate lowers the deposit rate and induces households to shift consumption toward the present, thereby increasing aggregate demand and, all else equal, raising inflationary pressures.

The model therefore boils down to a dynamic system in two variables, the capital stock and the inflation rate, K_t and π_t. The steady-state equilibrium solutions for these variables can be determined directly from (3.32) and (3.33), and (3.34) and (3.35), by setting $dK_t/dt = d\pi_t/dt = 0$. These solutions are

$$KK(\tilde{K}, \tilde{\pi}; i^R) = I[J(\tilde{K}, \tilde{\pi}; i^R) - \tilde{\pi}] - \delta_K \tilde{K} = 0, \tag{3.36}$$

$$GG(\tilde{K}, \tilde{\pi}; i^R) = \frac{Y^s(\tilde{K}, i^R)}{[1 - \alpha_1(\tilde{\pi})]^{-1}} + \alpha_2[(1-\mu)i^R - \tilde{\pi}] - I[J(\tilde{K}, \tilde{\pi}; i^R) - \tilde{\pi}] = 0. \tag{3.37}$$

Equation (3.36) defines the combinations of the capital stock and inflation rate for which the stock of capital is constant and the financial market is in equilibrium; it is shown as curve *KK* in figure 3.1. Similarly, equation (3.37) defines the combinations of the same two variables for which aggregate supply is equal to aggregate demand and inflation is constant; it is shown as curve *GG* in the same figure. From (3.33) and (3.35), setting $dK_t/dt = d\pi_t/dt = 0$ yields

$$\left.\frac{dK_t}{d\pi_t}\right|_{KK} = -\frac{KK_\pi}{KK_K} < 0, \quad \left.\frac{dK}{d\pi_t}\right|_{GG} = -\frac{GG_\pi}{GG_K} < 0, \tag{3.38}$$

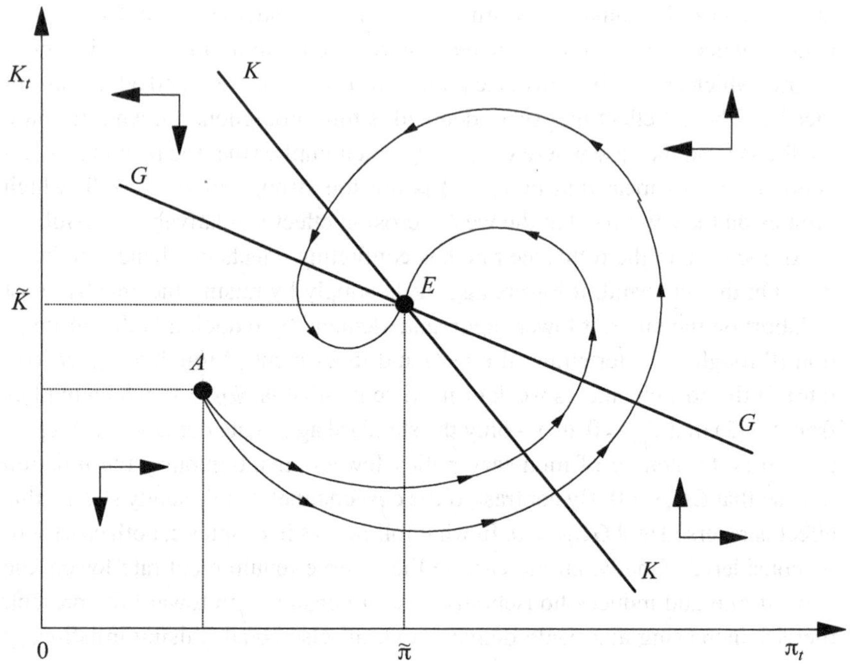

Figure 3.1
Macroeconomic equilibrium

which shows that, given that $KK_K, KK_\pi > 0$ and $GG_K, GG_\pi < 0$, both KK and GG have a negative slope.[11]

Equations (3.36) and (3.37) can be used to formally assess the long-run effects of a change in the refinance rate. Before doing so, however, the stability of the model and its implications for the relative position of curves KK and GG must be established.

In the vicinity of the steady state, a linear approximation to (3.33) and (3.35) gives

$$\begin{bmatrix} dK/dt \\ d\pi_t/dt \end{bmatrix} = \begin{bmatrix} KK_K & KK_\pi \\ \lambda^G GG_K & \lambda^G GG_\pi \end{bmatrix} \begin{bmatrix} K_t - \tilde{K} \\ \pi_t - \tilde{\pi} \end{bmatrix}. \tag{3.39}$$

Let $\mathbf{A}$ denote the matrix of coefficients in (3.39). Given that both the capital stock and the inflation rate adjust gradually, stability requires two negative eigenvalues. In turn, this requires that the determinant of $\mathbf{A}$, which is equal to the product of the eigenvalues, be positive (to exclude eigenvalues of opposite

11. In the particular case where $J_\pi = 1$, then $KK_\pi = 0$ and KK is a vertical curve.

signs) and that its trace, which is equal to the sum of the eigenvalues, be negative (to exclude two positive eigenvalues):[12]

$$\text{tr}\mathbf{A} = \overset{(+)}{KK_K} + \lambda^G \overset{(-)}{GG_\pi} < 0,$$

$$\det\mathbf{A} = \lambda^G(\overset{(+)}{KK_K}\overset{(-)}{GG_\pi} - \overset{(+)}{KK_\pi}\overset{(-)}{GG_K}) > 0.$$

Given the signs indicated earlier, both expressions are in general ambiguous. Given that $GG_\pi < 0$, if the speed of adjustment of inflation, λ^G, is sufficiently high or if the wealth erosion effect is very strong, tr**A** < 0. In addition, for det**A** > 0 it must be that $KK_K GG_\pi - KK_\pi GG_K > 0$, or equivalently $-KK_\pi/KK_K > -GG_\pi/GG_K$. Thus, given (3.38), the condition for det**A** > 0 is that KK be steeper than GG, as shown in figure 3.1. The adjustment process, starting from an initial point A at $t = 0$, is counter-clockwise and may involve repeated cycles, as also illustrated in the figure.[13] The system is asymptotically stable.

3.3 Monetary and Macroprudential Policies

To examine the transmission process of monetary and macroprudential policies, consider autonomous and permanent increases in the refinance rate, the required reserve ratio, and the tax on loans.

3.3.1 Monetary Policy

The effects of an increase in the refinance rate on the equilibrium levels of the capital stock and the inflation rate can be calculated by differentiating (3.36) and (3.37) and solving the system

$$\begin{bmatrix} KK_K & KK_\pi \\ GG_K & GG_\pi \end{bmatrix} \begin{bmatrix} d\tilde{K} \\ d\tilde{\pi} \end{bmatrix} = \begin{bmatrix} -KK_{i^R} \\ -GG_{i^R} \end{bmatrix} di^R. \tag{3.40}$$

To determine the sign of these steady-state effects, as in chapter 2 two cases must be considered: a weak cost channel (a low value of ψ_W, so that $GG_{i^R} < 0$) and a strong cost channel (with ψ_W large enough, in combination to other structural parameters, to ensure that $GG_{i^R} > 0$).

With $GG_{i^R} < 0$, recalling that $KK_{i^R} < 0$ and letting $\Delta = \det\mathbf{A}/\lambda^G = KK_K GG_\pi - KK_\pi GG_K > 0$, the solution of (3.40) gives

12. The condition to avoid cycles is det**A** $<$ (tr**A**)$^2/4$, which is difficult to evaluate analytically in terms of underlying parameters.

13. From the above conditions, it is clear that if $GG_\pi > 0$, the condition tr**A** < 0 cannot be satisfied. And if $GG_\pi < 0$ while at the same time $GG_K > 0$, then the condition det**A** > 0 cannot be satisfied.

$$\frac{d\tilde{K}}{di^R} = \frac{\overset{(+)}{KK_\pi}\overset{(-)}{GG_{i^R}} - \overset{(-)}{KK_{i^R}}\overset{(-)}{GG_\pi}}{\Delta} < 0, \tag{3.41}$$

$$\frac{d\tilde{\pi}}{di^R} = \frac{\overset{(-)}{KK_{i^R}}\overset{(-)}{GG_K} - \overset{(+)}{KK_K}\overset{(-)}{GG_{i^R}}}{\Delta} > 0. \tag{3.42}$$

By implication, using (3.31), the impact on the nominal loan rate is, given that $J_K < 0$, $J_\pi > 0$, and $J_{i^R} > 0$,

$$\frac{d\tilde{\imath}^L}{di^R} = J_K\left(\frac{d\tilde{K}}{di^R}\right) + J_\pi\left(\frac{d\tilde{\pi}}{di^R}\right) + J_{i^R} > 0,$$

whereas from (3.12), the impact on aggregate supply is

$$\frac{d\tilde{Y}^s}{di^R} = Y_K^s\left(\frac{d\tilde{K}}{di^R}\right) + Y_{i^R}^s < 0.$$

In addition, from (3.36), $\tilde{I} = \delta_K\tilde{K}$; thus, given (3.41),

$$\frac{d\tilde{I}}{di^R} = \delta_K\left(\frac{d\tilde{K}}{di^R}\right) < 0,$$

which implies also, given (3.7), that the real loan rate necessarily increases, as can be verified directly:

$$\frac{d(\tilde{\imath}^L - \tilde{\pi})}{di^R} = J_K\left(\frac{d\tilde{K}}{di^R}\right) + (J_\pi - 1)\left(\frac{d\tilde{\pi}}{di^R}\right) + J_{i^R} > 0.$$

Finally, as implied by (3.30),

$$\frac{d\tilde{C}}{di^R} = \frac{d\tilde{Y}^s}{di^R} - \frac{d\tilde{I}}{di^R} = (Y_K^s - \delta_K)\left(\frac{d\tilde{K}}{di^R}\right) + Y_{i^R}^s \gtrless 0.$$

Thus, in the standard case, an increase in the refinance rate leads not only to a contraction in investment, credit, and output, but also to an *increase* in inflation. The reason is that, in this model, the contraction in aggregate supply associated with the reduction in the capital stock (even in the absence of a working capital channel, so that $\psi_W = Y_{i^R}^s = 0$) must be matched by a reduction in aggregate demand. This is brought about by a higher steady-state inflation rate, which reduces consumption as a result of a strong wealth erosion effect. Because both output and investment fall, the net effect on consumption is in general ambiguous.

By contrast, with $GG_{i^R} > 0$, solving (3.40) gives

$$\frac{d\tilde{K}}{di^R} = \frac{\overset{(+)}{KK_{\pi}}\overset{(+)}{GG_{i^R}} - \overset{(-)}{KK_{i^R}}\overset{(-)}{GG_{\pi}}}{\Delta} \gtrless 0, \tag{3.43}$$

$$\frac{d\tilde{\pi}}{di^R} = \frac{\overset{(-)}{KK_{i^R}}\overset{(-)}{GG_K} - \overset{(+)}{KK_K}\overset{(+)}{GG_{i^R}}}{\Delta} \gtrless 0, \tag{3.44}$$

which implies that the effects on the nominal and real loan rates, and investment and output, are all ambiguous.

The transitional dynamics and steady-state effects associated with an increase in the refinance rate are illustrated in figures 3.2 and 3.3. In both cases, curve KK shifts outward or to the right. Indeed, from (3.36), $KK(\tilde{K}, \tilde{\pi}; i^R) = 0$; with $KK_K > 0$ and $KK_{i^R} < 0$, for a constant rate of inflation the capital stock must increase if the refinance rate rises. However, with $GG(\tilde{K}, \tilde{\pi}; i^R, \mu) = 0$ from (3.37) and $GG_K < 0$, curve GG may shift either outward or inward, depending on whether the cost channel is weak ($GG_{i^R} < 0$) or strong ($GG_{i^R} > 0$).

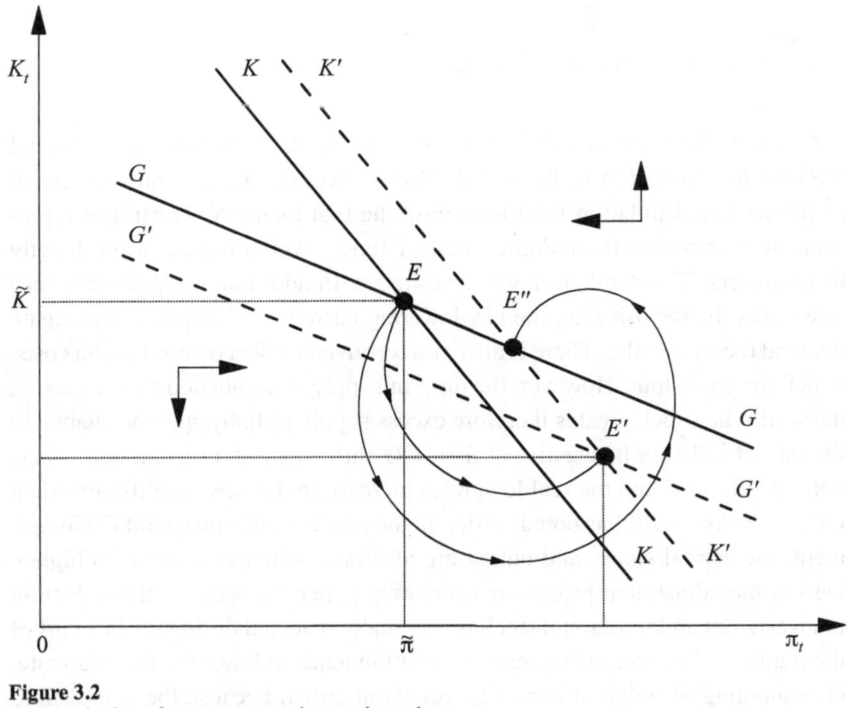

Figure 3.2
Increase in the refinance rate: weak cost channel

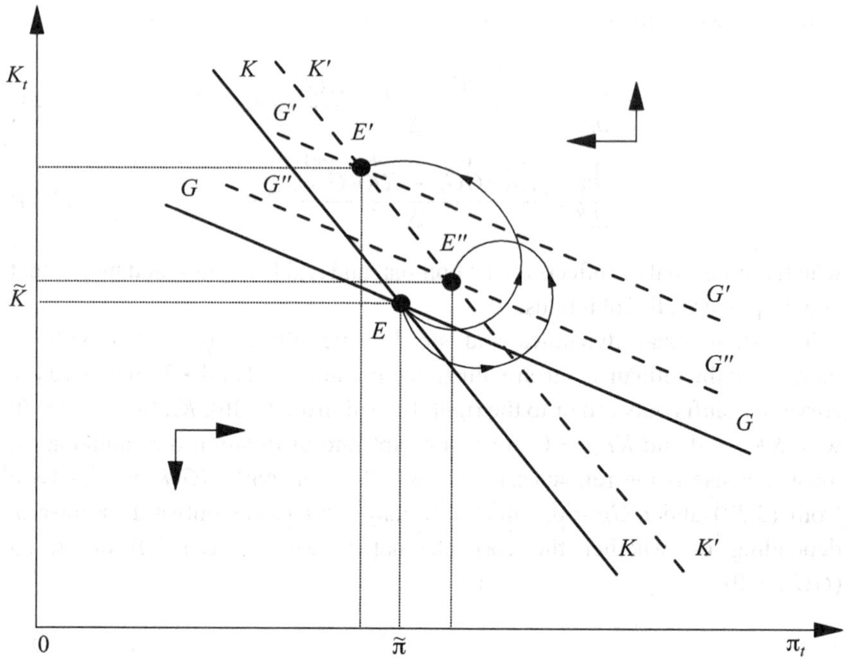

Figure 3.3
Increase in the refinance rate: strong cost channel

Consider first the standard case of a weak or inexistent cost channel ($GG_{i^R} < 0$), illustrated in figure 3.2. The immediate effect of an increase in i^R (at the initial inflation rate) is to raise the real loan rate, because it represents an increase in the marginal cost of funds, which is passed on directly to borrowers. This tends to lower investment. In addition, a higher refinance rate raises the deposit rate, thereby lowering current consumption. Aggregate demand therefore falls. There is also a direct adverse effect on production costs, which lowers output. However, the drop in supply is dominated by the drop in demand. The shock creates therefore excess supply initially, and the change in the rate of inflation is negative at first; *GG* shifts inward, or to the left. Thus, both the nominal and the real loan rates increase in the new equilibrium when $GG_{i^R} < 0$. As a result, as noted earlier, in the new equilibrium (point E') investment, the capital stock, and output are all lower, whereas inflation is higher. During the adjustment process overshooting generally occurs—the reduction in investment and the capital stock is eventually reversed during the last part of the transition because the increase in inflation tends to lower the real loan rate. Overshooting of inflation cannot be ruled out either, because the approach to point E' may involve repeated cycles. Note also that if the aggregate supply and aggregate demand effects of a change in the refinance rate exactly offset each other, so that $GG_{i^R} = 0$, curve GG will not shift; the long-run equilibrium will then be at point E'', as shown in figure 3.2, and would in general involve cycles in all variables.

Consider now the case of a strong cost channel ($GG_{i^R} > 0$), illustrated in figure 3.3. This time, curve GG shifts outward and to the right, and the initial change in the inflation rate is positive—reflecting the fact that there is excess demand on impact (even though both investment and consumption fall, output drops by even more). Excess demand continues to prevail during the early part of the transition to the new equilibrium. However, the steady-state effects, as shown earlier, are ambiguous and depend on how strong the cost channel is. Figure 3.3 illustrates two alternative scenarios. If the upward shift in GG is large (to $G'G'$), the initial increase in inflation lowers the collateral-loan ratio over time and leads to a higher nominal loan rate, as before. Excess demand prevails during the first part of the transition process. The economy converges to the equilibrium point E', characterized by *lower* inflation and a higher capital stock—but possibly also lower output; because $d\tilde{Y}^s/di^R = Y^s_K(d\tilde{K}/di^R) + Y^s_{i^R}$, even if $d\tilde{K}/di^R > 0$, the fact that $Y^s_{i^R} < 0$ may still dominate. The initial increase in the inflation rate is reversed beyond a certain point because higher inflation tends to reduce consumption (and aggregate demand) through the wealth erosion effect.

Alternatively, if the upward shift in GG is not too large (to $G''G''$), the economy may converge to point E''—an equilibrium characterized by a higher capital stock (but again, with an ambiguous effect on output) than initially but also a *higher* inflation rate. If the effect on output is negative, there may be a *price puzzle*, or *stagflation*, in the sense that a monetary contraction may lead in the long run to both higher inflation and lower activity.

3.3.2 Macroprudential Policy

As in chapter 2, both an increase in the required reserve ratio and a tax on loans can be analyzed in this setting.

Increase in required reserve ratio

The effects of an increase in the required reserve ratio on the equilibrium levels of the capital stock and the inflation rate can be calculated by differentiating (3.36) and (3.37), and solving the system

$$\begin{bmatrix} KK_K & KK_\pi \\ GG_K & GG_\pi \end{bmatrix} \begin{bmatrix} d\tilde{K} \\ d\tilde{\pi} \end{bmatrix} = \begin{bmatrix} 0 \\ -GG_\mu \end{bmatrix} d\mu,$$

which gives, with again $\Delta > 0$,

$$\frac{d\tilde{K}}{d\mu} = \frac{\overset{(+)}{KK_{\pi}}\overset{(+)}{GG_{\mu}}}{\Delta} > 0, \quad \frac{d\tilde{\pi}}{d\mu} = \frac{-\overset{(+)}{KK_{K}}\overset{(+)}{GG_{\mu}}}{\Delta} < 0,$$

so that, by implication, given that (as shown earlier) $J_K < 0$ and $J_\pi > 0$,

$$\frac{d\tilde{\imath}^L}{d\mu} = J_K\left(\frac{d\tilde{K}}{d\mu}\right) + J_\pi\left(\frac{d\tilde{\pi}}{d\mu}\right) < 0,$$

$$\frac{d\tilde{Y}^s}{d\mu} = Y_K^s\left(\frac{d\tilde{K}}{d\mu}\right) > 0,$$

$$\frac{d\tilde{I}}{d\mu} = \delta_K\left(\frac{d\tilde{K}}{d\mu}\right) > 0,$$

$$\frac{d\tilde{C}}{d\mu} = \frac{d\tilde{Y}^s}{d\mu} - \frac{d\tilde{I}}{d\mu} = (Y_K^s - \delta_K)\left(\frac{d\tilde{K}}{d\mu}\right) \gtrless 0,$$

$$\frac{d(\tilde{\imath}^L - \tilde{\pi})}{d\mu} = J_K\left(\frac{d\tilde{K}}{d\mu}\right) + (J_\pi - 1)\left(\frac{d\tilde{\pi}}{d\mu}\right) < 0,$$

where the last result must hold because investment can increase only if the real loan rate falls.

The transitional dynamics of an autonomous increase in the required reserve ratio are illustrated in figure 3.4. On impact, *KK* does not change whereas *GG* shifts outward, or to the right. The new equilibrium is at point *E'*, corresponding to a higher capital stock and a lower inflation rate. The adjustment path is again nonmonotonic, with an initial phase of higher inflation. Thus, in this setting, higher reserve requirements can be inflationary in the short run while at the same time reducing inflation and increasing investment, output, and the capital stock in the long run.[14] Put differently, as a policy aimed at mitigating credit expansion and promoting financial stability, an increase in the required reserve ratio does not operate in the direction expected. But again, it is worth emphasizing that under the monetary policy regime considered here, changes in reserve requirements have no direct effect on banks' marginal cost of funds.

14. In the static model of chapter 2, where macroeconomic equilibrium was defined in terms of the price level, rather than inflation, the policy led to both an expansion in output *and* higher prices with perfect substitutability between deposits and central bank borrowing. These static effects differ therefore from the steady-state effects obtained here.

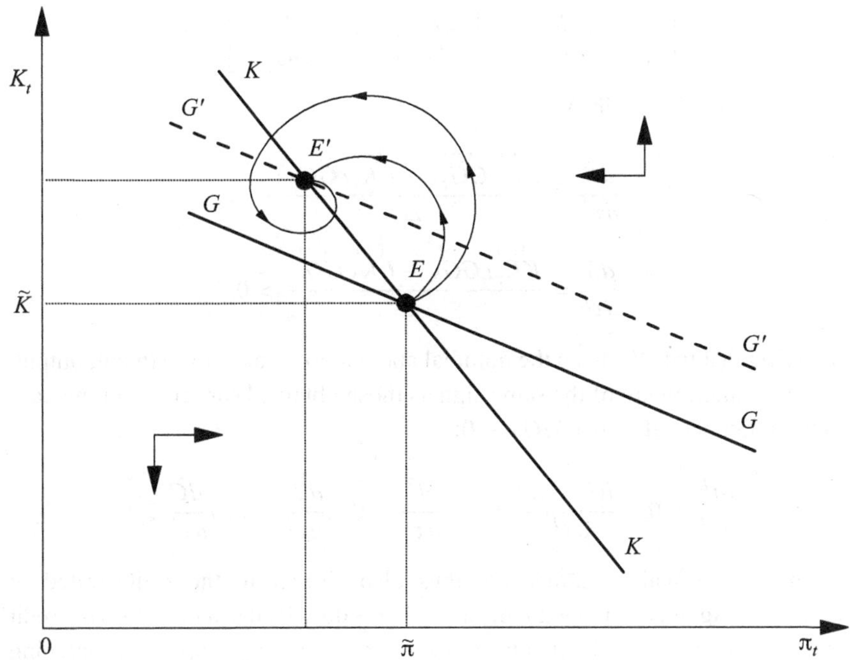

Figure 3.4
Increase in the required reserve ratio

Increase in tax rate on loans

As before, and in keeping with the idea of providing a simple analysis at first, macroprudential regulation is introduced as a tax on loans, at the rate $\tau^L \in (0, 1)$. From (3.31), the equilibrium loan rate is now

$$i_t^L = \theta\left[\frac{\kappa K_t}{I(i_t^L - \pi_t)}; i^R, \tau^L\right] = J(K_t, \pi_t; i^R, \tau^L),$$

where

$$J_{\tau^L} = \frac{\theta_{\tau^L}}{\Omega} > 0,$$

which shows that the direct effect of a higher tax rate on loans is again to raise the loan rate. By implication, from (3.33) and (3.35),

$$KK_{\tau^L} = GG_{\tau^L} = I' J_{\tau^L} < 0.$$

Given these results, the effects on the equilibrium levels of the capital stock and the inflation rate can be calculated by solving the system

$$\begin{bmatrix} KK_K & KK_\pi \\ GG_K & GG_\pi \end{bmatrix} \begin{bmatrix} d\tilde{K} \\ d\tilde{\pi} \end{bmatrix} = \begin{bmatrix} -KK_{\tau^L} \\ -GG_{\tau^L} \end{bmatrix} d\tau^L,$$

which gives, with again $\Delta > 0$,

$$\frac{d\tilde{K}}{d\tau^L} = \frac{\overset{(+)}{KK_\pi}\overset{(-)}{GG_{\tau^L}} - \overset{(-)}{KK_{\tau^L}}\overset{(-)}{GG_\pi}}{\Delta} < 0,$$

$$\frac{d\tilde{\pi}}{d\tau^L} = \frac{\overset{(-)}{KK_{\tau^L}}\overset{(-)}{GG_K} - \overset{(+)}{KK_K}\overset{(-)}{GG_{\tau^L}}}{\Delta} > 0,$$

implying that the effects on the nominal and real loan rates, investment, output, and consumption are of the same sign as those obtained earlier for an increase in the refinance rate when $GG_{i^R} < 0$:

$$\frac{d\tilde{\imath}^L}{d\tau^L} > 0, \quad \frac{d(\tilde{\imath}^L - \tilde{\pi})}{d\tau^L} > 0, \quad \frac{d\tilde{I}}{d\tau^L} < 0, \quad \frac{d\tilde{Y}^s}{d\tau^L} < 0, \quad \frac{d\tilde{C}}{d\tau^L} \gtrless 0.$$

The transitional dynamics are thus also similar to those illustrated in figure 3.2. Again, even though the tax on loans does lead to a reduction in credit and investment in the long run, it also lowers aggregate supply; a matching reduction in aggregate demand is brought about not only by lower investment but also lower consumption, through the wealth erosion associated with inflation. However, the implication now is that there is a long-run trade-off between financial stability and price stability, in the sense that while the policy leads to lower credit, it is accompanied by higher inflation. The issue now is whether this trade-off persists when the central bank is allowed to set the refinance rate endogenously, in response to both inflation and output developments.

3.4 Endogenous Refinance Rate

Consider the case where, as in Agénor and Pereira da Silva (2014), the refinance rate is endogenous and determined by a simple rule,

$$di_t^R/dt = \chi_1(\pi_t - \pi^T) + \chi_2(C_t + I_t - Y_t^s), \tag{3.45}$$

where $\chi_1, \chi_2 > 0$ and $\pi^T \geq 0$ is the central bank's inflation target. Thus, in line with the so-called *Taylor rule*—discussed by Svensson (2010), for instance, in the context of inflation targeting—the central bank raises the refinance rate in response to positive deviations in inflation from target (that is, the inflation gap) and excess demand for goods. One key difference with the standard specification of the Taylor rule is that the continuous-time specification (3.45) is in terms of the *change* in the refinance rate, which implies, implicitly, a persistence parameter of unity.[15]

The dynamic equations (3.33) and (3.35) remain the same as before, with the exception that i_t^R is endogenous; for convenience, they are repeated here:

$$dK_t/dt = KK(K_t, \pi_t, i_t^R; \tau^L), \tag{3.46}$$

$$\frac{d\pi_t}{dt} = \lambda^G GG(K_t, \pi_t, i_t^R; \mu, \tau^L), \tag{3.47}$$

where, under the same assumptions as before, $KK_K > 0$, $KK_\pi > 0$, $KK_{i^R} < 0$, and $KK_{\tau^L} < 0$, whereas $GG_K < 0$, $GG_\pi < 0$, $GG_{i^R} < 0$, $GG_\mu > 0$, and $GG_{\tau^L} < 0$.

Substituting (3.5), (3.7), (3.12), (3.17), and (3.31) for C_t, I_t, Y_t^s, i_t^D, and i_t^L in (3.45), with i_t^R now endogenous, yields

$$\frac{di_t^R}{dt} = \chi_1(\pi_t - \pi^T) + \chi_2\left\{-\alpha_2[(1-\mu)i_t^R - \pi_t] + I[J(K_t, \pi_t, i_t^R; \tau^L) - \pi_t]\right.$$
$$\left. -[1 - \alpha_1(\pi_t)]Y^s(K_t, i_t^R)\right\}. \tag{3.48}$$

In a more condensed form, equation (3.48) can be written as

$$\frac{di_t^R}{dt} = RR(K_t, \pi_t, i_t^R; \mu, \tau^L), \tag{3.49}$$

where, recalling that $\alpha_1' < 0$, $Y_{i^R}^s < 0$, $Y_K^s > 0$, $I' < 0$, $J_K < 0$, $J_{i^R} > 0$, $J_\pi > 0$, $J_{\tau^L} > 0$, and that by assumption $J_\pi < 1$,

$$RR_K = \chi_2\{I'J_K - [1 - \alpha_1(\tilde{\pi})]Y_K^s\} = \chi_2 GG_K \gtrless 0,$$
$$RR_\pi = \chi_1 + \chi_2[\alpha_2 + I'(J_\pi - 1) + \alpha_1'\tilde{Y}^s] = \chi_1 + \chi_2 GG_\pi \gtrless 0,$$
$$RR_{i^R} = \chi_2\{-\alpha_2(1-\mu) + I'J_{i^R} - [1 - \alpha_1(\tilde{\pi})]Y_{i^R}^s\} = \chi_2 GG_{i^R} \gtrless 0,$$
$$RR_\mu = \chi_2\alpha_2\tilde{i}^R = \chi_2 GG_\mu > 0,$$
$$RR_{\tau^L} = \chi_2 I'J_{\tau^L} = \chi_2 GG_{\tau^L} < 0.$$

Given that RR_h is proportional to GG_h, for $h = K, i^R, \mu$, and τ^L, the sign of these partial derivatives can be explained along the lines discussed earlier. For instance, an increase in the capital stock raises output and the value of collateral, thereby lowering the loan rate and stimulating investment. Because both aggregate supply and aggregate demand increase, the net effect on the change in the refinance rate is ambiguous. If the aggregate supply effect dominates, $GG_K < 0$

15. A more detailed discussion of the Taylor rule is provided in the discrete-time models considered in subsequent chapters.

and by implication $RR_K < 0$. Considering only the standard case where the cost channel is weak (that is, $GG_{\bar{\imath}^R}$) implies also that $RR_{\bar{\imath}^R} < 0$. The key difference is that now $RR_\pi = \chi_1 + \chi_2 GG_\pi$. If χ_1 (the weight attached to inflation deviations from target in the Taylor rule) is sufficiently high relative to χ_2 (the weight attached to excess demand), it is possible for a rise in inflation to lead to an increase in the refinance rate (so that $RR_\pi > 0$), even if the the wealth erosion effect is strong enough (as before) to ensure that $GG_\pi < 0$.

Equations (3.46), (3.47), and (3.49) determine jointly the dynamics of capital, inflation, and the refinance rate. In the vicinity of the steady state, they can be linearized to give

$$\begin{bmatrix} dK/dt \\ d\pi_t/dt \\ di_t^R/dt \end{bmatrix} = \begin{bmatrix} KK_K & KK_\pi & KK_{\bar{\imath}^R} \\ \lambda^G GG_K & \lambda^G GG_\pi & \lambda^G GG_{\bar{\imath}^R} \\ RR_K & RR_\pi & RR_{\bar{\imath}^R} \end{bmatrix} \begin{bmatrix} K_t - \tilde{K} \\ \pi_t - \tilde{\pi} \\ i_t^R - \tilde{\imath}^R \end{bmatrix}. \qquad (3.50)$$

The steady-state equilibrium solutions can be determined directly from (3.46), (3.47), and (3.49) by setting $dK_t/dt = d\pi_t/dt = di_t^R/dt = 0$; these solutions are

$$KK(\tilde{K}, \tilde{\pi}, \tilde{\imath}^R; \tau^L) = I[J(\tilde{K}, \tilde{\pi}, \tilde{\imath}^R; \tau^L) - \tilde{\pi}] - \delta_K \tilde{K} = 0, \qquad (3.51)$$

$$GG(\tilde{K}, \tilde{\pi}, \tilde{\imath}^R; \tau^L, \mu) = \frac{Y^s(\tilde{K}, \tilde{\imath}^R)}{[1 - \alpha_1(\tilde{\pi})]^{-1}} + \alpha_2[(1-\mu)\tilde{\imath}^R - \tilde{\pi}]$$
$$- I[J(\tilde{K}, \tilde{\pi}, \tilde{\imath}^R; \tau^L) - \tilde{\pi}] = 0, \qquad (3.52)$$

$$\tilde{\pi} = \pi^T. \qquad (3.53)$$

Equation (3.51) defines the combinations of the capital stock, the refinance rate, and the inflation rate for which the capital stock is constant, whereas equations (3.52) and (3.53) define the combinations of these variables for which aggregate supply is equal to aggregate demand, the refinance rate is constant, and inflation is equal to its target value. The system is now recursive: Equation (3.53) determines independently the steady-state inflation rate, whereas equations (3.51) and (3.52) determine the other two variables. In a sense, the Taylor rule helps to pin down inflation to the level desired by the central bank.

Establishing stability conditions is now more involved. Let **A** denote the matrix of coefficients in (3.50). Given that all three variables adjust gradually, stability requires three negative eigenvalues. These eigenvalues are the solutions of the characteristic equation

$$\lambda^3 - \text{tr}\mathbf{A}\lambda^2 - (\mathbf{A}_{11} + \mathbf{A}_{22} + \mathbf{A}_{33})\lambda - \det\mathbf{A} = 0,$$

where, as before, tr**A** is the trace of **A**, det**A** the determinant of **A**, and $\mathbf{A}_{ii}$ the ith diagonal cofactor of **A**. Beyond that, however, both tr**A** and det**A** are ambiguous in sign in general, so it is not possible to evaluate stability analytically in terms of underlying parameters.

Nevertheless, steady-state effects can readily be established. Consider an increase in the tax rate on loans. Differentiating equations (3.51) and (3.52) and setting $d\tilde{\pi}/d\tau^L = 0$, given (3.53), yields

$$\begin{bmatrix} KK_K & KK_{\tilde{i}^R} \\ RR_K & RR_{\tilde{i}^R} \end{bmatrix} \begin{bmatrix} d\tilde{K} \\ d\tilde{i}^R \end{bmatrix} = \begin{bmatrix} KK_{\tau^L} \\ -RR_{\tau^L} \end{bmatrix} d\tau^L.$$

Let Γ be defined as

$$\Gamma = \overset{(+)}{KK_K}\overset{(-)}{RR_{\tilde{i}^R}} - \overset{(-)}{KK_{\tilde{i}^R}}\overset{(-)}{RR_K} < 0,$$

then

$$\frac{d\tilde{K}}{d\tau^L} = \frac{\overset{(-)}{KK_{\tau^L}}\overset{(-)}{RR_{\tilde{i}^R}} + \overset{(-)}{KK_{\tilde{i}^R}}\overset{(-)}{RR_{\tau^L}}}{\Gamma} < 0,$$

$$\frac{d\tilde{i}^R}{d\tau^L} = -\frac{\overset{(-)}{RR_K}\overset{(-)}{KK_{\tau^L}} + \overset{(+)}{KK_K}\overset{(-)}{RR_{\tau^L}}}{\Gamma} \gtrless 0,$$

so that, by implication, given again that $Y^s_{\tilde{i}^R} < 0$, $J_K < 0$, and $J_{\tilde{i}^R} > 0$,

$$\frac{d\tilde{i}^L}{d\tau^L} = \frac{d(\tilde{i}^L - \pi^T)}{d\tau^L} = J_K\left(\frac{d\tilde{K}}{d\tau^L}\right) + J_{\tilde{i}^R}\left(\frac{d\tilde{i}^R}{d\tau^L}\right) > 0,$$

$$\frac{d\tilde{Y}^s}{d\tau^L} = Y^s_K\left(\frac{d\tilde{K}}{d\tau^L}\right) + Y^s_{\tilde{i}^R}\left(\frac{d\tilde{i}^R}{d\tau^L}\right) \gtrless 0,$$

$$\frac{d\tilde{I}}{d\tau^L} = \delta_K\left(\frac{d\tilde{K}}{d\tau^L}\right) < 0,$$

$$\frac{d\tilde{C}}{d\tau^L} = \frac{d\tilde{Y}^s}{d\tau^L} - \frac{d\tilde{I}}{d\tau^L} = (Y^s_K - \delta_K)\left(\frac{d\tilde{K}}{d\tau^L}\right) \gtrless 0,$$

which shows that the steady-state effects on output, investment, and credit are the same as before. In particular, the positive effect on the nominal (and real) loan rate must hold for investment to fall. In addition, if χ_2 (the weight attached to excess demand in the Taylor rule) is not too large, the condition $d\tilde{i}^R/d\tau^L > 0$ would also hold. Importantly, however, the policy now has no effect on inflation; thus, there is no trade-off in between price stability and financial stability, in the sense that lowering credit is not associated with higher inflation. This experiment illustrates well the importance of having two instruments when trying to achieve two targets—an issue that is explored in more detail in chapter 5.

3.5 Extensions

Despite its simplicity, the simple dynamic model with credit market imperfections and endogenous capital accumulation presented in this chapter provides some useful intuition regarding the transmission mechanism of monetary and macroprudential policies and the possibility of conflicts between these policies with regard to their short- and long-run effects. The model retains a key feature of the literature on financial frictions in the tradition of Bernanke et al. (1999)—namely, the possibility of a financial accelerator effect due to changes in collateral-loan ratios—but induced not by changes in asset prices *per se* but rather by endogenous adjustment in the capital stock.

The model could be extended in various directions. First, intertemporal optimizing households could be introduced, with or without a subset of agents subject to liquidity constraints. Second, a more thorough treatment of the labor market could be provided. Rather than assuming perfect wage indexation, a more elaborate approach would be to introduce unemployment (assuming an inelastic labor supply), which can be related to changes in wages through either a standard Phillips curve (an inverse relationship between wage *growth* and unemployment) or a wage curve (a negative relationship between the *level* of wages and unemployment). The latter specification can be implemented at relatively low cost, but the former would increase the order of the dynamic system characterizing the economy and would preclude an analytical characterization of the transitional dynamics. A numerical solution, based on a parameterized version of the model, would therefore be required. Third, although the case where the refinance rate is set on the basis of a Taylor-type rule was considered, countercyclical macroprudential rules were not. As a result, issues associated with the combination of monetary and macroprudential policies were not addressed. Doing so in purely analytical models is difficult and is best taken up with more elaborate, quantitative models of both closed and open economies, as in done in subsequent chapters.

4 A Core Closed-Economy DSGE Model with Financial Frictions

The simple static and dynamic models presented in the previous chapters are useful to gain insights on the macroeconomic effects of monetary and macroprudential policies with financial frictions. However, beyond the qualitative intuition, there is also a need to quantify these effects, examine how they affect the economy over time, assess the importance of different structural features in shaping outcomes through sensitivity analysis, and explore whether, and how, monetary policy and macroprudential regulation should be combined to promote macroeconomic and financial stability. Moreover, the components of aggregate demand specified in these models, although plausible and empirically based, were not derived from explicit microeconomic optimization problems.

To address these issues, this chapter and chapters 5 and 6 present full-blown, closed-economy dynamic stochastic general equilibrium models with financial frictions. These models belong to the class of DSGE-FF models discussed in chapter 1 and rely on the same underlying core features as the simpler models presented in chapters 2 and 3—namely, monopolistic competition in banking, collateral and balance sheet effects, and working capital needs. They are used to address a variety of issues. In this chapter, the focus is on a detailed description of the model, its parameterization, its numerical solution, and its properties in terms of its responses to a series of real and financial shocks that have commonly been analyzed in the literature. Chapters 5 and 6 will focus more specifically on macroprudential policies, and their interactions with monetary policy, in response to financial shocks. Implications for policy coordination will also be examined.

The chapter is organized as follows. The first section presents the model. Price rigidities are introduced through adjustment costs, and housing, rather than physical capital, is assumed to be used as collateral, in line with the evidence provided by Calomiris et al. (2017) on the use of movable assets by creditors in developing countries. It also combines the cost and balance sheet channels of monetary policy with an analysis of the link between collateralizable wealth and bank pricing behavior. As before, because of idiosyncratic risk, borrowers' ability to repay is uncertain, lending is collateralized, and borrowers' net worth affects the terms of credit through a premium that banks incorporate in lending rates. At the prevailing loan rate, the supply of funds by financial intermediaries is perfectly elastic. Thus, in contrast to models in the Kiyotaki-Moore (KM) tradition, reviewed in chapter 1, net worth does not impose a continuously binding constraint on borrowing.[1] At the same time, and despite significant modeling differences, the emphasis on balance sheet effects puts the model fundamentally in the Bernanke et al. (1999) tradition, hereafter BGG, also discussed in chapter 1. The central bank conducts monetary policy by fixing a policy interest rate on the basis of a simple instrument rule, and its supply of liquidity to the market is perfectly elastic at the target rate. As a result, banks are unconstrained in their lending operations. Loans, together with deposits and reserve requirements, determine residually their liquidity needs. The central bank policy rate represents the marginal cost of funds, upon which monopolistic banks set lending rates. But as in previous chapters, the equilibrium interest rate on investment loans (or loan rate, for short) accounts not only for the cost of borrowing from the central bank but also for the possibility of default by borrowers.

Next, the equilibrium conditions of the model are provided in section 2, whereas its steady-state properties and its log-linearization—essentially a first-order Taylor series approximation in the neighborhood of the steady state—are studied in sections 3 and 4. The model's parameterization and its solution procedure are discussed in section 5, whereas a series of experiments, related to both exogenous and policy shocks, are presented in section 6. Sensitivity tests with respect to some structural features of the model are presented in Section 7. The final section presents notes on the literature, which cover various extensions to the analysis—some of them fairly general and relatively easy to implement, others more complex and warranted only for specific purposes.

4.1 The Model

Consider a closed economy populated by eight types of agents: a continuum of infinitely lived households, a continuum of intermediate good (IG) producers indexed by $j \in (0, 1)$, a continuum of final good (FG) producers, a continuum of

1. Although the model does not account for endogenous credit rationing, as noted in chapter 1 it is compatible with *exogenous* rationing, to the extent that small-scale firms, which operate in the informal sector (as is often the case in developing countries), are rationed out of the financial system entirely. See Beck and Demirguc-Kunt (2006) and Beck et al. (2008) for a more detailed discussion and some evidence.

capital good (CG) producers indexed by $k \in (0, 1)$, a continuum of commercial banks indexed by $i \in (0, 1)$, the government, the central bank, and a financial regulator.[2] The final good is homogeneous and can be used either for consumption or investment, although in the latter case additional costs must be incurred. For ease of exposition, each household is matched to a single IG producer, a CG producer, and a bank and receives profits (if any) from all of them. Households make their housing stock available, free of charge, to their matched CG producer, who uses it as collateral against which it borrows from banks to buy the final good for investment purposes and to produce capital. Each CG producer then rents its capital to a randomly matched IG producer.

Banks supply credit to IG producers also, who use it to finance their short-term working capital needs. They do not lend to households. The supply of credit is perfectly elastic at the prevailing loan rate. In each period, loans are extended prior to activity (production or investment) and paid off at the end of the period. Banks pay interest on household deposits and the liquidity that they borrow from the central bank. Both categories of loans, as well as deposits, mature in one period.

Banks are also subject to idiosyncratic (borrower-specific) risk because of the possibility that investment loans to individual agents may not be repaid. They choose an unobservable monitoring effort, which (as in chapter 3) has a one-to-one relationship with the success probability of the projects that CG producers invest in.[3] At the end of each period, each bank closes its books and starts operations anew at the beginning of the next period; thus, all its profits are distributed. Finally, the central bank supplies liquidity elastically to banks and sets its policy rate in response to deviations of inflation to its target value and cyclical output.

The remainder of this section describes the decisions faced by each economic agent and solves, where warranted, the optimization problem that they face. Together with market-clearing conditions, these relationships completely characterize the equilibrium behavior of the economy.

4.1.1 Households

Households consume, hold financial assets, and supply labor to IG producers. The objective of the representative household is to maximize

2. The assumption of a group of agents being a continuum with unit mass is a common abstraction adopted for simplicity, to emphasize the fact that each agent is infinitesimal and has no effect on aggregates.

3. Because monitoring is unobservable, the level of effort cannot be set through the terms of a loan contract. And because it is costly, a moral hazard problem emerges—banks have a tendency to monitor less than they should, unless they are provided with adequate incentives to do so. As discussed in chapter 6, these incentives can take the form of binding capital requirements.

$$U_t = \mathbb{E}_t \sum_{s=0}^{\infty} \Lambda^s \left\{ \frac{C_{t+s}^{1-\varsigma^{-1}}}{1-\varsigma^{-1}} - \int_0^1 \frac{\eta_N (N_{t+s}^j)^{1+\psi_N}}{1+\psi_N} dj + \ln x_{t+s}^{\eta_x} + \ln H_{t+s}^{\eta_H} \right\}, \tag{4.1}$$

where C_t is consumption of the final good, N_t^j time allocated to IG firm j, x_t a composite index of real monetary assets, H_t the stock of housing, and $\Lambda \in (0, 1)$ the discount factor. $\mathbb{E}_t$ is the expectation operator conditional on the information available at the beginning of period t, $\varsigma > 0$ is the intertemporal elasticity of substitution in consumption, $\psi_N > 0$ is the inverse of the Frisch elasticity of labor supply, $\eta_N > 0$ is a preference parameter that measures the relative weight of the disutility of labor, and $\eta_x, \eta_H > 0$ are preference parameters that measure the utility benefits of monetary assets and housing, respectively.[4] As in Iacoviello (2005), Silos (2007), and Iacoviello and Neri (2010), for instance, housing services are assumed to be proportional to their stock, which enters directly in the period utility function.

Households derive utility, in the form of liquidity services, from holding a composite monetary asset in the same way that they derive utility from consuming real goods. Money is thus introduced directly, and additively, as an argument in the utility function.[5] In turn, the composite monetary asset is generated by combining real cash balances, m_t, and real bank deposits, d_t, respectively, through a Cobb-Douglas function,

$$x_t = m_t^{\nu} d_t^{1-\nu}, \tag{4.2}$$

where $\nu \in (0, 1)$. Both m_t and d_t are measured in terms of the price of the final good.

Real financial wealth of the representative household at the end of period t, a_t, is given by

$$a_t = m_t + d_t + b_t + p_t^H H_t, \tag{4.3}$$

where b_t denotes real holdings of one-period, noncontingent government bonds and p_t^H is the real price of housing services, both in terms of the price of the final good.

Each household enters period t with m_{t-1} holdings of cash and a stock H_{t-1} of housing. It also collects principal plus interest on bank deposits at the rate

4. The Frisch elasticity measures the substitution effect of a change in the wage rate on the supply of labor. It is the percent change in an individual's labor supply in response to a change in the real wage, holding the marginal utility of consumption constant.

5. Jones and Stracca (2006, 2008) found some empirical support for the assumption of additive separability between consumption and real money balances for the Euro area and the United Kingdom. But no such evidence appears to be available for developing countries.

contracted in $t-1$, $(1+i_{t-1}^D)d_{t-1}$, where i_{t-1}^D is the nominal interest rate on deposits at $t-1$, and principal and interest payments on maturing government bonds, $(1+i_{t-1}^B)b_{t-1}$, where i_{t-1}^B is the nominal bond rate at $t-1$.

At the beginning of the period, households choose the real levels of cash, deposits, government bonds, and labor supplied to IG firms, for which they receive factor payment of $\omega_t N_t$, where ω_t is the economy-wide real wage and $N_t = \int_0^1 N_t^j dj$ is total labor supply. Each household also receives the profits (if any) made by a matched IG producer, J_t^I, a CG producer, J_t^K, and a bank, J_t^B, in the form of lump-sum transfers.[6] It pays lump-sum taxes, whose real value is T_t. Households then purchase the final good for consumption and adjust their demand for housing services.

The representative household's flow budget constraint is thus

$$m_t + d_t + b_t + p_t^H \Delta H_t = \omega_t N_t - T_t - C_t \tag{4.4}$$
$$+ \frac{m_{t-1}}{1+\pi_t} + \left(\frac{1+i_{t-1}^D}{1+\pi_t}\right) d_{t-1} + \left(\frac{1+i_{t-1}^B}{1+\pi_t}\right) b_{t-1} + J_t^B + J_t^I + J_t^K,$$

where $\pi_t = (P_t - P_{t-1})/P_{t-1}$ denotes the inflation rate. For simplicity, housing does not depreciate. This assumption can be justified by the fact that, in real economies, the rate of depreciation of real estate (which matches the flow of new units in the steady state) is typically low at the frequency at which macroeconomic models operate.[7] Also for simplicity, and given the focus of this book, distortionary taxation is not explicitly accounted for.

The representative household chooses sequences of consumption, $\{C_{t+s}\}_{s=0}^{\infty}$, labor, $\{N_{t+s}^j\}_{s=0}^{\infty}$, $j \in (0,1)$, cash, $\{m_{t+s}\}_{s=0}^{\infty}$, deposits, $\{d_{t+s}\}_{s=0}^{\infty}$, bonds, $\{b_{t+s}\}_{s=0}^{\infty}$, and housing services, $\{H_{t+s}\}_{s=0}^{\infty}$, so as to maximize (4.1) subject to (4.2) and (4.4), taking the path of interest rates (i_t^B and i_t^D) as well as prices and inflation (ω_t, p_t^H, and π_t) and all lump-sum transfers and taxes (J_t^B, J_t^I, J_t^K, and T_t), as given.

The Lagrangian for this problem, $\mathcal{L}_t$, can be written as follows:[8]

6. As discussed later, FG producers make zero profits.

7. Note also that adjustment costs for housing are not allowed for. Housing investment is, of course, lumpy at the individual level and home purchases are subject to transactions costs, which are not convex in nature. In most cases, these costs involve a fixed fee and expenses that are proportional to the sale value of the house. While these features are clearly important at the individual level, it is hard to say whether lumpiness at the micro level has important implications for aggregate demand for housing. See Iacoviello and Neri (2010) for a more detailed discussion.

8. For an introduction to the dynamic optimization techniques used in this book, see Chiang (1992), for instance.

$$\mathcal{L}_t = \mathbb{E}_t \sum_{s=0}^{\infty} \Lambda^s \left\{ \frac{C_{t+s}^{1-\varsigma^{-1}}}{1-\varsigma^{-1}} - \int_0^1 \frac{\eta_N}{1+\psi_N} (N_{t+s}^j)^{1+\psi_N} dj + \ln x_{t+s}^{\eta_x} + \ln H_{t+s}^{\eta_H} \right.$$

$$-\lambda_{t+s} \left[m_{t+s} + d_{t+s} + b_{t+s} + p_{t+s}^H \Delta H_{t+s} - \omega_{t+s} N_{t+s} + T_{t+s} + C_{t+s} - \frac{m_{t+s-1}}{1+\pi_{t+s}} \right.$$

$$\left.\left. - \left(\frac{1+i_{t+s-1}^D}{1+\pi_{t+s}} \right) d_{t+s-1} - \left(\frac{1+i_{t+s-1}^B}{1+\pi_{t+s}} \right) b_{t+s-1} - (J_{t+s}^B + J_{t+s}^I + J_{t+s}^K) \right] \right\},$$

where λ_t is the Lagrange multiplier associated with the flow budget constraint (4.4).

The first-order conditions are given by

$$\frac{\partial \mathcal{L}_t}{\partial C_t} : C_t^{-1/\varsigma} - \lambda_t = 0, \tag{4.5}$$

$$\frac{\partial \mathcal{L}_t}{\partial N_t^j} : \eta_N (N_t^j)^{\psi_N} = \lambda_t \omega_t, \quad \forall j \in (0,1), \tag{4.6}$$

$$\frac{\partial \mathcal{L}_t}{\partial m_t} : \frac{\eta_x \nu}{m_t} - \lambda_t + \Lambda \mathbb{E}_t \left(\frac{\lambda_{t+1}}{1+\pi_{t+1}} \right) = 0, \tag{4.7}$$

$$\frac{\partial \mathcal{L}_t}{\partial d_t} : \frac{\eta_x (1-\nu)}{d_t} - \lambda_t + \Lambda \mathbb{E}_t \left\{ \lambda_{t+1} \left(\frac{1+i_t^D}{1+\pi_{t+1}} \right) \right\} = 0, \tag{4.8}$$

$$\frac{\partial \mathcal{L}_t}{\partial H_t} : \frac{\eta_H}{H_t} - \lambda_t p_t^H + \Lambda \mathbb{E}_t (\lambda_{t+1} p_{t+1}^H) = 0, \tag{4.9}$$

$$\frac{\partial \mathcal{L}_t}{\partial b_t} : -\lambda_t + \Lambda \mathbb{E}_t \left\{ \lambda_{t+1} \left(\frac{1+i_t^B}{1+\pi_{t+1}} \right) \right\} = 0, \tag{4.10}$$

for $t = 0, 1, \ldots \infty$, together with the sequence of budget constraints (4.4) and the transversality condition $\lim_{s \to \infty} \mathbb{E}_{t+s} \Lambda^s \lambda_{t+s} b_{t+s} = 0$.

These conditions yield a fully state-contingent plan for the household's choice variables—how much to consume (in terms of goods and housing services), work, and hold in the form of cash, deposits, and bonds—looking forward from the planning date t and into the indefinite future. At any point in time, households are naturally uncertain about the way in which the future will unfold. However, they are assumed to be aware of the kind of shocks that might affect their decisions and, crucially, to know the probability with which these shocks might occur. Households can therefore form expectations about future outcomes, which partly determine their current decisions. The optimal plan, then, is a series of rules on how to respond to the realization of each shock, given expectations about the future, rather than one-time decisions on each future date.

Combining equations (4.5) and (4.10) yields the standard Euler equation,

$$C_t^{-1/\varsigma} = \Lambda \mathbb{E}_t \left\{ C_{t+1}^{-1/\varsigma} \left(\frac{1+i_t^B}{1+\pi_{t+1}} \right) \right\}, \tag{4.11}$$

which essentially states that, at the optimum, households cannot gain from shifting consumption across periods. A one-unit reduction in period-t consumption lowers utility by $C_t^{-1/\varsigma}$. Abstracting from uncertainty, the same unit saved in period t can be converted through the bond market into $(1+i_t^B)/(1+\pi_{t+1})$ of period-$t+1$ consumption, raising utility by $(1+i_t^B)(1+\pi_{t+1})^{-1}C_{t+1}^{-1/\varsigma}$; this is discounted back to the present by Λ. Under uncertainty, naturally enough, it is the expected present value of tomorrow's marginal utility that must be equated to today's marginal utility.

Equation (4.6) captures the trade-off between consumption and leisure. It indicates that households work until the utility foregone by supplying an additional fraction of labor time is equalized to the utility gained from the consumption resulting from the increase in wage income. Using (4.5) to substitute out for λ_t yields, $\forall j$,

$$N_t^j = \left(\frac{\omega_t C_t^{-1/\varsigma}}{\eta_N} \right)^{1/\psi_N}, \tag{4.12}$$

which relates labor supply positively to the real wage and negatively to consumption. Households are willing to work more hours when wages are higher—at least for changes in wages modest enough to have no significant effect on their income. Large wage changes, in fact, would trigger an income effect and lead the now richer workers to *reduce* their supply of labor. The reason is that workers with higher income can afford more consumption, which would lead to a drop in the marginal utility of consumption and thus to a decrease in labor supply at any given wage level.

Condition (4.10) is the standard pricing formula for a one-period risk-free nominal bond. It can be rewritten as

$$\Lambda \mathbb{E}_t \left(\frac{\lambda_{t+1}}{1+\pi_{t+1}} \right) = \frac{\lambda_t}{1+i_t^B}. \tag{4.13}$$

Substituting this expression in (4.7) yields

$$\frac{\eta_x \nu}{m_t} = \lambda_t \left(1 - \frac{1}{1+i_t^B} \right) = \lambda_t \left(\frac{i_t^B}{1+i_t^B} \right),$$

which, using (4.5) to substitute out for λ_t, yields

$$m_t = \frac{\eta_x \nu C_t^{1/\varsigma}(1+i_t^B)}{i_t^B}. \tag{4.14}$$

Equation (4.14) relates the demand for cash positively to consumption and negatively to the opportunity cost of holding money, measured by the interest rate on government bonds.

Similarly, substituting (4.13) in (4.8) yields

$$\frac{\eta_x(1-\nu)}{d_t} = \lambda_t \left[1 - \left(\frac{1+i_t^D}{1+i_t^B}\right)\right] = \lambda_t \left(\frac{i_t^B - i_t^D}{1+i_t^B}\right),$$

which can be rearranged, using (4.5) again to substitute out for λ_t, to yield

$$d_t = \frac{\eta_x(1-\nu)C_t^{1/\varsigma}(1+i_t^B)}{i_t^B - i_t^D}. \tag{4.15}$$

Equation (4.15) relates the demand for bank deposits positively to consumption and the deposit rate, and negatively to the bond rate.

Using (4.5), equation (4.9) yields

$$\frac{p_t^H}{C_t^{1/\varsigma}} = \frac{\eta_H}{H_t} + \Lambda \mathbb{E}_t \left(\frac{p_{t+1}^H}{C_{t+1}^{1/\varsigma}}\right), \tag{4.16}$$

which represents the intertemporal condition for housing. It indicates that, at the margin, the benefit from consuming a flow of housing services must equate the cost in terms of foregone consumption.

4.1.2 Final Good Producers

The final good, Y_t, is produced by assembling a continuum of imperfectly substitutable intermediate goods, Y_t^j, with $j \in (0, 1)$,

$$Y_t = \left\{\int_0^1 (Y_t^j)^{(\theta-1)/\theta} dj\right\}^{\theta/(\theta-1)}, \tag{4.17}$$

where $\theta > 1$ is the elasticity of demand for each intermediate good. As long as the restriction on θ holds, intermediate goods are imperfectly substitutable with one another and production exhibits diminishing marginal returns in each of them.

The representative FG producer sells its output at a perfectly competitive price. Given the intermediate-goods prices, P_t^j $\forall j$, and the final-good price, P_t, it chooses the quantities of intermediate goods, Y_t^j, that maximize its profits. The producer's optimization problem is thus

$$Y_t^j = \arg\max \left[P_t \left\{ \int_0^1 (Y_t^j)^{(\theta-1)/\theta} dj \right\}^{\theta/(\theta-1)} - \int_0^1 P_t^j Y_t^j dj \right],$$

where $\int_0^1 P_t^j Y_t^j dj$ represents total production costs. The first-order condition is

$$P_t \left\{ \int_0^1 (Y_t^j)^{(\theta-1)/\theta} dj \right\}^{1/(\theta-1)} (Y_t^j)^{-1/\theta} - P_t^j = 0.$$

From (4.17), $\left\{ \int_0^1 (Y_t^j)^{(\theta-1)/\theta} dj \right\}^{1/(\theta-1)} = Y_t^{1/\theta}$. Substituting this result in the equation above yields

$$P_t \left(\frac{Y_t}{Y_t^j} \right)^{1/\theta} - P_t^j = 0,$$

so that

$$Y_t^j = \left(\frac{P_t^j}{P_t} \right)^{-\theta} Y_t, \tag{4.18}$$

which defines the demand for good $j \in (0, 1)$.

Given perfect competition, the zero-profit condition is $P_t Y_t = \int_0^1 P_t^j Y_t^j dj$. Substituting (4.18) for Y_t^j in that expression and simplifying gives the price of the final good:

$$P_t = \left\{ \int_0^1 (P_t^j)^{1-\theta} dj \right\}^{1/(1-\theta)}. \tag{4.19}$$

4.1.3 Intermediate Good Producers

Each IG firm $j \in (0, 1)$ produces, using capital and labor, a distinct, perishable good that is sold on a monopolistically competitive market. At the beginning of the period, each IG producer rents capital from a randomly matched CG producer, at the common price r_t^K.[9] Depreciated capital is returned to the CG producer after production has occurred. As in previous chapters, each firm must

9. The capital stock is predetermined in the aggregate, but profit maximization ensures that it is efficiently allocated across IG producers.

also borrow to pay wages in advance—that is, before production and sales have taken place.[10]

Production technology involves constant returns in labor and capital,

$$Y_t^j = \epsilon_t^Y (N_t^j)^{1-\alpha} (K_t^j)^\alpha, \tag{4.20}$$

where N_t^j is labor hours (defined earlier), $\alpha \in (0, 1)$, and ϵ_t^Y a common technology shock, which follows a first-order autoregressive process,

$$\epsilon_t^Y = (\epsilon_{t-1}^Y)^{\rho^Y} \exp(\xi_t^Y),$$

where $\rho^Y \in (0, 1)$ and $\xi_t^Y \sim \mathbf{N}(0, \sigma_{\xi^Y})$.[11]

At the beginning of the period, each firm j borrows from banks the real amount $l_t^{W,j}$, corresponding to a fraction $\psi_W \in (0, 1)$ of its wage bill, $\omega_t N_t^j$, to pay workers prior to the sale of output:

$$l_t^{W,j} = \psi_W \omega_t N_t^j. \tag{4.21}$$

As in chapters 2 and 3, loans contracted for the purpose of financing working capital are not subject to frictions. Because there is no risk of default, these loans are made at a rate that reflects only the marginal cost of borrowing from the central bank, i_t^R—that is, the refinance rate.[12] These loans are repaid at the end of the period. Total labor costs are thus $\psi_W i_t^R \omega_t N_t^j + (1 - \psi_W)\omega_t N_t^j = (1 + \psi_W i_t^R)\omega_t N_t^j$.

IG producers solve a two-stage problem. In the first stage, taking input prices as given, they rent labor and capital in perfectly competitive factor markets so as to minimize real costs of producing one unit of good. Thus, this static optimization problem can be specified as

$$N_t^j, K_t^j = \arg\min[(1 + \psi_W i_t^R)\omega_t N_t^j + r_t^K K_t^j],$$

subject to (4.20) with $Y_t^j = 1$.

10. DSGE models that account for working capital needs associated with the wage bill include Christiano et al. (2005, 2007*b*), Ravenna and Walsh (2006), Rabanal (2007), Tillmann (2008), Henzel et al. (2009), Hülsewig et al. (2009), Kaufmann and Scharler (2009), Agénor and Alper (2012), Chugh (2013), Pfajfar and Santoro (2014), Abo-Zaid (2015), Gersbach et al. (2017), and Airaudo and Olivero (2019). In some of these contributions, firms must also finance *capital* rental costs prior to the sale of output.

11. To ensure that profits of IG producers are zero in the steady state, some contributions introduce a fixed cost of production in (4.20). See Smets and Wouters (2003) and Christiano et al. (2005), for instance.

12. A similar assumption is also made in other contributions to the DSGE-FF literature; see, for instance, Christiano et al. (2011), Davis and Huang (2013), and Rannenberg (2016). Adding a fixed profit margin over and above the refinance rate would not affect the results qualitatively.

The Lagrangian for this problem can be written as

$$\mathcal{L}_t^I = (1+\psi_W i_t^R)\omega_t N_t^j + r_t^K K_t^j + \lambda_t^I[1-\epsilon_t^Y (K_t^j)^\alpha (N_t^j)^{1-\alpha}],$$

where λ_t^I is the Lagrange multiplier associated with (4.20). The first-order conditions equate the marginal product of capital and labor to their relative price, $\forall j$:

$$\frac{\partial \mathcal{L}_t^I}{\partial N_t^j} : (1-\alpha)\frac{Y_t^j}{N_t^j}\lambda_t^I = (1+\psi_W i_t^R)\omega_t, \tag{4.22}$$

$$\frac{\partial \mathcal{L}_t^I}{\partial K_t^j} : \alpha\frac{Y_t^j}{K_t^j}\lambda_t^I = r_t^K. \tag{4.23}$$

Dividing (4.22) by (4.23) yields

$$N_t^j = \left(\frac{1-\alpha}{\alpha}\right)\left[\frac{r_t^K}{(1+\psi_W i_t^R)\omega_t}\right]K_t^j. \tag{4.24}$$

Substituting this result in the constraint $Y_t^j = 1$ yields using (4.20),

$$\epsilon_t^Y \left(\frac{1-\alpha}{\alpha}\right)^{1-\alpha}\left\{\left[\frac{r_t^K}{(1+\psi_W i_t^R)\omega_t}\right]K_t^j\right\}^{1-\alpha}(K_t^j)^\alpha = 1,$$

which can be solved for K_t^j:

$$K_t^j = \frac{1}{\epsilon_t^Y}\left(\frac{\alpha}{1-\alpha}\right)^{1-\alpha}\left[\frac{(1+\psi_W i_t^R)\omega_t}{r_t^K}\right]^{1-\alpha}. \tag{4.25}$$

In turn, substituting this result in (4.24) gives

$$N_t^j = \frac{1}{\epsilon_t^Y}\left(\frac{\alpha}{1-\alpha}\right)^{-\alpha}\left[\frac{(1+\psi_W i_t^R)\omega_t}{r_t^K}\right]^{-\alpha}. \tag{4.26}$$

Dividing (4.25) by (4.26) shows that the optimal capital-labor ratio varies inversely with the effective wage-capital rental rate ratio:

$$\frac{K_t^j}{N_t^j} = \left(\frac{\alpha}{1-\alpha}\right)\left[\frac{(1+\psi_W i_t^R)\omega_t}{r_t^K}\right]. \tag{4.27}$$

Marginal cost can be defined as[13]

13. Adding (4.22) and (4.23) yields $[(1-\alpha)+\alpha]\lambda_t^I = \lambda_t^I = [(1+\psi_W i_t^R)\omega_t N_{jt} + r_t^K K_{jt}]/Y_{jt}$. Thus, λ_t^I is also equal to marginal cost.

$$mc_t^j = \frac{(1+\psi_W i_t^R)\omega_t N_t^j + r_t^K K_t^j}{Y_t^j}.$$

Substituting for Y_t^j from (4.20) yields

$$mc_t^j = \left\{ (1+\psi_W i_t^R)\omega_t \left(\frac{K_t^j}{N_t^j}\right)^{-\alpha} + r_t^K \left(\frac{K_t^j}{N_t^j}\right)^{1-\alpha} \right\} \frac{1}{\epsilon_t^Y},$$

that is, using (4.27),

$$mc_t^j =$$

$$\left\{ \left(\frac{\alpha}{1-\alpha}\right)^{-\alpha} \frac{[(1+\psi_W i_t^R)\omega_t]^{1-\alpha}}{(r_t^K)^{-\alpha}} + \left(\frac{\alpha}{1-\alpha}\right)^{1-\alpha} \frac{[(1+\psi_W i_t^R)\omega_t]^{1-\alpha}}{(r_t^K)^{-\alpha}} \right\} \frac{1}{\epsilon_t^Y},$$

or equivalently

$$mc_t^j = \left\{ \left(\frac{\alpha}{1-\alpha}\right)^{-\alpha} [(1+\psi_W i_t^R)\omega_t]^{1-\alpha} (r_t^K)^{\alpha} \left(1+\frac{\alpha}{1-\alpha}\right) \right\} \frac{1}{\epsilon_t^Y}.$$

Given that

$$\left(\frac{\alpha}{1-\alpha}\right)^{-\alpha} \left(1+\frac{\alpha}{1-\alpha}\right) = \frac{(1-\alpha)^{\alpha}}{\alpha^{\alpha}} \left(\frac{1-\alpha+\alpha}{1-\alpha}\right) = \frac{1}{\alpha^{\alpha}(1-\alpha)^{1-\alpha}},$$

the above expression for marginal cost can be rewritten as

$$mc_t^j = \frac{[(1+\psi_W i_t^R)\omega_t]^{1-\alpha} (r_t^K)^{\alpha}}{\alpha^{\alpha}(1-\alpha)^{1-\alpha}\epsilon_t^Y}, \tag{4.28}$$

which does not depend on index j because all IG producers face the same technology shock and they all rent inputs at the same price.

In the second stage, each IG producer chooses a sequence of prices P_t^j so as to maximize discounted real profits. As in Rotemberg (1982), they all incur a cost in adjusting prices of the form[14]

$$PAC_t^j = \frac{\phi_I}{2}\left[\frac{P_t^j}{(1+\tilde{\pi})P_{t-1}^j} - 1\right]^2 Y_t, \tag{4.29}$$

where $\phi_I \geq 0$ is an adjustment cost parameter (or, equivalently, a measure of the degree of price stickiness) and $\tilde{\pi}$ is the steady-state inflation rate. As argued

14. An alternative, and perhaps more popular, approach to formalizing price stickiness in DSGE models is the Calvo approach, which is discussed later on.

by Rotemberg (1982), the adjustment cost seeks to account for variable costs such as managerial costs (related to information gathering and decision making) and customer costs (related to negotiation and communication), as well as the negative effects of price changes on the customer-firm relationship. These negative effects increase in size with the magnitude of the price change and with the overall scale of economic activity, Y_t.[15] The price adjustment cost makes each IG producer's problem dynamic; rather than maximizing its profits period-by-period, each firm acts to maximize its total market value. At the same time, specification (4.29) ensures that this cost is zero in the steady state, when $P^j_t/P^j_{t-1} = 1+\tilde{\pi}$.

Real profits of IG producer j, $J^{I,j}_t$, can be defined as

$$J^{I,j}_t = \left(\frac{P^j_t}{P_t}\right) Y^j_t - mc^j_t Y^j_t - PAC^j_t,$$

where $mc^j_t Y^j_t$ represents total production costs.[16]

The dynamic, second-stage optimization problem is thus

$$\{P^j_{t+s}\}^{\infty}_{s=0} = \arg\max \mathbb{E}_t \left[\sum_{s=0}^{\infty} \Lambda^s \lambda_{t+s} J^{I,j}_{jt+s}\right],$$

subject to constraint (4.18) on Y^j_t.

Note that because IG firms are owned by households (to whom they transfer their profits, if any), the firm's discount factor for period-$t+s$ profits is $\Lambda^s \lambda_{t+s}$, where from (4.5) $\lambda_{t+s} = C_{t+s}^{-1/\varsigma}$ can be viewed as the marginal utility value (in terms of consumption of the final good) of an additional currency unit of profits at $t+s$.

Taking $\{mc^j_{t+s}\}^{\infty}_{s=0}$, $\{P_{t+s}\}^{\infty}_{s=0}$, and $\{Y_{t+s}\}^{\infty}_{s=0}$ as given, the first-order condition for this maximization problem is

$$(1-\theta)\lambda_t \left(\frac{P^j_t}{P_t}\right)^{-\theta} \frac{Y_t}{P_t} + \theta\lambda_t \left(\frac{P^j_t}{P_t}\right)^{-\theta-1} \frac{mc^j_t Y_t}{P_t} \tag{4.30}$$

$$-\lambda_t \phi_I \left\{\left(\frac{P^j_t}{(1+\tilde{\pi})P^j_{t-1}} - 1\right) \frac{Y_t}{(1+\tilde{\pi})P^j_{t-1}}\right\}$$

15. See, for instance, Correa et al. (2016) for evidence on menu costs and the frequency of price adjustment in Brazil. See also Özmen and Sevinç (2016) for a study on the size, frequency, distribution, and synchronization of price changes in Turkey.

16. Thus, marginal cost equals average cost.

$$+\Lambda\phi_I\mathbb{E}_t\left\{\lambda_{t+1}\left[\frac{P^j_{t+1}}{(1+\tilde{\pi})P^j_t}-1\right]Y_{t+1}\left[\frac{P^j_{t+1}}{(1+\tilde{\pi})(P^j_t)^2}\right]\right\}=0,$$

which determines the adjustment process of the nominal price P^j_t. With $\phi_I=0$ (full price flexibility), this equation boils down to

$$P^j_t=\frac{\theta}{\theta-1}P_t mc^j_t. \tag{4.31}$$

In a symmetric equilibrium, IG firms are identical; they produce the same output and choose the same price. Thus, $P^j_t=P_t$, for all $j\in(0,1)$. Equation (4.30) becomes

$$(1-\theta)\lambda_t\frac{Y_t}{P_t}+\theta\lambda_t\frac{mc_tY_t}{P_t}-\lambda_t\phi_I\left\{\left(\frac{1+\pi_t}{1+\tilde{\pi}}-1\right)\left(\frac{1+\pi_t}{1+\tilde{\pi}}\right)\left(\frac{Y_t}{P_t}\right)\right\}$$
$$+\Lambda\phi_I\mathbb{E}_t\left\{\lambda_{t+1}\left(\frac{1+\pi_{t+1}}{1+\tilde{\pi}}-1\right)\left(\frac{1+\pi_{t+1}}{1+\tilde{\pi}}\right)\left(\frac{Y_t}{P_t}\right)\left(\frac{Y_{t+1}}{Y_t}\right)\right\}=0,$$

or equivalently, dividing by λ_tY_t/P_t,

$$1-\theta+\theta mc_t-\phi_I\left(\frac{1+\pi_t}{1+\tilde{\pi}}-1\right)\left(\frac{1+\pi_t}{1+\tilde{\pi}}\right) \tag{4.32}$$
$$+\Lambda\phi_I\mathbb{E}_t\left\{\frac{\lambda_{t+1}}{\lambda_t}\left(\frac{1+\pi_{t+1}}{1+\tilde{\pi}}-1\right)\left(\frac{1+\pi_{t+1}}{1+\tilde{\pi}}\right)\left(\frac{Y_{t+1}}{Y_t}\right)\right\}=0,$$

which determines implicitly the behavior of the inflation rate. Note that inflation at t depends on its expected value at $t+1$. The fundamental reason is that a choice for P^j_t today has consequences for the menu costs that will be incurred tomorrow, in period $t+1$.

In addition, there is no persistence in inflation, despite the strong evidence to the contrary for a range of countries, including MICs (Agénor and Bayraktar 2010). A simple way to account for lagged inflation would be to assume that price adjustment costs are given by, instead of (4.29),

$$PAC^j_t=\frac{\phi_I}{2}\left[\frac{P^j_t}{(1+\tilde{\pi})^{\phi_{II}}(1+\pi_{t-1})^{1-\phi_{II}}P^j_{t-1}}-1\right]^2Y_t,$$

where $\phi_{II}\in(0,1)$. Thus, with this specification, past inflation would also appear in (4.32) as a determinant of current inflation as long as $\phi_{II}>0$.

Alternatively, as in Ireland (2001), for instance, it could be assumed that firms incur adjustment costs with respect to changes in *both* the level of prices and their rate of change. Thus, equation (4.29) would be replaced by

$$PAC_t^j = \frac{\phi_I}{2}\left[\frac{P_t^j}{(1+\tilde{\pi})P_{t-1}^j} - 1\right]^2 Y_t + \frac{\phi_{II}}{2}\left[\frac{P_t^j/P_{t-1}^j}{(1+\tilde{\pi})P_{t-1}^j/P_{t-2}^j} - 1\right]^2 Y_t,$$

where now $\phi_{II} > 0$. The issue of inflation persistence is further discussed in the appendix to this chapter, together with an alternative model of price formation.

4.1.4 Capital Good Producers

CG producers own the capital in the economy and use a linear technology to produce capital goods. At the beginning of the period, the representative firm buys a real amount I_t of the final good from the representative FG producer. These goods must be paid in advance; to purchase final goods, the representative CG producer must therefore borrow the amount

$$l_t^K = I_t. \tag{4.33}$$

The assumption that investment is fully paid for by bank loans is consistent with the evidence reported by Ayyagari et al. (2012, fig. 1), and discussed in chapter 1, which shows that in developing countries up to three-quarters of fixed asset investment by larger firms—those presumably with unrestricted access to the financial system—is financed by bank borrowing. It is also consistent with the evidence for Latin America provided by Kawamura and Ronconi (2015), according to which large firms—which, again, tend to be less subject to strict borrowing constraints—rely less on retained earnings to finance investment in fixed capital assets.[17]

As stated earlier, each household is matched to (or rather, owns) a single CG-producing firm and makes its housing stock, H_t, available free of charge to that firm, which uses it as collateral against which to borrow from banks.[18] However, repayment is uncertain. If loans are repaid in full—an event that occurs with probability $q_t \in (0, 1)$—the total cost faced by the CG producer at the end of period t is $(1+i_t^L)l_t^K$, where $1+i_t^L$ is the gross interest rate charged by banks. If there is default, which occurs with probability $1-q_t$, the CG producer loses the collateral that it pledged to secure the loan; lenders have no claim on the residual income (if any) of the borrower. Collateral is given by $\kappa \mathbb{E}_t p_{t+1}^H H_t$, where $\kappa = \int_0^1 \kappa^i di \leq 1$ and $\kappa^i \in (0, 1)$ is the fraction of the

17. Keen (2009) assumed that capital good suppliers finance investment only partially through bank borrowing. In the same vein, Jermann and Quadrini (2012) and Kamber et al. (2017) develop DSGE-FF models in which firms can finance investment by either borrowing or issuing equity. In these models, the choice between financing options is itself subject to frictions.

18. Because all profits (if any) made by the matched CG producer are returned lump sum to its owner, the assumption that the housing stock is made available free of charge is immaterial.

housing stock pledged as collateral to each bank i. Thus, expected repayment is $q_t(1+i_t^L)l_t^K + (1-q_t)\kappa \mathbb{E}_t p_{t+1}^H H_t$.[19]

Thus, in contrast to much of the discussion in chapters 2 and 3 (where physical capital was used as collateral), producers here use housing to secure loans. Again, this assumption is well suited for countries where the bulk of production is by medium-size firms, often owned by a single entrepreneur, who can only pledge the asset that banks are willing to take—the entrepreneur's own real estate property (see chapter 1).[20] As also discussed in previous chapters, coefficient κ can be viewed as a measure of the efficiency of enforcement of debt contracts, or an inverse measure of anti-creditor bias in the judicial system.

To produce new capital the representative CG firm combines gross investment with the existing stock of capital, adjusted for depreciation and adjustment costs,

$$K_{t+1} = I_t + (1-\delta_K)K_t - \frac{\Theta_K}{2}\left(\frac{K_{t+1}}{K_t} - 1\right)^2 K_t, \tag{4.34}$$

where $\delta_K \in (0,1)$ denotes the constant rate of depreciation and $\Theta_K > 0$ is an adjustment cost parameter.[21] The new capital stock built at t is then rented in $t+1$ to a randomly matched IG producer at the rate r_{t+1}^K.[22]

The representative CG producer chooses the level of the capital stock so as to maximize the value of the discounted stream of expected dividend payments to the matched household:

$$\{K_{t+s+1}\}_{s=0}^{\infty} = \arg\max \sum_{s=0}^{\infty} \mathbb{E}_t(\Lambda^s \lambda_{t+s} J_{t+s+1}^K),$$

subject to (4.34) and taking $\{i_{t+s}^L\}_{s=0}^{\infty}$, $\{p_{t+s+1}^H\}_{s=0}^{\infty}$, $\{q_{t+s}\}_{s=0}^{\infty}$, and $\{r_{t+s}^K\}_{s=0}^{\infty}$ as given. In this expression, $\lambda_t = C_t^{-1/\varsigma}$ is again the marginal utility value (in terms of units of consumption) of an additional currency unit of real profits and

19. As discussed later, to ensure that banks have an incentive to monitor, the return on lending must be at least equal to the value of collateral net of monitoring costs.

20. Note also that collateral depends on the expected market price of housing, a specification that (as discussed later) tends to magnify procyclicality in leverage. Indeed, in ways similar to the BGG and KM models, as well as Iacoviello (2005), this is one of the key channels through which the financial accelerator effect operates in the model.

21. Alternative specifications of investment or capital adjustment costs involve replacing the term $(K_{t+1}/K_t - 1)^2 K_t$ in (4.34) by either $(I_t/I_{t-1} - 1)^2 I_t$, as in Smets and Wouters (2003) and Christiano et al. (2005), for instance, or $(I_t/K_t - \delta_K)^2 K_t$, as in Erceg and Levin (2003) and Christensen and Dib (2008), or again $(I_t/K_t - \delta_K)^2 I_t$, as in Ireland (2003). In all three cases, as in (4.34), adjustment costs are nil in the steady state—in the third alternative case because in equilibrium investment is a fraction δ_K of the capital stock. In general, one would expect the model's transitional dynamics to depend on the exact specification chosen. Yet there is little comparative evidence to support a particular choice.

22. Hristov and Hülsewig (2017), for instance, use a similar assumption.

$\mathbb{E}_t(\Lambda^s \lambda_{t+s} J^K_{t+s+1})$ denotes expected profits at the end of period $t+s$, discounted at the rate $\Lambda^s \lambda_{t+s}$. Using (4.33), this term is defined as

$$\mathbb{E}_t(\Lambda^s \lambda_{t+s} J^K_{t+s+1})$$
$$= \Lambda^s \mathbb{E}_t\{\lambda_{t+s}[r^K_{t+s} K_{t+s} - q_{t+s}(1+i^L_{t+s}) I_{t+s} - (1-q_{t+s})\kappa p^H_{t+s+1} H_t]\}. \tag{4.35}$$

Substituting (4.34) in (4.35) for I_t, the unconstrained maximization problem becomes

$$\{K_{t+s+1}\}_{s=0}^{\infty} = \arg\max \sum_{s=0}^{\infty} \Lambda^s \mathbb{E}_t \left(\lambda_{t+s} \left\{ r^K_{t+s} K_{t+s} - (1-q_{t+s})\kappa p^H_{t+s+1} H_t \right.\right.$$
$$\left.\left. - q_{t+s}(1+i^L_{t+s}) \left[K_{t+s+1} - (1-\delta_K) K_{t+s} + \frac{\Theta_K}{2} \left(\frac{K_{t+s+1}}{K_{t+s}} - 1 \right)^2 K_{t+s} \right] \right\} \right).$$

The first-order condition is

$$-\frac{\lambda_t q_t}{(1+i^L_t)^{-1}} \mathbb{E}_t \left\{ 1 + \Theta_K K_t \left(\frac{K_{t+1}}{K_t} - 1 \right) \frac{1}{K_t} \right\} + \Lambda \mathbb{E}_t \lambda_{t+1} r^K_{t+1}$$
$$- \Lambda \mathbb{E}_t \left[\frac{\lambda_{t+1} q_{t+1}}{(1+i^L_{t+1})^{-1}} \times \left\{ -(1-\delta_K) + \frac{\Theta_K}{2} \left(\frac{K_{t+2}}{K_{t+1}} - 1 \right)^2 \right.\right.$$
$$\left.\left. + \frac{\Theta_K}{2} 2 \left(\frac{K_{t+2}}{K_{t+1}} - 1 \right) \left[-\frac{K_{t+2}}{(K_{t+1})^2} \right] K_{t+1} \right\} \right] = 0,$$

which can be rearranged to give

$$-\lambda_t q_t (1+i^L_t) \mathbb{E}_t \left\{ 1 + \Theta_K \left(\frac{K_{t+1}}{K_t} - 1 \right) \right\} + \Lambda \mathbb{E}_t \lambda_{t+1} r^K_{t+1} \tag{4.36}$$
$$- \Lambda \mathbb{E}_t \left[\lambda_{t+1} q_{t+1} (1+i^L_{t+1}) \left\{ -1 + \delta_K + \frac{\Theta_K}{2} \left(\frac{K_{t+2}}{K_{t+1}} - 1 \right)^2 \right.\right.$$
$$\left.\left. - \Theta_K \left(\frac{K_{t+2}}{K_{t+1}} - 1 \right) \frac{K_{t+2}}{K_{t+1}} \right\} \right]$$
$$= 0.$$

Now, note that

$$\frac{\Theta_K}{2} \left(\frac{K_{t+2}}{K_{t+1}} - 1 \right)^2 - \Theta_K \left(\frac{K_{t+2}}{K_{t+1}} - 1 \right) \left(\frac{K_{t+2}}{K_{t+1}} \right)$$
$$= \frac{\Theta_K}{2} \left\{ \left(\frac{K_{t+2}}{K_{t+1}} - 1 \right)^2 - 2 \left[\left(\frac{K_{t+2}}{K_{t+1}} \right)^2 - \frac{K_{t+2}}{K_{t+1}} \right] \right\}$$

$$= \frac{\Theta_K}{2}\left\{\left(\frac{K_{t+2}}{K_{t+1}}\right)^2 - 2\left(\frac{K_{t+2}}{K_{t+1}}\right) + 1 - 2\left(\frac{K_{t+2}}{K_{t+1}}\right)^2 + 2\left(\frac{K_{t+2}}{K_{t+1}}\right)\right\}$$

$$= -\frac{\Theta_K}{2}\left[\left(\frac{K_{t+2}}{K_{t+1}}\right)^2 - 1\right].$$

Substituting this result in (4.36) yields

$$\Lambda \mathbb{E}_t \lambda_{t+1} r^K_{t+1} - \lambda_t q_t (1 + i^L_t)\mathbb{E}_t \left\{1 + \Theta_K\left(\frac{K_{t+1}}{K_t} - 1\right)\right\}$$
$$- \Lambda \mathbb{E}_t \left[\lambda_{t+1} q_{t+1}(1 + i^L_{t+1})\left\{-1 + \delta_K - \frac{\Theta_K}{2}\left[\left(\frac{K_{t+2}}{K_{t+1}}\right)^2 - 1\right]\right\}\right] = 0,$$

or equivalently, ignoring covariance terms for simplicity,[23]

$$\mathbb{E}_t r^K_{t+1} \simeq \mathbb{E}_t\left(\frac{\lambda_t}{\Lambda \lambda_{t+1}}\right) q_t(1 + i^L_t)\left\{1 + \Theta_K\left(\frac{K_{t+1}}{K_t} - 1\right)\right\}$$
$$- \mathbb{E}_t\left[q_{t+1}(1 + i^L_{t+1})\left\{1 - \delta_K + \frac{\Theta_K}{2}\left[\left(\frac{K_{t+2}}{K_{t+1}}\right)^2 - 1\right]\right\}\right].$$

Ignoring again covariance terms, equation (4.13) can be rearranged to give $\mathbb{E}_t(\lambda_t/\Lambda\lambda_{t+1}) \simeq \mathbb{E}_t[(1 + i^B_t)/(1 + \pi_{t+1})]$. Substituting this result in the above expression gives therefore

$$\mathbb{E}_t r^K_{t+1} \simeq q_t(1 + i^L_t)\mathbb{E}_t\left[\left\{1 + \Theta_K\left(\frac{K_{t+1}}{K_t} - 1\right)\right\}\left(\frac{1 + i^B_t}{1 + \pi_{t+1}}\right)\right] \tag{4.37}$$
$$- \mathbb{E}_t\left[q_{t+1}(1 + i^L_{t+1})\left\{1 - \delta_K + \frac{\Theta_K}{2}\left[\left(\frac{K_{t+2}}{K_{t+1}}\right)^2 - 1\right]\right\}\right].$$

Equation (4.37) shows that the expected rental rate of capital is a function of the current and expected loan rates, the latter through its indirect impact on adjustment costs in $t+1$. Without borrowing in advance (so that profits are simply $r^K_t K_t - I_t$), and with no adjustment costs ($\Theta_K = 0$, so that $K_{t+1} = I_t + (1 - \delta_K)K_t$), this equation boils down to the standard arbitrage condition $\mathbb{E}_t r^K_{t+1} - \delta_K \simeq i^B_t - \mathbb{E}_t \pi_{t+1}$, which shows that the CG firm produces capital up to the point where the (expected) rental rate, adjusted for depreciation, is equal

23. With x^1_{t+1} and x^2_{t+1} being random variables, this implies using the approximation $\mathbb{E}_t(x^1_{t+1}x^2_{t+1}) \simeq \mathbb{E}_t(x^1_{t+1})\mathbb{E}_t(x^2_{t+1})$, even though the variables are not necessarily independent.

to the opportunity cost of investing, as measured by the (expected) real interest rate on government bonds.

As in previous chapters, the amount borrowed by the representative CG producer is a Dixit-Stiglitz basket of differentiated loans, each supplied by a bank i, with a constant elasticity of substitution $\zeta^L > 1$:

$$l_t^K = \left[\int_0^1 (l_t^{K,i})^{(\zeta^L - 1)/\zeta} di \right]^{\zeta^L/(\zeta^L - 1)}.$$

The demand for type-i loan, $l_t^{K,i}$, is thus given by the downward-sloping curve

$$l_t^{K,i} = \left(\frac{1 + i_t^{L,i}}{1 + i_t^L} \right)^{-\zeta^L} l_t^K, \tag{4.38}$$

where $i_t^{L,i}$ is the rate on the loan extended by bank i and i_t^L is the aggregate loan rate, defined as

$$i_t^L = \left[\int_0^1 (1 + i_t^{L,i})^{1-\zeta^L} di \right]^{1/(1-\zeta^L)} - 1.$$

4.1.5 Commercial Banks

Banks are risk-neutral and are indexed by $i \in (0, 1)$. They collect deposits from households and provide funding to IG producers to pay workers and differentiated loans to CG producers in an environment of monopolistic competition.[24] The supply of credit is perfectly elastic at the prevailing loan rate and therefore the total amount of bank lending is given by the sum of (4.21) and (4.33)—that is, the sum of loans for working capital needs and for investment. To fund any shortfall in resources, banks borrow a real amount $l_t^{B,i}$ from the central bank at the gross cost $1 + i_t^R$.

Bank i's balance sheet is thus

$$l_t^i + RR_t^i = V_t^i + d_t^i + l_t^{B,i}, \tag{4.39}$$

24. DSGE-FF models with monopolistic competition in banking include Aslam and Santoro (2009), Henzel et al. (2009), Hülsewig et al. (2009), Gerali et al. (2010), Güntner (2011), Angelini et al. (2014), Anand et al. (2015), Gambacorta and Karmakar (2018), and Jacob and Munro (2018). In all of these models, as is the case here, banks provide differentiated loans. Other models focus instead on spatial competition (Andrés and Arce 2012), *deep habits* or switching costs (Aliaga-Díaz and Olivero 2010*b*, 2019), strategic limit pricing (Mandelman 2010), and staggered loan contracts (Fujiwara and Teranishi 2011; Teranishi 2015). However, none of these models accounts at the same time for the presence of collateral and how it affects both the possibility of default and the premium embedded in loan rates.

where $l_t^i = l_t^{K,i} + l_t^{W,i}$, V_t^i is bank capital (taken as given in this chapter and chapter 5),[25] and RR_t^i denotes required reserves that are held permanently at the central bank and do not pay interest—a common practice, at least until the global financial crisis, as documented by Gray (2011), for instance. As in previous chapters, required reserves are determined as a fraction of deposits,

$$RR_t^i = \mu d_t^i, \tag{4.40}$$

where $\mu \in (0, 1)$ is again the required reserve ratio, assumed constant in this chapter.[26]

As before, the balance sheet constraint (4.39), together with (4.40), can be used to determine residually the level of bank i's borrowing from the central bank:

$$l_t^{B,i} = l_t^i - V_t^i - (1-\mu)d_t^i. \tag{4.41}$$

The market for deposits is competitive, and from the perspective of banks deposits and central bank liquidity are perfect substitutes. This ensures therefore that, $\forall i$, the following no-arbitrage condition holds:

$$i_t^{D,i} = (1-\mu)i_t^R. \tag{4.42}$$

Once again monopolistic competition prevails in the market for investment loans. The demand for these loans from bank i, $l_t^{K,i}$, is given by the downward-sloping curve (4.38). In addition, banks also choose optimally their level of monitoring. Specifically, as in chapter 3, each bank can affect the repayment probability on its investment loans, q_t^i, by expending effort; the higher the monitoring effort, the safer the loan. Although it is not observable, monitoring is also desirable from the borrower's perspective. Again, as in the micro-banking models of Allen et al. (2011), De Nicolò and Lucchetta (2012), Dell'Ariccia et al. (2014), and Cordella et al. (2018), for instance, the financial intermediation technology is such that the probability of repayment itself, rather than monitoring effort *per se*, is taken to be the choice variable.

Formally, each bank sets its (gross) loan rate and the repayment probability in order to maximize its end-of-period expected real profits, $\mathbb{E}_t J_{t+1}^{B,i}$:

25. Chapter 6 will provide a detailed discussion of the bank capital regime.

26. A marginal reserve requirement regime could be modeled as $RR_t = \mu_1 d_t + \mu_2(d_t - d_{t-1})$, with $\mu_1 \in (0, 1)$ and $\mu_2 > 0$. This regime would be equivalent to (4.40) in the steady state. Note also that banks do not hold bonds; as discussed later, in equilibrium they have no incentive to do so in the present setting.

$$1+i_t^{L,i}, q_t^i = \arg\max \mathbb{E}_t J_{t+1}^{B,i},$$

where $\mathbb{E}_t J_{t+1}^{B,i}$ is defined as

$$\mathbb{E}_t J_{t+1}^{B,i} = q_t^i(1+i_t^{L,i})l_t^{K,i} + (1-q_t^i)\kappa^i \mathbb{E}_t p_{t+1}^H H_t + (1+i_t^R)l_t^{W,i} \\ + \mu d_t^i - (1+i_t^D)d_t^i - (1+i_t^R)l_t^{B,i} - x_t^{M,i}. \tag{4.43}$$

Equation (4.43) defines expected profits as the difference between expected bank revenues, given by the sum of repayments on investment loans if there is no default, $q_t^i(1+i_t^{L,i})l_t^{K,i}$, the value of collateral seized in case of default, $(1-q_t^i)\kappa^i \mathbb{E}_t p_{t+1}^H H_t$, repayment of working capital loans, $(1+i_t^R)l_t^{W,i}$, augmented by the reserve requirements returned by the central bank to the bank, $\mu_t d_t^i$, and bank expenses, given by the sum of principal and interest payments on deposits, $(1+i_t^D)d_t^i$, and central bank borrowing, $(1+i_t^R)l_t^{B,i}$, and the pecuniary cost of monitoring investment loans, $x_t^{M,i}$.[27]

In turn, the monitoring costs faced by bank i are defined as

$$x_t^{M,i} = \Phi_t \frac{(q_t^i)^2}{2} l_t^{K,i} = \Phi\left(\frac{\kappa \mathbb{E}_t p_{t+1}^H H_t}{l_t^K}, \frac{Y_t}{\tilde{Y}}\right) \frac{(q_t^i)^2}{2} l_t^{K,i}, \tag{4.44}$$

where Φ_t is a unit cost function, taken to depend on the economy's *average* collateral-loan ratio and cyclical output, $Y_t/\tilde{Y}$, with $\tilde{Y}$ the steady-state value of final production. Both variables have a negative effect on monitoring costs. First, as noted in chapter 3, collateral exerts a *disciplining effect*, because it induces borrowers to take less risk and expend more effort in ensuring that their investments are successful, while at the same time leading to greater compliance with bank monitoring requirements. This tends to reduce (unit) monitoring costs. Second, in boom times, when profits and cash flows are high, (unit) monitoring costs tend to fall because borrowers are more diligent and the risk of default abates.[28] These effects, which are also noted by Atta-Mensah and Dib (2008, p. 166) and Athanasoglou et al. (2014, p. 61), are consistent with the evidence on the negative impact of operating costs, which include monitoring costs *per se*, on bank profitability (Dietrich and Wanzenried 2014). For

27. To avoid a corner solution in which banks have no incentive to provide investment loans, the condition $\kappa^i \mathbb{E}_t p_{t+1}^H H_t \leq \left(1+i_t^{L,i}\right) l_t^{K,i} - x_t^{M,i}$ is required.

28. Hansen (2018) introduced countercyclical verification costs in a BGG-type model. As discussed in chapter 1, however, these costs are more akin to state-contingent bankruptcy costs, as opposed to the noncontingent monitoring costs considered in most of this book.

tractability, the cost of monitoring is assumed to be quadratic in the intensity of monitoring.[29]

Bank i maximizes expected profits subject to the downward-sloping loan demand curve of the representative CG producer (4.38), the balance sheet constraint (4.39), the definition of required reserves (4.40), and monitoring costs (4.44), taking as given working capital loans, the value of collateral, bank capital, the unit cost function, Φ_t, deposits and the deposit rate, and the refinance rate.[30]

Substituting (4.41) for $l_t^{B,i}$ in (4.43) yields

$$\begin{aligned}\mathbb{E}_t J_{t+1}^{B,i} = & q_t^i(1+i_t^{L,i})l_t^{K,i} + (1-q_t^i)\kappa^i \mathbb{E}_t p_{t+1}^H H_t + (1+i_t^R)l_t^{W,i} \\ & + \mu d_t^i - (1+i_t^D)d_t^i - (1+i_t^R)[l_t^i - V_t^i - (1-\mu)d_t^i] - x_t^{M,i}.\end{aligned}$$

Using (4.44) and solving, the first-order conditions with respect to q_t^i and $1+i_t^{L,i}$ are

$$(1+i_t^{L,i})l_t^{K,i} - \kappa^i \mathbb{E}_t p_{t+1}^H H_t - \Phi_t q_t^i l_t^{K,i} = 0, \tag{4.45}$$

$$q_t^i l_t^{K,i} + q_t(1+i_t^{L,i})\left[\frac{\partial l_t^{K,i}}{\partial(1+i_t^{L,i})}\right] - (1+i_t^R)\left[\frac{\partial l_t^{K,i}}{\partial(1+i_t^{L,i})}\right] = 0. \tag{4.46}$$

Consider first condition (4.45). It can be rearranged to give, in a symmetric equilibrium,

$$q_t = \min\left\{\Phi_t^{-1}\left(\frac{\kappa \mathbb{E}_t p_{t+1}^H H_t}{l_t^K}, \frac{Y_t}{\tilde{Y}}\right)\left[1+i_t^L - \left(\frac{\kappa \mathbb{E}_t p_{t+1}^H H_t}{l_t^K}\right)\right], 1\right\}. \tag{4.47}$$

This condition shows that, all else equal, a higher loan rate, or a higher level of cyclical output, tends to increase incentives to monitor borrowers. Intuitively, as in Allen et al. (2011), a higher loan rate increases incentives to monitor because it raises the bank's payoff if there is no default. The effect of cyclical output operates through monitoring costs, as explained earlier; it is consistent as well with the evidence—such as Marins and Eiras das Neves (2013)

29. A similar assumption is adopted by Allen et al. (2011), Dell'Ariccia et al. (2014), and Martinez-Miera and Repullo (2019). An alternative approach, as in Kopecky and VanHoose (2006), for instance, is to assume that intensity is constant and that the cost of monitoring is quadratic in the level of loans.

30. As noted earlier, loans to IG producers carry no risk and are extended at the marginal cost of funds, the refinance rate. In principle, the interest rate on these loans could also be determined as part of the banks' optimization problem. However, this would not affect the analysis in any substantive manner as long as the solution takes the form of a fixed markup over the refinance rate.

for Brazil—with suggests that the business cycle, in addition to firm-specific financial variables, has a negative impact on the probability of bankruptcy of nonfinancial firms.

Equation (4.47) also shows that, as discussed in chapter 3, the collateral-loan ratio exerts conflicting effects on monitoring and the repayment probability. On the one hand, there is a negative *hedging* or *lazy bank effect*, due to the fact that by mitigating the loss that banks incur in case of default, collateral can induce them to monitor less—thereby reducing the probability of repayment. On the other, there is a positive *disciplining effect*, alluded to earlier (reduced incentives for borrowers to take risks and lower unit monitoring costs). In what follows, as in chapter 3 and consistent with evidence of a negative correlation between collateral and a borrower's risk, it is assumed that the effect disciplining dominates. Thus, the net effect of an increase in the collateral-loan ratio is to raise the probability of repayment.

For tractability, equation (4.47) can be written in the form

$$q_t = \varphi_0 \left(\frac{\kappa \mathbb{E}_t p^H_{t+1}/\tilde{p}^H}{l^K_t/\tilde{l}^K} \right)^{\varphi_1} \left(\frac{Y_t}{\tilde{Y}} \right)^{\varphi_2} \left(\frac{1+i^L_t}{1+\tilde{\imath}^L} \right)^{\varphi_3}, \tag{4.48}$$

where $\varphi_0 > 0$ is a scale parameter that ensures an interior solution and $\varphi_1, \varphi_2, \varphi_3 > 0$.[31]

Consider next condition (4.46). From (4.38),

$$\frac{\partial l^{K,i}_t}{\partial (1+i^{L,i}_t)} = -\varsigma^L \left(\frac{1+i^{L,i}_t}{1+i^L_t} \right)^{-\varsigma^L - 1} \left(\frac{l^K_t}{1+i^L_t} \right). \tag{4.49}$$

Substituting (4.38) and (4.49) in (4.46) yields

$$q^i_t \left(\frac{1+i^{L,i}_t}{1+i^L_t} \right)^{-\varsigma^L} l^K_t - q^i_t (1+i^{L,i}_t) \varsigma^L \left(\frac{1+i^{L,i}_t}{1+i^L_t} \right)^{-\varsigma^L - 1} \left(\frac{l^K_t}{1+i^L_t} \right)$$
$$+ (1+i^R_t) \varsigma^L \left(\frac{1+i^{L,i}_t}{1+i^L_t} \right)^{-\varsigma^L - 1} \left(\frac{l^K_t}{1+i^L_t} \right) = 0.$$

In a symmetric equilibrium, $i^{L,i}_t = i^L_t$ and $q^i_t = q_t$ $\forall i$, and this expression becomes

31. To ensure that the default probability lies between zero and one, this functional form should be properly scaled. However, this is inconsequential for a local analysis in the vicinity of the steady state, as is the case when the model is (log) linearized. See the discussion in section 4.

$$q_t l_t^K - q_t(1+i_t^L)\zeta^L\left(\frac{l_t^K}{1+i_t^L}\right) + (1+i_t^R)\zeta^L\left(\frac{l_t^K}{1+i_t^L}\right) = 0.$$

Multiplying both sides by $-(1+i_t^L)/l_t^K$ yields

$$-q_t(1+i_t^L) + q_t(1+i_t^L)\zeta^L - (1+i_t^R)\zeta^L = 0,$$

which gives the equilibrium loan rate as

$$1+i_t^L = \frac{\zeta^L}{(\zeta^L-1)q_t}(1+i_t^R)\epsilon_t^L. \tag{4.50}$$

As in chapters 2 and 3, equation (4.50) shows that the loan rate is a markup over the marginal cost of central bank liquidity. It also incorporates a premium, given by the inverse of the repayment probability. Thus, the model accounts for a direct link between credit spreads and the risk of default, as in a number of analytical contributions.[32] It is also consistent with the evidence, discussed in chapter 1, which suggests that secured loans carry spreads that are lower than unsecured loans. Moreover, (4.48) and (4.50) imply that the default rate, as measured by $1-q_t$, and credit spreads are countercyclical, in line with the evidence discussed by Pesaran et al. (2006), for instance.

The random variable ϵ_t^L is added to capture credit spread shocks, which reflect, as in Airaudo and Olivero (2019), for instance, shocks to the elasticity of substitution across loan varieties—or, equivalently, a bank markup shock. This shock is assumed to follow an $AR(1)$ process,

$$\epsilon_t^L = (\epsilon_{t-1}^L)^{\rho^L}\exp(\xi_t^L),$$

where $\rho^L \in (0,1)$ and $\xi_t^L \sim \mathbf{N}(0, \sigma_{\xi^L})$.[33]

At the end of the period, banks pay interest on deposits, redeem their debt, and repay with interest the loans that they received from the central bank. Because banks close their books, there are no retained earnings and no changes in their net worth; profits (if any) are rebated lump-sum to households.

32. See Wickens (2017), for instance.

33. By assumption, banks are able to instantaneously set the loan rate to its equilibrium level. Interest rate stickiness can be introduced either through a simple partial adjustment process, as in Agénor and Alper (2012), for instance, or through explicit adjustment costs, as is the case in some models with monopolistic competition in banking (Dib 2010*a*; Gerali et al. 2010). In the latter case, today's loan rate would depend not only on its lagged value, i_{t-1}^L, but also on its expected future value, $\mathbb{E}_t i_{t+1}^L$.

4.1.6 Central Bank and Regulator

The central bank's assets consist of holdings of government bonds, b_t^C, and loans to commercial banks, $l_t^B = \int_0^1 l_t^{B,i} di$, whereas its liabilities consist of currency in circulation, m_t^s, and required reserves, RR_t. These liabilities make up the monetary base. The balance sheet of the central bank is thus

$$b_t^{CB} + l_t^B = m_t^s + RR_t + nw_t, \tag{4.51}$$

where nw_t is the central bank's net worth.

Changes in the central bank's holdings of government bonds are specified as

$$b_t^{CB} - \frac{b_{t-1}^{CB}}{1+\pi_t} = -\kappa^{CB}\left(l_t^B - \frac{l_{t-1}^B}{1+\pi_t}\right), \tag{4.52}$$

where $\kappa^{CB} \in (0, 1)$. Combining (4.51) and (4.52) and assuming that the central bank's net worth is constant in real terms yields

$$m_t^s = \frac{m_{t-1}^s}{1+\pi_t} + (1-\kappa^{CB})\left(l_t^B - \frac{l_{t-1}^B}{1+\pi_t}\right) - \left(RR_t - \frac{RR_{t-1}}{1+\pi_t}\right). \tag{4.53}$$

This equation allows a distinction between two monetary policy regimes: open-market operations ($\kappa^{CB} = 1$), whereby provision of liquidity by the central bank are fully sterilized by offsetting changes in bond holdings and therefore have no impact on the supply of currency, and a standing facility ($\kappa^{CB} = 0$), where changes in central bank lending fully translate into changes in the supply of cash. As in previous chapters, the focus will be on $\kappa^{CB} = 0$.

Specifically, monetary policy is operated by setting the refinance rate, i_t^R, and providing uncollateralized loans at the discretion of commercial banks.[34] The refinance rate depends on a base policy rate, i_t^T, and a penalty rate, θ_t^{CB}:

$$1 + i_t^R = (1 + i_t^T)(1 + \theta_t^{CB}). \tag{4.54}$$

In turn, the base policy rate is set on the basis of a Taylor-type policy rule,

$$\frac{1+i_t^T}{1+\tilde{\imath}^T} = \left(\frac{1+i_{t-1}^T}{1+\tilde{\imath}^T}\right)^{\chi} \left\{\left(\frac{1+\pi_t}{1+\pi^T}\right)^{\varepsilon_1} \left(\frac{Y_t}{\tilde{Y}}\right)^{\varepsilon_2}\right\}^{1-\chi} \epsilon_t^T, \tag{4.55}$$

where $\tilde{\imath}^T$ is the steady-state value of the policy rate, $Y_t/\tilde{Y}$ is the cyclical component of output (as defined earlier), $\pi^T \geq 0$ is the central bank's inflation target,

34. Again, for simplicity, collateral requirements (typically low-risk and low-yield assets, such as government securities) are ignored, and a zero-width band around the target interest rate is assumed.

$\chi \in (0, 1)$ is a coefficient measuring the degree of interest rate smoothing, $\varepsilon_1, \varepsilon_2 > 0$, and ϵ_t^T is a stochastic shock that follows a first-order autoregressive process,

$$\epsilon_t^T = (\epsilon_{t-1}^T)^{\rho_{\xi^T}} \exp(\xi_t^T),$$

where $\rho_{\xi^T} \in (0, 1)$ and $\xi_t^T \sim \mathbf{N}(0, \sigma_{\xi^T})$ is a serially uncorrelated random shock with zero mean.

The rule specified in (4.55) implies that, if inflation and output rise above their target or steady-state levels, the nominal policy rate is raised over time above its own steady-state value by amounts dictated by the parameters ε_1 and ε_2 and at a speed that depends on the coefficient χ. A higher policy rate—which feeds into the refinance rate, as implied by (4.54), and eventually market interest rates, as implied by (4.42) and (4.50)—aims to dampen aggregate demand and mitigate pressure on marginal cost and inflation. Such a reaction function—or variants of it, where, for instance, expected inflation, $\mathbb{E}_t\pi_{t+1}$, rather than current inflation, appears—has been shown to be a key building block to ensure stability in DSGE models.[35] To ensure that the *Taylor principle*, discussed in chapter 1, holds, the restriction $\varepsilon_1 > 1$ must be imposed. Even though the debate continues regarding its analytical relevance in relatively complex macroeconomic models, this restriction, as discussed later on, is well supported by the empirical evidence.

In some analytical contributions, rather than cyclical output, it is the *output gap* that is used in interest rate rules such as (4.55). The output gap is generally defined as the percent deviation between actual output and *potential output*, with the latter defined as output in the efficient equilibrium without monopoly power and price rigidity—that is, when prices are fully flexible. However, while this definition of the output gap is conceptually appealing as an indicator to help guide policy, it is difficult to translate it into an operational measure (Billi 2011; Kiley 2013). In practice, due to measurement problems and data revisions, policymakers often prefer to rely on *output growth*. Some DSGE contributions, such as Liu (2006), have also relied on that measure in specifying the policy interest rate rule. Nevertheless, for the remainder of this book, when discussing monetary policy the focus will be on cyclical output; the distinction between steady-state deviations and growth rates will be addressed mainly when defining triggering variables in simple macroprudential policy rules.

35. See Woodford (2003) and Christiano et al. (2010*b*). Some contributions, such as Smets and Wouters (2003) and Christiano et al. (2010*a*), also include the *change* in inflation in the policy rule.

To create the possibility of a countercyclical role for reserve requirements, a specification similar in spirit to the *liability composition effect* discussed in chapter 2 is used to define the penalty rate imposed by the central bank,

$$1+\theta_t^{CB} = \left(\frac{l_t^B/\tilde{l}^B}{d_t/\tilde{d}}\right)^{\varphi^{CB}}, \tag{4.56}$$

where $\varphi^{CB} \geq 0$ and $\tilde{l}^B$ and $\tilde{d}$ are the steady-state values of l_t^B and d_t. Thus, the penalty rate increases with the amount borrowed, scaled by the bank's core liabilities—household deposits. This helps to capture the fact that, from the perspective of the central bank, the composition of bank liabilities matters when setting borrowing terms.[36] Indeed, in normal times central banks prefer to have commercial banks raise deposits to fund their operations rather than borrow from them, so when the ratio l_t^B/d_t is too high they raise the cost of refinancing to discourage further borrowing and induce commercial banks to offer higher deposit rates, thereby improving incentives for households to increase their deposit holdings. In a sense, an l_t^B/d_t ratio that is too high creates a "stigma" effect, which raises the cost of funds borrowed either directly from the central bank, as is modeled here, or indirectly through the interbank market, as may be the case in practice (Ennis and Weinberg 2013; Armantier et al. 2015). The case discussed in the previous chapters corresponds to $\varphi^{CB}=0$, which implies that $\theta_t^{CB}=0$, $\forall t$; there is no distinction between the policy rate and the refinance rate. When $\varphi^{CB}>0$, this condition also holds but only in the steady state, given that $\tilde{\theta}^{CB}=0$. In general, therefore, the model makes a clear distinction between the policy rate (set to stabilize fluctuations in output and inflation) and the refinance rate (the marginal cost of liquidity for banks).[37]

Any income made by the central bank from holding government bonds and providing loans to commercial banks is transferred in full to the government at the end of each period. Its net worth is thus constant over time, as assumed

36. A conceptually similar idea is developed in Alper et al. (2018), although in a very different setting. They also provided evidence that central bank liquidity and household deposits are imperfect substitutes as bank funding sources in Turkey.

37. An alternative specification would be to relate the penalty rate to ratio of central bank borrowing to required reserves, l_t^{CB}/RR_t. Thus, the penalty rate increases with the amount that banks borrow from the central bank (as before) and falls now with the amount of reserves held there, RR_t, rather than deposits, d_t. These reserves operate essentially as a form of (implicit) collateral, in line with, for instance, Barnea et al. (2015)—with the difference that collateral here determines not the *amount* that can be borrowed from the central bank but rather the *cost* at which such borrowing occurs. However, as implied by (4.40), $RR_t=\mu_t d_t$; given (4.15) and (4.42), an increase in the required reserve ratio has an ambiguous on total reserves, and thus the penalty rate, which makes that policy less potent as a countercyclical instrument (see chapter 5).

earlier. Finally, for the moment, the financial regulator plays no specific role; an explicit policy mandate will be discussed in chapters 5 and 6.

4.1.7 Government

The government purchases the final good and issues nominal riskless one-period bonds. Its budget constraint is given by, in nominal terms,

$$B_t^G = (1+i_{t-1}^B)B_{t-1}^G + P_t(G_t - T_t) - P_t i_{t-1}^B b_{t-1}^{CB} - P_t i_{t-1}^R l_{t-1}^B, \tag{4.57}$$

where $B_t^G = P_t b_t^{CB} + P_t b_t$ is the nominal stock of government bonds, G_t is government spending, and T_t is lump-sum tax revenues. The terms $P_t i_{t-1}^B b_{t-1}^{CB}$ and $P_t i_{t-1}^R l_{t-1}^B$ on the right-hand side of (4.57) come from the assumption that all interest income that the central bank earns is transferred to the government. Put differently, and consistent with the distinction made by Buiter (2007), what appears in the government budget is not seigniorage but *central bank revenue*, which represents the interest earned by investing the resources obtained through the issuance of base money—in the form of loans to commercial banks and the acquisition of government bonds.

In real terms, this expression becomes

$$b_t^G - \frac{b_{t-1}^G}{1+\pi_t} = G_t - T_t + \frac{i_{t-1}^B b_{t-1}}{1+\pi_t} - \frac{i_{t-1}^R l_{t-1}^B}{1+\pi_t}, \tag{4.58}$$

where $b_t^G = b_t + b_t^{CB}$.

In the remainder of the book, the government is assumed to keep its real stock of debt constant and to balance its budget by adjusting lump-sum taxes, T_t. Thus, because it can always be satisfied through a change in these taxes, the government budget constraint does not impose any restrictions on equilibrium allocations.

Government purchases are a constant fraction of output of the final good,

$$G_t = \psi_G Y_t, \tag{4.59}$$

where $\psi_G \in (0, 1)$.

Flows between agents are summarized in figure 4.1.

4.2 Equilibrium Conditions

In this economy, equilibrium conditions must be satisfied for the credit, deposit, cash, labor, housing, and final good markets. Because the supply of loans by commercial banks and the supply of deposits by households are perfectly

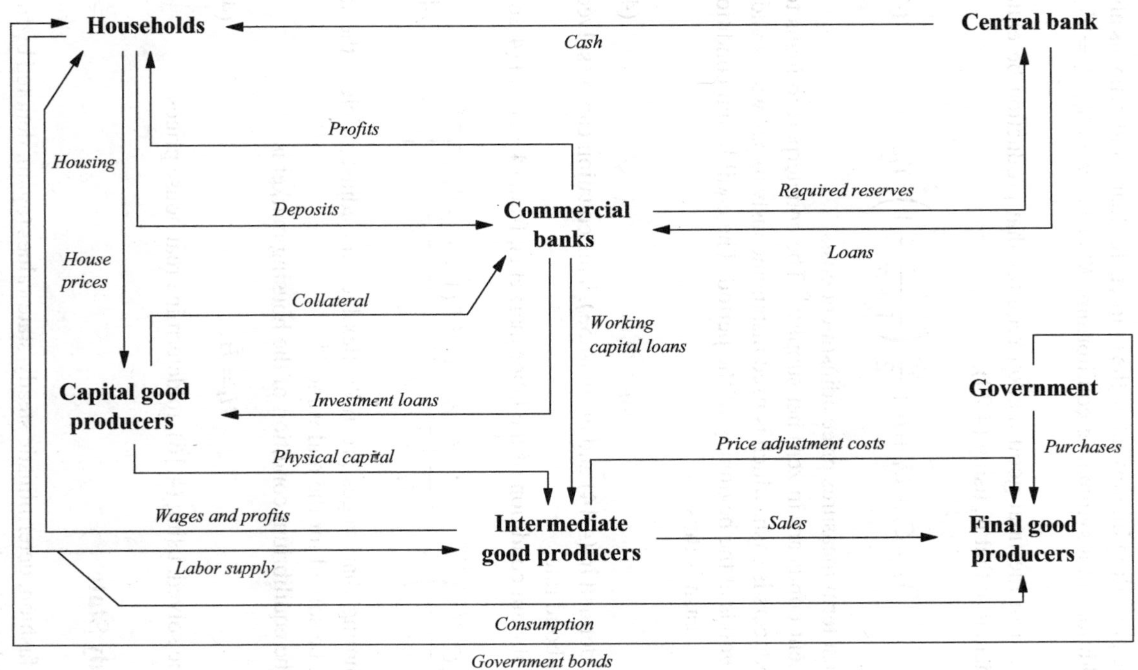

Figure 4.1 Structure of the core closed-economy DSGE-FF model

elastic at the prevailing interest rates, the markets for loans and deposits always clear. In addition, in a symmetric equilibrium, $K_t^j = K_t$, $N_t^j = N_t$, $Y_t^j = Y_t$, and $P_t^j = P_t$.

Equilibrium in the final good market requires that production be equal to aggregate demand; that is, using (4.29),

$$Y_t = C_t + G_t + I_t + \frac{\phi_I}{2}\left(\frac{1+\pi_t}{1+\tilde{\pi}} - 1\right)^2 Y_t, \tag{4.60}$$

where the last term measures price adjustment costs.

Government bonds are in zero net supply.[38] The counterpart to loans to IG and CG producers is cash, which is used instantaneously to pay wages and buy investment goods at the beginning of the period. The equilibrium condition of the market for cash is thus

$$m_t = m_t^s, \tag{4.61}$$

where m_t is defined in (4.14) and m_t^s in (4.53). This equation can be solved for the nominal bond rate.

The equilibrium condition of the labor market is, from (4.12) and (4.26),

$$\left(\frac{\omega_t C_t^{-1/\varsigma}}{\eta_N}\right)^{1/\psi_N} = \frac{1}{\epsilon_t^Y}\left(\frac{\alpha}{1-\alpha}\right)^{-\alpha}\left[\frac{(1+\psi_W i_t^R)\omega_t}{r_t^K}\right]^{-\alpha}, \tag{4.62}$$

which, assuming that wages are fully flexible and adjust to clear the labor market, can be solved for the real wage.[39]

Finally, the equilibrium condition of the housing market is

$$H_t = \bar{H}, \tag{4.63}$$

which can be solved, using (4.16), to determine real house prices.

4.3 Steady State

In standard fashion, deterministic steady-state values (again, denoted by tildes) can be calculated by dropping all time subscripts from the relevant variables. First, note that as in the simpler model of chapter 3 the policy rule (4.55)

38. By Walras' law, the equilibrium condition of the bond market can be eliminated.

39. The assumption of full wage flexibility at the aggregate level is a reasonable approximation for many developing countries with a large informal economy; see Agénor (2006*b*). Horvath (2018) presents an open-economy DSGE model with an explicit informal sector. However, it is not an appropriate assumption for countries where open unemployment is high.

implies, by construction, that in the steady state, inflation must be equal to its target value:

$$\tilde{\pi} = \pi^T.$$

In the remainder of the book the focus will be on a steady state where the target rate of inflation π^T is zero. Thus, by implication $\tilde{\pi} = 0$.

The steady-state value of the bond rate is determined by setting $C_t = C_{t+1}$ and $\tilde{\pi} = 0$ in (4.11). This gives

$$\tilde{\imath}^B = \Lambda^{-1} - 1. \tag{4.64}$$

From (4.55) and (4.56), and given that the penalty rate $\tilde{\theta}^{CB} = 0$ in the steady state, the refinance rate is equal to the policy rate:

$$\tilde{\imath}^R = \tilde{\imath}^T.$$

It must also be that

$$\tilde{\imath}^R = \tilde{\imath}^T = \tilde{\imath}^B,$$

to ensure that in equilibrium banks have no incentives to borrow from the central bank to purchase government bonds.

From (4.12), (4.14), (4.15), and (4.16), the representative household's labor supply and demand for real cash balances, bank deposits, and housing services are

$$\tilde{N} = \left(\frac{\tilde{\omega}(\tilde{C}^{-1/\varsigma}}{\eta_N} \right)^{1/\psi_N},$$

$$\tilde{m} = \frac{\eta_x \nu \tilde{C}^{1/\varsigma}(1 + \tilde{\imath}^B)}{\tilde{\imath}^B},$$

$$\tilde{d} = \frac{\eta_x (1 - \nu) \tilde{C}^{1/\varsigma}(1 + \tilde{\imath}^B)}{\tilde{\imath}^B - \tilde{\imath}^D},$$

$$\tilde{H} = \frac{\eta_H \tilde{C}^{1/\varsigma}}{(1 - \Lambda)\tilde{p}^H}.$$

From (4.20), steady-state output of intermediate goods is given by

$$\tilde{Y} = \tilde{N}^{1-\alpha} \tilde{K}^{\alpha},$$

whereas from (4.27) the steady-state value of the capital-labor ratio is

$$\frac{\tilde{K}}{\tilde{N}} = \left(\frac{\alpha}{1 - \alpha} \right) \left[\frac{(1 + \psi_W \tilde{\imath}^R)\tilde{\omega}}{\tilde{r}^K} \right].$$

From (4.21), the steady-state level of borrowing for working capital needs is

$$\tilde{l}^W = \psi_W \tilde{\omega} \tilde{N}.$$

By construction, price adjustment costs, as defined in (4.29), are zero in the steady state. From the price adjustment equation (4.32),

$$(1-\theta) + \theta \widetilde{mc} - \phi_I \left(\frac{\tilde{\pi}}{\tilde{\pi}} - 1 \right) \left(\frac{\tilde{\pi}}{\tilde{\pi}} \right) + \Lambda \phi_I \frac{\tilde{\lambda}}{\tilde{\lambda}} \left(\frac{\tilde{\pi}}{\tilde{\pi}} - 1 \right) \left(\frac{\tilde{\pi}}{\tilde{\pi}} \right) \left(\frac{\tilde{Y}}{\tilde{Y}} \right) = 0,$$

which can be solved for the steady-state value of marginal cost:

$$\widetilde{mc} = \frac{\theta - 1}{\theta}. \tag{4.65}$$

This equation relates marginal cost to the inverse of the markup, $\theta/(\theta-1)$, imposed by IG producers. As θ increases, the markup falls, and in the limit case of $\theta \to \infty$, both the markup and marginal cost tend to unity. The parameter θ is thus a measure of the steady-state distortion arising from monopolistic competition.

From (4.33), the equilibrium amount of loans demanded by CG producers is

$$\tilde{l}^K = \tilde{I}.$$

In the steady state, with $K_{t+1} = K_t$, capital adjustment costs in (4.34) are also zero. The equation implies therefore that steady-state investment is

$$\tilde{I} = \delta_K \tilde{K}.$$

From the optimality condition (4.37), the steady-state value of the rental rate of capital is given by

$$\tilde{r}^K = \tilde{q}(1+\tilde{\imath}^L) \left(\frac{1+\tilde{\imath}^B}{1+\tilde{\pi}} \right) - \tilde{q}(1+\tilde{\imath}^L)(1-\delta_K),$$

that is, using (4.64) and given that $\tilde{\pi} = 0$,

$$\tilde{r}^K = \tilde{q}(1+\tilde{\imath}^L) \left(\frac{1}{\Lambda} - 1 + \delta_K \right),$$

which relates the steady-state rental rate of capital to the expected cost of borrowing and the bond rate.[40]

40. Without borrowing in advance, as noted earlier the standard no-arbitrage condition $\tilde{r}^K - \delta_K = \Lambda^{-1} - 1$ would hold: in equilibrium the capital rental rate, adjusted for depreciation, must be equal to the real bond rate.

From (4.42) the steady-state deposit rate is

$$\tilde{\imath}^D = (1-\mu)\tilde{\imath}^R,$$

which implies, given that $\tilde{\imath}^R = \tilde{\imath}^B$, that $\tilde{\imath}^B > \tilde{\imath}^D$. Intuitively, the return on bonds must be higher than the return on deposits to compensate for the fact that bonds, unlike money, do not provide liquidity services.

Using (4.50), the steady-state loan rate is given by

$$\tilde{\imath}^L = \frac{\zeta^L}{\tilde{q}(\zeta^L - 1)}(1+\tilde{\imath}^R) - 1.$$

Because $\zeta^L > 1$ and $\tilde{q} < 1$, the condition $\zeta^L/\tilde{q}(\zeta^L - 1) > 1$ holds. Thus $\tilde{\imath}^L > \tilde{\imath}^R$. This condition ensures that banks have an incentive to borrow from the central bank (if needed) in order to satisfy the demand for credit. Because it also guarantees that $\tilde{q}(1+\tilde{\imath}^L) > 1+\tilde{\imath}^B$, it implies that in equilibrium banks have no incentive to hold government bonds.[41]

From (4.48), the steady-state value of the repayment probability is

$$\tilde{q} = \varphi_0 \kappa^{\varphi_1}.$$

From (4.39) and (4.40), the steady-state level of bank borrowing from the central bank is

$$\tilde{l}^B = \tilde{l} - V - (1-\mu)\tilde{d}.$$

The equilibrium condition of the final good market, equation (4.60), together with (4.59), yields the steady-state level of output:

$$\tilde{Y} = \frac{\tilde{C} + \tilde{I}}{1 - \psi_G}.$$

From (4.58) and (4.59), and given that $\tilde{\pi} = 0$, the steady-state value of lump-sum taxes is

$$\tilde{T} = \psi_G \tilde{Y} + \tilde{\imath}^B \tilde{b} - \tilde{\imath}^R \tilde{l}^B.$$

Finally, from (4.61), (4.62), and (4.63), the steady-state equilibrium conditions of the currency, labor, and housing markets are given by

$$\tilde{m}^s = \tilde{m},$$

41. To account for bank holdings of government bonds in equilibrium it could be assumed that the regulator imposes a statutory liquidity ratio, as in Anand et al. (2015), for instance. However, in the present setting this role is played by reserve requirements.

$$\tilde{\omega}^{\alpha+\psi_N^{-1}} = \left(\frac{\eta_N}{\tilde{C}^{-1/\varsigma}}\right)^{1/\psi_N} \left(\frac{\alpha}{1-\alpha}\right)^{-\alpha} \left[\frac{1+\psi_W(\Lambda^{-1}-1)}{\tilde{r}^K}\right]^{-\alpha},$$

$$\tilde{p}^H = \frac{\eta_H \tilde{C}^{1/\varsigma}}{(1-\Lambda)\bar{H}}. \tag{4.66}$$

The above equations form a static system that defines the nonstochastic steady state of the model. It can be solved numerically, based on the parameterization provided next. This solution is obtained under the assumption that policymakers have no access to lump-sum subsidies to correct the distortions created by monopolistic competition and financial frictions. In that sense, the nonstochastic steady state is *inefficient*. Although not without its problems—it rules out achieving the first-best allocation—this assumption is fairly common in the DSGE literature.[42]

4.4 Log-Linearization

To analyze the response of the economy to shocks, the model is log-linearized around the nonstochastic, zero-inflation steady state defined earlier. This solution technique is still widely used to solve DSGE models, despite the fact that (as discussed later) nonlinear techniques have become increasingly popular in recent years.

Before presenting the results, a brief reminder of the basic rules of log-linearization are provided.[43]

4.4.1 Basic Rules

For a variable x_t, log-linearization involves calculating $\widehat{x}_t = \ln x_t - \ln \tilde{x}$, where $\tilde{x}$ is the steady-state value of x_t. Equivalently,

$$\widehat{x}_t = \ln\left(\frac{x_t}{\tilde{x}}\right) = \ln\left[1+\left(\frac{x_t-\tilde{x}}{\tilde{x}}\right)\right] \simeq \frac{x_t-\tilde{x}}{\tilde{x}},$$

which corresponds to the percent deviation of x_t from its steady state.

42. See Benigno and Woodford (2005), for instance. To obtain an efficient steady state, it must be assumed that the government provides subsidies to monopolistic agents (IG producers and banks here) so that output in the nonstochastic steady state of the economy corresponds to a situation in which prices are fully flexible and financial frictions are neutralized. It must also be assumed that these subsidies—which could take the form of credit subsidies, as in Correia et al. (2016)—are financed with lump-sum taxes on households, to abstract from distortionary effects. See Carrillo et al. (2017), for instance.

43. Canova (2007) and Zietz (2008) provide a more detailed description of logarithmic approximations.

For an equation of the form $g(x_t) = 0$, log-linearization involves using a first-order Taylor series approximation in the vicinity of the steady state so that $g(x_t) \simeq g(\tilde{x}) + g'(\tilde{x})(x_t - \tilde{x})$. Because $g(\tilde{x}) = 0$, this expression can be rewritten as

$$g(x_t) \simeq \tilde{x}g'(\tilde{x})\left(\frac{x_t - \tilde{x}}{\tilde{x}}\right) = \tilde{x}g'(\tilde{x})\widehat{x}_t.$$

This approximation, of course, is valid if x_t does not drift too far from $\tilde{x}$ in response to shocks.

For more general models with variables x_t^1 and x_t^2, for instance, there are three basic rules:

$$(x_t^1)^\alpha \simeq (\tilde{x}^1)^\alpha(1 + \alpha\widehat{x}_t^1),$$
$$x_t^1 x_t^2 \simeq \tilde{x}^1\tilde{x}^2(1 + \widehat{x}_t^1 + \widehat{x}_t^2),$$
$$(x_t^1)^{\alpha_1}(x_t^2)^{\alpha_2} \simeq \tilde{x}^1\tilde{x}^2(1 + \alpha_1\widehat{x}_t^1 + \alpha_2\widehat{x}_t^2),$$

where α_1 and α_2 are parameters. The second and third results follow because the term $\widehat{x}_t^1\widehat{x}_t^2$ is (by assumption) the product of two small numbers and hence negligible. By implication,

$$x_t^1 \simeq \tilde{x}^1(1 + \widehat{x}_t^1), \quad \frac{x_t^1}{x_t^2} \simeq \frac{\tilde{x}^1}{\tilde{x}^2}(1 + \widehat{x}_t^1 - \widehat{x}_t^2).$$

For instance, consider the simple GDP identity $Y_t = C_t + I_t$, where Y_t is output, C_t is consumption, and I_t is investment. It can be written as $\tilde{Y}(1 + \hat{Y}_t) = \tilde{C}(1 + \hat{C}_t) + \tilde{I}(1 + \hat{I}_t)$, that is,

$$\tilde{Y} + \tilde{Y}\hat{Y}_t = \tilde{C} + \tilde{C}\hat{C}_t + \tilde{I} + \tilde{I}\hat{I}_t,$$

or equivalently, because $\tilde{Y} = \tilde{C} + \tilde{I}$,

$$\tilde{Y}\hat{Y}_t = \tilde{C}\hat{C}_t + \tilde{I}\hat{I}_t.$$

Similarly, the Cobb-Douglas production function $Y_t = Y_0 N_t^\alpha K_t^{1-\alpha}$, where $\alpha \in (0, 1)$, can be written as

$$\tilde{Y}(1 + \hat{Y}_t) = Y_0\tilde{N}^\alpha\tilde{K}^{1-\alpha}[1 + \alpha\hat{N}_t + (1 - \alpha)\hat{K}_t],$$

or equivalently, given that $\tilde{Y} = Y_0\tilde{N}^\alpha\tilde{K}^{1-\alpha}$,

$$\hat{Y}_t = \alpha\hat{N}_t + (1 - \alpha)\hat{K}_t.$$

Finally, the capital accumulation equation $K_{t+1} = (1 - \delta_K)K_t + I_t$, where $\delta_K \in (0, 1)$, can be written as $\tilde{K}(1 + \hat{K}_{t+1}) = (1 - \delta_K)\tilde{K}(1 + \hat{K}_t) + \tilde{I}(1 + \hat{I}_t)$, or equivalently

$$\tilde{K}+\tilde{K}\hat{K}_{t+1}=(1-\delta_K)\tilde{K}+(1-\delta_K)\tilde{K}\hat{K}_t+\tilde{I}+\tilde{I}\hat{I}_t,$$

or

$$\tilde{K}\hat{K}_{t+1}=(1-\delta_K)\tilde{K}-\tilde{K}+\tilde{I}+(1-\delta_K)\tilde{K}\hat{K}_t+\tilde{I}\hat{I}_t,$$

or again, noting that $\tilde{I}=\delta_K\tilde{K}$ and dividing by $\tilde{K}$,

$$\hat{K}_{t+1}=(1-\delta_K)\hat{K}_t+\left(\frac{\tilde{I}}{\tilde{K}}\right)\hat{I}_t=\hat{K}_t+\delta_K(\hat{I}_t-\hat{K}_t).$$

As discussed in chapter 5, when the objective of policymakers is to maximize social welfare, a second-order approximation of the model characterizing the economy becomes necessary.

4.4.2 Log-Linearized Equations

Dwelling on the basic rules presented earlier, the log-linearized equations of the model can now be presented. Variables with a hat denote percentage-point deviations of the related variables for interest rates and inflation, and log-deviations for the others, from steady-state levels.[44]

From the Euler equation (4.11), household consumption is given by[45]

$$\mathbb{E}_t\hat{C}_{t+1}\simeq\hat{C}_t+\varsigma(\hat{\imath}_t^B-\mathbb{E}_t\hat{\pi}_{t+1}),$$

where $\mathbb{E}_t\hat{\pi}_{t+1}$ is defined as, given that $\tilde{\pi}=0$,

$$\mathbb{E}_t\hat{\pi}_{t+1}=\mathbb{E}_t\hat{P}_{t+1}-\hat{P}_t.$$

From (4.12), labor supply is

$$\hat{N}_t=\frac{1}{\psi_N}\left(\hat{\omega}_t-\frac{\hat{C}_t}{\varsigma}\right),$$

whereas from (4.14), (4.15), (4.16), and (4.64), the demand functions for cash, deposits, and housing services, are given by

44. Net interest rates are thus used as approximations of the log gross interest rates.

45. In principle, taking logs of an equation and then subtracting the log terms of the steady-state solution of that equation is not a procedure that should be used on equations that involve expectational terms—even when all variables enter multiplicatively, as in (4.11). This is because, due to Jensen's inequality, the expectation of a log term is not the same as taking the log of an expectation term ($\ln\mathbb{E}_tx_t\geq\mathbb{E}_t\ln x_t$). However, it is used here for illustrative purposes.

$$\hat{m}_t = \frac{\hat{C}_t}{\varsigma} - \left(\frac{\Lambda}{1-\Lambda}\right)\hat{\imath}^B_t,$$

$$\hat{d}_t = \frac{\hat{C}_t}{\varsigma} + \left[\frac{1}{(1-\Lambda)\mu} - 1\right](\hat{\imath}^D_t - \hat{\imath}^B_t),$$

$$\hat{H}_t = \left[\frac{\eta_H}{\tilde{C}^{-1/\varsigma}(1-\Lambda)\tilde{H}\tilde{p}^H}\right]\hat{\imath}^B_t - \hat{p}^H_t - \hat{\imath}^B_t + \frac{\hat{C}_t}{\varsigma} + \frac{\Lambda}{1-\Lambda}\mathbb{E}_t\hat{\pi}^H_{t+1},$$

where

$$\mathbb{E}_t\hat{\pi}^H_{t+1} = \mathbb{E}_t\hat{p}^H_{t+1} - \hat{p}^H_t.$$

The $\hat{H}_t$ equation can be further manipulated to give

$$\hat{H}_t = \frac{\Lambda}{1-\Lambda}(\mathbb{E}_t\hat{\pi}^H_{t+1} - (\hat{\imath}^B_t - \mathbb{E}_t\hat{\pi}_{t+1})],$$

which relates housing demand to the difference between the expected rate of increase in house prices and the expected real bond rate.

The production function (4.20) yields output of intermediate goods as

$$\hat{Y}_t = \hat{\epsilon}^Y_t + (1-\alpha)\hat{N}_t + \alpha\hat{K}_t,$$

whereas from (4.24) labor demand by IG producers is given by

$$\hat{N}_t = \hat{K}_t - \psi_W\hat{\imath}^R_t - \hat{\omega}_t + \left(\frac{1+\Lambda\delta_K}{1+\Lambda\delta_K-\Lambda}\right)\hat{r}^K_t.$$

To derive the log-linear approximation of the price adjustment equation (4.32), note first that, with zero inflation in the steady state ($\tilde{\pi}=0$), it becomes

$$\theta(1-mc_t) = 1 - \phi_I\pi_t(1+\pi_t) + \Lambda\phi_I\mathbb{E}_t\left\{\frac{\lambda_{t+1}}{\lambda_t}\pi_{t+1}(1+\pi_{t+1})\left(\frac{Y_{t+1}}{Y_t}\right)\right\},$$

which upon log-linearization gives

$$(1-\widetilde{mc})\theta - \widetilde{mc}\theta\widehat{mc}_t = 1 - \phi_I\hat{\pi}_t + \Lambda\phi_I\mathbb{E}_t\hat{\pi}_{t+1}.$$

Using (4.65), this equation becomes

$$\hat{\pi}_t = \left(\frac{\theta-1}{\phi_I}\right)\widehat{mc}_t + \Lambda\mathbb{E}_t\hat{\pi}_{t+1}, \tag{4.67}$$

where

$$\hat{\pi}_t = \hat{P}_t - \hat{P}_{t-1}.$$

From (4.28), the log-linearized equation for marginal cost is

$$\widehat{mc}_t = (1-\alpha)(\psi_W \hat{\imath}_t^R + \hat{\omega}_t) + \alpha \hat{r}_t^K. \tag{4.68}$$

The combination of (4.67) and (4.68) illustrates well the cost channel of monetary policy discussed in a simpler framework in chapter 2—that is, the direct effect of (deviations in) the policy rate $\hat{\imath}_t^R$ on (deviations in) inflation, $\hat{\pi}_t$, through its impact on (deviations in) marginal cost.

From (4.34), investment is driven by

$$\hat{I}_t = \left(\frac{1}{\delta_K}\right)[\mathbb{E}_t\hat{K}_{t+1} - (1-\delta_K)\hat{K}_t].$$

The log-linearized law of motion for the marginal product of capital is derived from the first-order condition for the profit maximization problem of capital good producers, equation (4.37):

$$\mathbb{E}_t\hat{r}_{t+1}^K = \tilde{q}\frac{(1+\tilde{\imath}^L)(1+\tilde{\imath}^B)}{1+\tilde{r}^K}\left[\hat{\imath}_t^L + \hat{\imath}_t^B - \mathbb{E}_t\hat{\pi}_{t+1} + \Theta_K(\mathbb{E}_t\hat{K}_{t+1} - \hat{K}_t) + \hat{q}_t\right]$$
$$-\tilde{q}\left(\frac{1+\tilde{\imath}^L}{1+\tilde{r}^K}\right)\left\{(1-\delta_K)\mathbb{E}_t\hat{\imath}_{t+1}^L + \Theta_K(\mathbb{E}_t\hat{K}_{t+2} - \mathbb{E}_t\hat{K}_{t+1}) + (1-\delta_K)\mathbb{E}_t\hat{q}_{t+1}\right\}.$$

From (4.42), the fact that $\tilde{\imath}^R = \tilde{\imath}^B$, and (4.64), the deposit rate is given by

$$\hat{\imath}_t^D = (1-\mu)\hat{\imath}_t^R.$$

From (4.50), the equation for the lending rate takes the form

$$\hat{\imath}_t^L = \hat{\imath}_t^R - \hat{q}_t + \hat{\epsilon}_t^L.$$

From (4.48), the equation for the probability of repayment is

$$\hat{q}_t = \varphi_1(\mathbb{E}_t\hat{p}_{t+1}^H - \hat{l}_t^K) + \varphi_2\hat{Y}_t + \varphi_3\hat{\imath}_t^L.$$

From (4.21), the demand for working capital loans by IG producers is given by

$$\hat{l}_t^W = \hat{\omega}_t + \hat{N}_t,$$

whereas from (4.33), the demand for investment loans by CG producers is

$$\hat{l}_t^K = \hat{I}_t.$$

By implication, total credit demanded by firms is given by

$$\hat{l}_t = \left(\frac{1}{\tilde{l}}\right)(\tilde{l}^W\hat{l}_t^W + \tilde{l}^K\hat{l}_t^K).$$

From (4.41), bank borrowing from the central bank is

$$\hat{l}_t^B = \frac{1}{\tilde{l}^B}[\tilde{l}\hat{l}_t - (1-\mu)\tilde{d}\hat{d}_t)].$$

From (4.55), the central bank base policy rate is determined by

$$\hat{\imath}_t^T = \chi \hat{\imath}_{t-1}^T + (1-\chi)(\varepsilon_1 \hat{\pi}_t + \varepsilon_2 \hat{Y}_t) + \zeta_t^T,$$

whereas the refinance is given by

$$\hat{\imath}_t^R = \hat{\imath}_t^T + \varphi^{CB}\left(\frac{\tilde{l}^B}{\tilde{d}}\right)(\hat{l}_t^B - \hat{d}_t).$$

The equilibrium condition of the market for cash, equation (4.61), yields

$$\hat{m}_t = \hat{m}_t^s.$$

The equilibrium condition of the final good market, equation (4.60), yields, using (4.59),[46]

$$\hat{Y}_t = \left[\frac{\tilde{C}}{(1-\psi_G)\tilde{Y}}\right]\hat{C}_t + \frac{\delta_K \tilde{K}}{(1-\psi_G)\tilde{Y}}\hat{I}_t.$$

Finally, given constant supply, the equilibrium condition of the housing market requires that

$$\hat{H}_t = 0.$$

4.5 Parameterization

The estimation and validation of DSGE models is increasingly conducted in a Bayesian framework.[47] This approach assumes that parameters are random variables, about which prior information (in the form of theoretical ranges, empirical studies, or educated guesses) may be available. Combined with the likelihood function, this then forms the posterior density from which one

46. The quadratic specification of price adjustment costs in (4.29) implies that these costs are of second order. Thus, to a first-order approximation, they disappear from the log-linearized version of the resource constraint, and final output (adjusted for the share of government spending) depends only on household consumption and investment.

47. See Cantore et al. (2011) for a simple example of Bayesian estimation of a DSGE model. Validating DSGE models has also taken the form of matching impulse response functions with those estimated by vector autoregression models. See Christiano et al. (2010*b*) for a discussion and applications of this procedure. Guerron-Quintana et al. (2017) discussed Bayesian impulse response matching techniques.

can draw inferences about the parameters. The Bayesian approach constrains the parameter space, thus reducing the possibility of obtaining outliers—a possibility that cannot be excluded when classical maximum likelihood estimation techniques are used (Herbst and Schorfheide 2016). At the same time it provides more flexibility to the extent that several potential values of a parameter (rather than just one) can be considered, weighted by the relevant prior density.[48]

However, even in the Bayesian framework some parameters are typically not estimated, but rather imposed based on extraneous information. Moreover, in defining priors, the researcher must consider both the theoretical domain of each parameter (whether or not the parameter is bounded, strictly positive, larger than a specific value, and so on) and the shape of the prior distribution. Usually, inverse gamma distributions are used for parameters constrained to be positive (such as variances or standard deviations), the beta distribution for parameters constrained to be between 0 and 1 (such as probabilities and fractions), while the normal distribution is specified for nonbounded parameters. But these choices themselves are priors.

Among studies focusing on MICs, contributions that have used Bayesian estimation techniques include Elekdag et al. (2006), Lee and Rhee (2013), Palma and Portugal (2014), García-Cicco and Kirchner (2015), Carvalho and Castro (2016), Gabriel et al. (2016), and Gupta and Sun (2016). This is an important step for a model whose purpose eventually is to provide concrete policy advice for a particular country. However, as noted in this book's introduction and overview, as well as chapter 1, the focus here is on exploring analytical issues—especially transmission channels and the scope for coordination among policymakers—that arise in the context of modeling monetary and macroprudential policies in macroeconomic models with financial frictions, rather than trying to design models that reproduce a particular set of quantitative facts for a specific country or group of countries. At the same time, given the complexity of the issues involved, going beyond the qualitative predictions of the simple static and dynamic models presented in chapters 2 and 3 requires numerical solutions. Accordingly, the focus is on parameterization, rather than econometric estimation or a rigorous calibration exercise based on moment matching. To do so, a variety of data and a wide range of contributions are dwelt on. The goal, in a sense, is to characterize key features of a "typical" middle-income economy rather than a country in particular. In addition, for some of the parameters that are deemed critical (in this chapter and the subsequent ones),

48. As illustrated in Levine et al. (2012), for instance, the use of Bayesian techniques is also of great importance to design policy rules that are robust to model uncertainty.

sensitivity analysis is reported—although, to avoid making the exercise too repetitive and cumbersome, such analysis is not pursued systematically and thoroughly.

Parameter values are summarized in table 4.1.[49] The discount factor Λ is set at 0.95, which gives a steady-state annualized bond rate (real and nominal, given zero steady-state inflation) of 5.3 percent—a fairly common value for studies focusing on developing countries where real rates of return tend to be significantly higher than in advanced economies. The intertemporal elasticity of substitution, ς, is set at 0.5, in line with estimates for MICs (Ogaki et al. 1996; Agénor and Montiel 2015, chap. 2).[50] The relative weight of the disutility of working, η_N, is set at 25 to ensure that in the steady state, households devote about one-third of their time endowment to market activity, consistent with the available data for Mexico and other countries (Boz et al. 2015). This target value for time allocated to market work is also a standard benchmark in the literature, including for advanced economies as considered, for instance, by Christoffel and Schabert (2015). The Frisch elasticity of labor supply is set at 0.71, which implies that $\psi_N = 1.4$. This value is close to the one used, for instance, by Anand et al. (2015) for the Philippines, and consistent with the value recommended by Chetty et al. (2011), on the basis of a review of the micro-macro evidence. The parameter for composite monetary assets, η_x, is set at 0.001, a low value that aims to capture the common assumption in the literature that their weight in household preferences is negligible (see, for instance, Christiano et al. 2010*a*; Christoffel and Schabert 2015). The housing prefer ence parameter, η_H, is also set at a low value of 0.02. Normalizing the physical housing stock to unity, and given the other parameters and initial values equation (4.66) can be solved for the real price of housing services.[51] The share parameter in the index of money holdings, ν, which corresponds to the relative share of cash in narrow money, is set at 0.35. This value is consistent with available data for several MICs, where the use of cash remains significant.

The elasticity of substitution between intermediate goods, θ, is set equal to 6. This value is fairy close to those used, for instance, by Medina and Soto (2007) for Chile and by Demirel (2010). It gives a steady-state estimate of the markup

49. In line with standard practice, the model is parameterized so that time periods represent quarters.

50. See also the discussion of the evidence by Braun and Nakajima (2012) and Thimme (2017), which focuses on advanced economies.

51. Setting $\tilde{H} = 1$ in (4.66) yields $\tilde{p}^H = \eta_H \tilde{C}^{1/\varsigma}/(1-\Lambda)$. As noted earlier, $\Lambda = 0.95$ and $\varsigma = 0.5$; in addition, steady-state household consumption is set at 65 percent of GDP, which is itself normalized to unity. Thus, $\tilde{p}^H = 0.02(0.65)^{1/0.5}/(1-0.95) \simeq 0.17$.

Table 4.1
Benchmark Parameterization, Closed Economy

Parameter	Value	Description
Households		
Λ	0.95	Discount factor
ς	0.5	Elasticity of intertemporal substitution
η_N	25.0	Relative weight of the disutility of labor
ψ_N	1.4	Inverse of Frisch elasticity of labor supply
η_x	0.001	Preference parameter for money holdings
η_H	0.02	Preference parameter for housing
ν	0.35	Share parameter in index of money holdings
Production		
θ	6.0	Elasticity of demand, intermediate goods
α	0.35	Share of capital, intermediate goods
ϕ_I	25.0	Adjustment cost parameter, prices of intermediate goods
δ_K	0.025	Depreciation rate of capital
Θ_K	14	Adjustment cost parameter, investment
ψ_W	0.0	Share of labor costs financed in advance
Commercial banks		
κ	0.2	Effective collateral share
ζ^L	4.5	Elasticity of substitution, loans to CG producers
φ_1	0.05	Elasticity of repayment probability, collateral-loan ratio
φ_2	0.4	Elasticity of repayment probability, cyclical output
φ_3	0.0	Elasticity of repayment probability, loan rate
Central bank		
μ	0.2	Required reserve ratio
χ	0.8	Degree of interest rate smoothing
ε_1	2.0	Response of policy rate to inflation deviations
ε_2	0.4	Response of policy rate to output deviations
φ^{CB}	0.0	Sensitivity of penalty rate to borrowing-deposit ratio
Government		
ψ_G	0.22	Share of government spending in output
Shocks		
ρ^L	0.8	Persistence parameter, productivity shock
ρ^L	0.8	Persistence parameter, credit spread shock
ρ^T	0.8	Persistence parameter, base policy rate shock

rate, $\theta/(\theta-1)$, which corresponds to the inverse of marginal cost in the steady state, as defined in (4.65), equal to 20 percent.

The share of capital in output of intermediate goods, α, is set at 0.35, a fairly standard value. The adjustment cost parameter for prices of intermediate goods, ϕ_I, is set at 25, to capture a relatively low degree of persistence in price stickiness in developing economies, as documented in some studies (Kiley 2000; Klenow and Malin 2011). The rate of depreciation of private capital, δ_K, is set equal to 0.025, a fairly standard value for both developed and developing countries—see Cook and Devereux (2006), for instance—which implies an annualized depreciation rate of 10.4 percent. In the absence of a well-established benchmark in the literature, the adjustment cost incurred by CG producers for transforming investment into capital, Θ_K, is set at 14 to generate an investment path in response to shocks that is of the order of three to four times more volatile than output, as documented in several studies of macroeconomic fluctuations (see, for instance, Neumeyer and Perri 2005, table 1; Hnatkovska and Koehler-Geib 2018, table 2). The share of labor costs financed in advance, ψ_W, is set initially at 0.0 to study the behavior of the model in the absence of a cost channel. In line with the evidence discussed in chapter 1, the case where ψ_W is positive will also be examined later on.

Regarding commercial banks, the effective collateral-loan ratio, κ, is set at 0.2—a significantly lower number than the value used by Cavalcanti (2010), for instance, but which better captures the difficulty of seizing collateral in most developing countries, due to weak legal systems and inefficient debt enforcement procedures (see chapter 1). The elasticities of the repayment probability with respect to the effective collateral-loan ratio and to deviations in output from its steady state are set at $\varphi_1 = 0.05$ and $\varphi_2 = 0.4$, respectively. The value of φ_1 is close to the one used for the elasticity of the external finance premium with respect to borrowers' leverage in a number of BGG-type DSGE applications, such as Anand et al. (2015) for the Philippines. Under the reasonable assumption that the direct effect of the repayment probability on the loan rate dominates the indirect effect of the latter on the former, parameter φ_3 is set at 0.0. For the elasticity of substitution ζ^L, which measures the degree of monopoly power in the market for loans, direct estimates for MICs are scant. However, there is ample evidence to suggest that the spread between bank funding costs and loan rates (as well as net interest margins) in MICs are much higher than in advanced economies, especially in Latin America and the Caribbean (see, for instance, Gelos 2009; Birchwood et al. 2017). A key factor that helps to account for these spreads is bank market power. Accordingly, ζ^L is set at 4.5, as in Dib (2010*b*) for instance, to generate a relatively large spread (as shown later) between the loan rate and the refinance rate.[52] Bank capital, V, is set as a fixed share of 12 percent of investment loans so that $V = 0.12l^K$. This share is consistent with data on ratios of total capital to risk-weighted asset for MICs, as documented in Fonseca et al. (2010).

Regarding the central bank, the required reserve ratio μ is set at 0.2, consistent with the data reported by Montoro (2011), Montoro and Moreno (2011),

52. By way of comparison, the value used by Anand et al. (2015) for the Philippines is 2.5. To ensure that (4.50) holds in the steady state, a multiplicative constant is added to the expression on the left-hand side.

Table 4.2
Initial Steady-State Values: Key Variables
(In proportion of final output, unless indicated otherwise)

Variable	Description	Value
C	Household consumption	0.65
$I = l^K$	Investment loans to CG producers	0.13
K	Capital stock	5.2
r^K	Rental rate of capital (percent)	0.079
G	Public expenditure	0.22
q	Repayment probability, loans to CG producers (percent)	0.935
i^B, i^R	Government bond rate, central bank refinance rate (percent)	0.053
i^D	Bank deposit rate (percent)	0.042
i^L	Loan rate, investment lending to CG producers (percent)	0.095
l^B	Central bank borrowing	0.098
d/x	Share of deposits in money holdings (in percent)	0.65

and Cordella et al. (2014) for a group of large economies in Latin America. Responses of the base policy rate to inflation and output deviations, ε_1 and ε_2, and the degree of persistence in the central bank's policy response, χ, are set at 2.0, 0.4, and 0.8, respectively. These values are consistent with estimates of Taylor-type rules for MICs, including those of Medina and Soto (2007) for Chile, Palma and Portugal (2014) for Brazil, and Armas et al. (2014) for Peru, and some of the results obtained by Moura and Carvalho (2010) for a broad sample of Latin American countries. The elasticity of the penalty rate to the bank borrowing-deposits ratio, φ^{CB}, is set to 0.0 in order to focus initially on the case where there is no liability composition effect. The case $\varphi^{CB} > 0$ will be examined in chapter 5.

The share of noninterest government spending in output, ψ_G, is set at 0.22, a value consistent with the evidence for a number of MICs, such as South Africa and Brazil, for instance (Liu and Seeiso 2012; Carvalho and Castro 2016). Finally, the degree of persistence of all shocks (productivity, credit spread, and base policy rate) is set at the uniform value of 0.8, which implies a reasonably high degree of inertia.

Using these parameter values, the steady-state solution is obtained. Solved values for some of the key variables of the model are displayed in table 4.2. They indicate that household consumption represents 65 percent of final output, investment 13 percent, and government spending (as noted earlier) 22 percent. The repayment probability is 93.5 percent, to capture a higher incidence of default in MICs compared to advanced economies. The bond and refinance rates are both equal to 5.3 percent, the deposit rate is 4.2 percent, and the lending rate is 9.5 percent—a spread of 420 basis points relative to the marginal cost of funding.

4.6 Solution and Experiments

To study the properties of the model, three experiments are conducted: a productivity shock, a credit spread shock, and a monetary policy shock involving a nonsystematic change in the base policy rate. As is clear from this list, the focus in this chapter is, as it is indeed elsewhere in the book, largely on financial shocks. Although in the real world, shocks often occur concurrently (making them therefore difficult to disentangle), to understand how they are transmitted it is naturally easier to study them independently. But before presenting the results, a brief discussion of solution methods for DSGE models is in order.

4.6.1 Solving DSGE Models

A standard method for solving DSGE models is the first-order perturbation approach, which requires linearization or log-linearization (Fernández-Villaverde et al. 2016). Its key feature is that the solution displays the *certainty equivalence* property, whereby the first-order approximation to the unconditional means of the endogenous variables coincides with their nonstochastic steady-state values.[53] Second-order local approximations are commonly used (especially for welfare evaluation, as discussed in chapter 5), but this is less so for higher-order approximations—despite the fact that, in general, higher-order terms improve accuracy and may be required to study specific issues.[54]

Perturbation methods are generally accurate around the point where a model is approximated and often display good global properties.[55] In addition, diagnostic procedures can be used to gauge the reliability of any specific approximation, as discussed by Jin and Judd (2002), for instance. However, these methods have been criticized from a number of perspectives (Aruoba et al. 2006). For the issue at stake, the use of first- or second-order local approximations can be problematic because important features of the procyclicality of the financial system, which may hinge on global, nonlinear effects of financial frictions, are not accurately captured. In particular, the magnitude of the amplification effects generated by the financial accelerator, and thus the effects of both financial frictions and macroprudential policies, could differ significantly

53. The reason is that in a linear approximation, only the first moments of the shocks enter the equations of the model. And because the processes driving these shocks are assumed to be of zero mean, these moments drop out when expectations are taken. Consequently, the distribution of the shocks has no impact on the solution.

54. In solving their model, Laséen et al. (2017), for instance, rely on a third-order perturbation method to capture changes in risk premia.

55. As noted by Fernández-Villaverde et al. (2016), perturbation methods were widely used already in physics in the nineteenth century.

from those generated by the global solution of the same model. As noted by Mendoza (2016), if perturbation methods underestimate the magnitude of the financial amplification, they are also likely to underestimate the magnitude of the distortions that macroprudential policies should address.

Several alternative solution methods have been proposed by Aruoba et al. (2006), Kim et al. (2008), Fernández-Villaverde et al. (2016), and Pesaran and Xu (2016). For instance, Pesaran and Xu (2016) developed a method that relates the steady-state values to their means as well as their standard deviations, without using second- or higher-order perturbation techniques.[56] More generally, projection methods, which exploit the global behavior of the functional equations of the model to approximate its solution, have also been used as an alternative to perturbation techniques. These methods require finding iteratively roots of nonlinear equations and work fairly well with small models. However, the *curse of dimensionality* hampers significantly the ability to apply them (as well as other global, nonlinear methods) to even reasonably rich models, such as the one described earlier.

Throughout this book, and given that only modest shocks are considered, the focus will remain therefore on perturbation methods. First-order approximations are used to calculate impulse response functions, whereas (as discussed in chapter 5) second-order approximations are used when assessing welfare effects. Specifically, using the parameter and steady-state values provided in tables 4.1 and 4.2, the model's response to the three transitory shocks identified earlier is obtained with DYNARE, a widely used software platform for the solution of DSGE models.[57] In light of the discussion in chapter 1, the focus of the analysis is on both the quantitative and qualitative features of the transmission process of each shock.

4.6.2 Productivity Shock

Consider a positive productivity disturbance, taking the form of a 1 percentage point increase in the technology shock ϵ_t^Y that characterizes the production function of intermediate goods. The impulse response functions for some of they key macroeconomic variables—output, consumption, real house prices, the repayment probability, the loan rate, investment, the expected real bond rate, inflation, and the refinance rate—are reported in figure 4.2.

56. As a result, they are able to study the link between credit shocks and volatility in the steady state as well as over the business cycle.

57. Specifically, the system of linear difference equations consisting of the log-linearized expressions described earlier is solved using the Schur decomposition, as described in Soderlind (1999). See https://www.dynare.org/.

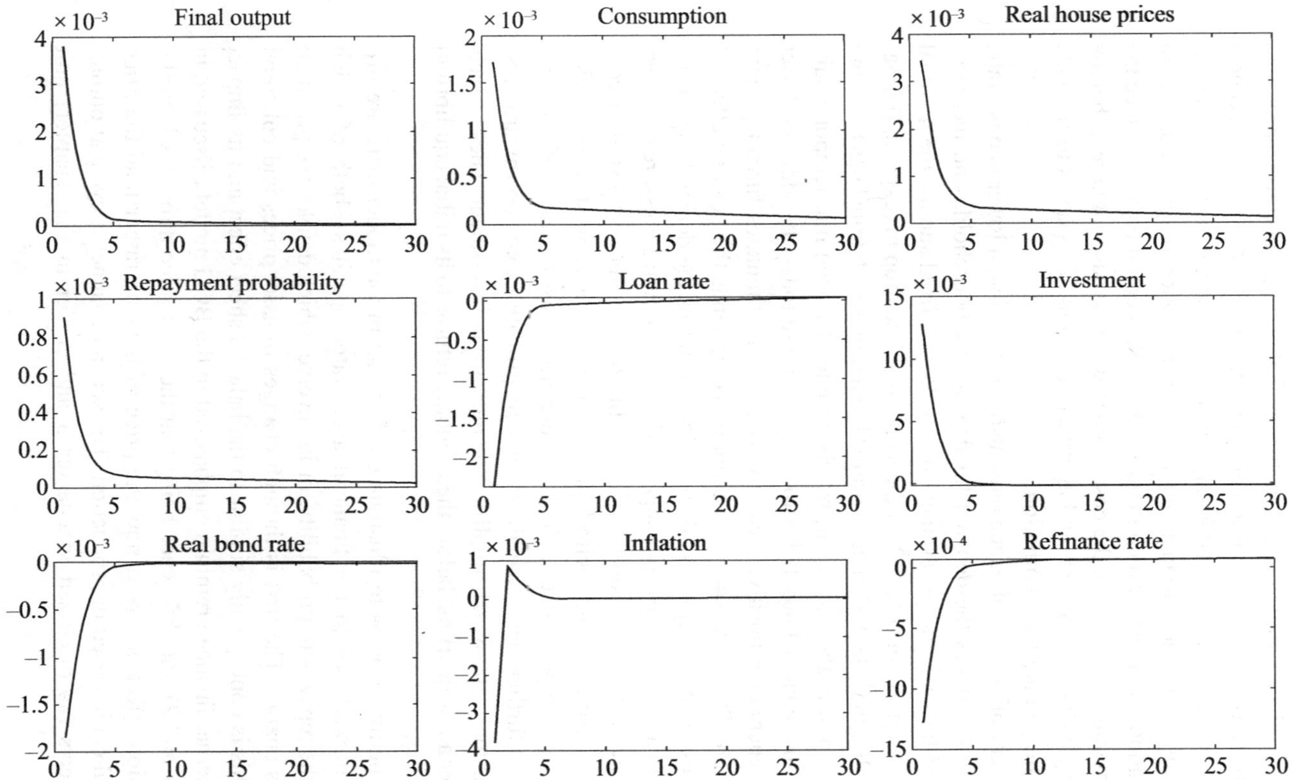

Figure 4.2
Positive productivity shock: impulse response functions
Note: The response of consumption, investment, output, and real house prices are expressed as percent deviations from their steady-state values. The response of the lending rate, the refinance rate, the expected real bond rate, the repayment probability, and the inflation rate are expressed as absolute deviations (or percentage points) from their steady-state values.

The direct effect of the shock is a higher level of output. This raises the repayment probability (through the mitigating effect, alluded to earlier, of cyclical output on unit monitoring costs) and lowers the loan rate, which in turn stimulates investment. Higher productivity also tends to reduce marginal cost and to lower inflation on impact, which in turn induces the central bank to reduce the base policy rate. The drop in the cost of borrowing is thus magnified, thereby stimulating further investment and aggregate demand. This tends to mitigate over time the initial drop in inflation.

The lower policy and refinance rates also translate into a lower deposit rate, which in turn reduces the demand for deposits by households and increases the demand for cash and government bonds. With a fixed supply, the nominal bond rate therefore must fall.[58] At the same time, the drop in (expected) inflation is smaller than the fall in the nominal bond rate, which translates therefore into a reduction in the (expected) real bond rate. Through intertemporal substitution, this induces households to consume more today. In addition, lower inflation generates a positive wealth effect, which stimulates further current consumption. The increase in consumption compounds the positive effect of higher investment on aggregate demand. It also raises the demand for leisure and leads to a reduction in labor supply, which puts upward pressure on wages and mitigates the initial drop in inflation. In addition, the expansion of consumption is also associated with higher demand for housing services, which tends to raise their price. In turn, higher house prices raise the value of collateral and induce a further increase in the repayment probability and downward pressure on the loan rate, which amplifies the increase in investment. These effects persist over a few quarters, before the economy returns to its initial equilibrium position.

This experiment helps to illustrate the fact that in the model there are *two channels* through which the financial accelerator operates—both of which affecting the repayment probability, or its inverse, which defines the premium that banks charge. The first is through changes in asset prices and collateral values. This is conceptually similar to the balance sheet effect and its impact on the external finance premium emphasized in the BGG model (discussed in chapters 1 and 2), the difference being that the asset price through which the amplification effect occurs is now the price of housing rather than the price of physical capital used in production. The second channel is cyclical output, which affects (as discussed in chapter 3 and earlier in this chapter) unit

58. The reduction in holdings of bank deposits also translates (at the initial level of loans) into an increase in bank borrowing from the central bank and—in the absence of offsetting open-market operations—an expansion in the money supply. This increase must be matched by a higher demand for cash, which is brought about by a reduction in the nominal bond rate.

monitoring costs. For the shock under consideration, these channels reinforce each other; the initial increase in output affects positively the repayment probability not only through its indirect, general equilibrium effect on house prices but also directly by lowering the cost of monitoring in good times. As a result, the loan rate falls by more than it would in response to the drop in the refinance rate (which results from the Taylor rule) and in the absence of endogenous default risk (which implies a constant repayment probability).

4.6.3 Credit Spread Shock

Consider a transitory reduction in the credit spread, which translates on impact into a 1 percentage point drop in the loan rate. The results are displayed in figure 4.3, for the same set of variables shown in figure 4.2.

The immediate impact of the shock is an increase in investment, which raises aggregate demand and inflation. The effects on output and prices combine to induce the central bank to raise the policy and refinance rates, which therefore mitigates the initial reduction in the loan rate. The deposit rate also increases, which induces households to switch away from cash and bonds. Given that the supply of bonds is fixed, the nominal bond rate must therefore increase.[59]

The increase in the nominal bond rate exceeds the rise in (the one-period ahead) inflation and, as a result, the (expected) real bond rate also increases. Intertemporal substitution induces households to shift consumption from the present to the future, which in turn leads to a reduction in demand for housing services. The fall in consumption dampens the initial increase in aggregate demand associated with higher investment, whereas the drop in house prices lowers the value of collateral that CG producers can pledge to lenders. The reduction in collateral values is large enough to induce initially a drop in the repayment probability (despite the increase in cyclical output and its mitigating effect on unit monitoring costs), but this indirect effect, which induces banks to raise the loan rate, is not large enough to dominate the direct effect of the negative spread shock on the market cost of borrowing.

The drop in consumption also reduces the marginal utility of leisure and induces households to supply more labor, thereby mitigating the upward pressure on real wages and marginal cost associated with the increase in labor demand. At the same time, higher investment raises the capital stock, which tends to reduce gradually the rental rate of capital as well as marginal cost.

59. In addition, the increase in deposits tends to reduce (all else equal) central bank borrowing by commercial banks and therefore the supply of cash. Thus, the nominal bond rate must also rise to reduce the demand for cash and maintain market equilibrium.

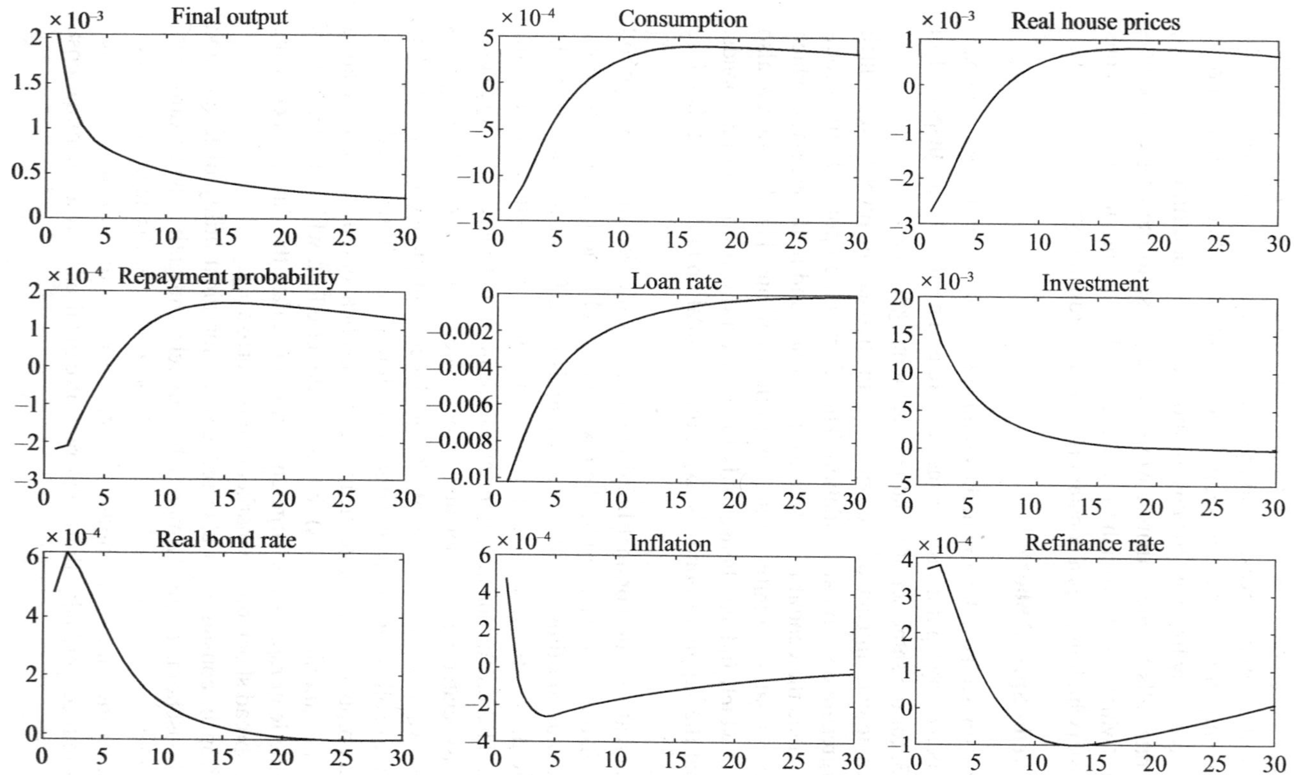

Figure 4.3
Negative credit spread shock: impulse response functions
Note: See note to figure 4.2.

The combination of both effects tends to mitigate inflationary pressures, but in nonmonotonic fashion. This also translates into nonmonotonic behavior in the refinance rate and the bond rate, as well as consumption and real house prices.

This experiment shows therefore that the two channels through which the financial accelerator operates work now in opposite directions: The drop in the collateral-loan ratio (resulting both from lower collateral values and an increase in investment loans) tends to lower the repayment probability, whereas the increase in cyclical output tends to increase it. Given the model's parameterization, the net effect is negative. As a result, the shock is associated with a financial *decelerator* effect: The fall in the repayment probability dampens the initial drop in the loan rate. However, an accelerator effect could also emerge with a different parameterization in which the impact of the loan-collateral ratio on the repayment probability is relatively small, or equivalently, the impact of cyclical output is relatively large.

4.6.4 Monetary Policy Shock

Consider a temporary, 1 percentage point reduction in the policy rate—and thus the refinance rate, given that the penalty rate is nil in the benchmark case. The results are reported in figure 4.4.

The immediate effect of this shock is a concomitant fall in the deposit rate, which lowers the demand for bank deposits and raises the demand for cash and bonds. With zero net supply of bonds, the nominal bond rate must fall as well.[60] At the same time, the reduction in the policy rate lowers directly the loan rate, which leads to an expansion of investment. Thus, aggregate demand increases, which puts upward pressure on prices. The rise in (expected) inflation, combined with the fall in the nominal bond rate, result in a reduction in the expected real bond rate. This induces households to shift consumption to the present, which therefore contributes to a further expansion in aggregate demand and output. At the same time, the increase in consumption induces households to supply less labor, which puts upward pressure on wages and marginal cost. It is also associated with higher house prices; in turn, higher prices, combined with a positive movement in cyclical output, lead to an increase in the repayment probability and therefore a further reduction in the loan rate. Thus, as in the case of the productivity shock, the two channels through which the financial accelerator operates are pulling in the same direction: They both combine to increase the repayment probability or, equivalently, to reduce the premium that

60. All else equal, the reduction in the level of deposits raises bank borrowing from the central bank and the monetary base; to increase the demand for cash and maintain equilibrium of the currency market, the bond rate (the opportunity cost of cash) must fall.

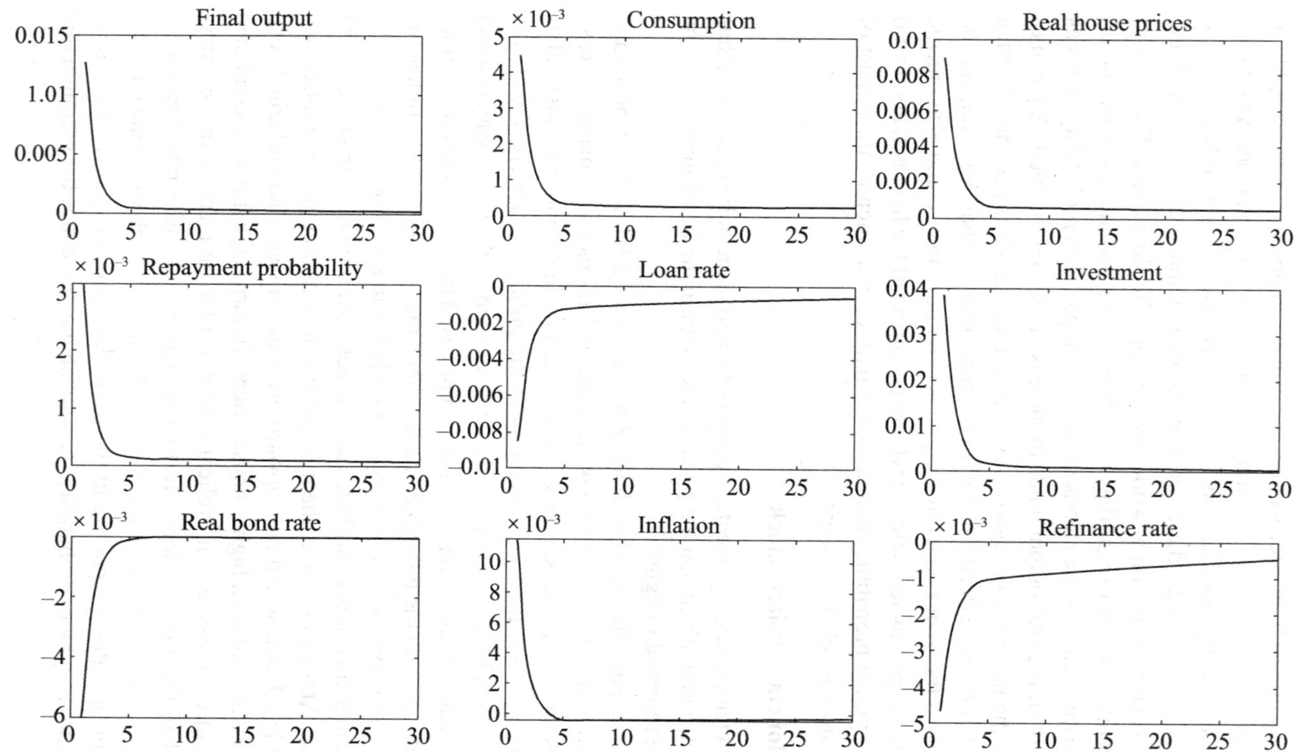

Figure 4.4
Negative base policy rate shock: impulse response functions
Note: See note to figure 4.2.

banks impose on borrowers. The expansion in investment, and consequently output, is therefore magnified compared to a situation where the repayment probability is constant.

The foregoing analysis helps to illustrate a potential trade-off between monetary and macroprudential policies and how it depends on the origin of shocks affecting the economy. As discussed in chapter 1, monetary and macroprudential policies tend to operate in a complementary manner in response to a demand shock—both being eased in response to a negative shock, for instance, to stimulate output and credit and prevent deflation. In response to a credit spread shock, as shown earlier, output and inflation also move in the same direction, implying that these policies would be complements as well. However, a trade-off may emerge between price and financial stability in response to a supply shock. Indeed, the positive productivity shock discussed earlier raises output while reducing inflation. In response to lower inflation, the central bank tends to reduce the refinance rate, which stimulates lending.[61] To mitigate the increase in credit, a macroprudential regulator would need instead to tighten its policy (by setting a higher tax rate on loans, for instance, as in chapters 2 and 3) in order to raise the cost of borrowing and dampen the drop in the loan rate. Moreover, if the tightening of macroprudential policy is too aggressive and the financial accelerator effect is weak, the result could be a contraction in spending and aggregate demand. This would tend to magnify downward pressure on inflation—which would call for the central bank to reduce further the policy interest rate, and so on. In this scenario, monetary and macroprudential policies would be in conflict and partially offset each other: Lower inflation requires a more accommodative monetary policy, whereas credit expansion necessitates a tightening of macroprudential policy. However, the issue here is fundamentally one of *joint calibration*; by solving simultaneously for the two policies, the trade-off between price stability and financial stability can be internalized—independently of whether the policy authorities choose to coordinate or to act independently.

4.7 Sensitivity Analysis

To further illustrate the properties of the model, two additional experiments are conducted: the first involves the use of physical capital, instead of housing, as collateral for loans, and the second the existence of a cost channel.

61. The accelerator effect operating through the increase in cyclical output amplifies, as noted earlier, the initial drop in the loan rate by increasing the repayment probability.

4.7.1 Physical Capital as Collateral

To account for the possibility that physical capital, rather than housing, is used as collateral pledged to lenders (in line with the simple analytical models discussed in chapters 2 and 3), equation (4.48) is now replaced by

$$q_t = \varphi_0 \left(\frac{\kappa K_t / \tilde{K}}{l_t^K / \tilde{l}^K} \right)^{\varphi_1} \left(\frac{Y_t}{\tilde{Y}} \right)^{\varphi_2} \left(\frac{1+i_t^L}{1+\tilde{\imath}^L} \right)^{\varphi_3},$$

where the interpretation of the parameters is the same as before. In addition, all three parameters are kept at the same values as those reported in table 4.1.[62]

To illustrate the implications of this alternative formulation, consider again the case of a spread shock. The results are shown in figure 4.5. The continuous line corresponds to the benchmark case (as shown in figure 4.3), and the dotted line to the case where physical capital is used as collateral. Although changes in house prices no longer have a direct effect on collateral values and the repayment probability, the results are qualitatively very similar to those described earlier. Movements in the repayment probability mitigate the drop in the loan rate, but given the magnitude of that effect, it exerts no discernible effects on investment and other macroeconomic variables.

4.7.2 Cost Channel

In the benchmark case considered earlier, the cost channel was shut down by assuming that IG producers do not need to pay wages in advance ($\psi_W = 0$). Consider now the opposite case, where these firms must borrow to finance their wage bill in its entirety, prior to the sale of output ($\psi_W = 1$). The results of a monetary policy shock of the same magnitude as considered earlier are displayed in figure 4.6.

In principle, the key implication of the cost channel is that the initial reduction in the refinance rate mitigates the impact of the increase in investment and aggregate demand on inflation. Indeed, the *effective* cost of labor falls by more than in the benchmark case.[63] However, impact effects are relatively weak; over time they become more potent, but only marginally so. The increase in output is more persistent, whereas the rise in inflation is smaller.[64] As a result,

62. See Agénor et al. (2013). Liu et al. (2013) also considered a DSGE-FF model, in the KM tradition, where both land and physical capital are used as collateral assets.

63. Recall that, with a full cost channel ($\psi_W = 1$), the effective cost of labor for IG producers is the gross refinance rate, $1 + i_t^R$, times the real wage, ω_t.

64. Conversely, in the presence of a strong cost channel a contractionary monetary policy (a higher base policy rate) would tend to raise inflation and reduce output over time.

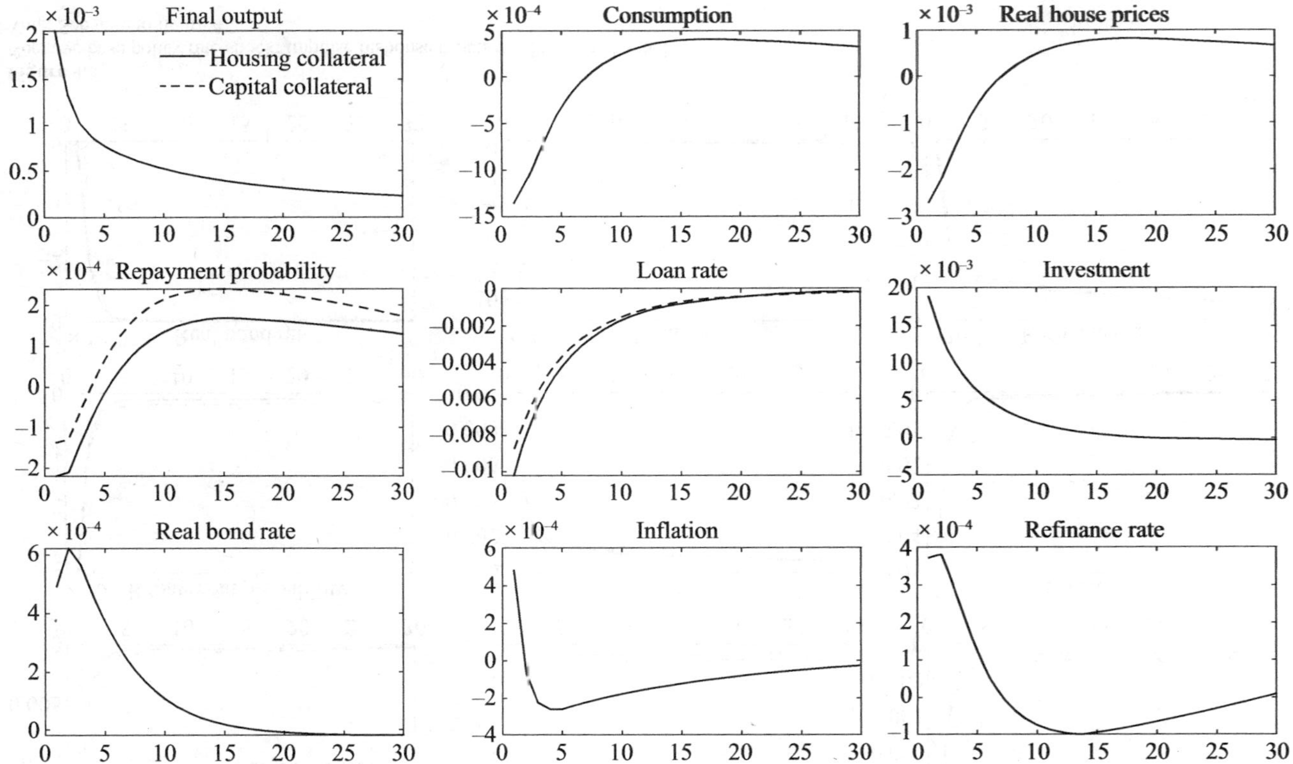

Figure 4.5
Negative credit spread shock: impulse response functions, capital as collateral
Note: See note to figure 4.2.

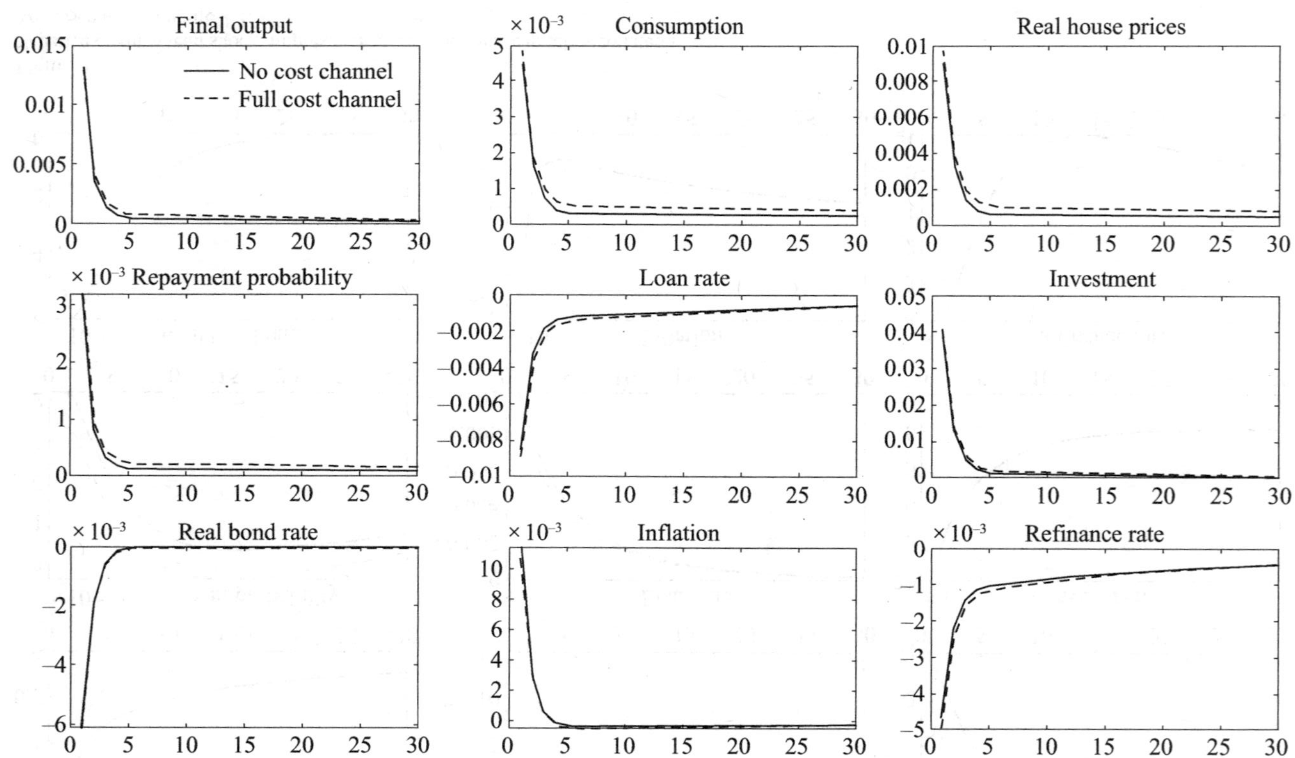

Figure 4.6
Negative base policy rate shock: impulse response functions, full cost channel
Note: See note to figure 4.2.

the central bank reacts less through the Taylor rule. The general equilibrium effect on the loan rate is now larger—it falls by more than in the benchmark case, which has a positive effect on investment. Because the deposit rate also falls by more, so does the nominal bond rate. The net effect of lower values of both the nominal bond rate and inflation is a larger reduction in the (expected) real bond rate. Consequently, incentives to shift consumption to the future are weaker, which translates into a larger increase, and greater persistence, in current household spending (and thus house prices) and output. In turn, the effects on house prices and output combine to amplify the increase in the repayment probability over time, which gradually reinforces the reduction in the loan rate and the expansion of investment. Overall, however, the magnitude of these effects is very modest. Put differently, the cost channel does not appear to be a major source of amplification of monetary policy shocks. However, it may play a larger role for different parameterizations and for different shocks, such as cost-push disturbances.

4.8 Notes on the Literature

The core DSGE model presented in this chapter can be extended in a number of directions in order to provide either a better understanding of specific analytical issues or a better match of the model's predictions with the data. Many of these extensions have been already explored in the literature and can be introduced in the core model at minimal cost in terms of additional complexity. Others, however, are more involved and may depart in some fundamental ways from the general approach adopted in this book. In addition, several of the building blocks of the model described earlier have been specified in alternative ways in the literature. This section offers a brief review of some of these issues, including the case where both monitoring and verification costs are accounted for in a more general specification of bank behavior.[65]

4.8.1 Household Preferences

Regarding the specification of household preferences in (4.1), there are three notable differences that are commonly found in the literature: the treatment of money, habit formation in consumption, and the separability of consumption and labor supply.

First, in (4.1), money is introduced directly as an argument in the utility function, for the reasons explained earlier. Alternatively, it could be assumed

65. Given that this chapter is already long, some additional extensions are considered in chapters 5 and 6.

that money is necessary for transactions and held before purchases of consumption goods take place, thereby leading to a cash-in-advance constraint as in Stockman (1989), Calvo and Végh (1995), Li (2000), or Ravenna and Walsh (2006), for instance. Furthermore, money could be viewed as facilitating transactions; by reducing shopping time and thus acting as a substitute for leisure, this would lead to the specification of a transactions technology directly in the representative household's budget constraint (Kimbrough 1992). The money-in-the-utility-function approach is used here mainly for tractability.[66]

Second, period utility, u_t, could be changed to reflect persistence in consumption habits. Habit formation can be introduced as being either internal (with period utility depending on the household's own lagged consumption) or external (with period utility depending on aggregate lagged consumption). Both specifications can generate, through aggregation, consumption persistence in the economy. With internal habits, for instance, a standard formulation of period utility is

$$u_t = \frac{(C_{t+s} - \chi_C C_{t+s-1})^{1-\varsigma^{-1}}}{(1-\chi_C)^{-\varsigma^{-1}}(1-\varsigma^{-1})} - \int_0^1 \frac{\eta_N (N^j_{t+s})^{1+\psi_N}}{1+\psi_N} dj + \ln x^{\eta_x}_{t+s} + \ln H^{\eta_H}_{t+s},$$

where $\chi_C \in (0, 1)$ measures the degree of habit formation.[67] The term $(1-\chi_C)^{-\varsigma^{-1}}$ is a scaling factor, which ensures that changing χ_C does not affect consumption in the steady state.

Accounting for habit formation has proved useful for estimation purposes and in policy-oriented DSGE models. It has helped to better match predictions from these models with the persistence in consumption observed in the data. From the perspective of this book, however, this is less of a concern.

Third, an alternative specification of household preferences involves using a period utility function that makes consumption and leisure nonseparable, such as

$$u_t = \frac{1}{1-\varsigma^{-1}} \left\{ C_{t+s} - \eta_N \int_0^1 \frac{(N^j_{t+s})^{1+\psi_N}}{1+\psi_N} dj \right\}^{1-\varsigma^{-1}} + \ln x^{\eta_x}_{t+s} + \zeta^H_t \ln H^{\eta_H}_{t+s},$$

66. In addition, the cash-in-advance constraint imposes a zero-interest-rate elasticity of money demand—a fairly restrictive assumption.There are conditions under which choosing a particular operational formulation matters little (Feenstra 1986), but in general alternative assumptions about the role of money do affect the predictions of macroeconomic models. See Obstfeld (1985) for an instructive example.

67. Estimates of χ_C vary significantly across countries. Caputo et al. (2007), for instance, found a value of about 0.14 for Chile, whereas Carvalho and Castro (2016) found values as high as 0.87 for Brazil. See Havranek et al. (2017) for broader evidence on habit formation in consumption and Turnovsky (2011, p. 1611) for a more critical discussion of consumption externalities in a representative agent framework.

which follows Greenwood et al. (1988). With $\varsigma = 1$, the first term on the right-hand side of this expression is therefore $\ln[C_{t+s} - \eta_N(1+\psi_N)^{-1} \int_0^1 (N^j_{t+s})^{1+\psi_N} dj]$. This specification—usually referred to as GHH preferences, after the three authors from Greenwood et al. (1988)—eliminates wealth effects on labor supply by making the marginal rate of substitution between consumption and labor independent of consumption. Thus, unlike (4.12), the labor supply schedule would depend on the real wage only and not on consumption ($N^j_t = (\eta_N^{-1}\omega_t)^{1/\psi_N}$, $\forall j$). GHH preferences have been used in a number of contributions, including Neumeyer and Perri (2005), Fornaro (2015), and Devereux and Yu (2019), for instance.

4.8.2 Liquidity-Constrained Consumers

As noted in chapter 2, there is significant evidence (for both high-income and middle-income countries) that households may face liquidity constraints and therefore be unable to smooth consumption over time. As a result, consumption tends to follow closely changes in current income, rather than being driven by intertemporal considerations.

The existence of liquidity-constrained consumers has been accounted for in a number of DSGE models. Typically, there are two types of households in these models, unconstrained and constrained, in proportion $\varkappa \in (0, 1)$ and $1 - \varkappa$, respectively. Constrained households supply labor inelastically, do not hold any assets, have no claims on firm or bank profits, and follow a rule of thumb that involves consuming all their available income in each period. By contrast, unconstrained households operate as described previously—they can trade in asset markets and optimize in a forward-looking manner and are therefore able to smooth consumption over time. They usually also own banks and firms and receive profits from them.[68]

The rule of thumb that constrained households follow can take several forms; in the simplest case, it consists of setting consumption expenditure, C^R_t, equal to after-tax disposable wage income,

$$C^R_t = \omega_t N^R_t - T^R_t, \tag{4.69}$$

where T^R_t is lump-sum taxes and N^R_t labor supply by that category of households, which is assumed to be inelastic. For tractability, N^R_t is often assumed to

68. DSGE models in which liquidity-constrained and intertemporal optimizing households are distinguished include, for instance, Galí et al. (2004), Agénor et al. (2013), Díaz (2013), and Lozej et al. (2016). In some models all households can borrow, but they are subject to a credit constraint: the amount borrowed is limited by the expected value of their real estate assets, as in Iacoviello (2005), or labor income, as in Carvalho and Castro (2016) and Valencia et al. (2017).

follow a first-order autoregressive process,

$$N_t^R = (N_{t-1}^R)^{\rho^R} \exp(\xi_t^R), \tag{4.70}$$

where $\rho^R \in (0, 1)$ and $\xi_t^R \sim \mathbf{N}(0, \sigma_{\xi^R})$ is a random shock. Thus, with liquidity-constrained households, when wages fall consumption falls also.

The equilibrium of the final good market, equation (4.60), involves now aggregate consumption, which given (4.69) is defined as $\varkappa C_t + (1-\varkappa)C_t^R$. Similarly, the equilibrium condition of the labor market, equation (4.62), must be adjusted as well, in light of (4.70). In the simplest case, constrained households are also assumed to hold no financial assets.[69] As a result, beyond the changes associated with (4.69) and (4.70), the model remains largely the same.

In terms of the transmission of shocks discussed earlier, the implications of these changes are rather straightforward: For shocks leading to changes in output and consumption by unconstrained households that operate in the same direction (as is the case for the monetary policy shock discussed earlier), adding consumption by constrained households will magnify output and price effects. This is because when consumption, for instance, increases, so does the demand for leisure; all else equal, the reduction in the supply of labor by unconstrained households will tend to exert upward pressure on wages, which will benefit constrained households and lead them to increase spending. By contrast, for shocks where output and consumption by unconstrained households operate in opposite directions (as is the case for the credit spread shock), these effects will be mitigated.

4.8.3 Monopolistic Competition in the Deposit Market

In the core model presented earlier, just as in chapters 2 and 3, it was assumed that the deposit market is competitive. It is straightforward to extend the analysis to account for monopolistic competition in the deposit market, as in a number of contributions to the DSGE-FF literature (Gerali et al. 2010; Dib 2010*a*, 2010*b*; Angelini et al. 2014; Agénor and Pereira da Silva 2017).

Suppose that the supply of deposits by the representative household is now a basket of differentiated deposits, each supplied to a bank *i*, with a constant elasticity of substitution $\zeta^D > 1$ between them:

$$d_t = \left[\int_0^1 (d_t^i)^{(1+\zeta^D)/\zeta^D} di \right]^{\zeta^D/(1+\zeta^D)}.$$

69. The analysis could be made somewhat less restrictive by assuming that constrained households are subject to a cash-in-advance constraint. However, usually this assumption does not add much to the analysis.

The supply of type-i deposit, d_t^i, is thus given by the upward-sloping curve

$$d_t^i = \left(\frac{1+i_t^{D,i}}{1+i_t^D} \right)^{\varsigma^D} d_t, \tag{4.71}$$

where $1+i_t^{D,i}$ is the deposit rate set by bank i and $1+i_t^D = [\int_0^1 (i_t^{D,i})^{1+\varsigma^D} di]^{1/(1+\varsigma^D)}$ the aggregate deposit rate.

Banks must therefore maximize profits, as given in (4.43), by setting also the gross deposit rate, $1+i_t^{D,i}$. The relevant first-order condition can be shown to be given by

$$-d_t^i - [1+i_t^{D,i} - (1-\mu)(1+i_t^R)] \left[\frac{\partial d_t^i}{\partial (1+i_t^{D,i})} \right] = 0. \tag{4.72}$$

From (4.71),

$$\frac{\partial d_t^i}{\partial (1+i_t^{D,i})} = \varsigma^D \left(\frac{1+i_t^{D,i}}{1+i_t^D} \right)^{\varsigma^D - 1} \left(\frac{d_t}{1+i_t^D} \right). \tag{4.73}$$

Substituting (4.71) and (4.73) in (4.72) yields

$$-\left(\frac{1+i_t^{D,i}}{1+i_t^D} \right)^{\varsigma^D} d_t - [1+i_t^{D,i} - (1-\mu)(1+i_t^R)]\varsigma^D \left(\frac{1+i_t^{D,i}}{1+i_t^D} \right)^{\varsigma^D - 1} \left(\frac{d_t}{1+i_t^D} \right)$$
$$= 0,$$

which implies that, in a symmetric equilibrium,

$$-1 - [1+i_t^D - (1-\mu)(1+i_t^R)]\varsigma^D \left(\frac{1}{1+i_t^D} \right) = 0,$$

so that

$$i_t^D = \frac{\varsigma^D}{1+\varsigma^D}(1-\mu)(1+i_t^R) - 1. \tag{4.74}$$

Thus, the main difference between the no-arbitrage condition (4.42) and equation (4.74), aside from the fact that one is in net terms and the other in gross terms, is the presence of the constant ratio $\varsigma^D/(1+\varsigma^D) < 1$, which tends to unity as $\varsigma^D \to \infty$. Otherwise, both specifications show that the deposit rate is equal to the marginal cost of borrowing from the central bank, adjusted downward for the implicit tax associated with reserve requirements. Adjustment costs to deposit rates may also be introduced in this framework, as in

Scharler (2008) and Kwapil and Scharler (2010), for instance, or Gerali et al. (2010), to account for the link between concentration in banking (a proxy for market power) and price rigidity. Evidence of this link is indeed provided by Berstein and Fuentes (2005) for Chile, Alencar (2012) for Brazil, and Gelos (2009) for a broader sample of countries in Latin America. Similar evidence is also reported by Tan (2012) for a group of Asian countries.

4.8.4 Calvo's Model of Staggered Prices

In DSGE models, with and without financial frictions, two time-dependent, workhorse models of nominal inertia have been commonly adopted to formalize the price formation mechanism and generate a meaningful role for monetary policy: the approach proposed by Rotemberg (1982) and that proposed by Calvo (1983), which was complemented by Yun (1996) to characterize the loss of output due to relative price dispersion among firms. The former, used throughout this book, emphasizes menu costs whereas the latter assumes that firms change prices infrequently due to staggered contracts and fixed costs.[70]

In Rotemberg's model, as discussed earlier, firms can change their price in each period, subject to the payment of the adjustment cost. Therefore, all firms face the same problem and thus will choose the same price and output. In other words, the equilibrium is symmetric. Given this symmetry, in the Rotemberg approach the aggregate production function features no inefficiency due to price dispersion. However, the adjustment cost associated with nominal rigidities enters the aggregate resource constraint as shown in (4.60). Thus, as long as $\phi_I > 0$, it creates an inefficiency wedge between aggregate expenditure and aggregate output. Part of the economy's production is absorbed by the price adjustment cost.

By contrast, in Calvo's model, prices are staggered because firms changing prices at different periods will set different prices. Then, in each given period t, there will be a distribution of prices. Price dispersion, which is caused by the interaction of inflation with price-setting frictions, results in an inefficiency loss in aggregate production. The reason is that with price dispersion, the price mechanism ceases to allocate resources efficiently, as too much production is done in firms with low prices and too little in the firms with high prices.[71] Indeed, in Calvo's model, condition (4.60) takes the standard form

70. A third approach involves abandoning altogether time-dependent models, in which firms set their prices for fixed periods of time, and focusing instead on *state-contingent* adjustment rules, as in Dotsey et al. (1999). In these models, firms change prices when underlying determinants (such as demand and costs) reach some prespecified upper or lower bounds. Partly for tractability and partly for conceptual reasons, this approach has not proved to be as popular in the literature.

71. Yun (1996) derived a simple formula that characterizes the loss of output due to price dispersion.

$Y_t = C_t + G_t + I_t$; the cost of nominal rigidities (price dispersion) takes instead the form of a wedge between aggregate employment and aggregate output, which makes aggregate production less efficient. Wedges in both the Rotemberg and Calvo models are nonlinear functions of inflation. They are minimized at one when steady-state inflation is zero, but they both increase as trend inflation rises above zero.

As shown by Roberts (1995), the Rotemberg and Calvo approaches generate isomorphic linearized Phillips curves and, if the steady state is efficient, the same policy conclusions. However, when using nonlinear solution techniques the implications of these models can be quite different (Ascari and Rossi 2011; Leith and Liu 2016). In addition, their welfare implications are also different (Lombardo and Vestin 2008). In particular, the fact that in Calvo's model there may be a large degree of persistence in the price level after shocks—given that some firms may not be able to change prices for an extended period of time—may affect significantly its welfare properties. Thus, the form of nominal inertia adopted in a particular model is not innocuous. On balance, there appears to be strong empirical support for Rotemberg's specification (Richter and Throckmorton 2016), although the evidence relates more to advanced economies.

The DSGE literature has also emphasized a practical connection between the key parameters of the Calvo and Rotemberg models. In general, it is difficult to attach a structural interpretation to the Rotemberg adjustment cost parameter, ϕ_I in (4.29), because there is no natural equivalent in the data. In contrast, for the Calvo model, it is relatively easy to compute average price durations (Nakamura and Steinsson 2013). Modelers have therefore often made use of the first-order equivalence of Rotemberg- and Calvo-type price specifications—under zero trend inflation or full indexation to inflation, as discussed by Ascari and Sbordone (2014)—by translating the Rotemberg adjustment cost parameter to an implied Calvo price duration coefficient via the slope of the inflation equation derived from these models. Indeed, under log-linearization, equation (4.67) indicates that the coefficient of marginal cost under Rotemberg pricing is $(\theta - 1)/\phi_I$, whereas (as shown in the appendix to this chapter) the relevant coefficient under Calvo pricing is $\xi^{-1}(1-\xi)(1-\xi\Lambda)$, where $1-\xi$ denotes the random fraction of firms that are able to reset their price each period. Setting these two coefficients equal to each other and solving for ϕ_I yields the following relationship between ϕ_I and ξ:

$$\phi_I = \frac{(\theta - 1)\xi}{(1-\xi)(1-\xi\Lambda)}.$$

For given assumptions about the steady-state markup, $(\theta - 1)^{-1}\theta$—which, from (4.65), is the inverse of marginal cost—and parameter ξ, this expression can be used to determine ϕ_I. In particular, the price adjustment cost is higher when the average markup is lower (θ is higher) and the mean time between price reoptimizations in Calvo's model is longer (ξ is higher). Conversely, for a given price adjustment cost parameter and average markup, the average time firms wait to reoptimize can be calculated. In either case, however, the resulting range of estimates is quite wide (Keen and Wang 2007).

4.8.5 Multi-Period Loans

In the model presented earlier, as is common in the DSGE-FF literature, all loans are one-period loans and carry an interest rate that is reset to a new equilibrium level in every period. In reality, loans are typically multi-period in nature and their interest rate is reset infrequently. Accounting for these features of the credit market are potentially important for understanding the transmission mechanism of monetary and macroprudential policies. In particular, accounting for multi-period loans may help to study how the term structure of interest rates interacts with financial frictions in response to real and financial shocks and to assess the extent to which the maturity transformation role of financial intermediaries affects the propagation of these shocks.

Tractable DSGE models with multi-period loans include Benes and Lees (2010), Montoro (2011), Andreasen et al. (2012), and Brzoza-Brzezina et al. (2014). In Montoro (2011), for instance, as in Benes and Lees (2011), banks collect short-term deposits and provide long-term loans. Thus, bank activity entails a maturity transformation problem. The fact that future interest payments are uncertain generates a maturity risk and an endogenous wedge between the loan rate and the policy or interbank market rate. Linking short- and long-term interest rates also helps to smooth out fluctuations in short-term rates. The result is a greater degree of interest rate persistence without resorting to *ad hoc* interest rate adjustment costs, as, for instance, in Gerali et al. (2010) or Agénor and Alper (2012). As a result, changes in credit and output induced by shocks are attenuated. In the model of Andreasen et al. (2012), which dwells on the Gertler-Kiyotaki-Karadi approach discussed in chapter 1, banks also use short-term deposits by households to provide longer-term credit to firms. As in the other contributions, maturity transformation imparts inertia to quantities and prices in the credit market and dampens the response of output in response to both real and financial shocks.

4.8.6 Sticky Wages and Labor Market Frictions

In many DSGE models (especially for advanced economies) sticky wages have been introduced to help these models provide a better match to the empirical evidence on wage behavior over the business cycles. In particular, it has been argued that wage stickiness may be a more important force than price stickiness in generating output persistence.[72]

A specification commonly used in these models to introduce wage stickiness is the one proposed by Erceg et al. (2000), which dwells on Calvo's model of price inertia discussed earlier. Individual households supply differentiated labor services to domestic firms, and domestic firms combine these labor services to produce domestic goods. Monopolistically competitive households also set nominal wages in staggered fashion. This approach has been used in a number of contributions, in both closed and open economies—see, for instance, Christiano et al. (2005), Adolfson et al. (2011), Davis and Huang (2013), and Galí (2015, chap. 6).[73] However, the existence of a large informal sector in MICs, as noted in chapter 1, makes the degree of wage stickiness a less plausible factor in generating persistence in output. Moreover, the evidence, as discussed in Agénor (2006*b*), for instance, suggests that the main sources of wage rigidity in the formal sector in these countries is often related to the presence of trade unions, strong signaling effects of wage settlements in the public sector for wage formation in the private sector, or efficiency wage considerations, rather than monopolistic labor suppliers.

Other types of labor market frictions have also been introduced in DSGE-FF models. Mumtaz and Zanetti (2016), for instance, focused on assessing how interactions between search and matching frictions, as in Walsh (2005) and Blanchard and Galí (2010), and financial frictions alter the response of the economy to real and financial shocks.[74] Their analysis suggests that these interactions operate through two main channels: inflation, which affects firms' net worth and the cost of bank borrowing, and firms' hiring decisions, which affect the persistence of employment, the return to capital, and investment. Depending on the nature of shocks, labor market frictions may either attenuate or amplify the effect of financial frictions on aggregate fluctuations. However, the robustness of these results needs to be further explored in more general settings.

4.8.7 Collateral, Monitoring and Verification Costs

As noted in chapter 1, in the models presented in this book the focus is on *noncontingent* monitoring costs, which vary with the net collateral pledged

72. See Riggi (2010) for a discussion.

73. Some contributions have also introduced nominal wage rigidity based on the Rotemberg approach to price stickiness. See Jacob and Munro (2018), for instance.

74. Garín (2015) also developed a model with both financial frictions and search frictions in the labor market. More general theoretical contributions include, for instance, Wasmer and Weil (2004), who studied the effect of endogenous search frictions (in the Diamond-Mortensen-Pissarides tradition) in both credit and labor markets on macroeconomic volatility.

by borrowers and the state of the economy. By contrast, as also noted in that chapter, the literature that has followed in the BGG tradition, which itself builds on the seminal contribution of Townsend (1979), has focused instead on *state-contingent* costs, which are incurred by lenders when borrowers choose to default—that is, verification costs. Moreover, in the model presented earlier, the underlying stochastic structure of the loan contract between banks and CG producers was not made explicit, and no distinction was made between the probability of default and bank monitoring intensity. Both issues can be addressed by adapting the approach followed in Agénor and Aizenman (1998), and subsequently Agénor et al. (2014*b*), which also dwells on Townsend (1979).

Suppose that in every period, each CG producer $k \in (0, 1)$ faces an idiosyncratic and uninsurable shock ζ_t^k to its capital stock, which affects the efficiency (or quality) of the services that capital produces. Effective capital is thus given by $(1+\zeta_t^k)K_t^k$. In addition, suppose that ζ_t^k is identically and independently distributed across producers on the interval $(-\zeta_m, \zeta_m)$, with mean 0 and standard deviation σ_ζ, and with density and cumulative distribution functions denoted $f(\zeta_t^k)$ and $F(\zeta_t^k)$, respectively.[75] Thus, in standard fashion, idiosyncratic shocks have no direct aggregate effects (given that their mean is zero) but they introduce heterogeneity among CG producers. Information is asymmetric, in the sense that while the quality shock ζ_t^k is observed costlessly by CG producer k, lenders can do so only at a cost.

As discussed earlier, CG producers cannot self-finance; they borrow from banks all the funds needed to invest, in quantity I_t^k, at the gross rate $1+i_t^{L,k}$. Thus, producer k must repay $(1+i_t^{L,k})I_t^k$. However, borrowers do not necessarily comply with their debt obligations and they are subject to limited liability. With capital rented to IG producers earning a gross return $1+r_t^K$, profits of a CG producer k who chooses to repay, once ζ_t^k is realized (which occurs *after* loans have been contracted), are given by $(1+r_t^K)(1+\zeta_t^k)K_t^k-(1+i_t^{L,k})I_t^k$. If, instead, CG producer k chooses to default, it must turn over both a fraction $\theta^C \in (0, 1)$ of the gross return on the realized value of its capital stock plus the collateral pledged to lenders, denoted by CC_t^k. Thus, the CG producer's realized profits in that case are $(1-\theta^C)(1+r_t^K)(1+\zeta_t^k)K_t^k-CC_t^k$.

CG producer k will choose to default whenever

$$\theta^C(1+r_t^K)(1+\zeta_t^k)K_t^k+CC_t^k<(1+i_t^{L,k})I_t^k, \tag{4.75}$$

which implies that the threshold value of ζ_t^k below which the producer chooses to default, $\zeta_t^{C,k}$, is

75. Rather than being constant, it could be assumed that the standard deviation σ_ζ is itself the realization of a stochastic process. Contributions such as Christiano et al. (2010*a*) refer to that process as a *risk shock*, which captures the notion that the riskiness of borrowers varies over time.

$$1+\zeta_t^{C,k} = \frac{(1+i_t^{L,k})I_t^k - CC_t^k}{\theta^C(1+r_t^K)K_t^k}. \tag{4.76}$$

This expression shows that $\zeta_t^{C,k}$ is increasing in the contractual loan rate (a higher loan rate makes default more likely) and decreasing in the revenue generated from renting capital and pledged collateral.

The expected profit of CG producer k is thus given by

$$\int_{\zeta_t^{C,k}}^{\zeta_m} [(1+r_t^K)(1+\zeta_t^k)K_t^k - (1+i_t^{L,k})I_t^k] f(\zeta_t^k)d\zeta_t^k$$

$$+\int_{-\zeta_m}^{\zeta_t^{C,k}} [(1-\theta^C)(1+r_t^K)(1+\zeta_t^k)K_t^k - CC_t^k] f(\zeta_t^k)d\zeta_t^k,$$

or equivalently, given that $F(\zeta_t^{C,k}) = \int_{-\zeta_m}^{\zeta_t^{C,k}} f(\zeta_t^k)d\zeta_t^k = 1 - \int_{\zeta_t^{C,k}}^{\zeta_m} f(\zeta_t^k)d\zeta_t^k$,[76]

$$(1+r_t^K)K_t^k - [1-F(\zeta_t^{C,k})](1+i_t^{L,k})I_t^k - F(\zeta_t^{C,k})[\theta^C(1+r_t^K)K_t^k + CC_t^k]. \tag{4.77}$$

As a result of asymmetric information and limited liability, a CG producer may be tempted to default on its loan repayment by claiming falsely to be bankrupt due to a bad realization of ζ_t^k. The solution to this problem involves costly state verification.[77] Dropping from this point on the superscript k to economize on notation, default is declared if and only if $\zeta_t \in (-\zeta_m, \zeta_t^C)$, in which case bank i's return per unit of loan is

$$\theta^C(1+r_t^K)(1+\zeta_t)\frac{K_t}{I_t^i} + \frac{CC_t^i}{I_t^i} - (\phi_t^K + \chi).$$

In this expression $\phi_t^K \in (0,1)$ is as before the (noncontingent) monitoring cost, whereas $\chi \in (0,1)$ is the constant (state-contingent) verification cost. For simplicity, and in line with the theoretical literature, both types of cost are taken to be proportional to the size of the loan (that is, investment).[78] By contrast, if $\zeta_t \in (\zeta_t^C, \zeta_m)$, the bank is paid back in full, earning a return of $1+i_t^L - \phi_t^K$ per unit of loan.

76. Note that if all the realized value of the gross return on the capital stock can be seized by lenders ($\theta^C = 1$) and if there is no collateral ($CC_t^k = 0$), equation (4.77) yields the standard expression in the costly state verification model, $(1+r_t^K)\int_{\zeta_t^{C,k}}^{\zeta_m}(1+\zeta_t^k)K_t^k f(\zeta_t^k)d\zeta_t^k - [1-F(\zeta_t^{C,k})](1+i_t^{L,k})I_t^k$.

77. See Townsend (1979) and Gale and Hellwig (1985).

78. Alternatively, in line with the BGG framework, the verification cost could be made a fraction of the realized value of the borrower's capital stock. Note also that if verification involves using up final goods, the aggregate resource constraint for the economy would be affected as well. See Bernanke et al. (1999, app. B) for a discussion.

From (4.75), holding with equality,

$$1+i_t^L = \frac{\theta^C(1+r_t^K)(1+\zeta_t^C)K_t + CC_t}{I_t} = (1+\zeta_t^C)x_t^K + cc_t, \tag{4.78}$$

where x_t^K is the fraction of the return to capital seized in proportion of the loan, and cc_t is the collateral-loan ratio:

$$x_t^K = \frac{\theta^C(1+r_t^K)K_t}{I_t}, \quad cc_t = \frac{CC_t}{I_t}. \tag{4.79}$$

To simplify the exposition, suppose now that bank i's balance sheet is, instead of (4.39),

$$l_t^{K,i} + RR_t^i = d_t^i, \tag{4.80}$$

where loans consist only of investment loans and there is no bank capital and no borrowing from the central bank. Assuming also that the market for loans is competitive, the equilibrium loan contract is one in which, prior to the realization of ζ_t, bank i's expected return from lending must be equal to its deposit repayment obligations. Thus, the break-even condition of the representative bank (or, equivalently, its participation constraint) is given by

$$(1+i_t^D)d_t^i = \int_{-\zeta_m}^{\zeta_t^C} [\theta^C(1+r_t^K)(1+\zeta_t)K_t + CC_t^i - (\phi_t^K+\chi)I_t^i]f(\zeta_t)d\zeta_t$$

$$+ \int_{\zeta_t^C}^{\zeta_m} (1+i_t^L - \phi_t^K)I_t^i f(\zeta_t)d\zeta_t, \tag{4.81}$$

where, as implied by (4.33), $I_t^i = l_t^{K,i}$.

As defined in equation (4.40), required reserves are given by $RR_t^i = \mu d_t^i$, and the no-arbitrage condition (4.42) between the deposit rate and the refinance rate gives again $i_t^D = (1-\mu)i_t^R$. From the balance sheet condition (4.80), $l_t^{K,i} = (1-\mu)d_t^i$, so that

$$(1+i_t^D)d_t^i = \left[\frac{1+(1-\mu)i_t^R}{1-\mu}\right]I_t^i.$$

Thus, dropping the superscript i for simplicity, using (4.79) and given that by definition $\int_{-\zeta_m}^{\zeta_m} f(\zeta_t)d\zeta_t = 1$, the break-even condition (4.81) can be written as

$$x_t^L = \int_{-\zeta_m}^{\zeta_t^C} [(1+\zeta_t)x_t^K + cc_t - \chi]f(\zeta_t)d\zeta_t + \int_{\zeta_t^C}^{\zeta_m} (1+i_t^L)f(\zeta_t)d\zeta_t, \qquad (4.82)$$

where

$$x_t^L = \frac{1+(1-\mu)i_t^R}{1-\mu} + \phi_t^K.$$

For any given ζ_t^C, condition (4.82) determines the contractual interest rate. Note that with $\mu = \phi_t^K = 0$, the term x_t^L is simply $1+i_t^R$—that is, the gross marginal cost of borrowing from the central bank. In general, given that monitoring costs are noncontingent, x_t^L can be viewed as measuring the marginal cost of producing a unit of loans—regardless of whether the borrower defaults or not. This cost depends therefore on the refinance rate, the required reserve ratio, and unit monitoring costs. Again, reserve requirements operate essentially as a tax, which raises the cost of financial intermediation.

Given again that $\int_{-\zeta_m}^{\zeta_m} f(\zeta_t)d\zeta_t = 1$, equation (4.82) can be rewritten as

$$x_t^L = 1 + i_t^L + \int_{-\zeta_m}^{\zeta_t^C} [(1+\zeta_t)x_t^K + cc_t - \chi]f(\zeta_t)d\zeta_t - \int_{-\zeta_m}^{\zeta_t^C} (1+i_t^L)f(\zeta_t)d\zeta_t, \qquad (4.83)$$

whereas from (4.78), summing over $(-\zeta_m, \zeta_t^C)$,

$$\int_{-\zeta_m}^{\zeta_t^C} (1+i_t^L)f(\zeta_t)d\zeta_t = \int_{-\zeta_m}^{\zeta_t^C} (1+\zeta_t^C)x_t^K f(\zeta_t)d\zeta_t + \int_{-\zeta_m}^{\zeta_t^C} cc_t f(\zeta_t)d\zeta_t. \qquad (4.84)$$

Substituting (4.84) in (4.83) implies that terms in cc_t cancel out so that

$$1 + i_t^L = x_t^L + \int_{-\zeta_m}^{\zeta_t^C} [(1+\zeta_t^C)x_t^K - (1+\zeta_t)x_t^K + \chi]f(\zeta_t)d\zeta_t. \qquad (4.85)$$

This expression measures the spread between the contractual loan rate and the marginal cost of producing loans, x_t^L. In particular, the magnitude of the spread depends on how much a bank expects to lose when a borrower goes bankrupt and is unable to make his full loan repayment—that is, when $\zeta_t \in (-\zeta_m, \zeta_t^C)$. Indeed, observe that by using (4.78) again the first integral term on the right-hand-side of (4.85) is equal to

$$\int_{-\zeta_m}^{\zeta_t^C} (1+\zeta_t^C)x_t^K f(\zeta_t)d\zeta_t = (1+i_t^L - cc_t)\int_{-\zeta_m}^{\zeta_t^C} f(\zeta_t)d\zeta_t = (1+i_t^L - cc_t)p_t^D, \qquad (4.86)$$

where p_t^D is the probability of default, defined as

$$p_t^D = F(\zeta_t^C) = \int_{-\zeta_m}^{\zeta_t^C} f(\zeta_t) d\zeta_t. \tag{4.87}$$

Thus, the term on the right-hand side of (4.86) measures the expected amount of non-repayment (adjusted for collateral) per unit of loan as a result of bankruptcy. Conversely, (minus) the second and third integral terms on the right-hand side of (4.85), $\int_{-\zeta_m}^{\zeta_t^C} [x_t^K(1+\zeta_t) - \chi] f(\zeta_t) d\zeta_t$, give the expected amount of income per unit of loan that is claimed from a bankrupt borrower, net of verification costs. Accordingly, (4.85) implies that the contractual interest rate on loans is set as a markup over the marginal cost of producing loans, where the size of the markup is equal to the expected *net* income lost due to bankruptcy.

It is worth noting that higher collateral increases the cost of default, reducing thereby the frequency of defaults; all else equal, an increase in CC_t leads to a drop in ζ_t^C, as can be inferred from (4.76). Consequently, higher collateral reduces the interest spread, as in the model presented earlier. Note also that in (4.85), an increase in the unit monitoring cost or the required reserve ratio (through x_t^L) raises the contractual lending rate. Thus, macroprudential regulation raises the cost of lending (just as a direct tax on loans would), whereas if unit monitoring costs vary inversely with the cycle, as discussed earlier, the cost of borrowing would tend to fall during upturns.

To make further progress, suppose that ζ_t is uniformly distributed over the interval $(-\zeta_m, \zeta_m)$, and $\zeta_m < 1$.[79] The shock therefore has a zero mean and a probability density function $f(\zeta_t) = 1/2\zeta_m$. Equation (4.85) can be rewritten as follows:

$$1 + i_t^L = x_t^L + x_t^K \int_{-\zeta_m}^{\zeta_t^C} [(1+\zeta_t^C) - (1+\zeta_t)] f(\zeta_t) d\zeta_t + \chi \int_{-\zeta_m}^{\zeta_t^C} f(\zeta_t) d\zeta_t.$$

Because

$$\int_{-\zeta_m}^{\zeta_t^C} f(\zeta_t) d\zeta_t = \frac{1}{2\zeta_m} \, \zeta_t \Big|_{-\zeta_m}^{\zeta_t^C} = \frac{\zeta_t^C + \zeta_m}{2\zeta_m},$$

the expression above becomes

$$1 + i_t^L = x_t^L + x_t^K \int_{-\zeta_m}^{\zeta_t^C} (\zeta_t^C - \zeta_t) f(\zeta_t) d\zeta_t + \left(\frac{\zeta_t^C + \zeta_m}{2\zeta_m} \right) \chi. \tag{4.88}$$

79. Because ζ_m is strictly less than unity, CG producers always have *some* capital, even in the worst case of nature, to rent to IG producers.

By definition,

$$\int_{-\zeta_m}^{\zeta_t^C} (\zeta_t^C - \zeta_t) f(\zeta_t) d\zeta_t = \zeta_t^C \int_{-\zeta_m}^{\zeta_t^C} f(\zeta_t) d\zeta_t - \int_{-\zeta_m}^{\zeta_t^C} \zeta_t f(\zeta_t) d\zeta_t,$$

or equivalently

$$\int_{-\zeta_m}^{\zeta_t^C} (\zeta_t^C - \zeta_t) f(\zeta_t) d\zeta_t = \left(\frac{\zeta_t^C + \zeta_m}{2\zeta_m} \right) \zeta_t^C - \int_{-\zeta_m}^{\zeta_t^C} \zeta_t f(\zeta_t) d\zeta_t. \tag{4.89}$$

Now, the last integral term in (4.89) gives

$$\int_{-\zeta_m}^{\zeta_t^C} \zeta_t f(\zeta_t) d\zeta_t = \frac{1}{2\zeta_m} \left. \frac{\zeta_t^2}{2} \right|_{-\zeta_m}^{\zeta_t^C} = \frac{(\zeta_t^C)^2 - \zeta_m^2}{4\zeta_m} = \frac{(\zeta_t^C - \zeta_m)(\zeta_t^C + \zeta_m)}{4\zeta_m}.$$

Thus, (4.89) becomes

$$\int_{-\zeta_m}^{\zeta_t^C} (\zeta_t^C - \zeta_t) f(\zeta_t) d\zeta_t = \left(\frac{\zeta_t^C + \zeta_m}{2\zeta_m} \right) \zeta_t^C - \frac{(\zeta_t^C - \zeta_m)(\zeta_t^C + \zeta_m)}{4\zeta_m},$$

so that

$$\int_{-\zeta_m}^{\zeta_t^C} (\zeta_t^C - \zeta_t) f(\zeta_t) d\zeta_t = \left(\frac{\zeta_t^C + \zeta_m}{4\zeta_m} \right) (2\zeta_t^C - \zeta_t^C + \zeta_m) = \frac{(\zeta_t^C + \zeta_m)^2}{4\zeta_m}. \tag{4.90}$$

Substituting (4.90) in (4.88) yields

$$1 + i_t^L = x_t^L + \frac{(\zeta_t^C + \zeta_m)^2}{4\zeta_m} x_t^K + \left(\frac{\zeta_t^C + \zeta_m}{2\zeta_m} \right) \chi. \tag{4.91}$$

Equivalently, given that the probability of default, defined in (4.87), is now

$$p_t^D = \int_{-\zeta_m}^{\zeta_t^C} f(\zeta_t) d\zeta_t = \frac{\zeta_t^C + \zeta_m}{2\zeta_m}, \tag{4.92}$$

expression (4.91) can also be written as:

$$1 + i_t^L = x_t^L + \zeta_m (p_t^D)^2 x_t^K + p_t^D \chi. \tag{4.93}$$

Equations (4.76) and (4.91) define a simultaneous system in $1 + i_t^L$ and ζ_t^C. Its solution is derived as follows. Using (4.78) to substitute for $1 + i_t^L$ in (4.91) yields

$$(1 + \zeta_t^C) x_t^K + cc_t = x_t^L + \frac{(\zeta_t^C + \zeta_m)^2}{4\zeta_m} x_t^K + \left(\frac{\zeta_t^C + \zeta_m}{2\zeta_m} \right) \chi,$$

which can be rearranged to give a quadratic equation in the equilibrium value of ζ_t^C, denoted $\tilde{\zeta}_t^C$:

$$x_t^K(\tilde{\zeta}_t^C)^2 - 2(x_t^K\zeta_m - \chi)\tilde{\zeta}_t^C - [4\zeta_m(x_t^K + cc_t - x_t^L) - x_t^K\zeta_m^2 - 2\zeta_m\chi] = 0. \tag{4.94}$$

The solution to this equation is

$$\tilde{\zeta}_t^C = \frac{2(x_t^K\zeta_m - \chi) \pm \sqrt{16x_t^K\zeta_m(x_t^K + cc_t - x_t^L - \chi) + 4\chi^2}}{2x_t^K},$$

or equivalently

$$\tilde{\zeta}_t^C = \zeta_m - \frac{\chi}{x_t^K} \pm \frac{\sqrt{4x_t^K\zeta_m(x_t^K + cc_t - x_t^L - \chi) + \chi^2}}{x_t^K}. \tag{4.95}$$

A sufficient, although not necessary, condition for ruling out complex eigenvalues is that

$$x_t^K + cc_t \geq x_t^L + \chi. \tag{4.96}$$

Given that condition, because it must be that $\tilde{\zeta}_t^C \leq \zeta_m$ (as implied by the assumed distribution of ζ_t), the positive eigenvalue in (4.95) can be ruled out because it would imply $\tilde{\zeta}_t^C > \zeta_m$.[80] Thus, the only viable solution to (4.94) is the one given by

$$\tilde{\zeta}_t^C = \zeta_m - \frac{\chi + \sqrt{4x_t^K\zeta_m(x_t^K + cc_t - x_t^L - \chi) + \chi^2}}{x_t^K}. \tag{4.97}$$

To ensure that $\tilde{\zeta}_t^C \geq -\zeta_m$ as well requires

$$2\zeta_m \geq \frac{\chi + \sqrt{4x_t^K\zeta_m(x_t^K + cc_t - x_t^L - \chi) + \chi^2}}{x_t^K},$$

or equivalently

80. To see this, note that equation (4.95) can be written as, for the positive eigenvalue, $\tilde{\zeta}_t^C = \zeta_m - (\chi/x_t^K) + (1/x_t^K)\sqrt{\chi^2 + Z}$, where $Z = 4x_t^K\zeta_m(x_t^K + cc_t - x_t^L - \chi)$. If $Z = 0$ then $\sqrt{\chi^2} = \chi$ and $\tilde{\zeta}_t^C = \zeta_m$, whereas if $Z > 0$ (which rules out complex eigenvalues, as stated in condition (4.96), $\sqrt{\chi^2 + Z} > \chi$. Then the sum of the last two terms in the expression for $\tilde{\zeta}_t^C$ is positive, which implies that $\tilde{\zeta}_t^C > \zeta_m$.

$$(2\zeta_m x_t^K - \chi)^2 \geq 4x_t^K \zeta_m (x_t^K + cc_t - x_t^L - \chi) + \chi^2,$$

which can be simplified to

$$x_t^K \leq \frac{x_t^L - cc_t}{1 - \zeta_m}. \tag{4.98}$$

Combining conditions (4.96) and (4.98) shows that, therefore, to ensure that the solution is feasible—that is, $\tilde{\zeta}_t^C \in (-\zeta_m, \zeta_m)$ $\forall t$—and unique, the restriction is

$$x_t^L + \chi < x_t^K < \frac{x_t^L - cc_t}{1 - \zeta_m}.$$

Assuming that this condition holds, equations (4.91) and (4.97) can be used to study analytically the effects of changes in monitoring costs, verification costs, the required reserve ratio, and the collateral-loan ratio on the equilibrium bankruptcy threshold and the loan rate. In particular, it can be established that a reduction in the verification cost, χ, lowers the bankruptcy threshold and the equilibrium loan rate—a standard result in this class of models (Agénor and Aizenman 1998). By contrast, an increase in the required reserve ratio, μ, or in the unit monitoring cost, ϕ_t^K, raises the bankruptcy threshold and the equilibrium loan rate. Finally, a higher collateral-loan ratio, cc_t, raises the cost of default, thereby reducing the frequency of defaults, as noted earlier. This, in turn, reduces the default probability and the lending rate.

These results are fairly consistent with those derived in the core approach used in this book—despite the fact that the banking structure is fundamentally different, with banks being perfectly competitive instead of monopolistic competitive as before.[81] But the analysis could be extended to consider in the same setting, along the lines of Afanasyeva and Güntner (2018), for instance, the case of monopolistic banking.

Appendix Calvo Pricing and Inflation Persistence

As noted in the text, the dynamics of price adjustment in DSGE models are often based on the formulation proposed by Calvo (1983) and extended by Yun (1996), rather than the specification developed by Rotemberg (1982) and

81. In terms of the model presented earlier, $q_t = 1 - p_t^D$. Thus, the effect of higher collateral (which, again, raises $\tilde{\zeta}_t^C$ and lowers p_t^D) has the same effect as discussed earlier. By contrast, the unit monitoring cost, ϕ_t^K, affects now the loan rate directly, rather than the default or repayment probability as before. The key reason is that monitoring effort is no longer a direct choice variable for lenders. Nevertheless, this effect operates in the same direction.

used throughout this book. This appendix provides a brief presentation of Calvo's model and discusses how it has been modified to account for inflation persistence.

To illustrate Calvo's model of price adjustment in the simplest possible terms, consider an economy characterized by a continuum of identical monopolistic competitive firms indexed by $j \in (0, 1)$, each of which producing a nonstorable differentiated intermediate good. The production function of each firm is linear in labor, N_t^j, so that

$$Y_t^j = \epsilon_t^Y N_t^j, \tag{A4.1}$$

where ϵ_t^Y denotes an aggregate productivity shock. If labor is paid a common nominal wage, W_t, nominal marginal cost of production—the ratio of the nominal wage rate to the marginal product of labor—is identical across firms and given by

$$MC_t^N = W_t/\epsilon_t^Y, \tag{A4.2}$$

or, in logs,

$$mc_t^N = w_t - \varepsilon_t, \tag{A4.3}$$

where $w_t = \ln W_t$ and $\varepsilon_t = \ln \epsilon_t^Y$.

In a closed economy, with no government and no investment, household consumption equals production ($Y_t = C_t$). Each firm is assumed to face an isoelastic demand curve for its product of the form

$$Y_t^j = \left(\frac{P_t^j}{P_t}\right)^{-\theta} Y_t, \tag{A4.4}$$

where the parameter $\theta > 1$ is again the Dixit-Stiglitz elasticity of substitution between differentiated goods (or the common price elasticity of demand facing each firm), P_t the aggregate price level, and Y_t aggregate output, defined as

$$P_t = \left\{\int_0^1 (P_t^j)^{1-\theta} di\right\}^{1/(1-\theta)}, \quad Y_t = \left\{\int_0^1 (Y_t^j)^{(\theta-1)/\theta} di\right\}^{\theta/(\theta-1)}.$$

These equations are similar to those discussed in the text—see (4.17), (4.18), and (4.19).

Real profits of the jth firm are given by, using (A4.1) and (A4.4),

$$J_t^j = \frac{(P_t^j Y_t^j - W_t N_t^j)}{P_t} = \left(\frac{P_t^j}{P_t} - \frac{MC_t^N}{P_t}\right)\left(\frac{P_t^j}{P_t}\right)^{-\theta} Y_t, \tag{A4.5}$$

where the second result obtains by combining (A4.1) and (A4.2) to give $W_t N_t^j = W_t Y_t^j / \varepsilon_t^Y = MC_t^N Y_t^j$.

In the absence of pricing frictions, the jth firm will choose its price to maximize its real profits. From (A4.5), the first-order condition is

$$\frac{\partial J_t^j}{\partial P_t^j} = \frac{\theta - 1}{\theta}\left(\frac{P_t^j}{P_t}\right)^{1-\theta} Y_t - \frac{MC_t^N}{P_t}\left(\frac{P_t^j}{P_t}\right)^{-\theta} Y_t = 0,$$

which can be simplified to give the (log) equilibrium price

$$p_t^O = \Theta + mc_t^N, \tag{A4.6}$$

where $\Theta = \ln[\theta/(\theta - 1)]$ is the (log) markup.[82] Thus, in the absence of frictions, all firms set their price as a fixed markup over marginal cost. Equation (A4.6) corresponds also to the result obtained with the Rotemberg model under symmetry when there are no costs to adjusting prices—$\phi_I = 0$, see equation (4.31) in logarithmic form.

Calvo's model price adjustment involves assuming that in each period a random fraction $1 - \xi$ of firms—where $\xi \in (0, 1)$—reset their price (regardless of how much time has elapsed since the last update), whereas all other firms keep their prices unchanged. The hazard rate, or the probability that any given price posted at time t will be adjusted at $t + 1$, is thus constant and the average duration of nominal price stickiness—or, equivalently, the expected waiting time for the next price adjustment—is $1/(1 - \xi)$. The evolution of the (log) price level, p_t, is given by

$$p_t = \xi p_{t-1} + (1 - \xi) p_t^O, \tag{A4.7}$$

where p_t^O is now the optimal price chosen by those who can reset their prices.

At time t, price-adjusting firms can set their price to maximize a discounted sum of current and future profits. Using (A4.5), the maximization problem can be specified as

$$P_t^j = \arg\max \mathbb{E}_t \left\{ \sum_{s=0}^{\infty} (\xi\Lambda)^s \left(\frac{\lambda_{t+s}}{\lambda_t}\right) \left[\left(\frac{P_t^j}{P_{t+s}} - \frac{MC_{t+s}^N}{P_{t+s}}\right)\left(\frac{P_t^j}{P_{t+s}}\right)^{-\theta} Y_{t+s} \right] \right\}, \tag{A4.8}$$

82. The index j is dropped in (A4.6) because the equilibrium price is the same for all firms.

where Λ is the firm's discount factor and λ_{t+s}/λ_t is the intertemporal marginal rate of substitution of the representative household between t and $t+s$.[83] Note that in (A4.8) P_t^j is not moved forward to P_{t+s}^j because firms choose their price in the current period t under the constraint that they might not be able to change that price in future periods.

Assuming that firms take the processes driving marginal cost (or, equivalently, W_t and ϵ_t^Y) as given, the first-order condition is given by

$$\mathbb{E}_t\left\{\sum_{s=0}^{\infty}(\xi\Lambda)^s\left(\frac{\lambda_{t+s}}{\lambda_t}\right)\left[\left(\frac{1-\theta}{P_{t+s}}\right)\left(\frac{P_t^{j,O}}{P_{t+s}}\right)^{-\theta}+\theta\frac{MC_{t+s}^N}{P_{t+s}^2}\left(\frac{P_t^{j,O}}{P_{t+s}}\right)^{-\theta-1}\right]Y_{t+s}\right\}$$
$$=0,$$

where $P_t^{j,O}$ is firm j's optimal price. Multiplying this expression by $P_t^{j,O}$, dividing by $1-\theta$, and simplifying yields

$$\mathbb{E}_t\left\{\sum_{s=0}^{\infty}(\xi\Lambda)^s\left(\frac{\lambda_{t+s}}{\lambda_t}\right)\left[\left(\frac{P_t^{j,O}}{P_{t+s}}\right)\left(\frac{P_t^{j,O}}{P_{t+s}}\right)^{-\theta}\right.\right.$$
$$\left.\left.-\left(\frac{\theta}{\theta-1}\right)\left(\frac{MC_{t+s}^N}{P_{t+s}}\right)\left(\frac{P_t^{j,O}}{P_{t+s}}\right)^{-\theta}\right]Y_{t+s}\right\}=0,$$

or equivalently

$$\mathbb{E}_t\left\{\sum_{s=0}^{\infty}(\xi\Lambda)^s\left(\frac{\lambda_{t+s}}{\lambda_t}\right)\left(\frac{P_t^{j,O}}{P_{t+s}}\right)^{1-\theta}Y_{t+s}\right\}$$
$$=\left(\frac{\theta}{\theta-1}\right)\mathbb{E}_t\left\{\sum_{s=0}^{\infty}(\xi\Lambda)^s\left(\frac{\lambda_{t+s}}{\lambda_t}\right)\left(\frac{MC_{t+s}^N}{P_{t+s}}\right)\left(\frac{P_t^{j,O}}{P_{t+s}}\right)^{-\theta}Y_{t+s}\right\}.$$

Multiplying and dividing the right-hand side of this expression by $P_t^{j,O}$ (which, again, does not depend on time s) gives

$$\mathbb{E}_t\left\{\sum_{s=0}^{\infty}(\xi\Lambda)^s\left(\frac{\lambda_{t+s}}{\lambda_t}\right)\left(\frac{P_t^{j,O}}{P_{t+s}}\right)^{1-\theta}Y_{t+s}\right\}$$

83. As noted in the text, because firms distribute all profits to their owners at the end of each period, the discount factor depends also on the intertemporal marginal rate of substitution of the representative household.

$$= \left(\frac{\theta}{\theta-1}\right) \mathbb{E}_t \left\{ \sum_{s=0}^{\infty} (\xi\Lambda)^s \left(\frac{\lambda_{t+s}}{\lambda_t}\right) \left(\frac{MC^N_{t+j}}{P^{j,O}_t}\right) \left(\frac{P^{j,O}_t}{P_{t+s}}\right)^{1-\theta} Y_{t+s} \right\},$$

or, moving $P^{j,O}_t$ on the right-hand side to the left and dropping the term $(P^{j,O}_t)^{1-\theta}$ on both sides,

$$P^{j,O}_t \mathbb{E}_t \left\{ \sum_{s=0}^{\infty} (\xi\Lambda)^s \left(\frac{\lambda_{t+s}}{\lambda_t}\right) \left(\frac{1}{P_{t+s}}\right)^{1-\theta} Y_{t+s} \right\} \tag{A4.9}$$

$$= \left(\frac{\theta}{\theta-1}\right) \mathbb{E}_t \left\{ \sum_{s=0}^{\infty} (\xi\Lambda)^s \left(\frac{\lambda_{t+s}}{\lambda_t}\right) MC^N_{t+s} \left(\frac{1}{P_{t+s}}\right)^{1-\theta} Y_{t+s} \right\},$$

so that

$$P^{j,O}_t = \left(\frac{\theta}{\theta-1}\right) \frac{\mathbb{E}_t \left[\sum_{s=0}^{\infty} (\xi\Lambda)^s (\lambda_{t+s}/\lambda_t)(1/P_{t+s})^{1-\theta} MC^N_{t+s} Y_{t+s}\right]}{\mathbb{E}_t \left[\sum_{s=0}^{\infty} (\xi\Lambda)^s (\lambda_{t+s}/\lambda_t)(1/P_{t+s})^{1-\theta} Y_{t+s}\right]},$$

or again

$$P^{j,O}_t = \left(\frac{\theta}{\theta-1}\right) \mathbb{E}_t \left[\sum_{s=0}^{\infty} \varrho_{t,t+s} MC^N_{t+s} \right], \tag{A4.10}$$

where

$$\varrho_{t,t+s} = \frac{(\xi\Lambda)^s (\lambda_{t+s}/\lambda_t) P^{\theta-1}_{t+s} Y_{t+s}}{\mathbb{E}_t \left[\sum_{s=0}^{\infty} (\xi\Lambda)^s (\lambda_{t+s}/\lambda_t) P^{\theta-1}_{t+s} Y_{t+s}\right]}.$$

Equation (A4.10) defines firm j's optimal reset price as a markup over a weighted average of expected future nominal marginal costs; in equilibrium, it is the same for all firms.

To get the log-linearized price equation, begin by dividing both sides of equation (A4.9) by P_t so that, after dropping superscript j,

$$\frac{P^O_t}{P_t} \mathbb{E}_t \left\{ \sum_{s=0}^{\infty} (\xi\Lambda)^s (\lambda_{t+s}/\lambda_t) P^{\theta-1}_{t+s} Y_{t+s} \right\} \tag{A4.11}$$

$$= \left(\frac{\theta}{\theta-1}\right) \mathbb{E}_t \left\{ \sum_{s=0}^{\infty} (\xi\Lambda)^s (\lambda_{t+s}/\lambda_t) \frac{MC^N_{t+s}}{P_t} P^{\theta-1}_{t+s} Y_{t+s} \right\}.$$

Taking a first-order, log-linear approximation of the left-hand side (and thus dropping the product of two or more variables) in the neighborhood of a zero-inflation steady state yields

$$lfs \simeq \tilde{P}^{\theta}\tilde{Y}\sum_{s=0}^{\infty}(\xi\Lambda)^s\mathbb{E}_t[(\hat{P}_t^O - \hat{P}_t) + \hat{Y}_{t+s} + (\theta-1)\hat{P}_{t+s} + (\hat{\lambda}_{t+s} - \hat{\lambda}_t)].$$

Similarly, a log-linear approximation of the right-hand side of (A4.11) gives

$$rhs \simeq \tilde{P}^{\theta}\tilde{Y}\left[\sum_{s=0}^{\infty}(\xi\Lambda)^s\right]\mathbb{E}_t[(\widehat{MC_{t+s}^N} - \hat{P}_t) + \hat{Y}_{t+s} + (\theta-1)\hat{P}_{t+s} + (\hat{\lambda}_{t+s} - \hat{\lambda}_t)].$$

Equating the two expressions above and simplifying yields, given that $\sum_{s=0}^{\infty}(\xi\Lambda)^s = 1/(1-\xi\Lambda)$,

$$\hat{P}_t^O = (1-\xi\Lambda)\sum_{s=0}^{\infty}(\xi\Lambda)^s\mathbb{E}_t\widehat{MC_{t+s}^N}. \tag{A4.12}$$

Intuitively, firms take into account the fact that their prices will likely be fixed over some period of time by setting their price equal to a weighted average of expected future nominal marginal costs. The parameter ξ (which is inversely related to the expected duration of the currently determined price) affects how fast the weights decline over time. If $\xi = 0$, all prices are flexible and all firms would set their price as described in (A4.6).

Now, equation (A4.7) in log-linearized form can be rewritten as

$$\hat{P}_t^O = \frac{1}{1-\xi}(\hat{P}_t - \xi\hat{P}_{t-1}), \tag{A4.13}$$

whereas (A4.12), in quasi-differenced form, gives, with $\widehat{MC_t^N} = \widehat{mc_t} + \hat{P}_t$, and $\widehat{mc_t}$ denoting deviation of real marginal cost from its steady-state value $\theta/(\theta-1)$,

$$\hat{P}_t^O = (1-\xi\Lambda)(\widehat{mc_t} + \hat{P}_t) + (\xi\Lambda)\mathbb{E}_t\hat{P}_{t+1}^O.$$

Substituting (A4.13) for $\hat{P}_t^O$ in this expression yields

$$\frac{\hat{P}_t - \xi\hat{P}_{t-1}}{1-\xi} = (1-\xi\Lambda)(\widehat{mc_t} + \hat{P}_t) + \left(\frac{\xi\Lambda}{1-\xi}\right)(\mathbb{E}_t\hat{P}_{t+1} - \xi\hat{P}_t),$$

which can be easily rearranged to give, with $\hat{\pi}_t = \hat{P}_t - \hat{P}_{t-1}$ and $\mathbb{E}_t\hat{\pi}_{t+1} = \mathbb{E}_t\hat{P}_{t+1} - \hat{P}_t$,

$$\hat{\pi}_t + (1-\xi)\hat{P}_{t-1} = (1-\xi)(1-\xi\Lambda)\widehat{mc_t} + (1-\xi)(1-\xi\Lambda)\hat{P}_t$$
$$+ \xi\Lambda[\mathbb{E}_t\hat{\pi}_{t+1} + (1-\xi)\hat{P}_t].$$

The coefficient of $\hat{P}_t$ on the right-hand side of this expression is $(1-\xi)(1-\xi\Lambda)+\xi\Lambda(1-\xi)=1-\xi$. Using this result, and rearranging terms yields

$$\hat{\pi}_t-(1-\xi)(\hat{P}_t-\hat{P}_{t-1})=(1-\xi)(1-\xi\Lambda)\widehat{mc_t}+\xi\Lambda\mathbb{E}_t\hat{\pi}_{t+1},$$

so that

$$\hat{\pi}_t=\Lambda\mathbb{E}_t\hat{\pi}_{t+1}+\frac{(1-\xi)(1-\xi\Lambda)}{\xi}\widehat{mc_t}. \tag{A4.14}$$

Equation (A4.14) defines an alternative formulation of the *New Keynesian Phillips curve*. It relates (deviations in) inflation to next period's (deviations in) expected inflation rate and the current deviation of real marginal cost from its frictionless optimal level.[84] The higher the degree of price rigidity, as measured by ξ, the less sensitive is inflation with respect to movements in marginal cost.

This result can easily be generalized to alternative assumptions about the production technology; for instance, with a Cobb-Douglas production function of the form $Y_t^j=\epsilon_t^Y(N_t^j)^{1-\alpha}(K_t^j)^{\alpha}$ as in (4.20), where K_t^j is capital and $\alpha\in(0,1)$, the coefficient of the second term on the left-hand side of (A4.14) would be multiplied by $(1-\alpha)[1+\alpha(\theta-1)]$, as discussed by Galí et al. (2001, 2003), Sbordone (2002), and Lawless and Whelan (2011), for instance.

Note also that in this setting, where production is linear in labor and firms hire workers in a common economy-wide labor market, all firms face the same marginal cost, which is independent of their level of output. Consequently, the firm's marginal cost is equal to average marginal cost, which equals the labor share.[85] By contrast, as shown by Gagnon and Khan (2005), if the production technology takes a Cobb-Douglas or constant-elasticity-of-substitution form with overhead labor, and if capital cannot be instantly reallocated across firms, real marginal cost will depend not only on unit labor costs but also on a *strategic complementarity* parameter, which depends essentially on the elasticity of firms' real marginal cost with respect to their own output—a parameter that is now different from zero. This parameter affects also estimates of the average duration of nominal price stickiness.

Abstracting from these complications and from capital in production, it can be shown that the deviation in the labor share from its steady state (and thus the deviation in average real marginal cost) is proportional to the gap between

84. In the steady state, as implied by (A4.6), real marginal cost corresponds to the inverse of the markup (in log terms, $-\Theta$), because then nominal marginal cost and output are constant, and so all firms charge the same price.

85. Because, from (A4.1), $\varepsilon_t^Y=y_t-n_t$, real (average) marginal cost $mc_t^N-p_t$ is equal to $w_t-\varepsilon_t^Y-p_t=w_t+n_t-(y_t+p_t)$—that is, the (log) labor income share, or unit labor cost.

output and its potential level—that is, the output gap $\hat{Y}_t$ (Rotemberg and Woodford 1997). Using this result, the dynamics of inflation are given by, instead of (A4.14),

$$\hat{\pi}_t = \Lambda \mathbb{E}_t \hat{\pi}_{t+1} + \frac{(1-\xi)(1-\xi\Lambda)}{\xi}\hat{Y}_t, \qquad \text{(A4.15)}$$

which shows, in particular, that the longer prices are held fixed (on average), the less responsive is inflation to cyclical fluctuations in output.[86]

Galí and Gertler (1999), and subsequently Steinsson (2003), derived a hybrid Phillips curve from a price adjustment model à la Calvo and the additional assumption that although a mass of firms of measure $1-\xi$ is allowed to reset prices, only a fraction $1-\kappa$ of these firms, where $\kappa \in (0,1)$, does so optimally (that is, in a forward-looking manner). Perhaps as a result of information-processing costs, the remaining firms set their price according to a rule of thumb. Specifically, a fraction κ of price-resetting firms chooses the (log) price p_t^B according to the backward-looking rule

$$p_t^B = p_{t-1}^M + \pi_{t-1},$$

where p_{t-1}^M is the average price set in $t-1$, across both backward- and forward-looking firms, which depends therefore on both p_{t-1}^O and p_{t-1}^B.

As derived by Galí and Gertler (1999, pp. 209–211), the hybrid equation takes the form

$$\hat{\pi}_t = \left(\frac{\kappa}{\phi}\right)\pi_{t-1} + \left(\frac{\Lambda\xi}{\phi}\right)\mathbb{E}_t\hat{\pi}_{t+1} + \frac{(1-\kappa)(1-\xi)(1-\xi\Lambda)}{\phi}\hat{Y}_t, \qquad \text{(A4.16)}$$

where $\phi = \xi + \kappa[1-\xi(1-\Lambda)]$. This equation corresponds to (A4.15) if $\kappa = 0$. A similar result would obtain if instead, as in Christiano et al. (2005), firms that are unable to reset their prices optimally do so by indexing them to last period's inflation, as follows:

$$p_t^B = p_{t-1} + \vartheta(p_{t-1} - p_{t-2}), \qquad \text{(A4.17)}$$

where $\vartheta \in (0,1)$ measures the degree of indexation. To ensure a vertical Phillips curve in the long run, one can set $\vartheta = \xi$, as in Liu (2006), for instance.

Equation (A4.16) is a second-order difference equation. Let $\mu_1 \leq 1$ and $\mu_2 \geq 1$ denote, respectively, the stable and unstable roots of this equation. The

86. See Kozicki and Tinsley (2002) for a more general result in the presence of trend deviations in output.

stable forward solution of (A4.16) is

$$\hat{\pi}_t = \mu_1 \hat{\pi}_{t-1} + \Gamma \sum_{s=0}^{\infty} \left(\frac{1}{\mu_2} \right)^s \mathbb{E}_t \hat{Y}_{t+s}, \quad \Gamma = \frac{(1-\kappa)(1-\xi)(1-\xi\Lambda)}{\mu_2 \Lambda \xi},$$

which shows that current inflation depends on past inflation and on expected future values of the output gap.

A common criticism of the Galí-Gertler specification and its variants involving backward-looking indexation, as in (A4.17), is that it dwells on an *ad hoc* behavioral assumption by some agents. However, this outcome is consistent with the existence of a sufficiently large fraction of myopic agents (Orland and Roos 2013). Moreover, as shown by Kozicki and Tinsley (2002), a virtually identical form to the Galí-Gertler specification (which includes not only a term in lagged inflation but also an additional lead term $E_t \hat{\pi}_{t+2}$) can arise from optimizing behavior if the dynamics of pricing frictions are more complex than in the pure forward-looking version. Sheedy (2010) derived a similar result. He showed that, under the plausible assumption that newer prices are stickier than older prices, the hazard function of the Calvo model would be upward-sloping rather than constant. Essentially, a hazard function that increases with time implies that if there has been inflation in the recent past, so that older prices are lower than more recent prices, the average price will automatically increase when prices are reoptimized—even if the new prices are no higher than the average current price. There is therefore inflation inertia and the Phillips curve takes a form that includes both past and future values of inflation. In the same vein, Calvo et al. (2007) provided a generalization of Calvo's staggered pricing model that also generates inflation inertia. In their framework, once a firm gets the opportunity to change its pricing plan, it optimally chooses *both* an initial price level and a rate at which it will update its price in the future.

Finally, Mankiw and Reis (2002) proposed a model in which information is costly and disseminated gradually. Each period a fraction of firms sets prices based on outdated information, whereas the other fraction sets the optimal price path based on new information about the state of the economy. Thus, while prices adjust continuously, information does not. Empirical studies for advanced economies suggest that the sticky-information model is also consistent with the evidence on inflation persistence.

5 Reserve Requirements, Policy Evaluation, and Coordination

Beyond their role as a structural liquidity management tool, reserve requirements have often been used in middle-income countries (MICs) for a broader set of purposes—including as an alternative to interest rate management and as a countercyclical macroprudential tool in response to external shocks. Both Brazil and Turkey, for instance, lowered required reserve ratios in response to the collapse of Lehman Brothers in September 2008—a time of considerable turmoil in financial markets around the world—and increased them again in the period of large capital inflows that occurred between 2010 to mid-2011, following the implementation of quantitative easing policies in the United States.[1] In the first episode the goal was to inject liquidity quickly into the financial system to prevent disruptions in the interbank market and a credit crunch, whereas in the second the goal was to prevent excessive credit growth—a phenomenon, as documented in chapter 1, that has often accompanied sudden floods in capital flows. Other Latin American countries, such as Colombia and Peru, have also used reserve requirements aggressively. Prior to the global financial crisis the central banks of both countries managed reserve requirements as a prudential tool to contain pressures on credit growth associated with large capital inflows. Both of them raised marginal reserve requirements during those episodes. In addition, in the case of Peru, a highly dollarized economy, marginal reserve requirements were also imposed on foreign-currency deposits. More generally, the evidence shows that central banks in MICs have time and again raised reserve requirements in response to capital inflows (Hoffmann and Löffler 2014) and rapid credit growth (Cerutti et al. 2017*a*). In countries where excess liquidity prevails, reserve requirements also play a critical role as an instrument of monetary policy, given the possible asymmetric effects associated with changes in policy interest rates (see the discussion later on).

1. See Robitaille (2011) and Mimir et al. (2013) for a discussion of these experiences.

This chapter uses the core closed-economy DSGE model developed in chapter 4 to study the role of reserve requirements as a countercyclical macroprudential instrument—an important issue on the policy agenda for many MICs.[2] As background to the analysis, section 1 provides a broad discussion of the role of reserve requirements, in both closed and open economies. Section 2 discusses the scope for using reserve requirements to conduct countercyclical policy and identifies two settings in which the policy can prove effective: imperfect substitutability between bank funding sources and economies of scope in banking. Section 3 considers a simple, arbitrary countercyclical reserve requirement rule and illustrates its functioning in response to financial shocks. For comparative purposes, results obtained with a tax rate on loans—a generic instrument that captures well the cost effects associated with instruments like capital requirements, as noted in chapters 2 and 3—and an interest rate policy that reacts directly to credit developments, are also provided. Section 4 focuses on optimal countercyclical rules. It begins by discussing alternative approaches to optimal policy evaluation, which involve the central bank (regulator) either minimizing a policy loss function that reflects macroeconomic (financial) stability concerns or maximizing social welfare (namely, the utility of the representative household). The role of instrument manipulation costs is discussed as well. Section 5 focuses on the issue of coordination between monetary policy and macroprudential regulation, whereas section 6 examines the optimal determination of these policies, both independently and jointly, in response to financial shocks. Both the loss-minimization approach and the welfare-maximization approach are considered. The benefit of coordination is also assessed. Section 7 discusses the Ramsey optimal policy and the relative performance of simple countercyclical macroprudential rules. The last section provides some notes on the literature.

5.1 Background

As noted by Gray (2011), reserve requirements usually serve three purposes, depending on circumstances: a microprudential function, a monetary policy role (through their impact on market interest rates and monetary aggregates), and a liquidity management function (including, in some countries, as a tool for sterilization of excess bank reserves). The microprudential function relates to protection against liquidity and solvency risks; from that perspective, reserve requirements help to ensure that adequate liquidity is available in the event of a

2. In chapters 7 and 9, this issue will also be discussed in the context of an open economy.

sudden drop in market funding. This role is particularly important in countries where the lack of development of financial markets translates into an inadequate supply of liquid assets.[3]

Regarding the monetary policy and liquidity management functions, the evidence suggests that in MICs reserve requirements have proved to be particularly useful during episodes of large capital inflows associated with changes in world interest rates or risk perceptions. As noted in chapter 1, these episodes have often been accompanied by an expansion in credit, an increase in aggregate demand, and in some cases (if the pass-through associated with the initial exchange rate appreciation is weak) inflationary pressures. In such conditions, although interest rate hikes could dampen activity and restrain inflation, they may also attract more capital, which in turn may fuel further increases in credit. By contrast, an increase in reserve requirements would induce banks to *lower* deposit rates. Suppose that, as is often the case in practice, the central bank intervenes to buy foreign exchange and prevent an appreciation of the exchange rate, in response to a large inflow of capital (see chapter 8). Concurrently, to avoid an expansion in the money supply, they often engage not only in open-market operations (sales of government bonds) but also in increases in reserve requirements.[4] The incentive to do so is particularly strong if the use of open-market operations to sterilize capital flows is costly, due to large differentials between the interest rate on assets used for these operations and the interest earned on foreign reserves. Because, as noted in previous chapters, reserve requirements represent fundamentally a tax on bank intermediation, they drive a wedge between the rate that a bank pays its depositors and its cost of funding. If bank deposits offer special transaction and liquidity services to households, the cost of higher reserve requirements would normally be passed on in full to depositors in the form of lower deposit rates. A similar outcome, albeit with a less than complete pass-through, would occur if banks can partly substitute reservable liabilities with other funding sources as a result, for instance, of information frictions or a less than perfectly elastic supply of liquidity from the central bank. In either case, the policy may lead to an increase in bank intermediation spreads through lower deposit rates, higher lending rates, or both.

3. In dollarized economies, differentiated reserve requirement rates are also used as instruments to mitigate the risks associated with financial dollarization, most notably by building foreign exchange liquidity buffers. See, for instance, Armas et al. (2014) for a discussion of the Peruvian case and Camors et al. (2019) for the Uruguayan case.

4. Higher reserve requirements on bank deposits have been used to sterilize the effects of capital inflows not just on the monetary base but also on the broader money supply, as was the case, for instance, in China, India, and Morocco, among others, in recent years. See, for instance, Ma et al. (2013) for a discussion of China's experience.

In an early contribution, Reinhart and Reinhart (1999) found indeed that increases in reserve requirements in developing countries tend to reduce deposit rates and to raise lending rates, whereas Gelos (2009) found that high reserve requirements are a key determinant of the comparatively high intermediation spreads observed in Latin America. In subsequent studies, Montoro and Moreno (2011), Tovar et al. (2012), Izquierdo et al. (2013), Armas et al. (2014), Cordella et al. (2014), Federico et al. (2014), Glocker and Towbin (2015), and Fendoglu (2017) all found that increases in reserve requirements tend to mitigate the expansion of credit in Latin America. In effect, during the global financial crisis, reserve requirements were used as a substitute to monetary policy in a number of MICs, not only to curb lending growth (as noted earlier) but also to dampen inflationary pressures.[5]

More recent thinking on the use of reserve requirements has focused on their role as a *systematic*—as opposed to sporadic—countercyclical macroprudential instrument, aimed at mitigating systemic risks to the financial system. By requiring banking institutions to hold permanently a fraction of their deposits (in the form of cash earning no interest, or deposits at the monetary authority remunerated at below-market rates), mandatory reserves act as an implicit tax on financial intermediation; and by altering the cost of funding, they may be useful to reduce the volatility of credit. In addition, increasing reserve requirements can restrain credit growth during expansions while reducing them during downturns can provide additional resources to banks to limit credit contractions, as noted earlier in the case of Brazil and Turkey. Thus, reserve requirements may potentially play a significant role in managing *both* the financial and the business cycles.

Analytical contributions on the countercyclical macroprudential role of reserve requirements, in both closed and open economies, include Prada (2008), Vargas et al. (2010), Montoro (2011), Glocker and Towbin (2012), Kashyap and Stein (2012), Mimir et al. (2013), Escudero et al. (2014), Alper et al. (2018), Leduc and Natal (2018), and Medina and Roldós (2018). In all of these contributions an increase in reserve requirements turns deposits into a more expensive source of funding for commercial banks, which induces them to reduce the interest rate that they offer on these liabilities. In Prada's model, for instance, this reduction leads not only to a drop in the demand for deposits but also to a reduction in credit as well, because deposits and credit are complements (as discussed next) due to joint production costs. Thus, the policy

5. Over a broader period, Mora (2014) also found evidence that increases in reserve requirements were contractionary for Lebanon. See Agénor and Pereira da Silva (2016) for a detailed review of the literature and some country experiences.

is countercyclical. Glocker and Towbin (2012) considered required reserves as an additional policy instrument and variations in loans as an additional target in an open-economy model with nominal rigidities and financial frictions. Their findings show that reserve requirements favor the price stability objective only if financial frictions are significant, and they are more effective if there is a financial stability objective and debt is denominated in foreign currency. In their model, due to the endogeneity of the monetary base, an increase in the reserve requirement ratio raises loan-to-deposit spreads only if the remuneration of reserves is below the market rate. However, because they obtain opposite impact effects on consumption and investment, the net effect on aggregate demand and inflation is ambiguous. Kashyap and Stein (2012) showed that the central bank can exploit a nonzero and time-varying scarcity value of reserves to tax the negative systemic externality associated with credit booms. Essentially, the use of time-varying reserve requirements on short-term debts acts as a Pigouvian tax on financial institutions engaged in maturity transformation.

5.2 Active Use of Reserve Requirements

In models where monetary policy targets a short-term interest rate, bank funding sources (deposits and central bank liquidity, abstracting from market borrowing at home or abroad) are perfect substitutes, and there are no disincentives from accessing central bank facilities, an increase in the required reserve ratio has no impact on lending rates—despite making deposits more expensive. Banks simply borrow more from the central bank at the prevailing refinance rate while reducing the deposit rate. There is no direct impact on the lending rate. But without a change in the lending rate, it is difficult to generate a countercyclical role for reserve requirements; if anything, the opposite may occur—if intertemporal substitution effects are strong, the drop in the deposit rate tends to reduce savings today and to *increase* current consumption—thereby generating a *procyclical* movement in aggregate demand.[6] This section discusses two channels through which reserve requirements can play a countercyclical role.

5.2.1 Imperfect Substitution between Funding Sources

The liability composition effect defined in chapters 2 and 4 provides a particularly simple way to introduce imperfect substitutability between deposits and

6. See the discussion in chapter 2 as well as Evandro and Takeda (2013), Agénor and Pereira da Silva (2014), and Escudero et al. (2014).

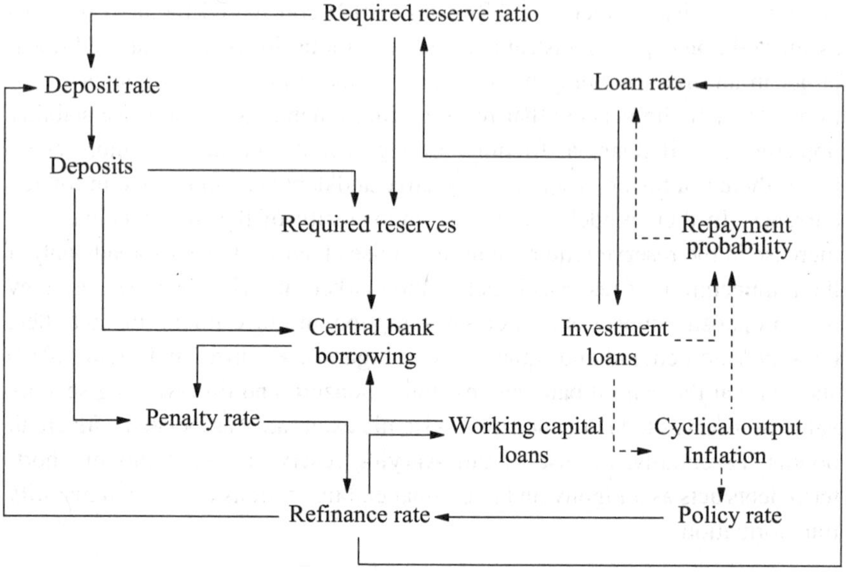

Figure 5.1
Reserve requirements, refinance rate, and bank interest rates

central bank borrowing, from the perspective of the monetary authority (or, in a more general setting, the interbank market), while retaining the no-arbitrage condition between the deposit rate and the refinance rate. Figure 5.1 provides a simplified description of the link between reserve requirements, policy rates, and market interest rates, based on the closed-economy model presented in chapter 4. Commercial banks have access to two sources of funding only: deposits (which are determined by household optimization behavior) and central bank borrowing. They set market interest rates and lend for investment, with a perfectly elastic credit supply curve at the prevailing loan rate. The central bank operates a standing facility, with a perfectly elastic supply of liquidity at the prevailing refinance rate. Thus, for given amounts of deposits and investment loans, central bank borrowing is determined residually from the balance sheet of financial institutions.

As shown in the figure, the required reserve ratio has no direct impact on the lending rate; it affects only the deposit rate, which is essentially a markdown over the cost of borrowing from the central bank. As in previous chapters, suppose that required reserves are set as a fixed fraction of deposits. Thus, an increase in the required reserve ratio may either raise or reduce the level of required reserves, depending on the sensitivity of deposits to interest rates. Suppose then that this sensitivity is low, because the demand for deposits is essentially related to real transactions. All else equal, therefore, an increase in the required reserve ratio raises the level of reserves.

If deposits and central bank borrowing are perfect substitutes, from the perspective of both commercial banks and the central bank, a change in the required reserve ratio would have (as noted earlier) no effect on the loan rate and investment; deposit rates fall, but all that happens is a switch in funding sources. However, suppose instead that, as in chapter 4, above and beyond a base policy rate (determined on the basis of standard macroeconomic objectives, inflation and output) the central bank charges a penalty rate that increases with the ratio of actual borrowing to deposits. Put differently, the supply of liquidity by the monetary authority is no longer perfectly elastic at the base policy rate. Because the central bank borrowing-deposit ratio unambiguously increases (as noted earlier), the refinance rate rises following a hike in the required reserve ratio. While this increase mitigates the initial drop in the deposit rate, it also leads to a higher loan rate, which tends to lower investment. All else equal, cyclical output and inflation also fall.[7] Both effects contribute to a reduction in the base policy rate, which mitigates the contractionary effect associated with the increase in the penalty component of the refinance rate. Nevertheless, if the impact on the penalty rate is sufficiently strong, the liability composition effect, viewed as a simple way to capture imperfect substitutability between deposits and central bank borrowing from the perspective of the monetary authority (or, more generally, from the perspective of banks lending at a premium to each other), is capable of generating a countercyclical role for reserve requirements through their impact on credit and investment—even if their effect on consumption can be, as noted earlier, procyclical.

5.2.2 Economies of Scope in Banking

An alternative way to generate a countercyclical role for reserve requirements is to introduce economies of scope in banking, as in Agénor and Pereira da Silva (2017), for instance. Consider the same market structure as in chapter 4 —perfect competition in the deposit market, and monopolistic competition in the credit market, with banks setting the loan rate to maximize expected profits. Formally, and given that the optimization problem is static, it can be written as

$$1 + i_t^{L,i}, q_t^i = \arg\max \mathbb{E}_t J_{t+1}^{B,i},$$

7. In the full model discussed in chapter 4, the fall in investment tends to increase the collateral-loan ratio, which raises the probability that loans are repaid, whereas the drop in output (through a cyclical effect on cash flows) lowers that probability. Depending on the net effect on the repayment probability, this may either magnify or mitigate the change in the loan rate. These effects are shown in figure 5.1 as dotted lines.

where $\mathbb{E}_t J^{B,i}_{t+1}$ is defined as

$$\mathbb{E}_t J^{B,i}_{t+1} = q^i_t(1+i^{L,i}_t)l^{K,i}_t + (1-q^i_t)\kappa^i \mathbb{E}_t p^H_{t+1}\bar{H} + (1+i^R_t)l^{W,i}_t \tag{5.1}$$
$$+ \mu d^i_t - (1+i^D_t)d^i_t - (1+i^R_t)l^{B,i}_t - x^{M,i}_t - \Gamma(l^{K,i}_t, d^i_t),$$

where all expressions and variables are as defined in chapter 4, and $\Gamma(l^{K,i}_t, d^i_t)$ measures now the nonseparable cost of producing investment loans and deposits. The function $\Gamma(l^{K,i}_t, d^i_t)$ is assumed to be strictly increasing and convex in its two arguments, so that $\Gamma_{l^K}, \Gamma_d > 0$, $\Gamma_{l^K l^K}, \Gamma_{dd} > 0$; in addition, it is also assumed to be linearly homogeneous. By implication of linear homogeneity, $\Gamma_{l^K d} < 0$, that is, a higher volume of deposits lowers the cost of lending by providing more information on (potential) borrowers. There is therefore *cost complementarity* or economies of scope—that is, lower costs of producing a combined set of products than the sum of costs incurred when producing them individually—a well-documented feature of banking.[8]

To be more specific, consider the case where $\Gamma(l^{K,i}_t, d^i_t)$ can be represented by the Diewert cost function

$$\Gamma(l^{K,i}_t, d^i_t) = \gamma_D d^i_t + \gamma_L l^{K,i}_t - 2\gamma\sqrt{d^i_t l^{K,i}_t}, \tag{5.2}$$

where $\gamma_D, \gamma_L, \gamma > 0$.[9]

As in chapter 4, bank i maximizes expected profits (5.1) subject to its balance sheet constraint, the downward-sloping loan demand equation by the representative producer of capital goods, as well as now the cost function (5.2), and given the value of collateral, deposits and the deposit rate, monitoring costs, and the refinance rate. In a symmetric equilibrium, the solution to this optimization problem leads now to the following first-order condition with respect to the loan rate:

$$1 + i^L_t = \frac{\varsigma^L}{q_t(\varsigma^L - 1)}\left\{1 + i^R_t + \gamma_L - \gamma\left(\frac{d_t}{l^K_t}\right)^{0.5}\right\}, \tag{5.3}$$

8. See Carvallo and Kasman (2005) for evidence on economies of scope in banking in Latin America. Dijkstra (2013) provides a review of the evidence for European countries.

9. Claus (2007, eq. (19)) used a similar specification. An alternative formulation, which has the same properties as (5.1) and generalizes the functional form suggested by Edwards and Végh (1997, fn 14), is $\Gamma(l^{K,i}_t, d^i_t) = \sqrt{\gamma_L(l^{K,i}_t)^2 + \gamma_D(d^i_t)^2}$, where $\gamma_L, \gamma_D > 0$. Kopecky and VanHoose (2012) and Abo-Zaid (2015) proposed yet another formulation, based on quadratic changes in deposits and loans.

which shows that the loan rate depends not only on the repayment probability and the marginal cost of borrowing, as before, but also on the marginal cost of producing loans.

Equation (5.3) helps to illustrate, in partial equilibrium, how changes in the required reserve ratio may operate in countercyclical fashion. Consider, for instance, an unanticipated increase in collateral values, which raises the repayment probability q_t. From (5.3), the result is a fall in the loan rate, which stimulates credit and investment. If, in response, the required reserve ratio is increased, the deposit rate will fall (as implied by the no-arbitrage condition $i_t^D = (1-\mu)i_t^R$ discussed in chapter 4), and this will reduce bank deposits. At the initial level of loans, the fall in the ratio d_t/l_t^K tends to *increase* the loan rate, which therefore mitigates the initial drop in that rate and the expansion of investment. Thus, the policy is countercyclical. However, there are also broader effects at play, including the feedback effect of changes in the supply of credit on the deposit-investment loan ratio, the effect of output fluctuations on the repayment probability, and so on. To understand these general equilibrium effects and the extent to which they either mitigate or magnify the partial equilibrium effects, a numerical analysis of the complete model is required.

5.3 Simple Countercyclical Rules

In chapter 4, it was assumed that the required reserve ratio, μ, is constant. As noted earlier, in practice policymakers in MICs have often used reserve requirements as part of a countercyclical toolkit to mitigate aggregate fluctuations—either as a substitute to monetary policy (in the form of changes in policy rates) or to promote financial stability. Even though in practice central banks almost never announce specific instrument rules, from an analytical perspective it is instructive to study their performance in isolation. Accordingly, this section considers some simple policy rules based on both the required reserve ratio and, for comparative purposes, a generic tax on loans.

5.3.1 Required Reserve Ratio

Suppose that the regulator implements a countercyclical reserve requirement rule that relates changes in μ_t endogenously to steady-state deviations in a trigger variable, Z_t. This rule takes the form

$$\frac{1+\mu_t}{1+\tilde{\mu}} = \left(\frac{1+\mu_{t-1}}{1+\tilde{\mu}}\right)^{\chi_1} Z_t^{\chi_2^R(1-\chi_1)}, \tag{5.4}$$

where $\chi_1 \in (0, 1)$ is a persistence parameter and $\chi_2^R > 0$ is the response parameter—that is, the degree of aggressiveness of the policy. As is clear from (5.4), the response parameters do not affect the steady-state level of the required reserve ratio, only its cyclical properties.

In line with the evidence (reviewed in chapter 1), which suggests that rapid credit expansion is a robust predictor of episodes of financial instability, it is natural to view the trigger variable Z_t in the policy rule (5.4) as representing either a credit aggregate or a credit-related measure. Thus, in a sense, credit represents an *intermediate target* for countercyclical macroprudential regulation—even though, as discussed later, credit fluctuations are not always the manifestation of a fundamental distortion (related to the inherent procyclicality of the financial system, in particular) that needs to be corrected.

Two commonly used measures of Z_t are (deviations in) the credit-to-output ratio and real credit growth:

$$Z_t = \frac{l_t^K / Y_t}{\tilde{l}^K / \tilde{Y}}, \quad Z_t = \frac{l_t^K}{l_{t-1}^K}. \tag{5.5}$$

In either definition, what appears is not total credit but investment loans only, which contribute in the present setting to aggregate demand fluctuations, as opposed to working capital loans, which affect the supply side.[10] In general, choosing between these two definitions involves both analytical and operational considerations. For instance, some observers have argued that using credit growth is preferable because in practice it is less prone to the type of errors of measurement that typically occur with final output or gross domestic product (GDP), especially when early estimates of these variables are used in real time. In addition, the credit-to-output ratio can be a misleading indicator in the early stages of a recession—as noted by Drehmann and Tsatsaronis (2014), for instance, it may rise not because of an increase in the numerator (credit) but rather as a result of a fall in the denominator (output).

Alternative specifications are of course possible. Montoro (2011) used a contemporaneous rule in terms of steady-state deviations in the *level* of credit. Rather than defining Z_t in terms of contemporaneous values, expected future values could also be used. A forward-looking credit-growth rule is studied in Mimir et al. (2013) and Escudero et al. (2014), for instance. Another measure, in the context of the present model, is (deviations in) *uncollateralized credit*, or equivalently the loan-collateral ratio, $l_t^K / \kappa \mathbb{E}_t p_{t+1}^H H_t$. The view in this case is

10. Recall that in the benchmark case there are no working capital needs ($\psi_W = 0$); there is therefore no distinction between investment loans and total loans. In a more general setting, however, the distinction is meaningful.

that the fragility of the financial system depends on the extent to which loans are collateralized or not—that is, whether lenders can mitigate the cost of default by seizing a fraction of a borrower's assets.[11] As discussed later, the very fact that the trigger variable can be defined in several alternative (and seemingly equally plausible) ways makes it important to define a clear benchmark to assess the performance of simple rules.

Before examining how this rule performs, recall from chapter 4 that the refinance rate is set as

$$1+i_t^R=(1+i_t^T)(1+\theta_t^{CB})=(1+i_t^T)\left(\frac{l^B/\tilde{l}^B}{d/\tilde{d}}\right)^{\varphi^{CB}}, \tag{5.6}$$

where i_t^T is the base policy rate (determined through a Taylor rule), θ_t^{CB} the penalty rate, and $\varphi^{CB}\geq 0$. The penalty rate is thus positively related to (deviations in) the ratio of central bank borrowing to deposits.

Suppose that φ^{CB} is set at 0.02, and that the parameters χ_1 and χ_2^R are set at 0.8 and 1.5, respectively. Thus, the case considered is that of a relatively aggressive policy but with significant inertia. Although arbitrary, these values help to illustrate the mechanisms at play.[12] All other parameters and initial values are the same as those listed in tables 4.1 and 4.2. In particular, the steady-state value of the required reserve ratio, $\tilde{\mu}$, is equal to 0.2. The trigger variable Z_t is defined for now in terms of (deviations in) the loan-to-output ratio, as defined in (5.5); experiments with a credit growth-based rule are discussed subsequently.

Impulse response functions associated with a negative credit spread shock are displayed in figure 5.2, with and without the countercyclical rule (5.4). As noted in chapter 4, the immediate impact of the shock is a reduction in the loan rate and an expansion in credit, investment, and output. The investment loan-to-output ratio also increases. With the rule (5.4) in place, this increase induces the regulator to raise the required reserve ratio. This lowers the deposit rate and raises the central bank borrowing-deposit ratio, which leads to an increase in the penalty rate and therefore a higher refinance rate. The effect on the loan rate and investment is fairly muted, but because the real bond rate increases by less (due to the shift away from deposits), consumption drops by less and output expands by more than in the benchmark case. Inflationary pressures are stronger, and the central bank reacts by raising the base policy rate, which exerts two conflicting effects on the refinance rate: On the one hand, it tends to

11. Other examples of trigger variables, in the context of studies focusing on monetary policy and countercyclical capital requirements, are discussed in the next section and in chapter 6.

12. Using an alternative value of 0.1 for χ_1 did not affect qualitatively the results. To simplify matters, therefore, the persistence parameter is kept constant throughout.

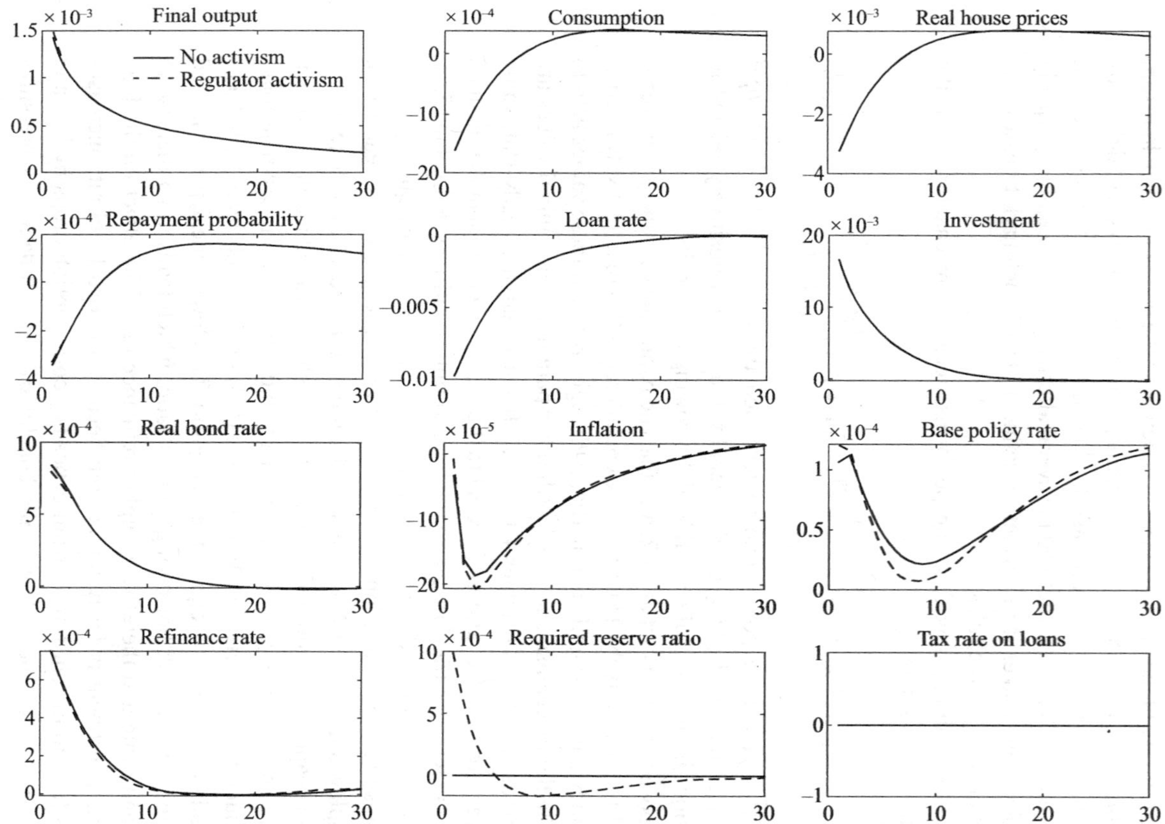

Figure 5.2 Negative credit spread shock: countercyclical required reserve ratio. *Note*: The responses of consumption, investment, output, and real house prices are expressed as percent deviations from their steady-state values. The responses of the lending rate, the refinance rate, the expected real bond rate, the repayment probability, and the inflation rate are expressed as absolute deviations (or percentage points) from their steady-state values.

increase it directly, but on the other, by mitigating the drop in the deposit rate due to the higher required reserve ratio, it tends to lower it indirectly. The net effect, nevertheless, is a higher refinance rate compared to the benchmark case. In turn, the higher refinance rate mitigates the initial drop in the loan rate. The policy response also stabilizes consumption (by mitigating the initial increase in the real bond rate, which attenuates incentives to cut spending today) and house prices. Put differently, the endogenous response of the required reserve ratio is unambiguously countercyclical, in the sense that it mitigates the initial expansion in output, credit, and asset price pressures, even though the policy has more limited effects on inflation. At the same time, given the degree of aggressiveness of the policy ($\chi_2^R = 1.5$), these effects are fairly muted.

5.3.2 Tax on Loans

For comparative purposes, it is useful to compare the performance of the countercyclical reserve requirement rule (5.4) with a rule based on a time-varying tax on loans. As noted in chapter 2, such a tax captures in a generic fashion the cost effect associated with some commonly used macroprudential instruments, such as capital requirements and loan loss provisions. In fact, several contributions to the DSGE literature with financial frictions have accounted for macroprudential regulation in the form of a tax on loans; see, for instance, Kannan et al. (2012), Gertler et al. (2012), Quint and Rabanal (2014), Levine and Lima (2015), Carrillo et al. (2017), and Agénor and Pereira da Silva (2018*b*).[13] More generally, the stylized characterization of macroprudential regulation as a tax can be related to the broader literature—which includes Farhi et al. (2014)—that highlights the equivalence of allocations attained under different sets of policy instruments.

Instead of (5.1), bank *i*'s profits are now given by

$$\mathbb{E}_t J_{t+1}^{B,i} = q_t^i (1 + i_t^{L,i})(1 - \tau_t^L) l_t^{K,i} + (1 - q_t^i)\kappa^i \mathbb{E}_t p_{t+1}^H H_t + (1 + i_t^R) l_t^{W,i} \quad (5.7)$$
$$+ \mu d_t^i - (1 + i_t^D) d_t^i - (1 + i_t^R) l_t^{B,i} - x_t^{M,i} + \Omega_t^i,$$

where $\tau_t^L \in (0, 1)$ is the tax rate on loans and Ω_t^i represents the proceeds of the tax. In order to abstract from the fiscal effects of macroprudential policy, these proceeds are assumed to be rebated to each bank in lump-sum fashion.

Solving the bank's optimization problem in the same way as in chapter 4, it can readily be established that in a symmetric equilibrium the first-order

13. Other contributions focusing on a tax-like instrument of macroprudential regulation include De Paoli and Paustian (2017), who considered a tax (or subsidy) on firms' borrowing costs, and Kiley and Sim (2017), who studied a tax on bank leverage.

condition with respect to the loan rate is now given by

$$i_t^L = \frac{\varsigma^L}{(\varsigma^L - 1)(1 - \tau_t^L)q_t}(1 + i_t^R), \tag{5.8}$$

which shows that the wedge between the refinance rate and the loan rate depends now also on the regulatory regime. A higher tax rate on loans raises the lending rate.

The countercyclical rule takes now a form similar to (5.4),

$$\frac{1+\tau_t^L}{1+\tilde{\tau}^L} = \left(\frac{1+\tau_{t-1}^L}{1+\tilde{\tau}^L}\right)^{\chi_1} Z_t^{\chi_2^L(1-\chi_1)}, \tag{5.9}$$

where again $\chi_1 \in (0, 1)$, $\chi_2^L > 0$, and Z_t is a trigger variable.[14] From (5.8) and (5.9), borrowing is more costly during episodes of credit booms and this helps to stabilize the financial cycle and dampen macroeconomic fluctuations. Thus, to the extent that it helps to mitigate the negative externality associated with what is perceived to be excessive lending (which, again, is often highly correlated with financial instability, as documented in chapter 1), a tax on loans is essentially Pigouvian in nature.[15]

Suppose that parameter χ_1 is set at 0.8 as before, and χ_2^L at 1.5 for illustrative purposes. The steady-state value of τ^L is set at 0. All other parameters and initial values are kept the same as in chapter 4. Once again, the focus is on the investment loan-to-output ratio as the trigger variable (see (5.5)).

Results are displayed in figure 5.3, for the same negative credit spread shock as before. They show that the countercyclical tax rule is quite effective; it mitigates significantly the drop in the loan rate and the expansion in investment and output. The increase in the expected real bond rate is also muted, which leads to consumption falling by less than in the case with no macroprudential activism. The smaller reduction in the demand for housing services associated with the reduction in spending also attenuates pressure on house prices, which dampens the drop in the repayment probability associated with the increase in cyclical output. At the same time, because the drop in consumption is now smaller, the increase in labor supply is weaker; as a result, wages fall by less than in the benchmark case, thereby amplifying the increase in inflation and the base policy rate. This, in turn, also mitigates the drop in the loan rate.

14. Again, as is clear from (5.9), the response parameters do not affect the steady-state level of the macroprudential tax rate, only its cyclical properties.

15. See Jeanne and Korinek (2019) for a more formal discussion of the Pigouvian nature of a countercyclical tax on borrowing in a model with booms and busts in credit and asset prices. Note also that while rules (5.4) and (5.9) imply a symmetric response of the policy instrument, it could be made *contingent* on both the direction and magnitude of the change in the trigger variable.

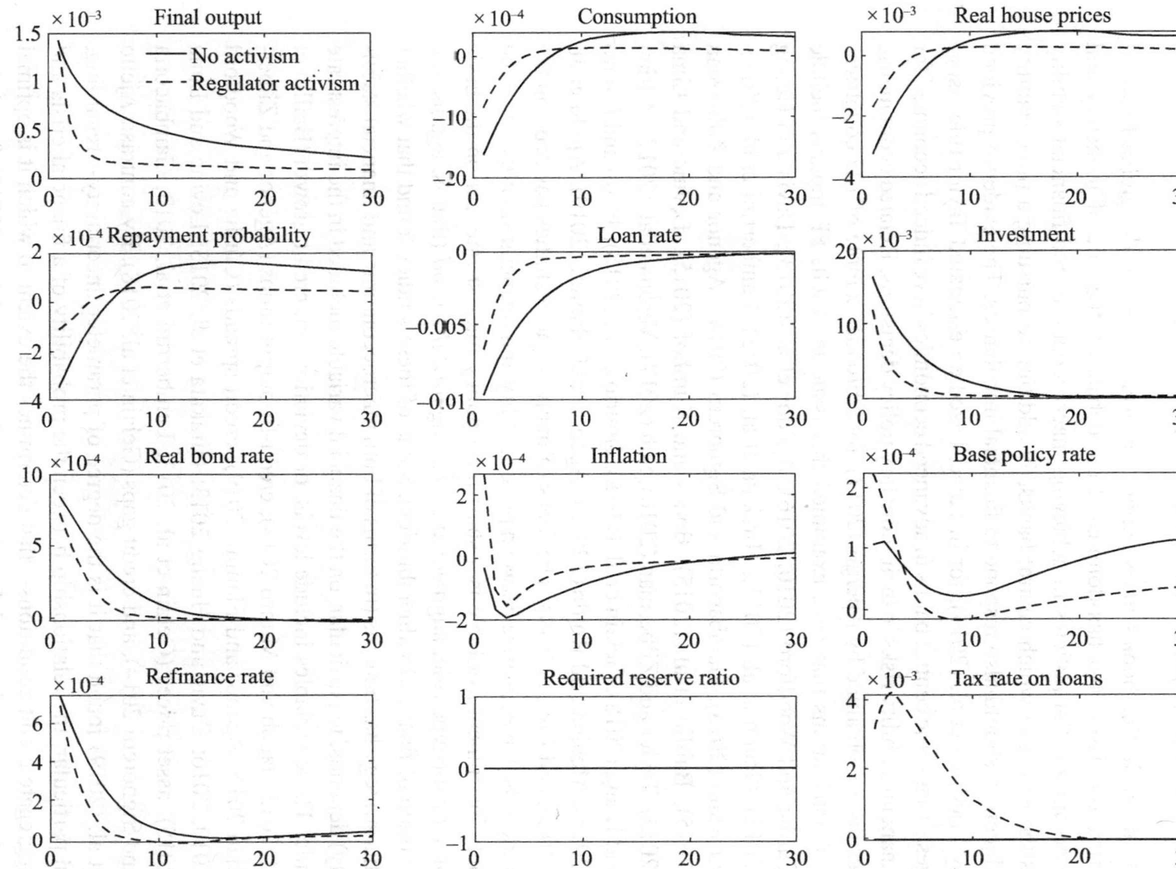

Figure 5.3 Negative credit spread shock: countercyclical tax on loans. *Note*: See note to figure 5.2.

5.3.3 Leaning against the Wind

As noted in this book's introduction and overview, since the global financial crisis one issue that has dominated the debate on the role of monetary and macroprudential policies in achieving macroeconomic and financial stability is the extent to which central banks, in addition to pursuing a price stability objective, should also respond to financial imbalances. The evidence provided by Friedrich et al. (2019), for instance, based on estimated Taylor rules, suggests that some central banks in advanced economies have indeed accounted for financial stability risks in their monetary policy decisions. Related econometric results are obtained by Apergis (2017), for a broader sample of 127 countries.

Contributions that have examined this issue in DSGE-FF models include Cúrdia and Woodford (2010, 2016), Agénor et al. (2013), Davis and Huang (2013), Gelain et al. (2013), Hirakata et al. (2013), Lambertini et al. (2013), Pirovano (2013), Gambacorta and Signoretti (2014), Agénor and Zilberman (2015), Bailliu et al. (2015), Benes and Kumhof (2015), Levine and Lima (2015), Tayler and Zilberman (2016), Suh (2017), Verona et al. (2017), Adrian and Liang (2018), Gelain et al. (2018), Gourio et al. (2018), Jacob and Munro (2018), Medina and Roldós (2018), Agénor and Flamini (2019), Ajello et al. (2019), and Rubio (2019). The focus of many of these studies has been on the trade-offs that may arise between price stability and financial stability when the only instrument available is a short-term policy interest rate, set on the basis of a Taylor-type rule, augmented to *lean against the wind* (that is, against the buildup of financial vulnerabilities). Some of these studies found that whether this strategy has benefits (in terms of both macroeconomic and financial stability) depends, in particular, on the financial variable included in the interest rate rule. These variables include levels, or deviations in, credit growth (Bailliu et al. 2015; Jacob and Munro 2018), credit-to-output ratios (Agénor and Zilberman 2015; Agénor and Flamini 2019), credit spreads (Cúrdia and Woodford 2010, 2016; Davis and Huang 2013; Hirakata et al. 2013; Levine and Lima 2015), asset prices (Gelain et al. 2013; Lambertini et al. 2013; Gambacorta and Signoretti 2014), and credit gaps (Gelain et al. 2018). By contrast, Ajello et al. (2019) found that it is the degree of parameter uncertainty—regarding, in particular, the relationship between the probability of a financial crisis and aggregate credit conditions—that determines the extent to which it is optimal to *lean against the wind*. For their part, Adrian and Liang (2018) found that tightening interest rates can mitigate financial vulnerabilities if it reduces the degree of risk-taking of financial intermediaries. In both cases, the central bank can achieve higher welfare by responding more strongly early on to avoid future unfavorable outcomes.

Other contributions have centered on the case where standard Taylor-type rules are complemented by countercyclical macroprudential rules, which respond to an operational target for financial stability, such as, again, credit growth or the credit-to-output ratio. Carrillo et al. (2017), De Paoli and Paustian (2017), Gelain and Ilbas (2017), and Agénor and Flamini (2019), for instance, all studied interactions and coordination between instruments in models where separate monetary and prudential authorities operate, with potentially different objectives. Some of these contributions focus more specifically on the interaction between monetary policy and countercyclical capital buffers, which is discussed in chapter 6. A common finding of the literature is that, in responding to financial shocks, countercyclical capital requirements may yield significant gains in terms of lower macroeconomic and financial volatility or higher welfare—regardless of the way monetary and capital requirements policies interact. In addition, several studies also found that when monetary policy also leans against the financial cycle, larger gains can be achieved in terms of either reduced volatility or higher welfare. At the same time, as is made clear later, most of these studies do not account for instrument manipulation costs and may therefore overstate the gains associated with more aggressive policies.

In the context of the model presented in chapter 4, *leaning against the wind* can be implemented by augmenting the Taylor rule to account for credit developments, in terms of investment loans:

$$\frac{1+i_t^T}{1+\tilde{\imath}^T} = \left(\frac{1+i_{t-1}^T}{1+\tilde{\imath}^T}\right)^{\chi} \left\{ \left(\frac{1+\pi_t}{1+\pi^T}\right)^{\varepsilon_1} \left(\frac{Y_t}{\tilde{Y}}\right)^{\varepsilon_2} \left(\frac{l_t^K}{l_{t-1}^K}\right)^{\varepsilon_3} \right\}^{1-\chi}, \tag{5.10}$$

where $\varepsilon_3 \geq 0$. In line with most of the literature on leaning against the wind, credit developments are measured in the central bank response function in terms of credit growth, rather than the loan-to-output ratio.[16]

Impulse response functions associated with the same negative credit spread shock as before and $\varepsilon_3 = 0.2$ (for illustrative purposes) are displayed in figure 5.4. The higher loan-to-output ratio induces the central bank to increase the policy and refinance rates, which mitigates the drop in the loan rate, the increase in investment, and the expansion of output. Initially inflation falls by a lot more (relatively speaking) than in the benchmark case, which implies that the expected real bond rate rises by more on impact, thereby magnifying somewhat the initial contraction in consumption and further dampening the rise in

16. Note also that credit growth, just like the other variables, enters contemporaneously in (5.10). In practice, data on credit flows are usually available at a higher frequency than data on inflation and output. However, this is not accounted for, to avoid biasing the results toward the inclusion of a credit variable in the reaction function of the central bank.

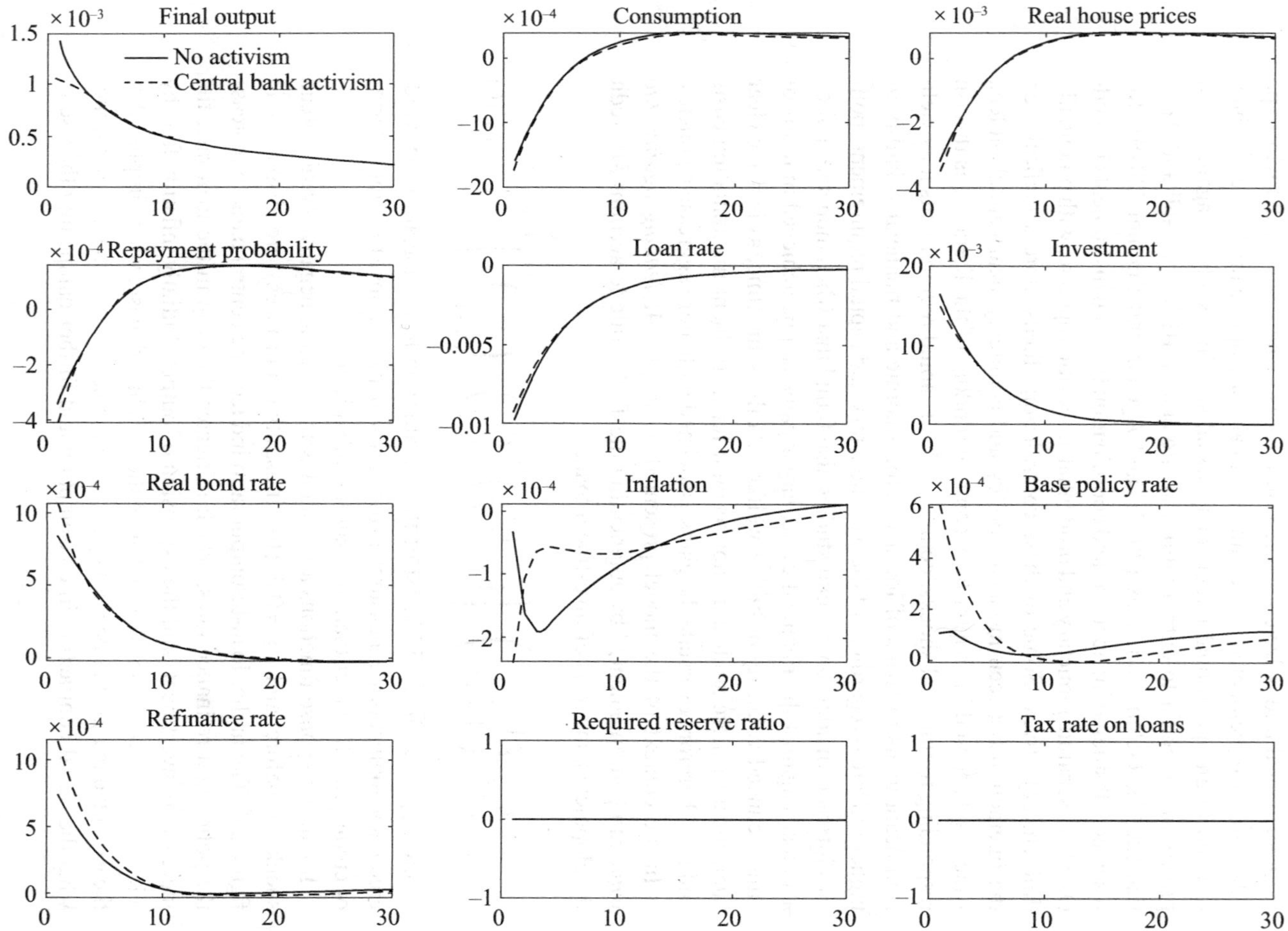

Figure 5.4 Negative credit spread shock: augmented Taylor rule. *Note*: See note to figure 5.2.

output. Thus, making monetary policy directly responsive to credit developments appears to generate stabilization gains in terms of both macroeconomic and financial variables. Yet, some of these effects appear to be fairly small—at least for the specific value of ε_3 used to illustrate the performance of the rule.

5.4 Optimal Simple Countercyclical Rules

In the foregoing discussion arbitrary values of the parameters characterizing the simple instrument rules (5.4) and (5.9), as well as the credit variable in the augmented Taylor rule (5.10), were considered for illustrative purposes. In principle, of course, these parameters should be set on the basis of an explicit criterion. This section begins with a general discussion of alternative approaches to policy optimization in DSGE models. It then considers the case where response parameters in simple countercyclical rules are solved for optimally, either by minimizing a policy loss function or by maximizing social welfare. The role of instrument adjustment costs is also examined.

5.4.1 Alternative Approaches to Policy Evaluation

Three approaches have been used in the DSGE literature to study optimal policies. The first focuses on using simple, implementable rules as defined in Schmitt-Grohé and Uribe (2007)—rules whereby macroeconomic or financial policy instruments are set (without violating standard nonnegativity constraints) on the basis of a few number of observable, aggregate variables to minimize a policy loss function attributed to the central bank or the regulator. The second consists of choosing simple instrument rules to maximize social welfare, generally defined in terms of the utility function of the representative household.[17] In the first case a linear approximation of the model is sufficient, whereas in the second a second-order approximation is necessary. The third approach is the Ramsey optimal policy (or Ramsey policy, for short), under which a social planner sets directly the path of some policy instrument, or instruments, so as to maximize social welfare, subject to the constraints imposed by the competitive market equilibrium.[18] In what follows the pros and

17. In models where there are several categories of households, such as models with patient and impatient borrowers following Iacoviello (2005) and possibly entrepeneurs who also consume, the welfare criterion is generally based on a weighted average of each group's utility function.

18. See Christiano et al. (2007*a*) for an explicit characterization of the Ramsey policy in some simple DSGE models, and Andrés et al. (2013) and Fujiwara and Teranishi (2017) for DSGE-FF applications. The latter contribution, in particular, provides a full derivation of the Ramsey policy in a model with monopolistic banking and staggered loan contracts.

cons of these different approaches are briefly discussed, from the perspective of both central banks and regulators.[19]

The first approach typically involves, for the central bank, minimizing an intertemporal loss function, defined as a discounted sum of current and expected future losses, with a quadratic period loss function in terms of the (squared) inflation gap and the (squared) output gap. The period loss function is generally justified as being consistent with flexible inflation targeting (Agénor 2002; Svensson 2010; Adolfson et al. 2011). The underlying rationale is that the central bank has a *dual mandate* or *extended simple mandate*, with inflation stability taking precedence over output stability as an objective. This is captured by imposing a higher weight on the former relative to the latter.[20]

As discussed by Svensson (2010), Agénor and Flamini (2019), and Lazopoulos and Gabriel (2019), simple mandates are appealing for a number of reasons. First, they facilitate communication of policy decisions. Second, to the extent that they are implemented by choosing robust instrument rules, simple mandates may perform well in a range of settings—including cases where there is some degree of model uncertainty. Third, the degree of accountability of policy authorities is enhanced when objectives are simple and measurable (Committee on the Global Financial System 2016). Fourth, should central banks, in particular, be mandated to maximize social welfare, there would be multiple distortions (such as those related to price distortions under monopolistic competition) that monetary policy would be called on to address—making communication, accountability, and implementation difficult in practice. Finally, although the Ramsey policy provides a rigorous benchmark as to what *can* (or *should*) be achieved by policy, offering as such a normative view of policy evaluation, from the perspective of policymakers it is an abstract construct that may not be easily implementable.

Indeed, although in theory society could design a mandate corresponding to the Ramsey policy, in practice, it does not. Instead, the mandate typically bestowed on central banks involves only a few specific target variables, such as price and output stability. Similarly, the institutional mandate that society delegates to regulators is generally focused on financial stability. Household welfare is hardly an operational objective for these institutions.

19. Throughout this book, and as in Svensson (2010), for instance, the term "optimal" is used to refer in general to optimization-based policies. In addition, where needed the term "mandate optimal" is used to refer to loss-minimizing policies and "Ramsey optimal" (or simply "Ramsey") to the Ramsey policy.

20. However, as noted by Debortoli et al. (2019), assigning a high weight to output in the loss function could be beneficial, as economic activity serves as an overall proxy for welfare-relevant variables not included in an extended simple mandate. In their analysis, the high weight on the output gap stems from a low elasticity of substitution between monopolistic goods, price indexation to lagged inflation by nonoptimizing firms, and a low interest rate sensitivity of demand.

These approaches are not necessarily incompatible. In the core DSGE model with frictionless financial markets, as shown by Rotemberg and Woodford (1997) and Woodford (2003), quadratic approximations of the welfare of a representative household result in a period loss function that also incorporates inflation and output gaps, with the relative weight of the output gap being a function of the underlying deep parameters in the economy—such as those governing the degree of price stickiness. The derivation of a microfounded loss function is also feasible in more elaborate DSGE models. For instance, in an open-economy setting without financial frictions, De Paoli (2009) showed that the utility-based loss function can be written as a quadratic expression of domestic inflation, the output gap, and the real exchange rate. More generally, Debortoli et al. (2019) discussed how simple loss functions for central banks can be viewed as parsimonious approximations to social welfare.

Similarly, in small-scale DSGE models with both nominal and financial frictions, social welfare can be related not only to inflation and output gap volatility but also to the volatility of financial wedges (Andrés et al. 2013; De Fiore and Tristani 2013; De Paoli and Paustian 2017). Andrés et al. (2013), for instance, in a model with (constrained) borrowers and savers, showed that the microfounded loss function contains additional terms capturing some aspects of heterogeneity between households. These terms include a *housing gap* and a *consumption gap*, with the former measuring the distortion in the distribution of collateralizable assets between household groups (savers and borrowers) and the latter measuring the gap between the consumption of these groups. In effect, the consumption gap represents the welfare loss due to imperfect risk-sharing, given that borrowers cannot smooth consumption as easily as they would want. De Fiore and Tristani (2013), for their part, derived a utility-based loss function that depends on the volatility of the nominal interest rate and credit spreads, in addition to inflation and output gap volatility. In the same vein, De Paoli and Paustian (2017), in a setting where credit market imperfections and macroprudential regulation are explicitly modeled, derived a quadratic utility-based welfare criterion in which appear not only the typical terms in standard central bank loss functions (the variability of inflation and the output gap) but also a measure of changes in credit market conditions. Some studies, such as Laureys et al. (2017), have shown that these insights carry over to more policy-relevant models of the type used to guide decision-making in central banks. Specifically, they found that (*a*) an extended monetary policy mandate that includes measures of bank credit availability leads to welfare-superior outcomes, compared to flexible inflation targeting, and (*b*) extended mandates are robust in the sense of producing similar levels of social welfare regardless of policymakers' relative preference for inflation stability versus output stability.

However, such approximations of household welfare remain to a very significant extent *model dependent* and reflect the particular distortions assumed in any given model. In addition, it is not clear that in any of the models where these approximations are derived that volatility in the credit-to-output ratio, in particular, is actually welfare-reducing. In fact, in any model that does not have an indeterminate financial structure (because, for instance, the financial system helps to overcome an agency problem), there typically are some fluctuations in the credit-to-output ratio that are efficient (or at least constrained efficient) in response to some shocks. Kiley and Sim (2017), for instance, provided an example where a tax-like macroprudential instrument rule—of the type used throughout this book—can adversely constrain efficient credit expansion, in contrast to the Ramsey policy. Similarly, Medina and Roldós (2018) found that if the source of a credit boom is a productivity shock, and the macroprudential authority reacts mechanically to credit (rather than to the effects of the shock) through a simple operational rule, then welfare might decrease. Under these conditions, minimizing measures of (macroeconomic and financial) volatility instead of maximizing welfare itself may give misleading results. Finally, there is a need to study further the design of policy objective functions and simple instrument rules in an environment where central banks face uncertainty about the structure of the underlying economy, as considered in Ajello et al. (2019), for instance, or cannot implement their desired policies because of lags or credibility problems.

In sum, the debate on whether policy evaluation should be based on loss function minimization and welfare maximization, and whether focusing on simple, implementable rules is preferable to the Ramsey policy, has not been settled. The policy loss minimization approach is more consistent with the existence in the real world of delegated mandates, but it does not account for the fact that fluctuations in the variable on which the instrument rule is based can be, to some extent at least, efficient. The welfare maximization approach is more normative in nature and consistent with the fundamental principles of economics. It is therefore important to examine how household welfare is affected by central bank policy and prudential regulation. However, in its standard form it does not account for the possibility that society may also want particular policymakers to attach more weight to a specific objective, consistent with separate institutional mandates.[21] As noted earlier, there are conditions under which

21. An intermediate approach, involving maximization of a welfare criterion that adjusts the utility of the representative household by an institution-specific target variable (for instance, inflation volatility for the central bank and volatility of the loan-to-output ratio for the regulator) is discussed in Bodenstein et al. (2019) and Agénor and Jackson (2019). The latter contribution also examines the determination of the optimal weight on that additional target.

the policy loss function can be derived directly from a second-order approximation of household utility. But the solution tends to be model-specific and yields loss functions that are relatively complex, especially when financial frictions are introduced. The Ramsey policy provides a rigorous and conceptually sound approach to policy evaluation, but it is often difficult to derive in richer models—the so-called *curse of dimensionality*, as discussed by Maliar et al. (2011)—and when a solution is obtained it may generate implausibly volatile instrument paths. In addition, there are cases where optimized simple instrument rules—especially interest rate rules that respond aggressively to inflation fluctuations—can generate levels of welfare that are reasonably close to those obtained with the Ramsey policy, as shown, for instance, by Levin et al. (2006), Schmitt-Grohé and Uribe (2007), Adjemian et al. (2008), Galí (2015, chap. 4), Cúrdia and Woodford (2016), and Kiley and Sim (2017). In Kiley and Sim (2017), in particular, this is the case even when monetary policy is set on the basis of a standard Taylor rule and macroprudential regulation is set on the basis of the Ramsey policy.

However, as noted in this book's introduction and overview, the set of policy rules that can be deemed to be "simple" and "implementable" may be fairly broad. In particular, while it is reasonable (as noted earlier) to consider credit as a proximate target for macroprudential regulation, an operational definition of "excessive credit expansion" is not straightforward. Such a definition could be based, in equally plausible ways, on credit growth, the credit-to-output ratio, the risky credit-to-bank capital ratio, credit spreads, total credit or only *uncollateralized* credit (conceptually a more relevant indicator of financial fragility), and so on, all in terms of deviations from a reference value or benchmark. Which indicator and which reference value is chosen could affect significantly the performance of any particular instrument rule. The implications are twofold: Instrument rules should be evaluated systematically across a range of variables that can be used to trigger their activation, and choosing across alternative specifications should involve not only operational considerations (frequency of observation of the triggering variable, reliability of first estimates, and so on), which are clearly important in practice, but also a normative comparison with a benchmark.

The view in this book is that the Ramsey policy (if it can be computed) provides a natural benchmark for assessing the performance of alternative specifications of simple instrument rules. Thus, later on in this chapter, after considering first how simple rules (both individually and jointly) operate and studying outcomes under both policy loss minimization and welfare maximization, the performance of these rules will be compared to the Ramsey policy. The use of alternative triggering variables will also be discussed, although to avoid a cumbersome taxonomy, not as comprehensively as the foregoing discussion suggests.

5.4.2 Policy Loss Minimization

Consider first the case where the central bank is concerned with macroeconomic stability and the regulator with financial stability. Macroeconomic (in)stability can be defined in terms of a *macroeconomic stability index*, which is specified as a weighted average of the asymptotic conditional variances (that is, subject to the initial state of the economy being the nonstochastic steady state) of inflation deviations, σ_{π}^2, and cyclical output deviations, σ_Y^2:

$$\mathcal{LF}_t^M = \sigma_{\pi}^2 + \gamma^M \sigma_Y^2, \tag{5.11}$$

where $\gamma^M > 0$ is the weight on output deviations. In general, γ^M is set to a value significantly less than unity, to reflect a greater concern with price stability. This is consistent with the evidence aimed at assessing the revealed preferences of central banks. In addition, as noted earlier, under certain conditions a loss function similar to (5.11) can be derived as a second-order approximation to a representative household utility function.

Similarly, financial (in)stability can be defined in terms of a *financial stability index*. In the literature, two specifications are commonly adopted. The first is in terms of a *narrow* index, denoted $\mathcal{LF}_t^{F,N}$, which in the present case can be specified in terms of the variance of the ratio of investment loans to output, l_t^K/Y_t.[22] The second is in terms of a *broad* index, denoted $\mathcal{LF}_t^{F,B}$, which can be specified here in terms of a weighted average of the variances of the investment loan-to-output ratio and the variance of real house prices, p_t^H. Thus,

$$\mathcal{LF}_t^F = \begin{cases} \mathcal{LF}_t^{F,N} = \sigma_{l^K/Y}^2 & \text{Narrow index} \\ \mathcal{LF}_t^{F,B} = \gamma^F \sigma_{l^K/Y}^2 + (1-\gamma^F)\sigma_{p^H}^2 & \text{Broad index} \end{cases}, \tag{5.12}$$

where $\gamma^F \in (0, 1)$ reflects the relative weight attached to the volatility of the loan-to-output ratio. In general, γ^F is set to a value greater than 0.5, to reflect the fact that, as discussed in chapter 1, the evidence on fluctuations in asset prices prior to financial crises appears to be less robust than that on credit.

Finally, as in Agénor et al. (2013) for instance, a composite *economic stability index*, $\mathcal{LF}_t$, which combines the objectives of the central bank and the regulator, can be defined as a weighted average of the two indexes,

$$\mathcal{LF}_t = \gamma \mathcal{LF}_t^M + (1-\gamma)\mathcal{LF}_t^F, \tag{5.13}$$

22. The volatility of credit growth is also used in a number of contributions.

where $\gamma \in (0, 1)$. If society values equally macroeconomic stability and financial stability, for instance, the weight γ would be at 0.5.[23]

5.4.3 Welfare Maximization

Alternatively, suppose that the central bank's objective is to maximize social welfare, defined in terms of the utility of the representative household. To do so welfare calculations must be based on a second-order approximation to the household's period utility function around the deterministic steady state. Indeed, as demonstrated in several contributions (Kim and Kim 2003, 2007; Schmitt-Grohé and Uribe 2004; Benigno and Woodford 2005), in a stochastic environment a first-order approximation is not adequate to perform welfare comparisons accurately. Moreover, a correct second-order approximation of the equilibrium welfare function requires also a second-order approximation to the model characterizing the economy.

The first step therefore is to solve for the second-order approximation of the utility function. From equation (4.1) in chapter 4, the present discounted value of the household's expected utility function is

$$U_t = \mathbb{E}_t \sum_{s=0}^{\infty} \Lambda^s u_{t+s},$$

where u_t is the period utility function defined as

$$u_t = \frac{C_t^{1-\varsigma^{-1}}}{1-\varsigma^{-1}} - \int_0^1 \frac{\eta_N (N_t^j)^{1+\psi_N}}{1+\psi_N} dj + \ln x_t^{\eta_x} + \ln H_t^{\eta_H}, \qquad (5.14)$$

and all variables and parameters are as defined previously.

Given that the housing market is always in equilibrium and that the supply of housing is constant, the utility benefit from housing services is also constant and can be ignored. Further, following common practice (see, for instance, Bergin et al. 2007; Berger 2008; Lartey 2008; De Fiore and Tristani 2013), real money balances are ignored when evaluating welfare. This procedure is sometimes justified by the fact that the preference parameter for liquidity services is set at a small value, that is, $\eta_x \rightarrow 0$; see, for instance, Obstfeld and Rogoff (1996, p. 684). This is indeed the case here, as discussed in chapter 4 ($\eta_x = 0.001$). However, as noted in Agénor et al. (2018*b*), this practice can be rationalized at a deeper level by noting that there is a well-established *functional equivalence* between using money as an argument of the utility function and either entering it into liquidity costs or a shopping-time technology (Feenstra 1986; Croushore

23. Agénor et al. (2014*a*, 2018*a*) considered different weights to macroeconomic and financial stability in a related analysis for an open economy. See also chapter 9.

1993). Given this equivalence, accounting for money in the utility function, as is done in (5.14), is mainly a matter of convenience rather than a reflection of a firm belief that it provides proper microfoundations for why money is used. Ignoring it when evaluating welfare would therefore be a sensible approach.

In any case, the truncated period utility function can be written as

$$u_t = u(C_t, N_t) \simeq \frac{C_t^{1-\varsigma^{-1}}}{1-\varsigma^{-1}} - \eta_N \frac{N_t^{1+\psi_N}}{1+\psi_N}. \tag{5.15}$$

Taking a second-order approximation to $u()$ in the vicinity of the initial, deterministic steady state yields

$$u_t \simeq \tilde{u} + u_C(\tilde{C},\tilde{N})(C_t - \tilde{C}) + u_N(\tilde{C},\tilde{N})(N_t - \tilde{N}) + \frac{u_{CC}(\tilde{C},\tilde{N})}{2}(C_t - \tilde{C})^2$$
$$+ \frac{u_{NN}(\tilde{C},\tilde{N})}{2}(N_t - \tilde{N})^2 + u_{CN}(\tilde{C},\tilde{N})(C_t - \tilde{C})(N_t - \tilde{N}) + \mathcal{O}(3),$$

where

$$\tilde{u} = \frac{\tilde{C}^{1-\varsigma^{-1}}}{1-\varsigma^{-1}} - \frac{\eta_N \tilde{N}^{1+\psi_N}}{1+\psi_N},$$

and $\mathcal{O}(3)$ denotes terms of third order or higher. Ignoring these higher-order terms, and noting that $u_{CN}(\tilde{C},\tilde{N}) = 0$, this approximation can be rewritten as

$$u_t \simeq \tilde{u} + \tilde{C}^{-\varsigma^{-1}}(C_t - \tilde{C}) - \eta_N \tilde{N}^{\psi_N}(N_t - \tilde{N}) - \frac{\tilde{C}^{-\varsigma^{-1}-1}}{2\varsigma}(C_t - \tilde{C})^2$$
$$- \eta_N \psi_N \frac{\tilde{N}^{\psi_N - 1}}{2}(N_t - \tilde{N})^2,$$

or again

$$u_t \simeq \tilde{u} + \tilde{C}^{1-\varsigma^{-1}}\left(\frac{C_t - \tilde{C}}{\tilde{C}}\right) - \eta_N \tilde{N}^{1+\psi_N}\left(\frac{N_t - \tilde{N}}{\tilde{N}}\right) - \frac{\tilde{C}^{1-\varsigma^{-1}}}{2\varsigma}\left(\frac{C_t - \tilde{C}}{\tilde{C}}\right)^2$$
$$- \eta_N \psi_N \frac{\tilde{N}^{1+\psi_N}}{2}\left(\frac{N_t - \tilde{N}}{\tilde{N}}\right)^2.$$

Equivalently, with $\widehat{x}_t = \ln(x_t/\tilde{x}) \simeq (x_t - \tilde{x})/\tilde{x}$, this expression becomes

$$u_t \simeq \tilde{u} + \tilde{C}^{1-\varsigma^{-1}}\hat{C}_t - \eta_N \tilde{N}^{1+\psi_N}\hat{N}_t - \frac{\tilde{C}^{1-\varsigma^{-1}}}{2\varsigma}\hat{C}_t^2 - \eta_N \psi_N \frac{\tilde{N}^{1+\psi_N}}{2}\hat{N}_t^2,$$

where $\hat{C}_t$ and $\hat{N}_t$ denote, as in chapter 4, log-deviations of C_t and N_t from their steady-state values.

Thus, the conditional expectation of the present discounted value of the household's expected utility function can be approximated by

$$\mathcal{U}_t \simeq \frac{1}{1-\Lambda}\left\{\tilde{u} - \frac{\tilde{C}^{1-\varsigma^{-1}}}{2\varsigma}\text{Var}(\hat{C}_t) - \eta_N\psi_N\frac{\tilde{N}^{1+\psi_N}}{2}\text{Var}(\hat{N}_t)\right\}, \tag{5.16}$$

where $\text{Var}(x_t)$ denotes the conditional variance of x_t, calculated from period t to infinity. In deriving (5.16), the fact that the conditional expectation of log-deviations from steady state is zero, that is, $\mathbb{E}_t(\widehat{x}_t) = 0$, was used.

Thus, to compute welfare under alternative instrument rules (all of which consistent with the same nonstochastic steady-state equilibrium), it is sufficient to compute the conditional variances of consumption and employment in the model and plug them into equation (5.16). If, for instance, the welfare of a countercyclical instrument rule is calculated as $\mathcal{U}_t^c$ and that associated with the status quo is $\mathcal{U}_t^b < \mathcal{U}_t^c$, countercyclical policy welfare dominates the no-activism regime. To measure how much better countercyclical policy is, compared to no policy intervention, a basic measure is thus the percentage change in welfare associated with activism, which can be defined as $\mathcal{U}_t^c/\mathcal{U}_t^b - 1$.

A more general approach to quantifying the relative welfare gain associated with pursuing a given policy relative to no intervention is the one proposed by Lucas (1987, 1990). It is based on calculating the percentage of the consumption stream under no activism that ensures that households are as well off under no policy intervention than under activism—that is, by calculating *welfare compensating variations*. Specifically, consider the welfare gain under an active countercyclical rule of the type (5.4), for instance, associated with $\chi_2^R > 0$, relative to the case where no countercyclical policy is implemented so that $\chi_2^R = 0$. This can be calculated as the percentage change in consumption along its path under the status quo that would leave the representative household indifferent between living in an economy where the countercyclical policy rule is under operation, $\chi_2^R > 0$, and an economy with no policy activism. Thus, using the truncated utility function (5.15), the welfare gain associated with intervention relative to no activism is measured by the constant β, which is solved from the condition

$$\mathbb{E}_t\sum_{s=0}^{\infty}\Lambda^s u[(1+\beta)C_{t+s}^b, N_{t+s}^b] = \mathbb{E}_t\sum_{s=0}^{\infty}\Lambda^s u(C_{t+s}^c, N_{t+s}^c), \tag{5.17}$$

or equivalently, using (5.15),

$$\mathbb{E}_t\sum_{s=0}^{\infty}\Lambda^s\left\{\frac{[(1+\beta)C_{t+s}^b]^{1-\varsigma^{-1}}}{1-\varsigma^{-1}} - \frac{\eta_N(N_{t+s}^b)^{1+\psi_N}}{1+\psi_N}\right\} \tag{5.18}$$

$$= \mathbb{E}_t \sum_{s=0}^{\infty} \Lambda^s \left\{ \frac{(C^c_{t+s})^{1-\varsigma^{-1}}}{1-\varsigma^{-1}} - \frac{\eta_N (N^c_{t+s})^{1+\psi_N}}{1+\psi_N} \right\},$$

where $\{C^h_{t+s}\}_{s=0}^{\infty}$ and $\{N^h_{t+s}\}_{s=0}^{\infty}$ are solution paths under the status quo ($h=b$) and activism ($h=c$)—that is, $\chi_2^R = \chi_2^{R,c}$. In the particular case where $\varsigma \to 1$, the term $[(1+\beta)(C^h_t)]^{1-\varsigma^{-1}}/(1-\varsigma^{-1})$ tends to $\ln(1+\beta)C^h_t$ (by application of L'Hôpital's rule) and the above expression can be written as

$$\mathbf{U}^b + \mathbb{E}_t \sum_{s=0}^{\infty} \Lambda^s \ln(1+\beta) = \mathbf{U}^b + \frac{\ln(1+\beta)}{1-\Lambda} = \mathbf{U}^c,$$

where $\mathbf{U}^h = \mathbb{E}_t \sum_{s=0}^{\infty} \Lambda^s \left\{ \ln C^h_{t+s} - \eta_N (1+\psi_N)^{-1} (N^h_{t+s})^{1+\psi_N} \right\}$. Thus, β can be written as a function of the difference between two infinite sums:

$$\beta = \exp[(1-\Lambda)(\mathbf{U}^c - \mathbf{U}^b)] - 1 \simeq (1-\Lambda)(\mathbf{U}^c - \mathbf{U}^b).$$

In the general case, the fraction β can be computed from the solution of the second-order approximation to the truncated utility function, given in (5.16), and the model's equilibrium around the deterministic steady state. From (5.16) and (5.18),

$$\frac{1}{1-\Lambda} \left\{ \tilde{u} - (1+\beta)^{1-\varsigma^{-1}} \frac{\tilde{C}^{1-\varsigma^{-1}}}{2\varsigma} \text{Var}(\hat{C}^b_t) - \eta_N \psi_N \frac{(\tilde{N})^{1+\psi_N}}{2} \text{Var}(\hat{N}^b_t) \right\}$$
$$= \frac{1}{1-\Lambda} \left\{ \tilde{u} - \frac{\tilde{C}^{1-\varsigma^{-1}}}{2\varsigma} \text{Var}(\hat{C}^c_t) - \eta_N \psi_N \frac{\tilde{N}^{1+\psi_N}}{2} \text{Var}(\hat{N}^c_t) \right\},$$

or again

$$(1+\beta)^{1-\varsigma^{-1}} \frac{\tilde{C}^{1-\varsigma^{-1}}}{2\varsigma} \text{Var}(\hat{C}^b_t) + \eta_N \psi_N \frac{\tilde{N}^{1+\psi_N}}{2} \text{Var}(\hat{N}^b_t)$$
$$= \frac{\tilde{C}^{1-\varsigma^{-1}}}{2\varsigma} \text{Var}(\hat{C}^c_t) + \eta_N \psi_N \frac{\tilde{N}^{1+\psi_N}}{2} \text{Var}(\hat{N}^c_t),$$

or equivalently

$$(1+\beta)^{1-\varsigma^{-1}} \Gamma^C \text{Var}(\hat{C}^b_t) + \Gamma^N \text{Var}(\hat{N}^b_t) = \Gamma^C \text{Var}(\hat{C}^c_t) + \Gamma^N \text{Var}(\hat{N}^c_t),$$

where the weights on the variances of consumption and employment are, respectively,

$$\Gamma^C = \frac{\tilde{C}^{1-\varsigma^{-1}}}{2\varsigma}, \quad \Gamma^N = \eta_N \psi_N \frac{\tilde{N}^{1+\psi_N}}{2}.$$

This expression can be solved for β:

$$\beta = \left\{ \frac{\Gamma^C \text{Var}(\hat{C}_t^c) + \Gamma^N[\text{Var}(\hat{N}_t^c) - \text{Var}(\hat{N}_t^b)]}{\Gamma^C \text{Var}(\hat{C}_t^b)} \right\}^{1/(1-\varsigma^{-1})} - 1. \tag{5.19}$$

Thus, a positive value of β denotes a welfare gain.

The same approach can be followed to compare the performance of a simple countercyclical rule relative to the Ramsey policy. In that case, the benchmark is no longer the no-activism regime but the Ramsey-optimal allocation. Thus, analogously to (5.17), the welfare loss associated with a particular countercyclical rule relative to that allocation is measured by the constant β', which is defined as the percentage change in consumption under the simple rule necessary to make the level of welfare under that rule identical to that achieved under the Ramsey policy:

$$\mathbb{E}_t \sum_{s=0}^{\infty} \Lambda^s u[(1-\beta')C_{t+s}^r, N_{t+s}^r] = \mathbb{E}_t \sum_{s=0}^{\infty} \Lambda^s u(C_{t+s}^c, N_{t+s}^c), \tag{5.20}$$

where $\{C_{t+s}^h\}_{s=0}^{\infty}$ and $\{N_{t+s}^h\}_{s=0}^{\infty}$ are solution paths under the Ramsey policy ($h=r$) and activism ($h=c$). A positive value of β' indicates therefore that society is now worse off by adopting the simple rule.[24] Alternatively, the performance of the simple rule can also be assessed, as noted earlier, by calculating the percentage change in welfare with respect to the Ramsey policy. Using the approximation (5.16), this expression is $\mathcal{U}_t^c/\mathcal{U}_t^r - 1$.

Finally, it is worth noting that an alternative approach followed in the literature—including Kollmann (2002), Straub and Tchakarov (2004), Bergin et al. (2007), and Kolasa and Lombardo (2014)—is to solve for *unconditional* welfare. In that case the welfare gain under activism is expressed in terms of the additional proportion of each period's *steady-state* consumption that the representative household would need to receive in a deterministic world (under no activism) to ensure that its welfare is equal to the expected conditional utility in the stochastic world (when the countercyclical rule is implemented). Thus, the solution of β is now such that

$$\sum_{s=0}^{\infty} \Lambda^s u[(1+\beta)\tilde{C}^b, \tilde{N}^b] = \mathbb{E}_t \sum_{s=0}^{\infty} \Lambda^s u(C_{t+s}^c, N_{t+s}^c),$$

24. In the particular case where $\varsigma \to 1$, derivations simillar to those conducted before give $\beta' = 1 - \exp[(1-\Lambda)(\mathbf{U}^c - \mathbf{U}^r)]$, where $\mathbf{U}^h = \mathbb{E}_t \sum_{s=0}^{\infty} \Lambda^s \left\{ \ln C_{t+s}^h - \eta_N (1+\psi_N)^{-1} (N_{t+s}^h)^{1+\psi_N} \right\}$ and $h = c, r$. To obtain a numerical estimate of β', $\mathbf{U}^c$ and $\mathbf{U}^r$ can again be approximated up to second-order accuracy.

which implies again that $\beta > 0$ corresponds to a welfare gain. Thus, while conditional welfare captures changes in utility during the transition period (given that it is defined as a discounted sum of period utilities), unconditional welfare captures only the long-run steady-state changes in expected utility. However, even though the type of simple rules considered in this book do not have any first-order effects—implying that the deterministic steady state of the model is the same across activism and no activism—the two policy regimes are associated with different stochastic steady states. Neglecting welfare effects occurring during the transition from one steady state to another could therefore be misleading.[25]

5.4.4 Accounting for Instrument Adjustment Costs

A common justification for the high degree of statistical significance of the lagged endogenous variable in estimating interest rate policy reaction functions, in developed and developing countries alike, is the existence of adjustment costs. These costs, which relate to *changes* in interest rates, are often explicitly introduced in policy loss functions to reflect an interest rate smoothing incentive for the monetary authority. Indeed, in practice central banks rarely change policy rates by more than a quarter of a percentage point at a time in normal circumstances. In turn, this smoothing incentive is a fairly broad rationale and applies to the use of policy instruments in general: It is sensible to assume that policymakers internalize the potential costs of acting too aggressively. In theoretical models, ignoring these costs may lead to a corner solution in which the optimal policy involves full stabilization.[26]

In the present setting, to account for instrument smoothing the policy loss functions and the welfare function defined earlier can be adjusted to reflect a cost associated with changes in the relevant policy tool—the interest rate for the central bank and the macroprudential instrument for the regulator. Specifically, assuming that the macroprudential policy instrument is the required reserve ratio, equations (5.11) and (5.12) can be replaced by

$$\mathcal{LF}_t^M = \gamma^M \sigma_\pi^2 + (1-\gamma^M)\sigma_Y^2 + \varkappa_C \sigma_{\Delta i^R}^2, \tag{5.21}$$

25. See Kim and Kim (2003, 2018) for a further discussion.

26. Examples of analytical contributions where changes in policy instrument are accounted for in the central bank's policy loss function include Woodford (2003, chap. 6), Taylor and Williams (2010), Adolfson et al. (2011), De Fiore and Tristani (2013), and Debortoli et al. (2019), with respect to monetary policy, and Angelini et al. (2014) and Binder et al. (2018), with respect to both monetary and macroprudential policies. Söderström et al. (2005) and Givens (2012) provided evidence on the preference for interest rate smoothing (in terms of changes in policy rates) for the United States. However, their estimates vary significantly across policy regimes.

$$\mathcal{LF}_t^F = \begin{cases} \mathcal{LF}_t^F = \sigma_{l^K/Y}^2 + \varkappa_R \sigma_{\Delta\mu}^2 & \text{Narrow index} \\ \mathcal{LF}_t^F = \gamma^F \sigma_{l^K/Y}^2 + (1-\gamma^F)\sigma_{p^H}^2 + \varkappa_R \sigma_{\Delta\mu}^2 & \text{Broad index} \end{cases}, \tag{5.22}$$

where $\varkappa_C, \varkappa_R \geq 0$ are cost parameters. Similar expressions hold when the macroprudential tool is the tax rate on loans. The composite stability index remains as defined in (5.13).

For the welfare approach, the objective of the central bank is now no longer to maximize U_t but to maximize instead

$$W_t^C = \mathbb{E}_t \sum_{s=0}^{\infty} \Lambda^s u_{t+s} - \varkappa_C \mathbb{E}_t \sum_{s=0}^{\infty} \Lambda^s (i_{t+s}^R - i_{t+s-1}^R)^2, \tag{5.23}$$

whereas for the regulator, the objective becomes, with the required reserve ratio used as a macroprudential instrument,

$$W_t^R = \mathbb{E}_t \sum_{s=0}^{\infty} \Lambda^s u_{t+s} - \varkappa_R \mathbb{E}_t \sum_{s=0}^{\infty} \Lambda^s (\mu_{t+s} - \mu_{t+s-1})^2. \tag{5.24}$$

Using the second-order approximation of discounted utility based on the truncated utility function (5.15), as defined in (5.16), and using the approximation

$$\mathbb{E}_t \sum_{s=0}^{\infty} \Lambda^s (i_{t+s}^R - i_{t+s-1}^R)^2 \simeq \frac{\text{Var}(\Delta i_t^R)}{1-\Lambda},$$

the adjusted welfare function of the central bank, equation (5.23), can be approximated by

$$\mathcal{W}_t^C \simeq \frac{1}{1-\Lambda} \left\{ \tilde{u} - \frac{\tilde{C}^{1-\varsigma^{-1}}}{2\varsigma} \text{Var}(\hat{C}_t) - \eta_N \psi_N \frac{\tilde{N}^{1+\psi_N}}{2} \text{Var}(\hat{N}_t) \right\} - \frac{\varkappa_C}{1-\Lambda} \text{Var}(\Delta i_t^R). \tag{5.25}$$

Similarly, for the regulator, using the approximation

$$\mathbb{E}_t \sum_{s=0}^{\infty} \Lambda^s (\mu_{t+s} - \mu_{t+s-1})^2 \simeq \frac{\text{Var}(\Delta \mu_t)}{1-\Lambda},$$

the adjusted welfare objective (5.24) can be approximated by

$$\mathcal{W}_t^R \simeq \frac{1}{1-\Lambda} \left\{ \tilde{u} - \frac{\tilde{C}^{1-\varsigma^{-1}}}{2\varsigma} \text{Var}(\hat{C}_t) - \eta_N \psi_N \frac{\tilde{N}^{1+\psi_N}}{2} \text{Var}(\hat{N}_t) \right\} - \frac{\varkappa_R}{1-\Lambda} \text{Var}(\Delta \mu_t), \tag{5.26}$$

and similarly when the macroprudential instrument is the tax rate on loans.

Thus, while under the loss minimization approach the two authorities have objectives that differ both in terms of their mandate and in the effect of instrument adjustment costs, under the welfare maximization approach the difference is only in terms of the latter. In the absence of these costs ($\varkappa_C = \varkappa_R = 0$), the objective function would be the same.[27]

5.5 Tinbergen's Principle and Coordination

A common policy prescription, referred to as *Tinbergen's effective assignment principle*, or simply *Tinbergen's principle*, is that achieving n policy objectives requires n instruments. In this particular case, achieving both macroeconomic stability and financial stability requires two instruments—the base policy rate and a macroprudential instrument, be it the required reserve ratio, a tax on loans, or (as discussed in chapter 6) a countercyclical capital adequacy ratio. Indeed, in the debate that followed the global financial crisis, some observers argued, based on Tinbergen's principle—or what Stein (2013) referred to as the *decoupling philosophy*—that monetary policy should remain squarely focused on macroeconomic stability whereas macroprudential policy should focus solely on financial stability. This is the view adopted by Svensson (2017) and Kockerols and Kok (2019), for instance.[28]

The application of Tinbergen's principle allows policymakers to achieve exactly and continuously (in the case of dynamic rules) its two targets. In that sense, the two instruments are necessarily *complements*. However, strictly speaking, the principle holds only in a deterministic environment and only if targets must be achieved precisely; in practice, policymakers that carry a mandate imposed by society aim to minimize deviations from their assigned targets rather than realize them exactly and (in a dynamic setting) continuously. Moreover, in a stochastic environment, if the goal is to minimize deviations from targets over time rather than achieve them exactly and continuously, it is possible that each instrument may affect both targets in the same direction (in terms of lower volatility, for instance). A similar result may hold if the goal of

27. As noted earlier, different welfare objectives could be related to asymmetric preferences, themselves related to different institutional mandates. See Agénor and Jackson (2019) for a discussion.

28. However, other observers have argued that some of the assumptions underlying this line of analysis—in particular, in Svensson's analysis, the fact that the policy response does not affect the cost of financial crises and that crises occur with a given frequency and do not result in permanent output losses—tend to underestimate the costs of crises and limit the potential benefits of a monetary policy response (Filardo and Rungcharoenkitku 2016; Gourio et al. 2018). In addition, incorporating the role of asset prices, credit, and bank risk-taking may significantly alter the cost-benefit analysis of the use of monetary policy (Adrian and Liang 2018).

policymakers is more normative in nature and involves maximizing social welfare as a single objective: A combination of instruments may generate higher welfare than the use of a single instrument, although this may not hold when (as discussed earlier) the cost of instrument manipulation is accounted for. At the same time, when the use of policy tools is costly and the social welfare function is adjusted to reflect that cost—as in (5.25) and (5.26), for instance—the aggressive use of a single instrument may entail rapidly decreasing marginal returns. As a result, a combination of instruments may help to achieve higher welfare.

An important question, therefore, is whether monetary policy can be a (partial) *substitute* to macroprudential policy by making it responsive to (some measure of) financial (in)stability—a rationale for the *leaning against the wind* policy discussed earlier. Due to decreasing marginal returns to each instrument, they may reinforce each other. It is therefore important to study jointly augmented monetary policy rules and macroprudential rules to understand whether they should be combined. A related question, of course, is whether by *leaning against the wind* policymakers are better off in terms of their specific goals, or welfare, compared to the case where both policy instruments are used.

5.6 Results for a Credit Spread Shock

This section considers the optimal determination of response parameters in both the augmented monetary policy and the simple macroprudential rules taken independently, as well as when these policies are used jointly in response to the same negative credit spread shock considered earlier in this chapter. By doing so, the scope and validity of Tinbergen's principle and the benefit of coordination can be assessed. At the same time, for comparative purposes, both policy minimization and welfare maximization criteria are considered.

To perform the calculations, in the macroeconomic stability index (5.11) coefficient γ^M is set at 0.3, to reflect a greater concern with price stability. This is consistent with the evidence on central bank preferences in a flexible inflation-targeting regime, as documented by Adolfson et al. (2011), Palma and Portugal (2014), Paez-Farrell (2015), and Carney (2017), in both middle- and high-income countries. In the broad financial stability index (5.12), the weight on the volatility of the loan-to-output ratio in the broad index is set at 0.7, which implies therefore a weight of 0.3 on the volatility of real house prices. This captures the evidence on credit as a more robust predictor of episodes of severe financial stress.

The performance of simple rules, both independently and jointly, and the relevance of Tinbergen's principle for the conduct of monetary and macroprudential policies can be evaluated by comparing the policy losses and welfare gains across three regimes:

Regime A: Leaning against the wind, where the central bank uses the augmented Taylor rule (5.10), so that $\varepsilon_3 \geq 0$, and the regulator does not act at all, so that $\chi_2^R = 0$ in (5.4) or $\chi_2^L = 0$ in (5.9).

Regime B: Separate mandates, in which the central bank uses the standard Taylor rule and therefore focuses on inflation and output stability, so that $\varepsilon_3 = 0$ in (5.10), and the regulator responds as needed to credit fluctuations, with either $\chi_2^R \geq 0$ in (5.4) or $\chi_2^L \geq 0$ in (5.9). This separation of mandates is consistent with the fact that, as noted earlier, in practice distinct institutions are often made responsible for achieving narrower goals on the grounds of transparency and accountability.

Regime C: Coordination, in which the central bank uses an augmented Taylor rule and the regulator responds to credit fluctuations, with the response parameters $\varepsilon_3 \geq 0$ in (5.10) and either $\chi_2^R \geq 0$ in (5.4) or $\chi_2^L \geq 0$ in (5.9), solved for jointly.

It is important to note that coordination does not necessarily imply that *both* institutions should respond to financial stability considerations; it is possible, for instance, that the optimal policy requires an aggressive monetary (regulatory) response to credit fluctuations, with the regulator (central bank) not acting at all. If so, coordination would work against (in favor of) Tinbergen's principle. In general, this will depend on the structure of the model, the nature of the shocks affecting the economy, and the cost of instrument manipulation for both types of policymakers.

In all three cases, the optimal values are calculated so as to either minimize the adjusted economic stability index (5.13), with its components defined in (5.21) and (5.22), or maximize the composite welfare function, defined as

$$\mathcal{W}_t = \gamma \mathcal{W}_t^C + (1-\gamma)\mathcal{W}_t^R, \tag{5.27}$$

where $\mathcal{W}_t^C$ and $\mathcal{W}_t^R$ correspond to the second-order approximations in (5.25) and (5.26), and $\gamma \in (0,1)$ is the weight attached to the central bank's welfare function. As noted earlier, $\mathcal{W}_t^C = \mathcal{W}_t^R$ when $\varkappa_C = \varkappa_R = 0$.

Finding that under regime B χ_2^R or $\chi_2^L > 0$ (strictly positive) would provide support for Tinbergen's principle, given that, by construction, $\varepsilon_3 = 0$ under that regime. The two instruments are then complements. Alternatively, finding that χ_2^R or $\chi_2^L = 0$ under regime B, while $\varepsilon_3 > 0$ under regime A, would work against the principle—in that case the instruments can be described as substitutes. In addition, if under complementarity the difference in policy losses between regimes B and A is negative, or the difference in welfare between the two is positive, a narrow application of Tinbergen's principle (in the form of a strict separation of mandates) would generate superior outcomes compared to *leaning against the wind* (regime A).

Comparing the results under Regime C with those obtained under B, and finding that *both* $\varepsilon_3 > 0$ and χ_2^R or $\chi_2^L > 0$ under C while $\varepsilon_3 = 0$ (by construction) and χ_2^R or $\chi_2^L > 0$ under B, would imply that coordination is not consistent with Tinbergen's principle. The instruments can be viewed as *partial* substitutes. In addition, if the difference in policy losses between C and B is negative, or the difference in welfare between the two is positive, that would imply that coordination performs better than a narrow application of Tinbergen's principle. By contrast, if the solution yields $\varepsilon_3 > 0$ and χ_2^R or $\chi_2^L = 0$, the instruments can be viewed as *full* substitutes, whereas if $\varepsilon_3 = 0$ and χ_2^R or $\chi_2^L > 0$, they would again be viewed as complements.[29]

For all policy parameters, the grid search is conducted at a degree of accuracy of one decimal point and a step of 0.1. Optimal policy responses, as well as percent changes (relative to the no-activism case) in the loss functions and welfare, are reported. In all cases, it is assumed that society attaches equal importance to each mandate so that $\gamma = 0.5$. Policies are computed under *commitment*—that is, under the assumption that policy authorities (whether they act individually and jointly) have the ability to deliver on past promises, no matter what the current situation is today.[30] In line with the foregoing discussion, a second-order approximation of the model is used when the policy goal is welfare maximization.

Tables 5.1 and 5.2 present the results for the required reserve ratio and the tax on loans, respectively, when $\varkappa_C = \varkappa_R = 0.1$.[31] Results for both the loan-to-output ratio as the trigger variable in the regulatory policy rules (5.4) and (5.9), as well as, alternatively, the growth rate of investment loans, l_t^K / l_{t-1}^K, as in the Taylor rule (5.10), are also reported. As noted earlier, the literature has been rather unsettled as to which credit variable specifically the regulator should respond to, so considering both the loan-to-output ratio and credit growth is informative.[32]

29. Of course, in all of these cases the comparison is not absolute but applies solely to the set of instruments (and specific trigger variables) under consideration.

30. Under discretion, policy announcements are not credible; agents understand each policymaker's incentive to depart from the stated policy once expectations are formed. However, current policy choices can still affect future expectations. See, for instance, Airaudo and Olivero (2019) for a discussion of optimal time-consistent monetary policy under discretion.

31. It would be plausible to assume that policymakers incur a higher cost of instrument manipulation under coordination, but for a benchmark comparison it is preferable to keep that cost identical across regimes.

32. Of course, other combinations are possible. However, given that the goal of these experiments is largely illustrative, throughout this book only a limited set of alternatives is discussed.

Relative broad loss and relative welfare—the value of the broad loss function or welfare under each policy regime defined earlier, divided by the value of the broad loss function or welfare under no activism—are also reported in figures 5.5 and 5.6 for the required reserve ratio, and figures 5.7 and 5.8 for the tax on loans (in both cases when the instrument responds to the loan-to-output ratio), together with the optimal response parameters, ε_3 and χ_2^R, under the three policy regimes. By construction, the optimal value of ε_3 under A is shown on the right-hand edge of the 3D surface (along which either $\chi_2^R = 0$ or $\chi_2^L = 0$), the optimal value of χ_2^R or χ_2^L under B is shown on the left-hand edge (along which $\varepsilon_3 = 0$), and the optimal values of ε_3 and either χ_2^R or χ_2^L under C are inside the 3D surface, if they are both strictly positive.

Consider first the case where the required reserve ratio is used as the macroprudential instrument (table 5.1) and the rule is specified in terms of the loan-to-output ratio. With *leaning against the wind*, the optimal response parameter ε_3 is positive under both the loss minimization approach (either with the narrow or broad definition of financial stability) and the welfare maximization approach. In all three cases, there is also a substantial gain for both authorities (and thus for the economy at large) relative to the case of no activism. When the required reserve ratio only is active, it is optimal for the regulator to respond only when the objective is to maximize welfare. This reflects the fact the cost of manipulating the instrument outweighs its benefits under the loss minimization approach. Thus, according to the definitions provided earlier, monetary policy and macroprudential regulation are substitutes when policymakers focus on policy losses, whereas they are complements when the focus is on welfare maximization. Moreover, because the response is relatively strong (with an optimal value $\chi_2^R = 2.3$, and therefore a higher cost of instrument manipulation) the welfare gain is more substantial for the central bank than it is for the regulator.

Under coordination, in all cases it is optimal for both authorities to respond to the shock. The gains are substantially higher than in the case of *leaning against the wind* only or separate mandates.[33] These results can be viewed as providing partial refutation for Tinbergen's principle: Two instruments are better than one, but it is optimal for the central bank to be also concerned with financial developments—beyond their indirect effect on output fluctuations and inflation. The instruments are partial substitutes. Put differently, a clear separation of mandates—whereby the central bank uses the policy interest rate

33. In the tables, gains and losses across regimes are all measured with respect to the same case of no activism. Thus, comparing the three regimes with one another can be done directly by looking at the relevant entries.

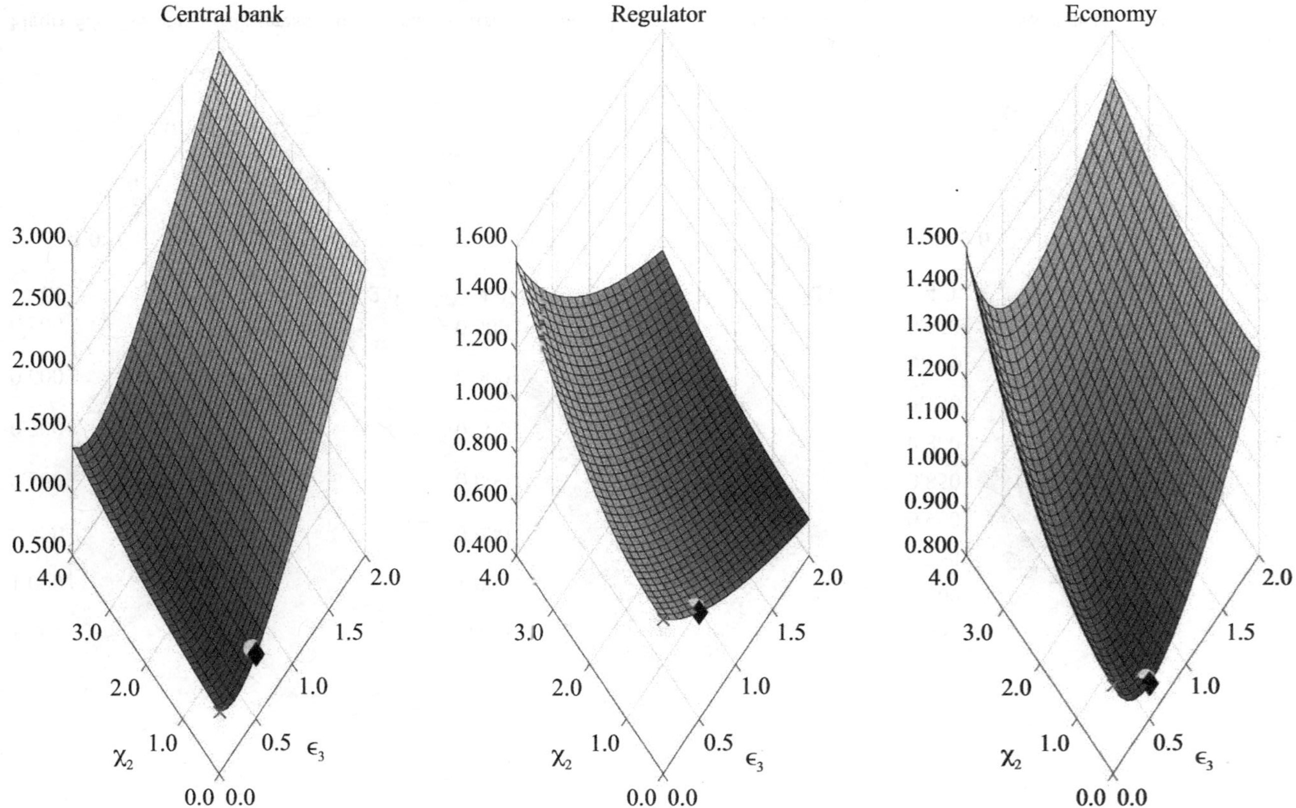

Figure 5.5 Negative credit spread shock: relative broad loss function and optimal policy responses, required reserve ratio. *Note*: The diamond corresponds to leaning against the wind only, the cross to macroprudential regulation only, and the circle to coordination.

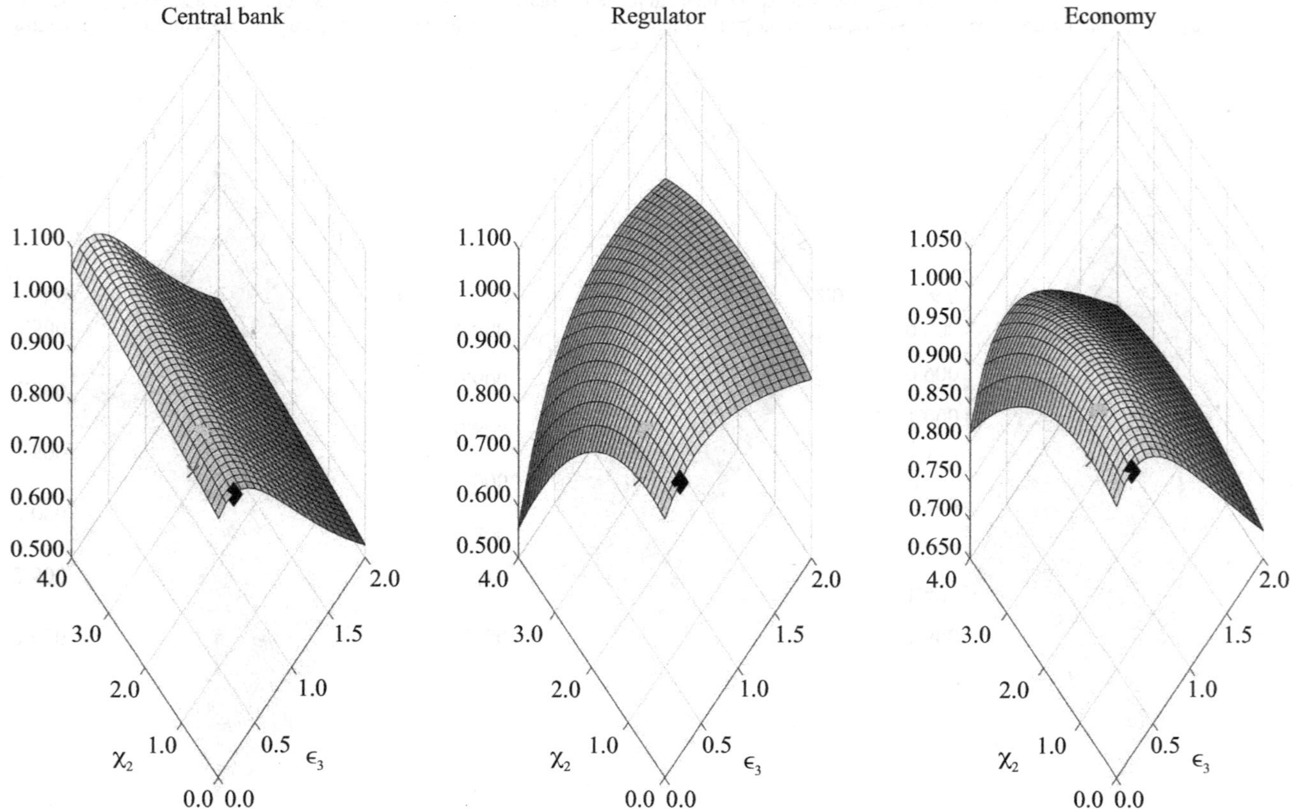

Figure 5.6 Negative credit spread shock: relative welfare and optimal policy responses, required reserve ratio. *Note*: See note to figure 5.5.

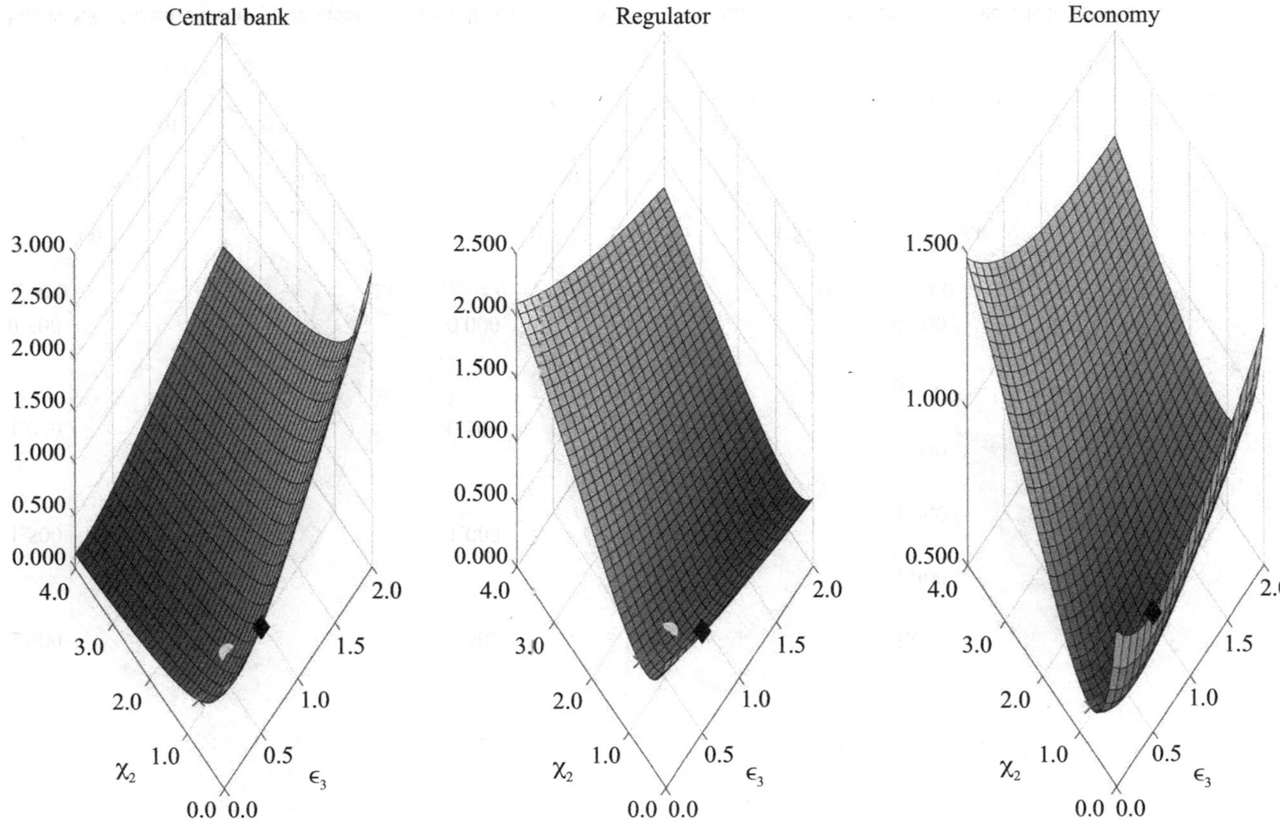

Figure 5.7 Negative credit spread shock: relative broad loss function and optimal policy responses, tax rate on loans. *Note*: See note to figure 5.5.

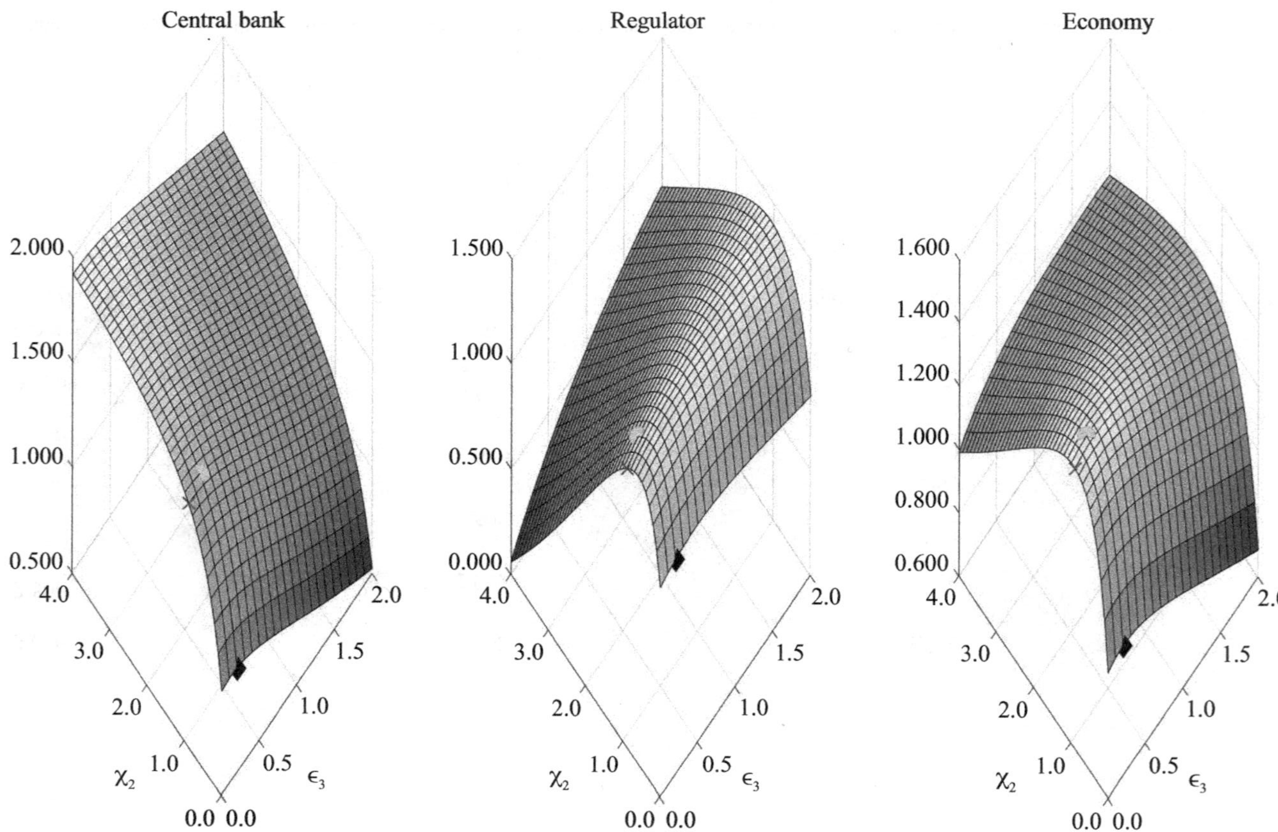

Figure 5.8 Negative credit spread shock: relative welfare and optimal policy responses, tax rate on loans. *Note*: See note to figure 5.5.

Table 5.1
Negative Credit Spread Shock: Optimal Responses and Gains from Coordination, Required Reserve Ratio, $\varkappa_C = \varkappa_R = 0.1$[a]

	Narrow Loss	Broad Loss	Welfare
Loan-to-Output Ratio in Macroprudential Rule			
Leaning against the wind ($\varepsilon_3 \geq 0, \chi_2^R = 0$)			
Optimal response parameter, ε_3	0.9	0.7	0.3
Percent change in policy loss or welfare[a,b]			
Central bank	0.089	−0.042	0.024
Financial regulator	−0.306	−0.240	0.035
Economy[c]	−0.207	−0.178	0.029
Macroprudential regulation ($\varepsilon_3 = 0, \chi_2^R \geq 0$)			
Optimal response parameter, χ_2^R	0.0	0.0	2.3
Percent change in policy loss or welfare[a,b]			
Central bank	0.0	0.0	0.051
Financial regulator	0.0	0.0	0.010
Economy[c]	0.0	0.0	0.030
Coordination ($\varepsilon_3 \geq 0, \chi_2^R \geq 0$)			
Optimal response parameters, ε_3, χ_2^R	0.9, 1.1	0.7, 0.8	0.6, 4.0
Percent change in policy loss or welfare[a,b]			
Central bank	0.063	−0.053	0.120
Financial regulator	−0.308	−0.242	0.071
Economy[c]	−0.215	−0.183	0.095
Credit Growth in Macroprudential Rule			
Leaning against the wind ($\varepsilon_3 \geq 0, \chi_2^R = 0$)			
Optimal response parameter, ε_3	0.9	0.7	0.3
Percent change in policy loss or welfare[a,b]			
Central bank	0.089	−0.042	0.024
Financial regulator	−0.306	−0.240	0.035
Economy[c]	−0.207	−0.178	0.029
Macroprudential regulation ($\varepsilon_3 = 0, \chi_2^R \geq 0$)			
Optimal response parameter, χ_2^R	0.0	0.1	0.0
Percent change in policy loss or welfare[a,b]			
Central bank	0.0	0.0	0.0
Financial regulator	0.0	0.0	0.0
Economy[c]	0.0	0.0	0.0
Coordination ($\varepsilon_3 \geq 0, \chi_2^R \geq 0$)			
Optimal response parameters, ε_3, χ_2^R	0.9, 0.4	0.7, 0.2	0.4, 0.6
Percent change in policy loss or welfare[a,b]			
Central bank	0.085	−0.043	0.023
Financial regulator	−0.305	−0.239	0.037
Economy[c]	−0.208	−0.178	0.030

Notes: a. Includes the cost of instrument adjustment. b. With respect to no activism. c. Equal weights to each policy authority.

to respond to fluctuations in inflation and output, whereas the regulator uses reserve requirements to stabilize fluctuations in credit—does not minimize stabilization losses or maximize welfare, compared to a setting where monetary policy also responds to movements in credit. Tinbergen's principle is not optimal. This result is consistent with those obtained by Glocker and Towbin (2012) and Leduc and Natal (2018), for instance. In particular, Glocker and Towbin (2012) found that reserve requirements can contribute to both price and financial stability in the presence of financial frictions.[34] At the same time, while both policy authorities gain under the broad loss and welfare approaches, this is not the case with the narrow loss function approach: The central bank is worse off. Thus, coordination is not Pareto-improving in that case.

When the macroprudential rule is based on credit growth, the results under *leaning against the wind* are obviously the same as before. However, when macroprudential policy alone is used, even under welfare maximization it is optimal for the regulator not to react. Under coordination it is optimal once again for both policymakers to react, regardless of whether the objective is to minimize the policy loss or to maximize welfare. Nevertheless, the reaction of the regulator is muted, compared to its response when the loan-to-output ratio is the trigger variable. Consequently, the gain from coordination is lower, especially so when welfare is maximized. This comparison illustrates well the differences in outcomes that alternative trigger variables can lead to, and it is an important point for researchers to keep in mind.

Consider now the results when the tax on loans is used as the macroprudential tool (table 5.2) and the trigger variable in the rule is again the loan-to-output ratio. In contrast to those reported earlier, the regulator reacts now strongly under regimes B and C, and in both cases the gains relative to no activism—regardless of whether the objective is to minimize policy losses or maximize welfare—are significantly larger. In addition, under coordination, each authority reacts at least as strongly as under the other regimes. In particular, the central bank follows a more aggressive policy under coordination than when it leans against the wind and the regulator does not react (regime A). Moreover, under welfare maximization, both authorities react more strongly than when they act independently; in that sense, coordination does not involve *burden sharing*—that is, a situation where one authority reacts *less* when there is

34. In the foregoing analysis, the impact of reserve requirements on inflation is only indirect, through its effect on the loan rate, investment, and aggregate demand. The policy rule does *not* depend directly on inflation (or cyclical output, for that matter), as in Glocker and Towbin (2012). While some observers have argued that macroprudential policy may need to be concerned with output stability, very few support the view that it should also be explicitly concerned with price stability.

Table 5.2
Negative Credit Spread Shock: Optimal Responses and Gains from Coordination, Tax on Loans, $\varkappa_C = \varkappa_R = 0.1$[a]

	Narrow Loss	Broad Loss	Welfare
Loan-to-Output Ratio in Macroprudential Rule			
Leaning against the wind ($\varepsilon_3 \geq 0, \chi_2^L = 0$)			
Optimal response parameter, ε_3	0.9	0.7	0.3
Percent change in policy loss or welfare[a,b]			
Central bank	0.089	−0.042	0.024
Financial regulator	−0.306	−0.240	0.035
Economy[c]	−0.207	−0.178	0.029
Macroprudential regulation ($\varepsilon_3 = 0, \chi_2^L \geq 0$)			
Optimal response parameter, χ_2^L	2.4	2.0	2.4
Percent change in policy loss or welfare[a,b]			
Central bank	−0.787	−0.752	0.860
Financial regulator	−0.602	−0.545	0.573
Economy[c]	−0.648	−0.610	0.717
Coordination ($\varepsilon_3 \geq 0, \chi_2 \geq 0$)			
Optimal response parameters, ε_3, χ_2^L	1.2, 2.4	1.0, 2.0	0.7, 2.8
Percent change in policy loss or welfare[a,b]			
Central bank	−0.724	−0.731	0.859
Financial regulator	−0.727	−0.672	0.625
Economy[c]	−0.726	−0.691	0.742
Credit Growth in Macroprudential Rule			
Leaning against the wind ($\varepsilon_3 \geq 0, \chi_2^L = 0$)			
Optimal response parameter, ε_3	0.9	0.7	0.3
Percent change in policy loss or welfare[a,b]			
Central bank	0.089	−0.042	0.024
Financial regulator	−0.306	−0.240	0.035
Economy[c]	−0.207	−0.178	0.029
Macroprudential regulation ($\varepsilon_3 = 0, \chi_2^L \geq 0$)			
Optimal response parameter, χ_2^L	3.0	1.8	4.0
Percent change in policy loss or welfare[a,b]			
Central bank	−0.234	−0.188	0.486
Financial regulator	−0.225	−0.157	−0.002
Economy[c]	−0.228	−0.167	0.242
Coordination ($\varepsilon_3 \geq 0, \chi_2^L \geq 0$)			
Optimal response parameters, ε_3, χ_2^L	1.2, 4.0	0.8, 2.0	0.8, 4.0
Percent change in policy loss or welfare[a,b]			
Central bank	−0.046	−0.116	0.450
Financial regulator	−0.455	−0.357	0.124
Economy[c]	−0.353	−0.282	0.287

Notes: a. Includes the cost of instrument adjustment. b. With respect to no activism. c. Equal weights to each policy authority.

a joint response, compared to when it acts alone, as considered by Agénor and Pereira da Silva (2018*b*). On the contrary, it involves *burden deepening*, with both policymakers reacting more aggressively. And despite the more aggressive responses, which raises the cost of instrument manipulation, the gains associated with coordination, relative to either one of the other two regimes, is always greater—both at the level of each policymaker and at the level of the economy. Thus, coordination is Pareto-improving.

As also shown in table 5.2, the results remain qualitatively similar when (as in the monetary policy rule) credit growth is used as the triggering variable in the macroprudential policy rule. Thus, a *leaning against the wind* policy regime in which the central bank alone responds to financial stability considerations is inferior to a regime where the regulator acts alone (the *separate mandates* regime, in which the central bank follows a standard Taylor rule), and both are in fact inferior to the *coordination* regime, where both authorities act jointly. Coordination generates superior outcomes compared to a strict application of Tinbergen's principle.

Tables 5.3 and 5.4 show the results for the two macroprudential instruments when the cost adjustment parameters are $\varkappa_C = \varkappa_R = 0.4$. Policy responses are now of course less aggressive, regardless of the policy regime, and relative gains are significantly lower. Yet, some of the key results, and their interpretation, remain broadly similar to those discussed earlier. In particular, when the loan-to-output ratio is the variable that triggers changes in the tax rate on loans, it is always optimal—regardless of whether the policy objective is specified in terms of a loss function or welfare—to coordinate an augmented monetary policy rule with countercyclical macroprudential regulation. Again, these results provide partial refutation of Tinbergen's principle: Using macroprudential policy improves over the use of monetary policy alone to address financial stability issues (so two instruments are necessary to achieve two targets), but coordination when both policymakers react to credit developments improves over a regime of strictly separate mandates.

Tables 5.5 and 5.6 report the asymptotic standard deviations for a range of macroeconomic and financial variables, for $\varkappa_C = \varkappa_R = 0.4$ and for macroprudential policy rules based on either the loan-to-output ratio or credit growth. The results indicate that outcomes under activism, especially coordination, are always at least as favorable as under no activism. However, among the activist regimes, the results are not uniformly better. In particular, when the required reserve ratio is used as the countercyclical regulatory instrument, the refinance rate is more variable under coordination than under *leaning against the wind*, given that (as noted earlier) when policymakers act jointly they both respond

Table 5.3
Negative Credit Spread Shock: Optimal Responses and Gains from Coordination, Required Reserve Ratio, $\varkappa_C = \varkappa_R = 0.4$[a]

	Narrow Loss	Broad Loss	Welfare
Loan-to-Output Ratio in Macroprudential Rule			
Leaning against the wind ($\varepsilon_3 \geq 0, \chi_2^R = 0$)			
Optimal response parameter, ε_3	0.6	0.5	0.2
Percent change in policy loss or welfare[a,b]			
Central bank	0.098	0.023	0.006
Financial regulator	−0.228	−0.185	0.028
Economy[c]	−0.146	−0.120	0.017
Macroprudential regulation ($\varepsilon_3 = 0, \chi_2^R \geq 0$)			
Optimal response parameter, χ_2^R	0.0	0.0	0.7
Percent change in policy loss or welfare[a,b]			
Central bank	0.0	0.0	0.017
Financial regulator	0.0	0.0	0.002
Economy[c]	0.0	0.0	0.010
Coordination ($\varepsilon_3 \geq 0, \chi_2^R \geq 0$)			
Optimal response parameters, ε_3, χ_2^R	0.6, 0.1	0.5, 0.1	0.2, 0.9
Percent change in policy loss or welfare[a,b]			
Central bank	0.099	0.024	0.027
Financial regulator	−0.228	−0.186	0.032
Economy[c]	−0.146	−0.120	0.030
Credit Growth in Macroprudential Rule			
Leaning against the wind ($\varepsilon_3 \geq 0, \chi_2^R = 0$)			
Optimal response parameter, ε_3	0.6	0.5	0.2
Percent change in policy loss or welfare[a,b]			
Central bank	0.098	0.023	0.006
Financial regulator	−0.228	−0.185	0.028
Economy[c]	−0.146	−0.120	0.017
Macroprudential regulation ($\varepsilon_3 = 0, \chi_2^R \geq 0$)			
Optimal response parameter, χ_2^R	0.0	0.0	0.0
Percent change in policy loss or welfare[a,b]			
Central bank	0.0	0.0	0.0
Financial regulator	0.0	0.0	0.0
Economy[c]	0.0	0.0	0.0
Coordination ($\varepsilon_3 \geq 0, \chi_2^R \geq 0$)			
Optimal response parameters, ε_3, χ_2^R	0.6, 0.0	0.5, 0.0	0.2, 0.1
Percent change in policy loss or welfare[a,b]			
Central bank	0.098	0.023	0.006
Financial regulator	−0.228	−0.185	0.028
Economy[c]	−0.146	−0.120	0.017

Notes: a. Includes the cost of instrument adjustment. b. With respect to no activism. c. Equal weights to each policy authority.

Table 5.4
Negative Credit Spread Shock: Optimal Responses and Gains from Coordination, Tax on Loans, $\varkappa_C = \varkappa_R = 0.4$[a]

	Narrow Loss	Broad Loss	Welfare
Loan-to-Output Ratio in Macroprudential Rule			
Leaning against the wind ($\varepsilon_3 \geq 0, \chi_2^L = 0$)			
Optimal response parameter, ε_3	0.6	0.5	0.2
Percentage change in policy loss or welfare[a,b]			
Central bank	0.098	0.023	0.006
Financial regulator	−0.228	−0.185	0.028
Economy[c]	−0.146	−0.120	0.017
Macroprudential regulation ($\varepsilon_3 = 0, \chi_2^L \geq 0$)			
Optimal response parameter, χ_2^L	0.8	0.7	0.9
Percentage change in policy loss or welfare[a,b]			
Central bank	−0.545	−0.514	0.652
Financial regulator	−0.355	−0.299	0.324
Economy[c]	−0.402	−0.366	0.488
Coordination ($\varepsilon_3 \geq 0, \chi_2^L \geq 0$)			
Optimal response parameters, ε_3, χ_2^L	0.5, 0.8	0.4, 0.7	0.2, 1.0
Percentage change in policy loss or welfare[a,b]			
Central bank	−0.463	−0.487	0.662
Financial regulator	−0.477	−0.408	0.345
Economy[c]	−0.474	−0.432	0.504
Credit Growth in Macroprudential Rule			
Leaning against the wind ($\varepsilon_3 \geq 0, \chi_2^L = 0$)			
Optimal response parameter, ε_3	0.6	0.5	0.2
Percentage change in policy loss or welfare[a,b]			
Central bank	0.098	0.023	0.006
Financial regulator	−0.228	−0.185	0.028
Economy[c]	−0.146	−0.120	0.017
Macroprudential regulation ($\varepsilon_3 = 0, \chi_2^L \geq 0$)			
Optimal response parameter, χ_2^L	0.4	0.3	0.4
Percent change in policy loss or welfare[a,b]			
Central bank	−0.075	−0.059	0.096
Financial regulator	−0.056	−0.039	0.005
Economy[c]	−0.061	−0.045	0.051
Coordination ($\varepsilon_3 \geq 0, \chi_2^L \geq 0$)			
Optimal response parameters, ε_3, χ_2^L	0.7, 0.5	0.5, 0.4	0.3, 0.6
Percent change in policy loss or welfare[a,b]			
Central bank	0.081	−0.045	0.127
Financial regulator	−0.289	−0.209	0.016
Economy[c]	−0.197	−0.158	0.071

Notes: a. Includes the cost of instrument adjustment. b. With respect to no activism. c. Equal weights to each policy authority.

Table 5.5
Negative Credit Spread Shock: Asymptotic Standard Deviations, Alternative Policy Regimes, Required Reserve Ratio and $\varkappa_C = \varkappa_R = 0.4$[a]

	No Activism	LAW Only	MaP Only	Coord.
	Loan-to-Output Ratio in Macroprudential Rule			
Output	0.0032	0.0030	0.0032	0.0030
Employment	0.0011	0.0009	0.0011	0.0010
Consumption	0.0020	0.0020	0.0020	0.0020
Investment	0.0034	0.0033	0.0034	0.0033
Inflation	0.0005	0.0004	0.0005	0.0003
Refinance rate	0.0012	0.0017	0.0014	0.0019
Loan rate	0.0167	0.0161	0.0166	0.0159
Real house prices	0.0010	0.0011	0.0010	0.0010
Repayment probability	0.0010	0.0010	0.0009	0.0010
Loan-to-output ratio	0.0031	0.0030	0.0031	0.0030
Required reserve ratio	—	—	0.0023	0.0028
	Credit Growth in Macroprudential Rule			
Output	0.0032	0.0030	0.0032	0.0030
Employment	0.0011	0.0009	0.0011	0.0009
Consumption	0.0020	0.0020	0.0020	0.0020
Investment	0.0034	0.0033	0.0034	0.0033
Inflation	0.0005	0.0004	0.0005	0.0004
Refinance rate	0.0012	0.0017	0.0012	0.0017
Loan rate	0.0167	0.0161	0.0167	0.0161
Real house prices	0.0010	0.0011	0.0010	0.0011
Repayment probability	0.0010	0.0010	0.0010	0.0010
Loan-to-output ratio	0.0031	0.0030	0.0031	0.0030
Required reserve ratio	—	—	0.0001	0.0001

Note: a. No Activism corresponds to $\varepsilon_3 = \chi_2^R = 0$, LAW to leaning against the wind, $\varepsilon_3 \geq 0, \chi_2^R = 0$, MaP Only to $\varepsilon_3 = 0, \chi_2^R \geq 0$ and Coord. to coordination $\varepsilon_3, \chi_2^R \geq 0$.

more aggressively than when they act independently. The opposite occurs when the tax rate on loans is used as the regulatory tool. Overall, the results corroborate the fact that the best outcomes are obtained when the tax rate on loans reacts to the credit-to-output ratio—although the benefits of coordination do not appear to be particularly strong compared to the case where the regulator acts alone. This is consistent with the results reported earlier on relative policy losses and welfare.

Intuitively, and regardless of the policy regime, the reason optimal response values exist is because a more aggressive policy tends at first to reduce volatility but, subsequently, as the policy becomes more aggressive, it becomes more costly. With *leaning against the wind*, the increase in the base policy rate dampens initially the expansion of credit (by raising borrowing costs), and this helps to stabilize investment and aggregate demand. Greater output stability tends to

Table 5.6
Credit Spread Shock: Asymptotic Standard Deviations Alternative Policy Regimes, Tax on Loans and $\varkappa_C = \varkappa_R = 0.4$[a]

	No Activism	LAW Only	MaP Only	Coord.
	Loan-to-Output Ratio in Macroprudential Rule			
Output	0.0032	0.0030	0.0020	0.0018
Employment	0.0011	0.0009	0.0008	0.0007
Consumption	0.0020	0.0020	0.0011	0.0011
Investment	0.0034	0.0033	0.0022	0.0020
Inflation	0.0005	0.0004	0.0004	0.0003
Refinance rate	0.0012	0.0017	0.0010	0.0014
Loan rate	0.0167	0.0161	0.0100	0.0094
Real house prices	0.0010	0.0011	0.0006	0.0005
Repayment probability	0.0010	0.0010	0.0005	0.0005
Loan-to-output ratio	0.0031	0.0030	0.0020	0.0018
Tax rate on loans	—	—	0.0076	0.0079
	Credit Growth in Macroprudential Rule			
Output	0.0032	0.0030	0.0030	0.0028
Employment	0.0011	0.0009	0.0010	0.0008
Consumption	0.0020	0.0020	0.0019	0.0019
Investment	0.0034	0.0033	0.0032	0.0029
Inflation	0.0005	0.0004	0.0005	0.0005
Refinance rate	0.0012	0.0017	0.0010	0.0016
Loan rate	0.0167	0.0161	0.0158	0.0147
Real house prices	0.0010	0.0011	0.0010	0.0010
Repayment probability	0.0010	0.0010	0.0009	0.0010
Loan-to-output ratio	0.0031	0.0030	0.0029	0.0027
Tax rate on loans	—	—	0.0015	0.0020

Note: a. No Activism corresponds to $\varepsilon_3 = \chi_2^L = 0$, LAW to leaning against the wind, $\varepsilon_3 \geq 0, \chi_2^L = 0$, MaP Only to $\varepsilon_3 = 0, \chi_2^L \geq 0$ and Coord. to coordination $\varepsilon_3, \chi_2^L \geq 0$.

mitigate the response of the base policy rate, through the Taylor rule. However, as the policy response becomes forceful, thereby magnifying the increase in the policy rate, it raises the volatility of the deposit rate, which leads to a portfolio reallocation between deposits, cash, and bonds. As a result, the higher volatility of the deposit rate translates into higher volatility of the bond rate—nominal and real, given sticky prices. This, in turn, leads to higher volatility in consumption and labor supply. At first, the stabilizing effect on credit and investment dominates and the volatility of aggregate demand (and thus inflation) tends to fall, but eventually, higher consumption volatility becomes relatively more important and the volatility of aggregate demand and inflation tends to increase. At the same time, as the policy becomes more aggressive, the cost of instrument manipulation rises as well, thereby mitigating the net benefits of the policy adjustment. The optimal value is the point at which volatility is the lowest, either because the objective is directly to minimize economic volatility (which depends on the volatility of output and inflation) or to maximize welfare (which depends on the volatility of consumption and labor supply).

For reserve requirements, the reasoning is very similar. A higher required reserve ratio raises the cost of borrowing (through its impact on the penalty rate imposed by the central bank) and dampens the volatility of investment, but at the same time it induces more volatility in deposit and bond rates, which affects consumption and labor supply. This trade-off, once again, is internalized by setting optimally the response parameter in the policy rule.

However, for the tax on loans, there are no direct effects on the deposit rate, and subsequently the (expected) bond rate, and therefore no direct impact on consumption volatility. This means that when the instrument cost is zero ($\varkappa_R = 0$), the optimal value of the response parameter χ_2^L in (5.9) tends to infinity: It is optimal to fully stabilize the loan-to-output ratio. This is indeed corroborated numerically. At the same time, of course, the marginal gain, in terms of lower policy loss or higher welfare, becomes very small once χ_2^L is high enough. Because the assumption of costly instrument manipulation matches well with the evidence—as noted earlier, central banks usually refrain from large and abrupt changes in the refinance rate, and regulators tend to act in the same way—whenever warranted the focus in subsequent chapters will be on the case where $\varkappa_C, \varkappa_R > 0$.

It is worth noting also that the foregoing analysis was conducted under the assumption that the standard Taylor rule, having been found in a number of studies to perform "nearly" as well as the Ramsey policy (as noted earlier), had fixed parameters across regimes. This is a reasonable way to proceed, given the focus of this chapter. However, a more general exercise would involve solving for *all* the parameters of the augmented Taylor rule; that is, not only ε_3 but also ε_1, ε_2, and possibly χ, the degree of persistence.[35] This would help to assess, in particular, the extent to which a more forceful response to credit developments by the central bank may weaken its aggressiveness toward stabilizing inflation and output. If so, the use of a single instrument could exacerbate the trade-off between price stability and financial stability—thereby restoring the fundamental validity of Tinbergen's principle. However, it is still possible for coordination to generate better outcomes compared to a strict separation of mandates.

Finally, the focus in this chapter, as elsewhere in this book, has been on financial shocks. However, it is intuitively clear that the optimal policy depends also on the origin of the shock. Consider, for instance, a positive productivity

35. See, for instance, Davis and Huang (2013).

shock, which raises output. In the model, as discussed in chapter 4, this leads to a direct increase in the repayment probability, a reduction in the loan rate, and an expansion of credit and investment. If the macroprudential instrument rule, of the type given by (5.4) or (5.9), involves a mechanical response to credit growth, it may reduce welfare.[36] The risk of a policy mistake is less potent if the rule responds to the loan-to-output ratio (given that both increase) but it is, nevertheless, also present.

5.7 Ramsey Policy and Simple Rules

As noted earlier, although there are a number of reasons for focusing on simple instrument rules (including implementability, transparency and communication, robustness with respect to the origin of shocks, and accountability), the Ramsey policy provides a natural benchmark to assess what policy *can* (or *should*) achieve and to help discriminate among alternative simple rules. Moreover, it is not subject to the possibility that fluctuations in the aggregate variables on which simple policy rules are based can be efficient—in which case intervention could reduce welfare. However, as also pointed out, the Ramsey policy (when it can be calculated) may lead in practice to excessively volatile instrument paths, and it is possible for optimized simple policy rules to achieve welfare levels that are comparable—at least to some degree. It is thus important to assess to what extent the simple regulatory rules discussed in this chapter compare to the Ramsey policy. In addition, it is essential to evaluate the performance of coordinated instrument rules, which involve both leaning against the wind and countercyclical macroprudential regulation, with the Ramsey policy. Before doing so, however, a brief outline of the methodology used to solve for the Ramsey policy is warranted.

5.7.1 Solving for the Ramsey Policy

Under the Ramsey optimal policy, the objective of the social planner is to set its policy instrument so as to maximize conditional welfare (that is, expected welfare conditional on the initial state being the nonstochastic steady state), subject to the constraints imposed by the competitive equilibrium. In this book the numerical procedure developed by Bodenstein et al. (2019), which relies on a Lagrangian approach, is used. In that approach, the exact nonlinear first-order conditions that characterize the optimal policy are obtained by symbolic differentiation of the Lagrangian with respect to each of the endogenous variables

36. See, for instance, Quint and Rabanal (2014) for a related example.

(including the policy instrument) and setting these derivatives to zero.[37] Thus, these first-order conditions take the place of a single policy reaction function, while the set of Lagrange multipliers is added to the list of the model's variables. Each system of equations is then approximated around its deterministic steady state using first-order perturbation methods (to compute impulse response functions) or second-order methods, of the type discussed in chapter 4, to evaluate conditional welfare.[38]

Formally, let y_t denote an $N \times 1$ vector of endogenous variables, which is partitioned as $y_t = [y_t^O \ \ \tau_t]'$. The variable τ_t is the policy instrument. Let also ξ_t denote a vector of exogenous shocks. For a given sequence of the policy instrument $\{\tau_t\}_{t=0}^{\infty}$, the remaining $N-1$ endogenous variables need to satisfy the $N-1$ structural equations—the private sector's behavioral equations and the market-clearing conditions—that characterize an equilibrium:

$$\mathbb{E}_t G(y_{t-1}, y_t^O, y_{t+1}, \tau_t; \xi_t) = 0, \tag{5.28}$$

where it is assumed (without loss of generality) that only one period lagged and future values of the endogenous variables appear in the system.

Suppose that the system of equations in $G()$ is differentiable up to the desired order of approximation. In terms of endogenous and exogenous variables, the present discounted value of the household's expected utility function can now be written in generic form as[39]

$$U_t = \mathbb{E}_t \sum_{s=0}^{\infty} \Lambda^s u(y_{t+s-1}^O, y_{t+s}^O; \xi_{t+s}).$$

Abstracting for the moment from the cost of instrument manipulation, under full commitment the Ramsey policy is the solution of the maximization problem

$$\max_{\{y_t^O, \tau_t\}_{t=0}^{\infty}} \mathbb{E}_t \sum_{s=0}^{\infty} \Lambda^s u(y_{t+s-1}^O, y_{t+s}^O; \xi_{t+s}), \tag{5.29}$$

37. These derivations use the symbolic MATLAB procedures developed initially by Levin and López-Salido (2004). In fact, the key innovation in Bodenstein et al. (2019) was to extend that contribution to discuss macroeconomic policy games involving two (or more) policymakers. See chapters 6 and 10.

38. Bodenstein et al. (2019) also discussed how their technique compares with the linear-quadratic (LQ) approach developed by Benigno and Woodford (2012), and used by Demirel (2010), for instance, which involves finding first a purely quadratic approximation to the policymaker's objective function. This function is then optimized subject to a linear approximation of the model's structural equations.

39. The lagged values of the other endogenous variables in the generic form of $u()$ may reflect habit formation, as discussed in chapter 4.

subject to

$$\mathbb{E}_t G(y_{t+s-1}, y_{t+s}, y_{t+s+1}, \tau_{t+s}; \xi_{t+s}) = 0 \quad \forall s.$$

Thus, given that the steady state of the model is inefficient—as noted in chapter 4, instruments that would allow a benevolent planner to achieve the socially efficient allocation in the absence of price and financial sector distortions are assumed not to be available—the solution to this problem yields a second-best constrained allocation.

The first-order conditions of this maximization problem can be obtained by differentiating the Lagrangian

$$\mathcal{L}_t = \mathbb{E}_t \sum_{s=0}^{\infty} \left\{ \Lambda^s u(y^O_{t+s-1}, y^O_{t+s}; \xi_{t+s}) + \boldsymbol{\lambda}'_{t+s} G(y_{t+s-1}, y_{t+s}, y_{t+s+1}; \xi_{t+s}) \right\}, \tag{5.30}$$

where $\boldsymbol{\lambda}_t$ is a vector of $N-1$ Lagrange multipliers associated with the structural conditions (5.28).

Taking derivatives of $\mathcal{L}_t$ with respect to the $N-1$ endogenous variables in y^O_t and τ_t gives N first-order conditions. In addition, taking derivatives with respect to the $\boldsymbol{\lambda}_t$ multipliers gives again the $N-1$ structural equations. Thus, in all, there are $2N-1$ conditions and $2N-1$ variables.

In summary, the (constrained) Ramsey solution $\{y^O_{t+s}, \tau_{t+s}, \boldsymbol{\lambda}_{t+s}\}_{s=0}^{\infty}$ satisfies the following conditions:

For $s \geq 1$:

$$\begin{aligned} &\boldsymbol{D}_y u(y^O_{t+s-1}, y^O_{t+s}; \xi_{t+s}) + \Lambda \mathbb{E}_t \boldsymbol{D}_{y^-} u(y^O_{t+s}, y^O_{t+s+1}; \xi_{t+s+1}) \\ &\quad + \mathbb{E}_t\{\boldsymbol{\lambda}'_{t+s} \boldsymbol{D}_y G(y_{t+s-1}, y_{t+s}, y_{t+s+1}; \xi_{t+s})\} \\ &\quad + \Lambda \mathbb{E}_t\{\boldsymbol{\lambda}'_{t+s+1} \boldsymbol{D}_{y^-} G(y_{t+s}, y_{t+s+1}, y_{t+s+2}; \xi_{t+s+1})\} \\ &\quad + \Lambda^{-1} \boldsymbol{\lambda}'_{t+s-1} \boldsymbol{D}_{y^+} G(y_{t+s-2}, y_{t+s-1}, y_{t+s}; \xi_{t+s-1}) = 0, \end{aligned} \tag{5.31}$$

$$\mathbb{E}_t G(y_{t+s-1}, y_{t+s}, y_{t+s+1}; \xi_{t+s}) = 0. \tag{5.32}$$

For $s = 0$:

$$\begin{aligned} &\boldsymbol{D}_y u(y^O_{t-1}, y^O_t; \xi_t) + \Lambda \mathbb{E}_t \boldsymbol{D}_{y^-} u(y^O_t, y^O_{t+1}; \xi_{t+1}) \\ &\quad + \mathbb{E}_t\{\boldsymbol{\lambda}'_t \boldsymbol{D}_y G(y_{t-1}, y_t, y_{t+1}; \xi_t)\} + \Lambda \mathbb{E}_t\{\boldsymbol{\lambda}'_{t+1} \boldsymbol{D}_{y^-} G(y_t, y_{t+1}, y_{t+2}; \xi_{t+1})\} = 0, \\ &\mathbb{E}_t G(y_{t-1}, y_t, y_{t+1}; \xi_t) = 0, \end{aligned}$$

where $\boldsymbol{D}_{y^-}$, $\boldsymbol{D}_y$, and $\boldsymbol{D}_{y+}$ denote vectors of partial derivatives of any of the functions with respect to the elements of y_{t+s-1}, y_{t+s}, and y_{t+s+1}, respectively.[40]

In this approach, the initial period $s=0$ is different from subsequent periods $s>0$ because the choice of policies at time t is not restricted by previous commitments. Although in general this system of equations can be solved, the equilibrium functions and the policy decision rule will not be time-invariant. Fundamentally, this is a reflection of the problem of *time inconsistency*, which arises when the behavior of agents today depends on their expectations of future policy and a policymaker has the incentive to renege on a previous commitment—see Wickens (2012, chap. 17), for instance.

To avoid this problem, Bodenstein et al. (2019) adopt the concept of optimality from a *timeless perspective*, proposed by Benigno and Woodford (2005), and further discussed by Woodford (2010), Benigno and Woodford (2012), and Kwon and Miao (2019). Intuitively, the timeless perspective requires an initial precommitment (promises) to suitably chosen values $\boldsymbol{\lambda}_{t-1}$ at time t, so that the first-order conditions of the optimization problem (5.29), as given in (5.31) and (5.32), apply to all subsequent dates $t+s$ as well, with $s \geq 0$. It therefore imposes additional constraints for time t on the policymaker's optimization problem. These constraints, which ensure that the optimal policy is time-consistent, can be accounted for directly by modifying the policymaker's objective function in (5.29):

$$\max_{\{y_t^O, \tau_t\}_{t=0}^{\infty}} \mathbb{E}_t \sum_{s=0}^{\infty} \Lambda^s \left\{ u(y_{t+s-1}^O, y_{t+s}^O; \xi_{t+s}) + \Lambda^{t-1} \boldsymbol{\lambda}_{t-1} G(y_{t-2}, y_{t-1}; \xi_t) \right\}. \tag{5.33}$$

The timeless perspective implies therefore that the optimal, deterministic steady-state solutions $(y, \boldsymbol{\lambda})$ must satisfy the conditions:

$$\begin{aligned} & \boldsymbol{D}_y u(y^O, y^O; \mathbf{0}) + \Lambda \boldsymbol{D}_{y^-} u(y^O, y^O; \mathbf{0}) \\ & \quad + \boldsymbol{\lambda}' [\Lambda \boldsymbol{D}_{y^-} G(y, y, y; \mathbf{0})\} + \boldsymbol{D}_y G(y, y, y; \mathbf{0}) + \Lambda^{-1} \boldsymbol{D}_{y+} G(y, y, y; \mathbf{0})] = 0, \\ & G(y, y, y; \mathbf{0}) = 0. \end{aligned}$$

The solution of these equations is obtained by exploiting the fact that the problem is linear in the Lagrange multipliers. Equations (5.30) and (5.31) can then be replaced by a local approximation around the steady state of the Ramsey equilibrium $(y, \boldsymbol{\lambda})$. The resulting system of difference equations can then be solved by standard perturbation methods, as discussed in chapter 4.

40. By implication, with m instruments, the system to be solved would involve $2N-m$ conditions and $2N-m$ variables.

Finally, in implementing the Bodenstein et al. algorithm, the cost of instrument manipulation is accounted for in (5.33), as in (5.23) and (5.24).

5.7.2 Approximating the Ramsey Policy

As discussed earlier, several contributions have shown that a Taylor-type monetary policy rule is "nearly" optimal, in the sense that it can generate levels of welfare that are relatively close to those associated with the Ramsey policy. In principle, it is also possible for the same result to hold with respect to (some) simple macroprudential rules, either taken individually or in combination, with and without an augmented Taylor rule. To conduct that assessment, a basic procedure, which builds on the analysis in Schmitt-Grohé and Uribe (2007) with respect to monetary policy, is proposed.

Consider the case where the central bank follows a standard interest rate rule and the macroprudential instrument is the tax on loans, τ_t^L, which is set according to the rule defined in (5.9). Assessing to what extent this simple, credit-based rule provides a good approximation to the Ramsey policy involves the following five steps:

Step 1: Solve for the optimal Ramsey allocation, including τ_t^L, conditional on the instrument cost parameter, $\varkappa_R$, and calculate the compensating variation, using a formula like (5.19), with respect to no activism, $\beta^r(\varkappa_R)$.

Step 2: Iterate over χ_1, the degree of inertia in the simple macroprudential policy rule, over the interval (0, 1[, and χ_2^L over a range $(0, \chi_M^L)$, where $\chi_M^L > 0$ is an upper bound, whose exact value may be based on computational considerations. Calculate the compensating variation associated with the simple rule with respect to no activism, $\beta^c(\chi_1, \chi_2^L; \chi_R)$, conditional on the instrument cost parameter.

Step 3: Determine the optimal response parameters as those for which the absolute difference between compensating variations, or *welfare gap*, is lower than a given threshold, $\xi\%$:[41]

$$\chi_1^O(\varkappa_R), \chi_2^{L,O}(\varkappa_R), \text{ such that } |\beta^r(\varkappa_R) - \beta^c(\chi_1, \chi_2^L; \varkappa_R)| \leq \xi\% \qquad (5.34)$$

Step 4: Repeat Step 3 for different values of $\xi\%$, the threshold parameter, to assess the sensitivity of the results.

Step 5: Repeat Steps 1 to 3 for different values of $\varkappa_R$, the cost of instrument manipulation, to assess the sensitivity of the results.

41. In the foregoing discussion of the optimality of simple macroprudential rules, for simplicity χ_1 was taken as given, in order to focus on the response parameter to the trigger variable. For the issue at stake, given that by definition the Ramsey policy does not have built-in inertia, iterating over χ_1 is important to assess the ability of the simple rule to replicate outcomes under that policy.

Thus, $\chi_1^O(\varkappa_R)$ and $\chi_2^{L,O}(\varkappa_R)$ are the parameter values that jointly ensure that the welfare gap between the Ramsey optimal allocation and the simple macroprudential rule is arbitrarily small, depending on the value of $\xi\%$. Of course, whether the optimal rule associated with (5.34) is *actually implementable* depends on the implied volatility of the macroprudential instrument itself, τ_t^L. In turn, this may depend on the origin and magnitude of shocks impinging on the economy. This is important because, as discussed later, all else being equal the Ramsey policy often tends to be more aggressive than a simple rule with built-in inertia. In addition, criterion (5.34) could yield a range of alternative parameter combinations, which would need to be ranked according to their implications for either instrument volatility or stability and uniqueness considerations.[42]

Rather than compensating variations, relative welfare could also be used; instead of differences with respect to no activism, compensating variations could be calculated directly by comparing outcomes under the Ramsey policy and the simple rule, as in (5.20). More generally, the above procedure could be extended to solve jointly for optimal monetary and macroprudential policy rules, with and without *leaning against the wind*, or for a combination of macroprudential policy rules—at the cost, however, of greater computational complexity. In addition, because the set of simple, implementable rules can be fairly broad (as argued previously), a systematic and thorough comparison would need to be performed to ensure that the results of these exercises, and the policy recommendations that they may lead to, are robust.

5.7.3 Application to the Tax Rate on Loans

As discussed earlier, the tax rate on loans performed significantly better than the required reserve ratio, whether it is used independently or jointly with monetary policy and both in terms of policy loss minimization and welfare maximization. It is therefore of particular interest to focus on that instrument and compare outcomes with the Ramsey policy, when there is no *leaning against the wind*. Thus, in studying that policy, the central bank is assumed to follow a standard Taylor rule. This is consistent with the evidence on the near optimality of that rule discussed earlier and helps to keep the analysis manageable. The case of a negative spread shock is again considered.

Asymptotic standard deviations relative to the Ramsey policy are shown in figure 5.9 for both (*a*) the optimal simple macroprudential rule (5.9) for the tax

42. Tightening the threshold parameter $\xi\%$ could also help to eliminate some parameter combinations. See Schmitt-Grohé and Uribe (2007) and Adjemian et al. (2008) for a further discussion in the context of monetary policy.

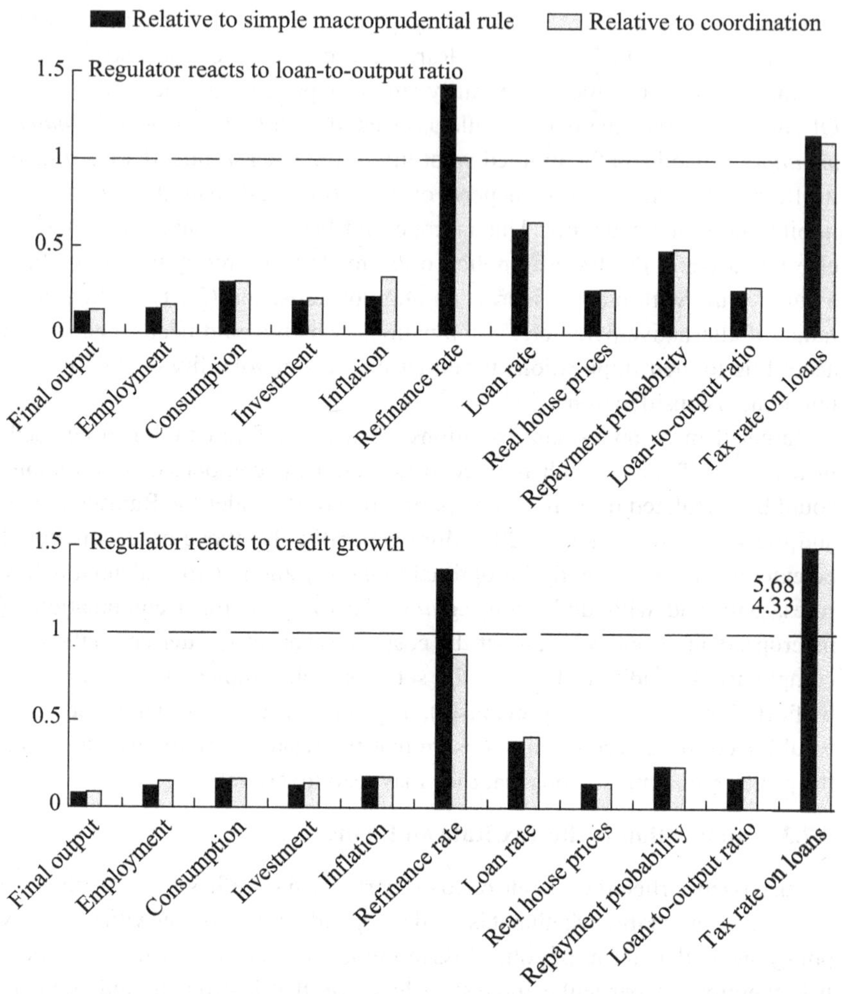

Figure 5.9
Negative credit spread shock: asymptotic standard deviations, Ramsey policy relative to simple macroprudential rule and coordination
Note: The cost of instrument manipulation is 0.4 in both graphs. The simple macroprudential rule relates to the tax on loans. Under coordination, the central bank reacts to credit growth. Optimal response parameters are those reported in table 5.4. The numbers 5.68 and 4.33 refer to the relative volatility of the tax on loans when only the regulator acts and under coordination, respectively. The vertical scale in both graphs is set at a maximum of 1.5 to facilitate comparison.

rate on loans, and assuming that there are separate mandates, so that $\varepsilon_3 = 0$, and (*b*) outcomes under coordination, in which both the central bank and the regulator react, the former to credit growth and the latter to either the loan-to-output ratio or credit growth as well, and for instrument cost parameters $\varkappa_C = \varkappa_R = 0.4$. The optimal values of the response parameters are those displayed in table 5.4. Thus, if the Ramsey policy delivers a superior outcome for a particular variable, compared to the simple instrument rule used independently or in coordination with monetary policy, the ratio for that variable in the figure should be less than unity.[43]

The results show that under the Ramsey policy, both policy instruments exhibit a high degree of volatility. The reason is that the tax rate on loans under that policy increases significantly on impact, by up to four times more compared to the other two regimes.[44] Although it stabilizes fairly rapidly afterward, the initial movement in the tax rate has a disproportionate effect on its asymptotic standard deviation. At the same time, the gains from the policy are almost uniformly better—in some cases substantially so (particularly for real sector variables, as well as inflation and real house prices). In fact, although the tax rate on loans and the refinance rate are both more variable under the Ramsey policy, the loan rate itself is not. The key reason is that the repayment probability is significantly less volatile. In terms of relative welfare, and depending on the trigger variable used in the simple macroprudential rule, the Ramsey policy generates a welfare gain (relative to no activism) of about 57 to 60 percent higher than the other regimes.

At the same time, however, the magnitude of this gain means that applying the approximation procedure described earlier would generate an equally volatile instrument path, for any reasonable value of the threshold parameter $\varepsilon\%$. This implies that any simple policy rule aimed at keeping the *welfare gap* low may be equally difficult to implement in practice. Thus, in contrast to some of the studies alluded to earlier, whose focus was on monetary policy, the welfare losses associated with simple, implementable macroprudential rules can be substantial relative to the Ramsey optimal policy. Nevertheless, it is important to note that, depending on the trigger variable used in the rule, the macroprudential instrument and the policy interest rate can be *both* highly volatile under that policy; such volatility could itself be a source of instability and lower

43. Note again that because monopoly power and frictions (real and financial) persist in equilibrium, the welfare analysis is conducted around a distorted steady state; thus, the constrained Ramsey planner can only achieve the second-best allocation.

44. A similar result is obtained in chapter 10, where a combination of countercyclical macroprudential instruments is used.

welfare. It is also possible that the positive outcomes reported in figure 5.9 are specific to the shock considered. A broader and more systematic analysis could lead to different conclusions.

5.8 Notes on the Literature

The analysis presented in this chapter can be extended in several directions. Three important ones are the treatment of excess liquid reserves, the modeling of lending restrictions and the degree of complementarity between macroprudential instruments, and the design of institutional arrangements for policy coordination.

5.8.1 Excess Liquid Reserves

Banks in developing countries often hold large excess liquid reserves. This decision may be *involuntary* (as a result, for instance, of a structural lack of opportunities to lend, inadequate collateral from potential borrowers, or large capital inflows driven by changes in world interest rates and intermediated by the banking system), or it can be *voluntary* (for precautionary reasons, for instance, as a result of a sudden shift in perceived risks to the economy).[45] If banks are unwilling, rather than unable, to extend loans, a contraction in credit can be attributed to supply, rather than demand, factors. Regardless of their cause, excess liquid reserves have important implications for the effectiveness of monetary policy (Agénor and El Aynaoui 2010): a liquidity glut may impart greater stickiness to the deposit rate in response to a monetary contraction and induce an easing of collateral requirements on borrowers—which in turn may translate into a lower premium and a drop in loan rates. Asymmetric price response under excess liquidity may therefore hamper the ability of a contractionary monetary policy to fight inflationary pressures. If required reserves are viewed as an instrument of (structural or countercyclical) prudential regulation, excess reserves may also have significant implications for policies aimed at promoting financial stability. DSGE models that have discussed these implications include Glocker and Towbin (2012), Dressler and Kersting (2015), and Primus (2017).

A simple way to introduce (voluntary) excess reserves in the model presented earlier is to distinguish between required reserves, defined as before as $RR_t^i = \mu d_t^i$, and *total reserves*, defined as $TR_t^i = \mu_t^T d_t^i$, where d_t^i denotes bank deposits and $\mu, \mu_t^{T,i} \in (0, 1)$. Thus, bank *i*'s total reserves include (voluntary)

45. Implicit bailout guarantees also affect the decision to hold excess liquid assets voluntarily.

excess reserves, which are defined as $TR_t^i - RR_t^i = (\mu_t^{T,i} - \mu)d_t^i$. Banks now choose $\mu_t^{T,i}$ and thus, indirectly, the level of excess reserves.

Suppose that excess reserves are held in the form of (short-term) government bonds at the gross rate $1 + i_t^B$. Thus, banks earn additional income in amount $(1 + i_t^B)(\mu_t^{T,i} - \mu)d_t^i$.[46] At the same time, as in Glocker and Towbin (2012), suppose that there is a convex cost of holding reserves,

$$\Phi(\mu_t^{T,i} - \mu) = -\Phi_1^R(\mu_t^{T,i} - \mu) + \frac{\Phi_2^R}{2}(\mu_t^{T,i} - \mu)^2, \tag{5.35}$$

where $\Phi_1^R, \Phi_2^R > 0$. In this expression, the first (linear) term determines steady-state deviations from the required reserve ratio. The second (quadratic) term measures the benefits from holding excess reserves, related, for instance, to the fact that it reduces the cost of liquidity management and the risk of penalties imposed by the central bank if the required level of reserves is not met. However, this benefit is subject to decreasing marginal returns.

Bank i's maximization problem (defined in chapter 4) involves now choosing $\mu_t^{T,i}$, in addition to the loan rate and the repayment probability. With the balance sheet constraint given now by

$$l_t^i + TR_t^i = V_t^i + d_t^i + l_t^{B,i},$$

and profits adjusted for the term $[(1 + i_t^B)(\mu_t^{T,i} - \mu) - \Phi(\mu_t^{T,i} - \mu)]d_t^i$, the first-order condition with respect to that variable is

$$(1 + i_t^B)d_t^i - (1 + i_t^R)d_t^i + \Phi_1 d_t^i - \Phi_2(\mu_t^{T,i} - \mu)d_t^i = 0,$$

or equivalently, in a symmetric equilibrium,

$$\mu_t^T - \mu = \frac{i_t^B + \Phi_1^R - i_t^R}{\Phi_2^R}, \tag{5.36}$$

which shows that the excess reserve ratio increases with its opportunity cost (the bond rate) and falls with the marginal cost of borrowing from the central bank. By holding an additional unit of excess reserves, banks benefit from a return on government bonds; however, all else equal, that additional unit must be borrowed at a cost from the monetary authority.

46. More generally, it could be assumed that banks hold a fraction $\gamma^R \in (0, 1)$ of their excess reserves at the central bank and earn the net rate $(1 - \theta^R)i_t^R$, with $\theta^R \in (0, 1)$, whereas the fraction $1 - \gamma^R$ is invested in government bonds. Then, the additional income for banks would be $\{\gamma^R[1 + (1 - \theta^R)i_t^R] + (1 - \gamma^R)(1 + i_t^B)\}(\mu_t^{T,i} - \mu)d_t^i$.

In the model presented in chapter 4, which assumed perfect competition in the market for deposits, the addition of an equation for excess reserves such as (5.36) does not have any substantive impact on the results. However, if the market for deposits is also monopolistically competitive, it can be shown that the deposit rate will also depend on the excess reserve ratio (Primus 2017). In addition, if deposits and central bank borrowing are imperfect substitutes from the perspective of the central bank, as captured through (5.6) with $\varphi^{CB} > 0$, the transmission channel of changes in the required reserve ratio would be more complex. Whether this affects the properties of a countercyclical reserve requirement rule, based either on credit as before or excess liquidity instead, depends on the model's parameterization. In the experiments performed by Primus (2017), combining an augmented Taylor rule with a countercyclical reserve requirement rule (with both responding to excess reserves) is more effective to mitigate macroeconomic and financial volatility associated with liquidity shocks, compared to a standard Taylor rule coupled with a countercyclical reserve requirement rule. These results are in line with those discussed earlier for the tax rate on loans. Thus, monetary and macroprudential policies are complements in addressing financial stability issues, which runs counter to Tinbergen's principle.

5.8.2 Lending Restrictions and Instrument Combination

As noted in chapter 1, in both high-income and middle-income countries there is a wide range of macroprudential instruments currently in use, whether they relate to capital requirements, liquidity requirements, provisioning requirements, or lending restrictions. In this book, the emphasis is explicitly on the first two sets of instruments. But the other two have also been studied in a number of contributions. Provisioning requirements are discussed in chapter 6. As for lending restrictions, they include loan-to-value (LTV) ratios, loan-to-income (LTI) ratios, debt-to-income (DTI) ratios, and debt service-to-income (DSTI) ratios. Since the global financial crisis, these restrictions have been used with greater intensity in a wide range of countries. As documented by Akinci and Olmstead-Rumsey (2018), this has been especially the case for LTV restrictions.

LTV regulation helps to address externalities arising both on the supply and the demand side of the credit market. From the perspective of lenders, LTV limits impose quantity restrictions on their asset allocation. This mitigates externalities connected to strategic interactions that could induce banks to weaken their lending standards (thereby creating an adverse selection problem) and engage in more risky activities. From the perspective of borrowers, LTV constraints link debt to asset prices and help to address two main externalities:

a *demand externality* and *pecuniary externalities*, which may affect systemic risk (Farhi and Werning 2016; Jeanne and Korinek 2019). Households taking on debt do not take into account how their behavior affects wealth distribution in the economy, the evolution of house prices, aggregate debt ratios, and output. When a negative shock hits the economy, foreclosures tend to increase, and this may lead to further drops in house prices, generating negative feedback loops (see chapter 1).

LTI and DSTI regulations impose a limit on borrowing or debt service in relation to disposable income, thereby directly targeting risky borrowers who might also raise macroprudential concerns in the presence of pecuniary and demand externalities. On the side of the lender, similarly to LTV regulation, these limits address the strategic interaction externality, preventing lenders from lowering their credit standards. Notably, DSTI limits, by directly linking interest rate expenses to debt, enhance the transmission mechanism from interest rates into credit growth, house prices, and aggregate demand. LTI and DSTI limits can coexist and they complement both LTV caps and capital adequacy requirements.

The performance of LTV regulation—in terms of its ability to reduce borrowers' leverage, mitigate the procyclicality of credit flows and promote financial stability—has been studied in a number of contributions to the DSGE literature. These contributions have generally found that stricter LTV limits are fairly effective in mitigating macroeconomic and financial volatility (Gelain et al. 2013; Mendicino and Punzi 2014; Rubio and Carrasco-Gallego 2014; Castillo et al. 2015; Rubio 2019), as well as stabilizing leverage of the nonfinancial sector (Iacoviello 2005; Carlstrom and Fuerst 2016; Chen and Columba 2016; Alpanda and Zubairy 2017; Falagiarda and Saia 2017; Funke et al. 2018). Rubio and Carrasco-Gallego (2014), for instance, examined the welfare implications of introducing a countercyclical macroprudential LTV rule that reacts to credit growth. They found that the rule is welfare-enhancing. In a related setup, Mendicino and Punzi (2014) studied welfare implications of countercyclical LTV rules in a two-country world where monetary policy may respond to household indebtedness or house prices. The LTV restriction that maximizes social welfare depends on the assumed behavior of the monetary authority. The largest welfare gains, compared to no activism, are obtained when the LTV ratio reacts countercyclically to house prices, whereas the policy interest rate reacts also to credit growth. Thus, there is complementarity between monetary and macroprudential policies—a result, once again, similar to the one established earlier with respect to the tax on loans.

Although the list of DSGE models considering LTV requirements is fairly extensive, the literature incorporating LTI or DSTI constraints is scant. This literature includes contributions by Gelain et al. (2013), Finocchiaro et al. (2016), and Greenwald (2016). In one of the experiments that they consider, Gelain et al. (2013) augmented an LTV borrowing constraint with an LTI limit and found that this additional rule is effective in decreasing the volatility of debt in the economy. For their part, Finocchiaro et al. (2016) found that lowering LTI (or LTV) limits reduces household indebtedness and lowers the volatility of house prices and credit in the economy, although this may come at the cost of lower output and consumption. Finally, in a model where a housing collateral constraint is augmented with a DSTI constraint, Greenwald (2016) found that DSTI limits may be more effective—in terms of mitigating credit fluctuations—than LTV regulation, because not all borrowers in the economy are continuously bound by that constraint.

Given that lending restrictions operate through mechanisms that differ from the other macroprudential instruments, a key question that arises is to what extent these various categories of tools are complementary. In fact, it is very possible that combining macroprudential policies (say, reserve requirements, as in this chapter, with an LTV restriction) generate higher welfare, or a lower policy loss, than combining either one of these instruments with an augmented monetary policy rule, along the lines discussed in this chapter and in chapter 6.

Some DSGE contributions have indeed considered the interactions (or lack thereof) and performance of a combined set of macroprudential instruments.[47] This is the case in Finocchiaro et al. (2016) and Greenwald (2016), as noted earlier. In addition, Agénor and Pereira da Silva (2017) considered interactions between loan loss provisions and reserve requirements, whereas Frache et al. (2018) and Krueger et al. (2018) focus on the interactions between loan loss provisions and capital requirements (see chapter 6). Agénor and Jia (2020) considered, in an open economy, the combination of a tax on bank foreign borrowing and reserve requirements (see chapter 9). However, a systematic comparison between the gains from combining multiple macroprudential instruments, on the one hand, and combining monetary policy with alternative individual macroprudential tools, on the other, is not yet available.

5.8.3 Institutional Arrangements for Coordination

The foregoing analysis has shown that, under some circumstances, coordination between monetary and macroprudential policymakers is desirable. However,

47. The finance literature has studied the interactions between different forms of banking regulation (Kashyap et al. 2014; Walther 2016; Mankart et al. 2018), but these aspects of regulation have not been discussed extensively in the macroeconomic literature.

this does not provide any guideline as to how such coordination should occur in practice. Questions that arise in this context are whether the macroprudential function of monitoring and mitigation of risks and vulnerabilities of the financial system as a whole should be carried jointly by the central bank and regulators, whether institutionally independent entities should be responsible for each policy instrument to improve transparency and accountability, or whether central bank charters should be changed to reflect explicitly the adoption of a financial stability objective.

Since the global financial crisis, there have been indeed a number of changes in the institutional organization of financial supervision and the role played by central banks beyond their traditionally narrow mandate of price stability. These changes have led to a variety of institutional arrangements, which differ essentially in two dimensions (Calvo et al. 2018): The first is their ability to exploit synergies across different functions by grouping them within a specific institution; the second is their capacity to minimize conflicts across objectives by assigning them to different authorities. The latter is, in principle, as important as the former, given that conflicting objectives within the same authority may lead to the subordination of one to the other in a way that may be socially suboptimal. These arrangements include a *goal-integrated* mandate, in which the central bank is responsible for both monetary policy and macroprudential regulation, and *partially integrated* mandates, which group responsibilities in different authorities according to different criteria, including the setting of objectives and the choice of instruments.

As discussed by Agénor and Pereira da Silva (2019), the debate is still open regarding the costs and benefits of alternative institutional arrangements—in developed and developing countries alike. In particular, it has been argued that a specific mandate to preserve financial stability may deter, in effect, the central bank from its fundamental goal (the pursuit of price stability) and may generate reputational or credibility costs that can jeopardize its ability to perform its core function effectively. Moreover, the accumulation of power within a single institution may raise issues of political legitimacy, which could end up being resolved by introducing excessive constraints on the monetary authority's mandates and operational procedures. At the other extreme, price and financial stability cannot be viewed as two different objectives that may be effectively pursued by different agencies, acting separately, using different instruments (interest rates for the central bank, macroprudential tools for the regulator). As noted earlier, a key argument in favor of an integrated mandate, with respect to objectives if not instruments, is the fact that there are close linkages between the transmission mechanisms of monetary and macroprudential policies. This close relationship is the fundamental reason why it is generally optimal, and beneficial in terms of outcomes, to solve jointly for these policies. Again, however, this argument is one for coordination, not necessarily for delegating responsibility for instrument setting and manipulation to a single institution. In practice, nevertheless, central banks have become the primary macroprudential authority in close to 60 percent of the jurisdictions surveyed by Calvo et al. (2018), although often other authorities are also involved by participating in interagency committees.

6 Capital Requirements and Monetary Policy

Capital requirements are a key aspect of bank regulation, both at the microprudential and macroprudential levels. The banking literature, in particular, has focused on two main functions of bank capital. First, because of limited liability and deposit insurance, banks have incentives to engage in excessively risky lending activities. Requiring banks to hold a minimum ratio of capital to assets reduces these incentives. As discussed by Bhattacharya et al. (1998) and Brunnermeier et al. (2009), for instance, capital requirements (especially when they are based on the degree of riskiness of bank assets) help to mitigate moral hazard on the part of lenders. Second, bank capital acts as a buffer that may offset losses due to unexpected default—unlike provisions, designed to cope with expected loan losses—and therefore helps to strengthen the resilience of the financial system.

Understanding the macroeconomic effects of bank capital requirements has also been the subject of a large literature in recent years. From the perspective of this book, critical issues include how regulatory capital affects the monetary transmission mechanism, how it contributes to aggregate fluctuations and financial volatility, and the extent to which it contributes to the attenuation or, on the contrary, amplification of real and financial shocks.

This chapter extends the core dynamic stochastic general equilibrium (DSGE) model presented in chapter 4 to account for bank capital requirements. In addition, it considers again whether, as discussed in chapter 5, central banks should more explicitly account for financial stability considerations in the conduct of monetary policy in order to prevent the buildup of financial imbalances. By implication, a natural question is the extent to which monetary policy and capital regulation should be combined to promote macroeconomic and financial stability.[1] In contrast to chapter 5, the case considered here assumes

1. Christensen et al. (2011), Agénor et al. (2013), Angelini et al. (2014), and Rubio and Carrasco-Gallego (2016) are some of the contributions that have focused on this issue.

that policy authorities can act strategically when they independently set their policy instrument.

To set the stage, section 1 provides a brief discussion, largely from a macroeconomic perspective, of the treatment of bank capital requirements under existing international accords. Section 2 presents the model. Importantly, it accounts for both required bank capital and excess capital—an important empirical regularity observed in advanced and middle-income economies alike. As in chapter 4, sections 3, 4 and 5 discuss the equilibrium conditions of the model, its steady-state properties and log-linearization, and its parameterization. Because the structure of the model is fundamentally the same, only differences with respect to previous developments are dwelt on. Section 6 considers the impact of a standard financial shock and briefly examines its transmission under capital regulation. Section 7 discusses alternative simple rules for promoting macroeconomic and financial stability: a credit-augmented interest rate rule, on the one hand, and a countercyclical capital requirements rule, on the other. The performance of each rule, implemented independently, is assessed, and so are outcomes under coordination. The last section offers further notes on the literature, with a focus on the treatment of bank capital in DSGE models.

6.1 Background

Bank capital requirements are the cornerstone of the Basel Accords, developed by the Basel Committee on Bank Supervision (BCBS), on international financial regulation. The 1988 Basel Accord, known as Basel I, was criticized for the fact that capital charges were not risk sensitive—that is, they did not reflect the degree of riskiness of the assets that banks were holding in their portfolios. Indeed, Basel I required banks to hold capital of at least 8 percent of their risk-weighted assets. Critics noted early on that it treated all corporate credits alike and thereby could promote regulatory arbitrage, and that it failed to take account of the distortions induced by capital regulation. In effect, the Basel I regulatory capital regime gave banks strong incentives to reduce required capital by shifting loans off their balance sheets. Over time, banks in advanced economies turned to an *originate and distribute* model in which standardized loans—mostly high-risk mortgages involving no money down, interest only or less as the initial payment with no documentation on borrowers' capacity to pay, and initial "teaser" interest rates that would adjust upward even if market rates remained constant—could be bundled and sold as securities, thereby leaving the originating bank free to use its capital elsewhere.[2]

2. In the United States, as the housing market started to deteriorate in 2006, and uncertainty about the underlying value of subprime mortgage-backed securities mounted, efforts to maintain adequate

To address this limitation, the Basel II Accord, implemented in 2004, introduced risk-based capital regulation. Under Basel II, capital requirements are based on asset *quality* and not only on asset *type*. In addition, banks were required to use mark-to-market accounting to price assets at fair value, rather than book value. The accord also introduced the *internal ratings-based* (IRB) approach, which allowed banks to use their internal models—once validated by the regulatory authority—to assess the riskiness of their portfolios and determine their required capital cushion. In effect, the amount of capital that a bank is required to hold against a given exposure depends on the estimated credit risk of that exposure, which in turn is determined by the probability of default (PD), loss given default (LGD), exposure at default (EAD), and maturity. Thus, riskier exposures carry a higher capital charge. The fundamental goal of risk-based capital regulation is to reduce bank failures and the associated systemic costs by holding the bank probability of default below some fixed target.[3] It is also consistent with the argument, alluded to earlier, that risk-based capital requirements help to mitigate moral hazard.

The adoption of Basel II prompted a broader debate as well on the procyclicality of regulatory rules and practices. Because these rules make bank capital requirements more sensitive to changes in the banks' risk exposure, and as the riskiness of loan portfolios changes over the business cycle, the required regulatory capital varies also. For instance, when asset prices start declining, banks may be forced to undertake write-downs (accompanied by increased loan-loss provisioning), and this raises their need for capital. Thus, capital requirements may increase in a cyclical downturn. If banks are highly leveraged, to maintain their capital ratio during a recession they must either raise capital (which is difficult and/or costly in bad times) or cut back their lending, which in turn tends to amplify the downturn by triggering a credit crunch. Thus, it became increasingly clear that risk-sensitive capital charges, along the lines proposed in the Basel II Accord, may not only increase the volatility of regulatory capital, but also (by limiting banks' ability to lend) exacerbate an economic downturn.[4] Kashyap and Stein (2004), for instance, argued that the IRB approach is largely microprudential in nature and ignores the importance of the function of bank lending for the aggregate economy. In line with the literature on capital crunches in banking, they argued that the shadow value

levels of capital led to massive deleveraging, liquidity shortages, and contractions in credit supply, with adverse consequences for the functioning of both real and financial markets. See Kashyap et al. (2008) and Calomiris (2009).

3. Basel II also acknowledged the importance of two complementary mechanisms to safeguard financial stability—namely, supervision and market discipline.

4. See, for instance, Agénor and Pereira da Silva (2012) and the references therein.

of bank capital increases during recessions and that imposing capital requirements that are too high when bank capital is scarce may result in insufficient funding of investments with positive net present value. By implication, if the regulator's objective is both to protect the financial system against the costs of large-scale bank defaults and sustain bank lending, capital requirements should be adjusted—for any degree of credit-risk exposure—to the state of the business cycle. More specifically, it has been argued that during good times banks should hold capital in excess of the minimum regulatory requirements in order to strengthen their balance sheets and increase their resilience to adverse shocks and prevent a credit crunch in bad times.

In response to these concerns, the Basel III Accord, which began to be implemented in 2011, introduced countercyclical capital buffers, which range from zero to 2.5 percent of risk-weighted assets (Basel Committee on Banking Supervision 2011, 2017). The goal of these buffers is to try to reduce the tension between micro and macro regulation mentioned earlier—that is, the need to maintain the risk sensitivity of capital requirements for different financial institutions while at the same time mitigating the procyclical effects of this type of regulation.[5] The Basel III Accord also proposed to adjust the level of the countercyclical capital buffer on the basis of the credit gap, defined as deviation from trend, even though it was acknowledged that in practice this gap may not be a good indicator of financial fragility in downturns (Drehmann et al. 2010; Drehmann and Tsatsaronis 2014). At an analytical level, the performance of countercyclical capital requirement rules is a key focus of this chapter.

6.2 The Model

As in the previous chapters, the economy is closed and populated by eight types of agents: infinitely lived households, intermediate good (IG) producers, final good (FG) producers, capital good (CG) producers, commercial banks, the government, the central bank, and a financial regulator. Each household makes its housing stock available, free of charge, to a matched CG producer, who uses it as collateral against which it borrows from banks to buy goods for investment and to produce capital. It then rents capital to IG producers. Banks also supply credit to IG producers, who use it to finance their short-term working capital needs. Their supply of loans is perfectly elastic at the prevailing loan rate. To satisfy capital regulations, each bank issues nominal debt at the beginning of

5. In addition, as argued by Dewatripont and Tirole (2012), countercyclical capital buffers aimed at neutralizing the effects of macroeconomic shocks may also be an optimal regulatory response when the goal is to keep the incentives of both bank managers and shareholders unchanged.

the period, once the level of (risky) loans is known.[6] Banks pay interest on household deposits, the liquidity that they borrow from the central bank, and the debt that they issue.

All assets and liabilities mature in one period. At the end of each period, banks close their books and reopen at the beginning of the next; thus, all their profits are distributed, bank debt is redeemed, and new debt is issued at the beginning of the next period to comply with prudential regulatory rules. As before, the central bank supplies all the liquidity that banks demand at the prevailing refinance rate and initially sets its base policy rate solely in response to deviations of inflation from its target value and cyclical output.

6.2.1 Households

Households consume, hold financial assets, and supply labor to IG producers. The objective of the representative household is to maximize

$$U_t = \mathbb{E}_t \sum_{s=0}^{\infty} \Lambda^s \left\{ \frac{C_{t+s}^{1-\varsigma^{-1}}}{1-\varsigma^{-1}} - \int_0^1 \frac{\eta_N (N_{t+s}^j)^{1+\psi_N}}{1+\psi_N} dj + \ln x_{t+s}^{\eta_x} + \ln H_{t+s}^{\eta_H} \right\}, \tag{6.1}$$

where C_t is final good consumption, N_t^j time allocated to IG firm j, x_t monetary assets, H_t the stock of housing, $\Lambda \in (0, 1)$ the discount factor, $\varsigma > 0$ the intertemporal elasticity of substitution, and $\eta_N, \psi_N, \eta_x, \eta_H > 0$ are preference parameters.

The monetary asset combines real cash balances, m_t, and real bank deposits, d_t:

$$x_t = m_t^{\nu} d_t^{1-\nu}, \tag{6.2}$$

where $\nu \in (0, 1)$.

Real financial wealth of the representative household, a_t, is

$$a_t = m_t + d_t + b_t + p_t^H H_t + V_t,$$

where b_t denotes real holdings of noncontingent government bonds, p_t^H the real price of housing services (in terms of the price of the final good), and V_t real holdings of bank debt.

Assuming that housing does not depreciate, the household's flow budget constraint is

6. Thus, in the Basel terminology, capital consists solely of "supplementary" or "tier 2" capital; there is no "core" or "tier 1" capital (that is, ordinary shares). In practice, to meet capital requirements banks have often issued hybrid securities that are more like debt than equity. Even though under Basel III the definition of capital in terms of common equity has been tightened, banks continue to have the ability to issue debt-like instruments to meet these requirements.

$$m_t + d_t + b_t + p_t^H \Delta H_t + V_t \tag{6.3}$$
$$= \omega_t N_t - T_t - C_t + \frac{m_{t-1}}{1+\pi_t} + \left(\frac{1+i_{t-1}^D}{1+\pi_t}\right) d_{t-1} + \left(\frac{1+i_{t-1}^B}{1+\pi_t}\right) b_{t-1}$$
$$+ J_t^B + J_t^I + J_t^K + \left(\frac{1+i_{t-1}^V}{1+\pi_t}\right) V_{t-1} - \Theta_V \frac{V_t^2}{2},$$

where $N_t = \int_0^1 N_t^j dj$ is total labor supply; T_t is lump-sum taxes; $\pi_{t+1} = (P_{t+1} - P_t)/P_t$ is the inflation rate; J_t^B, J_t^I, J_t^K are profits (if any) made by a matched bank, IG producer, and CG producer, respectively; and i_{t-1}^V is the rate of return on bank debt. The last term, $0.5\Theta_V V_t^2$, represents pecuniary transactions costs—such as costs paid to brokers, or costs of collecting information about the banks' balance sheet—that households incur when adjusting their stock of bank debt across periods, and $\Theta_V > 0$ is an adjustment cost parameter.[7]

The representative household chooses sequences $\{C_{t+s}\}_{s=0}^{\infty}$, $\{N_{t+s}^j\}_{s=0}^{\infty}$, $j \in (0,1)$, $\{m_{t+s},\ d_{t+s},\ b_{t+s},\ H_{t+s}\}_{s=0}^{\infty}$, and now also holdings of bank debt, $\{V_{t+s}\}_{s=0}^{\infty}$, so as to maximize (6.1) subject to (6.2) and (6.3), taking interest rates (i_t^B, i_t^D, and i_t^V), prices and inflation (ω_t, p_t^H, and π_t), and all lump-sum transfers and taxes (J_t^B, J_t^I, J_t^K, and T_t) as given at all times. The Lagrangian for this problem, $\mathcal{L}_t$, can be written as

$$\mathcal{L}_t = \mathbb{E}_t \sum_{s=0}^{\infty} \Lambda^s \left\{ \frac{C_{t+s}^{1-\varsigma^{-1}}}{1-\varsigma^{-1}} - \int_0^1 \frac{\eta_N}{1+\psi_N} (N_{t+s}^j)^{1+\psi_N} dj + \ln x_{t+s}^{\eta_x} + \ln H_{t+s}^{\eta_H} \right.$$
$$-\lambda_{t+s} \left\{ m_{t+s} + d_{t+s} + b_{t+s} + p_{t+s}^H \Delta H_{t+s} + V_{t+s} - \omega_{t+s} N_{t+s} + T_{t+s} \right.$$
$$+ C_{t+s} - \frac{m_{t+s-1}}{1+\pi_{t+s}} - \left(\frac{1+i_{t+s-1}^D}{1+\pi_{t+s}}\right) d_{t+s-1} - \left(\frac{1+i_{t+s-1}^B}{1+\pi_{t+s}}\right) b_{t+s-1}$$
$$\left. - (J_{t+s}^B + J_{t+s}^I + J_{t+s}^K) - \left(\frac{1+i_{t+s-1}^V}{1+\pi_{t+s}}\right) V_{t+s-1} + \Theta_V \frac{V_{t+s}^2}{2} \right\},$$

where λ_t is the Lagrange multiplier associated with constraint (6.3).

The first-order conditions with respect to C_t, N_t^j, m_t, d_t, b_t, and H_t are the same as those derived in chapter 4 and need not be repeated here. These

7. The presence of adjustment costs can be viewed as reflecting asymmetric information. As in Markovic (2006), for instance, the adjustment cost is taken to be a deadweight loss for society. Alternatively, in a manner similar to Andrés et al. (2004), for instance, portfolio adjustment costs could be entered directly in the period utility function.

conditions can be combined to give

$$C_t^{-1/\varsigma} = \Lambda \mathbb{E}_t \left\{ C_{t+1}^{-1/\varsigma} \left(\frac{1+i_t^B}{1+\pi_{t+1}} \right) \right\}, \tag{6.4}$$

$$N_t^j = \left(\frac{\omega_t C_t^{-1/\varsigma}}{\eta_N} \right)^{1/\psi_N}, \tag{6.5}$$

$$m_t = \frac{\eta_x \nu C_t^{1/\varsigma}(1+i_t^B)}{i_t^B}, \tag{6.6}$$

$$d_t = \frac{\eta_x (1-\nu) C_t^{1/\varsigma}(1+i_t^B)}{i_t^B - i_t^D}, \tag{6.7}$$

$$\frac{p_t^H}{C_t^{1/\varsigma}} = \frac{\eta_H}{H_t} + \Lambda \mathbb{E}_t \left(\frac{p_{t+1}^H}{C_{t+1}^{1/\varsigma}} \right). \tag{6.8}$$

Condition (6.4) is the Euler equation and condition (6.5) defines labor supply. Conditions (6.6), (6.7), and (6.8) define the demand functions for cash, deposits, and housing services, respectively. The properties of all these equations are the same as those discussed in chapter 4.

The condition with respect to V_t is given by

$$\frac{\partial \mathcal{L}_t}{\partial V_t} : -\lambda_t + \Lambda \mathbb{E}_t \left\{ \lambda_{t+1} \left(\frac{1+i_t^V}{1+\pi_{t+1}} \right) \right\} - \Theta_V \lambda_t V_t = 0, \tag{6.9}$$

for $t = 0, 1, \ldots \infty$.[8] It can be rewritten as

$$\Lambda \mathbb{E}_t \left\{ \frac{\lambda_{t+1}}{\lambda_t} \left(\frac{1+i_t^V}{1+\pi_{t+1}} \right) \right\} = 1 + \Theta_V V_t.$$

As shown in chapter 4, $\Lambda \mathbb{E}_t[\lambda_{t+1}/(1+\pi_{t+1})] = \lambda_t/(1+i_t^B)$. Substituting this result in the above expression yields

$$\frac{1+i_t^V}{1+i_t^B} = 1 + \Theta_V V_t,$$

which can be rearranged to give

$$V_t^d = \Theta_V^{-1} \left(\frac{i_t^V - i_t^B}{1+i_t^B} \right). \tag{6.10}$$

8. There is also an additional transversality condition, $\lim_{s \to \infty} \mathbb{E}_{t+s} \Lambda^s \lambda_{t+s} V_{t+s} = 0$.

Equation (6.10) shows that household demand for bank capital is positively (negatively) related to the rate of return on capital (bonds). Without adjustment costs ($\Theta_V = 0$) it boils down to the arbitrage equation $i_t^V = i_t^B$, which implies that households are indifferent between holding bank capital and government bonds.

6.2.2 Final Good Producers

The final good, Y_t, is produced by assembling a continuum of imperfectly substitutable intermediate goods Y_t^j, with $j \in (0, 1)$,

$$Y_t = \left\{ \int_0^1 (Y_t^j)^{(\theta-1)/\theta} dj \right\}^{\theta/(\theta-1)}, \tag{6.11}$$

where $\theta > 1$ is the elasticity of demand for each intermediate good.

The FG producer sells its output at a perfectly competitive price. Given the intermediate-good price P_t^j and the final-good price P_t, it chooses the quantities of intermediate goods, Y_t^j, that maximize its profits. Thus,

$$Y_t^j = \arg\max \left[P_t \left\{ \int_0^1 (Y_t^j)^{(\theta-1)/\theta} dj \right\}^{\theta/(\theta-1)} - \int_0^1 P_t^j Y_t^j dj \right].$$

The first-order conditions yield again the demand for each variety of good $j \in (0, 1)$,

$$Y_t^j = \left(\frac{P_t^j}{P_t} \right)^{-\theta} Y_t, \tag{6.12}$$

which can be combined as before with the zero-profit condition to give the final-good price

$$P_t = \left\{ \int_0^1 (P_t^j)^{1-\theta} dj \right\}^{1/(1-\theta)}. \tag{6.13}$$

6.2.3 Intermediate Good Producers

Each IG firm produces a differentiate good which is sold on a monopolistically competitive market. At the beginning of the period, each of them rents capital from a randomly matched CG producer, at a cost r_t^K.

Production of each intermediate good j, Y_t^j, requires labor, N_t^j, and capital, K_t^j,

$$Y_t^j = (N_t^j)^{1-\alpha}(K_t^j)^{\alpha}, \tag{6.14}$$

where $\alpha \in (0, 1)$.

Each firm j borrows an amount $l_t^{W,j}$ from the bank at the beginning of the period to pay a fraction $\psi_W \in (0, 1)$ of the wage bill in advance:

$$l_t^{W,j} = \psi_W \omega_t N_t^j. \tag{6.15}$$

Working capital loans are again risk-free and contracted at the refinance rate, i_t^R. These loans are repaid at the end of the period.

Intermediate goods are sold on a monopolistically competitive market. IG producers solve a two-stage problem. In the first stage, taking input prices as given, they rent labor and capital in perfectly competitive factor markets so as to minimize real costs. As shown in chapter 4, this yields the optimal capital-labor ratio

$$\frac{K_t^j}{N_t^j} = \left(\frac{\alpha}{1-\alpha}\right)\left[\frac{(1+\psi_W i_t^R)\omega_t}{r_t^K}\right], \quad \forall j \tag{6.16}$$

and marginal cost

$$mc_t = \frac{\left[(1+\psi_W i_t^R)\omega_t\right]^{1-\alpha}(r_t^K)^{\alpha}}{\alpha^{\alpha}(1-\alpha)^{1-\alpha}}. \tag{6.17}$$

In the second stage, each IG producer chooses a sequence of prices P_t^j so as to maximize discounted real profits

$$\{P_{t+s}^j\}_{s=0}^{\infty} = \arg\max \mathbb{E}_t \sum_{s=0}^{\infty} \Lambda^s \lambda_{t+s} J_{jt+s}^{I,j},$$

where real profits at t, $J_t^{I,j}$, are defined as

$$J_t^{I,j} = \left(\frac{P_t^j}{P_t}\right) Y_t^j - mc_t Y_t^j - PAC_t^j,$$

and PAC_t^j is a Rotemberg-type price adjustment cost defined as, assuming zero steady-state inflation,

$$PAC_t^j = \frac{\phi_I}{2}\left(\frac{P_t^j}{P_{t-1}^j} - 1\right)^2 Y_t. \tag{6.18}$$

In this expression, $\phi_I \geq 0$ is an adjustment cost parameter.

Taking $\{mc_{t+s}, P_{t+s}, Y_{t+s}\}_{s=0}^{\infty}$ as given, the first-order condition for this maximization problem gives, in a symmetric equilibrium where $P_t^j = P_t$ for all j, and with zero inflation in the steady state,

$$\phi_I \pi_t(1+\pi_t) = 1 - \theta + \theta mc_t + \Lambda\phi_I \mathbb{E}_t\left\{\frac{\lambda_{t+1}}{\lambda_t}\pi_{t+1}(1+\pi_{t+1})\left(\frac{Y_{t+1}}{Y_t}\right)\right\}. \tag{6.19}$$

6.2.4 Capital Good Producers

Capital goods are produced with a linear technology. At the beginning of the period, the representative CG producer buys a real amount I_t of the final good from the representative FG producer. These goods must be paid in advance, so investment loans are given by

$$l_t^K = I_t. \tag{6.20}$$

Each household makes its housing stock, H_t, available free of charge to the CG-producing firm that it owns, which uses it as collateral to borrow from banks, at the rate i_t^L. With $q_t \in (0, 1)$ denoting the probability that loans are repaid in full, expected repayment is $q_t(1+i_t^L)l_t^K + (1-q_t)\kappa\mathbb{E}_t p_{t+1}^H H_t$, where $(1+i_t^L)l_t^K$ is the contractual payment and $\kappa\mathbb{E}_t p_{t+1}^H H_t$ the value of collateral, where $\kappa = \int_0^1 \kappa^i di \leq 1$ and $\kappa^i \in (0, 1)$ is the fraction of the housing stock pledged to each bank i.

To produce new capital, K_{t+1}, requires combining gross investment with the existing stock of capital, adjusted for depreciation and adjustment costs:

$$K_{t+1} = I_t + (1-\delta_K)K_t - \frac{\Theta_K}{2}\left(\frac{K_{t+1}}{K_t} - 1\right)^2 K_t, \tag{6.21}$$

where $\delta_K \in (0, 1)$ is the rate of depreciation and $\Theta_K > 0$ an adjustment cost parameter. The new capital stock is then rented to a randomly matched IG producer.

The representative CG producer chooses the level of the capital stock so as to maximize the value of the discounted stream of dividend payments to the matched household:

$$\{K_{t+s}\}_{s=0}^{\infty} = \arg\max \sum_{s=0}^{\infty} \mathbb{E}_t(\Lambda^s \lambda_{t+s} J_{t+s+1}^K),$$

where $\mathbb{E}_t(\Lambda^s \lambda_{t+s} J_{t+s+1}^K)$ denotes expected profits at the end of period $t+s$, discounted at the rate $\Lambda^s \lambda_{t+s}$, and defined as

$$\mathbb{E}_t(\Lambda^s \lambda_{t+s} J^K_{t+s+1}) = \Lambda^s \mathbb{E}_t\{\lambda_{t+s}[r^K_{t+s} K_{t+s} - q_{t+s}(1+i^L_{t+s}) I_{t+s} - (1-q_{t+s})\kappa p^H_{t+s+1} H_t]\},$$

subject to equation (6.21) and taking $\{i^L_{t+s}\}^\infty_{s=0}$, $\{p^H_{t+s+1}\}^\infty_{s=0}$, $\{q_{t+s}\}^\infty_{s=0}$, and $\{r^K_{t+s}\}^\infty_{s=0}$ as given.

As shown in chapter 4, the solution of this problem gives

$$\mathbb{E}_t r^K_{t+1} \simeq q_t(1+i^L_t)\mathbb{E}_t\left[\left\{1+\Theta_K\left(\frac{K_{t+1}}{K_t}-1\right)\right\}\left(\frac{1+i^B_t}{1+\pi_{t+1}}\right)\right] - \mathbb{E}_t\left[q_{t+1}(1+i^L_{t+1})\left\{1-\delta_K+\frac{\Theta_K}{2}\left[\left(\frac{K_{t+2}}{K_{t+1}}\right)^2-1\right]\right\}\right], \tag{6.22}$$

which relates the expected rental rate of capital to the current and expected loan rates, the latter through its indirect effect on future adjustment costs.

The amount borrowed by the representative CG producer is a Dixit-Stiglitz basket of differentiated loans, each supplied by a bank i, with a constant elasticity of substitution $\zeta^L > 1$:

$$l^K_t = \left[\int_0^1 (l^{K,i}_t)^{(\zeta^L-1)/\zeta} di\right]^{\zeta^L/(\zeta^L-1)}.$$

The demand for type-i loan, $l^{K,i}_t$, is thus given by the downward-sloping curve

$$l^{K,i}_t = \left(\frac{1+i^{L,i}_t}{1+i^L_t}\right)^{-\zeta^L} l^K_t, \tag{6.23}$$

where $i^{L,i}_t$ is the rate on the loan extended by bank i and i^L_t is the aggregate loan rate, defined as $i^L_t = [\int_0^1 (1+i^{L,i}_t)^{1-\zeta^L} di]^{1/(1-\zeta^L)} - 1$.

6.2.5 Banks and Regulatory Regime

Balance sheet

Banks hold capital, collect deposits, and lend to IG and CG producers, respectively, to finance working capital needs and investment. They also hold required reserves at the central bank, RR^i_t. To fund any shortfall in resources, they borrow from the central bank, $l^{B,i}_t$.

Bank i's balance sheet is thus

$$l^i_t + RR^i_t = V^i_t + d^i_t + l^{B,i}_t, \tag{6.24}$$

where $l_t^i = l_t^{K,i} + l_t^{W,i}$ and

$$V_t^i = V_t^{E,i} + V_t^{R,i}, \tag{6.25}$$

with V_t^i denoting total capital, $V_t^{R,i}$ capital requirements, and $V_t^{E,i}$ excess capital.

Required reserves held at the central bank do not pay interest and are determined, as in previous chapters, as a fraction of deposits,

$$RR_t^i = \mu d_t^i, \tag{6.26}$$

where $\mu \in (0, 1)$ is again the required reserve ratio. Given the focus on capital requirements, μ is kept constant in what follows.

As before, the balance sheet constraint (6.24), together with (6.25) and (6.26), can be used to determine residually the level of bank i's borrowing from the central bank:

$$l_t^{B,i} = l_t^i - V_t^{E,i} - V_t^{R,i} - (1-\mu)d_t^i. \tag{6.27}$$

Because banks close all their operations at the end of each period, they do not accumulate capital through retained earnings. This is in contrast to Zhang (2009) and Gerali et al. (2010), for instance, and extensions of the latter contribution, such as Angelini et al. (2014).[9]

Capital regulation

Banks are subject to risk-based capital requirements, imposed by the regulator. In each period they must hold an amount of capital that covers an endogenous percentage of their risky loans. Working capital loans bear no risk and are therefore subject to a zero weight in calculating capital requirements. Thus, with σ_t^i denoting the risk weight on investment loans, required capital is given by

$$V_t^{R,i} = \rho_t \sigma_t^i l_t^{K,i}, \tag{6.28}$$

where $\rho_t \in (0, 1)$ is the overall capital ratio, defined later. As in Agénor and Pereira da Silva (2012), and in line with the *foundation* variant of the IRB approach of Basel II, the risk weight σ_t^i can be negatively related to the repayment probability, which reflects the possibility of default,[10]

$$\sigma_t^i = \left(\frac{q_t^i}{\tilde{q}}\right)^{-\phi_q}, \tag{6.29}$$

where $\phi_q \geq 0$ and $\tilde{q}$ is the steady-state value of q_t.

9. This issue is discussed further in the chapter's last section.

10. De Walque et al. (2010) and Mendicino et al. (2018) used a related specification.

Under the IRB approach, discussed earlier, the estimated credit risk—and the associated risk weights—is a function of four parameters: the probability of default *PD*, the loss given default, the exposure at default, and the loan's maturity. Banks adopting the *advanced* variant of this approach must provide all of these parameters from their own internal ratings models; those adopting the *foundation* variant provide only the *PD* parameter, with the other parameters set externally by regulators. The appendix to this chapter provides a justification for the reduced-form, constant elasticity specification shown in (6.29), based on the Basel formulas.

Equation (6.29) implies that in the steady state, the risk weight is normalized to unity.[11] Thus, if risk weights are insensitive to the possibility of default (as in a Basel I-type regime), $\phi_q = 0$ and $\sigma_t^i = 1$, $\forall i$. Moreover, given that in this model the only other assets that banks hold are required reserves and working capital loans (which are zero in the benchmark case, given that $\psi_W = 0$), the case where $\phi_q = 0$ also corresponds to the case where ρ_t^{-1} is the leverage ratio, defined as $l_t^{K,i}/V_t^{R,i}$.[12]

The overall capital ratio, ρ_t, can be decomposed into a deterministic component, ρ^D, and a cyclical component, ρ_t^C:

$$\rho_t = \rho^D + \rho_t^C. \tag{6.30}$$

Thus, the component ρ^D can be viewed as the minimum capital adequacy ratio (or *Cooke ratio*) imposed under the Basel arrangements, whereas the component ρ_t^C can be viewed as the discretionary component, that is, the countercyclical capital ratio that is now part of Basel III.

The market for deposits is competitive, and deposits and central bank liquidity are perfect substitutes from the perspective of commercial banks. This ensures therefore that $\forall i$, the deposit rate is given by

$$i_t^{D,i} = (1 - \mu) i_t^R. \tag{6.31}$$

11. The Standardized Approach in Basel II can be modeled by making the risk weight a function of the output gap, under the assumption that ratings are procyclical, in a manner similar to Zicchino (2006) and Angeloni and Faia (2013), for instance. See Drumond (2009) and Panetta and Angelini (2009) for a discussion of the evidence on this issue.

12. In a more general setting, the leverage ratio and the capital adequacy ratio would of course be different. Moreover, under Basel III, the leverage ratio is intended to act as a complement and a *backstop* to risk-based capital requirements. In principle, it should counterbalance the buildup of systemic risk by limiting the effects of lower risk weights during booms. Thus, the leverage ratio is expected to act (more) countercyclically than the risk-weighted asset ratio, being tighter in expansions and looser in recessions. See Gambacorta and Karmakar (2018) for an analysis.

Optimization problem

Monopolistic competition prevails again in the market for investment loans. Banks therefore set the loan rate, as well as holdings of excess capital, to maximize expected profits. For simplicity, and in contrast to chapter 4, the optimal intensity of monitoring (or, equivalently in this setting, the repayment probability) is not solved for explicitly; instead, the functional form for q_t^i used in that chapter is specified directly.

Given that banks do not accumulate capital through retained earnings (recall that books are closed at the end of each period), bank i's maximization problem is

$$\max_{1+i_t^{L,i},V_t^{E,i}} \mathbb{E}_t J_{t+1}^{B,i},$$

where $\mathbb{E}_t J_{t+1}^{B,i}$ is defined as

$$\mathbb{E}_t J_{t+1}^{B,i} = q_t^i(1+i_t^{L,i})l_t^{K,i} + (1-q_t^i)\kappa^i \mathbb{E}_t p_{t+1}^H H_t + (1+i_t^R)l_t^{W,i} \tag{6.32}$$

$$+\mu d_t^i - (1+i_t^{D,i})d_t^i - (1+i_t^R)l_t^{B,i} - (1+i_t^V)V_t^i$$

$$-\gamma_V V_t^i + \gamma_{VV}\frac{(V_t^{E,i})^{1-\phi_E}}{1-\phi_E},$$

with $\gamma_V > 0$, $\gamma_{VV} \geq 0$, and $\phi_E \in (0,1)$.

The first term on the right-hand side in (6.32), $q_t^i(1+i_t^{L,i})l_t^{K,i}$, represents expected repayment if there is no default, whereas the second, $(1-q_t^i)\kappa^i \mathbb{E}_t p_{t+1}^H H_t$, represents what bank i expects to earn in case of default. The third term, $(1+i_t^R)l_t^{W,i}$, represents gross income from working capital loans. The fourth term, $\mu_t d_t^i$, represents the reserve requirements held at the central bank and returned to the bank at the end of the period. The fifth and sixth terms, $(1+i_t^{D,i})d_t^i$ and $(1+i_t^R)l_t^{B,i}$, represent repayment to depositors and the central bank, respectively. The seventh term, $(1+i_t^V)V_t^i$, represents the value of bank debt redeemed at the end of the period, inclusive of interest. The linear term $-\gamma_V V_t^i$ captures the cost of issuing debt, which includes the cost of underwriting, issuing brochures, and so on.[13] By contrast, the last term, $2\gamma_{VV}(V_t^E)^{\phi_E}$, captures the view that maintaining a positive capital buffer generates a benefit—it represents a signal that the bank's financial position is strong, which mitigates

13. The cost of issuing equity could be defined in a more general way, to account for the fact that (*a*) a positive capital buffer provides a signal to markets that the bank is healthy, and (*b*) during recessions (expansions), market funding is more difficult (easier) to obtain. Formally, this would imply a cost term defined as $c_t^V = \gamma_V (V_t^E/V_t)^{-\phi_E^V}(Y_t/\tilde{Y})^{-\phi_Y^V}$, where $\phi_E^V, \phi_Y^V \geq 0$. The case of a fixed cost, as considered here, corresponds therefore to $\phi_E^V = \phi_Y^V = 0$.

the intensity of regulatory scrutiny. In turn, this reduces the pecuniary cost associated with complying with information requests from the regulator (Agénor et al. 2012). Related rationales are provided by Dib (2010*b*), who assumes that holding bank capital in excess of the required level generates a pecuniary benefit because it helps banks to signal their ability to withstand unexpected shocks, and by De Walque et al. (2010) and Darracq Pariès et al. (2011), who assume that banks keep a buffer above the required minimum in order to avoid penalties and reputational costs. Buffer capital serves therefore as an insurance against the failure to meet capital requirements.[14] The restriction $\phi_E < 1$ ensures that the marginal gain is decreasing.

Using (6.25) to substitute out for V_t and (6.27) for $l_t^{B,i}$, equation (6.32) becomes

$$\begin{aligned}\mathbb{E}_t J_{t+1}^{B,i} &= q_t^i(1+i_t^{L,i})l_t^{K,i} + (1-q_t^i)\kappa^i \mathbb{E}_t p_{t+1}^H H_t \\ &+ (1+i_t^R)l_t^{W,i} + \mu_t d_t^i - (1+i_t^{D,i})d_t^i \\ &- (1+i_t^R)[l_t^i - V_t^{E,i} - V_t^{R,i} - (1-\mu)d_t^i] - (1+i_t^V)(V_t^{E,i} + V_t^{R,i}), \\ &-\gamma_V(V_t^{E,i} + V_t^{R,i}) + \gamma_{VV}\frac{(V_t^{E,i})^{1-\phi_E}}{1-\phi_E}\Bigg\}.\end{aligned}$$

Banks maximize profits subject to the loan demand function (6.23), as before, as well as the capital requirement constraint (6.28), taking the repayment probability, the value of collateral, the refinance rate, and the risk weight σ_t^i as given.[15] The first-order conditions for maximization are

$$\begin{aligned}&q_t^i l_t^{K,i} + [q_t^i(1+i_t^{L,i}) - (1-\rho_t\sigma_t^i)(1+i_t^R) \\ &- \rho_t\sigma_t^i(1+i_t^V+\gamma_V)]\left[\frac{\partial l_t^{K,i}}{\partial(1+i_t^{L,i})}\right] = 0, \qquad (6.33)\end{aligned}$$

$$(1+i_t^R) - (1+i_t^V) - \gamma_V + \gamma_{VV}(V_t^E)^{-\phi_E} = 0. \qquad (6.34)$$

14. A related approach, which has yet to be implemented in DSGE models of the type discussed here, would be to introduce a precautionary demand for excess capital along the lines proposed by Repullo and Suarez (2013). In their framework, banks are unable to access equity markets in every period; by holding capital buffers today, they mitigate the possibility that their ability to lend in the future may be compromised by adverse shocks to their earnings or unfavorable aggregate economic conditions.

15. If it had been assumed that banks also solve for monitoring effort, the issue of whether banks internalize the fact that the risk weight depends on the repayment probability would also need to be addressed. The reason is that, under the IRB approach, banks are allowed to use their own internal models for risk assessment.

From (6.23),

$$\frac{\partial l_t^{K,i}}{\partial(1+i_t^{L,i})} = -\varsigma^L \left(\frac{1+i_t^{L,i}}{1+i_t^L}\right)^{-\varsigma^L-1} \left(\frac{l_t^K}{1+i_t^L}\right).$$

Substituting this result, together with (6.23), in (6.33) yields

$$q_t^i \left(\frac{1+i_t^{L,i}}{1+i_t^L}\right)^{-\varsigma^L} l_t^K - [q_t^i(1+i_t^{L,i}) - (1-\rho_t\sigma_t^i)(1+i_t^R) - \rho_t\sigma_t^i(1+i_t^V+\gamma_V)]$$

$$\times\varsigma^L \left(\frac{1+i_t^{L,i}}{1+i_t^L}\right)^{-\varsigma^L-1} \left(\frac{l_t^K}{1+i_t^L}\right) = 0,$$

that is, in a symmetric equilibrium,

$$q_t l_t^K - [q_t(1+i_t^L) - (1-\rho_t\sigma_t)(1+i_t^R) - \rho_t\sigma_t(1+i_t^V+\gamma_V)]\varsigma^L \left(\frac{l_t^K}{1+i_t^L}\right) = 0,$$

or, multiplying both sides by $-(1+i_t^L)/l_t^K$,

$$-q_t(1+i_t^L) + q_t(1+i_t^L)\varsigma^L - [(1-\rho_t\sigma_t)(1+i_t^R) + \rho_t\sigma_t(1+i_t^V+\gamma_V)]\varsigma^L = 0,$$

which can be rearranged to give

$$1+i_t^L = \frac{\varsigma^L}{q_t(\varsigma^L-1)}[(1-\rho_t\sigma_t)(1+i_t^R) + \rho_t\sigma_t(1+i_t^V+\gamma_V)]\epsilon_t^L. \quad (6.35)$$

This equation shows that the lending rate depends negatively on the repayment probability (as before), and positively now on a weighted average of the marginal cost of borrowing from the central bank (at the gross rate $1+i_t^R$) and the total cost of issuing equity, $1+i_t^V+\gamma_V$, which accounts for both the gross rate of return to be paid on bank debt and issuing costs. Weights on each component of funding costs are measured in terms of the ratio of required capital to (risky) loans, $\rho_t\sigma_t$ and $1-\rho_t\sigma_t$. Thus, to the extent that the capital adequacy ratio (through its cyclical component) can be influenced by the policy rate, and that the loan rate has a direct effect on investment, there is now a *bank capital channel* of monetary policy.[16]

16. See Markovic (2006) and Van den Heuvel (2007) for a broader discussion of the bank capital channel and its relation to balance sheet effects. Another channel, operating through the repayment probability, will be discussed later on.

As in previous chapters, the random variable ϵ_t^L is added in (6.35) to capture credit spread shocks and is assumed to follow an $AR(1)$ process:

$$\epsilon_t^L = (\epsilon_{t-1}^L)^{\rho^L} \exp(\xi_t^L),$$

where $\rho^L \in (0, 1)$ and $\xi_t^L \sim \mathbf{N}(0, \sigma_{\xi^L})$.

Equation (6.34) gives, in a symmetric equilibrium,

$$V_t^E = \left(\frac{\gamma_{VV}}{i_t^V + \gamma_V - i_t^R} \right)^{1/\phi_E}. \tag{6.36}$$

Equation (6.36) indicates that an increase in the direct or indirect cost of issuing debt (i_t^V or γ_V) reduces excess capital, whereas an increase in the benefit parameter γ_{VV} raises excess capital. With $\gamma_{VV} = 0$, holding capital beyond what is required brings no benefit, so $V_t^E = 0$ for all t. A similar result holds if the fixed cost of issuing debt, γ_V, is very high (technically, $\gamma_V \to \infty$). Finally, an increase in required capital, by raising in equilibrium the cost of issuing bank debt, i_t^V, has an indirect, negative effect on the desired level of excess capital. Thus, in this setting there is an inherent degree of substitutability between the two components of bank capital.

As noted earlier, to simplify matters the repayment probability q_t is specified directly as a function of the effective collateral-investment loan ratio and the cyclical position of the economy,

$$q_t = \varphi_0 \left(\frac{\kappa \mathbb{E}_t p_{t+1}^H / \tilde{p}^H}{l_t^K / \tilde{l}^K} \right)^{\varphi_1} \left(\frac{Y_t}{\tilde{Y}} \right)^{\varphi_2}, \tag{6.37}$$

with $\varphi_0, \varphi_1, \varphi_2 > 0$.

It is worth noting that as a result of a *monitoring incentive effect*, the repayment probability may depend also on the capital-risky assets ratio, as discussed in chapter 2. Both Allen et al. (2011) and Mehran and Thakor (2011) provide rigorous micro foundations for a link between bank capital and monitoring. In Allen et al. (2011), for instance, banks hold capital voluntarily because it strengthens their incentives to monitor (tantamount to a *skin in the game* effect) and increases the borrower's success probability. A similar result is established by Cordella et al. (2018). In a sense, capital plays a strategic role, to the extent that it induces banks to take actions that they might not otherwise find optimal. This effect is consistent with the evidence of a negative relationship between bank capital-risky asset ratios and bank lending spreads provided by Fonseca et al. (2010). In Mehran and Thakor (2011), in addition, bank capital increases the future survival probability of the bank, as considered in Repullo and Suarez

(2013), which in turn enhances the bank's monitoring incentives. Given the link between monitoring and the repayment probability in the models presented in this book, the monitoring incentive effect could be captured directly by adding the capital-risky assets ratio in (6.37), as in Agénor et al. (2012) and Agénor and Jackson (2019), for instance.

6.2.6 Central Bank

As in chapter 4, the central bank's balance sheet is

$$b_t^{CB} + l_t^B = m_t^s + RR_t + nw_t, \tag{6.38}$$

where b_t^C are holdings of government bonds, $l_t^B = \int_0^1 l_t^{B,i} di$ are loans to commercial banks, m_t^s is currency in circulation, RR_t is required reserves, and nw_t is the central bank's net worth.

In the absence of open-market operations, $b_t^{CB} - (1+\pi_t)^{-1} b_{t-1}^{CB} = 0$. Assuming also that the central bank's net worth is constant in real terms, changes in currency in circulation are therefore given by

$$m_t^s = \frac{m_{t-1}^s}{1+\pi_t} + \left(l_t^B - \frac{l_{t-1}^B}{1+\pi_t}\right) - \left(RR_t - \frac{RR_{t-1}}{1+\pi_t}\right). \tag{6.39}$$

Once again, the refinance rate depends on both a base policy rate, i_t^T, and a penalty rate, θ_t^{CB}:

$$1 + i_t^R = (1 + i_t^T)(1 + \theta_t^{CB}). \tag{6.40}$$

In turn, the base policy rate is set on the basis of a Taylor-type policy rule with inertia,

$$\frac{1+i_t^T}{1+\tilde{\imath}^T} = \left(\frac{1+i_{t-1}^T}{1+\tilde{\imath}^T}\right)^{\chi} \left\{(1+\pi_t)^{\varepsilon_1} \left(\frac{Y_t}{\tilde{Y}}\right)^{\varepsilon_2}\right\}^{1-\chi}, \tag{6.41}$$

where $\tilde{\imath}^T$ and $\tilde{Y}$ are the steady-state values of the policy rate and output of final goods, $\chi \in (0,1)$ and $\varepsilon_1, \varepsilon_2 > 0$. Given the focus of this chapter, $\theta_t^{CB} = 0$, $\forall t$; thus, the policy rate and the refinance rate are one and the same.

6.2.7 Government

The government purchases the final good and issues nominal riskless one-period bonds. As shown in chapter 4, assuming that the interest income that the central bank receives is transferred in its entirety to the government, its budget constraint in real terms is given by

$$b_t^G - \frac{b_{t-1}^G}{1+\pi_t} = G_t - T_t + \frac{i_{t-1}^B b_{t-1}}{1+\pi_t} - \frac{i_{t-1}^R l_{t-1}^B}{1+\pi_t}, \tag{6.42}$$

where $b_t^G = b_t + b_t^{CB}$.

Government purchases are again a constant fraction of output of the final good,

$$G_t = \psi_G Y_t, \tag{6.43}$$

where $\psi_G \in (0, 1)$.

As before also, the government keeps its real stock of debt constant ($b_t = b$, for all t) and balances its budget by adjusting lump-sum taxes.

Flows between agents, and the links between regulatory capital, the repayment probability, and the lending rate, are summarized in figures 6.1 and 6.2.

6.3 Equilibrium Conditions

As in chapter 4, equilibrium conditions must be satisfied for the credit, deposit, goods, cash, bank capital, labor, and housing markets.[17] Because the supply of loans by commercial banks, and the supply of deposits by households are perfectly elastic at the prevailing interest rates, the markets for loans and deposits always clear. Equilibrium in the final good market requires that production be equal to aggregate demand; that is, using (6.18) and assuming zero inflation in the steady state,

$$Y_t = C_t + G_t + I_t + \frac{\phi_I}{2}\pi_t^2 Y_t. \tag{6.44}$$

Again, government bonds are in zero net supply and the equilibrium condition of the market for cash is given by

$$m_t = m_t^s, \tag{6.45}$$

where m_t and m_t^s are defined in (6.6) and (6.39), respectively.

The equilibrium condition of the market for bank debt requires, from (6.10) and (6.25),

$$V_t^d = V_t^R + V_t^E, \tag{6.46}$$

which can be solved for i_t^V.

17. Again, by Walras' law, the equilibrium condition of the market for government bonds can be eliminated.

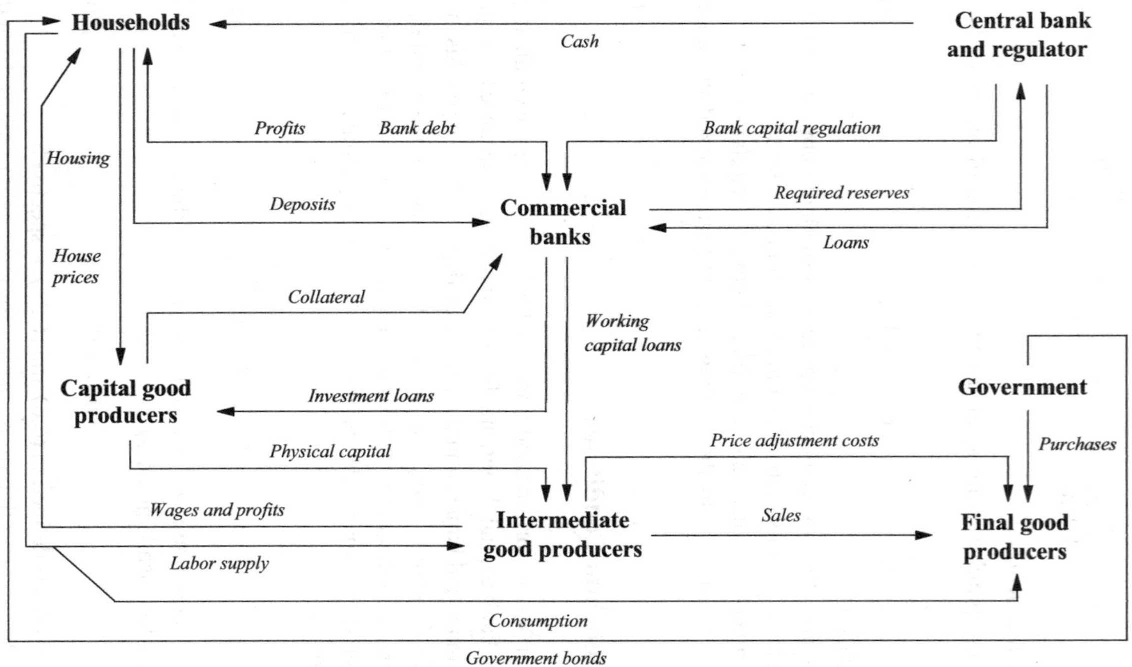

Figure 6.1 Core DSGE model structure: closed economy with bank capital regulation

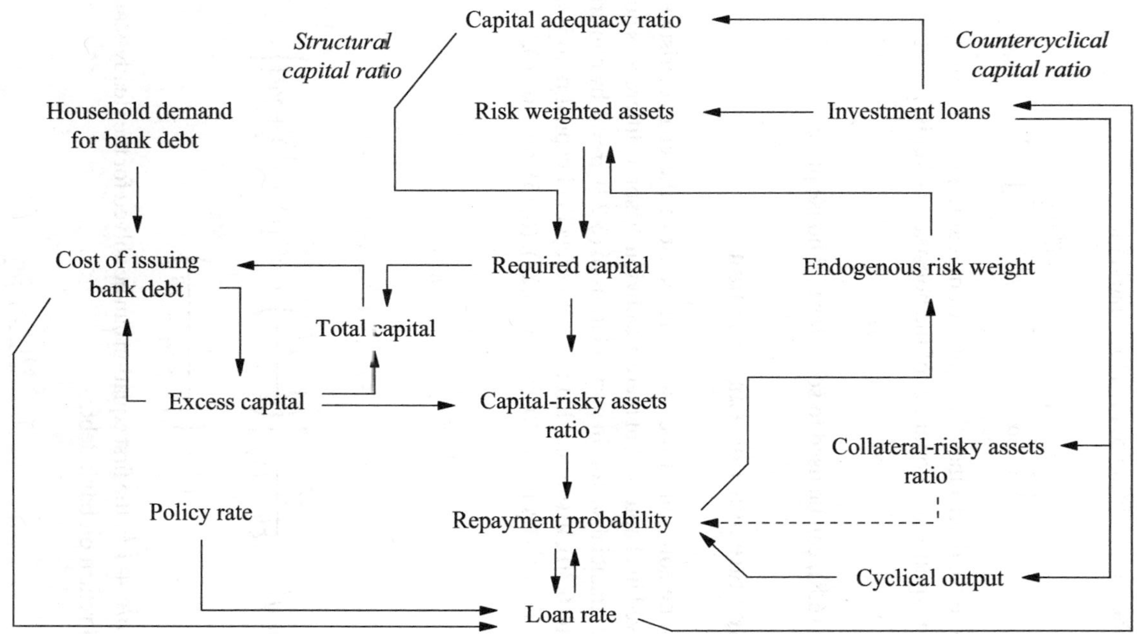

Figure 6.2 Bank capital, repayment probability, and the loan rate

The equilibrium condition of the labor market is

$$N_t = \left(\frac{\alpha}{1-\alpha}\right)^{-\alpha} \left[\frac{(1+\psi_W i_t^R)\omega_t}{r_t^K}\right]^{-\alpha}, \tag{6.47}$$

which, using (6.5), determines the equilibrium real wage.

Finally, the equilibrium condition of the housing market is

$$\bar{H} = H_t, \tag{6.48}$$

which, using (6.8), can be used to solve for real house prices.

6.4 Steady State and Log-Linearization

The steady-state solution of the model has most of the characteristics of the solution derived in chapter 4, but there are obviously some differences now with respect to the financial sector. In particular, from (6.29), $\tilde{\sigma} = 1$ by construction, whereas from (6.30), assuming that the countercyclical capital ratio is 0 in the steady state, $\tilde{\rho} = \rho^D$. From (6.10), (6.25), (6.28), (6.35), and (6.36),

$$\tilde{V} = \frac{1}{\Theta_V}\left(\frac{\tilde{\imath}^V - \tilde{\imath}^B}{1+\tilde{\imath}^B}\right),$$

$$\tilde{V} = \tilde{V}^R + \tilde{V}^E, \quad \tilde{V}^R = \rho\tilde{l}^K,$$

$$1 + \tilde{\imath}^L = \frac{\zeta^L}{(\zeta^L - 1)\tilde{q}}\left\{\left(\frac{1-\rho^D}{\Lambda}\right) + \rho^D\left[(1+\tilde{\imath}^V) + \gamma_V\right]\right\},$$

$$\tilde{V}^E = \left(\frac{\gamma_V V}{\tilde{\imath}^V + \gamma_V - \tilde{\imath}^B}\right)^{1/\phi_E}.$$

With $\tilde{V} = \rho\tilde{l}^K + \tilde{V}^E$, the first equation can be solved for the steady-state value of the rate of return on bank debt,

$$\tilde{\imath}^V = \frac{\Theta_V \tilde{V}}{\Lambda} + \tilde{\imath}^B,$$

which implies, given that $\tilde{V} > 0$, that $\tilde{\imath}^V > \tilde{\imath}^B$ as long as $\Theta_V > 0$. Because holding bank debt is subject to a cost, from the perspective of the household the rate of return on that debt must incorporate a premium above and beyond the rate of return on government bonds. Of course, $\tilde{\imath}^V = \tilde{\imath}^B$ when $\Theta_V = 0$. The above results also show that $\tilde{V}^E > 0$, given that $\tilde{\imath}^V > \tilde{\imath}^R$. Finally, because $\tilde{\imath}^B > \tilde{\imath}^D$ (as discussed in chapter 4), by implication $\tilde{\imath}^V > \tilde{\imath}^D$ for $\Theta_V > 0$ also holds. Bank capital is more costly than deposits (or, equivalently, households demand a liquidity premium), as in Aguiar and Drumond (2007) and various other contributions.

To analyze the response of the economy to shocks, the model is again log-linearized around the nonstochastic, zero-inflation steady state. Most of the log-linearized equations are the same as those presented in chapter 4, with some new equations now relating to the existence of regulatory capital. From (6.10), (6.25), (6.28), (6.29), (6.35), and (6.36), these equations are

$$\hat{V}_t = \left(1 + \frac{1}{\Theta_V \tilde{V}}\right)(\hat{\imath}_t^V - \hat{\imath}_t^B),$$

$$\hat{V}_t = \left(\frac{\tilde{V}^R}{\tilde{V}}\right)\hat{V}_t^R + \left(\frac{\tilde{V}^E}{\tilde{V}}\right)\hat{V}_t^E,$$

$$\hat{V}_t^R = \left(\frac{1+\rho^D}{\rho^D}\right)\hat{\rho}_t^C + \hat{\sigma}_t + \hat{\imath}_t^K,$$

$$\hat{\sigma}_t = -\phi_q \hat{q}_t,$$

$$\hat{\imath}_t^L = \frac{1}{(1+\tilde{\imath}^L)\tilde{q}}\left\{\frac{(1-\rho^D)}{\Lambda}\hat{\imath}_t^R + \rho^D(1+\tilde{\imath}^V)\hat{\imath}_t^V \right.$$
$$\left. -(1+\rho^D)\left(1+\tilde{\imath}^V + \gamma_V - \frac{1}{\Lambda}\right)\hat{\rho}_t^C + \rho^D\left[(1+\tilde{\imath}^V) + \gamma_V - \frac{1}{\Lambda}\right]\hat{\sigma}_t\right\} - \hat{q}_t,$$

$$\hat{V}_t^E = \left(\frac{1}{\phi_E}\right)\frac{\Lambda^{-1}\hat{\imath}_t^R - (1+\tilde{\imath}^V)\hat{\imath}_t^V}{1+\tilde{\imath}^V + \gamma_V - \Lambda^{-1}}.$$

6.5 Parameterization

Table 6.1 summarizes parameter values. The parameterization of the model is similar to the one presented in chapter 4; only new parameters are discussed here.

The portfolio adjustment cost parameter for holdings of bank debt, Θ_V, is set at a relatively high value, 0.3, to capture fairly inefficient debt markets in middle-income countries (MICs), as discussed in chapter 1). The elasticities of the risk weight with respect to the repayment probability, φ_q, as well as the cost parameters γ_V and γ_{VV}, are set at low values, 0.1, 0.05, and 0.001, respectively. The value of φ_q is the same as the benchmark value used by Angeloni and Faia (2013), for instance, to relate the risk weight and the output gap. The initial required capital ratio ρ^D (which is also equal to ρ, given that $\rho^C = 0$ in the steady state) is set to 0.08, which corresponds to the minimum value of the ratio of capital to risk-weighted assets under the current Basel regime.

Table 6.1
Benchmark Parameterization: Parameter Values

Parameter	Value	Description
Household		
Λ	0.95	Discount factor
ς	0.5	Elasticity of intertemporal substitution
η_N	25.0	Relative preference for leisure
ψ_N	1.4	Inverse of Frisch elasticity of labor supply
η_x	0.001	Relative preference for money holdings
η_H	0.02	Relative preference for housing
ν	0.35	Share parameter in index of money holdings
Θ_V	0.3	Adjustment cost parameter, holdings of bank debt
Production		
θ	6.0	Elasticity of demand, intermediate goods
α	0.35	Share of capital, domestic intermediate goods
ϕ_I	25.0	Adjustment cost parameter, prices of intermediate goods
δ	0.025	Depreciation rate of capital
Θ_K	14	Adjustment cost parameter, investment
ψ_W	0.0	Share of labor costs financed in advance
Commercial banks		
κ	0.2	Effective collateral share
ζ^L	4.5	Elasticity of substitution, loans to CG producers
φ_1	0.05	Elasticity of repayment probability, collateral-loan ratio
φ_2	0.4	Elasticity of repayment probability, cyclical output
γ_V	0.05	Linear cost of issuing bank capital
γ_{VV}	0.001	Linear benefit of holding excess bank capital
ϕ_E	0.1	Parameter, marginal benefit of holding excess bank capital
Regulator		
φ^Q	0.05	Elasticity of the risk weight with respect to the repayment probability
ρ^D	0.08	Capital adequacy ratio (deterministic component)
Central bank		
μ	0.2	Required reserve ratio
χ	0.8	Degree of interest rate smoothing by central bank
ε_1	2.0	Response of refinance rate to inflation deviations
ε_2	0.4	Response of refinance rate to output gap
φ^{CB}	0.0	Sensitivity of penalty rate to borrowing-deposit ratio
Government		
ψ_G	0.22	Share of government spending in domestic output sales
Shock		
ρ^C	0.8	Degree of persistence, credit spread shock

Table 6.2
Initial Steady-State Values: Key Variables
(In proportion of final output, unless indicated otherwise)

Variable	Description	Value
C	Household consumption	0.65
$I = l^K$	Investment loans to CG producers	0.13
K	Capital stock	5.2
r^K	Rental rate of capital (percent)	0.079
G	Public expenditure	0.22
q	Repayment probability, loans to CG producers (percent)	0.935
i^B, i^R	Government bond rate, central bank refinance rate (percent)	0.053
i^D	Bank deposit rate (percent)	0.042
i^L	Loan rate, investment lending to CG producers (percent)	0.095
i^V	Rate of return on bank capital (percent)	0.06
σ	Risk weight (percent)	1.0
V^E/l^K	Excess capital ratio (proportion of risky loans)	0.040
V^R/l^K	Required capital ratio (proportion of risky loans)	0.079
$(l^K + l^W)/V$	Leverage ratio (in terms of total loans)	8.3

The parameter that contributes to measuring the marginal benefit of holding excess bank capital, ϕ_E, is set at 0.1.

Table 6.2 shows the steady-state values of the key variables. Many of them (consumption, investment, and so on) are similar, if not identical, to those reported in previous chapters. The rate of return to bank debt is 6.0 percent, which indeed exceeds both the deposit and bond rates. From (6.28), and given that $\tilde{\sigma} = 1$ and $\tilde{\rho} = \rho^D$, the steady-state required capital-risky assets ratio, $\tilde{V}^R/\tilde{l}^K$, is equal to $\rho^D = 0.08$, as noted before, whereas the steady-state excess capital-risky assets ratio, $\tilde{V}^E/\tilde{l}^K$, is calibrated to 0.04.[18] This implies that the steady-state ratio of total bank capital to risky loans is equal to 12 percent, in line with the evidence reported in Agénor and Pereira da Silva (2012).

6.6 Experiment: Credit Spread Shock

To study the behavior of the economy under bank capital regulation, as in previous chapters a negative 1 percentage point credit spread shock is considered. The experiment assumes that $\rho_t^C = 0$ and $\rho_t = \rho^D$ $\forall t$, in (6.30). Both the cases of endogenous and exogenous excess capital are considered.[19]

18. This value is obtained by adding a multiplicative constant in (6.36).

19. A further comparison would be to contrast the case where the risk weight is exogenous ($\phi_q = 0$) with the case where it is endogenous ($\phi_q > 0$). See Agénor et al. (2012, 2013), for instance.

The results are displayed in figure 6.3. As in chapter 4, the direct effect of the shock is an expansion in investment and an increase in aggregate demand, which leads to higher inflation. The base policy and refinance rates therefore increase, thereby mitigating the initial drop in the cost of bank borrowing. At the same time, both the nominal deposit and bond rates increase.[20] The increase in the nominal bond rate exceeds the rise in the one-period ahead inflation, implying that the expected real bond rate also increases. This leads to a drop in current consumption and to a reduction in the demand for housing services.[21] As a result, house prices and collateral values fall. The effect of a reduction in the collateral-loan value dominates the effect of higher cyclical output and as a result the repayment probability falls on impact, which also contributes to dampening somewhat the initial drop in the loan rate. In addition, the fall in the repayment probability raises the risk weight; combined with the increase in investment loans, this translates into higher capital requirements. The rate of return on bank debt must therefore increase to induce households to hold more of that debt, and this further mitigates the initial downward effect on the market cost of borrowing and the initial boom in investment and output. Because the increase in the return on bank capital largely exceeds in magnitude the increase in the policy rate, banks tend to *reduce* their holdings of excess capital. But although required capital and excess capital move in opposite directions, the increase in the former exceeds the drop in the latter, so that total bank capital increases as well. This increase is less significant than the expansion of risky loans, implying that the bank leverage ratio also rises. Thus, the regulatory regime is countercyclical in response to a credit spread shock (due to its impact on the loan rate), but this effect is mitigated somewhat by the offsetting movement in excess capital held by banks.[22] However, as shown by the dotted lines in figure 6.3, this offsetting movement is relatively weak. While the increase in total capital is larger, and therefore that of the bank leverage ratio smaller, when excess capital is exogenous the impact on the other variables—including the loan rate, given that the return on bank debt increases by more than in the benchmark case—is fairly muted.

20. As discussed in chapter 4, the deposit rate rises *pari passu* with the refinance rate and leads to an increase in household demand for deposits and a reduction in the demand for cash, which is brought about (at the initial level of consumption) by a higher nominal bond rate.

21. The reduction in consumption also lowers the demand for leisure and raises labor supply, which mitigates the upward pressure on wages associated with the increase in activity.

22. Values of φ_q, γ_V, γ_{VV}, are ϕ_E are potentially all important parameters in assessing the role of the capital regulatory regime in the transmission of shocks. See Agénor and Jackson (2019) for sensitivity analysis along these lines in a related model. They also consider a shock to bank capital, as in Zhang (2009), for instance.

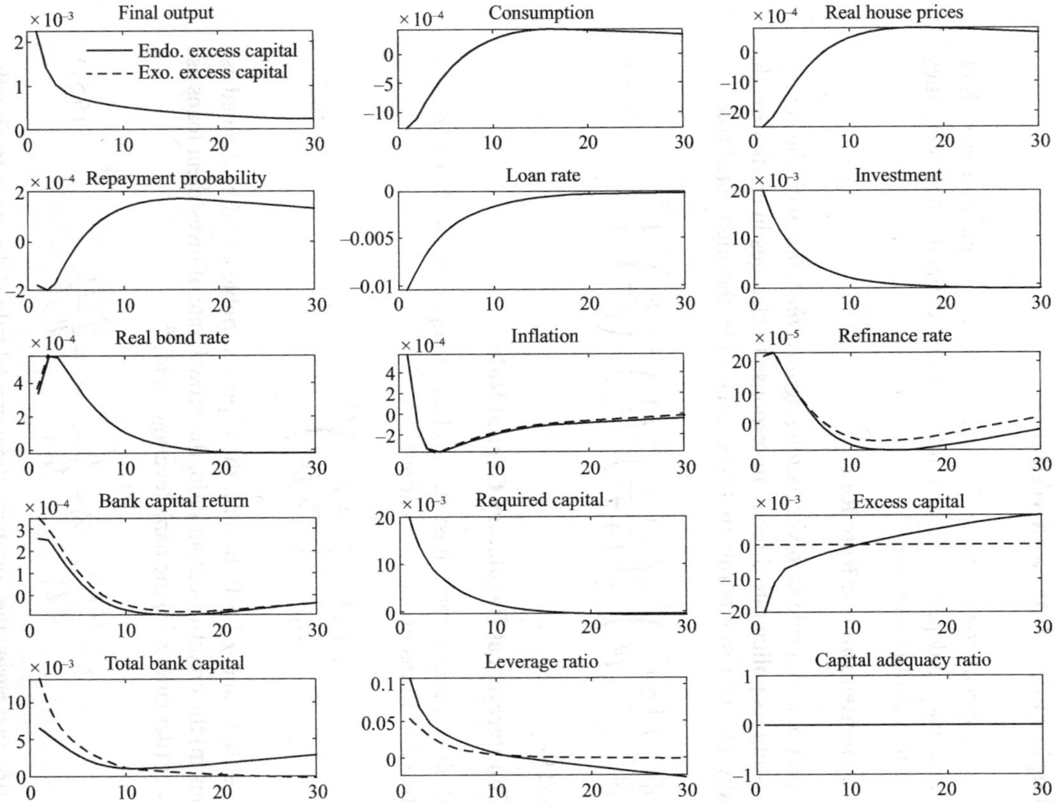

Figure 6.3 Negative credit spread shock: impulse response functions with endogenous and exogenous excess bank capital.
Note: The responses of consumption, investment, output, real house prices, required capital, excess capital, and total capital are expressed as percent deviations from their steady-state values. The responses of the lending rate, the refinance rate, the expected real bond rate, the repayment probability, the inflation rate, the bank capital return, the leverage ratio, and the capital adequacy ratio are expressed as absolute deviations (or percentage points) from their steady-state values.

6.7 Simple Policy Rules and Welfare

In line with the discussion in chapter 5, several alternative regimes under which simple rules, used independently or jointly, can be defined when the policy objective is to maximize welfare.[23]

6.7.1 Augmented Interest Rate Rule

As in chapter 5, a first rule involves *leaning against the wind*, with the central bank adjusting its policy rate directly in response to changes in credit growth. Specifically, the interest rate rule (6.41) is replaced by the augmented rule

$$\frac{1+i_t^R}{1+\tilde{\imath}^R} = \left(\frac{1+i_{t-1}^R}{1+\tilde{\imath}^R}\right)^{\chi} \left\{ \left(\frac{1+\pi_t}{1+\pi^T}\right)^{\varepsilon_1} \left(\frac{Y_t}{\tilde{Y}}\right)^{\varepsilon_2} \left(\frac{l_t^K}{l_{t-1}^K}\right)^{\varepsilon_3} \right\}^{1-\chi}, \tag{6.49}$$

where $\varepsilon_3 \geq 0$.

6.7.2 Countercyclical Regulatory Capital Rule

Similarly, the regulator can adjust the cyclical component in (6.30), ρ_t^C, to steady-state deviations in a trigger variable, Z_t,

$$\frac{1+\rho_t^C}{1+\tilde{\rho}^C} = \left(\frac{1+\rho_{t-1}^C}{1+\tilde{\rho}^C}\right)^{\chi_1} Z_t^{\chi_2^R(1-\chi_1)}, \tag{6.50}$$

where $\chi_1 \in (0, 1)$ and $\chi_2^R > 0$. In turn, the trigger variable could be defined as (deviations in) the credit-to-output ratio, the growth rate of investment loans as in (6.49), or (deviations in) the bank leverage ratio:[24]

$$Z_t = \frac{l_t^K/Y_t}{\tilde{l}^K/\tilde{Y}}, \quad Z_t = \frac{l_t^K}{l_{t-1}^K}, \quad Z_t = \frac{l_t^K/V_t}{\tilde{l}^K/\tilde{V}}. \tag{6.51}$$

In the first two cases, the countercyclical capital rule is designed to directly mitigate the easing of lending conditions that induces borrowers to take on more debt during upturns. The use of (deviations in) the risky loan-to-output ratio is consistent with the analysis in Drehmann et al. (2010) and Drehman and Tsatsaronis (2014) with regard to the buildup phase of capital buffers under Basel III. Similar contemporaneous rules have been studied in various contributions,

23. To keep the analysis tractable, the policy loss approach is not considered.

24. In all three cases, a forward-looking rule, involving expected future values instead of contemporaneous values, could also be used.

including Angelini et al. (2014), Benes and Kumhof (2015), Clerc et al. (2015), Clancy and Merola (2017), and Bekiros et al. (2018). As an alternative, credit growth has also been used as a trigger variable. As noted in chapter 5, some observers have argued that it should be preferred not only because it is less prone to measurement errors but also because the credit-to-output ratio can send the wrong signal in the early stages of a recession—it may increase not because of a rise in the numerator (credit) but instead because of a fall in the denominator (output). Finally, the countercyclical capital rule could also be based on deviations in the ratio of risky loans to bank capital, l_t^K/V_t. This would provide a direct link between financial regulation and lenders' propensity to engage in risky activities.

6.7.3 Alternative Policy Regimes

In line with the discussion in chapter 5, and based on the foregoing discussion, four policy regimes are now considered:

Regime A: Leaning against the wind, where the central bank uses the augmented Taylor rule (6.49), so that $\varepsilon_3 > 0$, and the regulator does not act, so that $\chi_2^R = 0$ in (6.50).

Regime B: Separate mandates, in which the central bank uses the standard Taylor rule, so that $\varepsilon_3 = 0$ in (6.49), and the regulator responds to credit fluctuations, so that $\chi_2^R \geq 0$ in (6.50).

Regime C: Nash equilibrium, in which each authority pursues policies independently (or noncooperatively) while being aware of the policy being pursued by the other authority. The equilibrium gives a solution (ε_3^N, $\chi_2^{R,N}$), and no authority has anything to gain by changing its own strategy.

Regime D: Coordination, in which the central bank uses an augmented Taylor rule and the regulator responds to credit fluctuations, with the response parameters $\varepsilon_3 \geq 0$ in (6.49) and $\chi_2^R \geq 0$ in (6.50) solved for jointly.

Specifically, as in chapter 5, suppose that the central bank's objective function accounts not only for household welfare but also for the cost associated with changes in the policy rate:

$$\mathcal{W}_t^C = \mathbb{E}_t \sum_{s=0}^{\infty} \Lambda^s u_{t+s} - \varkappa_C \mathbb{E}_t \sum_{s=0}^{\infty} \Lambda^s (i_{t+s}^R - i_{t+s-1}^R)^2, \tag{6.52}$$

where $\varkappa_C > 0$ and u_t is the truncated period utility function based on (6.1):

$$u_t \simeq \frac{C_t^{1-\varsigma^{-1}}}{1-\varsigma^{-1}} - \eta_N \frac{N_t^{1+\psi_N}}{1+\psi_N}. \tag{6.53}$$

Similarly, the objective function of the regulator accounts also for the cost to changes in the discretionary component of capital requirements:

$$\mathcal{W}_t^R = \mathbb{E}_t \sum_{s=0}^{\infty} \Lambda^s u_{t+s} - \varkappa_R \mathbb{E}_t \sum_{s=0}^{\infty} \Lambda^s (\rho_{t+s}^C - \rho_{t+s-1}^C)^2, \tag{6.54}$$

where $\varkappa_R > 0$.

Thus, under *leaning against the wind* the central bank sets $\varepsilon_3 = \arg\max \mathcal{W}_t^C$ with $\chi_2^R = 0$, under separate mandates the regulator sets $\chi_2^R = \arg\max \mathcal{W}_t^R$ with $\varepsilon_3 = 0$, under Nash each policymaker determines independently the optimal value of their response parameters ε_3^N and $\chi_2^{R,N}$ (taking into account each other's policy reaction) and under coordination policymakers jointly determine both response parameters so as to maximize a weighted sum of each policymaker's objective function:

$$\varepsilon_3^O, \chi_2^{R,O} = \arg\max[\gamma \mathcal{W}_t^C + (1-\gamma)\mathcal{W}_t^R], \tag{6.55}$$

where $\gamma \in (0, 1)$ reflects the relative weight attached to the central bank's objective function. It is important to note again that the optimal policy under coordination does not necessarily imply that *both* institutions should respond to financial stability considerations; this is also the case now under the Nash equilibrium.

As in chapter 5, the relevance of Tinbergen's principle for the conduct of monetary and macroprudential policies can be evaluated by comparing outcomes under regimes B and A, which helps to determine whether the instruments are complements or substitutes, and regimes C and D with B, which helps to determine whether the Nash equilibrium and coordination, given that both can generate $\varepsilon_3, \chi_2^R > 0$, improve over Tinbergen's principle. Indeed, finding that $\varepsilon_3 > 0$ under A and that $\chi_2^R = 0$ under B would militate against Tinbergen's principle; the instruments are substitutes. Alternatively, finding that $\chi_2^R > 0$ under B would work in favor of the principle (complementarity of instruments), given that, by construction, $\varepsilon_3 = 0$ in that regime. In addition, finding under complementarity that the difference in (adjusted) welfare between regimes B and A is positive would imply that a narrow application of Tinbergen's principle generates superior outcomes compared to *leaning against the wind*.

Comparing the results under regimes C and D with those obtained under B, and finding that both $\varepsilon_3 > 0$ and $\chi_2^R > 0$ under C and D while $\chi_2^R > 0$ under B would imply that neither the Nash equilibrium nor coordination is consistent with Tinbergen's principle. The instruments are substitutes, rather than complements. Furthermore, should the difference between welfare under regimes C and D and welfare under regime B be positive, it would mean that both Nash and coordination perform better than a strict separation of mandates.

To perform these calculations, the welfare gain is assessed in two ways: First, by calculating the percentage welfare change with respect to no activism ($\varepsilon_3 = \chi_2^R = 0$), as before, and second, by calculating compensating variations, compared to the case of no activism. In that case, the welfare gain from the perspective of each policymaker is obtained by solving for $\beta^j, j = C, R$, in the expression

$$\mathbb{E}_t \sum_{s=0}^{\infty} \Lambda^s \mathcal{W}_t^j[(1+\beta^j)C_{t+s}^b, N_{t+s}^b] = \mathbb{E}_t \sum_{s=0}^{\infty} \Lambda^s \mathcal{W}_t^j(C_{t+s}^c, N_{t+s}^c), \tag{6.56}$$

where $\{C_{t+s}^h\}_{s=0}^{\infty}$ and $\{N_{t+s}^h\}_{s=0}^{\infty}$ are solution paths under the status quo ($h = b$) and activism ($h = c$). Similarly, the welfare gain for the economy as a whole is calculated by solving for β in the expression

$$\mathbb{E}_t \sum_{s=0}^{\infty} \Lambda^s \left\{\gamma \mathcal{W}^C[(1+\beta)C_{t+s}^b, N_{t+s}^b] + (1-\gamma)\mathcal{W}^R[(1+\beta)C_{t+s}^b, N_{t+s}^b]\right\}$$

$$- \mathbb{E}_t \sum_{s=0}^{\infty} \Lambda^s \left\{\gamma \mathcal{W}^C(C_{t+s}^c, N_{t+s}^c) + (1-\gamma)\mathcal{W}^R(C_{t+s}^c, N_{t+s}^c)\right\}, \tag{6.57}$$

where β^j, $\beta > 0$ indicates a welfare gain.

In addition, independently of assessing the validity of Tinbergen's principle (through appropriate restrictions on ε_3 and χ_2), the *gain from coordination* can be assessed by comparing outcomes under regimes D and C. To do so a similar method as the one described earlier can be used, except that welfare gains are relative to the Nash equilibrium, rather than the case of no activism as in the previous calculations. Formally, one must solve for $\beta^j, j = C, R$, in the expression

$$\mathbb{E}_t \sum_{s=0}^{\infty} \Lambda^s \mathcal{W}_t^j[(1+\beta^j)C_{t+s}^N, C_{t+s}^N] = \mathbb{E}_t \sum_{s=0}^{\infty} \Lambda^s \mathcal{W}_t^j(C_{t+s}^O, C_{t+s}^O), \tag{6.58}$$

where $\{C_{t+s}^N\}_{s=0}^{\infty}$ and $\{N_{t+s}^N\}_{s=0}^{\infty}$ are solution paths under noncooperation, based once again on the maximized value of each policymaker's objective function (that is, at the optimal own response parameters ε_3^N and $\chi_2^{R,N}$), and $\{C_{t+s}^O\}_{s=0}^{\infty}$ and $\{N_{t+s}^O\}_{s=0}^{\infty}$ are solution paths under coordination (at the jointly determined optimal value ε_3^O and $\chi_2^{R,O}$). Similarly, the welfare gain from coordination for the economy as a whole is calculated by solving for β in the expression

$$\mathbb{E}_t \sum_{s=0}^{\infty} \Lambda^s \left\{\gamma \mathcal{W}^C[(1+\beta)C_{t+s}^N, N_{t+s}^N] + (1-\gamma)\mathcal{W}^R[(1+\beta)C_{t+s}^N, N_{t+s}^N]\right\}$$

$$= \mathbb{E}_t \sum_{s=0}^{\infty} \Lambda^s \left\{\gamma \mathcal{W}^R(C_{t+s}^O, N_{t+s}^O) + (1-\gamma)\mathcal{W}^R(C_{t+s}^O, N_{t+s}^O)\right\}. \tag{6.59}$$

Expressions (6.56) to (6.59) are evaluated using second-order approximations to the objective functions of both policy authorities, (6.52) and (6.54), and the model itself, conditional on the initial steady state being the deterministic steady state. Based on the discussion in chapter 5, the approximations of (6.52) and (6.54) involve using the truncated period utility function (6.53) and are given by, for the central bank,

$$\mathcal{W}_t^C \simeq \frac{1}{1-\Lambda}\left\{\tilde{u} - \frac{\tilde{C}^{1-\varsigma^{-1}}}{2\varsigma}\text{Var}(\hat{C}_t) - \eta_N \psi_N \frac{\tilde{N}^{1+\psi_N}}{2}\text{Var}(\hat{N}_t)\right\}$$

$$- \frac{\varkappa_C}{1-\Lambda}\text{Var}(\Delta i_t^R),$$

and for the regulator,

$$\mathcal{W}_t^R \simeq \frac{1}{1-\Lambda}\left\{\tilde{u} - \frac{\tilde{C}^{1-\varsigma^{-1}}}{2\varsigma}\text{Var}(\hat{C}_t) - \eta_N \psi_N \frac{\tilde{N}^{1+\psi_N}}{2}\text{Var}(\hat{N}_t)\right\}$$

$$- \frac{\varkappa_R}{1-\Lambda}\text{Var}(\Delta \rho_t^C),$$

where $\hat{C}_t$ and $\hat{N}_t$ are log-deviations of consumption and labor supply from their steady-state values.

Note that, if there are no adjustment costs so that $\varkappa_C = \varkappa_R = 0$, the central bank and the regulator maximize the same objective (the discounted utility of the representative household); in that case, outcomes under the Nash equilibrium and under coordination are the same, and there can be no gains from cooperation.

6.8 Results for a Credit Spread Shock

The benchmark results associated with a negative credit spread shock are shown in tables 6.3 and 6.4, again for equal weights to each authority (so that $\gamma = 0.5$) and two alternative assumptions about the magnitude of the instrument adjustment cost, $\varkappa_C = 0.1$ and 0.4 for the central bank (as in chapter 5), and $\varkappa_R = 0.001$ and 0.004 for the regulator.[25] Table 6.3 corresponds to the case of endogenous excess capital, whereas table 6.4 relates to exogenous excess capital. For all parameters the grid search is once again conducted at one decimal point and a step of 0.1. To keep the analysis manageable, only credit growth, as defined in (6.51), is used as the trigger variable in the regulatory rule (6.50). Relative welfare gains—the value of welfare under each regime, divided by the value of welfare under no activism—are shown in figure 6.4 (for $\varkappa_R = 0.004$), together with the optimal response parameters, ε_3 and χ_2^R, under all four of the policy regimes defined earlier. For simplicity, in the tables welfare results under Nash relative to no activism, are not reported.

The results show, first, that with endogenous excess capital it is always optimal for both policymakers to react, whether they do so independently or jointly. Moreover, the gain from an active response, compared to no activism, is generally substantial, regardless of whether the focus is on the relative welfare gain or compensating variations—with the latter showing, in general, larger gains when the regulator's instrument cost is relatively low.

Second, the comparison of regimes A and B suggests that Tinbergen's principle is not optimal; the gains under A are actually significantly larger than under B, regardless of how these gains are measured. In that sense, monetary policy and countercyclical capital buffers can be viewed as substitutes from the perspective of promoting financial stability.

Third, comparing policy regimes B and D shows that welfare gains are substantially higher when the two policies are used in coordination than when macroprudential policy alone is used to mitigate credit growth. This result goes therefore also against Tinbergen's principle and is consistent with the comparison of regimes A and B. Put differently, when policy authorities pursue different objectives (in the present case, welfare maximization but with a specific adjustment cost associated with instrument manipulation), it is optimal to use both tools in coordination.

25. Using the same values as $\varkappa_C$ for $\varkappa_R$ (as in chapter 5) yields optimal response parameters that are close to 0 for the regulator. The values used here provide more sensible results. This illustrates the importance of properly calibrating instrument manipulation costs when doing comparisons across instruments. See Agénor and Jackson (2019) for a more detailed discussion.

Table 6.3
Negative Credit Spread Shock: Optimal Policy Responses and Gains from Coordination Response to Credit Growth for the Regulator, Endogenous Excess Capital

	$\varkappa_C = 0.1, \varkappa_R = 0.001$		$\varkappa_C = 0.4, \varkappa_R = 0.004$	
	RWG	CV[a,b]	RWG	CV[a,b]
Leaning against the wind ($\varepsilon_3 \geq 0, \chi_2 = 0$)				
Optimal response parameter, ε_3	1.0		0.7	
Gain from activism				
Central bank	0.108	0.126	0.049	0.065
Financial regulator	0.136	0.154	0.012	0.147
Economy[c]	0.122	0.141	0.086	0.107
Macroprudential regulation ($\varepsilon_3 = 0, \chi_2 \geq 0$)				
Optimal response parameter, χ_2	3.8		1.0	
Gain from activism				
Central bank	0.034	0.048	0.010	0.014
Financial regulator	0.001	0.002	0.000	0.000
Economy[c]	0.018	0.025	0.005	0.007
Coordination ($\varepsilon_3 \geq 0, \chi_2 \geq 0$)				
Optimal response parameters, ε_3, χ_2	1.0, 1.1		0.7, 0.7	
Gain from activism				
Central bank	0.110	0.128	0.053	0.069
Financial regulator	0.136	0.154	0.123	0.145
Economy[c]	0.123	0.141	0.088	0.109
Nash equilibrium ($\varepsilon_3 \geq 0, \chi_2 \geq 0$)				
Optimal response parameters, $\varepsilon_3^N, \chi_2^N$	0.9, 0.6		0.5, 0.3	
Gain from coordination[a,d]				
Central bank	0.000	0.000	−0.005	−0.007
Financial regulator	0.002	0.002	0.020	0.026
Economy[c]	0.001	0.001	0.007	0.009

Notes: a. RWG refers to welfare gain relative to welfare under no activism. CV refers to compensating variations, which include the cost of instrument volatility and are calculated using the formulas provided in the text. b. With respect to the equilibrium with no activism. c. Equal weights to each policy authority. d. With respect to the Nash equilibrium.

Fourth, the gain from coordination (regime D), relative to Nash (regime C), is positive, albeit small—regardless of how welfare gains are evaluated. When the instrument cost parameter is relatively low ($\varkappa_C = 0.1$, $\varkappa_R = 0.001$), *both* authorities react more under coordination than under Nash. Thus, cooperation does not imply *burden sharing*—in the sense (as defined in chapter 5) of one authority reacting more while the other reacts less than under Nash—but rather *burden deepening*. Fifth, when the instrument cost parameter is relatively large ($\varkappa_C = 0.4$, $\varkappa_R = 0.004$), there is again *burden deepening* (both policymakers react more under coordination than under Nash), but now both measures of welfare gains show that the central bank is worse off under coordination, even if the economy (or society at large) gains. The implication is that coordination is not

Table 6.4
Negative Credit Spread Shock: Optimal Policy Responses and Gains from Coordination Response to Credit Growth for the Regulator, Exogenous Excess Capital

	$\varkappa_C = 0.1, \varkappa_R = 0.001$		$\varkappa_C = 0.4, \varkappa_R = 0.004$	
	RWG	CV[a,b]	RWG	CV[a,b]
Leaning against the wind ($\varepsilon_3 \geq 0, \chi_2 = 0$)				
Optimal response parameter, ε_3	1.1		0.8	
Gain from activism				
Central bank	0.109	0.128	0.040	0.052
Financial regulator	0.142	0.161	0.131	0.153
Economy[c]	0.126	0.145	0.085	0.106
Macroprudential regulation ($\varepsilon_3 = 0, \chi_2 \geq 0$)				
Optimal response parameter, χ_2	3.9		1.6	
Gain from activism				
Central bank	0.051	0.066	0.027	0.038
Financial regulator	0.021	0.028	0.004	0.005
Economy[c]	0.036	0.048	0.016	0.022
Coordination ($\varepsilon_3 \geq 0, \chi_2 \geq 0$)				
Optimal response parameters, ε_3, χ_2	1.1, 0.0		0.7, 0.5	
Gain from activism				
Central bank	0.109	0.128	0.050	0.065
Financial regulator	0.142	0.161	0.122	0.145
Economy[c]	0.126	0.145	0.086	0.106
Nash equilibrium ($\varepsilon_3 \geq 0, \chi_2 \geq 0$)				
Optimal response parameters, ε_3, χ_2	1.0, 0.0		0.5, 0.3	
Gain from coordination[a,d]				
Central bank	−0.001	−0.001	−0.006	−0.008
Financial regulator	0.003	0.003	0.021	0.028
Economy[c]	0.001	0.001	0.007	0.009

Note: See notes to table 6.3.

Pareto-improving. In addition, a comparison of regimes A, B, and D shows that coordination does involves *burden sharing* compared to when policymakers act on their own. Indeed, under coordination each policymaker reacts less compared with when it acts alone to address financial stability risks, while the other reacts more aggressively.

Table 6.4 displays the results when excess capital is exogenous. They are qualitatively similar to those reported earlier, except in two cases. First, under either Nash or coordination, it is optimal for the regulator not to react at all when the cost of instrument manipulation is relatively low; monetary policy alone is used to respond to credit growth. This invalidates Tinbergen's principle once again. However, when the cost of instrument manipulation is relatively high, there is *burden deepening*: Under coordination both policymakers react more aggressively. Second, the gain from coordination relative to Nash is negative

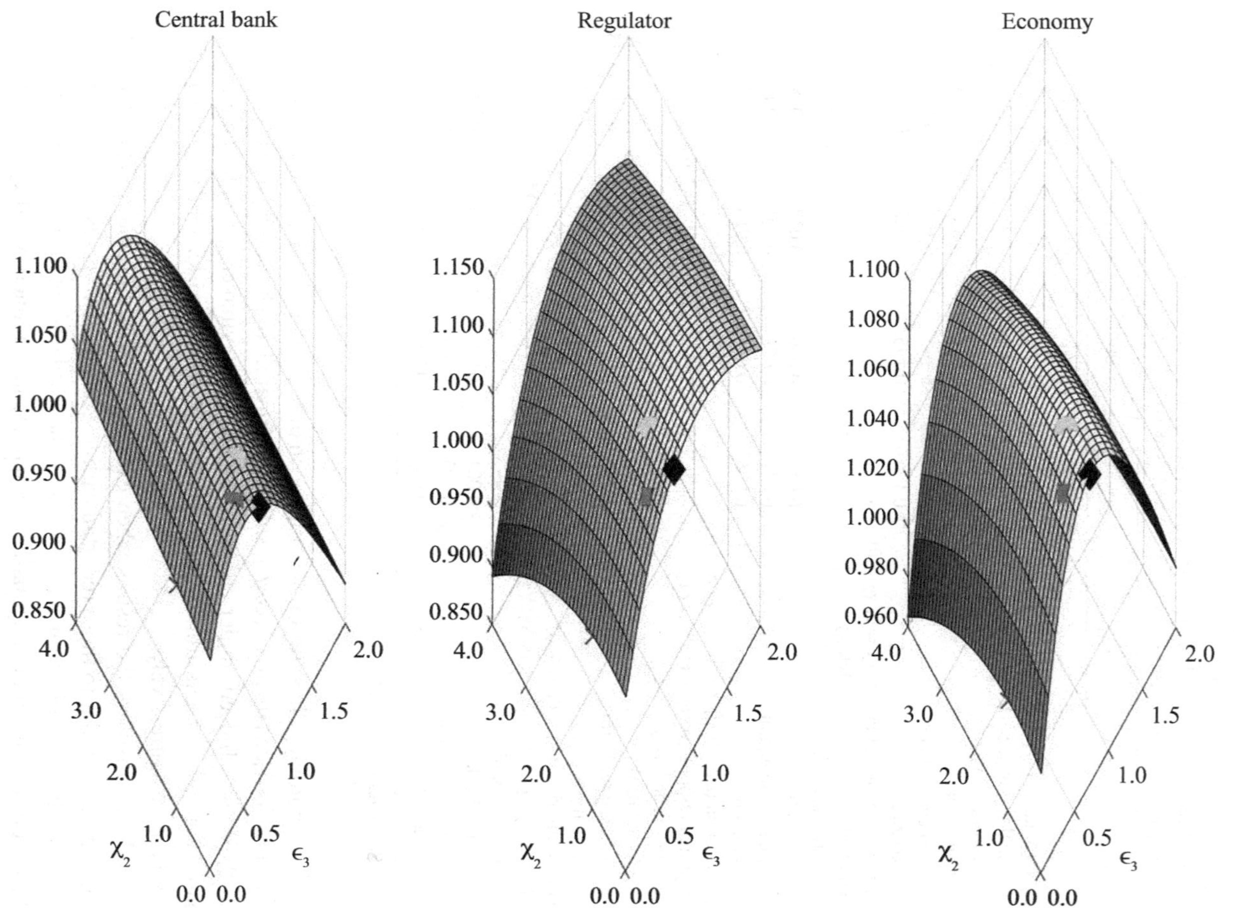

Figure 6.4 Negative credit spread shock: relative welfare and optimal policy responses. *Note*: The diamond corresponds to leaning against the wind only, the cross to macroprudential regulation only, the square to the Nash equilibrium, and the circle to coordination.

for the central bank, this time regardless of the cost of instrument manipulation and how welfare gains are measured. Intuitively, this is because (as discussed previously) the countercyclical capital requirement is less effective as a stabilization tool when excess capital is exogenous. The central bank must therefore intervene more aggressively to mitigate credit growth when policies are set jointly—incurring in the process a higher instrument manipulation cost. As a result, coordination, even though it benefits society at large, is not Pareto-improving. To enforce it may require an explicit institutional constraint on both policy authorities.

Finally, table 6.5 shows the asymptotic standard deviations for a range of macroeconomic and financial variables for the case where $\varkappa_C = 0.4$ and $\varkappa_R = 0.004$ only, and under both endogenous and exogenous excess capital. The results indicate that a *leaning against the wind* policy performs very well across a wide range of these variables, compared with the other regimes—including coordination. Again, this reflects the fact that the countercyclical capital requirement is not, in general, a particularly effective instrument in the model. As a result, when the macroprudential rule is used alone, it is only marginally better than no activism, in contrast to the other regimes. Of course, the volatility of the policy instruments (the refinance rate and the capital adequacy ratio) varies significantly across regimes. In general, results with endogenous and exogenous excess capital do not differ much, except with respect to a few bank-related variables (such as the leverage ratio), in line with the earlier analysis of impulse response functions.

As in chapter 5, the reason why an optimal policy exists (as illustrated in figure 6.4) is because of the trade-off that eventually emerges as the policy response becomes gradually more aggressive. At first, a more aggressive countercyclical capital rule tends to reduce volatility by raising the cost of borrowing and reducing investment. This stabilizes output and at first benefits the economy, because it stabilizes policy and market interest rates and therefore consumption and labor supply. However, as the capital rule becomes more and more responsive to credit growth, the cost of instrument manipulation rises. This effect eventually dominates, leading to more volatility in output, consumption, and employment. At the optimum, the response parameters ε_3 and χ_2^R are set so as to equate marginal benefits and costs. But here again, as was the case in chapter 5 with respect to the tax on loans, when there are no costs associated with instrument manipulation ($\varkappa_C = \varkappa_R = 0$) a corner solution is obtained: It is optimal to fully stabilize credit fluctuation so that $\chi_2^R \longrightarrow \infty$.[26] The reason

26. Note once more that, in that case, under welfare maximization both policy authorities have the same objective function (household welfare only). Thus, the solutions under Nash and coordination are the same, and the latter generates no gain with respect to the former.

Table 6.5
Negative Credit Spread Shock: Asymptotic Standard Deviations under Alternative Policy Regimes, Credit Growth for the Regulator, Cost Parameters $\varkappa_C = 0.4$, $\varkappa_R = 0.004$[a]

	No Activism	LAW	MaP Only	Nash Eq.	Coord.
			Endogenous Excess Capital		
Output	0.0038	0.0031	0.0038	0.0033	0.0031
Employment	0.0015	0.0010	0.0014	0.0011	0.0010
Consumption	0.0019	0.0020	0.0019	0.0020	0.0020
Investment	0.0038	0.0033	0.0038	0.0035	0.0033
Inflation	0.0011	0.0005	0.0011	0.0006	0.0005
Refinance rate	0.0008	0.0019	0.0008	0.0015	0.0019
Loan rate	0.0177	0.0162	0.0177	0.0166	0.0161
Real house prices	0.0010	0.0010	0.0010	0.0010	0.0010
Repayment probability	0.0009	0.0010	0.0009	0.0010	0.0010
Loan-to-output ratio	0.0034	0.0030	0.0034	0.0031	0.0030
Required capital	0.0003	0.0003	0.0009	0.0004	0.0006
Capital adequacy ratio	—	—	0.0048	0.0013	0.0028
Excess capital	0.0006	0.0004	0.0008	0.0005	0.0004
Total bank capital	0.0006	0.0006	0.0006	0.0006	0.0006
Leverage ratio	0.3546	0.2212	0.3300	0.2474	0.2306
			Exogenous Excess Capital		
Final output	0.0038	0.0031	0.0036	0.0033	0.0031
Employment	0.0015	0.0010	0.0014	0.0011	0.0010
Consumption	0.0019	0.0020	0.0019	0.0020	0.0020
Investment	0.0038	0.0033	0.0037	0.0034	0.0033
Inflation	0.0011	0.0004	0.0009	0.0005	0.0004
Refinance rate	0.0008	0.0020	0.0008	0.0015	0.0019
Loan rate	0.0177	0.0160	0.0174	0.0165	0.0161
Real house prices	0.0010	0.0010	0.0010	0.0010	0.0010
Repayment probability	0.0009	0.0010	0.0009	0.0010	0.0010
Loan-to-output ratio	0.0034	0.0030	0.0033	0.0031	0.0030
Required capital	0.0003	0.0003	0.0012	0.0004	0.0005
Capital adequacy ratio	—	—	0.0075	0.0013	0.0020
Excess capital	—	—	—	—	—
Total bank capital	0.0003	0.0003	0.0012	0.0004	0.0005
Leverage ratio	0.0815	0.0701	0.4668	0.0624	0.1028

Note: a. No Activism corresponds to $\chi_2 = \varepsilon_3 = 0$, LAW to leaning against the wind, $\varepsilon_3 \geq 0$, $\chi_2 = 0$, MaP Only to $\varepsilon_3 = 0$, $\chi_2 \geq 0$, Nash Eq. to the Nash equilibrium, and Coord. to coordination, with in both cases $\varepsilon_3, \chi_2 \geq 0$.

is that, in contrast to a countercyclical reserve requirement rule, the policy has no direct effect on the deposit and bond rates and therefore no direct impact on consumption and labor supply volatility as it becomes more aggressive.

6.9 Notes on the Literature

The treatment of capital requirements in DSGE models with financial frictions has followed a number of different paths. This section considers briefly five issues: the link between retained earnings and capital accumulation, the effect of capital requirements on the incidence of bank default, the complementarity between loan loss provisions and bank capital as instruments to strengthen the resilience of financial institutions, the link between bank capital and risk-taking, and the impact of capital regulation on the development of shadow banking.

6.9.1 Bank Capital and Retained Earnings

In the model presented in this chapter, two key simplifying assumptions were made: Banks satisfy capital requirements by issuing debt-like instruments rather than equity *per se* and do not accumulate capital over time—as they close their operations at the end of each period and start anew at the beginning of the next. At the same time, the cost effect of issuing debt was accounted for and was shown to affect directly the loan rate. Together with the endogeneity of the risk weight imposed on investment loans in calculating capital requirements, this created additional feedback loops between the real economy and the banking sector. An alternative approach in the literature, followed, for instance, by De Walque et al. (2010), Gerali et al. (2010), Meh and Moran (2010), Darracq Pariès et al. (2011), Angelini et al. (2014), and others is to assume that banks accumulate capital through retained earnings.[27] This assumption is equivalent to assuming that the cost of raising equity on financial markets is prohibitively high. For the most part, these models do not account directly for the demand for bank capital, how it depends on the rate of return on capital, and how the latter affects banks' decisions in setting the cost of borrowing. They do generate a positive relationship between increases in bank leverage and the loan spread, but only as long as leverage exceeds the targeted level. In addition, the share of profits that banks accumulate (or, equivalently, their dividend policy) is generally exogenous, and excess capital holdings—a common feature of banking

27. Kiley and Sim (2014) proposed a more complex framework, which also accounts for the dynamics of bank equity accumulation.

systems around the world, as noted earlier—is not accounted for. Indeed, the cost of the capital-assets ratio deviating from the target value imposed by the regulator is symmetric in most of these models, implying that there are no benefits from holding excess capital. Ideally, it would be desirable to have a model that accounts for both ways of accumulating bank capital and to determine endogenously how banks choose among them.

6.9.2 Bank Default and Capital Requirements

In most of the DSGE literature, the possibility of bank default, and the role of bank capital in that context, is not explicitly addressed.[28] In addition, models that allow for the possibility of default by borrowers (including those presented in this book) rule it out in equilibrium. The consequences of default (by either lenders or borrowers) for financial stability and for the real economy therefore cannot be explored.

Contributions that allow for default in equilibrium, either by borrowers or lenders, include Martinez-Miera and Suarez (2014), Angeloni and Faia (2013), Hirakata et al. (2013), Clerc et al. (2015), Pesaran and Xu (2016), and Mendicino et al. (2018). In several of these contributions, default and its costs impinge on the balance sheet of the lenders, influencing their optimal behavior and therefore macroeconomic outcomes. Angeloni and Faia (2013) and Mendicino et al. (2018), in particular, focused specifically on the role of capital requirements in mitigating the risk of bank default. The first contribution studied the benefits of capital regulation in a model where banks are fragile and subject to runs, and the main distortion arises from the fact that the projects funded by banks may be subject to costly early liquidation. In that setting, bank capital matters because it reduces the probability of the occurrence of a run. In the same vein, Mendicino et al. (2018) found that it is always optimal to impose capital requirements that keep the likelihood of bank default sufficiently low. In their model, more resilient banks helps to lower the deadweight cost of bank default and to weaken bank-related amplification channels, thereby stabilizing the response of the economy to aggregate shocks.

6.9.3 Capital Requirements and Loan Loss Provisions

Since the global financial crisis, the possibility that accounting standards may contribute to banking procyclicality and financial volatility has been the subject of renewed scrutiny. Under the so-called *incurred loss* model, which is

28. For a discussion of the importance of accounting explicitly for default in dynamic macroeconomic models, see Geanakoplos (2011) and Goodhart et al. (2013, 2016).

part of the current International Accounting Standard (IAS) 39, objective evidence that loans will not be repaid in their entirety—events that would have an impact on the estimated future cash flows of the loan—must be identified before any impairment losses are recognized.[29] Critics have argued that recognition *after* identification of evidence, such as a counterparty failing to meet its contractual obligations, is too late in the credit cycle because the expenses in the income statement for impairments then accumulate in downturns, when losses materialize. This provisioning regime therefore tends to exacerbate procyclicality. By contrast, under the so-called *expected loss* model, credit losses that are expected to occur are recognized *early* in the credit cycle, without first identifying a credit loss event; impairments are therefore made in a more timely manner, potentially dampening procyclicality in loan provisioning and providing a more accurate profit and loss account. Provisions set aside in good times serve as a buffer against risk and reduce the likelihood of banks becoming insolvent.

Elements of the expected loss model were adopted in the new International Financial Reporting Standards (IFRS) 9, which replaced IAS 39 in January 2018, and implemented in the so-called *dynamic* provisioning regime introduced in Spain in July 2000.[30] In recent years a number of countries in Latin America have implemented similar schemes. Although the details of these schemes differ in several ways from the Spanish system (Wezel et al. 2012), they all share a common goal—to ensure that banks are not required to increase the reserves that they must hold against loan losses at exactly the same time that their capacity to lend is needed to help promote, or sustain, an economic recovery. The fundamental goal therefore is similar to the one underlying the implementation of countercyclical capital buffers.

Empirical evidence on the performance of provisioning regimes is discussed by Burroni et al. (2009), Caprio (2010), Packer et al. (2014), Pool et al. (2015), and Murcia and Kohlscheen (2016) in cross-country studies, and by Levin et al. (2016) for Mexico, López et al. (2014) and Gómez et al. (2017) for Colombia, and Minaya et al. (2017) for Peru. A growing body of research has also focused on the countercyclical performance of these regimes, and their impact on financial stability, using DSGE-FF models. Contributions include Agénor and Zilberman (2015) and Agénor and Pereira da Silva (2017), which dwell in

29. See https://www.ifrs.org/.

30. Dynamic (also referred to as *statistical*) provisioning is an extension of through-the-cycle provisioning; the latter refers to provisions made on the basis of the expected loss-given default of a loan throughout its duration, whereas the former is calculated using time series on default probabilities. See Burroni et al. (2009) for a more detailed discussion.

part on the partial equilibrium model of Bouvatier and Lepetit (2012), as well as Frache et al. (2018) and Krueger et al. (2018). The first two contributions also considered the combination of provisions with either monetary policy or with other macroprudential instruments, namely, reserve requirements, as discussed in chapter 5. The last two focused instead on the interactions between loan loss provisions and capital requirements.

Agénor and Pereira da Silva (2017), in particular, established three key results. First, dynamic (or, more accurately from a macroeconomic perspective, cyclically adjusted) provisioning can be highly effective in mitigating procyclicality and financial volatility. However, the relationship between the parameter that characterizes the response of provisions to cyclical shifts in the possibility of default follows a U-shape pattern. At first, a more aggressive policy mitigates financial volatility—measured, in line with the policy loss approach discussed in chapter 5, in terms of a weighted average of the volatility of the credit-to-output ratio and the volatility of real house prices—because the policy stabilizes credit, investment, and economic activity. But beyond a certain point, market interest rates become more volatile, and so do lending and aggregate demand; financial volatility therefore begins to increase again. The optimal policy is obtained at the point where the volatility index is minimized. This result is similar to those discussed in chapter 5. Second, the optimal policy involves *excess smoothing*, in the sense that it entails a more than proportional reaction to cyclical movements in the share of nonperforming loans. Third, cyclically adjusted provisioning and countercyclical reserve requirements are not complements, in the sense that the use of either one of these instruments does not improve (at the margin) the ability of the other to mitigate financial volatility. At the same time, the optimal countercyclical provisioning rule performs significantly better than the optimal reserve requirement rule. In that sense, the two instruments are partial substitutes.

6.9.4 Capital Requirements and Bank Risk-Taking

In the model presented in this chapter, as in many other contributions in the literature, capital regulation does not affect the *ex ante* risk-taking behavior of lenders. However, there are good reasons to believe that this effect can be large and persistent, as documented by Altunbas et al. (2018), for instance, and may affect both the asset and liability sides of banks' balance sheets.

Recent micro-based banking models and DSGE-FF models that account for both the possibility of excessive risk-taking behavior and a role for capital requirements include Dell'Ariccia et al. (2014), Martinez-Miera and Suarez (2014), Begenau (2015), Nguyen (2015), Begenau and Landvoigt (2016), Boissay and Collard (2016), Acosta Smith et al. (2017), Collard et al. (2017),

Cordella et al. (2018), and Mendicino et al. (2019).[31] A common result from these contributions is that capital requirements may help to mitigate bank risk-taking, but only under certain conditions—a result established in an earlier analytical contribution by Blum (1999). Martinez-Miera and Suarez (2014), for instance, argued that countercyclical capital requirements may in fact increase systemic risk-taking and reduce welfare. This may occur because when bankers anticipate such countercyclical response after a systemic shock, they also anticipate lower gains from protecting their capital against it and, therefore, engage in more risky activities to begin with.

A related issue is the extent to which countercyclical capital requirements—or macroprudential regulation in general—can help to offset an adverse effect of monetary policy on bank risk-taking. Indeed, the literature on the risk-taking channel of monetary policy has argued that such policy may itself induce boom-bust cycles in asset prices—precisely when it is successful at maintaining low and stable prices. Low interest rates may encourage increased risk-taking and excessive leverage and promote a *search for yield* when banks' return target is sticky (Borio and Zhu 2012). When an expansionary monetary policy, for instance, causes a drop in the yield of safe assets, banks may be forced to hold a larger amount of risky assets in order to meet the fixed or targeted level of returns that was guaranteed on their liabilities.[32] Alternatively, as argued by Diamond and Rajan (2012), an anticipated expansionary monetary policy may serve as insurance against expected future liquidity risk and thus spur excessive lending today to finance investment in risky, long-term assets.[33] To the extent that this negative externality associated with the pursuit of price stability increases systemic risk and financial vulnerabilities, it may be essential to combine monetary policy with macroprudential regulation, either in the form of capital requirements (as in this chapter) or other instruments (as in chapters 5 and 9).

31. In the micro-banking literature, including Dell'Ariccia et al. (2014) and Cordella et al. (2018), a common approach to measuring bank risk-taking is to relate it inversely to bank monitoring effort—which corresponds, in the present modeling framework, to the inverse of the repayment probability. However, the DSGE-FF literature has taken a broader perspective on this issue.

32. As noted by Cociuba et al. (2016), low policy rates not only make riskier assets more attractive than safe bonds, they may also reduce the amount of safe bonds available for collateralized borrowing in interbank markets. Because collateral constraints tighten as a result, risk-taking may not be excessive, compared to the social optimum. However, the magnitude of this offsetting effect is difficult to establish in practice.

33. Evidence of a negative impact of low policy rates on bank risk-taking, both before and after the global financial crisis, is provided by Altunbas et al. (2014), Neuenkirch and Nöckel (2018), Abbate and Thaler (2019), and Gaggl and Valderrama (2019) for advanced economies. However, evidence for MICs is scant and less compelling; see Tabak et al. (2010), for instance.

6.9.5 Capital Regulation and Shadow Banking

Finally, some contributions have focused on the fact that regulatory capital measures that are too restrictive could generate incentives for economic agents to circumvent regulatory requirements, thereby creating unintended side-effects of regulation. Begenau and Landvoigt (2016), for instance, showed how these unintended effects could take the form of an expansion of alternative financing channels, such as the shadow banking system. Evidence to that effect is provided by Cizel et al. (2016), especially for advanced economies. However, it may be argued that this risk is stronger for the *structural* component of capital requirements (as discussed in chapter 11) rather than their countercyclical component which, by its very nature, involves transitory changes. In another contribution, Meeks et al. (2017) developed a model in which banks (which specialize in originating loans) can offload risky loans to shadow banks. These banks are economically valuable because, by transforming illiquid loans into tradable assets, they allow collateral to be used more efficiently. They showed, in particular, that interactions and spillover effects between the two types of financial institutions affect credit dynamics, in part because high leverage in the shadow banking system makes the economy excessively vulnerable to aggregate disturbances. However, this literature is still embryonic; much remains to be done to capture the full complexity of shadow banking activities and how regulation can affect them.

Appendix Risk Weight Formulas under the IRB Approach

The constant elasticity specification relating the risk weight σ_t to the repayment probability q_t, as shown in (6.29), can be derived as follows. Under the IRB approach of Basel II and III, capital requirements are calculated based on the probability of default PD_t (or $1 - q_t$ here), the loss given default, LGD_t (or the level of exposure that will *not* be recovered following default), the exposure at default (or the loan itself), and maturity for each loan, M_t (which is one period here).[34]

As derived by Gordy (2003), the IRB risk weight formula for a given loan (or unit of exposure) can be written as

34. Pillar I of Basel II also requires capital to be held against market and operational risk. In practice, however, the major contribution to the overall capital requirements still comes from credit risk, as emphasized here. For more details on the IRB formulas, see Basel Committee on Banking Supervision (2006).

$$\sigma_t = LGD_t \left\{ \Phi \left[\frac{\Phi^{-1}(1-q_t) + \sqrt{cor_t}\Phi^{-1}(0.999)}{\sqrt{1-cor_t}} \right] - (1-q_t) \right\} \quad \text{(A6.1)}$$
$$\times \frac{1+(M_t-\bar{m})b_t^M}{1-1.5+b_t^M},$$

where $\Phi(\cdot)$ is the cumulative distribution function for a standard normal random variable, $\bar{m}$ is average maturity of loans, $cor_t \in (0, 1)$ is an estimate of the correlation across borrowers, and b_t^M is a parameter that adjusts the maturity of the loan according to its risk (based on quantitative impact studies conducted by banks, as requested by supervisors).

Based on the results reported in Covas and Fujita (2010) and Darracq Pariès et al. (2011), it may be postulated that

$$co_t = co(1-q_t), \quad b_t^M = b^M(1-q_t), \quad \text{(A6.2)}$$

with $R' < 0$, $b' < 0$ and with co and b^M as positive constants. In addition, in a model where loan maturity is not explicitly accounted for, it is reasonable to set $M_t = \bar{m}$.

To calculate the behavior of LGD_t, two approaches are possible. The first is to assume, as in the *foundation* IRB approach, a fixed LGD value provided by the supervisory authority, as in Darracq Pariès et al. (2011), for instance, who set a value of 0.45. The second, which is more consistent with the *advanced* IRB approach of Basel II, is to recognize that in the present setting, and given the presence of collateral, the value of LGD_t for a CG producer k borrowing from bank i is essentially $l_t^{K,k,i} - \kappa^{k,i}\mathbb{E}_t p_{t+1}^H \bar{H}^{k,i}$. However, as shown in the text, this is already accounted for in the repayment probability through the collateral-loan ratio in equation (6.37). Thus, movements in LGD_t are also implicitly captured through the dependence of σ_t on q_t. Given (A6.2), formula (A6.1) boils down therefore to a relationship between σ_t and q_t only. Regression results in Angeloni and Faia (2013, app. 5) suggest that a constant elasticity relationship between these two variables, of the type postulated in (6.29), is consistent with the Basel II and III risk weight formulas.

7 A Simple Open-Economy Model with Financial Frictions

As discussed in chapter 1, a key feature of MICs is their high degree of vulnerability to external shocks, both real and financial. Swings in short-term capital flows, in particular, create major challenges to policymakers concerned with maintaining macroeconomic and financial stability. To design appropriate policy responses to these shocks and assess the performance of alternative policy instruments, it is essential to develop macroeconomic models that incorporate a range of open-economy features, including the nature of the exchange rate regime and impediments to trade in financial assets. This chapter and chapters 8 through 10 aim to address these issues using both simple and more advanced models.

To start with, this chapter extends the core static model of a closed economy with financial frictions developed in chapter 2 to an open-economy setting. As before, key features of the core model are the assumptions that banks' funding sources are perfect substitutes from the banks' perspective and that lending rates are set as a premium over the cost of borrowing from the central bank. The premium itself is a function of borrowers' collateralizable net worth. Thus, credit market imperfections in this setting imply that access to loans is more costly for firms with a weak financial position. Loan supply to firms and the provision of liquidity by the central bank to commercial banks are perfectly elastic at prevailing interest rates. Also as before, behavioral relations are not explicitly derived from first principles; instead, these relations are postulated and some background rationalization and intuitive arguments are provided. Again, the reason for doing so is that simple models can be viewed as a way to communicate basic intuition and results from other, more fully articulated, stochastic macroeconomic models where credit market imperfections play a prominent role—such as those discussed in chapters 4 through 6.[1]

1. Chapters 8, 9, and 10 will present full-blown open-economy DSGE-FF models, including a two-region model of the world economy.

In addition, capital mobility is imperfect, allowing domestic interest rates to be determined at home, rather than being tied to the world interest rate.

Section 1 presents the basic model under fixed exchange rates. After describing its structure and its solution, the impact of monetary and macroprudential policies are studied. Section 2 considers the case of a flexible exchange rate and illustrates, for comparative purposes, the behavior of the model with the same set of policy shocks. Section 3 discusses some extensions of the analysis, whereas the last section provides some notes on the literature.

7.1 Fixed Exchange Rates

7.1.1 Model Structure

Consider a small open economy producing a specialized, homogeneous good that is imperfectly substitutable for foreign goods. Because the economy is small, the world price of foreign goods is taken as exogenous. However, the domestic economy is assumed to exert significant market power over the price of the good that it produces. Thus, changes in domestic demand for the exportable good affect its relative price or level of production, and the economy's terms of trade—the relative price of the foreign good in terms of the domestic good, or equivalently here the real exchange rate—are endogenous. In effect, the production structure is in the tradition of Fleming (1962) and Mundell (1963).[2] There are now six markets in the economy (for cash, domestic-currency deposits, bank loans to firms, central bank loans to commercial banks, goods, and now foreign exchange), and as in chapter 2, five categories of agents: firms, households, commercial banks, the central bank, and a financial regulator. Their behavior is considered in turn, before market-clearing conditions are specified.

Firms

As before, firms must pay all wages in advance and to do so borrow a fraction of their wage bill from banks. Loans contracted for the purpose of financing working capital are not subject to the risk of default and are therefore made at a rate that reflects only the refinance rate, i^R. Firms repay these loans, with interest, at the end of the period, after goods have been produced and sold.

2. As discussed in Agénor and Montiel (2015, chap. 1), a dependent-economy framework (based on a tradable-nontradable distinction) or a three-good structure (dinstinguishing between importables and exportables in the production of tradables) would be a more appropriate starting point for developing countries. However, because the focus here is on the effects of monetary and macroprudential policies rather than the production structure *per se*, the Mundell-Fleming structure is adopted for simplicity.

Let W denote the nominal wage and N the quantity of labor employed. The wage bill, inclusive of borrowing costs, is thus $(1+\psi_W i^R)WN$, where $\psi_W \in (0,1)$ is the fraction of wage costs financed by bank borrowing. The maximization problem faced by the representative firm can be written as

$$N = \arg\max[P^D Y - (1+\psi_W i^R)WN], \tag{7.1}$$

where Y is output and P^D the price of the domestic good.

The production function takes again a Cobb-Douglas form,

$$Y = N^\alpha K_0^{1-\alpha}, \tag{7.2}$$

where K_0 is the stock of capital at the beginning of the period and $\alpha \in (0,1)$.

Substituting (7.2) in (7.1), and taking i^R, P^D and W as given, the first-order condition of the firm's maximization problem is

$$\alpha P^D N^{\alpha-1} K_0^{1-\alpha} - (1+\psi_W i^R)W = 0.$$

Defining the *product wage* as $\omega = W/P^D$, this condition yields the demand for labor as

$$N^d = \left[\frac{\alpha}{(1+\psi_W i^R)\omega}\right]^{1/(1-\alpha)} K_0, \tag{7.3}$$

which can be substituted in (7.2) to give the supply of domestic goods:

$$Y^s = \left[\frac{\alpha}{(1+\psi_W i^R)\omega}\right]^{\alpha/(1-\alpha)} K_0. \tag{7.4}$$

These equations show that, as in chapter 2, the demand for labor and the supply of domestic goods are inversely related to the effective cost of labor, $(1+\psi i^R)\omega$. They can be written as5

$$N^d = N^d(\omega; i^R), \quad Y^s = Y^s(\omega; i^R), \tag{7.5}$$

where

$$N^d_\omega = -\left(\frac{1}{1-\alpha}\right)\frac{N^d}{\omega} < 0, \quad Y^s_\omega = -\left(\frac{\alpha}{1-\alpha}\right)\frac{Y^s}{\omega} < 0,$$

$$N^d_{i^R} = -\left(\frac{\psi_W}{1-\alpha}\right)\frac{N^d}{1+\psi_W i^R} < 0, \quad Y^s_{i^R} = -\left(\frac{\alpha\psi_W}{1-\alpha}\right)\frac{Y^s}{1+\psi_W i^R} < 0.$$

Increases in the product wage or the cost of borrowing lead to a reduction in employment and a contraction in output.

Investment is again given by

$$I = I(i^L - \pi^e), \tag{7.6}$$

where π^e is the expected inflation rate (taken as given) and $I' < 0$.

Thus, total loans, L, are given by

$$L = \psi_W W N^d(\omega; i^R) + L_0^K + P^D I(i^L - \pi^e),$$

where L_0^K is the beginning-of-period stock of investment loans.

Households

In this open economy, households consume the domestic and foreign goods and their supply of labor is perfectly elastic at the going wage. They hold now three categories of assets: currency (which again bears no interest), domestic-currency deposits with the banking system, and foreign-currency deposits held abroad. All assets are imperfect substitutes in household portfolios.[3] Foreigners do not hold domestic assets. Household financial wealth, F^H, is thus defined now as

$$F^H = M + D + \bar{E}D^*, \tag{7.7}$$

where M is currency holdings, D (D^*) domestic- (foreign-) currency deposits, and $\bar{E}$ the nominal exchange rate, taken as fixed in this section. As a result, and because there is once again a distinction between beginning- and end-of-period stocks, total financial wealth at the beginning of the period, F_0^H, is predetermined.

As in chapter 2, the domestic deposit-cash ratio is increasing in the deposit rate, i^D:

$$\frac{D}{M} = \nu(i^D), \tag{7.8}$$

where $\nu' > 0$.

The foreign-domestic deposit ratio depends on the interest rate differential between these assets:

3. Substitution across assets can be impeded by a variety of factors, such as heterogeneous information, institutional constraints, and government-induced distortions. As discussed in Agénor and Montiel (2015, chap. 13), the empirical evidence for most developing countries suggests that the assumption of perfect substitutability between domestic and foreign assets is rejected—even for assets that differ only in a single dimension, such as the currency of denomination or maturity.

$$\frac{\bar{E}D^*}{D} = \chi(i^D - i^W - \varepsilon), \tag{7.9}$$

where i^W is the interest rate on deposits held abroad, ε the expected depreciation rate (assumed constant), and $\chi' < 0$. A reduction in the domestic deposit rate, or an increase in the world interest rate, raises the foreign-domestic deposit ratio.

Substituting (7.8) for M and (7.9) for $\bar{E}D^*$ in (7.7) yields

$$F^H = M + (1+\chi)D = [\nu^{-1} + (1+\chi)]D,$$

or equivalently,

$$\frac{D}{F^H} = \frac{\nu(i^D)}{1 + [1 + \chi(i^D - i^W - \varepsilon)]\nu(i^D)} = d(i^D, i^W), \tag{7.10}$$

where, given that $\nu' > 0$ and $\chi' < 0$,

$$d_{i^D} = \frac{\nu' - \chi'\nu^2}{[1 + (1+\chi)\nu]^2} > 0, \quad d_{i^W} = \frac{\chi'\nu^2}{[1 + (1+\chi)\nu]^2} < 0.$$

From (7.8), $D = \nu(i^D)M$. Substituting this result in (7.10) yields

$$\frac{M}{F^H} = \frac{1}{1 + [1 + \chi(i^D - i^W - \varepsilon)]\nu(i^D)} = m(i^D, i^W), \tag{7.11}$$

where

$$m_{i^D} = \frac{-[\chi'\nu + (1+\chi)\nu']}{[1 + (1+\chi)\nu]^2}, \quad m_{i^W} = \frac{\chi'\nu}{[1 + (1+\chi)\nu]^2} < 0.$$

Because a rise in the domestic deposit rate lowers the demand for foreign-currency deposits (as long as $\chi' \neq 0$), the net effect on the demand for cash is ambiguous in general.[4] To ensure that a higher domestic deposit rate also lowers the demand for cash, that is, $m_{i^D} < 0$, it must be that

$$-\chi'\nu - (1+\chi)\nu' < 0,$$

Given that $\nu' > 0$ and $\chi' < 0$, the following restriction must therefore be imposed:

$$\frac{\nu'}{\nu} > -\frac{\chi'}{1+\chi}. \tag{7.12}$$

4. Setting $\chi = \chi' = 0$ yields $m_{i^D} = -\nu'/(1+\nu)^2 < 0$, as established in chapter 2.

Multiplying both sides by the deposit rate shows that this condition requires the elasticity of the demand for domestic-currency deposits, $i^D \nu'/\nu$, to be sufficiently high.

Interest on deposits held at home or abroad is paid and profits are distributed at the end of each period. As in chapter 2, consumption expenditure, C, measured in units of the domestic good, depends positively on labor income, negatively on real interest rates, and positively on financial wealth at the beginning of the period, F_0^H. The effect of interest rates is now captured by making consumption a function of the expected real rates of return on both domestic- and foreign-currency deposits. For simplicity, the partial effects of each of these rates of return are assumed identical. Thus, consumption spending can be written as

$$C = \alpha_1 \omega N^d - \alpha_2[(i^D - \pi^e) + (i^W + \varepsilon - \pi^e)] + \alpha_3 \left(\frac{F_0^H}{P^D}\right), \qquad (7.13)$$

where $\alpha_1 \in (0, 1)$ is the marginal propensity to consume and $\alpha_2, \alpha_3 > 0$.

Because households consume both domestic and imported goods, the cost of living index, P, must be defined. Assuming that the foreign-currency price of imported goods is exogenous and normalized to unity, P can be written as

$$P = (P^D)^{1-\delta} \bar{E}^\delta = P^D z^\delta, \qquad (7.14)$$

where z is the *real exchange rate*, defined as $z = \bar{E}/P^D$, and $\delta \in (0, 1)$. Thus, the cost of living index is a geometrically weighted average of the price of the domestic good and the price of imported goods, with weights reflecting the share of each category of goods in household total expenditure. Specifically, the parameter δ $(1-\delta)$ is the share of consumption spending by households on imported (domestic) goods.

Commercial banks

Bank assets consist of loans to firms, L, and reserves held at the central bank, RR, whereas their liabilities consist of deposits held at home by households, D, and borrowing from the central bank, L^B. They cannot borrow abroad.[5] The balance sheet of the representative bank can therefore be written again as

$$L + RR = D + L^B. \qquad (7.15)$$

Reserves do not pay interest and are determined by

5. Bank borrowing abroad will be discussed in chapters 8 and 9, in the context of a full-blown DSGE-FF model.

$$RR = \mu D, \tag{7.16}$$

where $\mu \in (0, 1)$ is the required reserve ratio.

As in the core model of chapter 2, the deposit market is competitive and banks view domestic-currency deposits and loans from the central bank as perfect substitutes. Thus, the return on these deposits is equal to the cost of funds provided by the central bank, corrected for the (implicit) cost of holding unremunerated reserves:

$$i^D = (1 - \mu)i^R. \tag{7.17}$$

The loan rate, i^L, is set at a premium over the marginal cost of funds,

$$i^L = i^R + \theta + \gamma\tau^L, \quad \gamma > 0 \tag{7.18}$$

where $\tau^L \in (0, 1)$ is again the tax rate on loans and θ the premium, which is inversely related to the ratio of firms' assets (the value of their beginning-of-period physical capital stock, K_0, which is taken as given, times P^D, the price of the domestic good) over their liabilities (that is, beginning-of-period borrowing for investment, L_0^K),

$$\theta = \theta\left(\frac{\kappa P^D K_0}{L_0^K}\right), \tag{7.19}$$

where $\kappa \in (0, 1)$ is the proportion of assets that can effectively be used or pledged as collateral and $\theta' < 0$.

As discussed in previous chapters, the view that underlies this specification is that the premium charged by banks reflects the possibility of default on their loans to domestic firms faced with idiosyncratic risk. The higher the value of collateralizable wealth (which consists here of firms' physical assets, $\kappa P^D K_0$) that firms can pledge, relative to initial liabilities, L_0^K, the higher the proportion of their loans that banks can recoup in the event of default. This reduces the premium and the cost of borrowing. Because both K_0 and L_0^K are predetermined, the premium varies inversely with the price of the domestic good, P^D.

Given the commercial banks' interest rate-setting behavior, the outstanding stock of loans is determined by firms' demand for credit. Equation (7.15) combined with (7.16) implies as before that borrowing from the central bank is determined residually:

$$L^B = L - (1 - \mu)D. \tag{7.20}$$

Central bank and regulator

The central bank ensures the costless conversion of domestic-currency holdings into foreign currency at the officially determined exchange rate, $\bar{E}$. It also supplies liquidity elastically to commercial banks at the fixed refinance rate, i^R. As a result, the supply of cash is endogenous; it responds passively to shocks to banks' liquidity needs—which are themselves related to changes in household deposits held at home and firms' demand for credit.

The balance sheet of the central bank consists, on the asset side, of loans to commercial banks, L^B, and foreign reserves (in foreign-currency terms), R^*. On the liability side, it consists only of the monetary base, given by the sum of currency in circulation, M^s, and required reserves:

$$\bar{E}R^* + L^B = M^s + RR. \tag{7.21}$$

This equation, together with (7.16), determines residually the supply of currency. In contrast to chapter 2, changes in foreign reserves (which are now endogenous) also matter in an open economy with fixed exchange rates. Finally, the regulator sets the tax rate on loans, τ^L.

Market-clearing conditions

There are now six market equilibrium conditions to consider: five financial (cash, domestic-currency deposits, loans to firms, central bank loans to commercial banks, and foreign exchange) and one for the goods market. As in chapter 2, at the prevailing deposit, loan, and refinance rates, the markets for domestic-currency deposits, loans, and central bank credit adjust through quantities.

The equilibrium condition of the goods market, which determines the price of domestic goods, P^D, requires equality between the supply of domestic goods to the domestic market and aggregate demand,

$$Y^s - X(z) = (1-\delta)C + I, \tag{7.22}$$

where $X(z)$ denotes exports, which are positively related to the real exchange rate, so that $X' > 0$ and $(1-\delta)C$ is consumption spending on domestic goods.

The equilibrium condition of the market for foreign exchange is essentially the balance-of-payments equilibrium condition, which requires that

$$E^{-1}P^D[X(z) - \delta C] + i^W(D_0^* + R_0^*) - (D^* - D_0^*) = R^* - R_0^*, \tag{7.23}$$

where δC represents real imports in domestic-currency terms and D_0^* and R_0^* are the beginning-of-period stocks of household deposits held abroad and official reserves, respectively. This condition indicates that official foreign reserves must increase if the sum of the trade surplus, $E^{-1}P^D[X(z) - \delta C]$, and the services account, $i^W(D_0^* + R_0^*)$, exceeds capital outflows associated with the accumulation of deposits held abroad, $-(D^* - D_0^*)$.

The last equilibrium condition relates to the market for cash and (under the assumption that the counterpart to bank loans consists of currency, which is used instantly to buy goods for investment) involves (7.10) and (7.21). However, as discussed in chapter 2, there is no need to write this condition explicitly, given that by Walras' law it can be eliminated.

The elimination of the market for cash means also that changes in official foreign reserves play no direct role in determining the equilibrium. Given the balance sheet of the central bank (7.21), in the absence of sterilization changes in foreign reserves have a direct effect on changes in the supply of cash, given that $\Delta M^s = \bar{E}\Delta R^* + \Delta L^B - \Delta RR$.[6] However, given that the equilibrium condition of the market for currency can be eliminated by Walras' law, (7.21) plays no direct role in the solution of the model. Thus, end-of-period official reserves may take on any value required to ensure external balance (7.23). However, an equilibrium involving, say, very large losses in official reserves would not be feasible because it could lead to a collapse of the exchange rate regime, consistent with so-called first-generation models of currency crises.[7] In what follows, it will be assumed that the initial level of foreign reserves is sufficiently high to ensure that this scenario does not occur in response to shocks.

7.1.2 Macroeconomic Equilibrium

Suppose now that the wage rate is fully indexed on the cost of living index—an assumption that is consistent with the fact that, in this open economy, households (workers) consume both domestic and imported goods.[8] Thus, $W = P$, which means, using (7.14), that the product wage is now given by

$$\omega = \frac{P}{P^D} = z^\delta, \tag{7.24}$$

so that

$$d\omega = \delta z^{\delta-1} dz = \delta z^{\delta-1}\left[-\frac{\bar{E}}{(P^D)^2}\right] dP^D = -\delta\left(\frac{\omega}{P^D}\right) dP^D.$$

6. Sterilization is discussed in more detail in chapters 8 and 9. For the moment, the assumption is that there is no sterilization, which implies that changes in official reserves, $\bar{E}\Delta R^*$, have a one-to-one effect on money supply, ΔM^s.

7. See Agénor and Flood (1994) and Agénor and Montiel (2015, chap. 14), as well as references therein.

8. Partial indexation would not change qualitatively the results.

Substituting (7.24) in (7.3) and (7.4) gives

$$N^d = N^d(P^D; i^R), \quad Y^s = Y^s(P^D; i^R), \tag{7.25}$$

with

$$N^d_{PD} = \left(\frac{1}{1-\alpha}\right) N^d \left(\frac{\delta}{P^D}\right) > 0, \quad Y^s_{PD} = \left(\frac{\alpha}{1-\alpha}\right) Y^s \left(\frac{\delta}{P^D}\right) > 0,$$

with N^d_{iR} and Y^s_{iR} defined as before. Thus, an increase in the price of the domestic good lowers the product wage and raises employment and output.[9]

Combining (7.18) and (7.19) yields

$$i^L = FF(P^D; i^R, \mu, \tau^L), \tag{7.26}$$

where

$$FF_{PD} = \kappa \left(\frac{K_0}{L^K_0}\right) \theta' < 0,$$

$$FF_{iR} = 1,$$

$$FF_{\mu} = 0,$$

$$FF_{\tau^L} = \gamma.$$

Equation (7.26) defines the *financial sector equilibrium* condition. The interpretation of these derivatives is the same as that provided in chapter 2. In particular, the negative effect of the domestic price level on the equilibrium loan rate is the key source of the financial accelerator effect. An increase in the domestic price level raises the value of firms' collateralizable assets relative to their stock of outstanding loans, which are fixed in nominal value. Banks thus demand a lower premium and reduce the loan rate. An increase in the refinance rate by the central bank, or the tax rate on loans by the regulator, raise the cost of funds for banks and is reflected directly in the loan rate.

Suppose that the nominal exchange rate is credibly fixed so that the expected depreciation rate $\varepsilon = 0$. Substituting (7.6), (7.13), (7.17), (7.24), and (7.25) in the goods market equilibrium condition (7.22), with $\pi^e = 0$ as well, yields

9. Note that, if it had been assumed that the nominal wage is indexed solely on the price of the domestic good, P^D, both employment and output would be independent of the real exchange rate because in that case $\omega = 1$. Consequently, $N^d_{PD} = Y^s_{PD} = 0$. Alternatively, if it had been assumed that the nominal wage is fixed, as in chapter 2, a positive relationship between the domestic price and employment and output would also hold, as in (7.25).

$$Y^s(P^D; i^R)$$

$$= (1-\delta)\left\{\alpha_1\left(\frac{\bar{E}}{P^D}\right)^{\delta} N^d(P^D; i^R) - \alpha_2[(1-\mu)i^R + i^W] + \alpha_3\left(\frac{F_0^H}{P^D}\right)\right\}$$

$$+I(i^L) + X\left(\frac{\bar{E}}{P^D}\right),$$

which defines a set of combinations of the loan rate and the domestic price level that are consistent with equilibrium in the market for domestic goods. This equation can be totally differentiated and solved to give

$$i^L = GG(P^D; i^R, \mu, \tau^L), \tag{7.27}$$

where

$$GG_{P^D} = \frac{1}{I'}\left\{Y^s_{P^D} + \frac{\alpha_1(1-\delta)\omega}{P^D}(\delta N^d - P^D N^d_{P^D})\right.$$

$$\left. + \alpha_3(1-\delta)\left[\frac{F_0^H}{(P^D)^2}\right] + (\frac{z}{P^D})X'\right\},$$

$$GG_{i^R} = \frac{1}{I'}\left\{Y^s_{i^R} - \alpha_1(1-\delta)\omega N^d_{i^R} + \alpha_2(1-\delta)(1-\mu)\right\},$$

$$GG_{\mu} = -(1-\delta)\frac{\alpha_2 i^R}{I'} > 0,$$

$$GG_{\tau^L} = 0.$$

Equation (7.27) defines the *goods market equilibrium* condition.

As in chapter 2, it can be established that $GG_{P^D} < 0$. To do so, the first step consists again of showing that the sum of the supply and wage income effects, $Y^s_{P^D} + \alpha_1(1-\delta)(\omega/P^D)(\delta N^d - P^D N^d_{P^D})$, is positive. From (7.25), $\delta N^d - P^D N^d_{P^D} = -\alpha(1-\alpha)^{-1}\delta N^d$, which can be substituted in the previous expression, together with $Y^s_{P^D} = \alpha[(1-\alpha)P^D]^{-1}\delta Y^s$ from (7.25), to give $\alpha\delta[(1-\alpha)P^D]^{-1}[Y^s - \alpha_1(1-\delta)\omega N^d]$. From solutions (7.3) and (7.4),

$$Y^s - \alpha_1(1-\delta)\omega N^d = \frac{K_0}{\omega^{\alpha/(1-\alpha)}}\left(\frac{\alpha}{1+\psi_W i^R}\right)^{1/(1-\alpha)}\left[\frac{1+\psi_W i^R}{\alpha} - \alpha_1(1-\delta)\right].$$

The last term in brackets in this expression is positive because $\alpha^{-1}(1+\psi_W i^R) > \alpha^{-1} > 1 > \alpha_1(1-\delta)$. The second step is to note that, given that $\alpha_3(1-\delta)[F_0^H/(P^D)^2] + zX'/P^D > 0$, the expression in curly brackets in the definition of GG_{PD} is also positive. And because $I' < 0$, the result is indeed $GG_{PD} < 0$.

Also as in chapter 2, it can be established that $GG_{i^R} \gtrless 0$, due to the fact that a higher refinance rate leads to a contraction in both aggregate supply and aggregate demand. In what follows, the focus will be on the case where ψ_W is low enough, to ensure that the supply-side effect of an increase in the refinance rate is dominated by the demand side effect; as a result, $GG_{i^R} < 0$.

Equations (7.26) and (7.27) can be solved together for the equilibrium values of the loan interest rate, i^L, and the price of domestic goods, P^D, just as was the case with a closed economy. The solution can be depicted graphically as in figure 7.1. In the northeast quadrant both equations trace out curves FF and GG with negative slopes in i^L-P^D space. As discussed in chapter 2, it can be established that, under fairly standard dynamic assumptions, local stability requires GG to be steeper than FF. As in figure 2.2 also, the northwest quadrant shows the negative relationship between the lending rate and investment (7.6); this value is then reported in the southwest quadrant. The southeast quadrant shows now the relationship between domestic prices and the part of domestic production sold at home, $Y^s - X$, rather than total output; the slope of this relationship is positive because from (7.25) $Y^s_{PD} > 0$. And because $X' > 0$ and $dz/dP^D = d(\bar{E}/P^D)/dP^D = -\bar{E}/(P^D)^2 < 0$,[10]

$$\frac{d(Y^s - X)}{dP^D} = Y^s_{PD} - X'\left(\frac{dz}{dP^D}\right) > 0.$$

The difference between the part of domestic production sold at home and investment gives the equilibrium level of spending on domestic goods as a fraction of total expenditure, $(1-\delta)C$. The economy's equilibrium is determined at points E, D, H, and J.

7.1.3 Monetary and Macroprudential Policies

As in chapter 2, to illustrate the functioning of the model three experiments are considered: an increase in the official rate, i^R; an increase in the required reserve ratio, μ, which can be driven either by monetary policy or financial stability considerations; and an increase in the tax rate on loans, τ^L. The effects of these policy changes are very similar qualitatively to those obtained in a closed economy, and the description of how they operate is therefore kept short.

10. Note that, regardless of whether output is endogenous, sales of the domestic good on the domestic market $Y^s - X$ are negatively related to z, the real exchange rate, and thus positively to the price of the domestic good, P^D, through exports. Indeed, with exogenous output, $d(\bar{Y} - X)/dP^D = -X'(dz/dP^D) > 0$.

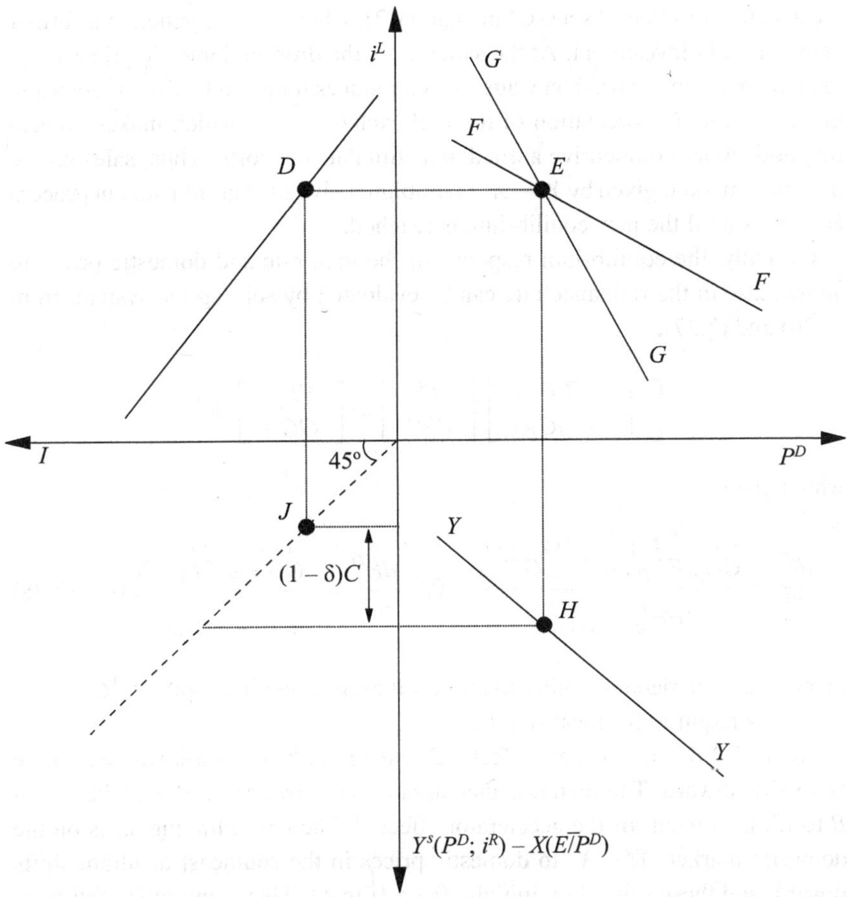

Figure 7.1
Macroeconomic equilibrium: fixed exchange rates

Increase in refinance rate

The direct effect of an increase in the refinance rate is to raise banks' borrowing costs, inducing them to increase the loan rate. This lowers investment. At the same time, it increases the deposit rate and reduces consumption through the intertemporal substitution effect. Thus, aggregate demand falls unambiguously on impact. At the same time, the increase in the refinance rate raises production costs. Under the assumption (stated earlier) that the share of these costs that must be financed by bank credit, ψ_W, is relatively small, the drop in the production of domestic goods is muted. Excess supply therefore prevails initially and domestic prices must fall. This tends to stimulate consumption (through the wealth effect) and to bring about further increases in the loan rate (through the accelerator effect discussed in chapter 2), which in turn generate a further contraction in investment. At the same time, the drop in domestic prices leads to an increase in the product wage, which reduces total production of domestic goods, and to a depreciation of the real exchange rate, which makes domestic goods more competitive abroad and stimulates exports. Thus, sales on the domestic market, given by $Y^s - X$, unambiguously fall. The adjustment process continues until the new equilibrium is reached.

Formally, the equilibrium response of the loan rate and domestic prices to an increase in the refinance rate can be evaluated by solving the system, from (7.26) and (7.27),

$$\begin{bmatrix} 1 & -FF_{PD} \\ 1 & -GG_{PD} \end{bmatrix} \begin{bmatrix} di^L \\ dP^D \end{bmatrix} = \begin{bmatrix} FF_{i^R} \\ GG_{i^R} \end{bmatrix} di^R,$$

which gives

$$\frac{di^L}{di^R} = \frac{\overset{(-)}{GG_{i^R}}\overset{(-)}{FF_{PD}} - \overset{(+)}{FF_{i^R}}\overset{(-)}{GG_{PD}}}{\underset{(-)}{FF_{PD}} - \underset{(-)}{GG_{PD}}} > 0, \quad \frac{dP^D}{di^R} = \frac{\overset{(-)}{GG_{i^R}} - \overset{(+)}{FF_{i^R}}}{\underset{(-)}{FF_{PD}} - \underset{(-)}{GG_{PD}}} < 0, \quad (7.28)$$

given that, in a manner similar to the result established in chapter 2, $|GG_{PD}| > |FF_{PD}|$ is required for local stability.

Figure 7.2 illustrates these effects. Curve FF shifts outward, whereas curve GG shifts inward. The loan rate increases initially from E to B, and then from B to E', as a result of the accelerator effect.[11] The curve linking sales on the domestic market, $Y^s - X$, to domestic prices in the southeast quadrant shifts inward, and these sales drop initially from H to M. They continue to fall from M to H', as domestic prices drop and the product wage increases, while at the same time exports keep rising, as the real exchange rate depreciates. Investment necessarily falls (from D to D') but consumption of domestic goods, $(1-\delta)C$, may either increase or fall; in the scenario depicted in figure 7.2, household expenditure falls as well to $(1-\delta)C'$. Once again, as in the more complex models of credit market imperfections discussed in the previous chapters, the financial accelerator magnifies the effect of monetary policy.

Increase in required reserve ratio

From (7.26) and (7.27), the equilibrium response of the loan rate and domestic prices to an increase in the required reserve ratio can be evaluated by solving the system

11. The case where $\alpha_2 = 0$ corresponds to the equiilibrium point E'', as in chapter 2.

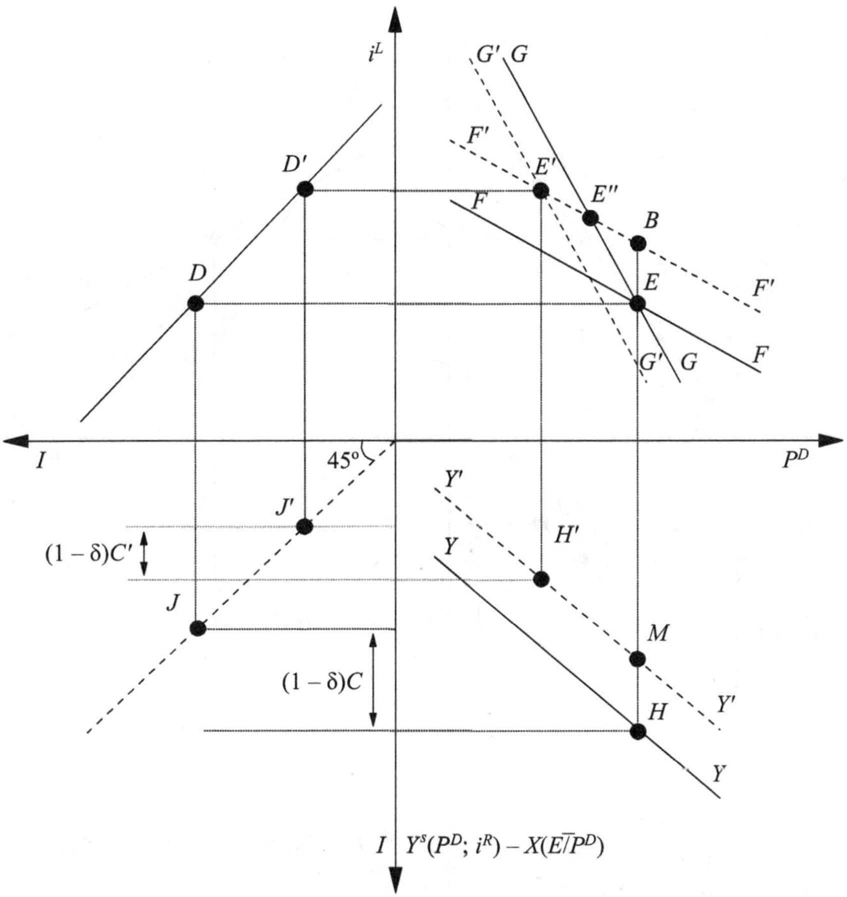

Figure 7.2
Fixed exchange rates: increase in refinance rate (weak cost channel)

$$\begin{bmatrix} 1 & -FF_{P^D} \\ 1 & -GG_{P^D} \end{bmatrix} \begin{bmatrix} di^L \\ dP^D \end{bmatrix} = \begin{bmatrix} 0 \\ GG_\mu \end{bmatrix} d\mu,$$

which gives

$$\frac{di^L}{d\mu} = \frac{\overset{(+)}{GG_\mu}\overset{(-)}{FF_P}}{\underset{(-)}{FF_P} - \underset{(-)}{GG_P}} < 0, \quad \frac{dP^D}{d\mu} = \frac{\overset{(+)}{GG_\mu}}{\underset{(-)}{FF_P} - \underset{(-)}{GG_P}} > 0, \tag{7.29}$$

given again the restriction $|GG_{P^D}| > |FF_{P^D}|$.

An increase in the required reserve ratio makes deposits less attractive to banks as a source of funding and causes them to lower the deposit interest

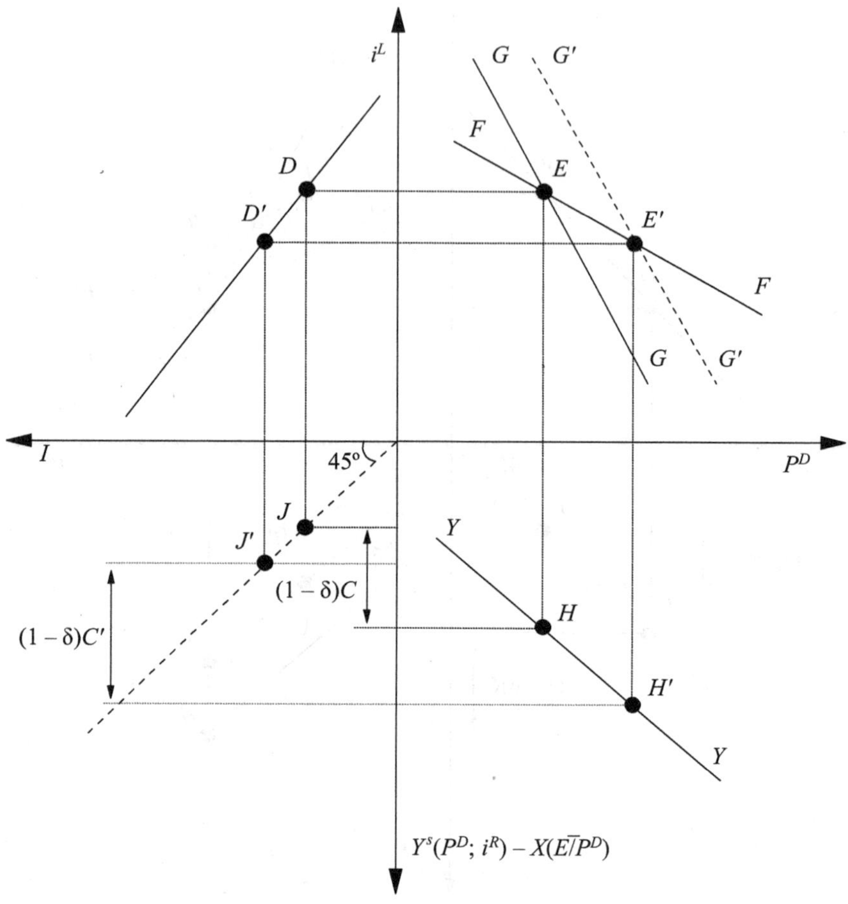

Figure 7.3
Fixed exchange rates: increase in required reserve ratio

rate. This affects the goods market directly, because the lower deposit rate discourages saving and stimulates current consumption. Because the demand for domestic goods increases, at the initial level of domestic prices a higher loan rate would be required to reduce investment and clear the goods market. Thus, curve *GG* shifts outward. By contrast, under the assumption that the central bank's supply of funds to banks is perfectly elastic at the refinance rate i^R, the increase in reserve requirements has no effect on banks' marginal cost of funds. Consequently, curve *FF* is unaffected by this policy. The upshot, as shown in figure 7.3, is that an increase in the required reserve ratio is inflationary.

As discussed in chapter 2, the explanation for this seemingly counterintuitive result is that, under the assumed monetary policy regime, changes in reserve requirements have no effect on banks' marginal cost of funds. Because the central bank stands ready to provide all the funds desired by banks at the prevailing refinance rate, increases in reserve requirements leave banks' borrowing costs—and therefore their lending rates—unaffected while lowering the interest rate that represents the opportunity cost of current versus future consumption. As also discussed in chapters 2 and 5, with imperfect substitutability between domestic-currency deposits and central bank liquidity (from the perspective of the monetary authority) it is possible for changes in the required reserve ratio to operate in countercyclical fashion.

Increase in the tax rate on loans

Consider now an increase in the tax rate on loans, τ^L. The effects of this policy are illustrated in figure 7.4. A higher τ^L raises the loan rate ($FF_{\tau^L} > 0$) and leads to an outward shift in FF. But because changes in τ^L have no direct effect on aggregate demand, GG does not change. The new equilibrium is at points E', D', H', and J' and is characterized by lower prices and output, as well as lower investment. The initial jump in the loan rate from point E to point B leads to a contraction in investment and thus excess supply of goods at the initial level of domestic prices. As prices begin to fall and collateral values drop, the premium rises, thereby inducing a further increase in the loan rate from B to E'. At the same time, the drop in prices raises the cost of labor, which induces a contraction in aggregate supply.

Once again, a financial accelerator effect is at play here because, fundamentally, the tax on loans operates via one of the key channels through which monetary policy is transmitted to the economy: It raises directly the cost at which firms can borrow from banks. The difference is that the tax on loans (unlike the refinance rate) has no direct effect on the deposit rate; consequently, at the initial level of prices, the contraction in aggregate demand is due entirely to a drop in investment.

7.2 Flexible Exchange Rates

The case of flexible exchange rates is now considered. Because the structure of the model remains very similar to the one presented earlier (which itself dwells significantly on the closed-economy version presented in chapter 2), only a parsimonious presentation of some of the equations that were previously introduced is provided; the focus instead is on explaining differences with the fixed-exchange-rate case.

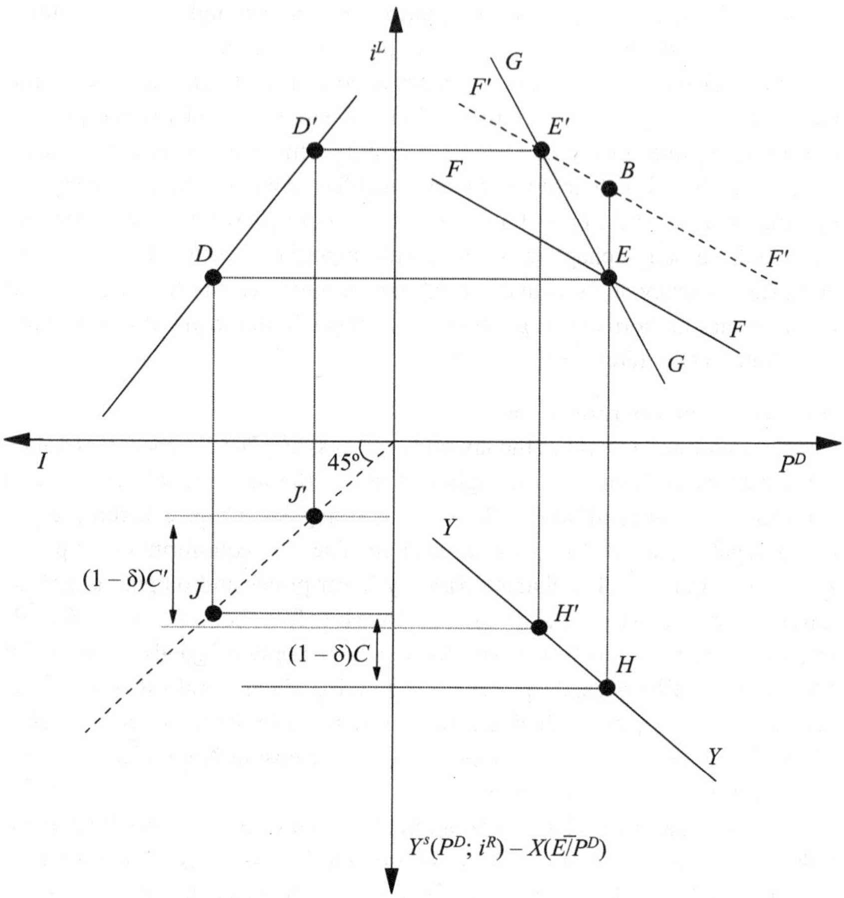

Figure 7.4
Fixed exchange rates: increase in tax rate on loans

7.2.1 Changes to Model Structure

The supply side of the model remains the same as before. But because the nominal exchange rate, denoted E, is now fully flexible, the real exchange rate is $z = E/P^D$. With again $\omega = W/P^D = z^\delta$ as in (7.24), equations (7.5) become

$$N^d = N^d(z; i^R), \quad Y^s = Y^s(z; i^R), \tag{7.30}$$

with

$$N_z^d = -\left(\frac{\delta}{1-\alpha}\right)\frac{N^d}{z} < 0, \quad Y_z^s = -\left(\frac{\alpha\delta}{1-\alpha}\right)\frac{Y^s}{z} < 0,$$

and as before N^d_{iR}, $Y^s_{iR} < 0$. Thus, a real depreciation (a rise in z), caused either by a nominal depreciation or a fall in domestic prices, tends to increase the product wage, which in turn lowers employment and the supply of domestic goods.

Household financial wealth is again defined as in (7.7),

$$F^H = M + D + ED^*, \tag{7.31}$$

which can be rewritten as

$$F^H = (M + D + E_0 D^*) + (E - E_0)D^*,$$

or, using (7.31),

$$F^H = F^H_0 + (E - E_0)D^*_0, \tag{7.32}$$

where E_0 and D^*_0 are the beginning-of-period values of the nominal exchange rate and the stock of foreign-currency deposits, respectively. As before, the term F^H_0 represents the predetermined component of household financial wealth, and $(E - E_0)D^*_0$ is now the endogenous component, due to the fact that the nominal exchange rate is flexible.

The cash-domestic deposit ratio and the foreign-domestic deposit ratio are given by the same equations (7.8) and (7.9), which are repeated here for convenience:

$$\frac{D}{M} = \nu(i^D), \tag{7.33}$$

$$\frac{ED^*}{D} = \chi(i^D - i^W - \varepsilon), \tag{7.34}$$

where $\nu' > 0$ and $\chi' < 0$.

For tractability, it will be assumed in what follows that households face costs in adjusting their stock of foreign-currency deposits. While these costs could be motivated in a variety of ways, a simple assumption is that the country in question maintains (imperfect) restrictions over capital outflows, which prevent households from adjusting instantaneously their holdings of foreign assets (see chapter 9). Specifically, suppose that these adjustments occur gradually over time, in such a way that capital outflows during each period, denoted ΔD^*, are proportional to the gap between households' desired stock of foreign-currency deposits and the actual stock at the beginning of the period (or inherited from the previous period):

$$\Delta D^* = \lambda^D (D^* - D_0^*),$$

that is, using (7.34),

$$\Delta D^* = \lambda^D \left[\frac{\chi(i^D - i^W - \varepsilon)D}{E} - D_0^* \right]. \tag{7.35}$$

The parameter $\lambda^D \geq 0$ is an indicator of the severity of adjustment costs, with $\lambda^D = 1$ indicating the absence of these costs and $\lambda^D = 0$ a situation where such costs are prohibitive, preventing capital flows altogether.

From (7.10), $D = d(i^D, i^W)F^H$. Using this result, together with (7.32), the actual stock of foreign-currency deposits evolves as

$$D^* = D_0 + \lambda^D \left\{ \frac{\chi(i^D - i^W - \varepsilon)}{E} d(i^D, i^W)[F_0^H + (E - E_0)D_0^*] - D_0^* \right\},$$

or equivalently, given that $z = E/P^D$, or $E = zP^D$,

$$\Delta D^* = \lambda^D d^*(z, P^D; i^D), \tag{7.36}$$

where, noting that $F_0^H - E_0 D_0^* = M_0 + D_0$,

$$d_z^* = \frac{-(M_0 + D_0)\chi d}{P^D z^2} < 0,$$

$$d_{P^D}^* = \frac{-(M_0 + D_0)\chi d}{z(P^D)^2} < 0,$$

$$d_{i^D}^* = \frac{1}{E}(\chi d_{i^D} + \chi' d)[F_0^H + (E - E_0)D_0^*].$$

A depreciation of the real exchange rate or an increase in domestic prices leads to a fall in the stock of foreign-currency deposits measured in foreign-currency terms. The same result obtains with an increase in the domestic deposit rate ($d_{i^D}^* < 0$) if the elasticity of the deposit ratio is higher than the elasticity of domestic-currency deposits with respect to that variable—that is, $-\chi' i^D/\chi > d_{i^D} i^D/d$. This assumption is imposed in what follows.

The equations characterizing the behavior of commercial banks are the same as before, as described by (7.16) to (7.19). They are summarized here for convenience:

$$RR = \mu D, \tag{7.37}$$

$$i^D = (1 - \mu)i^R, \tag{7.38}$$

$$i^L = i^R + \theta\left(\frac{\kappa P^D K_0}{L_0^K}\right) + \gamma\tau^L, \tag{7.39}$$

$$L^B = L - (1-\mu)D. \tag{7.40}$$

Once again equation (7.39) gives the financial sector equilibrium condition

$$i^L = FF(P^D; i^R, \mu, \tau^L), \tag{7.41}$$

which has the same properties as (7.26)—that is, $FF_{P^D} < 0$, $FF_{i^R} = 1 > 0$, $FF_\mu = 0$ and $FF_{\tau^L} = \gamma > 0$.

The central bank's balance sheet is now given by

$$ER^* + L^B = M^s + RR + (E - E_0)R^*, \tag{7.42}$$

where the term $(E - E_0)R^*$ on the liability side represents capital gains or losses on foreign exchange reserves arising from fluctuations in the market exchange rate relative to its value at the beginning of period, E_0. As before, equation (7.42) can be used to derive the supply of cash.

In addition to (7.30), equations needed to solve for the domestic goods market equilibrium are again (7.6), (7.13), (7.14), and (7.22), which are summarized here as well for convenience:

$$I = I(i_L - \pi^e), \tag{7.43}$$

$$C = \alpha_1 \omega N^d - \alpha_2[(i^D - \pi^e) + (i^W + \varepsilon - \pi^e)] + \alpha_3\left(\frac{F^H}{P^D}\right), \tag{7.44}$$

$$P = P^D z^\delta, \tag{7.45}$$

$$Y^s - X(z) = (1-\delta)C + I. \tag{7.46}$$

Regarding the balance of payments, suppose that the exchange rate is fully flexible (no intervention by the central bank, of the type discussed in chapter 8) and that consequently official foreign reserves are constant at $R_0^* = 0$. The model can then be closed by specifying the economy's balance-of-payments equilibrium condition as, instead of (7.23),

$$E^{-1}P^D[X(z) - \delta C] + i^W D_0^* - (D^* - D_0^*) = 0.$$

Given that $E/P^D = z$, this condition becomes

$$z^{-1}[X(z) - \delta C] + i^W D_0^* - \Delta D^* = 0. \tag{7.47}$$

7.2.2 Macroeconomic Equilibrium

In solving the model, the expected rate of inflation and the expected rate of depreciation are once again assumed constant and normalized to zero.[12] There are three key endogenous variables in the model: the banks' lending rate i^L, the price of domestic goods, P^D, and the real exchange rate z.[13] Correspondingly, there are three equilibrium conditions—equations (7.41), (7.45), and (7.47)—which relate to, respectively, the financial sector, the domestic goods market, and the balance of payments, respectively. However, (7.41) can be used to eliminate the lending rate, i^L, from the other equation where it appears, (7.45). As a result, the model collapses to two equations: an *internal balance condition*, which describes simultaneously equilibrium in the domestic goods market and the financial sector, and an *external balance condition*, which characterizes equilibrium of the balance of payments. These conditions can be solved jointly for the remaining two variables, z and P^D.

Internal balance

Substituting the investment function (7.43) and the consumption function (7.44), together with (7.30) for aggregate supply, in (7.46), the equilibrium condition of the domestic goods market becomes, with $\pi^e = \varepsilon = 0$,

$$Y^s(z; i^R) = (1-\delta)\left\{\alpha_1 \omega N^d(z; i^R) - \alpha_2(i^D + i^W) + \alpha_3\left(\frac{F^H}{P^D}\right)\right\} \tag{7.48}$$
$$+ I(i^L) + X(z).$$

From (7.32),

$$\frac{F^H}{P^D} = \frac{F_0^H}{P^D} + \left(\frac{E}{P^D} - \frac{E_0}{P^D}\right) D_0^*.$$

Substituting this result, together with (7.24), (7.38), and (7.39), in (7.48), yields

$$Y^s(z; i^R) = (1-\delta)\left\{\alpha_1 \frac{N^d(z; i^R)}{z^{-\delta}} - \alpha_2[(1-\mu)i^R + i^W]\right.$$

12. The assumption that the expected rate of depreciation is constant is much less tenable under flexible exchange rate compared to the fixed exchange rate case. This issue is further discussed later.

13. Under the fixed-exchange-rate regime considered earlier, the price of the domestic good and the real exchange rate vary in exact opposite directions, so there are only two key variables, i^L and P^D.

$$+\alpha_3\left[\frac{F_0^H}{P^D}+\left(z-\frac{E_0}{P^D}\right)D_0^*\right]\bigg\}+I\left\{i^R+\theta\left(\frac{\kappa P^D K_0}{L_0^K}\right)+\gamma\tau^L\right\}+X(z).$$

Differentiating totally this expression yields

$$\begin{aligned}Y_z^s dz+Y_{i^R}^s di^R &= (1-\delta)\alpha_1(z^\delta N_z^d dz+\delta z^{\delta-1}N^d dz+z^\delta N_{i^R}^d di^R)\\ &\quad -(1-\delta)\alpha_2[(1-\mu)di^R-i^R d\mu]\\ &\quad +(1-\delta)\alpha_3\left[-\frac{F_0^H}{(P^D)^2}dP^D+D_0^* dz+\frac{E_0 D_0^*}{(P^D)^2}dP^D\right]\\ &\quad +I' di^R+\left(\frac{\kappa K_0}{L_0^K}\right)I'\theta' dP^D+\gamma I' d\tau^L+X' dz,\end{aligned}$$

which implies that

$$z=NN(P^D;i^R,\mu,\tau^L). \tag{7.49}$$

where

$$NN_{P^D}=\Delta^{-1}\left\{-\frac{(1-\delta)\alpha_3}{(P^D)^2}(F_0^H-E_0D_0^*)+\left(\frac{\kappa K_0}{L_0^K}\right)I'\theta'\right\},$$

$$NN_{i^R}=\Delta^{-1}\left\{-Y_{i^R}^s+(1-\delta)[\alpha_1 z^\delta N_{i^R}^d-\alpha_2(1-\mu)]+I'\right\},$$

$$NN_\mu=\Delta^{-1}(1-\delta)\alpha_2 i^R,$$

$$NN_\tau=\Delta^{-1}I',$$

$$\Delta=Y_z^s-(1-\delta)\alpha_1(z^\delta N_z^d+\delta z^{\delta-1}N^d)-(1-\delta)\alpha_3D_0^*-X'.$$

Equation (7.49) expresses the *internal balance condition*, *NN*, as a relationship between the real exchange rate and the price of domestic goods.

Consider first the term Δ, which measures the total effect of a change in the real exchange rate on excess supply of domestic goods. As in chapter 2, and as shown earlier in the case of fixed exchange rates with a change in P^D, it can be established that the sum of the supply effect and the wage income effect of a change in the real exchange rate is negative, so that $Y_z^s-(1-\delta)\alpha_1(z^\delta N_z^d+\delta z^{\delta-1}N^d)<0$.[14] Given that $X'>0$, we also have $-(1-\delta)\alpha_3D_0^*-X'<0$. This

14. From (7.30), $z^\delta N_z^d+\delta z^{\delta-1}N^d=-\delta z^{\delta-1}(1-\alpha)^{-1}N^d+\delta z^{\delta-1}N^d=\delta z^{\delta-1}N^d[1-(1-\alpha)^{-1}]=-\alpha(1-\alpha)^{-1}\delta z^{\delta-1}N^d<0$. Again from (7.30), $Y_z^s=-(1-\alpha)^{-1}z^{-1}\alpha\delta Y^s$. Thus, $Y_z^s-(1-\delta)\alpha_1(z^\delta N_z^d+\delta z^{\delta-1}N^d)=(1-\alpha)^{-1}z^{-1}\alpha\delta[-Y^s+(1-\delta)\alpha_1 z^\delta N^d]$. Now, substituting

expression consists of two parts: a wealth effect on consumption of domestic goods, given by $(1-\delta)\alpha_3 D_0^*$, and a competitiveness effect, given by X'. The wealth effect arises from the fact that, given the price of domestic goods, a real exchange rate depreciation is equivalent to a depreciation in the *nominal* exchange rate. This nominal depreciation creates a capital gain on foreign-currency deposits. As stated, the sum of the wealth and competitiveness effects on aggregate demand is positive, and thus its impact on excess supply is negative. Put differently, a real exchange-rate depreciation, holding the price of domestic goods constant, lowers excess supply of domestic goods on the domestic market so that $\Delta < 0$.

The effect of an increase in the price of domestic goods on the excess demand for these goods, holding the real exchange rate constant, NN_{PD}, is more complicated. The first term, $-(1-\delta)\alpha_3(F_0^H - E_0 D_0^*)/(P^D)^2$, captures again a wealth effect on consumption. When the price of domestic goods rises at an unchanged value of the real exchange rate, the nominal exchange rate must depreciate in the exact same proportion, given that $E = zP^D$. As discussed earlier, this gives rise to a capital gain on foreign-currency deposits. But because $F_0^H - E_0 D_0^* = M_0 + D_0$ is predetermined, the net effect of an increase in P^D on the real value of household financial wealth is negative. This tends to *reduce* excess demand for domestic goods.

The second term, $(\kappa K_0/L_0^K)I'\theta'$, is the *financial accelerator effect*, discussed in detail in chapter 2. Recalling that $I' < 0$ and $\theta' < 0$, this term is positive: An increase in domestic prices raises firms' collateralizable net worth, thus lowering the premium and the loan rate and stimulating investment. This, in turn, tends to *increase* excess demand for domestic goods. In general, therefore, the sign of NN_{PD} is ambiguous. It will be assumed in what follows that the role of the financial accelerator effect is to mitigate but not reverse the negative effect on excess demand for (or, equivalently, excess supply of) domestic goods associated with an increase in the price of these goods that operates through the wealth effect. Thus, because $\Delta < 0$, $NN_{PD} > 0$.

An increase in the refinance rate lowers employment (and thus wage income) and aggregate supply, as well as consumption (by increasing incentives to save) and investment (by raising the lending rate). Assuming, as noted before, that the share of wage costs financed by bank borrowing is sufficiently low, the net effect on excess demand is negative. The real exchange rate—and thus the nominal exchange rate, given that P^D is held constant—must therefore depreciate

---

(7.24) in (7.3) and (7.4) yields $-Y^s + (1-\delta)\alpha_1 z^\delta N^d = z^{-\alpha\delta/(1-\alpha)} K_0[\alpha/(1+\psi_W i^R)]^{1/(1-\alpha)}[-\alpha^{-1}(1+\psi_W i^R) + \alpha_1(1-\delta)]$. The last term in brackets in this expression is negative because $\alpha^{-1}(1+\psi_W i^R) > \alpha^{-1} > 1 > \alpha_1(1-\delta)$. Thus, $Y_z^s - (1-\delta)\alpha_1(z^\delta N_z^d + \delta z^{\delta-1} N^d) < 0$.

to restore equilibrium by reducing the net supply of goods on the domestic market and increasing aggregate demand through a wealth effect on consumption. Thus, $NN_{i^R} > 0$.

An increase in the required reserve ratio lowers the deposit rate and mitigates incentives to save; by raising current consumption, it creates excess demand at the initial level of prices. Thus, the real exchange rate must appreciate to restore equilibrium so that $NN_{\mu} < 0$. Finally, an increase in the tax rate on loans raises the loan rate and lowers investment, thereby reducing excess demand at initial prices. The real (and, again, nominal) exchange rate must therefore depreciate to reduce net supply and increase demand so that $NN_{\tau^L} > 0$.

External balance

Substituting the capital flows equation (7.36) and the consumption function (7.44), together with (7.24) for ω, into the balance-of-payments equilibrium condition (7.47), and setting again $\pi^e = \varepsilon = 0$, the external balance condition can be written as

$$z^{-1}\left\{X(z) - \delta\left[\alpha_1 z^{\delta} N^d - \alpha_2(i^D + i^W) + \alpha_3\left(\frac{F^H}{P^D}\right)\right]\right\}$$
$$+ i^W D_0^* - \lambda^D d^*(z, P^D; i^D) = 0.$$

Substituting (7.30) for labor demand, (7.32) for household financial wealth, and (7.38) for the domestic deposit rate, and replacing the nominal exchange rate E by zP^D, this condition becomes

$$z^{-1}\left\{X(z) - \delta\left[\alpha_1 \frac{N^d(z; i^R)}{z^{-\delta}} - \alpha_2[(1-\mu)i^R + i^W] + \alpha_3\left[\frac{F_0^H}{P^D} + \left(z - \frac{E_0}{P^D}\right) D_0^*\right]\right]\right\}$$
$$+ i^W D_0^* - \lambda^D d^*[z, P^D; (1-\mu)i^R] = 0.$$

Differentiating totally this expression and rearranging terms yields

$$z^{-1}\left(X' - \frac{X - \delta C}{z}\right) dz - z^{-1}\delta\alpha_1(z^{\delta} N_z^d + \delta z^{\delta-1} N^d) dz - \delta\alpha_1 z^{\delta-1} N_{i^R}^d di^R$$
$$+ z^{-1}\delta\alpha_2(1-\mu) di^R - z^{-1}\delta\alpha_2 i^R d\mu + z^{-1}\delta\alpha_3 \frac{F_0^H}{(P^D)^2} dP^D - z^{-1}\delta\alpha_3 D_0^* dz$$
$$- z^{-1}\delta\alpha_3 \frac{E_0 D_0^*}{(P^D)^2} dP^D - \lambda^D[d_z^* dz + d_{P^D}^* dP^D + (1-\mu) d_{i^D}^* di^R - d_{i^D}^* i^R d\mu] = 0,$$

so that

$$z = XX(P^D; i^R, \mu, \tau^L), \tag{7.50}$$

where

$$XX_{PD} = \Omega^{-1}\left\{-\frac{z^{-1}\delta\alpha_3}{(P^D)^2}(F_0^H - E_0 D_0^*) + \lambda^D d_{PD}^*\right\},$$

$$XX_{iR} = \Omega^{-1}\left\{z^{-1}\delta[\alpha_1 z^\delta N_{iR}^d - \alpha_2(1-\mu)] + \lambda^D(1-\mu)d_{iD}^*\right\},$$

$$XX_\mu = \Omega^{-1}(z^{-1}\delta\alpha_2 i^R - \lambda^D d_{iD}^* i^R),$$

$$XX_{\tau L} = 0,$$

$$\Omega = z^{-1}\left(X' - \frac{X - \delta C}{z}\right) - z^{-1}\delta\alpha_1(z^\delta N_z^d + \delta z^{\delta-1}N^d) - z^{-1}\delta\alpha_3 D_0^* - \lambda^D d_z^*.$$

Equation (7.50) represents the *external balance condition*, which relates again the real exchange rate and the price of domestic goods.

Consider first Ω, which measures the total effect of a change in the real exchange rate on the balance of payments. This expression consists of four terms. The first term, $z^{-1}X' - z^{-2}(X - \delta C)$, where $X - \delta C$ is the initial trade balance, captures the conventional *expenditure-switching effect*, which captures shifts in exports as well as shifts in household expenditure away from imports and toward home-produced goods. The conventional positive sign is assumed here, so that $zX' - (X - \delta C) > 0$. In turn, for this condition to hold, the initial trade surplus cannot be too large ($X - \delta C < zX'$) or, equivalently, the sensitivity of the country's exports to the real exchange rate must be sufficiently high. Thus, the Marshall-Lerner condition is satisfied; a depreciation improves the trade balance.[15]

The second term, $-z^{-1}\delta\alpha_1(z^\delta N_z^d + \delta z^{\delta-1}N^d)$, relates to the impact of a change in the real exchange rate on the cost of labor and the demand for labor, which combine to affect the distribution of wage income. As shown earlier, $z^\delta N_z^d + \delta z^{\delta-1}N^d = -\alpha(1-\alpha)^{-1}\delta z^{\delta-1}N^d < 0$; thus, the second term is positive. A depreciation lowers consumption and imports, thereby improving the trade balance.

The third term, $-z^{-1}\delta\alpha_3 D_0^*$, captures an *expenditure-increasing effect* arising from the increase in wealth associated with a depreciation-induced capital

15. In the simplest case, where exports equal imports initially, the Marshall-Lerner condition states that for the trade balance to improve following a nominal devaluation the absolute sum of the elasticities of export supply and import demand must exceed unity; see Södersten and Reed (1999), for instance, for a detailed derivation. In the present setting, with δ given, and for a given level of total consumption, the elasticity of import demand is zero. Thus, if trade is balanced initially ($X = \delta C$), the condition for the trade balance to improve is simply $X' > 0$, which always holds. The case where δ is endogenous is discussed later on.

gain on foreign-currency deposits. An increase in household spending induced by these capital gains results in a rise in imports, which causes the trade balance to deteriorate.

The fourth term, $-\lambda^D d_z^*$, is positive (given that $d_z^* < 0$, as shown earlier) and arises from the valuation effect associated with exchange rate changes. A depreciation of the real exchange rate (and thus, given that domestic prices are held constant, the nominal exchange rate) raises proportionately the domestic-currency value of deposits held abroad.

In what follows, it will be assumed that the reference case is one in which the expenditure-switching effect dominates so that $\Omega > 0$.

The effect of an increase in the price of domestic goods on the balance of payments and the real exchange rate is captured by XX_{PD}. The first term in brackets in that expression, $-z^{-1}\delta\alpha_3(P^D)^{-2}(F_0^H - E_0 D_0^*)$, captures the *expenditure-reducing effect* of an increase in the price of domestic goods, operating through a negative wealth effect (given that $F_0^H - E_0 D_0^* = M_0 + D_0$), on the country's trade balance. This effect is the same as that described in the derivation of the *NN* curve: The reduction in consumption spending implies a contraction in imports, which therefore improves the balance of payments. The second term in brackets is also similar to that discussed earlier in deriving the effects of a real exchange-rate depreciation. Now, an increase in P^D, with z given, implies a concomitant nominal depreciation and a *reduction* in holdings of foreign-currency deposits. This effect is thus negative ($d_{PD}^* < 0$). Assuming that the wealth effect dominates the capital gain effect (or that λ^D is sufficiently small) implies that an increase in the price of domestic goods, at the initial value of the real exchange rate, improves the balance of payments. The real exchange rate must therefore appreciate to reduce exports and restore equilibrium. Thus, $XX_{PD} < 0$.

An increase in the refinance rate has three effects on the balance of payments. First, it lowers employment and wage income, as measured by $z^{-1}\delta\alpha_1 z^{\delta} N_{iR}^d$, which tends to reduce total consumption and imports. Second, it raises the domestic deposit rate, as measured by $-z^{-1}\delta\alpha_2(1-\mu)$, which also lowers expenditure on domestic and imported goods through the intertemporal substitution effect. Third, again through its effect on the domestic deposit rate, it makes domestic-currency deposits more attractive and reduces capital outflows, as measured by $\lambda^D(1-\mu)d_{iD}^*$. The sum of all three effects is negative. Given that $\Omega > 0$, the result is therefore $XX_{iR} < 0$.

An increase in the required reserve ratio lowers the deposit rate, which stimulates total consumption and imports and raises holdings of foreign-currency deposits ($z^{-1}\delta\alpha_2 i^R$, and $-\lambda^D d_{iD}^* i^R$). The net effect on the balance of payments is positive. Thus, given that $\Omega > 0$, $XX_{\mu} > 0$; the real exchange rate must depreciate to restore external equilibrium. Finally, an increase in the tax rate on loans,

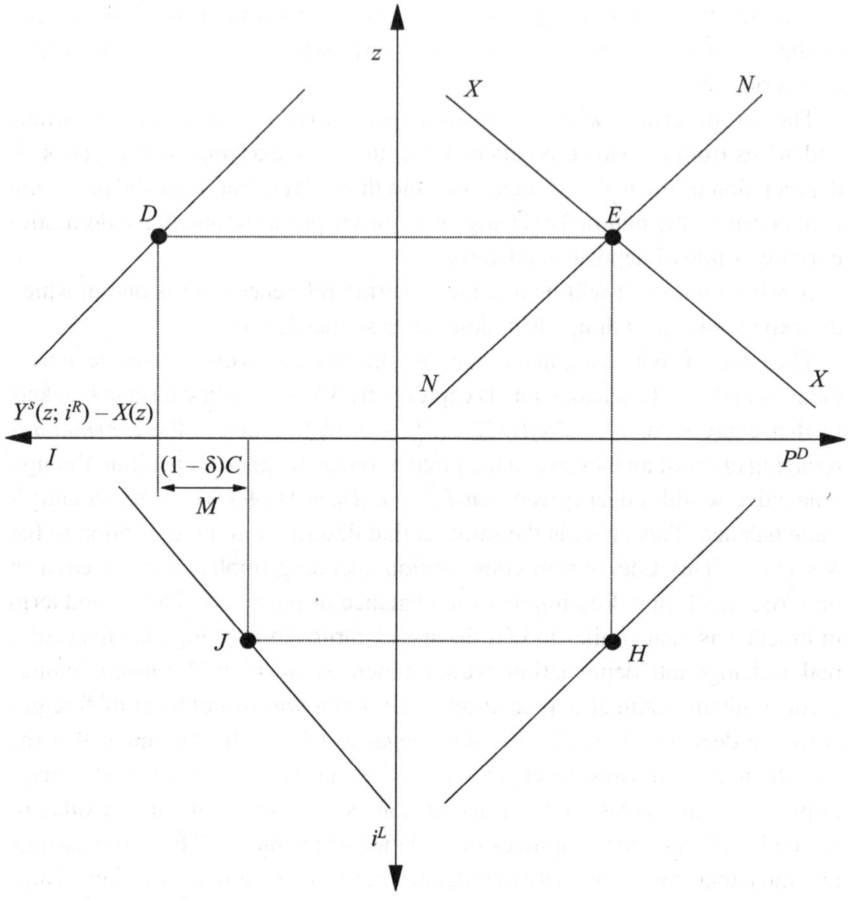

Figure 7.5
Macroeconomic equilibrium: flexible exchange rates

which operates only through the loan rate and investment, has no direct effect on the external balance condition.

Graphical illustration

Figure 7.5 presents the determination of macroeconomic equilibrium. Under the assumption stated earlier that wealth effects on consumption dominate financial accelerator effects on investment, the internal balance locus, labeled *NN* in the figure, has a positive slope, given by $NN_{P^D} > 0$; as noted earlier, this corresponds to the case where the negative wealth effect associated with an increase in the price of domestic goods outweighs the positive effect associated with the financial accelerator. Higher domestic prices reduce consumption and create excess supply of goods sold at home; the real exchange rate must depreciate to reduce production (through higher wages), stimulate exports, and restore equilibrium.[16] The external balance locus, labeled XX, has a negative slope, given that $XX_{P^D} < 0$. A rise in domestic prices lowers the demand for imports (through a negative wealth effect on total consumption) and improves the trade balance, requiring therefore a real appreciation to maintain equilibrium. Both curves are depicted in the northeast quadrant. The relationship between sales of domestic goods on the local market, or domestic sales for short, $Y^s(z; i^R) - X(z)$, and the real exchange rate is depicted in the northwest quadrant, whereas the relationship between investment and the loan rate, (7.43), is shown in the southwest quadrant. From the equilibrium condition of the goods market (7.46), the horizontal difference between domestic sales and investment gives private consumption—that is, $(1-\delta)C = Y^s - X - I$. This corresponds to the distance M in the figure. Finally, the southeast quadrant depicts the relationship between the loan rate and the price of domestic goods—that is, the financial sector equilibrium condition (7.41), which was substituted out in the goods market equilibrium condition (7.46) to solve the model in terms of z and P^D only. The economy's equilibrium is determined at points E, D, H, and J.

7.2.3 Monetary and Macroprudential Policies

To illustrate the functioning of the model under flexible exchange rates, the same set of experiments as those conducted under fixed exchange rates are conducted.

Increase in the refinance rate

From (7.49) and (7.50), the equilibrium response of the real exchange rate and domestic prices to an increase in the refinance rate can be evaluated by solving the system

$$\begin{bmatrix} 1 & -NN_{P^D} \\ 1 & -XX_{P^D} \end{bmatrix} \begin{bmatrix} dz \\ dP^D \end{bmatrix} = \begin{bmatrix} NN_{i^R} \\ XX_{i^R} \end{bmatrix} di^R,$$

which gives

$$\frac{dz}{di^R} = \frac{\overset{(-)}{XX_{i^R}}\overset{(+)}{NN_{P^D}} - \overset{(+)}{NN_{i^R}}\overset{(-)}{XX_{P^D}}}{\underset{(+)}{NN_{P^D}} - \underset{(-)}{XX_{P^D}}} \gtrless 0, \quad \frac{dP^D}{di^R} = \frac{\overset{(-)}{XX_{i^R}} - \overset{(+)}{NN_{i^R}}}{\underset{(+)}{NN_{P^D}} - \underset{(-)}{XX_{P^D}}} < 0. \quad (7.51)$$

16. Because the financial accelerator weakens the effects of increases in P^D on the excess demand for domestic goods, these effects make the internal balance locus flatter than it would otherwise be—that is, a larger increase in domestic prices is required to restore internal balance after a real depreciation than would be required if the financial accelerator effect was absent.

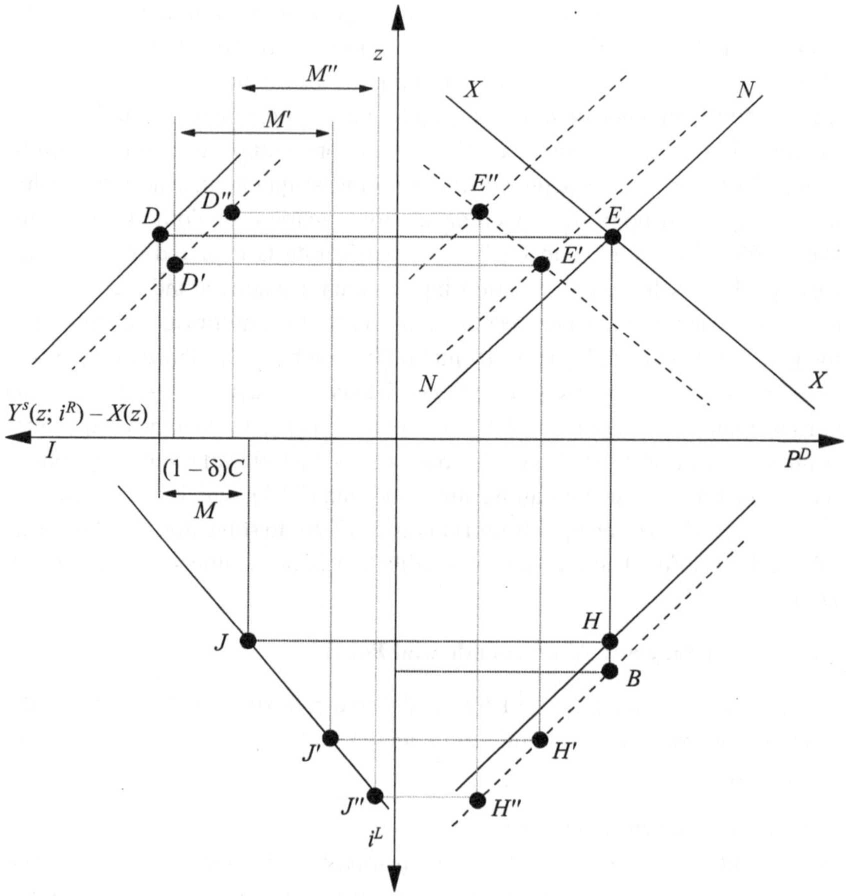

Figure 7.6
Flexible exchange rates: increase in refinance rate

As discussed in chapter 2 and earlier in this chapter, an increase in the refinance rate operates directly through changes in both the deposit rate and the loan rate. An increase in the deposit rate induces consumers to save more and thus reduce current spending on domestic goods. In addition, the higher refinance rate is passed on by banks to the loan rate, which reduces investment. It also lowers output (as a result of the cost channel), but this effect is dominated by the aggregate demand effect. The upshot is that to maintain internal balance at an unchanged value of P^D, the real exchange rate must depreciate. Thus, *NN* shifts inward, as illustrated in figure 7.6.

At the same time, an increase in the refinance rate has two effects on the external balance condition. First, through its impact on the deposit rate, it directly reduces consumption spending, thus lowering the demand for imports and improving the trade balance. Second, the higher return on domestic-currency deposits reduces household demand for foreign-currency deposits, which induces a capital repatriation. The resulting capital inflow also helps to improve the balance of payments. Consequently, to restore external balance, the real exchange rate has to appreciate at an unchanged value of P^D—that is, *XX* shifts also inward. Consequently, the price of the domestic good must fall—the increase in the refinance rate is deflationary—but the general equilibrium effect of this policy on the real exchange rate is ambiguous. As shown in figure 7.6, depending on the magnitude of the shift in *NN* for a given shift in *XX*, the economy may move from the initial position *E* to a point such as E' (corresponding to an appreciation) or E'' (corresponding to a depreciation).

Because the effect of the financial accelerator mechanism is to flatten out the *NN* curve, it is easy to show that the stronger the financial accelerator effect is, the more powerful will be the contractionary effect of the increase in the refinance rate on the domestic economy—that is, the larger the drop in domestic prices. A stronger financial accelerator effect, everything else equal, also makes it more likely that the real exchange rate will depreciate in response to an increase in the refinance rate.

In the southeast quadrant, the initial effect of an increase in the refinance rate is an outward shift in the curve linking i^L and P^D; at the initial level of domestic prices the loan rate jumps from *H* to *B*. Because domestic prices fall continuously during the transition, the loan rate continues to increase, reaching in equilibrium either H' or H''. In both cases, this movement corresponds to to the accelerator effect. By implication, investment falls continuously during the adjustment process. Because the increase in borrowing costs associated with the rise in the refinance rate also reduces (at the initial level of the exchange rate) sales on the domestic market on impact, the curve $Y^s(z; i^R) - X(z)$ shifts inward in the northwest quadrant, with a new equilibrium at either D' or D''. In either case, domestic sales of the domestic good are lower. However, with investment also falling to either J' or J'', whether consumption of domestic goods increases or falls cannot be determined a priori; in the case shown in figure 7.6 (as given by the distances M' or M'', compared to *M*) it increases, regardless of whether the real exchange rate appreciates or depreciates.

Increase in the required reserve ratio

From (7.49) and (7.50) again, the equilibrium response of the real exchange rate and domestic prices to an increase in the required reserve ratio can be evaluated by solving the system

$$\begin{bmatrix} 1 & -NN_{P^D} \\ 1 & -XX_{P^D} \end{bmatrix} \begin{bmatrix} dz \\ dP^D \end{bmatrix} = \begin{bmatrix} NN_\mu \\ XX_\mu \end{bmatrix} d\mu,$$

which gives

$$\frac{dz}{d\mu} = \frac{\overset{(+)}{XX_\mu}\overset{(+)}{NN_{P^D}} - \overset{(-)}{NN_\mu}\overset{(-)}{XX_{P^D}}}{\underset{(+)}{NN_{P^D}} - \underset{(-)}{XX_{P^D}}} \gtrless 0, \quad \frac{dP^D}{d\mu} = \frac{\overset{(+)}{XX_\mu} - \overset{(-)}{NN_\mu}}{\underset{(+)}{NN_{P^D}} - \underset{(-)}{XX_{P^D}}} > 0. \quad (7.52)$$

An increase in the required reserve ratio lowers the return on domestic-currency deposits, which discourages saving and stimulates consumption.[17] To eliminate excess demand at the initial level of domestic prices, the real (and nominal) exchange rate must appreciate—thereby reducing exports and raising sales of domestic goods on the local market. As shown in figure 7.7, curve *NN* therefore shifts outward.

At the same time, the rise in the required reserve ratio induces households to reallocate interest-bearing assets to holdings of foreign-currency deposits, which translates into a capital outflow and a deterioration of the balance of payments. To restore external equilibrium at the initial level of domestic prices, the real exchange rate must now depreciate. Thus, curve *XX* shifts outward, as also shown in figure 7.7. The net effect, as show in (7.52), is an increase in the price of domestic goods, but the effect on the real exchange rate is ambiguous and depends, in particular, on the elasticity of exports. If curve *XX* shifts relatively little, the equilibrium moves from E to E' and the final outcome is an appreciation; by contrast, if the shift in *XX* is relatively large, the new equilibrium is at E'', characterized by a depreciation. In both cases the loan rate falls, following the rise in domestic prices and the increase in collateral values to either H' or H'', whereas investment is higher at either J' or J''. Because domestic sales may either rise (to D', if the real exchange rate appreciates) or fall (to D'' if the real exchange rate depreciates), the impact on consumption is in general ambiguous (see distances M' and M'', compared to M). As shown in figure 7.7, if the real exchange rate appreciates (depreciates) in equilibrium consumption will fall (rise).

The explanation for the inflationary effect of an increase in μ is that, as discussed in chapter 2 and in the previous section, changes in required reserve

17. As before, the increase in the required reserve ratio has no direct effect on the loan rate—the marginal cost of funding for banks is the cost of borrowing from the central bank, whose supply of liquidity is perfectly elastic—and thus no immediate impact on investment.

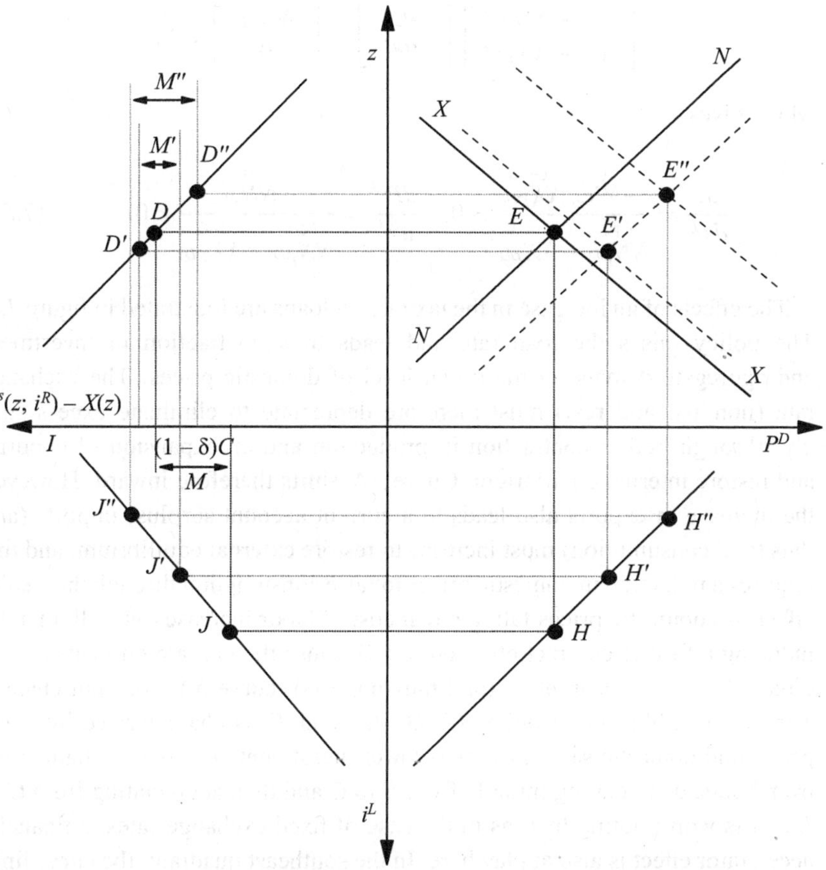

Figure 7.7
Flexible exchange rates: increase in required reserve ratio

ratios have no effect on banks' cost of funds. Because the central bank stands ready to provide all the funds desired by banks at the given refinance rate i^R, increases in reserve requirements leave banks' cost of funds—and therefore the loan rate—unaffected, while at the same time *lowering* the interest rate that represents the opportunity cost of current versus future consumption. As also discussed in chapter 2, in the presence of a *liability composition effect*, the increase in required reserves may instead be deflationary.

Increase in Tax rate on loans

From (7.49) and (7.50), the equilibrium response of the real exchange rate and domestic prices to an increase in the tax rate on loans, τ^L, can be evaluated by solving the system

$$\begin{bmatrix} 1 & -NN_{pD} \\ 1 & -XX_{pD} \end{bmatrix} \begin{bmatrix} dz \\ dP^D \end{bmatrix} = \begin{bmatrix} NN_{\tau L} \\ 0 \end{bmatrix} d\tau^L,$$

which gives

$$\frac{dz}{d\tau^L} = \frac{-\overset{(+)}{NN_{\tau L}}\overset{(-)}{XX_{pD}}}{\underset{(+)}{NN_{pD}} - \underset{(-)}{XX_{pD}}} > 0, \quad \frac{dP^D}{d\tau^L} = \frac{-\overset{(+)}{NN_{\tau L}}}{\underset{(+)}{NN_{pD}} - \underset{(-)}{XX_{pD}}} < 0. \tag{7.53}$$

The effects of an increase in the tax rate on loans are illustrated in figure 7.8. The policy raises the loan rate and leads to a contraction in investment and aggregate demand at the initial level of domestic prices. The exchange rate (nominal and real) must therefore depreciate to eliminate excess supply (through both a contraction in production and an expansion of exports) and restore internal equilibrium. Curve *NN* shifts therefore inward. However, the increase in exports also leads to a current account surplus; imports (and thus total consumption) must increase to restore external equilibrium, and this requires a reduction in domestic prices to raise consumption through the wealth effect. As domestic prices fall, the real cost of labor increases as well, thereby inducing a further contraction in output. Because the tax rate on loans has no direct effect on consumption (and thus imports), curve *XX* does not change. The new equilibrium, at points E', D', H', and J', is characterized by lower prices and domestic sales as well as lower investment. The real exchange rate overshoots, depreciating initially from *E* to *C* and then appreciating from *C* to E'. It is worth noting that, as in the case of fixed exchange rates, a financial accelerator effect is also at play here: In the southeast quadrant, the curve linking the loan rate and domestic prices shifts outward following the rise in the tax rate τ^L. The loan rate therefore jumps from *H* to *B* at the initial level of domestic prices. As these prices drop, so do collateral values; the premium therefore continues to rise, thereby inducing a further increase in the loan rate from *B* to H'. Because both domestic sales and investment fall (the first as a result of the real depreciation, the second as a result of the increase in the loan rate), the net effect on consumption is in general ambiguous. In the case shown in figure 7.8, household spending increases.

Finally, the foregoing discussion has assumed that the expected depreciation rate is constant. Under a fixed exchange rate regime where the national currency is credibly fixed, this assumption is reasonable; but under a flexible exchange rate regime, where the value of the currency fluctuates, possibly by large amounts, this is harder to justify. As noted in chapter 2, in the static framework considered here it is difficult to provide a satisfactory treatment of

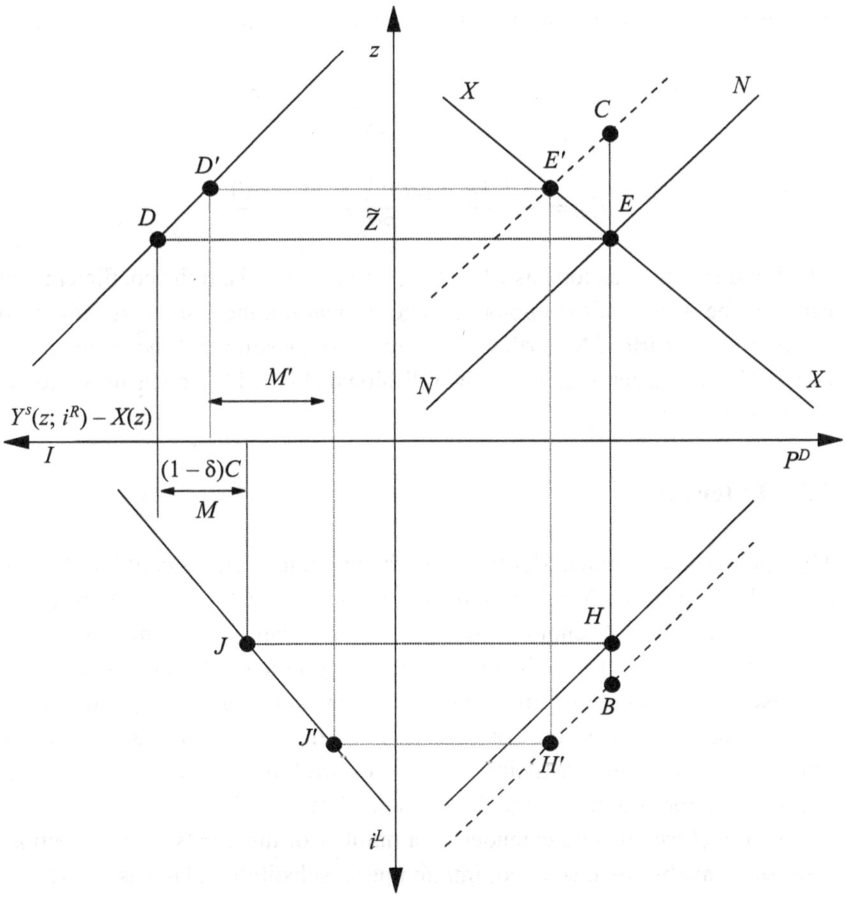

Figure 7.8
Flexible exchange rates: increase in tax rate on loans

expectations. However, suppose that exchange rate expectations are extrapolative and that the expected depreciation rate is given by $\varepsilon = \varkappa^E(E - E_0)$, where $\varkappa^E > 0$. Thus, a depreciation today raises the likelihood that the exchange rate will depreciate further tomorrow. In that case, and given again that $E = zP^D$, the actual stock of foreign-currency deposits would evolve as

$$D^* = D_0 + \lambda^D \left\{ \frac{\chi[i^D - i^W - \varkappa^E(zP^D - E_0)]}{zP^D} \right.$$

$$\left. d(i^D, i^W)[F_0^H + (zP^D - E_0)D_0^*] - D_0^* \right\},$$

and the partial derivatives d_z^* and d_{PD}^* in equation (7.36) would be given by

$$d_z^* = \frac{-d(M_0 + D_0)(\chi' \varkappa^E P^D + \chi)}{P^D z^2},$$

$$d_{PD}^* = \frac{-d(M_0 + D_0)(\chi' \varkappa^E P^D + \chi)}{z(P^D)^2},$$

which indicate that, as long as $\varkappa^E < (\chi' P^D/\chi)^{-1}$ (that is, if the coefficient that captures the degree of extrapolation is not too large), the results are similar to those reported earlier. Nevertheless, there is no question that the treatment of expectations is easier to tackle in the full-blown DSGE-FF models presented in the next chapters.

7.3 Extensions

The open-economy model developed in the previous sections could be used to assess the impact of other shocks, including a change in the world interest rate, i^W, as discussed in Agénor and Montiel (2015, chap. 6). An increase in i^W, for instance, has no direct effect on the economy's financial sector equilibrium because in this basic setting banks neither borrow nor lend abroad. Households, however, do have access to foreign assets, and the higher foreign deposit rate induces them to reallocate their portfolios toward foreign assets. This shift has implications for both the real and the financial sectors.[18]

The model can also be extended in a number of directions. In this section, four issues are briefly discussed: intratemporal substitution, land as a portfolio asset and collateral, dollarization, and bank foreign borrowing.

7.3.1 Intratemporal Substitution

In the foregoing analysis, changes in the exchange rate were shown to have an expenditure-reducing effect on the level of consumption and imports through their impact on financial wealth. At the same time, the share of total household spending on imports, δ, was assumed constant. More generally, it could be assumed that the share of spending on imported goods tends to fall when their real cost (measured in domestic currency) is higher (that is, when the real exchange rate depreciates); thus, $\delta = \delta(z)$, with $\delta' < 0$. Assuming that the weights δ and $1 - \delta$ appearing in (7.14) are kept constant at some base period to maintain tractability, the implications of this extension are fairly

18. Chapters 8 and 9 will study in detail the macroeconomic effects of shocks to world interest rates, using more elaborate models.

straightforward. A real exchange rate depreciation, by raising the domestic-currency price of imports, has now a direct expenditure-switching effect, which translates into lower imports and higher spending on domestic goods. There is therefore intratemporal substitution between domestically produced goods and foreign goods. As a result, under fixed exchange rates the term $\delta' C(z/P^D) < 0$ must be added to GG_{PD} in (7.27), whereas under flexible exchange rates the term $\delta' C < 0$ must be added to Δ in (7.49) and $-z^{-1}C\delta' > 0$ to Ω in (7.50). Consequently, the signs established previously, $GG_{PD} < 0$, $\Delta < 0$, and $\Omega > 0$, are not affected and the analysis remains qualitatively unchanged.

7.3.2 Land as Portfolio Asset and Collateral

The core open-economy model presented previously assumed that collateral consists of physical capital. However, as noted in chapter 1, in developing countries the most common asset used to secure loans is land or housing.

As in chapter 2, the analysis can be extended to account for land as an asset used to both diversify portfolios and pledge collateral. Total household wealth is now given by the sum of financial wealth, defined either in (7.7) or (7.31),

$$A^H = F^H + P^H \bar{H}, \tag{7.54}$$

where P^H is the price of land and $\bar{H}$ the fixed quantity of land. With flexible land prices, total wealth can change instantaneously, even though financial wealth remains predetermined—as is the case under fixed exchange rates.

Also as in chapter 2, the model can be modified to make consumption a function of total wealth (and therefore of capital gains or losses associated with changes in the relative price of land, P^H/P^D) and to account for the demand for land, through a simple portfolio equation. Moreover, if land is used as collateral, the premium embedded in the loan rate becomes a function of the price of land, rather than the price of domestic goods sold at home.[19] Solving for the equilibrium price of land would help to assess the implications of endogenous land prices on macroeconomic equilibrium, both in terms of curves *FF* and *GG* under fixed exchange rates and curves *NN* and *XX* under flexible exchange rates. However, as also noted in chapter 2, the combination of a simple portfolio structure and static expectations does not allow a full analysis of the macroeconomic effects of endogenous land prices. Thus, rather than pursue this extension here, a richer treatment, in the context of full-blown DSGE-FF models, will be provided in the next chapters.

19. Agénor and Montiel (2015, chap. 6) considered the intermediate case where land is a portfolio asset but the premium remains a function of the capital stock.

7.3.3 Dollarization

The model presented earlier can be extended to discuss the case of a dollarized economy under a flexible exchange rate (Alper 2007). To do so, suppose that now households also hold foreign-currency deposits in *domestic* banks, in quantity ED^*. Formally, the definition of household financial wealth remains the same as in (7.31), with only a different interpretation for D^*. While equation (7.33) continues to define the ratio D/M, the foreign-domestic deposit ratio is now given by, instead of (7.34),

$$\frac{ED^*}{D} = \chi(i^D - i^{D^*} - \varepsilon),$$

where i^{D^*} is the interest rate on foreign-currency deposits held in domestic banks.

In principle, households can also hold deposits abroad. In the absence of binding capital controls (an issue taken up in chapter 9), it is reasonable to assume that domestic banks internalize that possibility and would try to avoid losing a dependable source of funds by offering the same return on foreign-currency deposits held at home than what households would earn by holding deposits abroad. Abstracting also from transaction costs, and assuming that the expected depreciation rate ε is once again constant and normalized to zero, the net return on deposits held abroad would be equal to the world risk-free interest rate, i^W. Thus, although households have the possibility to make deposits abroad they would not do so as they earn the same return at home; $i^{D^*} = i^W$ and equation (7.36) would continue to hold.

For banks, their balance sheet would now be given by, instead of (7.15),

$$L + RR = D + ED^* + L^B,$$

which again can be used to solve residually for central bank borrowing.

However, because there are no capital flows, the balance-of-payments equilibrium condition (7.47) would become

$$X(z) - \delta C = 0,$$

which requires the trade balance to be in equilibrium at all times. Instead of (7.50), the external balance condition would now take the form

$$z = XX(P^D; i^R, \mu, \tau^L),$$

where

$$XX_{PD} = -\Omega^{-1}\frac{z^{-1}\delta\alpha_3}{(P^D)^2}(F_0^H - E_0D_0^*),$$

$$XX_{i^R} = \Omega^{-1}z^{-1}\delta[\alpha_1 z^{\delta}N_{i^R}^d - \alpha_2(1-\mu)],$$

$$XX_{\mu} = \Omega^{-1}z^{-1}\delta\alpha_2 i^R,$$

$$XX_{\tau^L} = 0,$$

$$\Omega = z^{-1}\left(X' - \frac{X-\delta C}{z}\right) - z^{-1}\delta\alpha_1(z^{\delta}N_z^d + \delta z^{\delta-1}N^d) - z^{-1}\delta\alpha_3 D_0^*,$$

which can be interpreted as before. Thus, when capital is *de facto* immobile, the introduction of dollarization does not fundamentally change the qualitative features of the transmission mechanism embedded in the model—even though it creates a host of other issues, including the measurement of monetary aggregates when the exchange rate is flexible; see, for instance, Savastano (1996).

7.3.4 Foreign Borrowing

In the framework described earlier, firms can borrow only from domestic banks. While this is appropriate for many lower middle-income countries, direct foreign borrowing by firms could also be accounted for in the present setting.[20] By endogenizing the foreign interest rate through a markup equation similar to the one used earlier, one could examine the net worth effects associated with changes in the domestic-currency value of foreign debt, in the presence of currency mismatches. A nominal depreciation, in this context, could trigger a vicious cycle: By increasing the domestic-currency value of foreign liabilities, it may lead to a deterioration in borrowers' net worth. The resulting increase in the premium on foreign borrowing, by raising the domestic cost of borrowing, would in turn exacerbate fluctuations in investment, activity, and capital flows.

Alternatively, it could be assumed that firms borrow directly only from domestic financial intermediaries, with these intermediaries in turn borrowing at a premium on world capital markets, as, for instance, in Agénor and Aizenman (1998).[21] This two-level financial intermediation structure may actually provide a better characterization of borrowing opportunities for countries for

20. Direct foreign borrowing by firms is accounted for in a number of contributions using full-blown DSGE models, including Tovar (2005), Elekdag et al. (2006), and Gertler et al. (2007).

21. Disyatat (2004) also considered foreign borrowing by domestic banks. Alper (2007) studied this issue in a similar setting to the one presented here.

which direct access to international capital markets is typically available to only a small group of large firms. This assumption is used in the more elaborate models presented in the next chapters.

7.4 Notes on the Literature

There are very few contributions focusing on simple, small open-economy models with financial frictions. Indeed, standard textbook models of the IS-LM-BP (or Mundell-Fleming) variety assume that financial markets function without impediments and that capital mobility is perfect.[22] A notable exception is a set of papers by Céspedes et al. (2003, 2004), which emphasized balance sheet constraints. The core model that they developed is fundamentally the IS-LM-BP model, modified to account for capital market imperfections (in the form of a risk premium) and balance sheet effects, through liability dollarization. When balance sheet effects are weak, their model behaves qualitatively just like the standard IS-LM-BP model—with the difference that, quantitatively, capital market imperfections magnify the effects of adverse external shocks. In that case, monetary and exchange rate policies operate in standard fashion. In particular, a devaluation stimulates output and exports, and possibly the trade balance, depending (in line with the previous discussion with respect to the Marshall-Lerner condition) on how high the elasticities of imports and exports are. By contrast, when balance sheet effects are strong and the country's foreign-currency debt is large, a devaluation can lead to a contraction in both investment and output. The model could be extended, along the lines pursued in this chapter, to address issues associated with macroprudential regulation.

22. Another workhorse model in open-economy macroeconomics is the AA-DD-XX model, where the AA curve represents the asset market equilibrium condition derived from the money market and foreign exchange markets, the DD curve represents goods market equilibrium, and XX represents combinations of the exchange rate and output at which the current account balance is equal to some desired level (Krugman et al. 2018, chap. 17). However, to my knowledge there have been no attempts to integrate financial frictions in that model (even in rudimentary ways) and use it to study macroprudential policy.

8 A Core Open-Economy DSGE Model with Financial Frictions

The static model presented in chapter 7 provided a simple, tractable framework for studying how financial frictions affect the transmission of monetary and macroprudential policies in an open economy. However, despite its usefulness to garner intuition, it is not rich enough to address some of the key challenges that policymakers must face in that context. Indeed, as discussed in chapter 1, a key feature of MICs is their high degree of vulnerability to external shocks, especially those that lead to large swings in short-term capital flows. To understand how these shocks are transmitted and how distortions in the financial system may magnify their impact, and to be able to evaluate policy options to respond to them, it is therefore essential to formulate more elaborate open-economy macroeconomic models.

This chapter takes a step in that direction by extending the core DSGE-FF model with financial frictions presented in chapter 4 to an open-economy setting.[1] The extensions considered cover several important structural and policy features of MICs, including a managed float regime and sterilized foreign exchange intervention. Indeed, managed floats, in which the central bank manipulates foreign reserves to mitigate exchange rate fluctuations, remain a common feature of MICs—even among those who adopted an inflation-targeting regime as a framework for conducting monetary policy and pursue price stability (Ilzetzki et al. 2019; Agénor and Pereira da Silva 2019). The evidence shows also that sterilized intervention—rather than the policy interest rate—is often the main instrument used by these countries to affect the exchange rate. Indeed, as discussed by Chang (2008), Aizenman and Glick (2009), Devereux and Yetman (2014*b*), and Ghosh et al. (2017), sterilization activity has played an important role in central bank policy responses to surges in capital inflows; its use has actually intensified in several countries since the global financial

1. The analysis dwells significantly on Agénor et al. (2014*a*, 2018*a*).

crisis.[2] Even though the feasibility and effectiveness of sterilization remain a matter of debate (as discussed later on), this may well have been the consequence of a greater weight attached by policymakers to mitigating exchange rate volatility. The model accounts not only for the fact that the central bank sterilizes the impact of its intervention on the domestic money supply (through offsetting changes in its holdings of government bonds) but also for the possibility that changes in official reserves may be driven by other considerations—namely, self-insurance motives. Importantly, the model also features imperfect capital mobility and a two-level financial intermediation system, which accounts for bank borrowing abroad—a key feature of cross-border capital flows in recent years, as documented, for instance, by Hoggarth et al. (2010), Reinhardt and Riddiough (2014), and the World Bank (2018).

This chapter is organized as follows. section 1 gives a formal description of the complete model. As in chapter 5, the model accounts for imperfect substitutability, from the perspective of the monetary authority, between deposits and central bank borrowing. This is captured as before by assuming that the rate at which banks can borrow from the central bank incorporates a penalty rate (above and beyond the base policy rate, determined again through a Taylor rule), which depends on the ratio of existing borrowing to deposits. Thus, because higher reserve requirements hamper the ability to attract deposits, they also lead (all else equal) to an increase in the cost of central bank liquidity, which in turn affects the cost at which private agents can borrow from commercial banks. This is again the key channel through which changes in reserve requirements may operate in countercyclical fashion. The equilibrium and some key features of the steady state are discussed in section 2. A benchmark parameterization, which extends the discussion in chapter 4, is presented in section 3. This parameterization is designed to reproduce the main stylized facts associated with episodes of large capital inflows induced by a drop in world interest rates, as identified in chapter 1: a real appreciation, current account deficit, lower domestic interest rates, a credit boom, output expansion, and asset price pressures. The results of the main experiment, a temporary reduction in the world safe interest rate, are described in section 4. The role of the degree of

2. Central bank intervention in the foreign exchange market consists of any official sale or purchase of foreign assets. Unsterilized operations involve a change in the domestic monetary base and are analogous to conventional open-market operations except that foreign, rather than domestic, assets are bought or sold. By contrast, sterilized operations involve an offsetting domestic asset transaction that restores the original size of the monetary base. For instance, an unsterilized purchase of foreign currency on the market for foreign exchange would result in an increase in the central bank's holdings of net foreign assets, say ΔR_t^F, and an expansion of the monetary base. This operation can be sterilized by an offsetting sale of domestic bonds that reduces the central bank's net domestic assets, say, Δb_t^{CB}, and returns the monetary base to its original level, so that, abstracting from exchange rate changes, $\Delta R_t^F + \Delta b_t^{CB} = 0$.

international financial integration in the transmission of this shock is discussed in section 5. The last section provides some notes on the literature.

8.1 The Model

Consider a small open economy populated again by eight categories of agents: a continuum of households with unit mass; a continuum of intermediate goods-producing (IG) firms, indexed by $j \in (0, 1)$; a representative final good (FG) producer; a continuum of capital good (CG) producers with unit mass; a continuum of commercial banks, indexed by $i \in (0, 1)$; the government; the central bank; and a regulator. As before, for simplicity each household is matched to an IG producer, a CG producer, and a bank and receives profits (if any) from them in lump-sum fashion.

The country produces a continuum of intermediate goods, which are imperfect substitutes to a continuum of imported intermediate goods. Both categories of goods are aggregated to produce a homogeneous, tradable final good. Thus, in line with the approach proposed by McCallum and Nelson (2000), imports are not treated as finished consumer goods but rather as intermediate goods, which are used (together with domestic intermediate goods) in the production of the domestic final good. This approach is highly relevant for MICs and consistent with the evidence on the increasing role of global value chains in international trade.[3] For instance, according to World Bank data, in 2014 the share of intermediate goods (broadly defined to include raw materials and fuels, in addition to manufactured products) was 58.1 percent for Brazil, compared to imports of consumption goods of 28.6 percent. Corresponding numbers for South Africa and Turkey are 59.7 and 29.1 percent, and 46.2 and 23.5 percent, respectively. Currently, more than two-thirds of international trade takes place within global value chains, up from 60 percent in 2001 (World Trade Organization 2019).

The final good is, in turn, either consumed by households and the government, used for investment (subject to additional costs) by CG producers, or exported.[4] Monopolistic competition prevails in the market for domestic

3. Kollmann (2001, 2002, 2004), Bergin et al. (2007), Huang and Liu (2007), Dib (2011), Gong et al. (2016), and Cuadra and Nuguer (2018), for instance, use a similar approach. As noted by McCallum and Nelson (2000), an advantage of this approach is that it avoids the assumption (implied by the standard tradable-nontradable dichotomy) that exportable and importable goods are perfectly substitutable in production. However, here the relevant price index for produced goods is *not* the same as the consumer price index.

4. Open-economy DSGE-FF models that are based on the standard Salter-Swan tradable-nontradable distinction on the production side, as opposed to a single tradable good sector as is the case here, include Kolasa and Lombardo (2014) and Castillo et al. (2015).

intermediate goods and each intermediate good is either produced or imported by a single firm. As in previous chapters banks are also monopolistically competitive in the credit market. While banks can borrow abroad, domestic firms can only borrow from local banks; they have no direct access to world capital markets. This two-level financial intermediation structure, which follows Agénor and Aizenman (1998), captures in stylized fashion the fact that foreign lenders are less able to enforce loan contracts in domestic courts, compared to domestic lenders.[5]

8.1.1 Households

The representative household consumes the final good, demands housing services, supplies labor, and holds imperfectly substitutable domestic assets (cash, deposits, and government bonds) as well as non contingent foreign bonds. As in chapter 4, the household's objective is to maximize

$$U_t = \mathbb{E}_t \sum_{s=0}^{\infty} \Lambda^s \left\{ \frac{C_{t+s}^{1-\varsigma^{-1}}}{1-\varsigma^{-1}} - \int_0^1 \frac{\eta_N (N_{t+s}^j)^{1+\psi_N}}{1+\psi_N} dj + \ln x_{t+s}^{\eta_x} + \ln H_{t+s}^{\eta_H} \right\}, \tag{8.1}$$

where C_t is final good consumption, N_t^j the number of hours of labor provided to IG producer j, x_t a composite index of real monetary assets, H_t the stock of housing, $\Lambda \in (0, 1)$ the subjective discount factor, $\varsigma > 0$ the intertemporal elasticity of substitution in consumption, ψ_N the inverse of the Frisch elasticity of labor supply, and $\eta_N, \eta_x, \eta_H > 0$ are preference parameters.

The composite monetary asset is again defined as a geometric average of real cash balances, m_t, and real bank deposits, d_t, both of which provide liquidity services,

$$x_t = m_t^{\nu} d_t^{1-\nu}, \tag{8.2}$$

where $\nu \in (0, 1)$. Both m_t and d_t are measured in terms of the price of domestically produced final goods sold at home, P_t^D.

The household's flow budget constraint is

$$m_t + d_t + b_t + z_t B_t^F + p_t^H \Delta H_t \tag{8.3}$$

5. Some contributions, both in the Kiyotaki-Moore and Bernanke et al. tradition, have assumed that domestic firms can borrow directly on foreign markets—consistent with the evidence for several large MICs on corporate borrowing abroad since 2005 (Bank for International Settlements 2019, chap. 2). These contributions include Céspedes et al. (2003, 2004), Elekdag et al. (2006), Gertler et al. (2007), and Castillo et al. (2015), among others.

$$= \omega_t N_t - T_t - C_t + \frac{m_{t-1}}{1+\pi_t^D} + \left(\frac{1+i_{t-1}^D}{1+\pi_t^D}\right) d_{t-1} + \left(\frac{1+i_{t-1}^B}{1+\pi_t^D}\right) b_{t-1}$$

$$+ (1+i_{t-1}^{FB}) z_t B_{t-1}^F + J_t^B + J_t^I + J_t^K,$$

where $N_t = \int_0^1 N_t^j dj$, $z_t = E_t / P_t^D$ is the real exchange rate (with E_t the nominal exchange rate), p_t^H the real price of housing, $1+\pi_t^D = P_t^D / P_{t-1}^D$, b_t (B_t^F) real (foreign-currency) holdings of one-period, non contingent domestic (foreign) government bonds, i_t^D the interest rate on bank deposits, i_t^B and i_t^{FB} interest rates on domestic and foreign government bonds, respectively, ω_t the economy-wide real wage (measured in terms of the price of final goods sold domestically), T_t real lump-sum taxes, and J_t^B, J_t^I, and J_t^K profits (if any) of the matched IG producer, CG producer, and commercial bank, respectively.[6] For simplicity, housing does not depreciate and domestic government bonds are held only at home.

The rate of return on foreign bonds is defined as

$$1+i_t^{FB} = (1+i_t^W)(1-\theta_t^{FB}), \tag{8.4}$$

where i_t^W is the risk-free world interest rate (in foreign currency units) and θ_t^{FB} an endogenous spread, defined as

$$\theta_t^{FB} = \frac{\theta_0^{FB}}{2} B_t^F, \tag{8.5}$$

with $\theta_0^{FB} > 0$.[7]

As discussed at length in Agénor (1997, 2006*a*) this specification reflects the view that the household is able to borrow (with $B_t^F < 0$, or lend) more on world capital markets only at a higher (lower) rate of interest; this captures the possibility of individual default. This treatment differs from the country risk specification often adopted in open-economy macroeconomics in general, and the open-economy DSGE literature in particular; see, for instance, Bhandari et al. (1990), Turnovsky (1997), and Heer and Schubert (2012) for deterministic models, as well as Gertler et al. (2007), Lindé et al. (2009), Adolfson et al. (2008, 2014), Chung and Turnovsky (2010), Demirel (2010), Aspachs-Bracons

6. The definition of the real exchange rate assumes that the foreign-currency price of final goods sold on markets abroad is normalized to unity. Note also that B_t^F is measured in foreign-currency terms.

7. To ensure that the premium is nil in the steady state, equation (8.5) could be written as $\theta_t^{FB} = 0.5\theta_0^{FB}(B_t^F/\tilde{B}^F - 1)$. However, this would have limited impact on the numerical analysis.

and Rabanal (2011), Fernández and Gulan (2015), Jacob and Munro (2018), and Brzoza-Brzezina and Kotłowski (2019), for stochastic models.[8] In this specification, the premium is symmetric; households pay a higher (receive a lower) rate on their foreign debt (savings) when their own liabilities (assets) increase. By contrast, with country risk, the spread depends (positively) on the country's net foreign liabilities or (negatively) on the economy's net foreign assets, defined later on as $R_t^F + B_t^F - L_t^{FC}$, where R_t^F denotes central bank reserves and L_t^{FC} bank borrowing abroad. Moreover, in the present setting the representative household internalizes the effect of its borrowing decisions on the premium that it faces, rather than taking it as given, as in models with country risk.[9]

The representative household chooses sequences of consumption, $\{C_{t+s}\}_{s=0}^{\infty}$, labor, $\{N_{t+s}^j\}_{s=0}^{\infty}$, $j \in (0,1)$, cash, $\{m_{t+s}\}_{s=0}^{\infty}$, deposits, $\{d_{t+s}\}_{s=0}^{\infty}$, domestic bonds, $\{b_{t+s}\}_{s=0}^{\infty}$, foreign bonds, $\{B_{t+s}^F\}_{s=0}^{\infty}$, and housing services, $\{H_{t+s}\}_{s=0}^{\infty}$, so as to maximize (8.1) subject to (8.2) to (8.5), taking the path of domestic interest rates (i_t^B and i_t^D), the world risk-free rate (i_t^W), prices and inflation (ω_t, p_t^H, z_t, and π_t^D), and all lump-sum transfers and taxes (J_t^B, J_t^I, J_t^K, and T_t), as given. The Lagrangian for this problem, $\mathcal{L}_t$, can be written as

$$\mathcal{L}_t = \mathbb{E}_t \sum_{s=0}^{\infty} \Lambda^s \left\{ \frac{C_{t+s}^{1-\varsigma^{-1}}}{1-\varsigma^{-1}} - \int_0^1 \frac{\eta_N}{1+\psi_N} (N_{t+s}^j)^{1+\psi_N} dj + \ln x_{t+s}^{\eta_x} + \ln H_{t+s}^{\eta_H} \right.$$

$$- \lambda_{t+s} \Bigg[m_{t+s} + d_{t+s} + b_{t+s} + z_{t+s} B_{t+s}^F + p_{t+s}^H \Delta H_{t+s} - \omega_{t+s} N_{t+s}$$

$$+ T_{t+s} + C_{t+s} - \frac{m_{t+s-1}}{1+\pi_{t+s}^D} - \left(\frac{1+i_{t+s-1}^D}{1+\pi_{t+s}^D} \right) d_{t+s-1} - \left(\frac{1+i_{t+s-1}^B}{1+\pi_{t+s}^D} \right) b_{t+s-1}$$

$$\left. -(1+i_{t+s-1}^W) z_{t+s} \left[B_{t+s-1}^F - \frac{\theta_0^{FB}}{2} (B_{t+s-1}^F)^2 \right] - J_{t+s}^B - J_{t+s}^I - J_{t+s}^K \Bigg] \right\},$$

where λ_t is the Lagrange multiplier associated with the household budget constraint.

8. Adolfson et al. (2008, 2014) also introduced the expected change in the exchange rate in the specification of the country risk premium, but this is somewhat arbitrary. See also Özbilgin (2017) for alternative specifications.

9. An alternative interpretation of (8.5) is to view θ_t^{FB} as reflecting transaction or intermediation costs, as in Kollintzas and Vassilatos (2000), Benigno (2009), Lartey (2012), and Liu and Spiegel (2015), for instance, which entail a proportional reduction in the return on foreign assets. See also Gabaix and Maggiori (2015) and Cavallino (2019), who model imperfect asset substitutability through financial frictions in the foreign exchange market. The important point here, however, is that households internalize the impact of their portfolio decisions on the spread.

The first-order conditions are

$$\frac{\partial \mathcal{L}_t}{\partial C_t}: C_t^{-1/\varsigma} - \lambda_t = 0, \tag{8.6}$$

$$\frac{\partial \mathcal{L}_t}{\partial N_t^j}: \eta_N (N_t^j)^{\psi_N} = \lambda_t \omega_t, \quad \forall j \in (0,1) \tag{8.7}$$

$$\frac{\partial \mathcal{L}_t}{\partial m_t}: \frac{\eta_x \nu}{m_t} - \lambda_t + \Lambda \mathbb{E}_t \left(\frac{\lambda_{t+1}}{1+\pi_{t+1}^D} \right) = 0, \tag{8.8}$$

$$\frac{\partial \mathcal{L}_t}{\partial d_t}: \frac{\eta_x (1-\nu)}{d_t} - \lambda_t + \Lambda \mathbb{E}_t \left\{ \lambda_{t+1} \left(\frac{1+i_t^D}{1+\pi_{t+1}^D} \right) \right\} = 0, \tag{8.9}$$

$$\frac{\partial \mathcal{L}_t}{\partial H_t}: \frac{\eta_H}{H_t} - \lambda_t p_t^H + \Lambda \mathbb{E}_t (\lambda_{t+1} p_{t+1}^H) = 0, \tag{8.10}$$

$$\frac{\partial \mathcal{L}_t}{\partial b_t}: -\lambda_t + \Lambda \mathbb{E}_t \left\{ \lambda_{t+1} \left(\frac{1+i_t^B}{1+\pi_{t+1}^D} \right) \right\} = 0, \tag{8.11}$$

$$\frac{\partial \mathcal{L}_t}{\partial B_t^F}: -\lambda_t z_t + (1+i_t^W) \Lambda \mathbb{E}_t [\lambda_{t+1} z_{t+1} (1 - \theta_0^{FB} B_t^F)] = 0, \tag{8.12}$$

for $t = 0, 1, \ldots \infty$ and $\forall j \in (0,1)$, together with the sequence of budget constraints (8.5) and the transversality conditions

$$\lim_{s\to\infty} \mathbb{E}_{t+s} \Lambda^s \lambda_{t+s} b_{t+s} = \lim_{s\to\infty} \mathbb{E}_{t+s} \Lambda^s \lambda_{t+s} B_{t+s}^F = 0.$$

From (8.11),

$$\lambda_t = \Lambda \mathbb{E}_t \left[\lambda_{t+1} \left(\frac{1+i_t^B}{1+\pi_{t+1}^D} \right) \right]. \tag{8.13}$$

Combining equations (8.6) and (8.13) yields the standard Euler equation:

$$C_t^{-1/\varsigma} = \Lambda \mathbb{E}_t \left\{ C_{t+1}^{-1/\varsigma} \left(\frac{1+i_t^B}{1+\pi_{t+1}^D} \right) \right\}. \tag{8.14}$$

Using (8.6) to substitute out for λ_t in (8.7) yields, in a symmetric equilibrium,

$$N_t = \left(\frac{\omega_t C_t^{-1/\varsigma}}{\eta_N} \right)^{1/\psi_N}, \tag{8.15}$$

which relates as before labor supply positively to the real wage and negatively to consumption.

Substituting (8.6) and (8.11) in (8.8) and (8.9) yields again the demand functions for cash and deposits:

$$m_t = \frac{\eta_x \nu C_t^{1/\varsigma}(1+i_t^B)}{i_t^B}, \tag{8.16}$$

$$d_t = \frac{\eta_x (1-\nu) C_t^{1/\varsigma}(1+i_t^B)}{i_t^B - i_t^D}. \tag{8.17}$$

Similarly, substituting (8.6) in (8.10) yields the intertemporal condition for housing services:

$$\frac{p_t^H}{C_t^{1/\varsigma}} = \frac{\eta_H}{H_t} + \Lambda \mathbb{E}_t\left(\frac{p_{t+1}^H}{C_{t+1}^{1/\varsigma}}\right). \tag{8.18}$$

Ignoring covariance terms for simplicity, equation (8.13) can be written as

$$\mathbb{E}_t\left(\frac{\Lambda\lambda_{t+1}}{\lambda_t}\right) \simeq \mathbb{E}_t\left(\frac{1+\pi_{t+1}^D}{1+i_t^B}\right). \tag{8.19}$$

At the same time, equation (8.12) can be written as

$$1 = (1+i_t^W)\mathbb{E}_t\left[\left(\frac{\Lambda\lambda_{t+1}}{\lambda_t}\right)\left(\frac{z_{t+1}}{z_t}\right)(1-\theta_0^{FB}B_t^F)\right],$$

so that, substituting (8.19), and given the definition of z_t,

$$1 \simeq (1+i_t^W)\mathbb{E}_t\left[\left(\frac{1+\pi_{t+1}^D}{1+i_t^B}\right)\left(\frac{E_{t+1}}{P_{t+1}^D}\frac{P_t^D}{E_t}\right)(1-\theta_0^{FB}B_t^F)\right],$$

or again, given that $1+\pi_{t+1}^D = P_{t+1}^D/P_t^D$,

$$1+i_t^B \simeq (1+i_t^W)\mathbb{E}_t\left[\frac{P_{t+1}^D}{P_t^D}\left(\frac{E_{t+1}}{P_{t+1}^D}\frac{P_t^D}{E_t}\right)(1-\theta_0^{FB}B_t^F)\right],$$

so that

$$1+i_t^B \simeq (1-\theta_0^{FB}B_t^F)(1+i_t^W)\mathbb{E}_t\left(\frac{E_{t+1}}{E_t}\right),$$

which relates the expected marginal rates of return on domestic and foreign assets under the assumption of imperfect world capital markets. This equation can be rearranged to give the demand for foreign bonds as

$$B_t^F \simeq \frac{(1+i_t^W)\mathbb{E}_t(E_{t+1}/E_t) - (1+i_t^B)}{\theta_0^{FB}(1+i_t^W)\mathbb{E}_t(E_{t+1}/E_t)}. \tag{8.20}$$

Equation (8.20) shows that optimal holdings of foreign bonds is a function of the difference between the expected, depreciation-adjusted world safe interest rate and the domestic bond rate. Perfect capital mobility prevails when $\theta_0^{FB} \to 0$, in which case $1+i_t^B \simeq (1+i_t^W)\mathbb{E}_t(E_{t+1}/E_t)$, corresponding to the standard uncovered interest parity condition under risk neutrality.

The risk-free world interest rate follows a first-order autoregressive process:

$$\frac{1+i_t^W}{1+\tilde{\imath}^W} = \left(\frac{1+i_{t-1}^W}{1+\tilde{\imath}^W}\right)^{\rho_W} \exp(\xi_t^W),$$

where $\rho_W \in (0,1)$ and $\xi_t^W \sim N(0, \sigma_{\xi^W})$.

8.1.2 Final Good Producers

The representative FG producer imports a continuum of differentiated intermediate goods from the rest of the world and combines them with a similar continuum of domestically produced intermediate goods to generate a final good, in quantity Y_t, which is sold both at home (for consumption and investment) and abroad:

$$Y_t = [\Lambda_I (Y_t^I)^{(\eta-1)/\eta} + (1-\Lambda_I)(Y_t^F)^{(\eta-1)/\eta}]^{\eta/(\eta-1)}, \tag{8.21}$$

where Y_t^I (Y_t^F) is a quantity index of domestic (imported) intermediate goods, $\Lambda_I \in (0,1)$ a measure of home bias (with $\Lambda_I \to 1$ corresponding to an economy closed to trade), and $\eta > 0$ the elasticity of substitution between baskets of domestic and imported composite intermediate goods. These baskets are defined as

$$Y_t^h = \left\{\int_0^1 (Y_t^{h,j})^{(\theta_h-1)/\theta_h} dj\right\}^{\theta_h/(\theta_h-1)}, \quad h = I, F, \tag{8.22}$$

where $\theta_h > 1$ is the elasticity of substitution between intermediate domestic goods among themselves ($h = I$) and imported goods among themselves ($h = F$), and $Y_t^{h,j}$ is the quantity of type-j intermediate good of category h (domestic or imported), with $j \in (0,1)$.[10]

10. For simplicity, the number of both domestic and imported intermediate goods is normalized to unity.

The FG producer sells its output at a perfectly competitive price. In the first stage, the producer first solves for the demand functions for each variety of domestic and imported intermediate goods, $Y_t^{h,j}$, taking as given their domestic-currency price $P_t^{h,j}$ as well as the aggregate quantities of these goods, Y_t^h, and their domestic-currency prices, P_t^h, for $h=I,F$. Let profits be defined as $P_t^h Y_t^h - \int_0^1 P_t^{h,j} Y_t^{h,j} dj$; using (8.22), the solution of the first-stage problem is thus determined by

$$Y_t^{h,j} = \arg\max \left[P_t^h \left\{ \int_0^1 (Y_t^{h,j})^{(\theta_h-1)/\theta_h} dj \right\}^{\theta_h/(\theta_h-1)} - \int_0^1 P_t^{h,j} Y_t^{h,j} dj \right],$$

which gives the demand functions for each variety of both types of intermediate goods:

$$Y_t^{h,j} = \left(\frac{P_t^{h,j}}{P_t^h} \right)^{-\theta_h} Y_t^h, \quad h=I,F. \tag{8.23}$$

Inserting this result in the zero-profit condition $P_t^h Y_t^h = \int_0^1 P_t^{h,j} Y_t^{h,j} dj$ yields the price indices for domestically produced and imported intermediate goods:

$$P_t^h = \left\{ \int_0^1 (P_t^{h,j})^{1-\theta_h} dj \right\}^{1/(1-\theta_h)}, \quad h=I,F. \tag{8.24}$$

In the second stage, the representative FG producer chooses the aggregate quantities of each type of intermediate goods, Y_t^h, so as to maximize its profits:

$$Y_t^I, Y_t^F = \arg\max(P_t Y_t - P_t^I Y_t^I - P_t^F Y_t^F),$$

where P_t is the price of final output. Using (8.21), the allocation of total demand between domestic and foreign goods is thus given by

$$Y_t^I = \Lambda_I^\eta \left(\frac{P_t^I}{P_t} \right)^{-\eta} Y_t, \quad Y_t^F = (1-\Lambda_I)^\eta \left(\frac{P_t^F}{P_t} \right)^{-\eta} Y_t. \tag{8.25}$$

Given perfect competition, the zero-profit condition is now $P_t Y_t = \sum_h P_t^h Y_t^h$. Substituting (8.25) in that expression and simplifying gives

$$P_t = \Lambda_I^\eta \frac{(P_t^I)^{1-\eta}}{P_t^{-\eta}} + (1-\Lambda_I)^\eta \frac{(P_t^F)^{1-\eta}}{P_t^{-\eta}},$$

which implies that the price of the final good is

$$P_t = [\Lambda_I^{\eta}(P_t^I)^{1-\eta} + (1-\Lambda_I)^{\eta}(P_t^F)^{1-\eta}]^{1/(1-\eta)}. \tag{8.26}$$

Imperfect exchange rate pass-through is accounted for with a simple partial adjustment mechanism, under the assumption that prices are set in the sellers' currency, or equivalently that producer currency pricing prevails. The domestic-currency price of imports of intermediate good j is thus given by

$$P_{jt}^F = E_t^{\mu^F} E_{t-1}^{1-\mu^F} WP_{jt}^F, \tag{8.27}$$

where WP_{jt}^F is the foreign-currency price of imported good j and $\mu^F \in (0, 1)$ measures the degree of exchange rate pass-through. Thus, $\mu^F = 1$ corresponds to complete pass-through. Regardless of the value of μ^F, full pass-through occurs in the long run.

The volume of goods sold abroad, Y_t^X, depends on the domestic-currency price of exports of the final good on world markets, P_t^X, relative to the price of domestic goods sold at home:

$$Y_t^X = \left(\frac{P_t^X}{P_t^D}\right)^{\varkappa_X}, \tag{8.28}$$

where $\varkappa_X > 0$. In evaluating the domestic-currency price of exports, domestic producers account for both the current exchange rate and its steady-state value

$$P_t^X = E_t^{\mu^X} \tilde{E}^{1-\mu^X} WP_t^X, \tag{8.29}$$

where WP_t^X denotes the foreign-currency price of exports. The dependence of P_t^X on the steady-state value of the exchange rate captures the view that exporters base their decisions on a longer-term perspective on the domestic currency's value, rather than how it fluctuates in the short term. In turn, this assumption is consistent with the evidence that suggests that greater integration in global value chains (a structural trend of the world economy, as indicated earlier) has weakened in the short run the trade channel associated with the exchange rate.[11]

Total output in volume terms is also given by

$$Y_t = Y_t^D + Y_t^X, \tag{8.30}$$

11. Another reason for exchange rate swings to have a weak impact on a country's export prices (measured in domestic-currency terms) in the short run may be because its trade is invoiced to a significant extent in foreign currency. See Bank for International Settlements (2019, chap. 2) for a discussion of these issues, together with some formal evidence.

where Y_t^D denotes the volume of domestically produced final goods sold at home.

8.1.3 Domestic Intermediate Good Producers

Domestic IG firms, indexed by $j \in (0, 1)$, produce intermediate goods by combining labor, N_t^j, and capital, K_t^j,

$$Y_t^{I,j} = (N_t^j)^{1-\alpha}(K_t^j)^\alpha, \tag{8.31}$$

where $\alpha \in (0, 1)$.[12]

Each IG producer rents capital from a randomly matched CG producer, at the rate r_t^K, and pays for it after the sale of output. However, a fraction $\psi_W \in (0, 1)$ of wages must be paid in advance. To do so, firm j borrows the amount $l_t^{W,j}$ from banks. The amount borrowed is therefore such that

$$l_t^{W,j} = \psi_W \omega_t N_t^j. \tag{8.32}$$

Loans contracted for the purpose of financing working capital do not carry any risk and are made (as in previous chapters) at a rate that reflects only the marginal cost of borrowing from the central bank, i_t^R. Total costs of firm j in period t, TC_t^j, are thus given by

$$TC_t^j = (1 + i_t^R)\psi_W \omega_t N_t^j + r_t^K K_t^j.$$

As in chapter 4, cost minimization yields the capital-labor ratio and marginal cost, mc_t^j, as

$$\frac{K_t^j}{N_t^j} = \left(\frac{\alpha}{1-\alpha}\right)\left[\frac{(1+\psi_W i_t^R)\omega_t}{r_t^K}\right], \tag{8.33}$$

$$mc_t^j = \left(\frac{r_t^K}{\alpha}\right)^\alpha \left[\frac{(1+\psi_W i_t^R)\omega_t}{1-\alpha}\right]^{1-\alpha}. \tag{8.34}$$

Also as in chapter 4, domestic IG producers incur a Rotemberg-type cost in adjusting prices, of the form $(\phi_I/2)[(P_t^{I,j}/P_{t-1}^{I,j}) - 1]^2 Y_t^I$, where $\phi_I \geq 0$.[13]

12. The analysis could be extended to account for the fact that the production of domestic intermediates also requires the use of imported intermediate goods (say, oil imports, O_t^j), by using a simple Leontief technology of the form $Y_t^{I,j} = \min[N_{jt}^{1-\alpha}K_{jt}^\alpha/(1-\kappa_Y), O_t^j/\kappa_Y]$, where $\kappa_Y \in (0, 1)$, a generalized Cobb-Douglas function, or a CES function, as in Medina and Soto (2005), Claus (2007), and Lombardo and Ravenna (2014).

13. For simplicity, and to maintain consistency with previous chapters, the adjustment cost is measured in terms of the total domestic production of intermediate goods, rather than final goods. The

Under monopolistically competitive markets, each firm j chooses a sequence of prices so as to maximize the discounted value of its current and future profits:[14]

$$\{P_{t+s}^{I,j}\}_{s=0}^{\infty} = \arg\max \mathbb{E}_t \sum_{s=0}^{\infty} \Lambda^s \lambda_{t+s} J_{t+s}^{I,j}, \tag{8.35}$$

where $J_t^{I,j}$ denotes real profits at t, defined as

$$J_t^{I,j} = \left(\frac{P_t^{I,j}}{P_t^I}\right) Y_t^{I,j} - mc_t^j Y_t^{I,j} - \frac{\phi_I}{2}\left(\frac{P_{jt}^{I,j}}{P_{t-1}^{I,j}} - 1\right)^2 Y_t^I. \tag{8.36}$$

Taking $\{mc_{t+s}\}_{s=0}^{\infty}$, $\{P_{t+s}^I\}_{s=0}^{\infty}$, and $\{Y_{t+s}^I\}_{s=0}^{\infty}$ as given, and using (8.23) with $h = I$, the first-order condition for this maximization problem is

$$(1-\theta_I)\left(\frac{P_t^{I,j}}{P_t^I}\right)^{-\theta_I} Y_t^I + \theta_I \left(\frac{P_t^{I,j}}{P_t^I}\right)^{-\theta_I - 1} mc_t Y_t^I$$

$$-\phi_I \left\{\left(\frac{P_t^{I,j}}{P_{t-1}^{I,j}} - 1\right)\frac{1}{P_{t-1}^{I,j}}\right\} Y_t^I + \Lambda\phi_I \mathbb{E}_t \left\{\frac{\lambda_{t+1}}{\lambda_t}\left(\frac{P_{t+1}^{I,j}}{P_t^{I,j}} - 1\right)\frac{P_{t+1}^{I,j}}{(P_t^{I,j})^2} Y_{t+1}^I\right\} = 0,$$

or, in a symmetric equilibrium, with $1 + \pi_t^I = P_t^I / P_{t-1}^I$,

$$1 - \theta_I + \theta_I mc_t - \phi_I \pi_t^I (1 + \pi_t^I) + \Lambda\phi_I \mathbb{E}_t \left\{\frac{\lambda_{t+1}}{\lambda_t}\pi_{t+1}^I (1 + \pi_{t+1}^I)\left(\frac{Y_{t+1}^I}{Y_t^I}\right)\right\} = 0, \tag{8.37}$$

which determines the path of inflation in domestic intermediates.

8.1.4 Capital Good Producers

The decision problem of the representative CG producer is the same as in chapter 4. It buys an amount I_t of the final good and combines it with the existing capital stock to produce new capital goods, K_{t+1}, which are rented in the next period to a randomly matched IG producer at the rate r_{t+1}^K. Aggregate capital accumulates as follows:

---

two now differ in a symmetric equilibrium. In addition, in this expression the steady-state inflation rate in the price of goods sold domestically is assumed to be zero.

14. As discussed in chapter 4, IG firms (which are owned by households) are assumed to value future profits according to the representative household's intertemporal marginal rate of substitution in consumption.

$$K_{t+1} = \left\{ \frac{I_t}{K_t} - \frac{\Theta_K}{2} \left(\frac{K_{t+1} - K_t}{K_t} \right)^2 \right\} K_t + (1 - \delta_K) K_t, \tag{8.38}$$

where $\delta_K \in (0, 1)$, and $\Theta_K > 0$.

Investment goods are paid for in advance. To do so the representative CG producer borrows from banks, at the rate i_t^L, the amount

$$l_t^K = I_t. \tag{8.39}$$

Let $\kappa = \int_0^1 \kappa^i di \leq 1$, where $\kappa^i \in (0, 1)$ is the fraction of the housing stock pledged as collateral to each bank i, and let $q_t \in (0, 1)$ denote the repayment probability. The representative CG firm chooses the level of capital K_{t+1} so as to maximize the value of the discounted stream of dividend payments to its owner's, subject to (8.38) and (8.39), and taking $\{i_{t+s}^L\}_{s=0}^{\infty}$, $\{p_{t+s+1}^H\}_{s=0}^{\infty}$, $\{q_{t+s}\}_{s=0}^{\infty}$, and $\{r_{t+s+1}^K\}_{s=0}^{\infty}$ as given, the equation is

$$\{K_{t+s+1}\}_{s=0}^{\infty} = \arg\max \sum_{s=0}^{\infty} \mathbb{E}_t(\Lambda^s \lambda_{t+s} J_{t+s+1}^K),$$

where $\mathbb{E}_t(\Lambda^s \lambda_{t+s} J_{t+s+1}^K)$ denotes expected profits at the end of period $t+s$, discounted at the rate $\Lambda^s \lambda_{t+s}$, given by

$$\begin{aligned} \mathbb{E}_t(\Lambda^s \lambda_{t+s} J_{t+s+1}^K) = \Lambda^s \mathbb{E}_t\{\lambda_{t+s}[r_{t+s}^K K_{t+s} - q_{t+s}(1 + i_{t+s}^L) I_{t+s} \\ - (1 - q_{t+s}) \kappa p_{t+s+1}^H H_t]\}, \end{aligned}$$

and $\lambda_{t+s} = C_{t+s}^{-1/\varsigma}$. As shown in chapter 4, the first-order condition for maximization can be approximated by

$$\begin{aligned} \mathbb{E}_t r_{t+1}^K \simeq q_t(1 + i_t^L) \mathbb{E}_t \left\{ \left[1 + \Theta_K \left(\frac{K_{t+1}}{K_t} - 1 \right) \right] \left(\frac{1 + i_t^B}{1 + \pi_{t+1}^D} \right) \right\} \qquad (8.40) \\ - \mathbb{E}_t \left\{ q_{t+1}(1 + i_{t+1}^L) \left\{ 1 - \delta_K + \frac{\Theta_K}{2} \left[\left(\frac{K_{t+2}}{K_{t+1}} \right)^2 - 1 \right] \right\} \right\}, \end{aligned}$$

which relates the expected rate of return on the capital stock to current and expected values of the repayment probability and the interest rate on investment loans (or loan rate, for short).

Again, the amount borrowed by the representative CG producer is a Dixit-Stiglitz basket of differentiated loans, each supplied by a bank i, with a constant elasticity of substitution $\zeta^L > 1$:

$$l_t^K = \left[\int_0^1 (l_t^{K,i})^{(\zeta^L - 1)/\zeta} di \right]^{\zeta^L/(\zeta^L - 1)}.$$

The demand for type-i loan, $l_t^{K,i}$, is thus given by the downward-sloping curve

$$l_t^{K,i} = \left(\frac{1 + i_t^{L,i}}{1 + i_t^L} \right)^{-\zeta^L} l_t^K, \tag{8.41}$$

where $i_t^{L,i}$ is the rate on the loan extended by bank i and the aggregate loan rate is defined as $i_t^L = [\int_0^1 (1 + i_t^{L,i})^{1-\zeta^L} di]^{1/(1-\zeta^L)} - 1$.

8.1.5 Commercial Banks

Banks behave in a similar fashion to the monopolistically competitive formulation adopted in chapter 4, with the exception that, in addition to borrowing from the central bank, they now also borrow on world capital markets. There are no markets that allow them to hedge against the foreign exchange risk that they incur as a result. At the end of each period, banks receive interest income from IG and CG producers, repay with interest household deposits and the liquidity borrowed from the central bank, and redeem in full their foreign debt. All profits are then distributed, books are closed, and operations start anew at the beginning of the next period.

Bank i's balance sheet is thus

$$l_t^i + RR_t^i = d_t^i + z_t L_t^{FC,i} + l_t^{B,i} + V_t^i, \tag{8.42}$$

where $l_t^i = l_t^{K,i} + l_t^{W,i}$, $L_t^{FC,i}$ is foreign borrowing (in foreign-currency terms), V_t^i is bank capital, and RR_t^i denotes required reserves held at the central bank, set as a fraction of deposits,

$$RR_t^i = \mu_t d_t^i, \tag{8.43}$$

where $\mu_t \in (0, 1)$ is again the required reserve ratio. Consistent with the parameterization discussed in chapter 6, capital requirements are a fixed fraction of investment loans, so that $V_t^i = 0.12 l_t^{K,i}$.

The market for deposits is competitive, so the no-arbitrage condition is again, $\forall i$,

$$i_t^{D,i} = (1 - \mu_t) i_t^R. \tag{8.44}$$

Bank i's cost of borrowing on world capital markets, $i_t^{FC,i}$, measured in foreign-currency terms, is defined as

$$1+i_t^{FC,i}=(1+i_t^W)(1+\theta_t^{FC,i}), \tag{8.45}$$

where, analogously to (8.5), $\theta_t^{FC,i}$ is a premium that increases with the amount borrowed:

$$\theta_t^{FC,i}=\frac{\theta_0^{FC}}{2}L_t^{FC,i}, \tag{8.46}$$

with $\theta_0^{FC}>0$.

Monopolistic competition prevails in the market for investment loans. Thus, each bank sets its loan rate and its foreign borrowing so as to maximize its end-of-period expected real profits, $\mathbb{E}_t J_{t+1}^{B,i}$. This equation is

$$\max_{1+i_t^{L,i},L_t^{FC,i}} \mathbb{E}_t J_{t+1}^{B,i},$$

where $\mathbb{E}_t J_{t+1}^{B,i}$ is defined as

$$\mathbb{E}_t J_{t+1}^{B,i}=(1+i_t^R)l_t^{W,i}+q_t^i(1+i_t^{L,i})l_t^{K,i}+(1-q_t^i)\kappa^i\mathbb{E}_t p_{t+1}^H H_t+\mu d_t^i$$
$$-(1+i_t^{D,i})d_t^i-(1+i_t^R)l_t^{B,i}-(1+i_t^{FC,i})\mathbb{E}_t\left(\frac{E_{t+1}}{E_t}\right)z_t L_t^{FC,i},$$

where $q_t^i(1+i_t^{L,i})l_t^{K,i}+(1-q_t^i)\kappa^i\mathbb{E}_t p_{t+1}^H H_t$ is expected repayment to bank i. As in chapter 6, the optimal repayment probability (or monitoring intensity) is not solved for explicitly. Instead, the functional form for q_t^i defined in that chapter is specified directly.

Solving this problem, subject to the loan demand curve (8.41) and the balance sheet constraint (8.42), taking as given collateral, deposits, the repayment probability, and the refinance rate and noting that from (8.45) and (8.46),

$$(1+i_t^{FC,i})L_t^{FC,i}=(1+i_t^W)\left(1+\frac{\theta_0^{FC}}{2}L_t^{FC,i}\right)L_t^{FC,i},$$

yields the first-order conditions

$$q_t^i\left(\frac{1+i_t^{L,i}}{1+i_t^L}\right)^{-\varsigma^L}l_t^K-q_t^i(1+i_t^{L,i})\varsigma^L\left(\frac{1+i_t^{L,i}}{1+i_t^L}\right)^{-\varsigma^L-1}\left(\frac{l_t^K}{1+i_t^L}\right)$$

$$+(1+i_t^R)\zeta^L \left(\frac{1+i_t^{L,i}}{1+i_t^L}\right)^{-\zeta^L-1} \left(\frac{l_t^K}{1+i_t^L}\right) = 0,$$

$$(1+i_t^R)z_t - (1+i_t^W)\mathbb{E}_t\left(\frac{E_{t+1}}{E_t}\right) z_t(1+\theta_0^{FC} L_t^{FC,i}) = 0,$$

so that, in a symmetric equilibrium,

$$i_t^L = \frac{\zeta^L}{q_t(\zeta^L - 1)}(1+i_t^R) - 1, \tag{8.47}$$

$$L_t^{FC} = \frac{1+i_t^R - (1+i_t^W)\mathbb{E}_t(E_{t+1}/E_t)}{\theta_0^{FC}(1+i_t^W)\mathbb{E}_t(E_{t+1}/E_t)}. \tag{8.48}$$

Equation (8.47) has the same interpretation as in chapter 4. It shows that the loan rate depends negatively on the repayment probability and positively on the marginal cost of borrowing from the central bank. Equation (8.48) states that foreign borrowing is decreasing in the (expected) cost of borrowing abroad and increasing in the cost of borrowing domestically from the central bank.

Based on the analysis in chapter 4, the repayment probability is related positively to the effective collateral-investment loan ratio and the cyclical position of the economy as

$$q_t = \varphi_0 \left(\frac{\kappa \mathbb{E}_t p_{t+1}^H / \tilde{p}^H}{l_t^K / \tilde{l}^K}\right)^{\varphi_1} \left(\frac{Y_t^D}{\tilde{Y}^D}\right)^{\varphi_2}, \tag{8.49}$$

with $\varphi_0, \varphi_1, \varphi_2 > 0$ and where $\tilde{Y}^D$ is the steady-state level of output sold domestically.

As in previous chapters, borrowing from the central bank, $l_t^{B,i}$, is determined residually from the balance sheet constraint (8.42).

8.1.6 Central Bank

The central bank supplies as before liquidity to commercial banks through a standing facility, at a price that reflects both a base policy rate and a penalty rate. It also engages in partial sterilization and reserve accumulation. Its balance sheet is given by

$$z_t R_t^F + b_t^{CB} + l_t^B = m_t^s + RR_t + nw_t, \tag{8.50}$$

where R_t^F denotes international reserves (measured in foreign-currency terms), b_t^{CB} denotes holdings of government bonds, m_t^s is the supply of cash to households and firms, and nw_t is the central bank's net worth.

Rather than a pure float as in chapter 7, the central bank is assumed now to operate a managed float regime and to self-insure against external shocks. Accordingly, foreign reserves depend on the expected change in the exchange rate and a target level of reserves, R_t^{FT}, which is given as

$$R_t^F = \left(\frac{\mathbb{E}_t E_{t+1}}{E_t}\right)^{-\varphi_1^R} (R_{t-1}^F)^{\varphi_2^R} (R_t^{FT})^{1-\varphi_2^R}, \tag{8.51}$$

where $\varphi_1^R \geq 0$ is the degree of exchange rate smoothing—that is, the extent to which the central bank leans against movements in the nominal exchange rate, and $\varphi_2^R \in (0, 1)$ is the degree of persistence.[15]

Consistent with the evidence on reserve accumulation for MICs, the reserve target is defined as a multiple $\phi_1^R \geq 1$ of the value of imports, $WP_t^F Y_t^F$, and a fraction $\phi_2^R \in (0, 1)$ of the net foreign-currency liabilities of the private sector, $L_t^{FC} - B_t^F$,

$$R_t^{FT} = (\phi_1^R WP_t^F Y_t^F)^{\varphi^R} [\phi_2^R (L_t^{FC} - B_t^F)]^{1-\varphi^R}, \tag{8.52}$$

where $\varphi^R \in (0, 1)$ measures the relative importance of the "trade" motive versus the "financial" motive. In that specification, self-insurance against trade shocks is captured through an import coverage ratio, as is often the case in practice.[16] The volatility of imports, or of reserves themselves, plays no direct role in determining the target level of foreign reserves.

The presence of the expected rate of depreciation in (8.51) is consistent with the evidence that MICs tend to intervene frequently and systematically in the foreign exchange market to stabilize currency fluctuations—even under an inflation targeting regime, where in principle the exchange rate should float freely. This evidence includes Kletzer and Spiegel (2004), Aizenman and Glick (2009), Vujanovic (2011), Palma and Portugal (2014) for Brazil, Daude et al. (2016), Ghosh et al. (2017), and Fratzscher et al. (2019).[17] An expected

15. In practice, exchange rate smoothing has also occurred through changes in policy rates; see the discussion in the last section of this chapter. Note also that, for the sake of simplicity, the possibility of a lower bound on the stock of foreign reserves—a key feature of so-called first-generation models of exchange rate crises, as discussed in Agénor and Flood (1994)—is ignored.

16. A more general measure would be the trade (or current account) balance, which would imply a positive relationship between external *deficits* and the level of reserves. At the same time, however, with a mercantilist motive instead of a self-insurance motive, the relationship could go in the opposite direction—the relationship between trade or current account *surpluses* and reserves could be positive.

17. See also the summary by Villamizar-Villegas and Perez-Reyna (2017, app. B) and the discussion in Agénor and Pereira da Silva (2019). As documented in the literature, the reasons the central bank may want to smooth exchange rate movements could be due to a *fear of floating*, itself

nominal depreciation, for instance, induces the central bank to sell foreign currency in the market for foreign exchange to stabilize the exchange rate. As a result, its stock of reserves falls. In the particular case where $\varphi_1^R = 0$ and $\varphi_2^R = 1$, the stock of reserves remains constant over time and the exchange rate is fully flexible.

Note that alternative intervention rules could be specified. For instance, as in Devereux and Yetman (2014*b*), the current rate of depreciation, E_t/E_{t-1}, could be used in (8.51) instead of $\mathbb{E}_t E_{t+1}/E_t$. Alternatively, if the central bank has a target exchange rate E^T, the term $\mathbb{E}_t E_{t+1}/E_t$ could be replaced by $\mathbb{E}_t E_{t+1}/E^T$ in (8.51). The central bank would therefore buy (sell) reserves to stabilize the exchange rate when it appreciates (depreciates) relative to target.

The central bank also adjusts its holdings of government bonds in order to sterilize the effects of its buying and selling of international reserves on the supply of cash.[18] Thus, its stock of bonds evolves according to

$$b_t^{CB} - \frac{b_{t-1}^{CB}}{1+\pi_t^D} = -\kappa^F z_t \Delta R_t^F, \tag{8.53}$$

where $\kappa^F \in (0, 1)$ measures the degree of sterilization.

All interest income earned by the central bank is transferred to the government. Thus, changes in the nominal value of the central bank's net worth, NW_t, are given by capital gains associated with exchange rate depreciation only ($\Delta NW_t = \Delta E_t R_t^F$). Using this result, taking first differences of (8.50) expressed in nominal terms and substituting (8.53) in the resulting expression yields[19]

related to concerns with competitiveness, the degree of exchange rate pass-through, and possibly financial stability, if foreign-currency risk is not fully hedged. At the same time, there may be a *fear of losing reserves,* which would militate in favor of less smoothing and induce instead the use of capital controls, as discussed in chapter 9.

18. To model sterilized intervention, some contributions have assumed that the central bank issues its own securities—see Vargas et al. (2013) and Prasad (2018), for instance. However, this would not make any significant difference if the interest rate on these bonds is set through a no-arbitrage condition with the government bond rate. What would be more consequential is the assumption that central bank securities are held by banks, and that changes in rates of return (including on loans) affect their portfolio allocation. See Agénor et al. (2020) for an analysis in this setting and its implications for the optimal degrees of exchange rate smoothing and sterilization.

19. In nominal domestic-currency terms, equation (8.50) can be written as $E_t R_t^F + B_t^{CB} + L_t^B = M_t^s + RR_t^N + NW_t$, where variable definitions are self-explanatory. Taking first differences of this expression gives $\Delta E_t R_t^F + E_t \Delta R_t^F + \Delta B_t^{CB} + \Delta L_t^B = \Delta M_t^s + \Delta RR_t^N + \Delta NW_t$. Setting $\Delta NW_t = \Delta E_t R_t^F$, and dividing by P_t^D yields $z_t \Delta R_t^F + (\Delta B_t^{CB} + \Delta L_t^B)/P_t^D = (\Delta M_t^s + \Delta RR_t^N)/P_t^D$. Using (8.53), $P_{t-1}^D/P_t^D = 1/(1+\pi_t^D)$, and $\Delta X_t\ /P_t^D = x_t - (X_{t-1}/P_t^D) = x_t - x_{t-1}/(1+\pi_t^D)$, for $X = L^B, M^s, RR^N$ yields (8.54).

$$m_t^s = \frac{m_{t-1}^s}{1+\pi_t^D} + (1-\kappa^F)z_t \Delta R_t^F + \left(l_t^B - \frac{l_{t-1}^B}{1+\pi_t^D}\right) - \left(RR_t - \frac{RR_{t-1}}{1+\pi_t^D}\right), \tag{8.54}$$

which shows that, with full sterilization ($\kappa^F = 1$), changes in the domestic-currency value of foreign-exchange reserves have no direct effect on the supply of cash.

As in previous chapters, the central bank sets its base policy rate, i_t^T, on the basis of an inertial Taylor rule,

$$\frac{1+i_t^T}{1+\tilde{\imath}^T} = \left(\frac{1+i_{t-1}^T}{1+\tilde{\imath}^T}\right)^{\chi} \left\{(1+\pi_t^D)^{\varepsilon_1} \left(\frac{Y_t^D}{\tilde{Y}^D}\right)^{\varepsilon_2}\right\}^{1-\chi}, \tag{8.55}$$

where $\chi \in (0, 1)$ and $\varepsilon_1, \varepsilon_2 > 0$.

The refinance rate, in addition to the base policy rate, incorporates a penalty rate, θ_t^{CB}:

$$1 + i_t^R = (1 + i_t^T)(1 + \theta_t^{CB}). \tag{8.56}$$

In turn, as in chapters 4 and 5, the penalty rate is positively related to the ratio of central bank borrowing to deposits,

$$1 + \theta_t^{CB} = \left(\frac{l_t^B / \tilde{l}^B}{d_t / \tilde{d}}\right)^{\varphi^{CB}}, \tag{8.57}$$

where $\varphi^{CB} \geq 0$. Note that the penalty rate relates to the composition of banks' *domestic* liabilities only. As discussed in chapter 9, a countercyclical tax on bank foreign borrowing will be considered separately.

8.1.7 Government

The government purchases the final good and issues nominal riskless one-period bonds to finance its deficit; it does not borrow abroad. In addition to lump-sum taxes, it also receives the interest income collected by the central bank on its foreign reserves and its loans to commercial banks. It pays interest on the share of government debt held by the private sector. Its budget constraint is given by

$$b_t^G - \frac{b_{t-1}^G}{1+\pi_t^D} = G_t - T_t + \frac{i_{t-1}^B b_{t-1}}{1+\pi_t^D} - \left(\frac{i_{t-1}^R l_{t-1}^B}{1+\pi_t^D} + z_t i_{t-1}^W R_{t-1}^F\right), \tag{8.58}$$

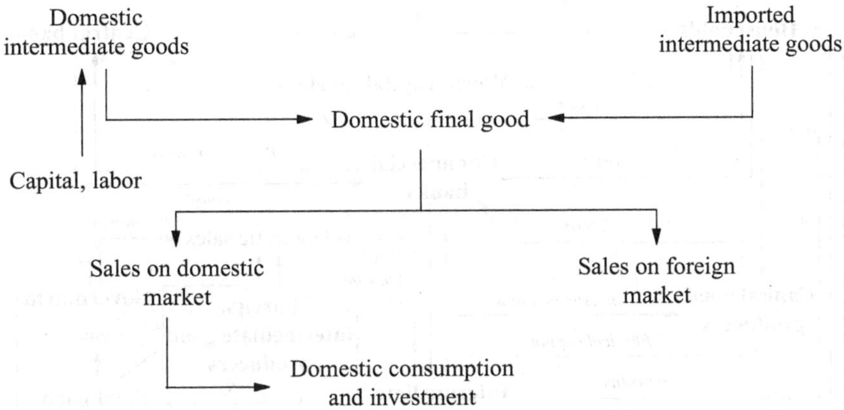

Figure 8.1
Production structure in the core open-economy DSGE-FF model

where $b_t^G = b_t^{CB} + b_t$ is the total stock of government bonds and G_t government spending. As before the government keeps its real stock of debt constant ($b_t = b$, for all t) and balances its budget by adjusting lump-sum taxes.

Government purchases represent a fraction $\psi_G \in (0, 1)$ of domestic sales of the final good:

$$G_t = \psi_G Y_t^D. \tag{8.59}$$

The production structure and the main real and financial flows between agents are summarized in figures 8.1 and 8.2.

8.2 Equilibrium and Steady State

As in the closed economy, equilibrium conditions must be satisfied for the credit, deposit, final good, cash, labor, and housing markets. To ensure equilibrium in the final good market, sales of the domestically produced final good at home must be now equal to domestic absorption, inclusive of price adjustment costs,

$$Y_t^D = C_t + G_t + I_t + \frac{\phi_I}{2}\left(\frac{P_t^I}{P_{t-1}^I} - 1\right)^2 \left(\frac{P_t^I}{P_t^D}\right) Y_t^I, \tag{8.60}$$

with the price of sales on the domestic market, P_t^D, determined through the identity

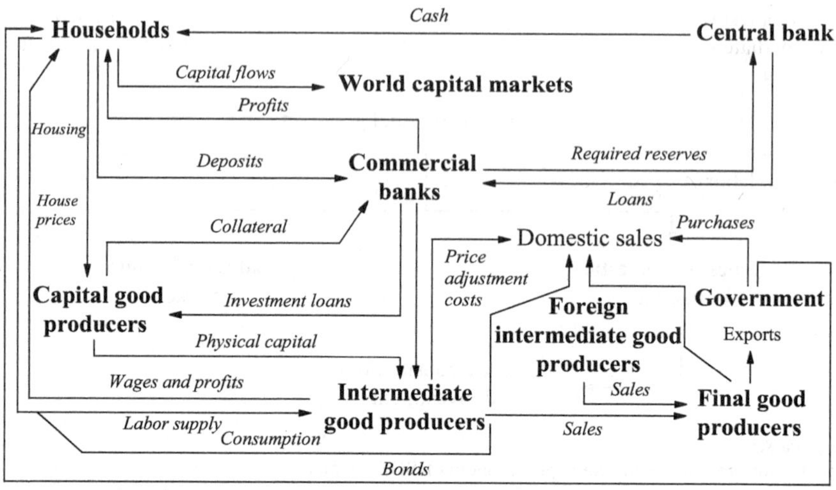

Figure 8.2
Structure of the core open-economy DSGE-FF model

$$P_tY_t = P_t^DY_t^D + P_t^XY_t^X. \tag{8.61}$$

As before, government bonds are in zero net supply and the equilibrium condition of the currency market is given once again by

$$m_t = m_t^s. \tag{8.62}$$

Similarly, the equilibrium condition of the housing market is

$$H_t = \bar{H}. \tag{8.63}$$

The equilibrium condition of the labor market is again

$$\left(\frac{\omega_t C_t^{-1/\varsigma}}{\eta_N}\right)^{1/\psi_N} = \left(\frac{\alpha}{1-\alpha}\right)^{-\alpha}\left[\frac{(1+\psi_W i_t^R)\omega_t}{r_t^K}\right]^{-\alpha}. \tag{8.64}$$

Finally, the balance of payments (or the equilibrium condition of the market for foreign exchange) is given by

$$WP_t^XY_t^X - WP_t^FY_t^F + i_{t-1}^W F_{t-1} - \theta_{t-1}^{FB}B_{t-1}^F - \theta_{t-1}^{FC}L_{t-1}^{FC} - \Delta F_t = 0, \tag{8.65}$$

where $F_t = R_t^F + B_t^F - L_t^{FC}$ is the economy's net foreign asset position.

Assuming again a zero inflation target, the key features of the steady-state solution of the model are similar to those described in chapter 4. From the Euler equation (8.14), the steady-state value of the bond rate is

$$\tilde{\imath}^B = \Lambda^{-1} - 1.$$

In the steady state, it must be also that

$$\tilde{\imath}^B = \tilde{\imath}^R,$$

which ensures that banks have no incentive to borrow from the central bank to buy government bonds.

From equations (8.15) to (8.20), the steady-state labor supply function and demand functions for cash, deposits, housing services, and foreign bonds are given by

$$\tilde{N} = \left(\frac{\tilde{\omega}\tilde{C}^{-1/\varsigma}}{\eta_N}\right)^{1/\psi_N},$$

$$\tilde{m} = \frac{\eta_x \nu \tilde{C}^{1/\varsigma}\Lambda^{-1}}{\Lambda^{-1} - 1},$$

$$\tilde{d} = \frac{\eta_x (1-\nu)\tilde{C}^{1/\varsigma}\Lambda^{-1}}{\Lambda^{-1} - 1 - \tilde{\imath}^D},$$

$$\tilde{p}^H \bar{H} = \frac{\eta_H \tilde{C}^{1/\varsigma}}{1-\Lambda},$$

$$\tilde{B}^F = \frac{\tilde{\imath}^W - \tilde{\imath}^B}{\theta_0^{FB}(1+\tilde{\imath}^W)}.$$

The last result implies that the steady-state value of the stock of foreign bonds held by the representative household is positive as long as the world risk-free interest rate exceeds the domestic bond rate. The greater the degree of imperfections on the world capital markets (the higher θ_0^{FB} is), the lower household holdings of foreign bonds are.

From (8.23) and (8.25)-(8.30), steady-state values of the demand for domestic and foreign intermediate goods, the price of final output, the price of foreign imported intermediate goods, the export price, exports, and the domestic final good are given by

$$\tilde{Y}^I = \Lambda_I^\eta \left(\frac{\tilde{P}^I}{\tilde{P}}\right)^{-\eta} \tilde{Y}, \quad \tilde{Y}^F = (1-\Lambda_I)^\eta \left(\frac{\tilde{P}^F}{\tilde{P}}\right)^{-\eta} \tilde{Y},$$

$$\tilde{P} = [\Lambda_I^\eta (\tilde{P}^I)^{1-\eta} + (1-\Lambda_I)^\eta (\tilde{P}^F)^{1-\eta}]^{1/(1-\eta)},$$

$$\tilde{P}^F = \tilde{E}WP^F,$$

$$\tilde{Y}^X = \left(\frac{\tilde{P}^X}{\tilde{P}^D}\right)^{\varkappa},$$

$$\tilde{P}^X = \tilde{E}WP^X,$$

$$\tilde{Y} = \tilde{Y}^D + \tilde{Y}^X.$$

From (8.31), (8.33) and (8.34), steady-state values of output of domestic intermediate goods, the capital-labor ratio, and marginal cost are defined as

$$\tilde{Y}^I = \tilde{N}^{1-\alpha}\tilde{K}^\alpha,$$

$$\frac{\tilde{K}}{\tilde{N}} = \left(\frac{\alpha}{1-\alpha}\right)\left[\frac{(1+\psi_W \tilde{\imath}^R)\tilde{\omega}}{\tilde{r}^K}\right],$$

$$\widetilde{mc} = \frac{\theta_I - 1}{\theta_I}.$$

From (8.38) and (8.40), the steady-state values of investment and the rental rate of capital are

$$\tilde{I} = \delta_K \tilde{K},$$

$$\tilde{r}^K = \tilde{q}(1+\tilde{\imath}^L)(\tilde{\imath}^B + \delta_K).$$

From (8.44) and (8.47) to (8.49), the steady-state values of the deposit rate, the loan rate, bank foreign borrowing, the repayment probability, and bank borrowing from the central bank are

$$\tilde{\imath}^D = (1-\tilde{\mu})\tilde{\imath}^R,$$

$$1+\tilde{\imath}^L = \left(\frac{\varsigma^L}{\varsigma^L - 1}\right)\frac{(1+\tilde{\imath}^R)}{\tilde{q}},$$

$$\tilde{L}^{FC} = \frac{\tilde{\imath}^B - \tilde{\imath}^W}{\theta_0^{FC}(1+\tilde{\imath}^W)},$$

$$\tilde{q} = \varphi_0 \kappa^{\varphi_1},$$

$$\tilde{l}^B = \tilde{l}^W + \tilde{l}^K - \tilde{z}\tilde{L}^{FC} - \tilde{V} - (1-\tilde{\mu})\tilde{d},$$

where from (8.32) and (8.39) $\tilde{l}^W = \psi_W \tilde{\omega}\tilde{N}$ and $\tilde{l}^K = \tilde{I}$.

From (8.52), (8.56) and (8.57), the steady-state levels of the central bank's foreign reserves and the refinance rate are

$$\tilde{R}^F = (\phi_1^R WP^F \tilde{Y}^F)^{\varphi^R} [\phi_2^R (\tilde{L}^{FC} - \tilde{B}^F)]^{1-\varphi^R},$$

$$\tilde{\imath}^T = \tilde{\imath}^R.$$

The equilibrium condition of the goods market, equation (8.60), combined with (8.59), yields the steady-state level of domestic sales,

$$\tilde{Y}^D = \frac{\tilde{C} + \tilde{I}}{1 - \psi_G},$$

whereas from (8.61), the steady-state price of sales on the domestic market is

$$\tilde{P}^D = (\tilde{P}\tilde{Y} - \tilde{P}^X \tilde{Y}^X)/\tilde{Y}^D.$$

From (8.62), the equilibrium condition of the market for cash yields

$$\tilde{m}^s = \tilde{m}.$$

Finally, the steady-state equilibrium condition of the market for foreign exchange, equation (8.65), yields

$$WP^X \tilde{Y}^X - WP^F \tilde{Y}^F + \tilde{\imath}^W \tilde{F} + \tilde{\theta}^{FB} \tilde{B}^F - \tilde{\theta}^{FC} \tilde{L}^{FC} = 0,$$

whereas the economy's net foreign asset position is

$$\tilde{F} = \tilde{R}^F + \tilde{B}^F - \tilde{L}^{FC}.$$

The static system of equations that defines the steady state is solved for numerically, based on the parameterization provided in the next section. To analyze the response of the economy to external shocks, once again the model is log-linearized around the nonstochastic, zero-inflation steady state. The log-linearized equations are summarized in the appendix to this chapter.

8.3 Parameterization

Parameter values are summarized in table 8.1, whereas initial steady-state values for key variables are displayed in table 8.2. The starting point for the parameterization is the material presented in chapter 4, extended to an

Table 8.1
Benchmark Parameterization, Open Economy

Parameter	Value	Description
Household		
Λ	0.95	Discount factor
ς	0.5	Elasticity of intertemporal substitution
η_N	25.0	Preference parameter for leisure
ψ_N	1.4	Inverse of Frisch elasticity of labor supply
η_x	0.001	Preference parameter for money holdings
η_H	0.1	Preference parameter for housing
ν	0.35	Share parameter in index of money holdings
θ_0^{FB}	0.2	Sensitivity of premium, household holdings of foreign bonds
Production		
Λ_I	0.7	Distribution parameter, final good
η	1.5	Elasticity of substitution, baskets of intermediate goods
μ^F	1.0	Exchange rate pass-through, imported goods
$\varkappa_X$	0.9	Price elasticity of exports
θ_I, θ_F	6.0	Elasticity of demand within groups, intermediate goods
α	0.35	Share of capital, domestic intermediate goods
ϕ_I	25	Adjustment cost parameter, domestic IG prices
δ_K	0.025	Depreciation rate of capital
Θ_K	14	Adjustment cost parameter, investment
ψ_W	0.0	Share of labor costs financed in advance
Commercial banks		
κ	0.2	Effective collateral-loan ratio
φ_1	0.05	Elasticity of repayment probability, collateral
φ_2	0.4	Elasticity of repayment probability, cyclical output
θ_0^{FC}	0.2	Sensitivity of premium, bank foreign borrowing
Central bank		
μ	0.2	Reserve requirement rate
χ	0.8	Degree of interest rate smoothing
ε_1	2.0	Response of base policy rate to inflation deviations
ε_2	0.4	Response of base policy rate to output deviations
φ^{CB}	0.02	Sensitivity of penalty rate to borrowing-deposit ratio
φ_1^R	0.0	Exchange rate smoothing parameter, foreign reserves rule
φ_2^R	1.0	Persistence parameter, foreign reserves rule
φ^R	0.8	Relative weight on trade motive, foreign reserves rule
κ^F	0.2	Sterilization coefficient
Government		
ψ_G	0.22	Share of government spending in domestic output sales
World interest rate		
ρ_W	0.8	Persistence parameter, shock to world risk-free rate

Table 8.2
Initial Steady-State Values: Key Variables
(In proportion of final output, unless indicated otherwise)

Variable	Description	Value
C	Household consumption	0.65
$I = l^K$	Investment loans to CG producers	0.13
K	Capital stock	5.2
r^K	Rental rate of capital (percent)	0.079
G	Public expenditure	0.22
q	Repayment probability, loans to CG producers (percent)	0.935
i^B, i^R	Government bond rate, central bank refinance rate (percent)	0.053
i^D	Bank deposit rate (percent)	0.042
i^L	Loan rate, investment lending to CG producers (percent)	0.095
L^{FC}	Foreign borrowing, commercial banks	0.162
l^B	Central bank borrowing, commercial banks	0.098

open-economy context. Supporting evidence is therefore provided only on a selective basis.

The sensitivity of the spread to household foreign bond holdings, θ_0^{FB}, is set at 0.2. This value is consistent with a wide range of estimates for MICs, although most studies are based on sovereign or total external debt as a determinant of sovereign spreads; see, for instance, Ferrucci (2003, table 4). With the world risk-free interest rate set equal to 2.0 percent and the steady-state bond rate equal again to 5.3 percent, as shown in table 8.2, the steady-state value of the stock of foreign assets held by households is equal to $\tilde{B}^F = (\tilde{\imath}^W - \tilde{\imath}^B)/[\theta_0^{FB}(1+\tilde{\imath}^W)] = -16.2$ percent of final output (which is normalized to unity). Thus, households are net debtors in the initial equilibrium.

The distribution parameter between domestic and imported intermediate goods in the production of the final good, Λ_I, is set at 0.7, to capture the case of a country where imports account for about a third of GDP, as in Cook (2004), Tomura (2010), Hwang (2012), and Medina and Roldós (2018), for instance. Thus, there is home bias in final good production. The elasticity of substitution between baskets of domestic and imported composite intermediate goods, η, is set at 1.5, a fairly standard value used, for instance, by Anand et al. (2015) for the Philippines and Cuadra and Nuguer (2018) for Mexico. This implies that these goods are substitutes in the production of the final good. By way of comparison, Kollmann (2001, 2002) uses a value $\eta = 0.6$, whereas Kollmann (2004), Gong et al. (2016), and Huang and Liu (2007) consider a production function for the final good that is Cobb-Douglas in domestic and foreign intermediates and therefore set $\eta = 1$. The elasticities of substitution between intermediate domestic goods among themselves, θ_I, and imported goods among themselves, θ_F, are set equal to the same value, 6. This is the same estimate as the one used in the closed-economy DSGE-FF models of the previous chapters and similar to the values used, for instance, by Medina and Soto (2007) for Chile and by Demirel (2010), Rhee and Turdaliev (2012), and Quint and Rabanal (2014). It gives a steady-state estimate of the domestic markup rate, $\theta_I/(\theta_I-1)$, equal to 20 percent. The instantaneous pass-through coefficient to import prices is set at $\mu^F=1.0$ in the benchmark case, which is consistent with the estimate for Turkey, for instance, obtained by Bussière et al. (2014, fig. 1). The price elasticity of exports, $\varkappa_X$, is set equal to 0.9, which is close to the value of unity used by Gertler et al. (2007) for Korea. It is also consistent with the estimates for a broad sample of countries obtained by Ahmed et al. (2015), as well as the lower range of estimates for developing countries reported by Imbs and Méjean (2017). The parameter μ^X is set at 0.5, which gives equal weights to the current exchange rate and its steady-state value in solving for the domestic-currency price of exports.

With respect to commercial banks, the only new parameter is θ_0^{FC}, which determines the sensitivity of bank foreign borrowing to the differential in the cost of domestic and foreign loans. It is also set at 0.2. With the values of $\tilde{\imath}^W$ and $\tilde{\imath}^B$ given earlier, this gives therefore a ratio of bank foreign debt to final output $\tilde{L}^{FC}=(\tilde{\imath}^B-\tilde{\imath}^W)/[\theta_0^{FC}(1+\tilde{\imath}^W)]=16.2$ percent.

Regarding the central bank, the parameter characterizing the degree of exchange rate smoothing in the foreign reserves targeting rule, φ_1^R, is set at 0.0 in the benchmark case, to reflect full exchange rate flexibility. The parameters ϕ_1^R and ϕ_2^R are set at 1.0 and 0.1, respectively; given that a period corresponds to one quarter, the assumption is that the target level of reserves is set so as to cover three months of imports and 10 percent of the economy's net foreign-currency liabilities. The relative weight attached to the trade motive for self insurance is assumed to be predominant (compared to the capital account motive) and accordingly the parameter φ^R is set at 0.8.[20] The degree of persistence in the rule, φ_2^R, is also set at 0.8. The sterilization coefficient, κ^F, is set at 0.2, but this has no effect in the benchmark case given that the exchange rate is fully flexible and the official stock of foreign reserves is kept constant. Setting that stock to zero, the economy's net stock of foreign assets $\tilde{F}=\tilde{R}^F+\tilde{B}^F-\tilde{L}^{FC}$ is

20. Given that the model is log-linearized and solved in terms of deviations from the steady state, parameters ϕ_1^R and ϕ_2^R (which relate the targeted stock of foreign reserves to imports and net private foreign-currency liabilities, respectively) are both normalized to unity.

thus initially −32.4 percent of final output. Thus, the country is a net debtor in the initial steady state. The sensitivity of the penalty rate to the central bank borrowing-deposit ratio, φ^{CB}, is set at 0.02, as in chapter 5, to capture some degree of imperfect substitutability (again, from the perspective of the monetary authority) between these two sources of funding for banks. Finally, the degree of persistence of the shock to the world risk-free rate, ρ_W, is set at 0.8, which implies a reasonably high degree of inertia.

8.4 Drop in the World Risk-Free Rate

To illustrate the impact of external financial shocks on capital flows and domestic economic fluctuations, consider a temporary drop in the world risk-free interest rate by 1 percentage point.[21] In analyzing the effects of this shock, the fact that changes in foreign interest rates could affect foreign output, and thus domestic exports, is not accounted for. This helps to isolate the pure financial effects of the shock.

The results of this experiment are shown in figure 8.3, for a set of key macroeconomic and financial variables. This set includes some of the same variables discussed in chapters 4 and 5 in a closed-economy context (consumption, real house prices, the repayment probability, the loan rate, investment, the expected real bond rate, inflation, and the base policy rate). In addition, final output is replaced by sales of final goods at home, and two important open-economy variables in the context of the model are added: bank foreign borrowing and the real exchange rate.

On impact, the shock lowers both the return on foreign assets and the bank's cost of borrowing abroad. Thus, households' net holdings of foreign bonds decline, whereas foreign borrowing by banks increases. These effects combine to generate an inflow of capital (a reduction in the economy's net foreign assets), which leads to a nominal appreciation. The domestic-currency price of imported intermediate goods falls as a result, thereby raising the demand for these goods. At the same time, the nominal appreciation lowers inflation (measured in terms of the price of domestic sales) initially, which induces the central bank to lower the base policy rate. As a result, the loan rate also falls, thereby stimulating investment. Because domestic prices are sticky, the nominal appreciation translates into a real appreciation.

21. See, for instance, Edwards (2010), Akinci (2013), Byrne and Fiess (2016), Eichengreen and Gupta (2016), and Sarno et al. (2016) for the importance of global interest rate shocks in explaining cross-border capital flows.

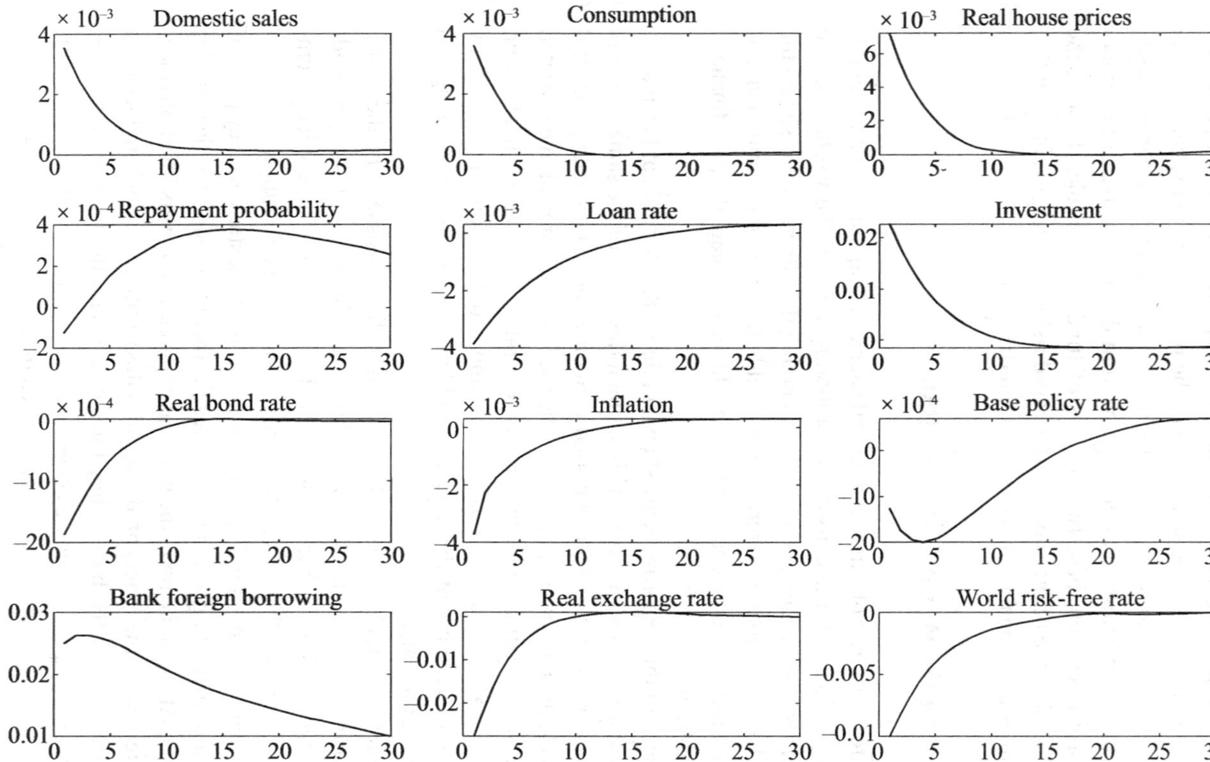

Figure 8.3 Negative shock to world safe interest rate: benchmark case. *Note*: The responses of consumption, investment, domestic sales, real house prices, bank foreign borrowing, and the real exchange rate are expressed as percent deviations from their steady-state values. The responses of the lending rate, the refinance rate, the expected real bond rate, the repayment probability, the inflation rate, and the world risk-free interest rate are expressed as absolute deviations (or percentage points) from their steady-state values.

The reduction in net holdings of foreign bonds by domestic households translates into higher demand for domestic cash and bonds, given that the deposit rate falls in response to the reduction in the refinance rate. Thus, the nominal bond rate also falls and, despite the drop in inflation on impact, the expected real bond rate falls as well.[22] The weaker incentive to save induces households to consume more today. In turn, the increase in consumption is accompanied by a reduction in the supply of labor (given that the marginal utility of leisure rises) and greater demand for housing services, which puts upward pressure on real estate prices and increases the value of the collateral that firms can pledge to secure investment loans. Nevertheless, the collateral-loan ratio *falls* initially, because the reduction in the cost of borrowing stimulates investment by more than the increase in the value of collateral. This tends to reduce the repayment probability on impact, despite the positive effect of the increase in cyclical output on monitoring costs. The two channels through which the financial accelerator effect operates once again work in opposite directions in terms of their impact on the repayment probability. Consequently, the reduction in the loan rate is dampened and so is the expansion in investment. There is therefore a *decelerator* effect, rather than an accelerator effect, despite the increase in real house prices. Nevertheless, domestic spending increases unambiguously on impact. At the same time, the real appreciation translates into a reduction in exports, which also contributes to the expansion of sales of the final good on the domestic market.

The results of this experiment show therefore that, consistent with the evidence, external shocks that lead to large inflows of capital (a *sudden flood*, as discussed in chapter 1) generate a domestic boom characterized by a credit expansion, asset price pressures, increases in aggregate demand, an expansion in output, and—over time only, given the initial exchange rate appreciation—inflationary pressures. Although the boom in domestic activity tends to raise the base policy rate, the drop in inflation induced by the appreciation tends to reduce it. Given the relative weights of inflation and output deviations in the Taylor rule, the net effect is a reduction in the policy and refinance rates. This, in turn, reduces the cost of borrowing for banks and their customers and contributes to an expansion in investment and output. Put differently, the endogenous response of monetary policy amplifies the domestic effects of a transitory drop in world interest rates.

22. Despite the increase in bank foreign borrowing, the expansion in investment loans raises also bank borrowing from the central bank. The monetary base therefore expands as well. At the initial level of consumption, the nominal bond rate must fall to raise the demand for cash and restore market equilibrium.

8.5 Greater International Financial Integration

To further examine the properties of the model, the case of greater international financial integration, is also considered, in the form of a simultaneous reduction of the parameters θ_0^{FB} and θ_0^{FC} from their common benchmark value of 0.2 to 0.15. The results are displayed in figure 8.4 (dotted lines), together with those corresponding to the benchmark case illustrated in figure 8.3. With greater financial integration, the initial increase in bank foreign borrowing is magnified on impact. With larger capital inflows, the nominal and real exchange rates appreciate by slightly more initially. In turn, the appreciation lowers the cost of imports of intermediate goods and stimulates domestic production. At the same time, exports drop by more as a result of the appreciation, and the effect on domestic output sales is now larger. However, despite the more significant appreciation, the larger increase in aggregate demand mitigates the initial drop in inflation, thereby dampening the fall in the policy and refinance rates. As a result, the reduction in the loan rate is smaller than in the benchmark case. At the same time, the combination of higher output and larger house prices leads now unambiguously to a rise in the repayment probability on impact, which tends to deepen the drop in the loan rate. The increase in investment is thus also amplified. The larger shift away from foreign bonds toward domestic bonds by households magnifies the drop in the nominal and real bond rates, despite the weaker downward effect on inflation. As a result, consumption expands by more, and so does aggregate demand. Overall, the results are fairly clear: In a more financially open economy, the macroeconomic and financial effects of external shocks tend to be magnified, both through trade and capital flows. Chapter 9 will discuss appropriate policy responses in this context.

8.6 Notes on the Literature

In line with the theoretical literature, open-economy DSGE models have followed a variety of approaches to model trade and financial linkages across countries. In the model presented in this chapter and in chapter 9, the economy considered was assumed to import intermediate goods only and to export final goods. In the two-region model presented in chapter 10, by contrast, each region will be assumed to import and export intermediate products only. But a number of alternative assumptions have been made about trade flows in the literature. This section begins by considering two other issues related to the production and trade structure—namely, the addition of imports of final goods and a more detailed treatment of the export and import sectors. It then discusses whether central banks should attempt to mitigate exchange rate fluctuations through

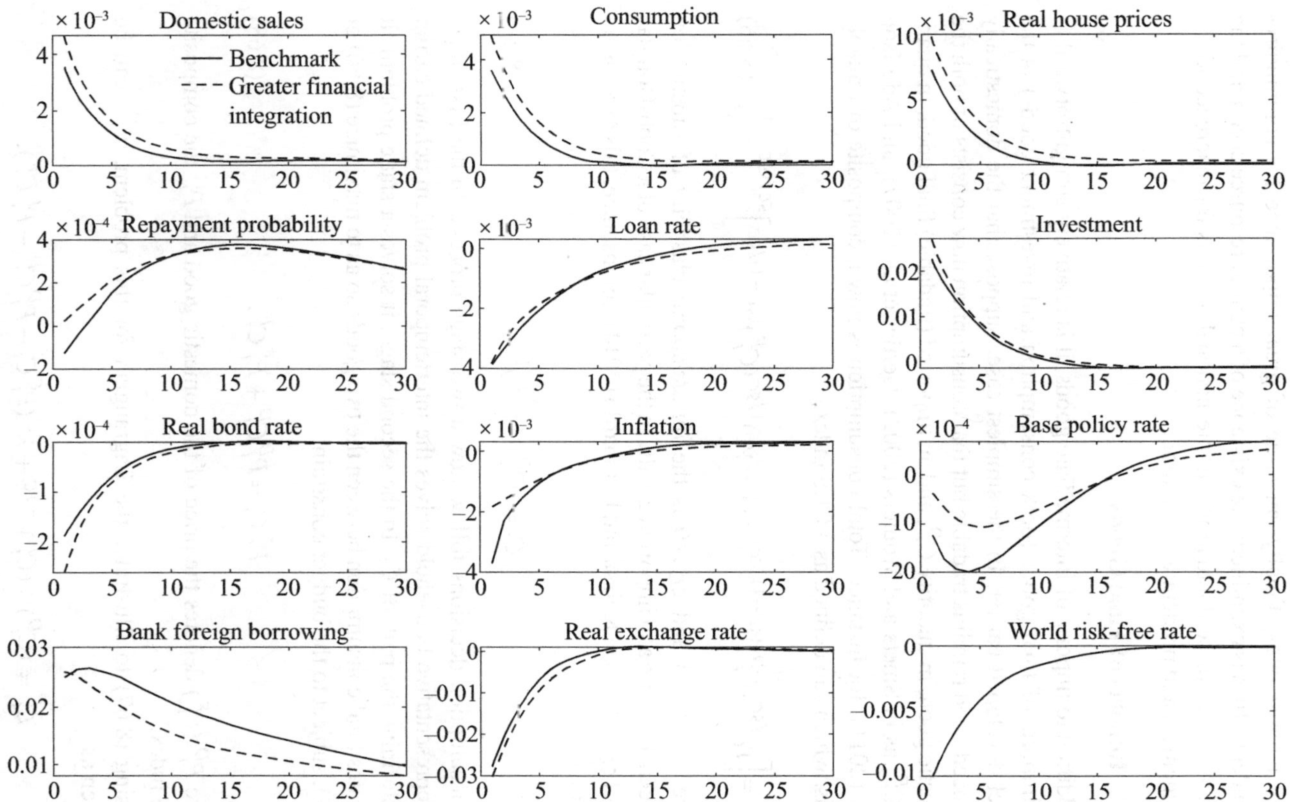

Figure 8.4 Negative shock to world safe interest rate: greater financial integration. *Note*: See note to figure 8.3.

policy interest rates. Finally, an issue of great importance for commodity-dependent MICs is examined: the existence of a natural resource sector and the implications of price fluctuations in international markets for macroeconomic management and prudential regulation.

8.6.1 Imports of Final Goods

In addition to imports of intermediate goods, it is relatively straightforward to add imports of final goods (both consumption and investment goods) in the model developed earlier. In the simplest case, suppose that the domestically produced good remains tradable but that consumption now consists of both the domestic good, in quantity C_t^D, and an imported (tradable) final good, in quantity C_t^F, as in Smets and Wouters (2002), Gertler et al. (2007), and Adolfson et al. (2011), for instance. Total consumption is now a composite of tradable goods, which can defined as a CES index,

$$C_t = \left[\gamma_C^{1/\varsigma_C}(C_t^D)^{(\varsigma_C-1)/\varsigma_C} + (1-\gamma_C)^{1/\varsigma_C}(C_t^F)^{(\varsigma_C-1)/\varsigma_C}\right]^{\varsigma_C/(\varsigma_C-1)}, \quad (8.66)$$

where $\gamma_C \in (0,1)$ and $\varsigma_C > 0$ is the *intratemporal* elasticity of substitution between domestic and imported goods. In the particular case of a Cobb-Douglas index ($\varsigma_C = 1$), as in Kolasa and Lombardo (2014), for instance, this expression becomes

$$C_t = (C_t^D)^{\gamma_C}(C_t^F)^{1-\gamma_C}. \quad (8.67)$$

Consumption decisions follow now a two-stage process. In the first stage, the representative household solves the intertemporal problem defined earlier to determine the path of C_t. In the second stage, it solves a static problem: It allocates total consumption between the two goods so as to maximize (8.66) or (8.67), subject to the budget constraint

$$P_t^C C_t = P_t^D C_t^D + P_t^F C_t^F, \quad (8.68)$$

where P_t^D (P_t^F) denotes the price of the domestic good and P_t^C the composite price index.

Using (8.67) to illustrate, the Lagrangian for this problem, $\mathcal{L}_t^C$, can be written as

$$\mathcal{L}_t^C = (C_t^D)^{\gamma_C}(C_t^F)^{1-\gamma_C} + \lambda^C(P_t^C C_t - P_t^D C_t^D - P_t^F C_t^F),$$

where λ^C denoting the Lagrange multiplier associated with (8.68). The first-order conditions are given by

$$\frac{\partial \mathcal{L}_t^C}{\partial C_t^D} : \gamma_C \left(\frac{C_t^F}{C_t^D}\right)^{1-\gamma_C} - \lambda^C P_t^D = 0,$$

$$\frac{\partial \mathcal{L}_t^C}{\partial C_t^F} : (1-\gamma_C) \left(\frac{C_t^F}{C_t^H}\right)^{-\gamma_C} - \lambda^C P_t^F = 0,$$

which can be combined to give

$$C_t^D = \gamma_C \left(\frac{P_t C_t}{P_t^D}\right), \quad C_t^F = (1-\gamma_C)\left(\frac{P_t C_t}{P_t^F}\right), \tag{8.69}$$

where the consumption-based price index is defined as[23]

$$P_t^C = \frac{(P_t^D)^{\gamma_C}(P_t^F)^{1-\gamma_C}}{(\gamma_C)^{\gamma_C}(1-\gamma_C)^{1-\gamma_C}}. \tag{8.70}$$

A similar approach can be adopted for total investment, I_t, it if is assumed to consist of domestic and imported goods as, for instance, in Gertler et al. (2007) and Kolasa and Lombardo (2014). In both cases, the composite tradable goods can be themselves defined as bundles of differentiated goods.

8.6.2 Trade Structure and Exchange Rate Pass-through

In the foregoing analysis a reduced-form approach was used to model imperfect exchange rate pass-through. A more formal analysis, as in a number of contributions in the literature, involves the explicit introduction of monopolistically competitive importing firms. These firms buy a homogeneous good on international markets, differentiate it costlessly (through brand naming, for instance), and sell the differentiated products to a domestic distributor, who combines them to produce the final imported good. Although importing firms have some degree of market power domestically, they incur costs in changing prices. This is consistent with the evidence which suggests that there are substantial distribution costs associated with imports, as documented by Burstein and Rebelo (2003), for instance. As a result of these costs—which can be modeled in Rotemberg fashion, as was done for IG producers earlier, or along the lines proposed by Calvo (1983), as discussed in chapter 4—there may be delays

23. The consumption-based price index measures the least expenditure that buys a unit of the consumption index. The highest value of the index C_t, given total spending $P_t^C C_t$, is obtained by substituting the demand functions in (8.69). The result is $C_t = (\gamma_C P_t C_t / P_t^D)^{\gamma_C}[(1-\gamma_C)P_t C_t / P_t^D)^{1-\gamma_C}$. Setting $C_t = 1$ in this expression yields the result shown in (8.70). The definition of P_t^C reflects the inverse relationship between expenditure and indirect utility functions.

between exchange rate changes and the adjustment of import prices locally. These delays can be magnified if prices are set in the currency of the buyer, rather than (as before) the sellers' currency. Thus, adjustment costs, possibly combined with local currency pricing, may generate stickiness in import prices and cause the law of one price to fail temporarily, implying that the exchange rate pass-through is incomplete in the short run. Contributions such as Smets and Wouters (2002), Caputo et al. (2007), Gertler et al. (2007), Coenen et al. (2009), Lindé et al. (2009), Shi and Xu (2010), Christiano et al. (2011), Adolfson et al. (2014), and Anand et al. (2015), as well as many others, have all accounted for imperfect exchange rate pass-through by introducing a monopolistically competitive import goods sector where nominal rigidities matter in setting prices.

Christiano et al. (2011) go one step further and account not only for the presence of domestic importers but also exporters. In their model, specialized domestic importers also purchase a homogeneous foreign good, which they turn into a specialized input and sell to domestic producers. They also generalize this approach by considering three groups of importers and by assuming that, before being passed on to final domestic users, imported goods must be combined with domestic inputs. One group uses the specialized import goods to create a homogeneous good used as an input into the production of specialized exports. The second uses the specialized import goods to create an input used in the production of investment goods. The third group uses specialized imports to produce a homogeneous input used in the production of consumption goods. In all three cases, pricing frictions help to generate a delayed and subdued pass-through of exchange rate shocks to domestic prices, consistent with the evidence discussed by Carrière-Swallow et al. (2016) and Ha et al. (2019). In addition, the model of Christiano et al. (2011) also accounts for price stickiness in the export sector. They assume that exports involve a continuum of monopolistic firms producing a specialized export good. Each monopolist produces the export good using a homogeneous domestically produced good and (as noted earlier) a homogeneous good derived from imports. The specialized export goods are sold to foreign, competitive retailers, who create a homogeneous good that is in turn sold to foreign consumers.

8.6.3 Leaning against Exchange Rate Changes

An issue much discussed in the literature on macroeconomic management in developing countries is the extent to which central banks should use monetary policy (in addition to, or in lieu of, foreign exchange intervention, as discussed earlier) to mitigate exchange rate volatility—in effect, lean against currency fluctuations. This discussion well predates the global financial crisis and took place in the context of the overall debate on the design of inflation targeting regimes and the extent to which the exchange rate should be allowed to float freely (Agénor 2002; Agénor and Pereira da Silva 2019). Aizenman et al. (2011), for instance, argued that it is optimal for the central bank to pursue an interest rate rule that accounts for movements in the real exchange rate. Céspedes et al. (2004), Morón and Winkelried (2005), Cavoli and Rajan (2006), and Cook and Devereux (2006) also suggested that there may be some benefit from including the exchange rate in the interest rate reaction function of an inflation-targeting central bank in *financially vulnerable* economies—that is, economies where external shocks can induce sudden reversals in capital flows and abrupt swings in the exchange rate, with adverse consequences for domestic agents with a large foreign debt and the economy's financial system. This leads therefore to a rule such as, instead of (8.55),

$$\frac{1+i_t^T}{1+\tilde{\imath}^T} = \left(\frac{1+i_{t-1}^T}{1+\tilde{\imath}^T}\right)^{\chi} \left\{ (1+\pi_t^D)^{\varepsilon_1} \left(\frac{Y_t^D}{\tilde{Y}^D}\right)^{\varepsilon_2} \left(\frac{E_t}{E_t^T}\right)^{\varepsilon_3} \right\}^{1-\chi},$$

where E_t^T is the nominal exchange rate target and $\varepsilon_3 > 0$. If the target is equal to last period's exchange rate, so that $E_t^T = E_{t-1}$, the policy aims to dampen the current nominal depreciation rate, as in Cook and Devereux (2006) and Devereux and Yetman (2014*b*), for instance. Alternatively, the term E_t/E_t^T could be replaced by the expected depreciation rate, $\mathbb{E}_t E_{t+1}/E_t$, if the central bank operates in a forward-looking fashion.[24]

Using numerical simulations, some studies have shown that the optimal weight on the exchange rate variable, ε_3, does not need to be very high. Indeed, Roger et al. (2009) and Garcia et al. (2011) found that in financially robust economies, putting a small weight on exchange rate smoothing is beneficial in managing risk premium shocks, with no significant adverse consequences for inflation or output performance. In financially vulnerable economies, some exchange rate smoothing may be even more beneficial, largely reflecting perverse effects of demand shocks on exchange rate movements.

In practice, the evidence regarding whether central banks in MICs respond explicitly, and systematically, to exchange rate movements is ambiguous.[25] More fundamentally, there are both limitations and risks associated with that policy. Roger et al. (2009), in particular, concluded that although having an

24. In some contributions, it is the real, rather than nominal, exchange rate that enters in the interest rate rule. See Morón and Winkelried (2005) and Aizenman et al. (2011), for instance.

25. See Agénor and Pereira da Silva (2019) for a review of the evidence and its limitations.

exchange rate term in the central bank interest rate rule may help to reduce volatility of the exchange rate, this may come at a cost in terms of price stability. This is especially so if the economy is exposed to demand and cost-push shocks. They also noted that any benefits tend to disappear fairly rapidly, as exchange rate targeting becomes more aggressive. Thus, using one instrument to achieve two targets does not generally improve welfare, particularly when the central bank can choose optimally its response to output and inflation (Adolfson 2007). This is in line with the discussion in chapter 5 regarding the use of credit-augmented interest rate rules alone to address financial stability concerns. Moreover, as discussed earlier, central banks may also intervene in the foreign exchange market—a more potent instrument (compared to interest rates) to stabilize the exchange rate when capital flows are driven by external financial shocks. This issue is taken up again in chapter 9.

8.6.4 Natural Resource Sector

Many developing countries (including MICs) are primary commodity exporters and, as such, highly dependent on resource revenue to fund public expenditure. In the absence of adequate hedging opportunities, they are therefore greatly exposed to commodity price fluctuations in international markets. In particular, shocks to world commodity prices may affect capital flows and the exchange rate, which in turn (depending on the magnitude of the pass-through, as discussed earlier) may have an impact on domestic inflation. Terms-of-trade shocks may also have significant effects on consumption and savings if households expect to face binding borrowing constraints in bad states of nature (Agénor and Aizenman 2004). These effects create major challenges for policymakers whose goals include maintaining fiscal stability, price stability, and financial stability (Agénor 2016; Agénor and Pereira da Silva 2019). A detailed discussion of the policy mix needed to address these challenges is beyond the scope of this book. Nevertheless, an important issue to consider from that perspective is how best to combine monetary and macroprudential policies in response to commodity price shocks.

Contributions that have gone some way toward addressing this issue include Vargas et al. (2013) and García-Cicco et al. (2017). In García-Cicco et al. (2017), for instance, the negative income effects associated with a fall in commodity prices reduce consumption, investment, and output. These effects are magnified in the presence of financial frictions. The resulting (nominal and real) depreciation tends to raise inflation due to higher prices of imported goods. Given the model's calibration, although lower demand dampens inflation, the net effect is still positive. The central bank therefore must increase the policy rate to contain the inflationary pressures. In addition, with financial frictions the negative impact of a commodity price shock is amplified because credit spreads (which depend on borrowers' leverage) widen. This creates some scope for macroprudential policy to react. However, in their model, exports of commodities are private and there is no direct link between these exports and the government budget constraint, as is often the case in MICs. Without a link between the commodity sector and the fiscal accounts, the effect of world commodity price shocks on domestic fluctuations cannot be accurately assessed. More generally, the most useful setting to study the effects of commodity price shocks is a three-sector model that accounts explicitly for a natural resource sector, a nonresource tradable sector, and a nontradable sector. In that framework a variety of policy options—including the combination of monetary and macroprudential policies with a fiscal rule designed to guide the allocation of resource windfalls to a stabilization fund, as discussed in Agénor (2016)—could be fully evaluated.

Appendix Log-Linearized Equations

Based on the results presented in the text, the log-linearized equations of the model are presented in this appendix. As in chapter 4, variables with a hat denote percentage point deviations of the related variables for interest rates and inflation, and log-deviations for the others, from steady-state levels.[26]

From the first-order condition (8.14), private consumption is driven by

$$\mathbb{E}_t\hat{C}_{t+1} = \hat{C}_t + \varsigma(\hat{\imath}_t^B - \mathbb{E}_t\hat{\pi}_{t+1}^D),$$

where $\hat{\pi}_{t+1}^D$ is defined as, given that $\tilde{\pi}^D = 0$,

$$\mathbb{E}_t\hat{\pi}_{t+1}^D = \mathbb{E}_t\hat{P}_{t+1}^D - \hat{P}_t^D.$$

From (8.15), labor supply is

$$\hat{N}_t = \frac{1}{\psi_N}\left(\hat{\omega}_t - \frac{\hat{C}_t}{\varsigma}\right).$$

From (8.16) the demand for cash is

$$\tilde{m}\hat{m}_t = \frac{\eta_x \nu \tilde{C}^{1/\varsigma}}{1-\Lambda}\left[\frac{\hat{C}_t}{\varsigma} - \left(\frac{\Lambda}{1-\Lambda}\right)\hat{\imath}_t^B\right],$$

26. Net interest rates are once again used as approximations of the log gross interest rates.

that is, by using the steady-state value of $\tilde{m}$ in the text,

$$\hat{m}_t = \frac{\hat{C}_t}{\varsigma} - \left(\frac{\Lambda}{1-\Lambda}\right)\hat{\imath}_t^B.$$

Similarly, from (8.17) and the steady-state value of $\tilde{d}$ in the text,

$$\hat{d}_t = \frac{\hat{C}_t}{\varsigma} + \left[\frac{1}{(1-\Lambda)\mu} - 1\right](\hat{\imath}_t^D - \hat{\imath}_t^B).$$

From equation (8.18), and in line with the derivations in chapter 4, the demand for housing services is

$$\hat{H}_t = \frac{\Lambda}{1-\Lambda}(\mathbb{E}_t\hat{\pi}_{t+1}^H - (\hat{\imath}_t^B - \mathbb{E}_t\hat{\pi}_{t+1}^D)],$$

where $\mathbb{E}_t\hat{\pi}_{t+1}^H = \mathbb{E}_t\hat{p}_{t+1}^H - \hat{p}_t^H$. From (8.20), the household demand for foreign bonds is

$$\hat{B}_t^F = \left(\frac{1-\theta_0^F\tilde{B}^F}{\theta_0^F\tilde{B}^F}\right)(\hat{\imath}_t^W + \mathbb{E}_t\hat{E}_{t+1} - \hat{E}_t - \hat{\imath}_t^B),$$

or equivalently, given that $\theta_0^F\tilde{B}^F = (\tilde{\imath}^W - \tilde{\imath}^B)/(1+\tilde{\imath}^W)$,

$$\hat{B}_t^F = \left(\frac{1+\tilde{\imath}^B}{\tilde{\imath}^W - \tilde{\imath}^B}\right)(\hat{\imath}_t^W + \mathbb{E}_t\hat{E}_{t+1} - \hat{E}_t - \hat{\imath}_t^B).$$

From (8.25) demand for domestic and foreign intermediate goods is

$$\hat{Y}_t^D = \eta(\hat{P}_t - \hat{P}_t^I) + \hat{Y}_t, \quad \hat{Y}_t^F = \eta(\hat{P}_t - \hat{P}_t^F) + \hat{Y}_t,$$

respectively, whereas from (8.26) the price of final good is derived as

$$\hat{P}_t = \left[\Lambda_I^\eta\left(\frac{\tilde{P}^I}{\tilde{P}}\right)^{1-\eta}\right]\hat{P}_t^I + \left[(1-\Lambda_I)^\eta\left(\frac{\tilde{P}^F}{\tilde{P}}\right)^{1-\eta}\right]\hat{P}_t^F.$$

From (8.27), and given that the world price of imported goods is constant, foreign intermediate good prices are given by

$$\hat{P}_t^F = \mu^F\hat{E}_t + (1-\mu^F)\hat{E}_{t-1}.$$

Exports can be derived from (8.28) as

$$\hat{Y}_t^X = \varkappa_X(\hat{P}_t^X - \hat{P}_t^D).$$

From (8.29), and given that the world price of exported goods is constant, the domestic-currency price of exported goods is simply

$$\hat{P}_t^X = \hat{E}_t.$$

From (8.30), final good production is

$$\hat{Y}_t = \left(\frac{\tilde{Y}^D}{\tilde{Y}}\right)\hat{Y}_t^D + \left(\frac{\tilde{Y}^X}{\tilde{Y}}\right)\hat{Y}_t^X.$$

From the production function (8.31), output of intermediate goods is

$$\hat{Y}_t^I = (1-\alpha)\hat{N}_t + \alpha\hat{K}_t.$$

From (8.33), labor demand by IG producers can be derived as

$$\hat{N}_t = \hat{K}_t - \psi_W \hat{\imath}_t^R - \hat{w}_t + \frac{(1+\tilde{r}^K)}{\tilde{r}^K}\hat{r}_t^K,$$

whereas, from (8.34), the behavior of marginal cost is given by

$$\widehat{mc}_t = (1-\alpha)(\psi_W \hat{\imath}_t^R + \hat{w}_t) + \alpha\hat{r}_t^K.$$

The price adjustment equation (8.37) yields, as in chapter 4,

$$\hat{\pi}_t^I = \left(\frac{\theta_D - 1}{\phi_I}\right)\widehat{mc}_t + \Lambda\mathbb{E}_t\hat{\pi}_{t+1}^I,$$

which implies that the price of domestic intermediate goods is solved backward as

$$\hat{P}_t^I = \hat{\pi}_t^I + \hat{P}_{t-1}^I.$$

From (8.38), investment is

$$\hat{I}_t = (1/\delta_K)[\mathbb{E}_t\hat{K}_{t+1} - (1-\delta_K)\hat{K}_t].$$

From (8.40), the rate of return of capital is given by

$$\hat{r}_{t+1}^K = \tilde{q}\frac{(1+\tilde{\imath}^L)(1+\tilde{\imath}^B)}{1+\tilde{r}^K}\left[\hat{\imath}_t^L + \hat{\imath}_t^B - \mathbb{E}_t\hat{\pi}_{t+1}^D + \Theta_K(\mathbb{E}_t\hat{K}_{t+1} - \hat{K}_t) + \hat{q}_t\right]$$

$$-\tilde{q}\left(\frac{1+\tilde{\imath}^L}{1+\tilde{r}^K}\right)\left\{(1-\delta_K)\mathbb{E}_t\hat{\imath}_{t+1}^L + \Theta_K(\mathbb{E}_t\hat{K}_{t+2} - \mathbb{E}_t\hat{K}_{t+1}) + (1-\delta_K)\mathbb{E}_t\hat{q}_{t+1}\right\}.$$

From (8.44), (8.47), and (8.48), together with the relevant steady-state expressions given in the text, the deposit rate, the loan rate, and foreign borrowing by the domestic bank are given by

$$\hat{\imath}_t^D = (1-\tilde{\mu})\hat{\imath}_t^R - \tilde{\imath}^R \tilde{\mu}\hat{\mu}_t,$$

$$\hat{\imath}_t^L = \hat{\imath}_t^R - \hat{q}_t,$$

$$\hat{L}_t^{FC} = \left(\frac{1+\theta_0^{FC}\tilde{L}^{FC}}{\theta_0^{FC}\tilde{L}^{FC}}\right)(\hat{\imath}_t^C - \hat{\imath}_t^W - \mathbb{E}_t\hat{E}_{t+1} + \hat{E}_t).$$

From the text, $\theta_0^{FC}\tilde{L}^{FC} = (\tilde{\imath}^R - \tilde{\imath}^W)/(1+\tilde{\imath}^W)$; substituting this result in the last expression yields

$$\hat{L}_t^{FC} = \left(\frac{1+\tilde{\imath}^R}{\tilde{\imath}^R - \tilde{\imath}^W}\right)(\hat{\imath}_t^C - \hat{\imath}_t^W - \mathbb{E}_t\hat{E}_{t+1} + \hat{E}_t).$$

The cost of foreign borrowing for banks is derived from (8.45) and (8.46):

$$\hat{\imath}_t^{FB} = \hat{\imath}_t^W + \mathbb{E}_t\hat{E}_{t+1} - \hat{E}_t + \frac{0.5\theta_0^{FC}\tilde{L}^{FC}}{1+0.5\theta_0^{FC}\tilde{L}^{FC}}\hat{L}_t^{FC}.$$

From (8.49), the probability of repayment is

$$\hat{q}_t = \varphi_1(\hat{p}_t^H - \hat{l}_t^K) + \varphi_2\hat{Y}_t.$$

The demand for credit for working capital needs is, from (8.32),

$$\hat{l}_t^W = \hat{\omega}_t + \hat{N}_t,$$

whereas the demand for investment loans is, from (8.39),

$$\hat{l}_t^K = \hat{I}_t.$$

Total credit demand is thus

$$\hat{l}_t = \left(\frac{\tilde{l}^W}{\tilde{l}}\right)\hat{l}_t^W + \left(\frac{\tilde{l}^K}{\tilde{l}}\right)\hat{l}_t^K.$$

From (8.42), bank borrowing from the central bank is

$$\hat{l}_t^B = \frac{1}{\tilde{l}^B}\left[\tilde{l}\hat{l}_t - \tilde{z}\tilde{L}^{FC}(\hat{z}_t + \hat{L}_t^{FC}) - (1-\tilde{\mu})\tilde{d}\hat{d}_t + \tilde{d}\hat{\mu}_t\right],$$

where

$$\hat{z}_t = \hat{E}_t - \hat{P}_t^D.$$

From (8.52), the accumulation of central bank reserves is determined by

$$\hat{R}_t^F = -\varphi_1^R(\hat{E}_t - \hat{E}_{t-1}) + \varphi_2^R \hat{R}_{t-1}^F$$

$$(1-\varphi_2^R)\left[\varphi^R \hat{Y}_t^F + (1-\varphi^R)\frac{\tilde{L}^{FC}\hat{L}_t^{FC} - \tilde{B}^F\hat{B}_t^F}{\tilde{L}^{FC} - \tilde{B}^F}\right].$$

From (8.54), the supply of cash evolves as

$$\hat{m}_t^s = \hat{m}_{t-1} + (1-\kappa^F)\tilde{z}\tilde{R}^F(\hat{R}_t^F - \hat{R}_{t-1}^F) + \frac{\tilde{l}^B}{\tilde{m}}(\hat{l}_t^B - \hat{l}_{t-1}^B)$$

$$-\frac{\tilde{\mu}\tilde{d}}{\tilde{m}}[(\hat{\mu}_t - \hat{\mu}_{t-1}) + (\hat{d}_t - \hat{d}_{t-1})].$$

From (8.55), the central bank base policy rate is determined by

$$\hat{i}_t^T = \chi \hat{i}_{t-1}^T + (1-\chi)(\varepsilon_1 \hat{\pi}_t^D + \varepsilon_2 \hat{Y}_t^S),$$

whereas from (8.56) and (8.57) the refinance rate is

$$\hat{i}_t^R = \hat{i}_t^T + \varphi^{CB}(\hat{l}_t^B - \hat{d}_t).$$

The equilibrium condition of the market for goods sold domestically—equation (8.60)—is, using (8.59),

$$\tilde{Y}^D \hat{Y}_t^D = \frac{\tilde{C}\hat{C}_t + \tilde{I}\hat{I}_t}{1-\psi_G}.$$

The identity (8.61) yields

$$\hat{P}_t^D = -\hat{Y}_t^D + \left(\frac{\tilde{P}\tilde{Y}}{\tilde{P}^D\tilde{Y}^D}\right)(\hat{P}_t + \hat{Y}_t) - \left(\frac{\tilde{P}^X\tilde{Y}^X}{\tilde{P}^D\tilde{Y}^D}\right)(\hat{P}_t^X + \hat{Y}_t^X).$$

The equilibrium condition of the market for cash, (8.62), yields

$$\hat{m}_t^s = \hat{m}_t^s.$$

With constant supply, the equilibrium condition for the housing market takes the form $\hat{H}_t^d = 0$, which implies, using the solution for housing demand given earlier,

$$\hat{p}_t^H = \frac{\tilde{\pi}^H(\mathbb{E}_t\hat{\pi}_{t+1}^H - \hat{\imath}_t^B)}{\tilde{\imath}^B - \tilde{\pi}^H} + \frac{\hat{C}_t}{\varsigma}.$$

From (8.65), the equilibrium condition of the balance of payments is given by

$$WP^X\tilde{Y}^X\hat{Y}_t^X + \tilde{F}\hat{\imath}_{t-1}^W + \tilde{F}\tilde{\imath}^W\hat{F}_{t-1} + 2\tilde{\theta}^F\tilde{B}^F\hat{B}_{t-1}^F$$
$$= 2\tilde{\theta}^{FC}\tilde{L}^{FC}\hat{L}_{t-1}^{FC} + \tilde{F}(\hat{F}_t - \hat{F}_{t-1}),$$

with

$$\tilde{F}\hat{F}_t = \tilde{R}^F\hat{R}_t^F + \tilde{B}^F\hat{B}_t^F - \tilde{L}^{FC}\hat{L}_t^{FC}.$$

9 External Shocks, Macroprudential Regulation, and Capital Controls

The experiments conducted in chapter 8 showed that the core open-economy DSGE-FF model was able to reproduce some of the well-documented facts (as reviewed in chapter 1) related to the transmission of interest rate shocks in advanced economies to developing countries: a surge in capital inflows, exchange rate appreciation, widening current account deficits, asset price increases, credit expansion, aggregate demand pressures, and, over time, higher inflation. The fact that a credit expansion and a real appreciation could create or exacerbate risks for financial stability was also noted. Moreover, these effects tend to be magnified in more financially open economies. They may create therefore severe challenges for policymakers.

As also pointed out in chapter 8, if a sudden flood in capital flows is associated with lower world interest rates, monetary policy may lose its effectiveness. Indeed, the scope for responding to the risk of macroeconomic and financial instability through monetary policy—above and beyond a "normal" response through a standard Taylor rule—becomes limited because higher domestic interest rates, relative to those abroad, may simply exacerbate the flood of private capital. The question that arises therefore is whether other instruments, used either individually or in combination, can be used to manage capital flows and mitigate their adverse effects (as described earlier) on the domestic economy. Indeed, if financial imbalances are related to excessive credit growth, and if credit growth is fueled by large capital inflows, a comprehensive policy response may require the use of both macroprudential tools and capital controls. In the aftermath of the global financial crisis, several MICs—including Brazil, Colombia, and Peru in Latin America, as well as Thailand—did impose or intensify restrictions on capital movements. More generally, temporary capital controls have been increasingly viewed by some economists and policymakers as a useful instrument for managing financial risks associated with large swings in capital flows, alongside macroprudential policies.[1]

This chapter extends the open-economy DSGE-FF model developed in chapter 8 to consider the effectiveness of countercyclical macroprudential policies (namely, a generic tax on loans, and reserve requirements) and capital controls in response to external financial shocks.[2] In line with previous chapters, the distortion that capital controls are aimed at correcting relates fundamentally to the fact that the financial system may behave procyclically in response to these shocks. Indeed, chapter 8 showed that when banks can borrow abroad, lower world interest rates may exacerbate financial risks at home. Capital controls, which essentially operate as a tax, may help therefore to mitigate these risks by dampening in the first place the increase in bank foreign borrowing. Moreover, by doing so the volatility of domestic interest rates, and thus the volatility of consumption and employment, can be significantly mitigated, thereby implying that capital controls may also enhance welfare. Reserve requirements, as discussed in chapter 5, can play fundamentally the same role under some circumstances—hence the issue of substitutability between these two instruments, which is also addressed later on.

The remainder of this chapter is organized as follows. Section 1 considers macroprudential policy responses in the form of countercyclical changes in the required reserve ratio and the tax rate on loans, as in chapter 5. Section 2 focuses instead on capital controls. It begins with a review of the case for capital controls in general and their interpretation as instruments of macroprudential regulation. It then studies the performance of capital controls on bank foreign borrowing, based on a simple implementable rule. In both sections, the focus is on macroprudential policies operating independently, in response to shocks to world interest rates. In all cases, the transmission process is characterized and the optimal policy response is discussed. A comparison with the Ramsey policy is also provided in the case of capital controls. In section 3, various policy combinations, including the joint determination of countercyclical rules based on reserve requirements and capital controls, are examined. The last section provides some notes on the literature regarding the effect of capital controls on the composition of capital flows, the cross-border spillover effects that these

1. After decades of opposition to all forms of restrictions on capital movements, the International Monetary Fund cautiously shifted in their favor and refers to them as *capital flow management* measures. See International Monetary Fund (2012, 2016).

2. Agénor et al. (2014*a*) studied the performance of a countercyclical capital requirements rule, of the type considered in chapter 6, in a related setting. Clancy and Merola (2017) also examined the ability of countercyclical capital regulation to promote macroeconomic and financial stability in small open economies.

controls may trigger when implemented unilaterally, and the so-called *financial trilemma*—that is, the view that unrestricted cross-border banking, national regulatory independence, and financial stability are incompatible.

9.1 Macroprudential Policy Responses

When the scope for using monetary policy to respond to surges in capital inflows induced by shocks to world interest rates is limited, policymakers may need to rely on a range of other instruments to promote price and financial stability. In line with the discussion in the previous chapters, this section focuses on reserve requirements and a tax on loans as policy tools, and assesses their ability to curb credit growth and fend off aggregate demand and inflationary pressures in an open economy. The next section will consider the case of capital controls.

9.1.1 Reserve Requirements

As discussed at length in chapter 5, in practice, policymakers in MICs have often used reserve requirements as part of a countercyclical toolkit to mitigate credit fluctuations caused by capital inflows. Consider now, again as in that chapter, the performance of a countercyclical reserve requirement rule that relates changes in the required reserve ratio, μ_t, to deviations in the loan-to-domestic sales ratio,

$$\frac{1+\mu_t}{1+\tilde{\mu}} = \left(\frac{1+\mu_{t-1}}{1+\tilde{\mu}}\right)^{\chi_1^R} \left\{ \left(\frac{l_t^K/Y_t^D}{\tilde{l}^K/\tilde{Y}^D}\right)^{\chi_2^R} \right\}^{1-\chi_1^R}, \tag{9.1}$$

where $\chi_1^R \in (0,1)$ and $\chi_2^R \geq 0$.

As in chapters 5 and 8, the refinance rate is given by

$$1+i_t^R = (1+i_t^T)(1+\theta_t^{CB}) = (1+i_t^T)\left(\frac{l_t^B/\tilde{l}^B}{d_t/\tilde{d}}\right)^{\varphi^{CB}}, \tag{9.2}$$

where i_t^T is the base policy rate, $\theta_t^{C,B}$ the penalty rate, and $\varphi^{CB} > 0$. The presence of imperfect substitution (from the perspective of the monetary authority) makes it once again more expensive for financial intermediaries to replace deposits with central bank borrowing, and this increase in cost tends to feed into the loan rate, given that, as derived in previous chapters, $1+i_t^L = \zeta^L/[q_t(\zeta^L - 1)](1+i_t^R)$, where q_t is the repayment probability and $\zeta^L > 1$ the elasticity of substitution between differentiated loans to capital good producers.

Impulse response functions

To illustrate the performance of the rule, consider as in chapter 8 a temporary drop in the world risk-free interest rate by 1 percentage point. Parameters χ_1 and χ_2^R in (9.1) are set at 0.8 and 20.0, respectively, and parameter φ^{CB} in (9.2) is kept at 0.02, as in chapters 5 and 8. Thus, although the sensitivity of the penalty rate is relatively low, the degree of aggressiveness of the rule is taken to be fairly high. At the same time, the implicit assumption is that there is no instrument manipulation cost.

The impulse response functions are shown in figure 9.1, together with the benchmark case of no activism (illustrated earlier in figure 8.3). On impact, as discussed in the previous chapter, both bank foreign borrowing and the country's net foreign liabilities increase. As a result of the capital inflow, the nominal (and real, given sticky prices) exchange rate appreciates. At the same time, the response of the required reserve ratio to the initial expansion in credit leads to a lower deposit rate and a drop in bank deposits, and to an increase in the central bank borrowing-deposit ratio; as a result, the penalty rate edges up, thereby mitigating the initial drop in the refinance rate and the loan rate. This dampens also the initial expansion in credit and investment. Because the drop in the real bond rate is also smaller, the incentive to consume today is weaker. As a result, aggregate demand also expands by less than in the benchmark case. The endogenous response of the required reserve ratio is unambiguously countercyclical, in the sense that it mitigates the initial expansion in output and credit, as well as asset price pressures. The real exchange rate appreciates slightly more than in the benchmark case because the smaller reduction in the cost of central bank liquidity induces banks to borrow more abroad, leading to a larger capital inflow. As a result of the appreciation, domestic inflation falls by more on impact—and so does the base policy rate. As expected, the instrument itself displays a significant degree of volatility. Related results are established in Agénor et al. (2018*a*), using a linear specification of the penalty rate.[3]

Welfare-maximizing policy

As in chapter 5, the optimal policy response parameter χ_2^R in the required reserve ratio rule (9.1) can be solved for either by minimizing a policy loss function for the regulator or by maximizing welfare, assuming either a positive or a zero instrument manipulation cost. With a focus on the latter, the goal is

3. The parametrization in Agénor et al. (2018*a*) differs slightly from the one presented in chapter 8, but these differences are not substantive. They also considered the case where credit growth is used instead in the rule.

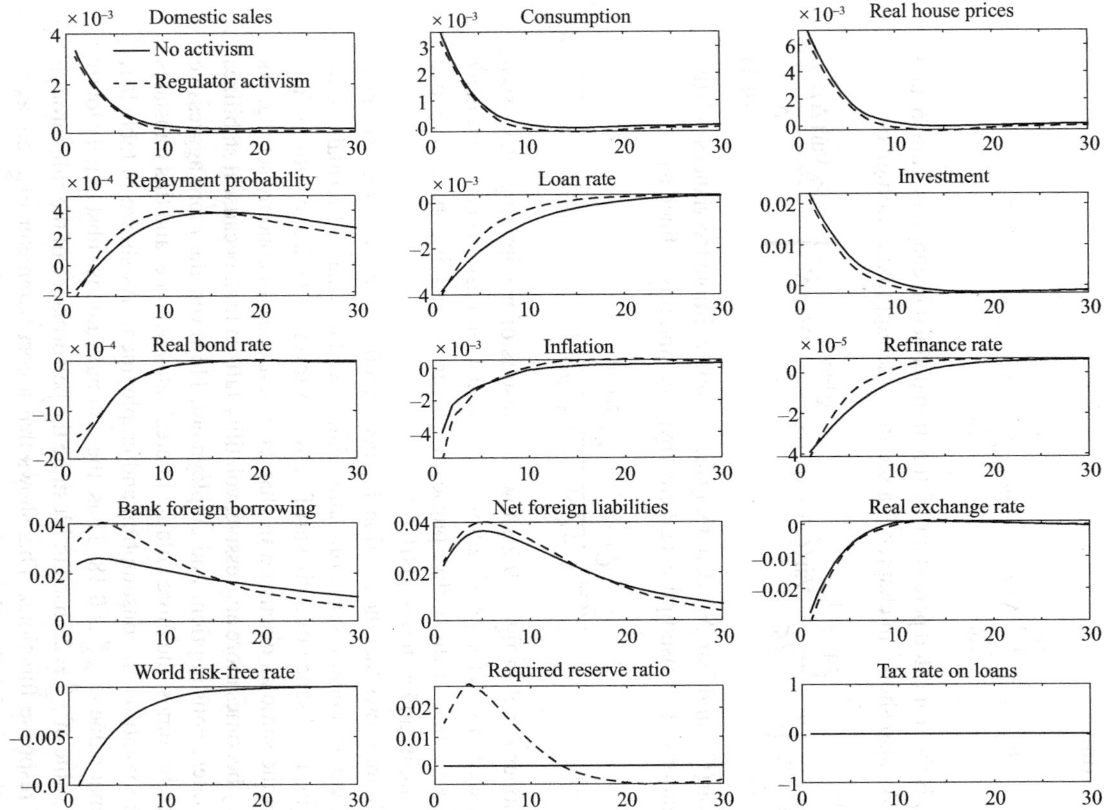

Figure 9.1 Negative shock to world safe interest rate: countercyclical required reserve ratio. *Note*: The responses of consumption, investment, domestic sales, real house prices, bank foreign borrowing, the real exchange rate, and net foreign liabilities are expressed as percent deviations from their steady-state values. The responses of the lending rate, the refinance rate, the expected real bond rate, the repayment probability, the inflation rate, the world risk-free rate, the required reserve ratio, and the tax rate on loans are expressed as absolute deviations (or percentage points) from their steady-state values.

thus to maximize

$$W_t^R = \mathbb{E}_t \sum_{s=0}^{\infty} \Lambda^s u_{t+s} - \varkappa_R \mathbb{E}_t \sum_{s=0}^{\infty} \Lambda^s (\mu_{t+s} - \mu_{t+s-1})^2,$$

where u_t is the truncated period utility function defined in chapters 5 and 6, and $\varkappa_R \geq 0$. As also shown in chapter 5, a second-order approximation gives

$$\mathcal{W}_t^R \simeq \frac{1}{1-\Lambda} \left\{ \tilde{u} - \frac{\tilde{C}^{1-\varsigma^{-1}}}{2\varsigma} \text{Var}(\hat{C}_t) - \eta_N \psi_N \frac{\tilde{N}^{1+\psi_N}}{2} \text{Var}(\hat{N}_t) \right\} - \frac{\varkappa_R \text{Var}(\Delta \mu_t)}{1-\Lambda}, \tag{9.3}$$

where $\text{Var}(\hat{C}_t)$ and $\text{Var}(\hat{N}_t)$ denote again the unconditional variances of (the log-deviations of) consumption and employment, and $\tilde{u}$ is defined as

$$\tilde{u} = \frac{\tilde{C}^{1-\varsigma^{-1}}}{1-\varsigma^{-1}} - \frac{\eta_N \tilde{N}^{1+\psi_N}}{1+\psi_N}. \tag{9.4}$$

The upper panel in figure 9.2 shows the results of maximizing (9.3), subject to a second-order approximation of the model, and using a cost parameter value of $\varkappa_R = 0.1$ for illustrative purposes. The grid search is conducted at two decimal points and a step of 0.01.[4]

The figure shows that the relationship between the degree of aggressiveness of the countercyclical reserve rule and relative welfare (that is, normalized by welfare in the absence of activism) follows an inverted U-shape pattern. The reason is the same as discussed in chapter 5 in a closed-economy setting. As the policy becomes more aggressive, volatility falls at first, because it stabilizes interest rates, consumption, and employment. However, the more aggressive the policy becomes, the more volatile interest rates become, and this translates into more volatility in consumption and employment. As shown in table 9.1, the optimal value of χ_2^R is 0.18. Thus, the optimal value is substantially lower than the value of $\chi_2^R = 20$ used to illustrate the performance of the rule through impulse response functions. This shows that a cost parameter of even $\varkappa_R = 0.1$, as before in the closed economy, may act as a significant deterrent to an aggressive use of reserve requirements as a countercyclical tool in response to

4. As discussed in previous chapters, lump-sum subsidies are not available to eliminate the distortions associated with nominal rigidities and financial frictions. Welfare is thus evaluated around a distorted steady state.

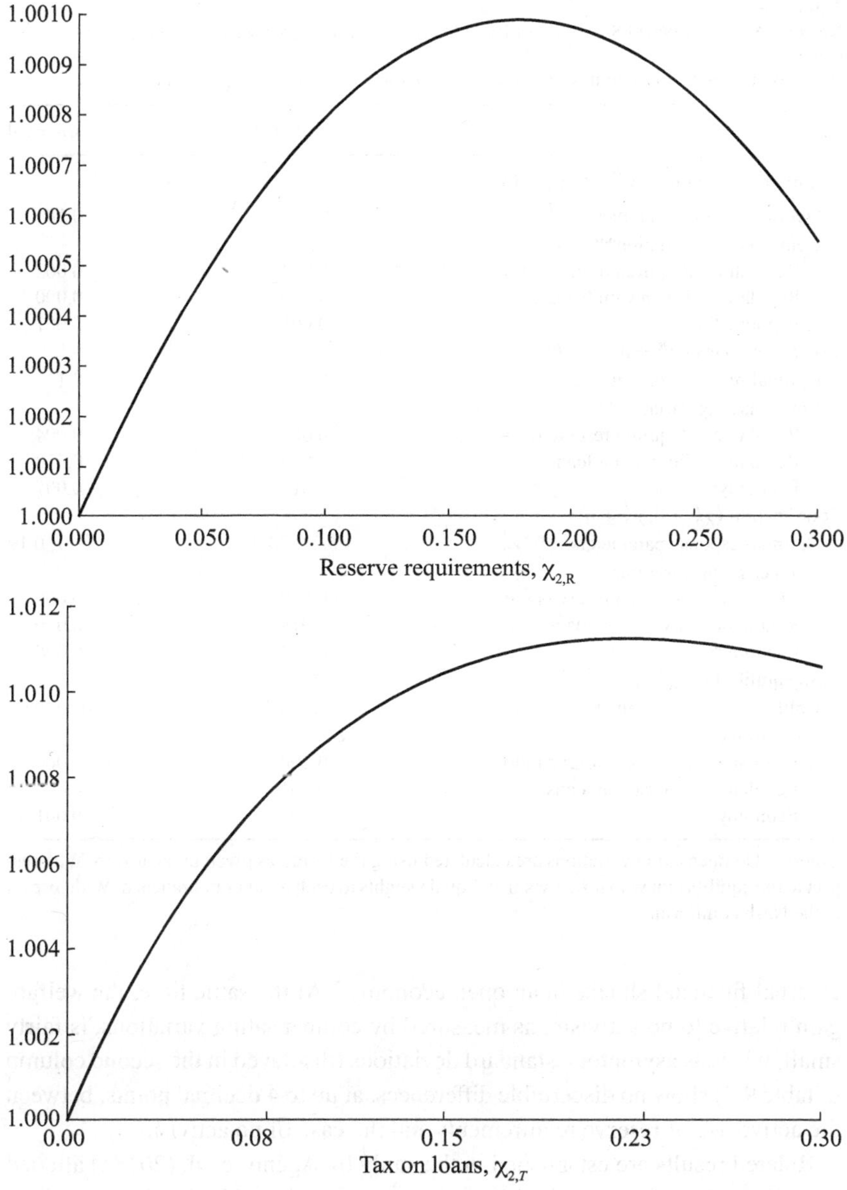

Figure 9.2
Negative shock to world safe interest rate: welfare-maximizing response parameter, required reserve ratio and tax rate on loans
Note: Values shown are those that maximize welfare, adjusted for an instrument manipulation cost parameter of 0.1. Relative welfare is scaled by the value of welfare in the absence of activism.

Table 9.1
Negative Shock to World Safe Interest Rate: Optimal Policy Responses and Gains from Coordination
Response to Credit-to-Output Ratio in both Regulatory Rules (Benchmark parameters)

	$\varkappa_R = 0.1$	$\varkappa_R = 0.4$
Required reserve ratio ($\chi_2^R \geq 0, \chi_2^L = 0$)		
Optimal response parameter, χ_2^R	0.18	0.18
Compensating variation[a,b]		
Regulator—Required reserve ratio	0.002	0.002
Regulator—Tax rate on loans	0.000	0.000
Economy[c]	0.001	0.001
Tax rate on loans ($\chi_2^R = 0, \chi_2^L \geq 0$)		
Optimal response parameter, χ_2^L	0.22	0.11
Compensating variation[a,b]		
Regulator—Required reserve ratio	0.008	0.004
Regulator—Tax rate on loans	0.014	0.010
Economy[c]	0.011	0.007
Coordination ($\chi_2^R \geq 0, \chi_2^L \geq 0$)		
Optimal response parameters, χ_2^R, χ_2^L	0.22, 0.20	0.11, 0.19
Compensating variation[a,b]		
Regulator—Required reserve ratio	0.010	0.006
Regulator—Tax rate on loans	0.014	0.010
Economy[c]	0.012	0.008
Nash equilibrium ($\chi_2^R \geq 0, \chi_2^L \geq 0$)		
Optimal response parameters, χ_2^R, χ_2^L	0.16, 0.10	0.07, 0.09
Gain from coordination[a,d]		
Regulator—Required reserve ratio	0.000	0.000
Regulator—Tax rate on loans	0.001	0.002
Economy[c]	0.001	0.001

Notes: a. Compensating variations are calculated using the formulas given in the text. b. With respect to the equilibrium with no activism. c. Equal weights to each regulatory branch. d. With respect to the Nash equilibrium.

external financial shocks in an open economy.[5] At the same time, the welfare gain relative to no activism, as measured by compensating variations, is fairly small, whereas asymptotic standard deviations (displayed in the second column of table 9.2) show no discernible differences, at up to 4 decimal points, between the active use of reserve requirements and the case of no activism.

Related results are established in the study by Agénor et al. (2018*a*) alluded to earlier, with a focus on the loss function approach and in the absence of any

5. Naturally, with a lower value of $\varkappa_R$ (say, 0.001), the optimal value of χ_2^R would be substantially higher than the one reported in table 9.1. This illustrates once again the inverse relationship, discussed in chapter 5, between the cost of instrument manipulation and the optimal degree of responsiveness in simple policy rules.

Table 9.2
Negative Shock to World Safe Interest Rate: Asymptotic Standard Deviations of Key Variables under Alternative Policy Regimes, $\varkappa_R = 0.1$

	No Activism	Reserve Req.	Tax on Loans	Nash Eq.	Coord.
Real variables					
Domestic final sales	0.0057	0.0057	0.0052	0.0053	0.0052
Employment	0.0011	0.0011	0.0011	0.0011	0.0011
Consumption	0.0033	0.0033	0.0033	0.0033	0.0033
Investment	0.0003	0.0003	0.0003	0.0003	0.0003
Real exchange rate	0.0643	0.0643	0.0640	0.0641	0.0641
Exports	0.0038	0.0038	0.0037	0.0038	0.0037
Inflation	0.0057	0.0057	0.0057	0.0057	0.0057
Financial variables					
Base policy rate	0.0068	0.0068	0.0067	0.0067	0.0067
Refinance rate	0.0075	0.0075	0.0074	0.0074	0.0074
Loan rate	0.0075	0.0075	0.0046	0.0052	0.0046
Government bond rate	0.0070	0.0070	0.0070	0.0070	0.0070
Real house prices	0.0017	0.0017	0.0017	0.0017	0.0017
Repayment probability	0.0020	0.0020	0.0018	0.0018	0.0018
Loan-to-output ratio	0.0003	0.0003	0.0003	0.0003	0.0003
Bank foreign borrowing	0.0168	0.0169	0.0166	0.0166	0.0166
Net foreign liabilities	0.0282	0.0282	0.0280	0.0280	0.0280
Policy instruments					
Required reserve ratio	—	0.0007	—	0.0003	0.0006
Tax rate on loans	—	—	0.0033	0.0026	0.0033

instrument manipulation cost. In their study, the central bank and the regulator determine the optimal value of χ_2^R so as to minimize the composite loss function

$$\mathcal{LF}_t = [\mathcal{LF}^M(\sigma_{\pi S}^2, \sigma_{YS}^2,)]^{\gamma}[\mathcal{LF}_t^F]^{1-\gamma}, \tag{9.5}$$

where $\mathcal{LF}_t^M$ is an index of macroeconomic (in)stability and $\mathcal{LF}_t^F$ an index of financial (in)stability. The first is defined, as in chapter 5, in terms of a weighted average of the volatility of inflation deviations and output deviations,

$$\mathcal{LF}_t^M = (1-\gamma^M)\sigma_\pi^2 + \gamma^M\sigma_Y^2, \tag{9.6}$$

where $\gamma^M \in (0, 1)$. The second is defined in terms of two composite measures. The first is a narrow index, $\mathcal{L}_t^{F,N}$, specified as a weighted average of the volatilities of the ratio of investment loans to domestic sales of the final good, l_t^K/Y_t^D; the ratio of net capital inflows to domestic sales, $(L_t^{FB} - B_t^F)/Y_t^D$; and the loan-refinance rate spread, $i_t^L - i_t^R$. The second measure is a broad index, $\mathcal{L}_t^{F,B}$, which adds to the variables included in the narrow index the volatility of real asset prices, measured by the volatility of real house prices and the volatility of the real exchange rate,

$$\mathcal{LF}_t^F = \begin{cases} \mathcal{LF}_t^{F,N} = \mathcal{LF}^{F,N}(\sigma^2_{l^K/Y^S}, \sigma^2_{(L^{F,B}-B^{F,P})/Y^S}, \sigma^2_{i^L-i^R}) & \text{Narrow index} \\ \mathcal{LF}_t^{F,B} = \gamma^F \mathcal{LF}^{F,N}() + (1-\gamma^F)\mathcal{LF}^{F,N}(\sigma^2_{p^H}, \sigma^2_z) & \text{Broad index} \end{cases}, \tag{9.7}$$

where $\gamma^F \in (0, 1)$. The focus on these variables is consistent with the large body of evidence suggesting that fluctuations in credit, capital flows, interest rate spreads, and asset prices have often been associated with episodes of financial stress, both in developed and developing countries (see chapter 1).

Agénor et al. (2018*a*) set $\gamma^M = 0.7$, which reflects greater concern with price stability, $\gamma^F = 0.8$, which attaches a lower weight to asset prices in the index of financial stability, and $\gamma = 0.5$, which indicates that the central bank and the regulator have equal concerns with the two objectives. To measure the volatility of real asset prices, equal weights are attached to the volatility of real house prices and the volatility of the real exchange rate. They also set the persistence parameter χ_1 at 0.1 and solved for χ_2^R in (9.1). As in chapter 5, the relationship between the degree of aggressiveness of the reserve rule and the narrow and broad indexes has a U-shape pattern. The optimal use of reserve requirements improves economic stability (compared to the benchmark case of no activism) by reducing both macroeconomic volatility and financial volatility, although the gains are relatively small in both cases—and despite the fact that volatility in the loan-to-output ratio, investment, and the loan rate all drop by about one-third and output volatility (which reflects mostly fluctuations in investment) by about a quarter. The benefit of the optimal policy in terms of financial stability stems fundamentally from its stabilizing effect on the loan-to-output ratio; with a greater weight attached to that variable in the financial stability index, the gains associated with the optimal policy are magnified.

These results illustrate again the important role of the interest rate volatility channel discussed earlier. In addition, in an open economy, the volatility in domestic interest rates induces more volatility in capital flows, and therefore increased exchange rate and financial volatility.

9.1.2 Tax on Loans

In response to capital inflows induced by shocks to world interest rates, another macroprudential instrument that policymakers can use is a countercyclical tax on loans $\tau_t^L \in (0, 1)$—that is, a tax on the *asset side* of the banks' balance sheets, which can be specified in the same manner as in chapter 5, with a focus on the loan-to-domestic sales ratio,

$$\frac{1+\tau_t^L}{1+\tilde{\tau}^L} = \left(\frac{1+\tau_{t-1}^L}{1+\tilde{\tau}^L}\right)^{\chi_1} \left\{\left(\frac{l_t^K/Y_t^D}{\tilde{l}^K/\tilde{Y}^D}\right)^{\chi_2^L}\right\}^{1-\chi_1}, \qquad (9.8)$$

where again $\chi_1 \in (0, 1)$ and $\chi_2^L \geq 0$. Thus, borrowing is more costly during periods of credit booms and this may help to smooth macroeconomic fluctuations.[6] The overall parameterization remains the same as discussed in chapter 8, and once again revenues from the tax are rebated in lump-sum fashion to banks.

Impulse response functions

To illustrate how the rule performs now in response to an external rather than domestic shock, consider again a 1 percentage point reduction in the world safe interest rate when the parameters in (9.8) are set at $\chi_1 = 0.8$ as before and $\chi_2^L = 0.4$. Impulse response functions are displayed as dotted lines in figure 9.3. Compared to the case where there is no activism (discussed in chapter 8), the countercyclical response clearly helps to stabilize investment, consumption, and output. But because the cost of borrowing from the central bank drops by less than before, banks borrow more abroad. The resulting appreciation (despite not being very large) helps to lower inflation by more than under no activism. At the same time, as expected, the instrument itself displays a significant degree of volatility.

Welfare-maximizing policy

To determine the optimal value of χ_2^L, consider again the welfare-maximizing approach discussed in chapter 5. Similar to (9.3), the goal of the regulator is to solve

$$\max_{\chi_2^L} \mathcal{W}_t^R \simeq \frac{1}{1-\Lambda}\left\{\tilde{u} - \frac{\tilde{C}^{1-\varsigma^{-1}}}{2\varsigma}\text{Var}(\hat{C}_t) - \eta_N \frac{\psi_N \tilde{N}^{1+\psi_N}}{2}\text{Var}(\hat{N}_t)\right\} - \frac{\varkappa_R \text{Var}(\Delta\tau_t^L)}{1-\Lambda},$$

where $\tilde{u}$ is defined as in (9.4), and subject to a second-order approximation of the model.

The results are shown in table 9.1 as well, for $\kappa_R = 0.1$ and 0.4, and in the lower panel of figure 9.2, for $\kappa_R = 0.1$. As before, the grid search is conducted at two decimal points and a step of 0.01.

6. As discussed earlier, the rule can also be specified in terms of credit growth rather than the loan-to-domestic sales ratio. However, results are broadly similar to those reported here and are omitted to save space.

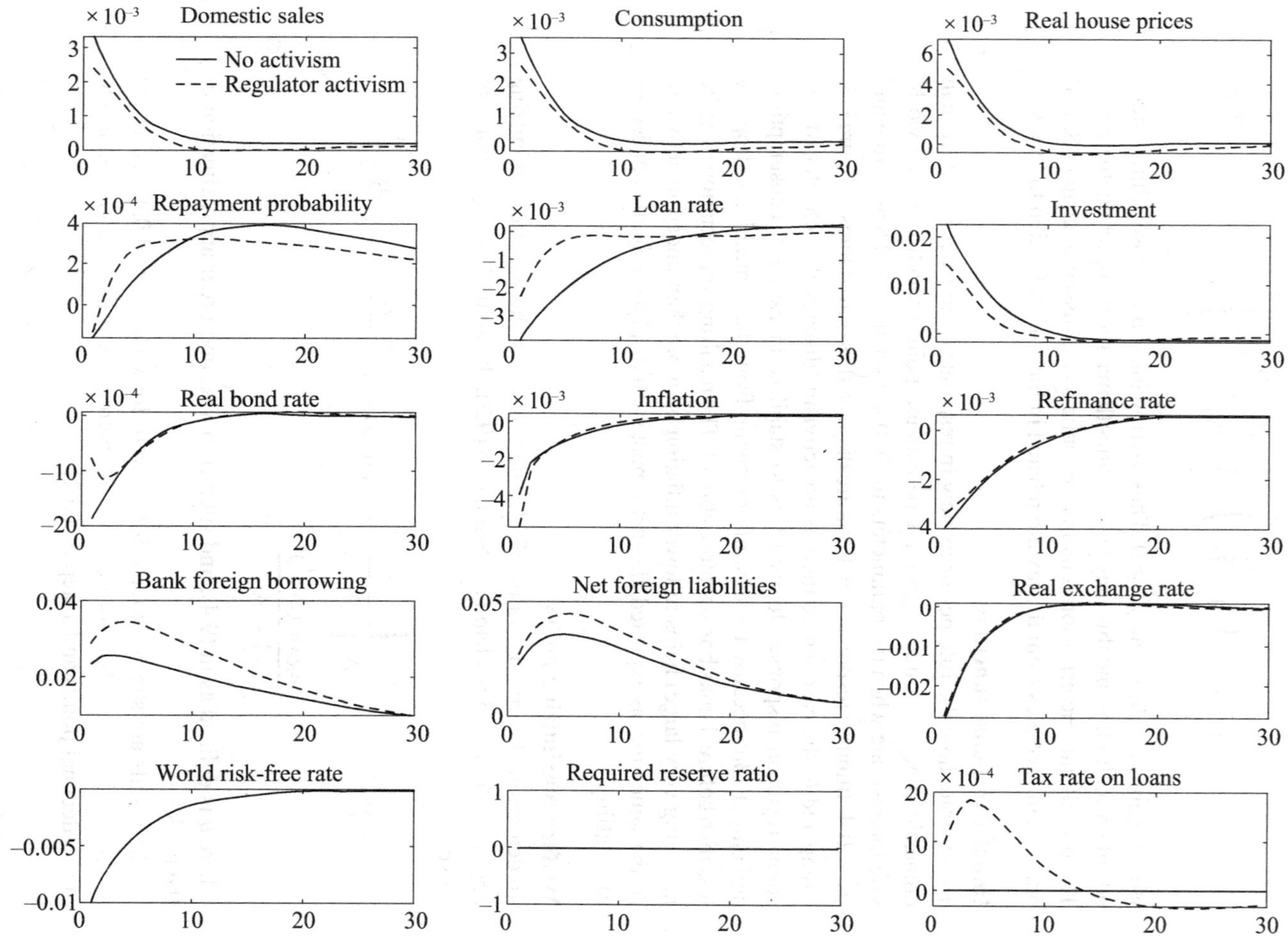

Figure 9.3 Negative shock to world safe interest rate: countercyclical tax rate on loans. *Note*: See note to figure 9.1.

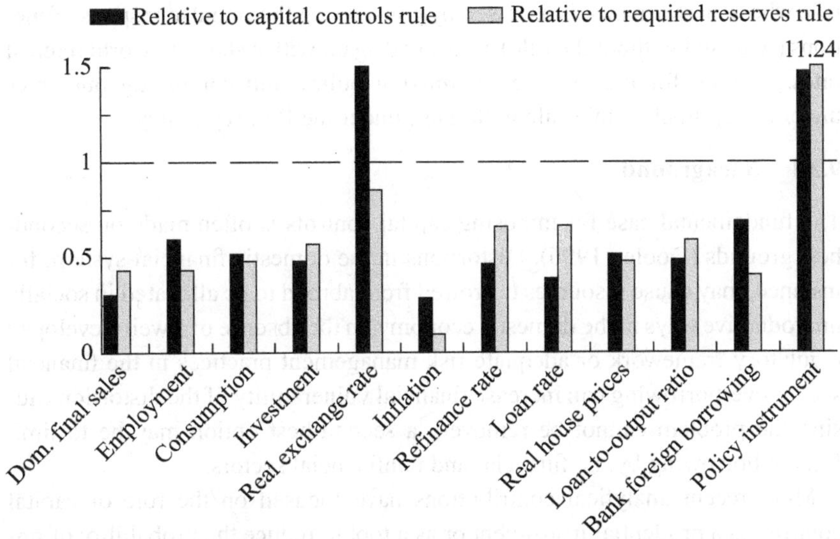

Figure 9.4
Negative shock to world safe interest rate: asymptotic standard deviations, Ramsey policy relative to simple rules for capital controls and reserve requirements.
Source: Agénor and Jia (2020).

In similar manner to the discussion in chapter 5, the inverted U-shape pattern observed in figure 9.2 results from the fact that as the tax on loans is increased, welfare increases at first because (as can be inferred from figure 9.3) it stabilizes interest rates, consumption, and labor supply. However, as the policy response becomes more aggressive, the cost of changing the instrument rises and mitigates the gain associated with lower volatility in consumption and employment. Eventually, welfare starts decreasing. Thus, there exists an optimal value for χ_2^R, which is equal to 0.22 when $\kappa_R = 0.1$ and 0.11 when $\kappa_R = 0.4$. At the same time, the welfare gain (relative to the case of no activism) is substantially higher than the gain associated with the countercyclical reserve requirement rule.

9.2 Capital Controls

To manage capital inflows and mitigate their destabilizing effects on the domestic economy, MICs have often resorted to unilateral capital controls. Indeed, since the global financial crisis, the use of these controls has become more widespread (Agénor and Pereira da Silva 2019). This section begins with a discussion of the rationale for capital controls. It then formulates a simple policy rule whose performance is assessed by considering the impulse response functions (with and without the rule) associated again with a shock to world interest rates, solving for the welfare-maximizing policy and comparing outcomes under the optimal simple rule with those under the Ramsey policy.

9.2.1 Background

The fundamental case for imposing capital controls is often made on second-best grounds (Dooley 1996). Distortions in the domestic financial system, for instance, may cause resources borrowed from abroad to be allocated in socially unproductive ways in the domestic economy. In the absence of a well-developed regulatory framework or adequate risk management practices in the financial sector, overborrowing can increase financial vulnerability. If the distortion causing the problem cannot be removed, a second-best option may be to limit foreign borrowing by the financial and nonfinancial sectors.

More recent analytical contributions have focused on the role of capital controls as a prudential instrument or as a tool to reduce the probability of financial distress. These contributions include Bianchi (2011), Farhi and Werning (2012), De Paoli and Lipinska (2013), Costinot et al. (2014), Devereux and Yetman (2014*a*), Brunnermeier and Sannikov (2015), Benigno et al. (2016), Heathcote and Perri (2016), Korinek and Sandri (2016), Davis and Presno (2017), Bengui and Bianchi (2018), and Kitano and Takaku (2018).

One strand of this literature motivates capital controls in the presence of aggregate demand externalities and frictions in the use of monetary policy. Farhi and Werning (2012), for instance, argued that, depending on the nature of shocks and the degree of price and wage stickiness, capital controls can be an effective stabilization instrument in a small open economy with a fixed exchange rate. They also argued that capital controls can mitigate significantly the effects of excess international capital movements caused by risk premium shocks on world capital markets. Using a two-country model, De Paoli and Lipinska (2013) showed that restricting international capital flows through capital controls can be beneficial for individual countries, although it would limit international risk sharing—that is, the ability to smooth consumption through cross-border borrowing and lending—independently of country-specific, idiosyncratic shocks. Devereux and Yetman (2014*a*) considered the desirability of capital controls for an economy, whose trading partner is in a liquidity trap. They found that capital controls can enhance the scope for monetary policy independence and improve welfare in the face of external shocks.

Another strand of this literature motivates capital controls on the basis of pecuniary externalities associated with financial constraints. Bianchi (2011) considered an economy where private agents can borrow on world capital markets but do not internalize the general equilibrium effects of their borrowing decisions on prices—thereby creating a potential pecuniary externality. They also face an occasionally binding constraint that limits borrowing. This constraint is denominated in tradable goods, whereas the value of collateral is in the form of output from both the tradable and nontradable sectors. Because the credit constraint is linked to market prices, changes in the relative price of nontradable goods (the real exchange rate) can induce sharp and sudden adjustments in access to foreign financing. In addition, markets are incomplete, so agents can only imperfectly insure themselves against shocks. Consequently, when indebted agents are faced with an adverse shock, consumption falls, putting downward pressure on the price of nontradables and inducing a real depreciation. This leads to a further tightening of the credit constraint, which amplifies the effects of the shock. But, by reducing the amount of borrowing *ex ante*, a social planner can lessen the contraction in consumption—thereby mitigating the magnitude of the real depreciation and preventing a further tightening of financial constraints, making everyone better off.

In the same vein, Benigno et al. (2016) developed a model in which foreign borrowing is subject to collateral constraints and pecuniary externalities associated with the exchange rate create a *prima facie* case for taxes on borrowing. They showed that a credible commitment to a price support policy in the event of a financial crisis always welfare-dominates prudential capital controls, because it can achieve the unconstrained allocation. For their part, Bengui and Bianchi (2018) considered the implication of an environment in which the ability to enforce capital controls is limited. They showed that while leakages create distortions that make capital controls undesirable, the social planner may find it optimal to tighten restrictions on the regulated households in order to achieve higher stabilization gains. They also argued that there are important benefits from capital controls, despite the presence of leakages. Brunnermeier and Sannikov (2015) studied the implications of pecuniary externalities in a two-country growth model with incomplete markets. Short-term capital flows can be excessive because individual firms do not internalize that an increase in production capacity undermines their output price, worsening their terms of trade. In such conditions, capital controls or domestic macroprudential measures that limit short-term borrowing can improve welfare.[7]

Yet another strand characterizes capital controls as a tool to manage a country's international terms of trade. De Paoli and Lipinska (2013) developed a model in which import and export taxes and subsidies are not available and

7. Devereux and Yu (2019) studied the performance of not only capital controls but also monetary policy in an economy subject to borrowing constraints and sudden stops in capital flows.

capital controls are instead tightened and loosened as competing concerns about output fluctuations gain and lose importance over the business cycle. Costinot et al. (2014) studied an infinite-horizon endowment economy with two countries in which one country chooses optimal taxes on capital flows while the other country is passive. They showed that it is optimal for the strategic country to tax capital inflows if it grows faster than the rest of the world and to tax capital outflows if it grows more slowly. Finally, Heathcote and Perri (2016) considered a two-country, two-good world in which international financial markets are incomplete, in the sense that the only asset traded internationally is a non contingent bond. This creates *prima facie* a potential role for policy intervention. The intervention that they consider is an extreme form of capital controls, in which asset trade is ruled out altogether. Thus, they compare welfare when countries only trade a non contingent, non defaultable one-period bond to welfare under financial autarky. In this setting, imposing capital controls can enhance welfare for *both* countries if terms-of-trade movements improve insurance against country-specific shocks.

By and large, therefore, the recent literature has identified a number of new channels through which capital controls can improve welfare—even though the empirical evidence on their benefits remains largely ambiguous. Fernández et al. (2015), for instance, examined the behavior of capital controls in 91 countries over the period 1995–2011. They found that these controls were largely acyclical, in the sense that policymakers did not seem to tighten capital controls on inflows or soften capital controls on outflows to curb expansions in aggregate activity, or overvaluations of the real exchange rate, or large current account deficits. By contrast, in a study of 33 countries over a similar period, Ben Zeev (2017) found that in countries with stricter controls on capital inflows output responded significantly less to global credit supply shocks, whereas bank foreign borrowing was significantly lower. Bruno et al. (2017), in a study of 12 Asia-Pacific economies over the period 2004–2013, also found that capital controls were effective in slowing down bank-related capital inflows.[8]

The core open-economy DSGE-FF model presented in chapter 8 is used next to study the benefits of time-varying capital controls. However, unlike most other contributions based on the DSGE approach, such as Escudé (2014), Davis and Presno (2017), and Kitano and Takaku (2018), the model incorporates

8. For other notable contributions and reviews of the evidence on the impact of capital controls, see Binici et al. (2010), International Monetary Fund (2010, chap. 4), Magud et al. (2011), Agénor (2012), Edwards (2012), Molnar et al. (2013), Eichengreen and Rose (2014), You et al. (2014), Forbes et al. (2015, 2016), and Li and Rajan (2015). However, as noted by Agénor and Pereira da Silva (2018*a*, 2019), few, if any, of these contributions have explicitly analyzed the impact of capital controls on financial stability.

financial frictions—an important feature to understand some of the negative externalities associated with capital flows from the perspective of financial volatility, such as rapid credit growth or asset price pressures. In addition, in contrast to existing contributions, which tend to focus on controls on households or the nonfinancial sector, the focus here is on bank-related capital flows. As noted in chapter 1, such flows have represented an important component of cross-border capital flows in recent years. Moreover, because in the base experiment capital controls are related to changes in bank foreign borrowing, they are tantamount to a macroprudential instrument.

9.2.2 Specification of the Simple Rule

Consider now the case where the regulator imposes a tax on foreign borrowing by domestic banks—that is, a tax on the *liability side* of the banks' balance sheets. This tax is once again essentially Pigouvian in nature, given that its fundamental goal is to mitigate the negative externality (increased systemic financial risks) associated with excessive borrowing on world capital markets.[9]

Specifically, the cost of borrowing abroad for domestic banks, i_t^{FC}, is now defined as, instead of (8.45) in chapter 8,

$$1+i_t^{FC}=(1+\tau_t^B)(1+i_t^W)(1+\theta_t^{FC}), \tag{9.9}$$

where $\tau_t^B \in (0, 1)$ is a tax imposed by the regulator and θ_t^{FC} is a premium which, as before, increases with the amount borrowed,

$$\theta_t^{FC}=\frac{\theta_0^{FC}}{2}L_t^{FC}, \tag{9.10}$$

with $\theta_0^{F,C}>0$. To abstract once again from fiscal effects, the proceeds of the tax are assumed to be rebated in lump-sum fashion to banks. Thus, the term $\Omega_t^{BC}=\tau_t^B z_t L_t^{FC}$ is added to their profits.

Bank *i*'s profit maximization problem takes the same form as in the previous chapter; each bank sets the loan rate and determines foreign borrowing so as to maximize expected profits, taking Ω_t^{BC} as given. The solution for the loan rate does not change, whereas the first-order condition with respect to L_t^{FC} becomes, in a symmetric equilibrium,

$$(1+i_t^R)z_t-(1+\tau_t^B)(1+i_t^W)\mathbb{E}_t\left(\frac{E_{t+1}}{E_t}\right)z_t(1+\theta_0^{FC}L_t^{FC})=0.$$

9. In a model that dwells on the Gertler-Kiyotaki-Karadi approach discussed in chapter 1, Aoki et al. (2018) also considered a tax on foreign borrowing by domestic banks as a macroprudential instrument.

Optimal foreign borrowing is thus given by

$$L_t^{FC} = \frac{1 + i_t^R - (1 + \tau_t^B)(1 + i_t^W)\mathbb{E}_t(E_{t+1}/E_t)}{\theta_0^{FC}(1 + \tau_t^B)(1 + i_t^W)\mathbb{E}_t(E_{t+1}/E_t)}, \tag{9.11}$$

which implies an inverse relationship between L_t^{FC} and τ_t^B. In the steady state, this equation gives

$$\tilde{L}^{FC} = \frac{1 + \tilde{\imath}^B - (1 + \tilde{\tau}^B)\tilde{\imath}^W}{\theta_0^{FC}(1 + \tilde{\tau}^B)(1 + \tilde{\imath}^W)}.$$

The countercyclical tax on borrowing is set by the regulator as a function of changes in the foreign-currency value of bank borrowing abroad,

$$\frac{1 + \tau_t^B}{1 + \tilde{\tau}^B} = \left(\frac{1 + \tau_{t-1}^B}{1 + \tilde{\tau}^B}\right)^{\chi_1} \left\{\left(\frac{L_t^{FC}}{L_{t-1}^{FC}}\right)^{\chi_2^B}\right\}^{1-\chi_1}, \tag{9.12}$$

where $\chi_1 \in (0, 1)$ and $\chi_2^B \geq 0$. To the extent that it raises the effective cost of foreign borrowing, this tax can be viewed as an unremunerated reserve requirement on banks' (net) foreign exchange liabilities, of the type used by Chile during the period 1991–1998 (Gallego et al. 2002) and more recently by Brazil and Thailand (Abhakorn and Tantisantiwong 2012; Chamon and Garcia 2016). It is also consistent with the *macroprudential levy* implemented in August 2011 by the Bank of Korea, in an attempt to dampen the growth in banks' foreign-currency liabilities, albeit without the maturity dimension (Bruno and Shin 2014).[10]

In practice, capital controls tend to take a permanent form or to be imposed during crisis (or pre crisis) periods, rather than a time-varying rule of the type described in (9.12). Nevertheless, focusing on a systematic policy provides a natural benchmark for a normative analysis of the benefits associated with market-based restrictions on cross-border, bank-related capital flows using simple, implementable rules.

The rest of the model is the same as in chapter 8, except for the assumption that foreign exchange intervention is fully sterilized through open-market operations. The parameterization is also essentially the same as in chapter 8.[11] In

10. Although this form of capital controls is viewed here as an attempt to mitigate the volatility of aggregate (bank-related) capital flows, and thus systemic financial risks, these tools could also be seen as microprudential in nature if their goal is to mitigate financial risks at the level of individua institutions. See Ostry et al. (2012) for a discussion.

11. There are some small differences, which are discussed in Agénor and Jia (2020).

addition, $\tilde{\tau}^B = 0$, so that the steady-state value of $\tilde{L}^{FC}$ is the same as in the case of no tax on foreign borrowing.

9.2.3 Impulse Response Functions

The impulse response functions presented in Agénor and Jia (2020), with both moderate and high persistence, and $\chi_2^B = 0.5$, indicate that the tax is highly effective in terms of dampening movements in cross-border bank borrowing, exchange rates, and the real economy. Intuitively, the increase in τ_t^B induced by the initial rise in bank foreign borrowing helps to mitigate the fall in the (premium exclusive) cost of foreign borrowing measured in domestic-currency terms—that is, the expression $(1+\tau_t^B)(1+i_t^W)\mathbb{E}_t(E_{t+1}/E_t)$ in (9.11). As a result, the increase in bank foreign borrowing is partially reversed. In turn, this mitigates the impact of capital inflows on the nominal exchange rate, the domestic-currency price of imported intermediate goods, and therefore the expansionary effect of the shock. At the same time, less foreign borrowing means (all else equal) more borrowing from the central bank, which in turn raises the cost at which commercial banks borrow domestically. The drop in the loan rate is thus mitigated, and so is the increase in investment. At the same time, a weaker appreciation mitigates on impact the downward effect of the exchange rate pass-through on inflation, which also contributes to a higher policy rate and thus a smaller drop in the loan rate.

9.2.4 Welfare-Maximizing Policy

Agénor and Jia (2020) also solved for the welfare-maximizing value of the reaction parameter χ_2^B, based again on a second-order approximation of expected lifetime utility and the model, conditional on the initial steady state being deterministic. They do so in the case where there is no cost to instrument adjustment ($\kappa_R = 0$), so that, instead of an objective like (9.3), the regulator's measure of welfare is now given by

$$\mathcal{W}_t^R \simeq \frac{1}{1-\Lambda}\left\{\tilde{u} - \frac{\tilde{C}^{1-\varsigma^{-1}}}{2\varsigma}\text{Var}(\hat{C}_t) - \eta_N\psi_N\frac{\tilde{N}^{1+\psi_N}}{2}\text{Var}(\hat{N}_t)\right\}.$$

The results show that, under high persistence, the optimal value of χ_2^B is 1.3. As in figure 9.2, relative welfare (welfare under activism, divided by welfare under no activism) has an inverted U-shape. Intuitively, the reason again is because a more aggressive capital controls rule reduces volatility in the economy, but only up to a certain point. As noted earlier, such a policy reduces incentives for banks to borrow abroad, thereby mitigating the impact of the world interest rate shock on capital inflows, the exchange rate, the domestic-currency price of imported intermediate goods, and the real economy.

However as the policy becomes more aggressive, it creates (given the degree of persistence in the policy rule) more inertia in all of these variables—at first through the refinance rate, and subsequently through market interest rates. As a result, beyond a certain degree of intervention, the net effect of a more aggressive capital controls policy is to increase the volatility of consumption and employment, and thus to reduce welfare relative to what can be achieved at more moderate responses.[12]

To assess the performance of the optimal simple capital controls rule, Agénor and Jia (2020) also solved for the Ramsey optimal policy, using the same methodology as described previously. Their results show that, as expected, the optimal simple rule does not performs particularly well relative to the Ramsey policy; the welfare gain associated with the latter is more than a third larger. In addition, asymptotic standard deviations are also significantly smaller for a wide range of variables under the Ramsey policy (see figure 9.4). However, the volatility of the tax on foreign borrowing is also considerably larger. If instrument volatility entails a cost, as in (9.3) for instance, the gain associated with the Ramsey policy could be significantly mitigated.

9.3 Policy Combinations

The foregoing analysis has focused on the case where the regulator sets instruments individually. This is important to assess the performance of, and the benefits associated with, each instrument separately. Alternatively, different combinations can be considered. In this section three such cases are examined: (*a*) the regulator sets both the tax rate on loans and the required reserve ratio; (*b*) the central bank sets the degree of sterilization whereas the regulator sets the required reserve ratio; and (*c*) the regulator sets both the required reserve ratio and the tax rate on bank foreign borrowing.[13] In the first case, the cost of intrument use is set at 0.1, whereas in the latter two cases it is set to zero. As a result, and as discussed earlier, the interest rate volatility channel is a key reason why an optimal policy (regardless of whether the policy goals are specified in terms of policy loss minimization or welfare maximization) exists.

12. Agénor and Jia (2020) also discussed the impact of a higher sensitivity of the penalty rate on the optimal policy rule.

13. Other combinations are of course possible. Those considered are sufficient to illustrate the issues at stake.

9.3.1 Tax on Loans and Reserve Requirements

Figure 9.5 illustrates the joint determination of the optimal response parameters in the required reserve ratio rule (9.1) and the tax rule (9.8). The solutions under Nash and under coordination are shown in the lower part of table 9.1, whereas asymptotic standard deviations under both regimes are displayed in the last two columns of table 9.2. The results show that both under Nash and coordination, it is optimal to use the two instruments together. In addition, regardless of the cost of instrument manipulation, coordination is always preferable to acting independently—even though the gain from doing so is not large, either in terms of welfare or in terms of the volatility of key macroeconomic and financial variables. Indeed, at up to 4 decimal points there are very few discernible differences in the asymptotic variances shown in the last two columns of table 9.2.

9.3.2 Reserve Requirements and Sterilization

Agénor et al. (2018*a*), using the loss function approach described earlier, considered the case where the central bank and the regulator determine jointly the optimal value of χ_2^R and the degree of sterilization, κ^F, in the notation of equation (8.53) in the previous chapter, so as to minimize the composite loss function (9.5), based on the index of macroeconomic (in)stability defined in (9.6) and the index of financial (in)stability defined in (9.7).

Using the same parameter values for γ^M, γ^F, γ, and $\chi_1 = 0.1$ noted earlier, Agénor et al. (2018*a*) solved jointly for χ_2^R in (9.1) and the degree of sterilization κ^F. The results show that, with endogenous reserves and a managed float, the optimal degree of sterilization is unity. By helping to insulate the money supply from the behavior of foreign reserves, sterilized intervention helps to stabilize movements in the exchange rate, market interest rates, and by implication, capital flows. This generates significant benefits in terms of financial stability and, to a lesser extent, macroeconomic stability.

When combined with an optimal use of reserve requirements, the benefits are magnified. In contrast with the case where only reserve requirements are used, at the optimal degree of sterilization both output and inflation volatility are lower. In terms of the overall index of financial stability, the benefit of optimal (full) sterilization results solely from its effect on reducing private capital flow volatility. This implies that, as can be expected, the marginal contribution of sterilization is higher in terms of macroeconomic stability than it is with respect to financial stability. Put differently, given two policy objectives, and the fact that macroprudential regulation generates some benefits in terms of macroeconomic stability as well, combining policy instruments is optimal. Moreover,

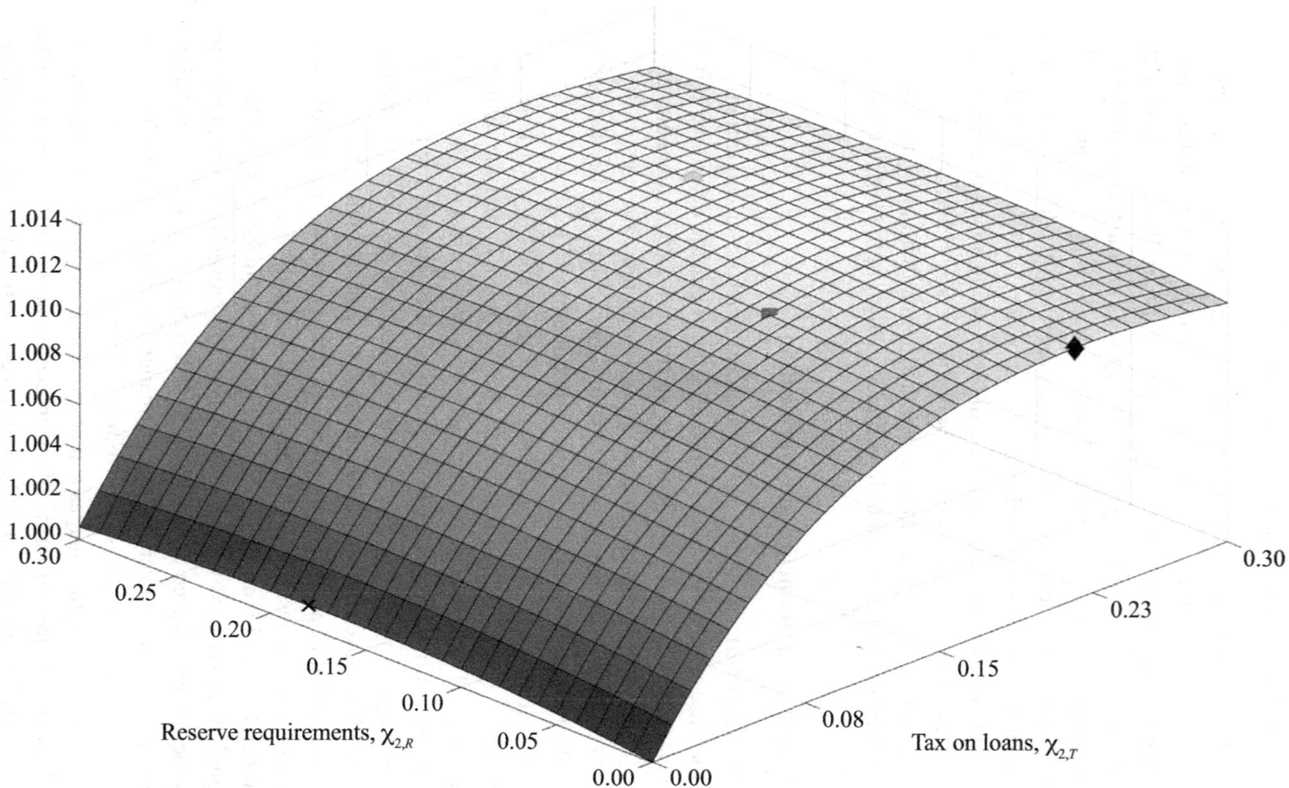

Figure 9.5 Negative shock to world safe interest rate: normalized welfare and optimal macroprudential rules. *Note*: The cross corresponds to the case where the regulator uses the required reserve ratio only, the diamond to the case where it uses the tax rate on loans only, the square to the Nash equilibrium, and the circle to coordination.

Agénor et al. (2018*a*) found that when the degree of sterilization increases from an arbitrary low value to its optimal value of unity, the countercyclical reserve requirement rule becomes less aggressive. The two instruments are therefore *partial substitutes* (at the margin). However, it is important to note that these results are based on the assumption that instrument manipulation entails no cost. In addition, the analysis does not consider the fact that sterilization entails a quasi-fiscal cost and can generate a number of unwelcome side effects (Agénor and Pereira da Silva 2019; Agénor and Jia 2020). Accounting for these features would help to provide a more thorough assessment of the benefits of combining sterilization and countercyclical macroprudential regulation.

9.3.3 Reserve Requirements and Capital Controls

Agénor and Jia (2020) focused on the case where, to mitigate fluctuations caused by external shocks, the regulator uses a countercyclical toolkit that involves the reserve requirement rule (9.1) and the capital controls rule (9.12). Their results show that there is indeed an optimal combination of the reaction parameters in the two rules that maximizes welfare. The reason is because, even though they operate through different channels, both policies help to mitigate real and financial volatility. Capital controls operate through their direct impact on bank foreign borrowing and ultimately, as noted earlier, through their dampening effect on the initial downward movement in the loan rate. Reserve requirements, by contrast, operate through the deposit rate and household portfolio allocation. A higher reserve requirement rate lowers the deposit rate and thus bank deposits. In the model, the drop in deposits is large enough to dominate the initial increase in foreign borrowing induced by lower world interest rates; as a result, commercial bank borrowing from the central bank increases, thereby raising the penalty rate, the refinance rate, and mitigating the initial drop in the loan rate. Thus, the two policies reinforce each other to the extent that they both contribute to maintaining market borrowing costs at a higher level than they would otherwise. These results provide therefore some rationale for the evidence suggesting that a number of MICs have in recent years used both instruments to respond to swings in capital flows, as discussed earlier and in chapter 5.

Agénor and Jia (2020) also found that when the response of both instruments is determined jointly, a more aggressive reserve requirement rule reduces reliance on capital controls. In that sense, there is *burden sharing* among instruments; countercyclical reserve requirements and capital controls can be viewed once again as partial substitutes (at the margin) in maximizing welfare. Intuitively, the capital controls rule generates faster decreasing marginal returns (in terms of welfare) than the reserve requirements rule; thus, combining the two instruments makes the relationship between the degree of policy aggressiveness and welfare less concave, thereby generating a superior outcome with less reliance on restrictions on bank foreign borrowing. However, although the joint policy performs better relative to no activism, as well as in comparison with reserve requirements only, the results also indicate that there is no discernible gain relative to capital controls only. Put differently, if the central bank can impose capital controls on bank foreign borrowing at its discretion, adding reserve requirements does not contribute much to improve welfare outcomes. Burden sharing generates fairly small gains.

9.4 Notes on the Literature

9.4.1 Leakages and Substitution Effects

A useful extension of the analysis presented in this chapter would be to study the role of distortions associated with leakages in implementing capital controls. By and large, the evidence suggests that incentives to evade restrictions on capital flows become stronger over time when they take a permanent form. The capital controls rule studied here operates at a business cycle frequency and is therefore less likely to induce this type of distortions. Nevertheless, it is possible that even in the short term, tighter restrictions on bank foreign borrowing (of the type defined earlier) may lead to a shift in the behavior of the nonfinancial private sector, which is such that it weakens the performance of these controls. A related issue is the possibility, as documented by Beirne and Friedrich (2017) and Bruno et al. (2017), that controls on some types of inflows may lead over time to *substitution effects* among capital movements. A key question then is whether gains from capital controls remain significant despite the existence of leakages—as discussed by Bengui and Bianchi (2018) in a different setting—especially in a context where policymakers are unable to respond quickly and effectively to attempts to circumvent regulatory and prudential standards.

9.4.2 Cross-Border Spillover Effects

Other leakages associated with capital controls relate to their cross-border effects in a multi-country world. A number of studies have documented the importance of this channel. Forbes et al. (2016), for instance, found indirect portfolio effects and externalities from capital controls in Brazil. Lambert et al. (2011) also found that a rise in Brazilian taxes on capital inflows had negative externalities on neighboring countries in Latin America. Similarly, Ghosh et al. (2014), Giordani et al. (2017), and Pasricha et al. (2018) found evidence that capital controls imposed by some countries are associated with larger flows to other countries where capital controls are not in place. Moreover, these cross-border spillovers can be highly significant. These studies naturally raise the issue of the extent to which the assessment of the performance of capital controls should consider more systematically their impact on other countries. In particular, an analysis of capital controls in a multi-country DSGE-FF model that internalizes cross-border spillover effects could help to define optimal rules for the global economy.

9.4.3 The Financial Trilemma

In a world where cross-border banking creates greater interconnectedness between countries, policymakers are confronted with a financial trilemma (Schoenmaker 2011; Obstfeld 2015): Financial integration, national control over financial supervision and regulation, and financial stability are not all mutually compatible. A country can attain any pair of these goals (financial stability and international integration, financial stability and independent financial regulation, or international integration and autonomous regulatory policies), but in general all three objectives cannot be achieved simultaneously.

In particular, the financial trilemma implies that, should countries choose to focus on domestic financial stability and to pursue an independent financial policy, a goal of internationally linked financial markets cannot be achieved. National regulators may face significant pressures to insulate their financial systems from international competition. Such a strategy may result in financial protectionism, or a race to the bottom, involving (as discussed earlier) unilateral capital controls, both of which are potentially detrimental to world welfare. To address the financial trilemma and avoid these risks, an alternative approach would be greater macroprudential policy coordination among national regulators. As discussed in chapter 10, in the context of a two-region DSGE-FF model, such coordination could also improve global welfare.

10 International Macroprudential Policy Coordination

As documented in a number of studies, financial globalization has proceeded at a rapid pace in the past thirty years. Key factors underlying this process include the deregulation of domestic financial markets, the dismantling of restrictions and controls on capital flows, international risk diversification by global asset managers, and improved economic environment and prospects through the introduction of market-oriented reforms in a wide range of previously heavily-managed economies.

At the same time, increased interconnectedness of financial institutions and markets, and more highly correlated financial shocks, have intensified cross-border spillovers and have led to renewed calls to strengthen prudential regulation and supervision of financial institutions across countries. These policies have been viewed by some observers as essential to mitigate the risks associated with international financial integration and the potentially large economic costs that countries may face when crises occur and are propagated across borders.[1] Indeed, when financial cycles are not well synchronized across countries, the combination of independent macroprudential policies may be suboptimal—even when each country's policy, when conducted on its own, is optimal at the national level. As a result, financial instability risks may worsen at the level of the global economy. The question arises therefore as to whether coordination of these policies across countries would not improve global financial stability and welfare.

This chapter extends the open-economy framework presented in chapter 8 to a two-region world. To quantify the gains (or lack thereof) associated with countercyclical macroprudential policy coordination, an explicit game-theoretic approach is used. This allows the analysis to account for strategic interactions between regulators when they choose their policies in the absence

1. See Agénor and Pereira da Silva (2018*a*) for a thorough discussion.

of cooperation.[2] The focus is on assessing whether cooperation in setting macroprudential policy helps to either reduce the magnitude of cross-border spillovers or mitigate their impact and generate more benefits than when policies are pursued independently.[3]

To set the stage for the subsequent analysis, section 1 discusses briefly the rationale for international policy coordination. Section 2, which dwells on Agénor and Pereira da Silva (2018*b*), describes the model. The model's equilibrium and some key features of its steady state are discussed in section 3, whereas its parameterization is presented in section 4. The results of asymmetric financial shocks are examined in section 5. A simple rule, linking (as in previous chapters) changes in the tax rate on loans to deviations in the credit-to-output ratio, is defined in section 6 and the optimal, welfare-maximizing policy is derived under independent policies and cooperation. The concluding section offers some comments on the literature and suggestions for further research.

10.1 Background

Recent analytical contributions have identified several channels through which international coordination of macroprudential policies could mitigate the adverse effects of cross-border spillovers and raise welfare. Some of these contributions, including those of Bengui (2014), Jeanne (2014), Korinek (2014, 2017), and Kara (2016*a*), are based on small analytical models. Korinek (2014), for instance, showed that international cooperation is not justified if small countries use prudential capital controls (of the type discussed in chapter 9) to respond to domestic externalities. Bengui (2014) studied the scope for international coordination in an open-economy model with public liquidity provision. He found that the noncooperative equilibrium between national regulators leads to an inefficiently low level of regulation, as national regulators do not internalize the benefits of their country's provision of liquidity to the rest of the world. Jeanne (2014) analyzed the case for international coordination of macroprudential policies in a model where both domestic macroprudential policies and prudential capital controls generate cross-border spillovers through their impact on capital flows. In this setting, the uncoordinated use of macroprudential

2. An older strand of literature focused on the scope for, and the benefits from, international coordination of *monetary* policies (Taylor 2013; Engel 2016). Even though many of these contributions do not account explicitly for financial frictions and regulatory regimes, several insights from that literature are relevant for the ongoing debate on macroprudential policy coordination across countries.

3. Agénor et al. (2018*d*), Dräger and Proaño (2019), and Palek and Schwanebeck (2019) discuss these issues in the specific context of currency unions.

policies may lead to a *capital war* that depresses global interest rates. However, international coordination of macroprudential policies is not warranted, unless there is unemployment in some countries. There is also scope for Pareto-improving international policy coordination when one part of the world (say, advanced economies) is in a liquidity trap while the rest of the world accumulates reserves for prudential reasons. Finally, Kara (2016*a*) focused on pecuniary externalities between national financial markets that operate through asset prices during times of distress. In his model, banks invest in a single country and are therefore regulated only in their national jurisdiction—although they interact with each other in global asset markets. He found that systemic risk in international financial markets arises as banks from two countries experience correlated liquidity shocks and financial amplification effects are triggered due to fire sales. His key result is that voluntary cooperation can exist only between sufficiently similar countries.

This brief review of the analytical literature suggests that there are various theoretical arguments to suggest that although coordinated macroprudential policies can potentially offer significant gains, this is not necessarily the case. At the same time, when there are gains, the contributions alluded to earlier are mostly silent as to the magnitude of these gains. A formal quantitative analysis is therefore essential to determine whether these gains exist, for the world as a whole and for national economies taken individually, and if so how large they are.

10.2 A Core-Periphery Model

The world economy consists of two regions, called core and periphery, of normalized economic size $n \in (0, 1)$ and $1 - n$, respectively. Population size in both parts of the world is normalized to unity. The distribution of agents in each region is the same as in the DSGE-FF models presented in previous chapters. In addition, a single global bank operates in the core economy, whereas a continuum of commercial banks operate in the periphery. In addition, banks in the periphery borrow at a premium from the global bank. Regions trade in (intermediate) goods and government bonds, but markets in cash and credit are segmented. In particular, firms in either region cannot directly lend or borrow internationally.

10.2.1 Core Economy

In what follows the behavior of the different categories of agents in the core economy is described. Because the real side is the same in the two regions, only the behavior of households, banks, and the central bank and regulator in the periphery is fully laid out.

Households

The representative household in the core economy maximizes the same function as in previous chapters,[4]

$$U_t = \mathbb{E}_t \sum_{s=0}^{\infty} \Lambda^s \left\{ \frac{(C_{t+s}^{1-\varsigma^{-1}}}{1-\varsigma^{-1}} - \eta_N \int_0^1 \frac{(N_{t+s}^j)^{1+\psi_N}}{1+\psi_N} dj + \ln[x_{t+s}^{\eta_x}(H_{t+s}^C)^{\eta_H}] \right\}, \tag{10.1}$$

where C_t is consumption, N_t^j denotes the hours provided to an intermediate good (IG) producer j, x_t is a composite index of monetary assets, H_t^C the stock of housing, $\Lambda \in (0, 1)$ a discount factor, $\varsigma > 0$ the intertemporal elasticity of substitution in consumption, ψ_N the inverse of the Frisch elasticity of labor supply, and $\eta_N, \eta_x, \eta_H > 0$ are preference parameters.

The composite monetary asset consists of real cash balances, m_t^C, and real bank deposits, d_t^C, both measured in terms of the price of core final output, P_t^C:

$$x_t = (m_t^C)^{\nu}(d_t^C)^{1-\nu}, \qquad \nu \in (0, 1). \tag{10.2}$$

The core household's flow budget constraint takes a similar form as in chapter 8,

$$\begin{aligned} &m_t^C + d_t^C + b_t^{CC} + z_t^{-1} b_t^{CP} + p_t^{CH} \Delta H_t^C \\ &= \omega_t^C N_t - T_t - C_t + \frac{m_{t-1}^C}{1+\pi_t^C} + \left(\frac{1+i_{t-1}^{CD}}{1+\pi_t^C}\right) d_{t-1}^C + \left(\frac{1+i_{t-1}^{CB}}{1+\pi_t^C}\right) b_{t-1}^{CC} \\ &+ (1+i_{t-1}^P) z_t^{-1} b_{t-1}^{CP} + J_t^I + J_t^K + J_t^B, \end{aligned} \tag{10.3}$$

where $N_t = \int_0^1 N_t^j dj$; p_t^{CH} is the real price of housing; $1+\pi_t^C = P_t^C/P_{t-1}^C$; b_t^{CC} ($z_t^{-1} b_t^{CP}$) real holdings of one-period, noncontingent core (periphery) government bonds; i_t^{CD} the interest rate on bank deposits; i_t^{CB} the interest rate on core government bonds; i_t^P the premium-adjusted interest rate on periphery government bonds measured in the core region's currency; E_t the nominal exchange rate; $z_t = E_t P_t^C / P_t^P$, the real exchange rate measured from the perspective of the periphery (with P_t^P the price of the periphery's final good); ω_t^C the economy-wide real wage; T_t lump-sum taxes; and J_t^B, J_t^I, and J_t^K

4. Superscripts C and P are used throughout to identify core and periphery, respectively. However, to further simplify, they are omitted when there is no risk of confusion.

end-of-period profits (if any) of the global bank, the IG producer, and the capital good (CG) producer, respectively.

The effective rate of return on periphery bonds is given by

$$1+i_t^P=(1+i_t^{PB})(1-\theta_t^{CP})\mathbb{E}_t\left(\frac{E_t}{E_{t+1}}\right), \tag{10.4}$$

where i_t^{PB} is the (unadjusted) periphery bond rate and θ_t^{CP} is an endogenous spread, which increases with the core household's own stock of periphery bonds,

$$\theta_t^{CP}=\frac{\theta_0^B}{2}b_t^{CP}, \tag{10.5}$$

with $\theta_0^B>0$ denoting a symmetric cost parameter.[5]

The representative household maximizes (10.1) with respect to sequences $\{C_{t+s}, N_{t+s}, m_{t+s}^C, d_{t+s}^C, b_{t+s}^{CC}, b_{t+s}^{CP}, H_{t+s}^C\}_{s=0}^{\infty}$, subject to (10.2) through (10.5), taking core interest rates, the periphery bond rate, as well as prices and inflation and all lump-sum transfers and taxes, as given. The first-order conditions give

$$C_t^{-1/\varsigma}=\Lambda\mathbb{E}_t\left\{C_{t+1}^{-1/\varsigma}\left(\frac{1+i_t^{CB}}{1+\pi_{t+1}^C}\right)\right\}, \tag{10.6}$$

$$N_t=\left(\frac{\omega_t^C C_t^{-1/\varsigma}}{\eta_N}\right)^{1/\psi_N}, \tag{10.7}$$

$$m_t^C=\frac{\eta_x\nu C_t^{1/\varsigma}(1+i_t^{CB})}{i_t^{CB}}, \tag{10.8}$$

$$d_t^C=\frac{\eta_x(1-\nu)C_t^{1/\varsigma}(1+i_t^{CB})}{i_t^{CB}-i_t^{CD}}, \tag{10.9}$$

$$\frac{p_t^{CH}}{C_t^{1/\varsigma}}=\frac{\eta_H}{H_t}+\Lambda\mathbb{E}_t\left(\frac{p_{t+1}^{CH}}{C_{t+1}^{1/\varsigma}}\right), \tag{10.10}$$

$$b_t^{CP}\simeq\frac{(1+i_t^{PB})\mathbb{E}_t(E_t/E_{t+1})-(1+i_t^{CB})}{\theta_0^B(1+i_t^{PB})\mathbb{E}_t(E_t/E_{t+1})}, \tag{10.11}$$

5. As discussed in chapter 8, θ_t^{CP} can also be viewed as an intermediation premium, related to transaction costs.

together with appropriate transversality conditions. These results are similar to those derived in chapter 8. Their interpretation is thus the same as before, with the exception that in (10.11) the exchange rate is defined from the perspective of the periphery region.

Final good production

To produce the core final good, Y_t^C, a basket of domestically produced differentiated intermediate goods sold domestically, Y_t^{CC}, is combined with a basket of imported intermediate goods produced abroad (that is, foreign exports), Y_t^{PC}:

$$Y_t^C = [\Lambda_I (Y_t^{CC})^{(\eta-1)/\eta} + (1-\Lambda_I)(Y_t^{PC})^{(\eta-1)/\eta}]^{\eta/(\eta-1)}, \tag{10.12}$$

where $\Lambda_I \in (0,1)$ and $\eta > 0$ is the elasticity of substitution between the two baskets, each of which defined as

$$Y_t^i = \left\{ \int_0^1 [Y_{jt}^i]^{(\theta^i-1)/\theta^i} dj \right\}^{\theta^i/(\theta^i-1)}, \quad i = CC, PC, \tag{10.13}$$

where $\theta^i > 1$ is the elasticity of substitution between intermediate core goods among themselves ($i = CC$) and imported goods among themselves ($i = PC$), and Y_{jt}^i is the quantity of type-j intermediate good of category i, with $j \in (0,1)$.

As before, cost minimization yields the demand functions for each variety j of intermediate goods,

$$Y_{jt}^i = \left(\frac{P_{jt}^i}{P_t^i} \right)^{-\theta^i} Y_t^i, \tag{10.14}$$

where P_{jt}^{CC} (P_{jt}^{PC}) is the domestic price of core (periphery) intermediate good j, and P_t^{CC} and P_t^{PC} are price indices, which are given by

$$P_t^i = \left\{ \int_0^1 (P_{jt}^i)^{1-\theta^i} dj \right\}^{1/(1-\theta^i)}. \tag{10.15}$$

Demand functions for baskets of core and periphery goods by the core final good producers are

$$Y_t^{CC} = \Lambda_I^\eta \left(\frac{P_t^{CC}}{P_t^C} \right)^{-\eta} Y_t^C, \quad Y_t^{PC} = (1-\Lambda_I)^\eta \left(\frac{P_t^{PC}}{P_t^C} \right)^{-\eta} Y_t^C, \tag{10.16}$$

where P_t^C is the price of core final output, given by

$$P_t^C = [\Lambda_I^\eta (P_t^{CC})^{1-\eta} + (1-\Lambda_I)^\eta (P_t^{PC})^{1-\eta}]^{1/(1-\eta)}, \tag{10.17}$$

with an analogous expression for the price of final output in the periphery, P_t^P.

Under the assumption of producer currency pricing (as in chapter 8), and assuming no transportation costs between regions and no rigidities, the law of one price implies that the price of imported periphery good j in the core economy is given by

$$P_{jt}^{PC} = E_t^{-1} P_{jt}^{PP}, \tag{10.18}$$

where P_{jt}^{PP} is the foreign-currency price of foreign intermediates, set in the periphery. However, because of home bias in production, $E_t P_t^C$ and P_t^P in general differ from each other; their ratio, as noted earlier, defines the real exchange rate.[6]

Production of intermediate goods

Core output of intermediate good j, Y_{jt}^{CI}, is sold on a monopolistically competitive market and is produced by combining labor, N_{jt}^C, and capital, K_{jt}^C, as follows:

$$Y_{jt}^{CI} = (N_{jt}^C)^{1-\alpha} (K_{jt}^C)^\alpha, \tag{10.19}$$

where $\alpha \in (0,1)$.

Assuming for simplicity that there are no working capital needs ($\psi_W = 0$), cost minimization yields the capital-labor ratio and the unit real marginal cost, mc_t^C:

$$\frac{K_{jt}^C}{N_{jt}^C} = \left(\frac{\alpha}{1-\alpha}\right)\left(\frac{\omega_t^C}{r_t^{CK}}\right) \quad \forall i, \tag{10.20}$$

$$mc_t^C = \frac{(\omega_t^C)^{1-\alpha} (r_t^{CK})^\alpha}{\alpha^\alpha (1-\alpha)^{1-\alpha}}. \tag{10.21}$$

Each firm j chooses a sequence of prices so as to maximize the discounted present value of its profits,

6. Defining the terms of trade for the core region as the price of imports relative to the price of exports as $tot_t = P_t^{PC}/P_t^{CC}$ yields $P_t^{PC} = tot_t P_t^{CC}$. Substituting this result in (10.17) yields $P_t^C = P_t^{CC}[\Lambda_I^\eta + (1-\Lambda_I)^\eta tot_t^{1-\eta}]^{1/(1-\eta)}$. A related definition holds for P_t^P. By log-linearizing these two equations, it can be shown that deviations in the real exchange rate, defined in the text as $z_t = E_t P_t^C / P_t^P$, are proportional to deviations in the terms of trade between the two regions.

$$\{P_{jt+s}^{CC}\}_{s=0}^{\infty} = \arg\max \mathbb{E}_t \sum_{s=0}^{\infty} \Lambda^s \lambda_{t+s}^I J_{jt+s}^{CI}, \tag{10.22}$$

where $\Lambda^s \lambda_{t+s}^I$ measures the marginal utility value to the representative core region household of an additional unit of real profits, J_{jt+s}^{CI}, received in the form of dividends at $t+s$. Assuming again price adjustment costs as in Rotemberg (1982), profits are defined as

$$J_{jt}^{CI} = \left(\frac{P_{jt}^{CC}}{P_t^{CC}}\right) Y_{jt}^{CI} - mc_t^C Y_{jt}^{CI} - \frac{\phi_I}{2}\left(\frac{P_{jt}^{CC}}{P_{jt-1}^{CC}} - 1\right)^2 Y_t^{CI}, \tag{10.23}$$

where $\phi_I \geq 0$.

Substituting (10.14) in (10.23), the first-order condition for problem (10.22) gives, under symmetry,

$$\begin{aligned} mc_t^C = {} & \frac{\theta^{CC} - 1}{\theta^{CC}} + \frac{\phi_I}{\theta^{CC}}[\pi_t^{CC}(1 + \pi_t^{CC})] \\ & - \frac{\phi_I}{\theta^{CC}} \mathbb{E}_t \left\{ \frac{\Lambda \lambda_t^I}{\lambda_{t+1}^I} \pi_{t+1}^{CC}(1 + \pi_{t+1}^{CC}) \frac{Y_{t+1}^{CI}}{Y_t^{CI}} \right\}. \end{aligned} \tag{10.24}$$

Under producer currency pricing, the law of one price implies once again that the price of core intermediate goods sold on the periphery market (that is, the price of core exports in the periphery), P_t^{CP}, is equal to the core price adjusted for the exchange rate:

$$P_t^{CP} = E_t P_t^{CC}. \tag{10.25}$$

As noted earlier, trade between the two regions occurs only at the level of intermediate goods.[7] The market-clearing condition equates therefore total output of core intermediate good j with world demand for that good—that is, the sum of the core and periphery demands for core good j,

$$Y_{jt}^{CI} = Y_{jt}^{CC} + Y_{jt}^{CP}, \tag{10.26}$$

with, similar to (10.14), $Y_{jt}^{CP} = (P_{jt}^{CP}/P_t^{CP})^{-\theta_i} Y_t^{CP}$ denoting core exports of good j. A similar condition holds for periphery production of each

7. By contrast, in chapters 8 and 9 it was assumed that while imports consisted of intermediate goods, exports took the form of final goods. In a two-region model of the world economy, a symmetric treatment requires imposing all trade flows to occur at the level of intermediate goods.

intermediate good j:

$$Y_{jt}^{PI} = Y_{jt}^{PP} + Y_{jt}^{PC}, \tag{10.27}$$

with Y_{jt}^{PC} (core region imports of good j) given by (10.14).

Note that we also have in value terms $P_t^{CI} Y_t^{CI} = P_t^{CC} Y_t^{CC} + P_t^{CP} Y_t^{CP}$, where P_t^{CI} is the implicit output price of intermediate goods. Given (10.25) and (10.26), this expression gives $P_t^{CI} = P_t^{CC}(Y_t^{CC} + E_t Y_t^{CP})/(Y_{jt}^{CC} + Y_{jt}^{CP})$.

Capital good production

The aggregate capital stock, $K_t^C = \int_0^1 K_{jt}^C dj$, is obtained by combining gross investment, I_t^C, with the existing capital stock, adjusted for depreciation and adjustment costs:

$$K_{t+1}^C = I_t^C + \left\{1 - \delta_K - \frac{\Theta_K}{2}\left(\frac{K_{t+1}^C - K_t^C}{K_t^C}\right)^2\right\} K_t^C, \tag{10.28}$$

where $\delta_K \in (0, 1)$ is the depreciation rate and $\Theta_K > 0$.

As in previous chapters, investment goods must be paid for in advance. The representative CG producer must therefore borrow from the core bank $l_t^{CK} = I_t^C$. The household makes its housing stock, H_t^C, available at no cost to the CG firm that it owns, which uses it as collateral to secure loans from commercial banks. Repayment is uncertain and occurs with probability $q_t^C \in (0, 1)$. Expected repayment is thus $q_t^C(1 + i_t^{CL})I_t^C + (1 - q_t^C)\kappa \mathbb{E}_t p_{t+1}^{CH} H_t^C$, where $\kappa \in (0, 1)$ is the share of the housing stock that can be effectively pledged as collateral.

Subject to equation (10.28), and taking $\{i_{t+s}^{CL}\}_{s=0}^{\infty}$, $\{p_{t+s+1}^{CH}\}_{s=0}^{\infty}$, $\{q_{t+s}^C\}_{s=0}^{\infty}$ and $\{r_{t+s+1}^{CK}\}_{s=0}^{\infty}$ as given, the representative CG firm chooses the path of capital $\{K_{t+s+1}^C\}_{s=0}^{\infty}$ so as to maximize the value of the expected, discounted stream of dividend payments to its owner:

$$\{K_{t+s+1}^C\}_{s=0}^{\infty} = \arg\max \sum_{s=0}^{\infty} \mathbb{E}_t(\Lambda^s \lambda_{t+s} J_{t+s+1}^{CK}),$$

where $\lambda_{t+s} = C_{t+s}^{-1/\varsigma}$ and $\mathbb{E}_t(\Lambda^s \lambda_{t+s} J_{t+s+1}^{CK})$ denotes expected profits at the end of period $t+s$, discounted at the rate $\Lambda^s \lambda_{t+s}$, given by

$$\begin{aligned}
&\mathbb{E}_t(\Lambda^s \lambda_{t+s} J_{t+s+1}^{CK}) \\
&= \Lambda^s \mathbb{E}_t\{\lambda_{t+s}[r_{t+s}^{CK} K_{t+s}^C - q_{t+s}^C(1 + i_{t+s}^{CL})I_{t+s}^C - (1 - q_{t+s}^C)\kappa p_{t+s+1}^{CH} H_t^C]\}.
\end{aligned}$$

As shown in chapter 4, the solution to this problem yields

$$\mathbb{E}_t r^{CK}_{t+1} \simeq q^C_t(1+i^{CL}_t)\mathbb{E}_t\left\{\left[1+\Theta_K\left(\frac{K^C_{t+1}}{K^C_t}-1\right)\right]\left(\frac{1+i^{CB}_t}{1+\pi^C_{t+1}}\right)\right\} \tag{10.29}$$

$$-\mathbb{E}_t\left[q^C_{t+1}(1+i^{CL}_{t+1})\left\{1-\delta_K+\frac{\Theta_K}{2}\left[\left(\frac{K^C_{t+2}}{K^C_{t+1}}\right)^2-1\right]\right\}\right].$$

Global bank

The balance sheet of the global bank is given by

$$l^{CK}_t + l^{CP}_t = d^C_t + l^{CB}_t + V^C_t, \tag{10.30}$$

where l^{CP}_t is lending to periphery banks, V^C_t is bank capital, and l^{CB}_t is borrowing from the core central bank. For simplicity, capital requirements are again set as a fixed fraction of investment loans so that $V^C_t = 0.12 l^{CK}_t$ (see chapter 4).

The global bank's expected real profits at the end of period t (or beginning of $t+1$), $\mathbb{E}_t J^C_{t+1}$, are defined as

$$\mathbb{E}_t J^C_{t+1} = q^C_t(1+i^{CL}_t)(1-\tau^{CL}_t)l^{CK}_t + (1-q^C_t)\kappa\mathbb{E}_t p^{CH}_{t+1}H^C_t \tag{10.31}$$

$$+q^{PC}_t(1+i^{CP}_t)l^{CP}_t - (1+i^{CD}_t)d^C_t - (1+i^{CR}_t)l^{CB}_t - \gamma^C\frac{(l^{CP}_t)^2}{2} + \Omega^C_t,$$

where i^{CR}_t is the marginal cost of borrowing from the central bank, i^{CP}_t the interest rate on loans to periphery banks, $\tau^{CL}_t \in (0,1)$ the tax rate on domestic loans imposed for macroprudential reasons (as in previous chapters), and $q^{PC}_t \in (0,1)$ the repayment probability of periphery banks on their loans, which is determined (as discussed later) by conditions in that region. The first term in (10.31) is expected repayment when there is no default by domestic firms, whereas the second term is the value of collateral seized in case of default, corresponding to a fraction $\kappa \in (0,1)$ of the expected value of the housing stock. The global bank cannot monitor perfectly periphery banks and cannot seize any collateral if they choose to default. In effect, these banks have limited liability so that when they default (which occurs with probability $1-q^{PC}_t$) the global bank gets nothing. Expected repayment—the third term in (10.31)—is therefore only $q^{PC}_t(1+i^{CP}_t)l^{CP}_t$. The fourth term is repayment to depositors and the fifth term is repayment to the central bank, neither of which is state contingent. The global bank also incurs a convex cost that increases with the amount of lending to periphery banks, as measured by $0.5\gamma^C(l^{CP}_t)^2$, where

$\gamma^C > 0$. The last term in equation (10.31), Ω_t^C, represents the proceeds of the loan tax. As in previous chapters, in order to abstract from the fiscal effects of macroprudential policy, these proceeds are assumed to be rebated in lump-sum fashion.

The bank sets the deposit and lending rates, as well as the amount of lending to periphery banks, so as to maximize expected profits:[8]

$$1+i_t^{CD}, 1+i_t^{CL}, l_t^{PC} = \arg\max \mathbb{E}_t J_{t+1}^C. \tag{10.32}$$

Solving (10.32) subject to (10.30), taking the repayment probabilities as given, yields

$$i_t^{CD} = \left(1+\frac{1}{\eta_D}\right)^{-1}(1+i_t^{CR})-1, \tag{10.33}$$

$$i_t^{CL} = \frac{(1+i_t^{CR})}{(1+\eta_L^{-1})(1-\tau_t^{L,C})q_t^C}-1, \tag{10.34}$$

$$l_t^{CP} = \frac{q_t^{PC}(1+i_t^{CP})-(1+i_t^{CR})}{\gamma^C}, \tag{10.35}$$

where $\eta_D > 0$ and $\eta_L < 0$ are interest elasticities of the supply of deposits and the demand for loans, respectively. The first equation shows that, under monopoly, the deposit rate is a markup over the refinance rate. The second equation has the same interpretation as the solution obtained under a symmetric equilibrium in previous chapters. In addition, equation (10.35) indicates that the supply of loans to periphery banks is increasing in the expected return on these loans, as measured by $q_t^{PC}(1+i_t^{CP})$.

As formally established in chapters 3 and 4, the repayment probability on loans to local firms depends positively on the expected value of collateral relative to the volume of loans and the cyclical position of the economy:

$$q_t^C = \varphi_0^C\left(\frac{\kappa\mathbb{E}_t p_{t+1}^{CH}/\tilde{p}^{CH}}{l_t^{CK}/\tilde{l}^{CK}}\right)^{\varphi_1^C}\left(\frac{Y_t^C}{\tilde{Y}^C}\right)^{\varphi_2^C}, \tag{10.36}$$

where $\varphi_0^C, \varphi_1^C, \varphi_2^C > 0$, and $\tilde{Y}^C$ is the steady-state level of core final output.

Borrowing from the central bank is again determined residually from (10.30).

8. One way to view this assumption is to think of a multitude of global banks in the core region being able to collude to set interest rates domestically, but unable to do so with respect to setting the cost of borrowing for periphery banks.

Central bank and regulator

As assumed in previous chapters, the core central bank operates a standing facility. It supplies cash in quantity m_t^{Cs}. Its balance sheet is thus

$$l_t^{CB} = m_t^{Cs}. \tag{10.37}$$

The core policy rate is set on the basis of a Taylor rule, assuming a zero target inflation rate,

$$\frac{1+i_t^{CT}}{1+\tilde{\imath}^{CT}} = \left(\frac{1+i_{t-1}^{CT}}{1+\tilde{\imath}^{CT}}\right)^{\chi^C} \left\{(1+\pi_t^C)^{\varepsilon_1^C}\left(\frac{Y_t^C}{\tilde{Y}^C}\right)^{\varepsilon_2^C}\right\}^{1-\chi^C}, \tag{10.38}$$

where $\chi^C \in (0,1)$ and $\varepsilon_1^C, \varepsilon_2^C > 0$. Abstracting from the liability composition effect implies therefore that $i_t^{CR} = i_t^{CT}$.

The tax on loans is set by the regulator on the basis of changes in the credit growth rate,

$$\frac{1+\tau_t^{CL}}{1+\tilde{\tau}^{CL}} = \left(\frac{1+\tau_{t-1}^{CL}}{1+\tilde{\tau}^{CL}}\right)^{\chi_1} \left\{\left(\frac{l_t^{CK}}{l_{t-1}^{CK}}\right)^{\chi_2^C}\right\}^{1-\chi_1}, \tag{10.39}$$

where $\chi_1 \in (0,1)$ and $\chi_2^C > 0$. Thus, from (10.34) and (10.39), borrowing is more costly during episodes of credit booms and this in turn helps to mitigate risks to financial stability.[9]

Government

Income received by the central bank on borrowing by the global bank, $i_t^{CR} l_t^{CB}$, is transferred to the government. The core government budget constraint is thus given by

$$b_t^C = G_t - T_t + (1+i_{t-1}^{CB})\frac{b_{t-1}^C}{1+\pi_t^C} - i_{t-1}^{CR}\frac{l_{t-1}^{CB}}{1+\pi_t^C}, \tag{10.40}$$

where $b_t^C = b_t^{CC} + b_t^{PC}$ is the real stock of riskless one-period bonds held by core (b_t^{PC}) and periphery (b_t^{PC}) households and G_t is real expenditure on core final goods, which represents a fraction $\psi_G \in (0,1)$ of final output:

$$G_t = \psi_G Y_t^C. \tag{10.41}$$

9. As in chapter 5, the credit-to-output ratio could also be used.

The government in each region keeps its real stock of debt constant and balances its budget by adjusting lump-sum taxes.

10.2.2 Periphery

Households

Periphery households face a resource allocation problem similar to the one faced by core households, with the effective rate of return on core government bonds i_t^C defined as, symmetrically to (10.4),

$$1 + i_t^C = (1 + i_t^{CB})(1 - \theta_t^{PC})\mathbb{E}_t\left(\frac{E_{t+1}}{E_t}\right), \tag{10.42}$$

where θ_t^{PC} is the spread faced by periphery households, defined analogously to (10.5):

$$\theta_t^{PC} = \frac{\theta_0^B}{2} b_t^{PC}. \tag{10.43}$$

The solution is therefore similar to (10.6) through (10.11). In particular, periphery demand for core government bonds is given by

$$b_t^{PC} \simeq \frac{(1 + i_t^{CB})\mathbb{E}_t(E_{t+1}/E_t) - (1 + i_t^{PB})}{\theta_0^B(1 + i_t^{CB})\mathbb{E}_t(E_{t+1}/E_t)}. \tag{10.44}$$

Equations (10.11) and (10.44) imply therefore that uncovered interest parity, $1 + i_t^{PB} \simeq (1 + i_t^{CB})\mathbb{E}_t(E_{t+1}/E_t)$, obtains when $\theta_0^B \to 0$.

Commercial banks

The balance sheet of periphery bank $i \in (0, 1)$ is given by

$$l_t^{PK,i} = (1 - \mu)d_t^{P,i} + z_t l_t^{PC,i} + l_t^{PB,i} + V_t^{P,i}, \tag{10.45}$$

where $l_t^{PK,i}$ is loans to periphery CG producers; $d_t^{P,i}$ denotes deposits which are determined analogously to (10.9); $\mu \in (0, 1)$ is the required reserve ratio on these deposits; $z_t l_t^{PC,i}$ is borrowing from the global bank (with $l_t^{PC,i}$ measured in foreign-currency terms) at the rate $i_t^{CP,i}$; $V_t^{P,i} = 0.12 l_t^{PK,i}$ is bank capital; and $l_t^{PB,i}$ is borrowing from the periphery central bank. Thus, periphery banks are exposed to exchange rate risk; currency fluctuations generate balance sheet effects.

As in previous chapters, the market for deposits is competitive and a no-arbitrage condition holds between the deposit rate and the refinance rate:

$$i_t^{PD,i} = (1 - \mu)i_t^{PR}. \tag{10.46}$$

By contrast, monopolistic competition prevails in the loan market. The demand for loans to bank i, $l_t^{PK,i}$, is given by the downward-sloping curve

$$l_t^{PK,i} = \left(\frac{1+i_t^{PL,i}}{1+i_t^{PL}}\right)^{-\zeta^L} l_t^{PK}, \tag{10.47}$$

where $l_t^{PK} = [\int_0^1 (l_t^{PK,i})^{(\zeta^L-1)/\zeta^L} di]^{\zeta^L/(\zeta^L-1)}$ is the amount borrowed by the representative CG producer (equal to investment) with $\zeta^L > 1$ denoting the elasticity of substitution between differentiated loans, $i_t^{PL,i}$ is the rate on the loan extended by bank i, and $1+i_t^{PL} = [\int_0^1 (1+i_t^{PL,i})^{1-\zeta^L} di]^{1/(1-\zeta^L)}$ is the aggregate loan rate.

Expected profits of bank i at the end of period t are given by

$$\mathbb{E}_t J_{t+1}^{PB,i} = q_t^{P,i}(1+i_t^{PL,i})(1-\tau_t^{PL})l_t^{PK,i} + (1-q_t^{P,i})\left(\kappa^i p_{t+1}^{PH} H_t^P\right) \tag{10.48}$$

$$-(1+i_t^{PD,i})d_t^{P,i} + \mu d_t^{P,i} - (1+i_t^{PR})l_t^{PB,i} - q_t^{PC}(1+i_t^{CP})\mathbb{E}_t\left(\frac{E_{t+1}}{E_t}\right) z_t l_t^{PC,i}$$

$$-\gamma^P z_t \frac{(l_t^{PC,i})^2}{2} + \Omega_t^{P,i},$$

where i_t^{PR} is the marginal cost of borrowing from the central bank, $\tau_t^{PL} \in (0,1)$ the macroprudential tax rate, and $q_t^{P,i} \in (0,1)$ the repayment probability of periphery firms. As before, the first two terms represent expected income (net of taxes) from lending, the third interest paid on deposits, the fourth reserve requirements held at the central bank and returned to bank i at the end of the period, the fifth repayment on loans from the central bank, and the sixth term the expected repayment to the global bank (given limited liability). In addition, periphery banks incur a convex cost that increases with the amount of borrowing abroad, as measured by $0.5\gamma^P z_t(l_t^{PC,i})^2$, where $\gamma^P > 0$. The last term $\Omega_t^{P,i}$ represents the revenue of the loan tax, which again is transferred in lump-sum fashion to bank i.

Each bank maximizes profits with respect to their loan rate, in addition to choosing their demand for foreign loans $z_t l_t^{PC,i}$:

$$i_t^{PL,i}, z_t l_t^{PC,i} = \arg\max \mathbb{E}_t J_{t+1}^{B,i}. \tag{10.49}$$

Solving (10.49) subject to (10.45), (10.47), and (10.48) yields, in a symmetric equilibrium,

$$i_t^{PL} = \left(\frac{\zeta^L}{\zeta^L - 1}\right)\frac{(1+i_t^{PR})}{(1-\tau_t^{PL})q_t^P} - 1, \tag{10.50}$$

$$l_t^{PC} = \frac{1}{\gamma^P}\left\{(1+i_t^{PR}) - q_t^{PC}(1+i_t^{CP})\mathbb{E}_t\left(\frac{E_{t+1}}{E_t}\right)\right\}. \tag{10.51}$$

Equation (10.50) shows once again that a tighter macroprudential policy response raises the cost of loans, whereas equation (10.51) indicates that a higher cost of borrowing from the global bank reduces the demand for foreign loans—and vice versa for an increase in the cost of borrowing domestically. Borrowing from the central bank is determined, as before, residually from (10.45).

The repayment probability of firms depends as before positively on the expected value of collateral relative to the volume of loans and the cyclical position of the economy,

$$q_t^P = \varphi_0^P\left(\frac{\kappa\mathbb{E}_t p_{t+1}^{PH}/\tilde{p}^{PH}}{l_t^{PK}/\tilde{l}^{PK}}\right)^{\varphi_1^P}\left(\frac{Y_t^P}{\tilde{Y}^P}\right)^{\varphi_2^P}, \tag{10.52}$$

where $\varphi_0^P, \varphi_1^P, \varphi_2^P > 0$, Y_t^P is the periphery's final output and $\tilde{Y}^P$ its steady-state value.

Although the global bank cannot effectively secure collateral against its loans to periphery banks, the existence of a reputational cost may create an incentive to repay. Yet, the more banks borrow, the greater the incentive to default. Accordingly the repayment probability on core loans is assumed to be negatively related to the bank debt-to-output ratio of the periphery,

$$q_t^{PC} = q_0^{PC}\left(\frac{z_t l_t^{PC}/Y_t^P}{\tilde{z}\tilde{l}^{PC}/\tilde{Y}^P}\right)^{-\varphi_Q}, \tag{10.53}$$

where $\varphi_Q > 0$.

Central bank and regulator

The balance sheet of the periphery central bank is given by

$$z_t R_t^{Pcb} + b_t^{Pcb} + l_t^{PB} - nw_t = m_t^{Ps}, \tag{10.54}$$

where $z_t R_t^{cb}$ denotes international reserves (which for simplicity carry no interest), b_t^{Pcb} holdings of government bonds, l_t^{PB} borrowing from the central bank, nw_t the central bank's real net worth, and m_t^{Ps} the supply of cash.

Consistent with the evidence for MICs discussed in chapter 8, the periphery central bank intervenes in the foreign exchange market to mitigate currency fluctuations,[10]

10. For simplicity, the existence of a target level of reserves is ignored.

$$\frac{R_t^{Pcb}}{R_{t-1}^{Pcb}} = \left(\frac{\mathbb{E}_t E_{t+1}}{E_t}\right)^{-\varphi^R}, \tag{10.55}$$

where $\varphi^R \geq 0$ is the degree of exchange rate smoothing. Thus, as long as $\varphi^R > 0$, the central bank buys (sells) reserves to stabilize the exchange rate when it appreciates (depreciates).

Foreign exchange intervention is fully sterilized through open-market operations:

$$z_t \Delta R_t^{Pcb} + b_t^{Pcb} - \frac{b_{t-1}^{Pcb}}{1+\pi_t^P} = 0. \tag{10.56}$$

All income received by the central bank is transferred to the government; thus, changes in the *nominal* value of the central bank's net worth are given by capital gains associated with exchange rate depreciation ($\Delta NW_t = R_t^{Pcb} \Delta E_t$). Combining this result with (10.54) and (10.56) yields

$$m_t^{Ps} = \frac{m_{t-1}^{Ps}}{1+\pi_t^P} + l_t^{PB} - \frac{l_{t-1}^{PB}}{1+\pi_t^P}. \tag{10.57}$$

The periphery central bank also operates a standing facility. Its supply of liquidity to local banks is perfectly elastic at the rate i_t^{PR}, which is set through a Taylor rule similar to (10.38),

$$\frac{1+i_t^{PT}}{1+\tilde{\imath}^{PT}} = \left(\frac{1+i_{t-1}^{PT}}{1+\tilde{\imath}^{PT}}\right)^{\chi^P} \left\{(1+\pi_t^P)^{\varepsilon_1^P} \left(\frac{Y_t^P}{\tilde{Y}^P}\right)^{\varepsilon_2^P}\right\}^{1-\chi^P}, \tag{10.58}$$

where $\chi^P \in (0, 1)$ and $\varepsilon_1^P, \varepsilon_2^P > 0$. Again, in the absence of a liability composition effect, $i_t^{PT} = i_t^{PR}$.

The tax on loans is also set according to a rule similar to (10.39),

$$\frac{1+\tau_t^{PL}}{1+\tilde{\tau}^{PL}} = \left(\frac{1+\tau_{t-1}^{PL}}{1+\tilde{\tau}^{PL}}\right)^{\chi_1} \left\{\left(\frac{l_t^{PK}}{l_{t-1}^{PK}}\right)^{\chi_2^P}\right\}^{1-\chi_1}, \tag{10.59}$$

where $\chi_2^P > 0$.

The periphery government budget constraint takes the same form as (10.40), with now $b_t^P = b_t^{PP} + b_t^{CP} + b_t^{Pcb}$ and net interest payments of $(1+\pi_t^P)^{-1}[(1+i_{t-1}^{PB})(b_{t-1}^{PP} + b_{t-1}^{CP}) - i_{t-1}^{PR} l_{t-1}^{PB}]$.

The production structure and the main real and financial flows between agents and regions are summarized in figure 10.1.

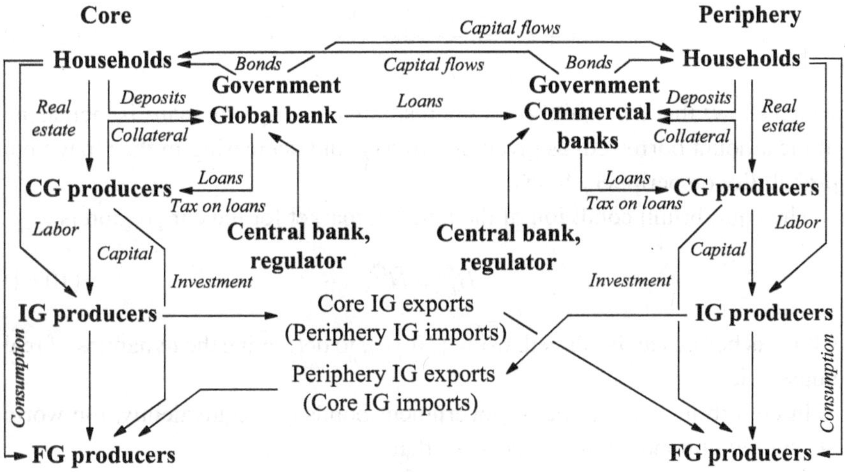

Figure 10.1
Structure of the core-periphery DSGE-FF model of the world economy
Source: Agénor and Pereira da Silva (2018*b*).

10.3 Equilibrium and Steady State

As in previous chapters, in a symmetric equilibrium all IG firms produce the same output and prices are the same across firms. Thus, the market-clearing conditions (10.26) and (10.27) for good j also imply that total output of core and periphery intermediate goods be equal to world demand for those goods:

$$Y_t^{CI} = Y_t^{CC} + Y_t^{CP}, \quad Y_t^{PI} = Y_t^{PP} + Y_t^{PC}. \tag{10.60}$$

Equilibrium in the market for final goods requires that output be equal to domestic absorption, inclusive of price adjustment costs,

$$Y_t^C = C_t + G_t + I_t^C + \frac{\phi_I}{2}\left(\frac{P_t^{CC}}{P_{t-1}^{CC}} - 1\right)^2 \left(\frac{P_t^{CC}}{P_t^C}\right) Y_t^{CI}, \tag{10.61}$$

and analogously for the periphery.

The equilibrium condition of the currency market in the core region is given by

$$m_t^C = m_t^{Cs}. \tag{10.62}$$

Equilibrium in the market for periphery loans requires equating (10.35) and (10.51)—that is, $l_t^{CP} = l_t^{PC}$, which can be solved for the equilibrium loan rate. Alternatively, equation (10.35) can be rewritten as

$$1+i_t^{CP}=\frac{(1+i_t^{CR})+\gamma^C l_t^{PC}}{q_t^{PC}}, \tag{10.63}$$

which shows that the equilibrium interest rate on periphery loans is increasing in the amount borrowed, as given by (10.51), and decreasing in the repayment probability on periphery loans.

The equilibrium condition of the housing market for the core region is

$$H_t^C=\bar{H}^C, \tag{10.64}$$

which as before can be solved, using (10.10), to determine the dynamics of real house prices.

In equilibrium, net trade in government bonds (or, equivalently, the world net supply of bonds) must be zero, so that

$$nb_t^{CC}+(1-n)b_t^{PC}=0, \quad (1-n)b_t^{PP}+nb_t^{CP}=0. \tag{10.65}$$

Analogously, in a two-region world, current account surpluses and deficits must be zero:

$$nCA_t^C+(1-n)E_t^{-1}CA_t^P=0, \tag{10.66}$$

with the core region's current account (in current local prices) defined in conventional manner as

$$\begin{aligned}CA_t^C=&P_t^{CC}Y_t^{CP}-P_t^{PC}Y_t^{PC}\\&+i_{t-1}^{CP}P_{t-1}^C l_{t-1}^{PC}+i_{t-1}^P E_{t-1}^{-1}P_{t-1}^P b_{t-1}^{CP}-i_{t-1}^C P_{t-1}^C b_{t-1}^{PC},\end{aligned} \tag{10.67}$$

where again P_t^{CC} is the price of core intermediate goods sold on the periphery market (that is, the price of core exports); Y_t^{CP} denotes core exports of intermediate goods, which correspond to the periphery's imports of these goods; $P_t^{PC}=E_t^{-1}P_t^{PP}$ is the price of periphery intermediate goods sold in the core region (equal to the price of periphery intermediate goods adjusted for the exchange rate); and Y_t^{PC} denotes core imports of intermediates, which correspond to the periphery's exports. The third term in (10.67) is the interest income from loans to the periphery by the global bank, and the fourth (fifth) term interest income (payment) on holdings of periphery (core) bonds by core (periphery) households. By definition, the current account is also given by (minus) the net change in foreign assets:[11]

11. Condition (10.67) also corresponds to the foreign exchange market equilibrium condition, which is solved for the exchange rate.

$$CA_t^C = (P_t^C l_t^{PC} - P_{t-1}^C l_{t-1}^{PC}) + (E_t^{-1} P_t^P b_t^{CP} - E_{t-1}^{-1} P_{t-1}^P b_{t-1}^{CP}) - (P_t^C b_t^{PC} - P_{t-1}^C b_{t-1}^{PC}). \tag{10.68}$$

The deterministic steady state of the model is described in the appendix to this chapter. Its key features are fundamentally similar to those described in chapter 8 for a small open economy.[12]

10.4 Parameterization

To assess its properties and evaluate the gains from coordination, the model is parameterized for two groups of countries, which represent the core and the periphery, respectively. The first group consists of *major advanced economies* (MAEs) and the second *systemically important middle-income countries* (SMICs). As defined in Agénor and Pereira da Silva (2018*a*), MAEs consist of the United States, the Euro area, and Japan, whereas SMICs consist of Brazil, China, India, Indonesia, Mexico, Russia, South Africa, and Turkey. These groups of countries represent those who have exerted and recorded the largest financial spillovers and spillbacks to each other in recent years. For SMICs, the benchmark parameterization uses for the most part the values used in previous chapters, whereas for MAEs a broader set of references, which includes the literature on two-country models discussed in Agénor and Pereira da Silva (2018*b*), is used.

The discount factor Λ is set at 0.98 for MAEs and 0.95 for SMICs, which gives a steady-state annualized real interest rate of about 2.1 percent in the first case and 5.3 percent in the second. The intertemporal elasticity of substitution is uniformly set at 0.5. The preference parameter for leisure, η_N, is set at 25, to ensure that in the steady state households in both regions devote about one-third of their time endowment to market activity. As in previous chapters, the Frisch elasticity of labor supply is set at 0.715 for both regions, implying that ψ_N is equal to 1.4.

The preference parameter for composite monetary assets, η_x, is set at the same low value as in previous chapters, 0.001. For the housing preference parameter, η_H, the same value as in Notarpietro and Siviero (2015), 0.1, is used. The share of currency in money holdings, ν, is set at 0.2 for MAEs and 0.35 for SMICs, to capture a more predominant use of cash in the latter group of countries. The parameter related to core (periphery) bond holdings

12. Once again subsidies are not available to correct the distortions created by monopolistic competition and financial frictions, implying therefore that the deterministic steady state is inefficient.

by core (periphery) households, θ_0^B, is set at 0.8, to capture imperfect capital mobility.

The distribution parameter between core and periphery intermediate goods in the production of the final good, Λ_I, is now set at 0.8 for MAEs and 0.6 for SMICs, to reflect the fact that the latter group is relatively more open than the former. The elasticity of substitution between baskets of domestic and imported composite intermediate goods, η, is set again at 1.5, which implies that these goods are substitutes in the production of the final good. The elasticities of substitution between core intermediate goods among themselves, θ^{CC}, and imported periphery goods among themselves, θ^{PP}, are both set equal to 6, as in the closed-economy case.

The share of capital in domestic output of intermediate goods, α, is set at the standard value 0.35. The adjustment cost parameter for prices of domestic intermediate goods, ϕ_I, is set at 74.5 for MAEs, to capture a relatively high degree of nominal price stickiness. This value is close to the average value initially estimated by Ireland (2001, table 3) and implies a Calvo-type probability of not adjusting prices—based on the formula discussed in chapter 4—of approximately 0.71 percent per period, or equivalently an average period of price fixity of about 3.5 quarters. These figures are consistent with the point estimates of Quint and Rabanal (2014, table 2) and Christoffel and Schabert (2015, table 2) for the Euro area. They are also in the range of values estimated by Gerali et al. (2010) and Darracq Pariès et al. (2011). For SMICs, the lower value $\phi_I = 25$ is used, as before. The capital depreciation rate, δ_K, is set at a quarterly rate of 0.025 for both regions. The adjustment cost incurred by the CG producer for transforming investment into capital, Θ_K, is set at 14 for both regions, in order to match once again the fact that the standard deviation of the cyclical component of investment is three to four times more volatile as output.

Regarding the global bank and the periphery banks, the parameter that determines the effective collateral-loan ratio, κ, is set at 0.4 for MAEs and at 0.2 for SMICs, to capture the relatively higher costs associated with debt enforcement procedures in the latter group of countries, as discussed in chapter 4. The elasticities η_D and η_L for the core region are set at 1.5 and −4.2, as in Dib (2010*a*), for instance, whereas the elasticity ς^L is set at the same value as in previous chapters, 4.5. For both regions, the elasticity of the repayment probability with respect to the effective collateral-loan ratio is set initially at $\varphi_1^C = 0.05$ for MAEs and $\varphi_1^P = 0.1$ for SMICs, whereas the elasticity with respect to cyclical output is set at $\varphi_2^C = 0.1$ for the core and $\varphi_2^P = 0.2$ for the periphery. The cost parameters γ^C and γ^P are set at 0.05 and 0.1, respectively. The parameter φ_Q, which measures the sensitivity of the repayment probability to the bank debt-to-output ratio, is set at 0.3.

The required reserve ratio in the periphery, μ, is set at 0.2, as in previous chapters. The degree of persistence in the core central bank's policy response, χ, is set at 0.7, whereas the responses of the base policy rate to inflation and output deviations, ε_1 and ε_2, are set at 1.7 and 0.1, respectively, as in Coenen et al. (2009). For the periphery central bank, the corresponding estimates are $\chi = 0.8$, $\varepsilon_1 = 2.0$, and $\varepsilon_2 = 0.5$, respectively, again as in previous chapters. The exchange rate is assumed to be fully flexible, so $\varphi^R = 0$. Finally, the share of noninterest government spending in final output, ψ_G, is set at 0.2 for MAEs, as in Coenen et al. (2009) and Alpanda and Aysun (2014), for instance, and 0.22 for SMICs, as before.

Parameter values are summarized in table 10.1, whereas initial steady-state values for some key variables are shown in table 10.2. In particular, they indicate that the shares of consumption and investment for both regions are in line with previous parameterizations, and that loans from the global bank to periphery banks are relatively large in proportion of the region's output.

10.5 Asymmetric Credit Spread Shocks

To characterize the properties of the model in terms of the cross-border transmission of financial disturbances, region-specific credit spread shocks under no activism ($\chi_2^C = \chi_2^P = 0$) are considered. To do so, as in previous chapters, a multiplicative markup shock—or, equivalently, a shock to the elasticity of substitution across loan varieties—is introduced in the loan rate equations (10.34) and (10.50), ϵ_t^{jL}, and is assumed to follow a first-order autoregressive process of the form $\epsilon_t^{j,L} = (\epsilon_{t-1}^{j,L})^{\rho^{j,L}} \exp(\xi_t^{j,L})$, where $\rho^{j,L} \in (0, 1)$ and $\xi_t^{j,L} \sim \mathbf{N}(0, \sigma_{\xi^{j,L}})$, with $j = C, P$. The autocorrelation coefficients ρ^j are both set at the same value as before, 0.8.

Figure 10.2 shows the results for a 1 percentage point negative shock to the loan rate in the core region, with both endogenous and exogenous global lending. In either case, the direct impact of the shock is a reduction in the loan rate and an increase in investment in that region. The resulting expansion in aggregate demand translates into higher marginal production costs and inflation. In response to the increase in cyclical output and higher inflation the central bank raises its base policy rate, which leads to a higher deposit rate and a shift toward deposits. To induce a reduction in the demand for cash, its opportunity cost, the nominal bond rate, must increase. In the benchmark calibration this increase dominates the rise in (one-period ahead) inflation so that the (expected) real bond rate increases, thereby inducing core households to reduce current consumption through intertemporal substitution. Gross complementarity between consumption and leisure implies that labor supply increases, but because labor

Table 10.1
Benchmark Parameterization, Two-Region World Economy

Parameter	Description	MAEs	SMICs
Households			
Λ	Discount factor	0.98	0.95
ς	Elasticity of intertemporal substitution	0.5	0.5
η_N	Preference parameter for leisure	25.0	25.0
ψ_N	Inverse of Frisch elasticity of labor supply	1.4	1.4
η_x	Preference parameter for money holdings	0.001	0.001
η_H	Preference parameter for housing	0.1	0.1
ν	Share parameter in index of money holdings	0.2	0.35
θ_0^B	Sensitivity of premium, household holdings of foreign bonds	0.8	0.8
Producers			
Λ_I	Share of own-region IG goods in final output	0.6	0.8
η	Elasticity of substitution, baskets of intermediate goods	1.5	1.5
θ^{CC}, θ^{PP}	Elasticity of own-region demand, intermediate goods	6.0	6.0
α	Share of capital, intermediate goods production	0.35	0.35
ϕ_I	Adjustment cost parameter, intermediate goods prices	74.5	25
δ_K	Depreciation rate of capital	0.025	0.025
Θ_K	Adjustment cost parameter, investment	14	14
Banks			
κ	Effective collateral-loan ratio	0.4	0.2
φ_1^C, φ_1^P	Elasticity of repayment probability, collateral	0.05	0.05
φ_2^C, φ_2^P	Elasticity of repayment probability, cyclical output	0.1	0.4
η_D	Elasticity of deposit supply by households	1.5	—
η_L, ζ^L	Elasticity of substitution, loan demand by CG producers	−4.2	4.5
γ^C	Cost parameter, loan supply by global bank	0.1	—
γ^P	Cost parameter, demand for global bank loans	—	0.1
φ_Q	Sensitivity of repayment probability, global bank loans	—	0.3
Central bank			
μ	Required reserve ratio	—	0.2
χ	Degree of interest rate smoothing	0.7	0.8
ε_1	Response of policy rate to inflation deviations	1.7	2.0
ε_2	Response of policy rate to cyclical output	0.1	0.4
φ^R	Degree of exchange rate smoothing	—	0.0
χ_1	Persistence parameter, tax on loans rule	0.8	0.8
Government			
ψ_G	Share of government spending in final output	0.2	0.22
Shocks			
ρ^L	Persistence parameter, credit spread shock	0.8	0.8

Table 10.2
Initial Steady-State Values: Key Variables
(In proportion of each region's output, or in percent; $j = C, P$)

Variable	Description	MAEs	SMICs
C^j	Private consumption	0.65	0.65
I^j, l^{jF}	Investment, loans to CG producers	0.15	0.13
r^{jK}	Rental rate of capital	0.046	0.081
l^{PC}	Loans from global bank to periphery banks	0.161	—
q^{jF}	Repayment probability, loans to CG producers	0.96	0.936
q^{PC}	Repayment prob., global bank loans to periphery banks	0.96	—
i^{jB}, i^{jR}	Government bond rate and refinance rate	0.020	0.053
i^{jD}	Bank deposit rate	0.015	0.042
i^{jL}	Loan rate, investment loans to CG producers	0.046	0.095
i^{CP}	Loan rate, global bank loans to periphery banks	0.08	—
τ^{jL}	Countercyclical tax rate on loans to CG producers	0.0	0.0
R^{Pcb}	Official reserves, periphery central bank	—	0.038

demand rises relatively more, wages tend to increase as well, thereby raising further marginal costs and inflation. The increase in the bond rate and the drop in current consumption also combine to reduce the demand for housing, which in turn translates into a fall in house prices—and thus a reduction in collateral values, which is large enough to induce a reduction in the repayment probability, despite the positive effect associated with the increase in cyclical output. This drop in the repayment probability mitigates somewhat the initial fall in the loan rate and the increase in investment.

The increase in the bond rate in the core region induces a drop in the demand for periphery bonds by core-region households, whereas the demand for core bonds by periphery-region households rises. At the same time, the increase in the marginal cost of borrowing from the core central bank induces the global bank to cut lending to periphery banks. From the perspective of the periphery, the net effect is thus a capital outflow and an initial depreciation of the nominal and real exchange rates. On the one hand, this makes imported intermediate goods from the core more expensive; on the other, it makes exports from the periphery cheaper. The result is a current account surplus for the periphery and a deficit for the core.

In addition, the increase in the domestic-currency price of imported inputs associated with the exchange rate depreciation translates into higher inflation in the periphery, which leads to an increase in the policy rate there as well. As a result, however, the loan rate increases now, and consequently investment falls in that region. At the same time, the increase in (expected) inflation is now larger than the increase in the nominal bond rate—which occurs through

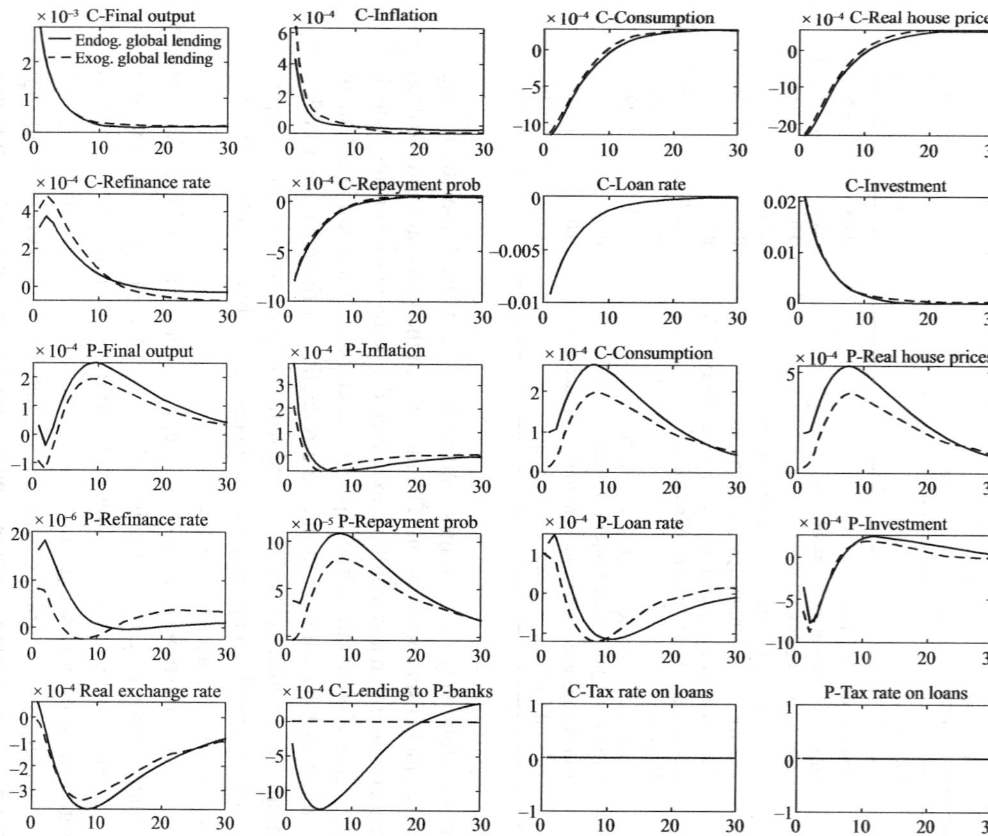

Figure 10.2 Negative credit spread shock: core region. *Note*: The responses of consumption, investment, output, real house prices, the real exchange rate, and core lending to periphery banks are expressed as percent deviations from their steady-state values. The responses of the lending rate, the refinance rate, the expected real bond rate, the repayment probability, and the inflation rate are absolute deviations (or percentage points) from their steady-state values.

the same mechanism described earlier, related to the shift away from cash and toward deposits—implying this time a fall in the real bond rate, which weakens incentives to save and induces households to spend more today. This tends to increase housing demand and real house prices which, through higher collateral values and a higher repayment probability, tends to mitigate the rise in the loan rate and the drop in investment. The net effect on aggregate demand is muted on impact but positive over time.

Figure 10.3 shows the results for a 1 percentage point negative credit spread shock in the periphery. The results are largely symmetric to those described earlier: The expansion in investment and output occurs initially in the periphery but is transmitted through an inflow of capital and a real appreciation of the periphery's currency (a depreciation for the core) to the core region. Inflation in the core region increases, inducing the central bank to raise the base policy rate; this, in turn, leads to a higher loan rate and a contraction in investment. The expected real bond rate rises as well, inducing households to reduce consumption today. Aggregate demand in the core region unambiguously falls. This time, lending by the global bank (after a short-lived dip) increases and serves in part to finance the investment boom that occurs in the periphery. The positive correlation between the policy rate in the periphery and borrowing by periphery banks is consistent with the empirical evidence provided by Avdjiev et al. (2018) on lending in global funding currencies.

A comparison of the cases where lending by the global bank is endogenous and exogenous (also shown as dotted lines in figures 10.2 and 10.3) suggests that for both types of shocks the effects described earlier are broadly similar qualitatively; however, they are significantly amplified when periphery banks borrow from the core region. This illustrates well the role of cross-border bank borrowing in the international transmission of shocks—a phenomenon that has been well documented in recent years, as noted earlier.

10.6 Gains from Coordination

In the absence of international coordination, each region's regulator determines its macroprudential policy instrument taking as given the reaction function of the other regulator. In doing so, each regulator $j = C, P$ seeks to maximize its own country's welfare only, adjusted (as discussed in chapter 5) for the cost of instrument manipulation,[13]

$$W_t^j = \mathbb{E}_t \sum_{s=0}^{\infty} \Lambda^s u(C_{t+s}, N_{t+s}) - \varkappa_R^j \mathbb{E}_t \sum_{s=0}^{\infty} \Lambda^s (\tau_{t+s}^{jL} - \tau_{t+s-1}^{jL})^2, \qquad (10.69)$$

13. As before, regulators discount the future at the same rate as households.

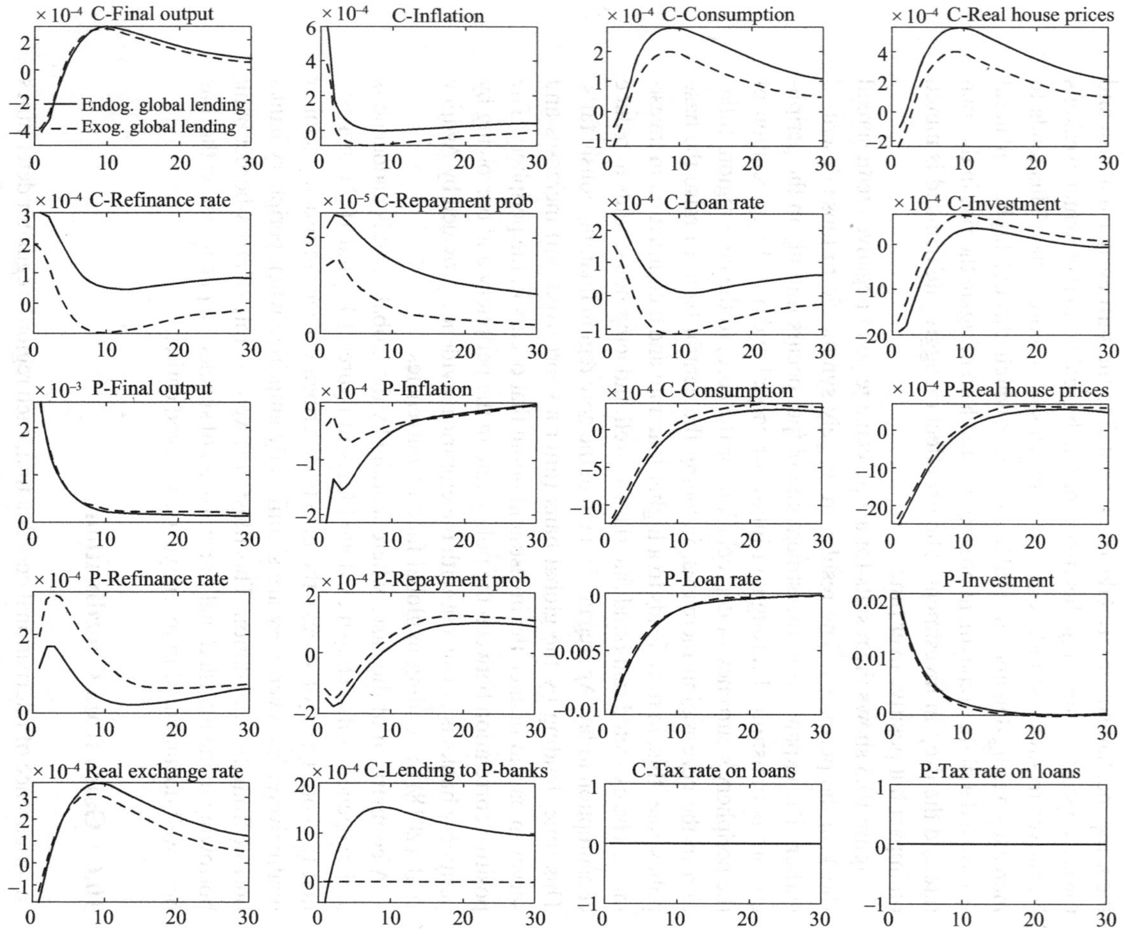

Figure 10.3 Negative credit spread shock: periphery region. *Note*: See note to figure 10.2.

where $\varkappa_R^j \geq 0$ and $u()$ is the truncated period utility function given by

$$u(C_t, N_t) \simeq \frac{C_t^{1-\varsigma^{-1}}}{1-\varsigma^{-1}} - \frac{\eta_N}{1+\psi_N} N_t^{1+\psi_N}.$$

Thus, under independent policies, the regulator in each region solves for the optimal value of the response parameter χ_2^j in the rules (10.39) and (10.59), denoted $\chi_2^{j,N}$, taking into account the reaction function of the other regulator:

$$\chi_2^{C,N} = \arg\max W_t^C|_{\chi_2^P = \chi_2^{P,N}}, \quad \chi_2^{P,N} = \arg\max W_t^P|_{\chi_2^C = \chi_2^{C,N}}. \tag{10.70}$$

In contrast, under coordination, regulators—or a benevolent global entity working on their behalf—jointly determine the optimal response parameters, denoted $\chi_2^{C,O}$ and $\chi_2^{P,O}$, so as to maximize a weighted sum of each region's welfare:

$$\chi_2^{C,O}, \chi_2^{P,O} = \arg\max[nW_t^C + (1-n)W_t^P], \tag{10.71}$$

where the persistence parameter χ_1 in (10.39) and (10.59) is assumed to remain the same under both regimes. Thus, a positive welfare gain for each region taken individually in the coordination regime relative to noncooperation is a sufficient, but not necessary, condition to generate a net gain for the world as a whole; this also depends on the magnitude of the relative gain (or loss) for each region and the relative weight of each of them, as measured by n, in the common welfare function.

As in previous chapters, policies are computed under commitment—that is, under the assumption that regulators (individually and jointly) can deliver on past promises regardless of what the situation is today. Thus, under noncooperation the model is solved for the closed-loop or feedback equilibrium. Given the predetermined nature of the feedback rules (10.39) and (10.59), each regulator has full knowledge of the other regulator's reaction function; the best responses reflect therefore this knowledge.[14]

As also discussed in chapter 5, welfare gains are evaluated in terms of compensating variations in consumption. Abstracting from the cost of instrument manipulation (so that $\varkappa_R^j = 0$), the welfare gain at the level of each region is

14. Coenen et al. (2009), Banerjee et al. (2016), and Agénor et al. (2018*c*) solve instead for the open-loop (Ramsey) optimal policy with commitment. In such conditions, each regulator chooses an instrument *path* at the beginning of time—as opposed to a *reaction function* under a closed-loop equilibrium—taking as given the whole future path of the other regulator's instrument. This is also considered later on.

thus obtained by solving for β^i, the fraction of the (expected) consumption stream that would make households equally well off in each period, under noncooperation as under cooperation:

$$\mathbb{E}_t \sum_{s=0}^{\infty} \Lambda^s W[(1+\beta^j)C_{t+s}^{j,N}, N_{t+s}^{j,N}] = \mathbb{E}_t \sum_{s=0}^{\infty} \Lambda^s W(C_{t+s}^{j,O}, N_{t+s}^{j,O}), \tag{10.72}$$

where $\{C_{t+s}^{j,N}\}_{s=0}^{\infty}$ and $\{N_{t+s}^{j,N}\}_{s=0}^{\infty}$ are solution paths under the Nash equilibrium, based once again on the maximized value of each region's welfare (that is, at the optimal own response parameter $\chi_2^{j,N}$) and $\{C_{t+s}^{j,O}\}_{s=0}^{\infty}$ and $\{N_{t+s}^{j,O}\}_{s=0}^{\infty}$ solution paths under coordination, based on the maximization of the weighted sum of each region's welfare. Thus, a positive value of β^j indicates that households in region *i* prefer the coordination regime—they would need additional consumption under noncooperation to be indifferent between the two regimes.

Similarly, the welfare gain for the world as a whole is calculated by solving for β in the expression

$$\mathbb{E}_t \sum_{s=0}^{\infty} \Lambda^s \left\{nW^C[(1+\beta)C_{t+s}^{C,N}, N_{t+s}^{C,N}] + (1-n)W^P[(1+\beta)C_{t+s}^{P,N}, N_{t+s}^{P,N}]\right\} \tag{10.73}$$

$$= \mathbb{E}_t \sum_{s=0}^{\infty} \Lambda^s \left\{nW^C(C_{t+s}^{C,O}, N_{t+s}^{C,O}) + (1-n)W^P(C_{t+s}^{P,O}, N_{t+s}^{P,O})\right\},$$

where again $\beta > 0$ indicates a welfare gain under coordination. Similar expressions hold when $\varkappa_R^j > 0$. As noted in the appendix to this chapter, and consistent with the discussion in chapter 5, (10.72) and (10.73) are evaluated using second-order approximations to both the household's (truncated) period utility function and the model, conditional on the initial steady state being the deterministic steady state.

Table 10.3 show the results for the asymmetric core and periphery shocks discussed earlier, for the benchmark set of parameters. The relative weight of each region in the joint welfare function is set at $n = 0.5$, to capture the case where although their economic weight may differ, equality prevails when it comes to evaluating the benefits of coordination.[15] The cost parameters $\varkappa_R^j$ are set at the same values as in previous chapters, 0.1 and 0.4, and so is the degree of persistence in the individual region and common countercyclical regulatory

15. Agénor and Pereira da Silva (2018*b*) considered the case where weights in the common welfare function are based on economic strength.

Table 10.3
Credit Spread Shock: Optimal Policy Responses and Gains from Coordination
Benchmark Parameters, $\varkappa_R = 0.1$ and $\varkappa_R = 0.4$[a]

	C-Shock	P-Shock	J-Shock
		$\varkappa_R = 0.1$	
Endogenous Lending by the Global Bank			
Nash: Optimal $\chi_2^{C,N}, \chi_2^{P,N}$	1.03, 0.40	0.11, 0.97	1.10, 1.00
Coord.: Optimal $\chi_2^{C,O}, \chi_2^{P,O}$	1.19, 0.00	0.00, 1.11	1.20, 1.20
Compensating variation			
Core	−0.0065	0.1134	0.0162
Periphery	0.0968	−0.0061	0.0014
World	0.0096	0.0077	0.0090
Exogenous Lending by the Global Bank			
Nash: Optimal $\chi_2^{C,N}, \chi_2^{P,N}$	1.02, 0.06	0.00, 1.03	1.00, 1.10
Coord.: Optimal $\chi_2^{C,O}, \chi_2^{P,O}$	1.11, 0.00	0.00, 1.09	1.20, 1.20
Compensating variation			
Core	−0.0031	0.0431	−0.0024
Periphery	0.0543	−0.0012	0.0126
World	0.0032	0.0012	0.0054
		$\varkappa_R = 0.4$	
Endogenous Lending by the Global Bank			
Nash: Optimal $\chi_2^{C,N}, \chi_2^{P,N}$	0.41, 0.44	0.28, 0.39	0.40, 0.50
Coord.: Optimal $\chi_2^{C,O}, \chi_2^{P,O}$	0.46, 0.00	0.16, 0.45	0.50, 0.50
Compensating variation			
Core	−0.0003	0.0806	−0.0046
Periphery	0.0338	−0.0063	0.0173
World	0.0051	0.0058	0.0061
Exogenous Lending by the Global Bank			
Nash: Optimal $\chi_2^{C,N}, \chi_2^{P,N}$	0.40, 0.09	0.00, 0.39	0.40, 0.40
Coord.: Optimal $\chi_2^{C,O}, \chi_2^{P,O}$	0.43, 0.00	0.00, 0.41	0.40, 0.50
Compensating variation			
Core	−0.0004	0.0201	0.0082
Periphery	0.0232	−0.0005	−0.0017
World	0.0022	0.0008	0.0031

Note: a. C-shock (P-shock) refers to the credit spread shock in the core (periphery) region, and J-shock to the credit spread shock occurring in both regions. Compensating variations are calculated using the formulas provided in the appendix to this chapter.

policy rules, χ_1, which is set at 0.8.[16] For both response parameters, χ_2^C and χ_2^P in (10.39) and (10.59), the grid search is again conducted at two decimal points and a step of 0.01. Compensatory variations with adjustment for the cost of changes in policy instruments are reported for both individual regions and the world. In addition, figures 10.4 and 10.5 show relative welfare levels (normalized by the level of welfare when there is no countercyclical response (that is, when $\chi_2^C = \chi_2^P = 0$) for both regions and the world, for the core and periphery shocks, respectively. The value of (relative) welfare at the Nash and cooperative solutions in these figures can therefore be interpreted as the gain from activism. Finally, table 10.4 shows the asymptotic standard deviations of a range of macroeconomic variables under the three policy regimes—no activism, Nash, and coordination—for both types of shocks. In tables 10.3 and 10.4, the results for the joint shock (credit spread shocks of the same magnitude occurring simultaneously in the two regions) are also shown for comparative purposes.

The results show first that, as in chapter 6, welfare has an inverted U-shape form, both under Nash and under coordination. Initially, as countercyclical regulatory policy is implemented, volatility falls at first, because it stabilizes credit, interest rates, aggregate demand, and employment. As a result, welfare increases. However, as the policy becomes more aggressive, its cost increases as well—so much so that it eventually dominates the initial gains, entailing therefore a marginal reduction in welfare. Thus, there exists an optimal value for the response parameters χ_2^j to credit growth, both under Nash and under coordination, whose magnitude varies inversely with the cost parameter $\varkappa_R$.

Second, when the instrument manipulation cost is relatively low ($\varkappa_R = 0.1$), it is optimal under the Nash equilibrium for both regulators to react, but under coordination it is optimal to react only for the regulator in the region where the shock originates. Moreover, under coordination, the regulator reacts more aggressively in the region where the shock occurs. Intuitively, under coordination regulators internalize the effects of credit fluctuations (occurring through spillovers and spillbacks) in both regions by pursuing a more aggressive policy, and this generates a superior outcome for the world as a whole. Thus, coordination does not involve *burden sharing*, a situation where the region where the shock occurs (say, the core) reacts less, whereas the other (say, the periphery) reacts more, or *burden deepening*, which involves (as noted in chapter 5) *both* policymakers reacting more than under Nash. In fact, it involves *free riding* by the periphery regulator. When the cost of adjusting policy instruments

16. As noted in chapter 5, a corner solution is obtained when there is no instrument adjustment cost ($\varkappa_R^C = \varkappa_R^P = 0$); full stabilization of the credit-to-output ratio is optimal.

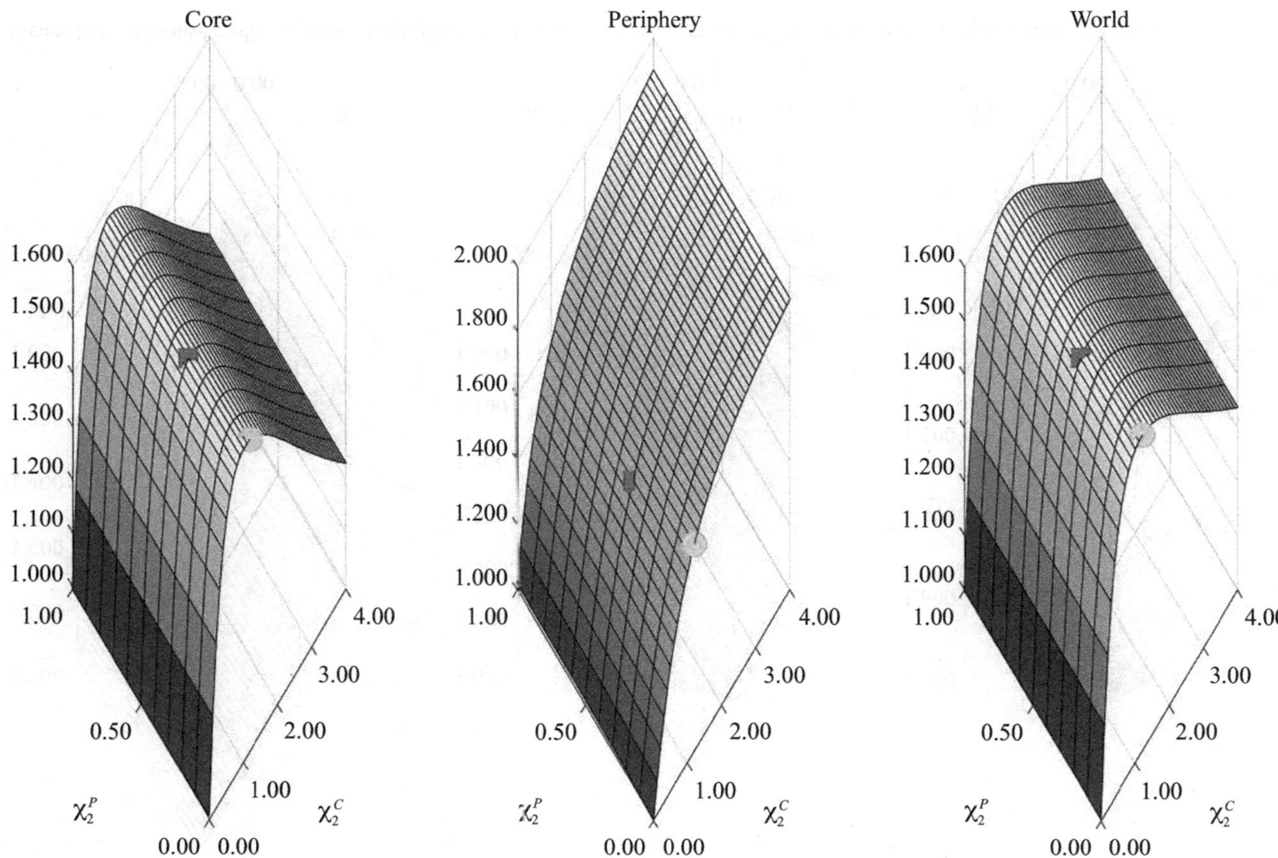

Figure 10.4 Negative credit spread shock, core region: normalized welfare and optimal policy response. *Note*: The square corresponds to the Nash equilibrium and the circle to the equilibrium under coordination.

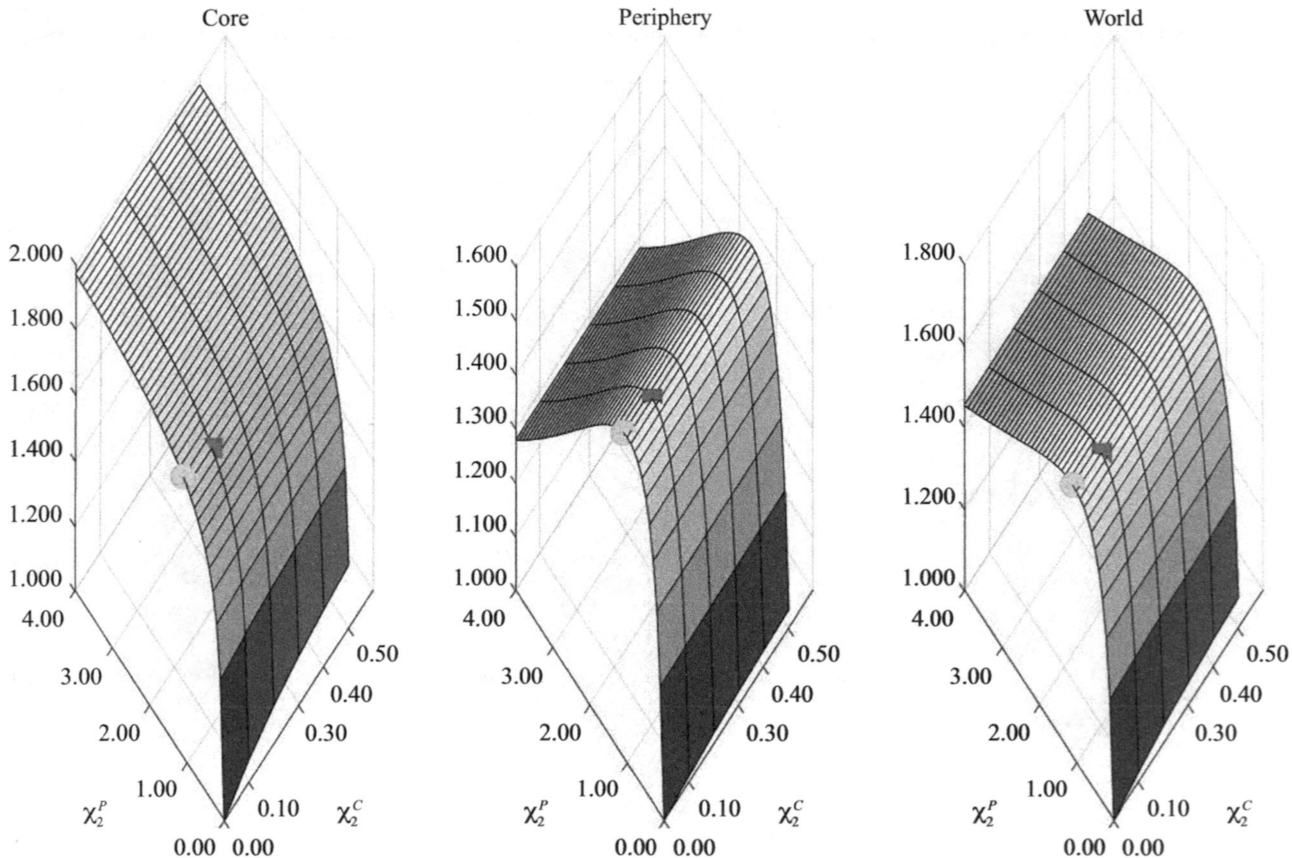

Figure 10.5 Negative credit spread shock, periphery region: normalized welfare and optimal policy response. *Note*: See note to figure 10.4.

Table 10.4
Asymptotic Standard Deviations of Key Variables under Alternative Policy Regimes, Endogenous Core Lending to Periphery Banks
Benchmark Parameters, $\varkappa_R = 0.4^a$

	No Activism		Nash Equilibrium		Coordination	
	C-Shock	P-Shock	C-Shock	P-Shock	C-Shock	P-Shock
			Core			
Final output	0.0042	0.0019	0.0035	0.0009	0.0034	0.0009
Employment	0.0012	0.0006	0.0010	0.0004	0.0010	0.0004
Consumption	0.0017	0.0011	0.0011	0.0005	0.0011	0.0005
Investment	0.0045	0.0006	0.0036	0.0003	0.0035	0.0003
Inflation	0.0005	0.0008	0.0004	0.0005	0.0004	0.0005
Refinance rate	0.0008	0.0009	0.0006	0.0006	0.0006	0.0005
Loan rate	0.0154	0.0009	0.0114	0.0003	0.0111	0.0003
Real house prices	0.0022	0.0014	0.0015	0.0007	0.0014	0.0007
Repayment probability	0.0013	0.0002	0.0009	0.0001	0.0009	0.0001
Loan-to-output ratio	0.0039	0.0004	0.0031	0.0003	0.0030	0.0003
Tax rate on loans	—	—	0.0049	0.0003	0.0054	0.0002
			Periphery			
Final output	0.0008	0.0034	0.0007	0.0029	0.0006	0.0028
Employment	0.0006	0.0011	0.0006	0.0008	0.0006	0.0008
Consumption	0.0006	0.0017	0.0004	0.0011	0.0004	0.0010
Investment	0.0002	0.0040	0.0001	0.0031	0.0001	0.0030
Inflation	0.0005	0.0004	0.0004	0.0003	0.0004	0.0003
Refinance rate	0.0003	0.0006	0.0003	0.0005	0.0002	0.0005
Loan rate	0.0004	0.0175	0.0004	0.0132	0.0003	0.0127
Real house prices	0.0003	0.0009	0.0002	0.0006	0.0002	0.0005
Repayment probability	0.0004	0.0007	0.0003	0.0004	0.0003	0.0004
Loan-to-output ratio	0.0002	0.0036	0.0001	0.0028	0.0001	0.0027
Tax rate on loans	—	—	0.0002	0.0049	0.0000	0.0054

Note: a. No Activism corresponds to no countercyclical policies. C-Shock (P-Shock) refers to a negative credit spread shock in the core (periphery) region.

is relatively high ($\varkappa_R = 0.4$), in the case of the periphery shock, coordination does involve *burden sharing* compared to what occurs when $\varkappa_R = 0.1$. In the case of a joint shock, as can be expected, coordination involves both regulators reacting (regardless of the instrument manipulation cost) and they do so more aggressively than under the Nash equilibrium. Coordination therefore involves *burden deepening*.

Third, the more aggressive response under coordination by the region where the shock originates means also that the cost of instrument manipulation is higher—so much so that, in fact, the country where the shock originates is worse off. This result holds regardless of the value of the cost parameter $\varkappa_R$, and independently of whether lending by global banks is endogenous or exogenous.

The gains from coordination are thus asymmetric. Put differently, policy coordination is not Pareto-improving—at least, in this setting, with respect to credit spread shocks. To the extent that these shocks are representative of those that tend to occur in practice, the results suggest that getting countries to engage in, and abide by, a formal arrangement to cooperate in setting countercyclical macroprudential policy instruments may be challenging.

Fourth, the results indicate that the gains from coordination, although positive, are not large—regardless of the value of the cost parameter $\varkappa_R$. For instance, with endogenous lending by global banks, the gain for the world economy is of the order of 0.96 percent when the shock originates in the core and $\varkappa_R = 0.1$, and 0.51 percent when $\varkappa_R = 0.4$. Put differently, a household with an annual consumption stream of \$50,000 would need to receive compensation of only \$480 or \$255 to be indifferent between cooperation and noncooperation. This gain is about \$385 or \$290 when the shock originates in the periphery. *Prima facie,* these relatively small gains create concerns regarding the ability to provide incentives for countries to join and remain voluntarily in a cooperative agreement. At the same time, however, it is important to keep in mind that in the real world, there could be a variety of financial shocks occurring simultaneously; the gain from coordination could be larger as a result.

Fifth, the results displayed in table 10.4 show that, regardless of the origin of the shock, the reduction in volatility is substantial between the last two regimes and the first (no countercyclical regulation). At the same time, for most variables there are no discernible differences between outcomes under Nash and under coordination. These results are broadly consistent with those reported in table 10.3, and discussed earlier, regarding the small welfare gain associated with coordination in response to a credit spread shock—regardless of where the shock originates.

10.7 Comparison with the Ramsey Policy

As in previous chapters, results with the simple countercyclical regulatory rule can be compared with those obtained with the Ramsey optimal policy to assess how well it performs. To do so, once again the numerical procedure proposed by Bodenstein et al. (2019) is used, assuming a common instrument cost parameter $\varkappa_R = 0.4$.

The impulse response functions corresponding to a credit spread shock are shown in figures 10.6 and 10.7 under no activism, coordination, and the Ramsey policy being implemented in both regions. Regardless of where the shock emanates, the policy response under the Ramsey policy is significantly more active. As a result, the path of most variables is in general much smoother in

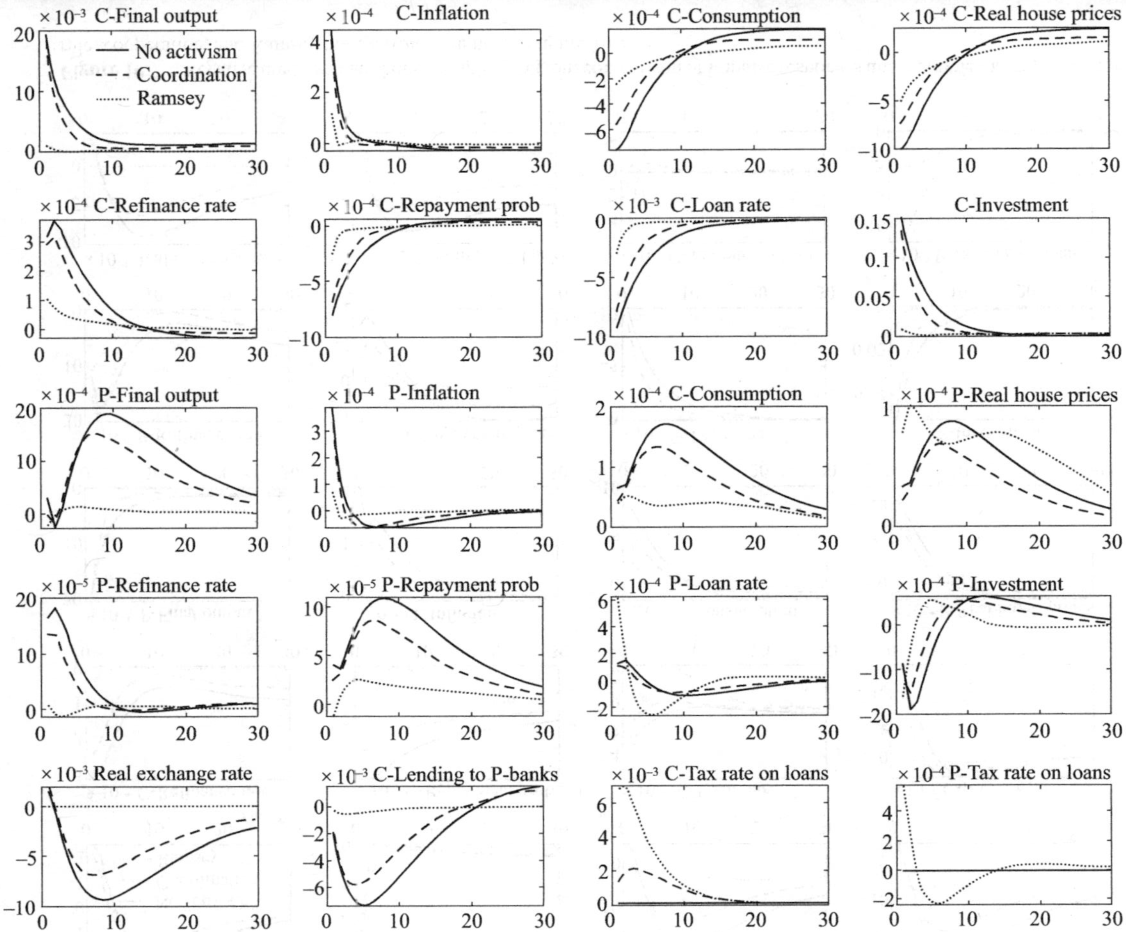

Figure 10.6 Negative credit spread shock, core region: comparison of impulse responses under simple macroprudential rule, cooperation, and Ramsey policy. *Note*: See note to figure 10.2.

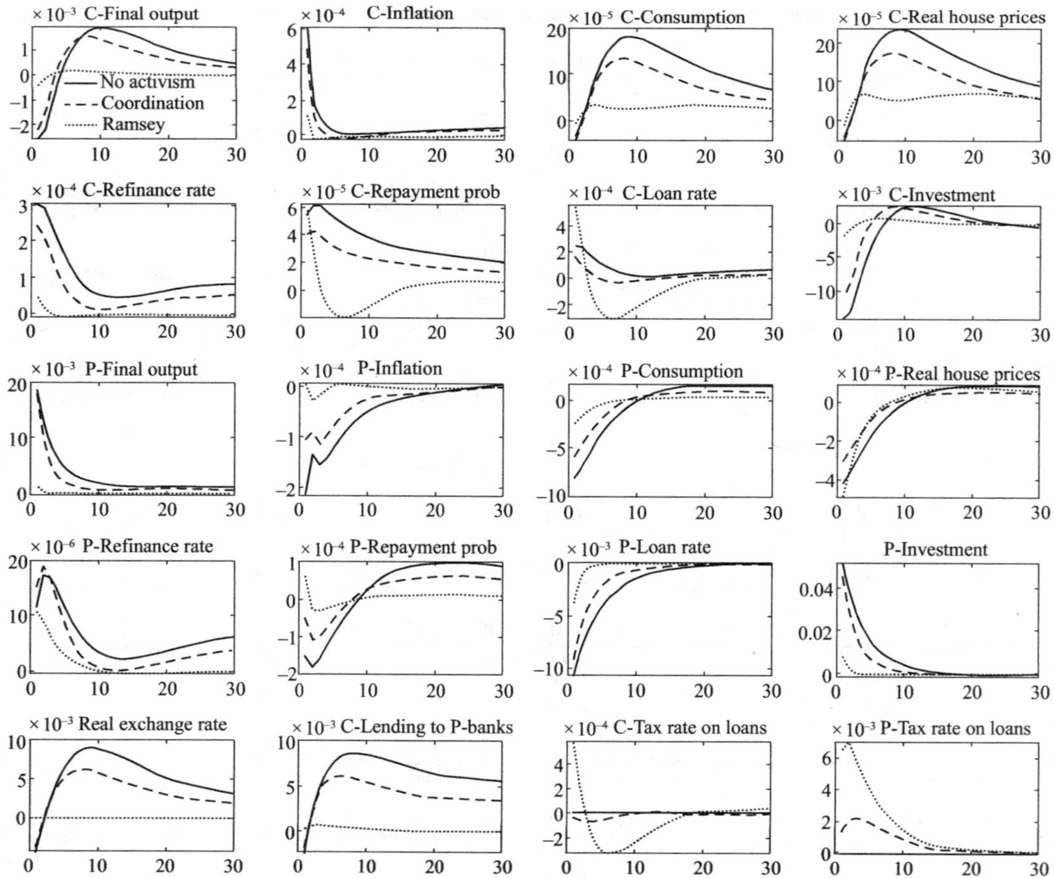

Figure 10.7 Negative credit spread shock, periphery region: comparison of impulse responses under simple macroprudential rule, cooperation, and Ramsey policy. *Note*: See note to figure 10.2.

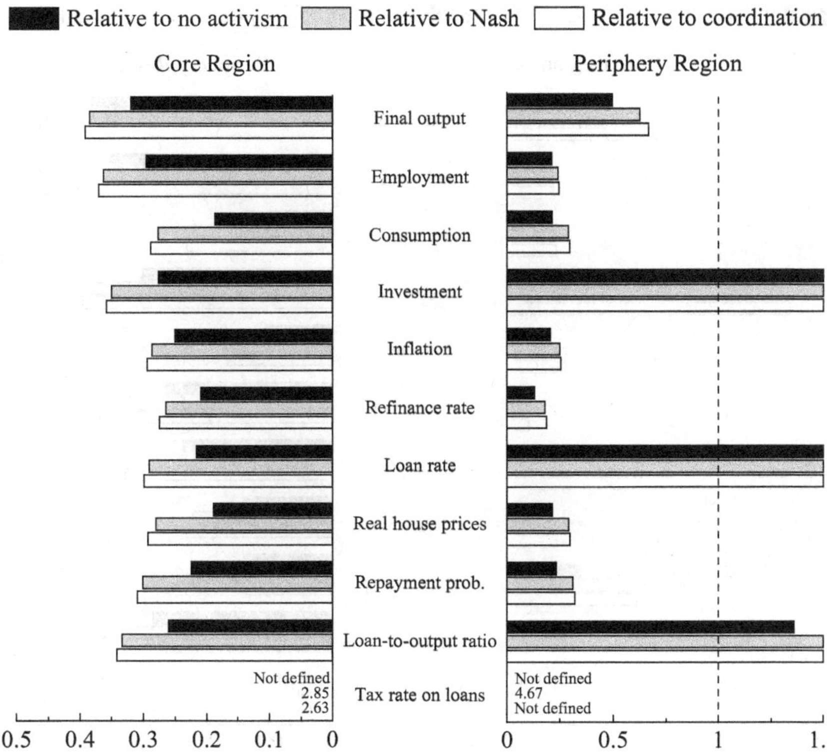

Figure 10.8
Core negative credit spread shock: asymptotic standard deviations, Ramsey policy relative to alternative regimes
Note: The simple macroprudential rule relates to the tax rate on loans, which reacts to the loan-to-output ratio.

the region where the shock occurs. This is in line with the results established in previous chapters. At the same time, results are not uniform in the other region, even though the policy instrument is also used more aggressively: There is a more stable path for most variables, but not for the repayment probability and the loan rate in the core region, for instance, when the shock occurs in the periphery. Under the Ramsey policy, the real exchange rate is almost fully stabilized, whatever the origin of the shock. Thus, this policy shuts down a key channel through which shocks are transmitted across borders.

Figures 10.8 and 10.9 show asymptotic standard deviations for the Ramsey policy relative to no activism, the Nash equilibrium, and coordination, for a range of real and financial variables. As noted in previous chapters, ratios lower than unity indicate that the Ramsey policy performs better for that

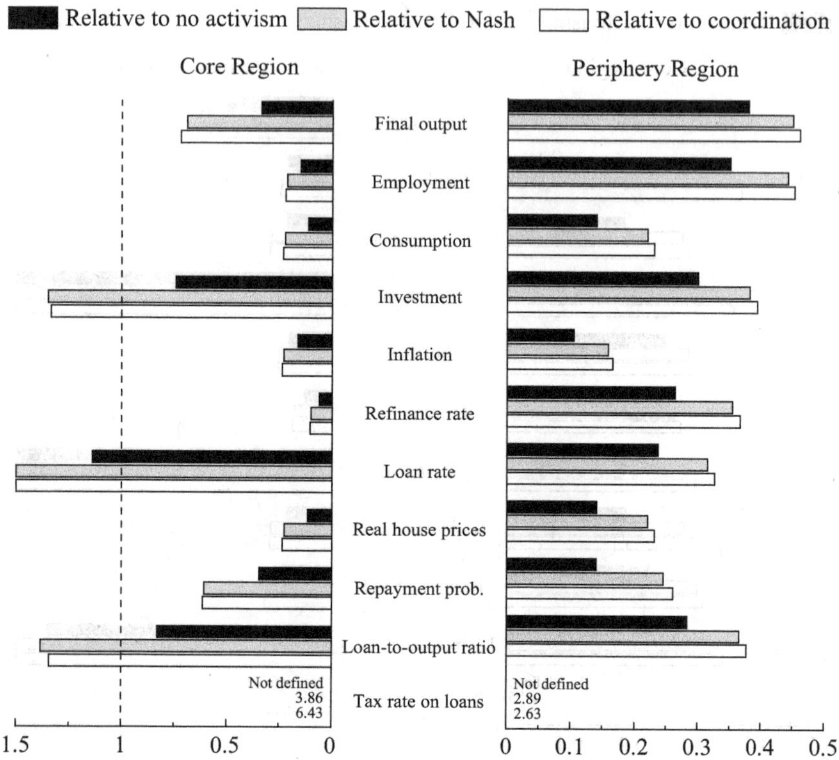

Figure 10.9
Periphery negative credit spread shock: asymptotic standard deviations, Ramsey policy relative to alternative regimes
Note: See note to figure 10.8.

particular variable. The results show that while the Ramsey policy does invariably better than the alternative regimes in the region where the shock originates, this is not always the case for the other region. This is the outcome in figure 10.8 (respectively, 10.9), for the loan rate, investment, and the loan-to-output ratio in the periphery (respectively, the core), especially with respect to the Nash equilibrium and coordination. In fact, it is possible also—depending on the magnitude of the instrument manipulation cost—that the Ramsey policy, applied *only* in the region where the shock originates dominates coordination of simple rules *across* regions.

There are two main lessons from the foregoing analysis. First, coordination—under which regulators internalize the consequences of policy interdependence—does not necessarily imply *burden sharing* (the regulator where the shock occurs reacting less, and the other reacting more) or *burden deepening* (both regulators reacting more). Depending on the nature of shocks and the cost of instrument manipulation, it may result in *free riding*, which entails a more aggressive response only from the region where the shock occurs, and the other region not reacting at all. Second, the welfare gains from macroprudential policy coordination, while positive, are not large, regardless of where the financial shock originates. They can also be asymmetric across regions (depending on where shocks occur), even when they are positive for the world economy as a whole. Thus, coordination is not necessarily Pareto-improving. Put differently, the existence of strong international financial spillovers may not be sufficient to ensure that coordination enables all parties to attain higher welfare, compared to when they act independently. Moreover, even if gains do exist for all parties, achieving and maintaining coordinated policies in pursuit of these gains may prove difficult in practice. In particular, assuming that a cooperative outcome can indeed be achieved and that regulators reach an agreement to coordinate, each of them almost invariably has an incentive to renege. Once one of the parties has set its instrument at the agreed level, the other typically can set its own instrument at a different value and attain an even lower policy loss or a higher welfare. The smaller the perceived *ex post* cost of reneging on a cooperative agreement, the stronger this incentive is.

10.8 Notes on the Literature

As noted in the introduction, research on international macroprudential policy coordination using two-country or two-region DSGE models and an explicit game-theoretic approach remains limited but is likely to attract considerably more attention in the coming years. One possible reason is the need to understand better the performance of the *principle of jurisdictional reciprocity* embedded in Basel III in the context of the use of countercyclical capital buffers, and ways to improve it.[17] In what follows, three broader modeling issues are considered under this agenda: leadership games, divergent views of the world among policymakers, and the existence of a global property market.

10.8.1 Leadership Games

As an alternative to the approach proposed here, the coordination issue could be cast in the context of leadership games, which would involve one regulator

17. Under this principle, foreign supervisors must apply (at least) the same additional capital buffers imposed by the host supervisor to their banks' lending to the host country. The goal is to ensure that all banks operate on a level playing field when lending to entities in the host country. See Agénor and Pereira da Silva (2018*a*) for a detailed discussion.

leading the decision-making process in the context of a cooperation agreement. Given that these games involve within-period timing, they are difficult to model fully in existing models—although leadership can be thought of as within-period commitment by one player, which clearly makes the leader better off (De Paoli and Paustian 2017). However, in general a leadership setup does not necessarily improve global welfare compared to the case where both players move simultaneously. Understanding the conditions under which gains may occur would be a significant contribution to the design of cooperative arrangements.

10.8.2 Divergent Views of the World

Multi-region theoretical models, such as the one presented in this chapter, often assume that policymakers in different countries share the same view of the world. However, in practice they often have fundamentally different economic models in mind. Regulators may therefore be unable to reach a consensus on the potential gains from coordination—which involves a systematic assessment of the costs and benefits of alternative policy choices—and how to achieve them. Indeed, as shown in an early contribution by Frankel and Rockett (1988) in the context of the debate on monetary policy coordination, if models are wrong, international coordination could make matters worse—by moving policies in the wrong direction—as easily as better. The same conclusion would surely apply to international coordination in the area of macroprudential regulation. Moreover, model perceptions could be *endogenous* with respect to individual-country interests. These difficulties may be compounded if policy coordination relates to countercyclical responses (as opposed to permanent, or structural, settings of macroprudential policy instruments) because agreement on the origin and nature of shocks (common or idiosyncratic, demand- or supply-related, permanent or transitory, and so on) also matters. Yet, identifying the origin and nature of shocks can be very difficult in real time, even in the absence of coordination. For these reasons, maintaining a macroprudential policy cooperation agreement is likely to be challenging in practice—even when, as noted earlier, all parties would benefit from it.

10.8.3 Global Property Market

Instead of assuming local housing markets, as in the model presented earlier, one could account for the existence of global property owners. With a globally integrated housing market, housing services are traded across regions, even though dwellings themselves are immovable assets. This would be consistent with the growing evidence that house price fluctuations have become highly synchronized across countries, as documented by Hirata et al. (2013),

Cesà-Bianchi (2013), Jordà et al. (2018), and in a comprehensive study by the International Monetary Fund (2018, chap. 3), which considered a large sample of high- and middle-income economies. Moreover, as documented by Bertay (2014) and Milcheva and Zhu (2016), house price spillovers could also occur through a global lending channel in which global banks intermediate wholesale funding to local banks. A preliminary attempt to capture these spillovers in a related model is proposed by Agénor and Pereira da Silva (2018*b*), but further research on this issue is warranted.

Appendix Steady-State Solution and Welfare Calculations

This appendix begins by presenting the steady-state solution for the core region. Results for the periphery region are symmetric, except where indicated.

From (10.38) and (10.58), with $Y_t^i = \tilde{Y}^i$, $i = C, P$, and assuming a zero inflation target,

$$\tilde{\pi}^i = 0. \tag{A10.1}$$

From the first-order condition (10.6), $1 + \tilde{\pi}^C = \Lambda(1 + \tilde{\imath}^{CB})$, which implies, given (A10.1), that the steady-state value of the bond rate is

$$\tilde{\imath}^{CB} = \Lambda^{-1} - 1. \tag{A10.2}$$

In the steady state, it must be also that

$$\tilde{\imath}^{CB} = \tilde{\imath}^{CR}, \tag{A10.3}$$

which implies that the global bank has no incentive to borrow from the central bank to buy domestic government bonds.

From (10.7), (10.8), (10.9), (10.10), and (10.11), the core household's labor supply and demand for cash, bank deposits, housing services, and periphery bonds are given by

$$\tilde{N} = \left(\frac{\tilde{w}^C \tilde{C}^{-1/\varsigma}}{\eta_N} \right)^{1/\psi_N}, \tag{A10.4}$$

$$\tilde{m}^C = \frac{\eta_x \nu \tilde{C}^{1/\varsigma}(1 + \tilde{\imath}^{CB})}{\tilde{\imath}^{CB}}, \tag{A10.5}$$

$$\tilde{d}^C = \frac{\eta_x (1 - \nu) \tilde{C}^{1/\varsigma}(1 + \tilde{\imath}^{CB})}{\tilde{\imath}^{CB} - \tilde{\imath}^{CD}}, \tag{A10.6}$$

$$\frac{\tilde{p}^H}{\tilde{C}^{1/\varsigma}} = \frac{\eta_H}{\tilde{H}^C} + \Lambda\left(\frac{\tilde{p}^H}{\tilde{C}^{1/\varsigma}}\right), \tag{A10.7}$$

$$\tilde{b}^{CP} = \frac{\tilde{\imath}^{PB} - \tilde{\imath}^{CB}}{\theta_0^B(1+\tilde{\imath}^{PB})}. \tag{A10.8}$$

Similarly, from (10.44), the demand for core government bonds by periphery households is

$$\tilde{b}^{PC} = \frac{\tilde{\imath}^{CB} - \tilde{\imath}^{PB}}{\theta_0^B(1+\tilde{\imath}^{CB})}. \tag{A10.9}$$

From (10.16), steady-state demand functions by core IG firms for core and periphery intermediate goods are given by

$$\tilde{Y}^{CC} = \Lambda_I^\eta\left(\frac{\tilde{P}^{CC}}{\tilde{P}^C}\right)^{-\eta}\tilde{Y}^C, \quad \tilde{Y}^{PC} = (1-\Lambda_I)^\eta\left(\frac{\tilde{P}^{PC}}{\tilde{P}^C}\right)^{-\eta}\tilde{Y}^C, \tag{A10.10}$$

where, from (10.17), the steady-state value of the price of final output is

$$\tilde{P}^C = [\Lambda_I^\eta(\tilde{P}^{CC})^{1-\eta} + (1-\Lambda_I)^\eta(\tilde{P}^{PC})^{1-\eta}]^{1/(1-\eta)}, \tag{A10.11}$$

with an analogous expression for $\tilde{P}^P$ in terms of $\tilde{P}^{PP}$ and $\tilde{P}^{CP}$.

From (10.18), the steady-state value of the price of imported intermediate goods is obtained as

$$\tilde{P}^{PC} = \tilde{E}^{-1}\tilde{P}^{PP}. \tag{A10.12}$$

From (10.19), steady-state output of domestic intermediate goods is given by

$$\tilde{Y}^{CI} = \tilde{N}^{1-\alpha}(\tilde{K}^C)^\alpha. \tag{A10.13}$$

From (10.20) and (10.21), the steady-state conditions for the capital-labor ratio and the unit real marginal cost can be written as

$$\frac{\tilde{K}^C}{\tilde{N}} = \left(\frac{\alpha}{1-\alpha}\right)\left(\frac{\tilde{w}^C}{\tilde{r}^{CK}}\right), \tag{A10.14}$$

$$\widetilde{mc}^C = \frac{\left(\tilde{w}^C\right)^{1-\alpha}\left(\tilde{r}^{CK}\right)^\alpha}{\alpha^\alpha\left(1-\alpha\right)^{1-\alpha}}. \tag{A10.15}$$

Price adjustment costs are zero in the steady state. From (10.24), the steady-state value of the marginal cost (the reciprocal of the markup) is also given by

$$\widetilde{mc}^C = \frac{\theta^{CC} - 1}{\theta^{CC}}. \tag{A10.16}$$

From (10.25), the steady-state value of the price of core exports in the periphery is

$$\tilde{P}^{CP} = \tilde{E}\tilde{P}^{CC}, \tag{A10.17}$$

whereas from (10.26), the steady-state value of intermediate exports is given by

$$\tilde{Y}^{CP} = \tilde{Y}^{CI} - \tilde{Y}^{CC}. \tag{A10.18}$$

In the steady state, with $K_{t+1}^C = K_t^C$, capital adjustment costs are zero; equation (10.28) therefore yields

$$\tilde{I}^C = \delta_K \tilde{K}^C. \tag{A10.19}$$

From (10.29), the steady-state value of the rental rate of capital is

$$\tilde{r}^{CK} = \tilde{q}^C(1+\tilde{\imath}^{CL})(1+\tilde{\imath}^{CL}) - \tilde{q}^C(1+\tilde{\imath}^{CL})(1-\delta_K),$$

that is, using (A10.2),

$$\tilde{r}^{CK} = \tilde{q}^C(1+\tilde{\imath}^{CL})(\Lambda^{-1} - 1 + \delta_K). \tag{A10.20}$$

From (10.33) and (10.34), the steady-state values of the core deposit and loan rates are

$$\tilde{\imath}^{CD} = \left(1 + \frac{1}{\eta^D}\right)^{-1} \tilde{\imath}^{CR}, \tag{A10.21}$$

$$\tilde{\imath}^{CL} = \frac{1+\tilde{\imath}^{CR}}{(1+1/\eta^L)(1-\tilde{\tau}^{L,C})\tilde{q}^C} - 1, \tag{A10.22}$$

$$1+\tilde{\imath}^{CP} = \frac{(1+\tilde{\imath}^{CR}) + \gamma^C \tilde{l}^{PC}}{\tilde{q}^{PC}}, \tag{A10.23}$$

where the last equation incorporates the equilibrium condition $\tilde{l}^{CP} = \tilde{l}^{PC}$.

From (10.36), the steady-state value of the repayment probability is

$$\tilde{q}^C = \varphi_0^C \kappa^{\varphi_1^C}. \tag{A10.24}$$

For the periphery, from (10.46), (10.50), (10.51), the equivalent expressions to (A10.21) through (A10.24) are

$$\tilde{\imath}^{PD} = (1-\mu)\tilde{\imath}^{PR}, \tag{A10.25}$$

$$\tilde{\imath}^{PL} = \left(\frac{\zeta^L}{\zeta^L - 1}\right)\frac{1+\tilde{\imath}^{PR}}{(1-\tilde{\tau}^{L,P})\tilde{q}^P} - 1, \tag{A10.26}$$

$$\tilde{l}^{PC} = \gamma^{-1}\left\{(1+\tilde{\imath}^{PR}) - \tilde{q}^{PC}(1+\tilde{\imath}^{CP})\right\}, \tag{A10.27}$$

$$\tilde{q}^P = \varphi_0^P \kappa^{\varphi_1^P}, \tag{A10.28}$$

together with, from (10.53) in equilibrium,

$$\tilde{q}^{PC} = q_0^{PC}.$$

The amount of loans demanded by the CG producer is $\tilde{l}^{CK} = \tilde{I}^C$. From (10.30), the steady-state level of the global bank's borrowing from the core central bank is

$$\tilde{l}^{CB} = (1-0.12)\tilde{l}^{CK} + \tilde{l}^{CP} - \tilde{d}^C, \tag{A10.29}$$

whereas from (10.45), the equivalent equation for the periphery banks is

$$\tilde{l}^{PB} = (1-0.12)\tilde{l}^{PK} - \tilde{z}\tilde{l}^{PC} - (1-\mu)\tilde{d}^P. \tag{A10.30}$$

The equilibrium condition of the final good market, equation (10.61), yields the steady-state condition $\tilde{Y}^C = \tilde{C} + \tilde{G} + \tilde{I}^C$, which can be rearranged, using (10.41) and (A10.19), to give

$$\tilde{Y}^C = \frac{\tilde{C} + \delta_K \tilde{K}^C}{1-\psi^G}. \tag{A10.31}$$

From (10.62), the equilibrium condition of the market for cash in the core yields

$$\tilde{m}^{Cs} = \tilde{m}^C, \tag{A10.32}$$

where, from (10.37), the supply of cash is $\tilde{m}^{Cs} = \tilde{l}^{CB}$. For the periphery, from (10.54),

$$\tilde{m}^{Ps} = \tilde{z}^{-1}\tilde{R}^{Pcb} + \tilde{b}^{Pcb} + \tilde{l}^{PB} - \widetilde{nw}.$$

From (10.64), the equilibrium condition of the housing market for the core is

$$\tilde{H}^C = \bar{H}^C, \tag{A10.33}$$

where $\tilde{H}^C$ is given in (A10.7).

Given (A10.8) and (A10.9), condition (10.65) gives

$$\tilde{b}^{CC} = -\frac{(1-n)\tilde{b}^{PC}}{n} = \left(\frac{1-n}{n}\right)\frac{\tilde{\iota}^{PB} - \tilde{\iota}^{CB}}{\theta_0^B(1+\tilde{\iota}^{PB})}, \tag{A10.34}$$

$$\tilde{b}^{PP} = -\frac{n\tilde{b}^{CP}}{1-n} = \left(\frac{n}{1-n}\right)\frac{\tilde{\iota}^{CB} - \tilde{\iota}^{PB}}{\theta_0^B(1+\tilde{\iota}^{PB})}.$$

Finally, from (10.68) the core region's current account is

$$\widetilde{CA}^C = \tilde{P}^{CC}\tilde{Y}^{CP} - \tilde{P}^{PC}\tilde{Y}^{PC} + \tilde{\iota}^{CP}\tilde{P}^C\tilde{l}^{PC} + \tilde{\iota}^P\tilde{E}^{-1}\tilde{P}^P\tilde{b}^{CP} - \tilde{\iota}^C\tilde{P}^C\tilde{b}^{PC}, \tag{A10.35}$$

which, from (10.66), implies that $\widetilde{CA}^P = -n(1-n)^{-1}\tilde{E}\widetilde{CA}^C$.

Consider now the welfare calculations. As noted in the text, the welfare criterion for each region $j = C, P$ is

$$W_t^j = \mathbb{E}_t \sum_{s=0}^{\infty} \Lambda^s u(C_{t+s}^j, N_{t+s}^j) - \varkappa_R \mathbb{E}_t \sum_{s=0}^{\infty} \Lambda^s (\tau_{t+s}^{jL} - \tau_{t+s-1}^{jL})^2, \tag{A10.36}$$

where the cost parameter $\varkappa_R > 0$ is taken to be the same for both regions.

As explained in chapter 5, the truncated period utility function is used:

$$u_t^j = u(C_t^j, N_t^j) \simeq \frac{(C_t^j)^{1-\varsigma^{-1}}}{1-\varsigma^{-1}} - \frac{\eta_N (N_t^j)^{1+\psi_N}}{1+\psi_N}. \tag{A10.37}$$

Taking a second-order approximation to u_t in the vicinity of the initial steady state yields

$$\begin{aligned} u_t^j \simeq{} & \tilde{u}^j + u_C(\tilde{C}^j, \tilde{N}^j)(C_t^j - \tilde{C}^j) + u_N(\tilde{C}^j, \tilde{N}^j)(N_t^j - \tilde{N}^j) \\ & + \frac{u_{CC}(\tilde{C}^j, \tilde{N}^j)}{2}(C_t^j - \tilde{C}^j)^2 + \frac{u_{NN}(\tilde{C}^j, \tilde{N}^j)}{2}(N_t^j - \tilde{N}^j)^2 \\ & + u_{CN}(\tilde{C}^j, \tilde{N}^j)(C_t^j - \tilde{C}^j)(N_t^j - \tilde{N}^j) + \mathcal{O}^j(3), \end{aligned}$$

where

$$\tilde{u}^j = \frac{(\tilde{C}^j)^{1-\varsigma^{-1}}}{1-\varsigma^{-1}} - \frac{\eta_N (\tilde{N}^j)^{1+\psi_N}}{1+\psi_N},$$

and $\mathcal{O}^j(3)$ denotes terms of the third order or higher. Ignoring once again these higher-order terms, and noting that $u_{CN}(\tilde{C}^j, \tilde{N}^j) = 0$, this approximation can be rewritten as

$$u_t^j \simeq \tilde{u}^j + (\tilde{C}^j)^{-\varsigma^{-1}}(C_t^j - \tilde{C}^j) - \eta_N \tilde{N}^{\psi_N}(N_t^j - \tilde{N}^j) - \frac{(\tilde{C}^j)^{-\varsigma^{-1}-1}}{2\varsigma}(C_t^j - \tilde{C}^j)^2$$
$$- \eta_N \psi_N \frac{(\tilde{N}^j)^{\psi_N - 1}}{2}(N_t^j - \tilde{N}^j)^2,$$

or equivalently, with $\widehat{x}_t^j = \ln(x_t^j/\tilde{x}^j) \simeq (x_t^j - \tilde{x}^j)/\tilde{x}^j$,

$$u_t^j \simeq \tilde{u}^j + (\tilde{C}^j)^{1-\varsigma^{-1}}\hat{C}_t^j - \eta_N(\tilde{N}^j)^{1+\psi_N}\hat{N}_t^j \tag{A10.38}$$
$$- \frac{(\tilde{C}^j)^{1-\varsigma^{-1}}}{2\varsigma}(\hat{C}_t^j)^2 - \eta_N \psi_N \frac{(\tilde{N}^j)^{1+\psi_N}}{2}(\hat{N}_t^j)^2,$$

where $\hat{C}_t^j$ and $\hat{N}_t^j$ denote log-deviations of C_t^j and N_t^j from their steady-state values.

Thus, the conditional expectation of the present discounted value of the household's expected utility function, $U_t^j = \mathbb{E}_t \sum_{s=0}^{\infty} \Lambda^s u_t^j$, can be approximated by

$$\mathcal{U}_t^j \simeq \frac{1}{1-\Lambda}\left\{\tilde{u}^j - \frac{(\tilde{C}^j)^{1-\varsigma^{-1}}}{2\varsigma}\text{Var}(\hat{C}_t^j) - \eta_N \psi_N \frac{(\tilde{N}^j)^{1+\psi_N}}{2}\text{Var}(\hat{N}_t^j)\right\}, \tag{A10.39}$$

where $\text{Var}(x_t^j)$ denotes the conditional variance of x_t^j, calculated from period t to infinity.

The second term on the right-hand side of equation (A10.36) can be approximated by

$$\mathbb{E}_t \sum_{s=0}^{\infty} \Lambda^s (\tau_{t+s}^{jL} - \tau_{t+s-1}^{jL})^2 \simeq \frac{\text{Var}(\Delta \tau_t^{jL})}{1-\Lambda}. \tag{A10.40}$$

Combining (A10.39) and (A10.40) implies that expression (A10.36) can be approximated by

$$\mathcal{W}_t^j \simeq \frac{1}{1-\Lambda}\left\{\tilde{u}^j - \frac{(\tilde{C}^j)^{1-\varsigma^{-1}}}{2\varsigma}\text{Var}(\hat{C}_t^j) - \eta_N \psi_N \frac{(\tilde{N}^j)^{1+\psi_N}}{2}\text{Var}(\hat{N}_t^j)\right\} \tag{A10.41}$$
$$- \frac{\varkappa_R}{1-\Lambda}\text{Var}(\Delta \tau_t^{jL}).$$

As discussed in the text, the welfare gains at the individual region level and for the world as a whole are obtained by solving for β^j and β in (10.72) and (10.73), the fractions of the (expected) consumption stream that would make households equally well off under noncooperation (Nash) as under cooperation. Suppose first that $\varkappa_R = 0$; these conditions are

$$\mathbb{E}_t \sum_{s=0}^{\infty} \Lambda^s u^j[(1+\beta^j)C_{t+s}^{j,N}, N_{t+s}^{j,N}] = \mathbb{E}_t \sum_{s=0}^{\infty} \Lambda^s u^j[(1+\beta^j)C_{t+s}^{j,O}, C_{t+s}^{j,O}], \tag{A10.42}$$

$$\mathbb{E}_t \sum_{s=0}^{\infty} \Lambda^s \left\{ nu^C[(1+\beta)C_{t+s}^{C,N}, N_{t+s}^{C,N}] + (1-n)u^P[(1+\beta)C_{t+s}^{P,N}, N_{t+s}^{P,N}] \right\} \tag{A10.43}$$

$$= \mathbb{E}_t \sum_{s=0}^{\infty} \Lambda^s \left\{ nu^C(C_{t+s}^{C,O}, N_{t+s}^{C,O}) + (1-n)u^P(C_{t+s}^{P,O}, N_{t+s}^{P,O}) \right\},$$

where $u^j()$ is defined in (A10.37) and $\{C_{t+s}^{j,h}\}_{s=0}^{\infty}$ and $\{N_{t+s}^{j,h}\}_{s=0}^{\infty}$ are solution paths under the Nash equilibrium ($h = N$) and coordination ($h = O$).

The fractions β^j and β are computed from the solution of the second-order approximation to the truncated utility function, as given in (A10.37), and the model equilibrium around the deterministic steady state. From (A10.39) and (A10.42), for instance,

$$\frac{1}{1-\Lambda}\left\{ \tilde{u}^j - (1+\beta^j)^{1-\varsigma^{-1}} \frac{(\tilde{C}^j)^{1-\varsigma^{-1}} \mathrm{Var}(\hat{C}_t^{j,N})}{2\varsigma} - \eta_N \psi_N \frac{(\tilde{N}^j)^{1+\psi_N} \mathrm{Var}(\hat{N}_t^{j,N})}{2} \right\}$$

$$= \frac{1}{1-\Lambda}\left\{ \tilde{u}^j - \frac{(\tilde{C}^j)^{1-\varsigma^{-1}}}{2\varsigma} \mathrm{Var}(\hat{C}_t^{j,O}) - \eta_N \psi_N \frac{(\tilde{N}^j)^{1+\psi_N}}{2} \mathrm{Var}(\hat{N}_t^{j,O}) \right\},$$

or

$$(1+\beta^j)^{1-\varsigma^{-1}} \frac{(\tilde{C}^j)^{1-\varsigma^{-1}}}{2\varsigma} \mathrm{Var}(\hat{C}_t^{j,N}) + \eta_N \psi_N \frac{(\tilde{N}^j)^{1+\psi_N}}{2} \mathrm{Var}(\hat{N}_t^{j,N})$$

$$= \frac{(\tilde{C}^j)^{1-\varsigma^{-1}}}{2\varsigma} \mathrm{Var}(\hat{C}_t^{j,O}) + \eta_N \psi_N \frac{(\tilde{N}^j)^{1+\psi_N}}{2} \mathrm{Var}(\hat{N}_t^{j,O}).$$

This expression can be rewritten as

$$(1+\beta^j)^{1-\varsigma^{-1}} \Gamma^{j,C} \mathrm{Var}(\hat{C}_t^{j,N}) + \Gamma^{j,N} \mathrm{Var}(\hat{N}_t^{j,N})$$

$$= \Gamma^{j,C} \mathrm{Var}(\hat{C}_t^{j,O}) + \Gamma^{j,N} \mathrm{Var}(\hat{N}_t^{j,O}),$$

where the weights on (deviations in) consumption and employment, respectively, are given as

$$\Gamma^{j,C} = \frac{(\tilde{C}^j)^{1-\varsigma^{-1}}}{2\varsigma}, \quad \Gamma^{j,N} = \eta_N \psi_N \frac{(\tilde{N}^j)^{1+\psi_N}}{2}. \tag{A10.44}$$

This expression can be solved for β^j:

$$\beta^j = \left\{ \frac{\Gamma^{j,C}\text{Var}(\hat{C}_t^{i,O}) + \Gamma^{j,N}[\text{Var}(\hat{N}_t^{j,O}) - \text{Var}(\hat{N}_t^{j,N})]}{\Gamma^{j,C}\text{Var}(\hat{C}_t^{j,N})} \right\}^{1/(1-\varsigma^{-1})} - 1. \tag{A10.45}$$

Similarly, from (A10.39) and (A10.43), and using the definitions of $\Gamma^{j,C}$ and $\Gamma^{j,N}$ provided in (A10.44),

$$\begin{aligned}
&\frac{n}{1-\Lambda}\left\{\tilde{u}^C - (1+\beta)^{1-\varsigma^{-1}}\Gamma^{C,C}\text{Var}(\hat{C}_t^{C,N}) - \Gamma^{C,N}\text{Var}(\hat{N}_t^{C,N})\right\}\\
&\quad + \frac{1-n}{1-\Lambda}\left\{\tilde{u}^P - (1+\beta)^{1-\varsigma^{-1}}\Gamma^{P,C}\text{Var}(\hat{C}_t^{P,N}) - \Gamma^{P,N}\text{Var}(\hat{N}_t^{P,N})\right\}\\
&\quad = \frac{n}{1-\Lambda}\left\{\tilde{u}^C - (1+\beta)^{1-\varsigma^{-1}}\Gamma^{C,C}\text{Var}(\hat{C}_t^{C,O}) - \Gamma^{C,N}\text{Var}(\hat{N}_t^{C,O})\right\}\\
&\quad + \frac{1-n}{1-\Lambda}\left\{\tilde{u}^P - (1+\beta)^{1-\varsigma^{-1}}\Gamma^{P,C}\text{Var}(\hat{C}_t^{P,O}) - \Gamma^{P,N}\text{Var}(\hat{N}_t^{P,O})\right\},
\end{aligned}$$

which, after simplifications can be rewritten as

$$\begin{aligned}
&n\left\{(1+\beta)^{1-\varsigma^{-1}}\Gamma^{C,C}\text{Var}(\hat{C}_t^{C,N}) + \Gamma^{C,N}\text{Var}(\hat{N}_t^{C,N})\right\} \\
&\quad + (1-n)\left\{(1+\beta)^{1-\varsigma^{-1}}\Gamma^{P,C}\text{Var}(\hat{C}_t^{P,N}) + \Gamma^{P,N}\text{Var}(\hat{N}_t^{P,N})\right\}\\
&\quad = n\left\{\Gamma^{C,C}\text{Var}(\hat{C}_t^{C,O}) + \Gamma^{C,N}\text{Var}(\hat{N}_t^{C,O})\right\}\\
&\quad + (1-n)\left\{\Gamma^{P,C}\text{Var}(\hat{C}_t^{P,O}) + \Gamma^{C,N}\text{Var}(\hat{N}_t^{P,O})\right\}.
\end{aligned} \tag{A10.46}$$

This expression can be solved for β, in a manner similar to (A10.45).

Related derivations apply for the case where the welfare function accounts for the cost of instrument volatility ($\varkappa_R > 0$), replacing $u^j()$ by $u^j() - \varkappa_R(\Delta\tau_{t+s}^j)^2$, as appropriate, in (A10.42) and (A10.43), combined with (A10.41) instead of (A10.39).

11 Macroprudential Regulation and Economic Growth

In the aftermath of the global financial crisis, much of the debate on regulatory reform focused on the implications of financial volatility for *short-term* economic stability and on the *short-run* benefits of countercyclical financial regulation. In large part as a reflection of these concerns, all the previous chapters in this book have focused on how macroprudential policy, whose focus in addressing financial vulnerabilities is systemic in nature, can mitigate the procyclicality of the financial system and dampen short-run fluctuations in credit and output—independently and jointly with monetary policy. In particular, as discussed in chapter 6, to the extent that higher capital adequacy ratios increase bankers' *skin in the game*, they may reduce risk-taking by improving incentives to screen and monitor borrowers and to exercise due diligence. In turn, this *monitoring incentive effect* can help to prevent excessive credit growth and dampen output fluctuations.[1]

By contrast, this last chapter presents an analysis of the links between financial stability, macroprudential regulation, and growth from a *longer-run* perspective. It also departs from the previous chapters in the sense that an alternative (but related) type of financial frictions is introduced. Specifically, it dwells on the double moral hazard model of Holmström and Tirole (1997), in which financial frictions result from the combination of an asymmetric information problem between borrowers and lenders (banks) and an incentive for banks to shirk. Borrowers are tempted to divert resources obtained from financial intermediaries toward privately beneficial activities. To mitigate this moral hazard problem, banks monitor borrowers' actions. However, monitoring is costly. Although it helps to alleviate the perverse incentives that borrowers face,

1. In Agénor and Pereira da Silva (2018*c*), as in Collard et al. (2017), capital requirements mitigate risks to the financial system by eliminating a specific *type* of credit (loans to risky borrowers) rather than the *amount* of credit that banks provide.

the fact that banks must pay interest on the resources that they use to fund their activities creates also an incentive for them to shirk.[2]

To begin with, section 1 provides a brief discussion of the links between financial stability, financial regulation, and growth from a longer-run perspective. Section 2 describes the model, taking the intensity of monitoring as well as the required reserve ratio as given. In the model, monitoring outlays are pecuniary in nature and their opportunity cost affects incentive constraints. The optimal financial contract is characterized in section 3. The equilibrium level of investment is then determined in section 4, whereas the balanced growth equilibrium path is characterized in section 5. Autonomous changes in monitoring intensity and the required reserve ratio are studied in section 6. Optimal monitoring is analyzed in section 7 and the growth- and welfare-maximizing values of the required reserve ratio are solved for numerically. The chapter concludes with some comments on the broader literature.

11.1 Background

Understanding the longer-run effects of financial regulation is essential because of a potential *dynamic trade-off*. Despite contributing to a more stable environment in which agents can assess risks and returns associated with their investment decisions, regulatory policies designed to reduce procyclicality and the risk of financial crises in the short run could well be detrimental to longer-run economic growth, due to their effect on risk-taking and incentives to borrow and lend.

In developing countries, where sustaining high growth rates is essential to increase standards of living and escape poverty, understanding the terms of this trade-off is particularly important. These countries are often characterized by an underdeveloped formal financial system (as discussed in chapter 1) and thus have limited opportunities to borrow and smooth shocks. The real effects of excessive financial volatility on firms and individuals can therefore be not only large but also highly persistent, thereby translating into not just transitory drops in the level of output but also adverse effects on the growth rate itself.[3] In such

2. In the previous chapters, (noncontingent) monitoring also played an important role. However, it was argued that it is the *combination* of monitoring and collateral requirements (both through their direct effect on the repayment probability) that helps to mitigate moral hazard on the part of borrowers. The decision to default on borrowed resources was also related to the state of nature rather than explicitly to the existence of privately beneficial activities.

3. These adverse growth effects are consistent with the evidence showing that financial liberalization, to the extent that it is accompanied by greater financial volatility, may not contribute significantly to promoting growth. See Loayza and Rancière (2006) for a discussion.

conditions, the benefits of regulatory measures aimed at promoting financial stability could be substantial.

At the same time, however, regulatory constraints may have a large and persistent effect on the risk-taking incentives of financial intermediaries. In particular, these constraints may induce structural shifts in banks' portfolio composition, in the form of a move away from risky (but potentially highly productive and beneficial in terms of longer-run growth) assets toward safer (but less productive) investments. More generally, they may unduly constrain their capacity to lend. The consequence may be high interest rate spreads (to reflect the cost of regulations), suboptimal levels of borrowing by entrepreneurs to finance privately and socially desirable investments, and (as noted in chapter 6) shifts in lending activity to less-regulated financial intermediaries—all of which exert potentially adverse effects on growth and welfare. A key question therefore is to determine the *optimal* degree of financial regulation that internalizes this trade-off.

The literature on these issues, however, remains scant. One of the first analytical contributions in this area is Van den Heuvel (2008), who studied the welfare effects of bank capital requirements in a standard growth setting. His analysis showed that capital adequacy requirements may have conflicting effects on welfare. On the one hand, by inducing banks to hold less risky portfolios, they mitigate the probability of a financial crisis, which enhances welfare. On the other, by inducing a shift in banks' portfolios away from risky but more productive investment projects toward safer but less productive projects, it may hamper economic growth (as noted earlier) and have an adverse effect on welfare. Capital requirements entail therefore a trade-off between banking efficiency and financial stability; as capital levels rise, there are costs in terms of increased lending spreads or reduced loan volumes. However, a crucial limitation of the paper is that, because growth is exogenous, the implications of this trade-off for long-run growth, and the extent to which policy can internalize it, cannot be fully explored.

Dwelling on Agénor (2019), this chapter discusses the growth and welfare effects of macroprudential regulation. It uses an overlapping generations (OLG) endogenous growth model where financial intermediation is carried out only by banks. In the model, the production of capital is subject to a dual moral hazard problem in the sense of Holmström and Tirole (1997).[4] Entrepreneurs, who need external funds to finance their investment projects, may be tempted to

4. Chakraborty and Ray (2006) extended the Holmström-Tirole model to a growth and financial development setting. However, they focused on the evolution of market- and bank-based financial systems, and did not discuss financial regulation or the optimal setting of policy instruments.

choose less productive projects (shirk) with higher non-verifiable returns. But although bank monitoring mitigates the moral hazard problem associated with the behavior of entrepreneurs, the fact that banks use deposits from households to fund their loans creates an incentive to shirk when monitoring is costly. In addition, banks have access to an imperfect monitoring technology, which can only detect high-shirking projects. Even when monitored by lenders, therefore, entrepreneurs may still choose to run a project with low-shirking intensity. The optimal financial contract ensures that they have the incentive to choose instead efficient (and socially valuable) projects only.[5]

However, the model presented here departs from the Holmström-Tirole paradigm in three important ways. First, households cannot lend directly to producers; finance is therefore fully intermediated through banks. Second, to mitigate the second source of moral hazard and increase incentives for depositors, banks are compelled to hold reserve requirements—a prudential instrument which, as noted in chapters 5 and 9, has been used extensively in developing countries and is now part of the liquidity requirement guidelines under the Basel III arrangement. In the context of the model, reserve requirements operate as partial deposit insurance. Third, the intensity of monitoring, which affects the private returns from shirking, is endogenously determined.

11.2 The Model

The economy consists of a continuum of risk-neutral agents who live for two periods, adulthood and old age. These agents are of two types: An exogenous fraction $n \in (0, 1)$ are workers and the remaining $1 - n$ are entrepreneurs. Without loss of generality, n is normalized to 0.5 and the measure of each type of agents is normalized to 1. Population is constant. Domestic agents can access the international capital market but such access is asymmetric: They can lend (deposit funds) but they cannot borrow.[6] There are two production sectors and a continuum of banks of measure 1, which channel funds from savers to borrowers. For simplicity, each worker and each entrepreneur are randomly matched with a single bank. There is also a financial regulator.

5. Rochet (2004) adapted the Holmström-Tirole model to study the comparative roles of market discipline and centralized supervision in a context where banks are vulnerable to macroeconomic shocks.

6. Foreign intermediaries do not lend directly to domestic agents because the terms of loan contracts cannot be legally enforced in domestic courts. This assumption is consistent with the evidence on limited access to world capital markets for many developing countries; see, for instance, Agénor (2012).

11.2.1 Workers and Entrepreneurs

A worker (or saver) is born with one unit of time in adulthood, which is supplied inelastically to the labor market. The entire wage income, w_t, is saved in adulthood; thus, a generation-t worker's lifetime utility depends only on second-period consumption. For simplicity, a worker's utility is linear in wage income. As in Gale (2004), for instance, workers do not have access to a monitoring technology and therefore do not lend directly to producers; they invest all their savings (or first-period income) either in bank deposits at home, d_t, or abroad. Arbitrage implies that both investments yield the same (gross) return, $R^D > 1$, which is set exogenously. In addition, there is a nonpecuniary benefit associated with holding deposits at home.

Each entrepreneur j, with $j \in (0, 1)$, is also born with one unit of labor time in adulthood, which is used to operate a technology that converts, after one period, units of the final good into a marketable capital good. Entrepreneurs therefore do not consume either in the period when they are born. They are altruists and derive utility from their old-age consumption, $c_{t+1}^{j,E}$, and bequests made to their offspring, b_{t+1}^{j}. Specifically, a generation-t entrepreneur's preferences are given by the *warm-glow* utility function

$$U_t^{j,E} = (c_{t+1}^{j,E})^{\beta}(b_{t+1}^{j})^{1-\beta}, \tag{11.1}$$

where $\beta \in (0, 1)$.

Let z_{t+1}^{j} denote entrepreneur j's realized income in old age, which is derived later. Given Cobb-Douglas preferences in (11.1), optimal decision rules are linear in z_{t+1}^{j}. Thus, entrepreneur j leaves to his offspring a constant proportion of his realized income in old age:

$$b_{t+1}^{j} = (1-\beta)z_{t+1}^{j}, \tag{11.2}$$

the remaining fraction being consumed so that $c_{t+1}^{j,E} = \beta z_{t+1}^{j}$.

11.2.2 Production Sectors

The production sectors in the economy consist of a final good sector, which produces a unique good (which can be either consumed or invested), and a capital good (CG) sector, which provides inputs used to produce the final good.

Final good

Competitive firms produce the final good by combining labor and capital goods. Entrepreneur j's production technology exhibits constant returns in private inputs, capital, K_t^{j}, and labor, N_t^{j}:

$$Y_t^j = A_t (N_t^j)^{1-\alpha} (K_t^j)^\alpha, \tag{11.3}$$

where $\alpha \in (0, 1)$ and A_t is a productivity index.

There is an Arrow-Romer type externality, associated with the (aggregate) capital-labor ratio $k_t = K_t/N_t$, where $N_t = \int_0^1 N_t^j$ is the number of workers in the economy and $K_t = \int_0^1 K_t^j dj$ is the aggregate capital stock,

$$A_t = A k_t^{1-\alpha}, \tag{11.4}$$

where $A > 0$. Thus, all firms benefit from an economy-wide increase in the capital-labor ratio.

Combining (11.3) and (11.4) yields, in a symmetric equilibrium, a linear relationship between production per worker, y_t, and capital per worker:

$$y_t = A k_t. \tag{11.5}$$

Final good producers operate in competitive output and input markets so that equilibrium capital rental and wage rates, R_t^K and w_t, are determined by their marginal product:

$$R^K = \alpha A, \quad w_t = (1-\alpha) A k_t. \tag{11.6}$$

To ensure that the gross return $R^K > 1$, the restriction $A > 1/\alpha$ is imposed.

Capital goods

Each capital good *j* is produced by a single entrepreneur. Because (as noted earlier) generations of entrepreneurs are interconnected through a bequest motive, firm *j* is effectively infinitely lived. At any given period in time, the adult member of entrepreneurial family *j* is the owner-manager of that firm, converting units of the final good into capital with a one-period lag. In each period, capital goods become available before production of final goods starts.

Each entrepreneur invests an indivisible amount I_t^j, which is taken as given for the moment. The investment is risky. When it fails, it yields nothing. When it succeeds, it produces a verifiable amount of capital equal to

$$K_{t+1}^j = I_t^j, \tag{11.7}$$

where for simplicity there is a one-to-one relationship between flows and stocks, and capital goods fully depreciate upon use.

As long as $I_t^j > b_t^j$, entrepreneur *j* has to raise the difference $l_t^j = I_t^j - b_t^j$ from banks. All entrepreneurs produce the same type of capital good and are price takers. The common return they earn from renting out their capital is $R^K > 1$, the (constant) marginal product of capital in a competitive equilibrium, given by (11.6).

11.2.3 The Financial Sector

Financial intermediaries consist of banks, which obtain their supply of loanable funds from workers' deposits and use them to lend to entrepreneurs for the purpose of building capital. However, deposits are subject to a reserve requirement imposed by the regulator. The reason for doing so is because there is no deposit insurance system (or, if it exists, it is not credible), so banks are required to hold liquid assets in order to provide partial insurance and maintain financial stability. This is the sense in which reserve requirements are macroprudential in nature. As noted earlier, for ease of exposition, each bank randomly receives deposits from one saver only and lends to one entrepreneur only.

Banks are endowed with a technology (specialized skills) that allows them to inspect entrepreneurs' cash flows and balance sheet, observe their activities, and ensure that they conform to the terms or covenants agreed on in the financial contract. Although imperfect, monitoring helps to address a standard agency problem that banks face in lending to entrepreneurs.

Specifically, as in Holmström and Tirole (1997), suppose that each entrepreneur is allowed to choose between three types of investment projects, which differ in their success probability and the nonverifiable private benefits that they bring.[7] As noted earlier, entrepreneurs must raise funds amounting to $l_t^j = I_t^j - b_t^j > 0$ for their investment. When the project succeeds, it realizes the amount of capital given in (11.7), with a verifiable return R^K. But when the project fails, it produces nothing; there is no remaining liquidation value.[8] The moral hazard problem arises from the fact that the probability of success depends on an unobserved action taken by the entrepreneur. The unobserved action can be interpreted as the entrepreneur's choice of how to spend I_t^j. Entrepreneurs can spend it on an *efficient* (good) project that succeeds with probability $\pi^H < 1$ (and returning therefore $R^K I_t^j$), but uses up all of I_t^j. Or, they can spend it on one of two *inefficient* projects that may not succeed. One of these alternatives, a low-moral hazard project, costs $I_t^j - \upsilon I_t^j$, where $\upsilon \in (0, 1)$, leaving υI_t^j for the entrepreneur to appropriate. The other inefficient choice, a high-moral hazard project, costs $I_t^j - VI_t^j$, where $V \in (0, 1)$, thereby leaving VI_t^j in private benefits. Inefficient projects carry the same probability of success, $\pi^L < \pi^H$, but it is assumed that $0 < \upsilon < V < 1$. Hence, entrepreneurs will

7. Private benefits are nontransferable and capture the idea that the entrepreneur gets some kind of nonpecuniary return from some projects. A common interpretation is that they capture effort. Lower effort is clearly a benefit to the entrepreneur, but (as discussed next) it also leads to a lower probability that projects will succeed.

8. Returns in this framework are verifiable at no cost.

always prefer the high-moral hazard project over the low-moral hazard one.[9] However, only the efficient project is economically viable and thus socially valuable; to ensure that this is indeed the case, the following standard conditions are imposed.

Assumption 11.1 $\pi^H \alpha A - R^D > 0 > \pi^L \alpha A + V - R^D$.

Intuitively, these conditions state that the expected net surplus per unit invested in a good project is positive, while that of a high-moral hazard project is negative—even after the private benefit is accounted for.[10]

Monitoring partially resolves the agency problem and reduces the entrepreneur's opportunity cost of being diligent. By monitoring borrowers, banks eliminate the high-moral hazard project but not the low-moral hazard one (Holmström and Tirole 1997). Thus, because misrepresenting high levels of effort can be achieved only by performing some level of effort, entrepreneurs are left with two choices under monitoring: Selecting the efficient and socially valuable project or the low-moral hazard project. At the same time, monitoring involves a pecuniary cost for the bank, representing a nonverifiable amount $\gamma \in (0, 1)$ per unit invested. Hence, bank monitoring will be an optimal arrangement only if the gain from resolving the agency problem outweighs the monitoring cost.

11.3 Optimal Financial Contract

In this setting, the structure of the optimal financial contract depends on whether or not entrepreneurs choose to be diligent, which in turn depends on their incentives to act that way and outside monitoring by the bank. For its part, the bank chooses either to lend the full amount needed to invest in the production of capital goods (net of the borrower's initial wealth, $I_t^j - b_t^j$) or not at all. In addition, because workers delegate to financial intermediaries the task of monitoring entrepreneurs, banks must ensure that the return that savers obtain is sufficiently high for them to deposit their funds in the first place. This section

9. While entrepreneurs consume in the second period of life only, they invest in the first. As in Chakraborty and Ray (2006), it is assumed that the private benefits generated by negligent behavior cannot be invested. Instead, they have to be stored away for one period in the form of goods. Such storage yields zero net return but is unobservable. As a result, stored goods cannot be seized by lenders if the investment project fails.

10. Because $\upsilon < V$, this restriction implies that the condition $0 > \pi^L \alpha A + \upsilon - R^D$ also holds. Note that a sufficient condition for Assumption 11.1 to hold is $1 \leq \pi^L \alpha A$, or equivalently that the highest benefit associated with the high-moral hazard project has a smaller value than the social cost that it imposes in the form of a lower success probability.

characterizes the optimal contract when entrepreneurs behave diligently and choose only good projects.

Specifically, the optimal contract is such that no party (given limited liability) earns anything when the project fails, whereas when it succeeds the gross return, R^K, is distributed so that

$$R_{t+1}^B + R_{t+1}^E + R_{t+1}^W = R^K, \tag{11.8}$$

where R_{t+1}^B, R_{t+1}^E and R_{t+1}^W denote the gross returns to the bank, the entrepreneur, and savers, respectively.

Entrepreneur j invests I_t^j in the good project as long as it yields an incentive compatible return. As noted earlier, given that the banker always monitors if it lends, entrepreneurs will not choose the high-moral hazard project. The good project returns $R_{t+1}^E I_t^j$ with probability π^H, whereas the expected return to the low-moral hazard project (if it succeeds) is $\pi^L R_{t+1}^E I_t^j + \upsilon I_t^j$—that is, the sum of the (expected) market return plus the private return. The incentive compatibility constraint for the entrepreneur is thus $\pi^H R_{t+1}^E I_t^j \geq \pi^L R_{t+1}^E I_t^j + \upsilon I_t^j$, or equivalently

$$R_{t+1}^E \geq \frac{\upsilon}{\Delta\pi}, \tag{11.9}$$

where $\Delta\pi = \pi^H - \pi^L$.

The incentive compatibility constraint for the bank relates to the fact that it engages in monitoring. The monitoring cost is proportional (at the rate γ, as noted earlier) to the size of the project. Thus, the bank's incentive constraint for monitoring, and thus to engage in lending, requires that its expected return on a good project, net of monitoring outlays (valued at their opportunity cost, R^D), be greater than or equal to the expected return of a low-moral hazard project without monitoring—that is, $\pi^H R_{t+1}^B I_t^j - \gamma R^D I_t^j \geq \pi^L R_{t+1}^B I_t^j$, or equivalently

$$R_{t+1}^B \geq \frac{\gamma R^D}{\Delta\pi}. \tag{11.10}$$

The participation constraint for workers requires that their expected return from the project, which is the weighted sum of the return when the project succeeds (and the bank is repaid, with probability π^H) and the value of reserve requirements, μd_t^j, when it fails (and so does the bank, with probability $1-\pi^H$), be at least equal to the risk-free return on deposits,

$$\pi^H R_{t+1}^W I_t^j + (1-\pi^H)\mu d_t^j \geq R^D d_t^j, \tag{11.11}$$

where $\mu \in (0, 1)$ is the required reserve ratio set by the financial regulator. Thus, in this setting, reserves can be used to compensate depositors if banks fail and operate fundamentally like a partial deposit insurance scheme—providing therefore, as discussed later, a rationale for prudential regulation.

Free entry and competition compel banks to offer contracts whose objective is to maximize the representative entrepreneur's expected share of the return, $\pi^H R^E_{t+1} I^j_t$, subject to the incentive compatibility constraints (11.9) and (11.10), the participation constraint (11.11), and the bank's resource constraint

$$l^j_t \leq (1-\mu)d^j_t - \gamma I^j_t, \tag{11.12}$$

and non-negativity constraints $R^i_{t+1} \geq 0$, where $i = E, B, W$. Equation (11.12) indicates that loans cannot exceed deposits (adjusted for required reserves), net of monitoring costs.

Given perfect competition, in equilibrium entrepreneurs earn just enough to choose the efficient project, and banks are paid just enough to have an incentive to monitor. The incentive constraints (11.9) and (11.10) therefore hold with equality,

$$R^E_{t+1} = \frac{\upsilon}{\Delta\pi}, \quad R^B_{t+1} = \frac{\gamma R^D}{\Delta\pi}, \tag{11.13}$$

so that, using (11.8),

$$R^W_{t+1} = R^K - \left(\frac{\upsilon + \gamma R^D}{\Delta\pi}\right). \tag{11.14}$$

Thus, when there is a greater incentive to divert funds (υ is larger), or when the monitoring activity is more costly (γ is higher), the payment share of the entrepreneur or the bank must be larger (and that of workers correspondingly smaller) to be incentive compatible—subject of course to $R^W_{t+1} > 0$.

Substituting (11.14) in (11.11), holding with equality, the value of deposits in bank j is given as

$$d^j_t = \frac{\pi^H}{R^D - (1-\pi^H)\mu}\left[R^K - \left(\frac{\upsilon + \gamma R^D}{\Delta\pi}\right)\right] I^j_t, \tag{11.15}$$

where $R^D - (1-\pi^H)\mu > 0$, given that $\pi^H, \mu < 1$. Assuming that deposits at home generate a nonpecuniary benefit, equation (11.15) also represents the supply of deposits, or gross loanable funds, by workers.

As noted earlier, workers save all their wage income in adulthood. To abstract from credit rationing and distributional considerations, it is assumed that $w_t \geq d^j_t$ for all i and that the difference (wage minus deposits) is invested abroad at the rate R^D. Thus, total income that workers consume in old age is always $R^D w_t$.

11.4 Equilibrium Investment

In equilibrium, only good projects are selected and all entrepreneurs obtain credit from a (matched) bank in period t. Using the bank's resource constraint (11.12), holding with equality, and $l_t^j = I_t^j - b_t^j$ to eliminate d_t^j in (11.15) yields

$$\frac{R^D - (1-\pi^H)\mu}{1-\mu}[(1+\gamma)I_t^j - b_t^j] = \pi^H \left[R^K - \left(\frac{\upsilon + \gamma R^D}{\Delta\pi}\right)\right] I_t^j,$$

which can be rewritten as

$$I_t^j = \left\{1 + \gamma - \frac{(1-\mu)\pi^H}{R^D - (1-\pi^H)\mu}\left[R^K - \left(\frac{\upsilon + \gamma R^D}{\Delta\pi}\right)\right]\right\}^{-1} b_t^j = \Phi b_t^j. \tag{11.16}$$

Equation (11.16) determines the equilibrium level of investment, for a given value of initial wealth, b_t^j. To ensure that Φ is positive, the following condition is imposed.

Assumption 11.2 $\pi^H R^K - (1+\gamma)[R^D - (1-\pi^H)\mu]/(1-\mu) < \pi^H(\upsilon + \gamma R^D)/\Delta\pi$.

This condition states that the expected per-unit surplus of a good project, $\pi^H R^K$, net of the cost of banking activity—which consists of interest paid to depositors and the opportunity cost of monitoring, with the deposit rate adjusted for the tax on financial intermediation imposed by reserve requirements, net of the return of these requirements if the bank defaults—must be less than the expected sum of the shares paid to the entrepreneur and the banker to ensure that they behave diligently. Put differently, Assumption 11.2 eliminates the incentive to engage in moral hazard behavior.

In addition, to guarantee that Φ is greater than unity (and thus ensure positive borrowing) the following restriction is also imposed.

Assumption 11.3 $\pi^H R^K - \gamma[R^D - (1-\pi^H)\mu]/(1-\mu) > \pi^H(\upsilon + \gamma R^D)/\Delta\pi$.

This condition requires essentially that the probability of success of the good project, π^H, be sufficiently large relative to the probability of success of the inefficient projects, π^L, which appears in $\Delta\pi$.

Using (11.16), the equilibrium level of loans is given by

$$l_j^j = (\Phi - 1)b_t^j. \tag{11.17}$$

From (11.16) and (11.17), the following proposition can be established.

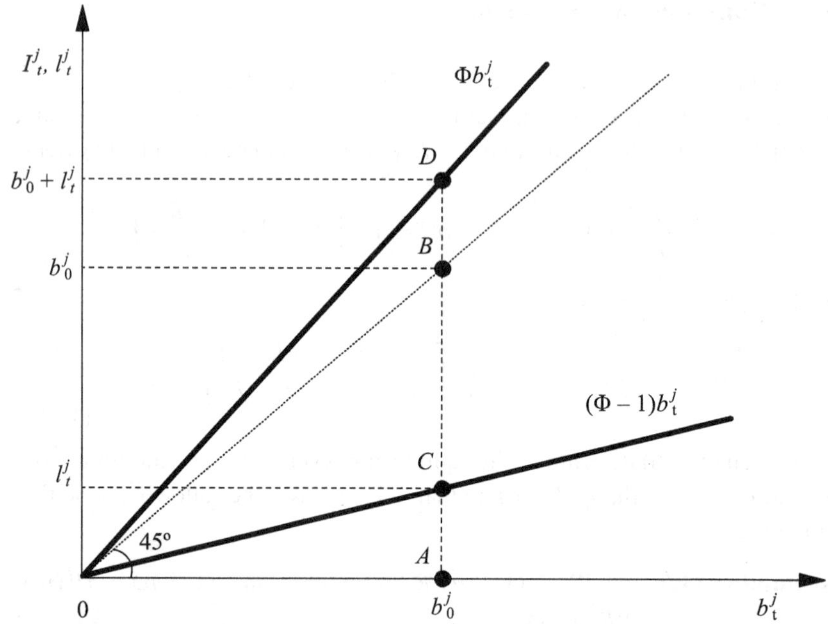

Figure 11.1
Equilibrium investment
Source: Agénor (2019).

Proposition 11.1 *With constant monitoring intensity, the equilibrium levels of investment and lending are decreasing in the required reserve ratio,* μ.

This proposition is easy to establish by showing that $\partial\Phi/\partial\mu < 0$. It results directly from the fact that higher required reserves reduce the bank's loanable funds and thus, all else equal, the (expected) income generated from lending. This occurs despite the fact that it raises incentives for savers, as can be inferred from (11.15)—an issue that is further discussed later.

Figure 11.1 shows the determination of the equilibrium, for an initial level of wealth equal to b^j_0. The equilibrium level of investment is at *D*, and the equilibrium level of loans at *C*. By construction, the distance *BD* is equal to the distance *AC* (or, equivalently, *AB* is equal to *CD*).

Let z^j_{t+1} denote entrepreneur *j*'s second-period income; in equilibrium, from (11.13) and (11.16),

$$z^j_{t+1} = \left(\frac{\upsilon\Phi}{\Delta\pi}\right) b^j_t. \tag{11.18}$$

which shows that entrepreneurial income is also linear in wealth.

11.5 Balanced Growth Equilibrium

Because the optimal loan contract ensures that all entrepreneurs behave diligently, they are all able to borrow from the banking system. In a symmetric equilibrium, the wealth of the representative entrepreneur—and thus aggregate wealth, given that all entrepreneurs behave in the same manner and their population is normalized to unity—evolves according to

$$b_{t+1} = (1+g)b_t, \tag{11.19}$$

where the constant growth rate $1+g$ is defined as, using (11.2) and (11.18),

$$1+g = \frac{(1-\beta)\upsilon\Phi}{\Delta\pi}. \tag{11.20}$$

As implied by (11.16), equilibrium investment is linear in entrepreneurial wealth. Because all entrepreneurs behave diligently, equations (11.7) and (11.16) imply that in a symmetric equilibrium the aggregate stock of capital in $t+1$ is given by

$$K_{t+1} = \Phi b_t, \tag{11.21}$$

which, using (11.19), yields $K_{t+1} = (1+g)K_t$. Aggregate capital grows at the same rate as entrepreneurial wealth. From (11.17), credit also grows at the same rate as investment and wealth.

From (11.5), because the aggregate production function is linear, the behavior of output mimics that of capital. Similarly, given that from (11.6) the equilibrium wage rate is linear in capital, and that second-period consumption of workers is equal to $R^D w_t$, worker consumption grows at the same rate as the rate of growth of the capital stock. For entrepreneurs, as noted earlier, in equilibrium all of them have access to the credit market and borrow from banks; from (11.18) and because $c_{t+1}^E = \beta z_{t+1}^j$, their consumption is linear in wealth and hence grows again at the same rate as workers' consumption and output.

11.6 Autonomous Policy Changes

Consider first the effect of a permanent reduction in the unit monitoring cost, γ, perhaps as a result of better contract enforcement, and suppose that the private benefit of the low-moral hazard project is decreasing and convex in monitoring intensity so that $\upsilon = \upsilon(\gamma)$, with $\upsilon' < 0$, $\upsilon'' \geq 0$ and $\lim_{\gamma\to\infty}\upsilon'(\gamma) = 0$. Thus, monitoring not only helps to eliminate the high-moral hazard project, it also reduces the private benefit that can be extracted from (and thus the incentives to invest in) low-moral hazard projects. The following proposition can then be easily established.

Proposition 11.2 *A reduction in monitoring intensity, γ, when the private benefit of the low-moral hazard project is decreasing and convex in γ, has ambiguous effects on investment and the steady-state growth rate.*

The direct impact of lower monitoring intensity can be gauged from (11.13) and (11.14). A reduction in γ raises $\upsilon(\gamma)$ and the per-unit project return R^E_{t+1} that must be promised to entrepreneurs, because it increases their ability to divert resources. At the same time it lowers R^B_{t+1}, the per-unit share of the project's return that must be allocated to bankers in order for them to find it worth monitoring as intensively as promised. Consequently, equation (11.14) shows that the change in the per-unit share of project return that accrues to workers is ambiguous in general, given that γ and $\upsilon(\gamma)$ move in opposite directions. The net effect depends on the efficiency of the monitoring technology. From (11.16) and (11.20), the effect on the optimal level of investment and output growth is thus also ambiguous. If υ' is relatively small, the impact on the banker's return will dominate. This would lead to higher deposits, greater borrowing, and higher investment. A lower unit monitoring cost would therefore increase the steady-state growth rate.

Consider now a permanent increase in the required reserve ratio, μ. In the present setting, the rationale for this policy is related to the fact that, by requiring banks to hold more reserves, the regulator provides partial deposit insurance to savers—thereby mitigating the bankruptcy risk that they incur. Indeed, the participation constraint of workers (11.11) accounts for the fact that required reserves are returned to savers when the bank fails, an event which occurs with probability $1-\pi^H$. As a result, and as can be directly inferred from (11.15), a higher required reserve ratio—for a given level of investment—improves savers' incentives to hold deposits in domestic banks.

At the same time, however, an increase in the required reserve ratio reduces the supply of loanable funds and leads to lower lending and investment (as noted in proposition 11.1) and consequently a lower steady-state growth rate. This can be inferred from (11.20), given that $\partial\Phi/\partial\mu < 0$. The drop in investment also mitigates the benefits of a higher reserve ratio in terms of increased incentives to depositors.[11] If the net effect on deposits is positive, a trade-off emerges

11. Substituting (11.16) in (11.15) and differentiating the resulting expression shows that $\partial d^j_t/\partial\mu \gtrless 0$; in principle, therefore, the net impact on deposits is ambiguous, although the indirect effect is unlikely to dominate, based on reasonable parameter values. Note also that in this setting changes in the required reserve ratio have no effect on the deposit rate, which is set on world capital markets.

between financial stability considerations and economic growth. These results can be summarized in the next proposition.

Proposition 11.3 *An increase in the required reserve ratio, μ, with constant monitoring intensity, unambiguously lowers investment and the steady-state growth rate, despite improving incentives (through partial deposit insurance) to hold deposits in domestic banks.*

A further potential benefit of regulation emerges in this model if it is assumed that systemic risk takes the form of a negative externality that relates the leverage ratio of borrowers to the probability of success of good projects—and thus the probability of bank failure. When entrepreneurs are highly leveraged, they may be less diligent in ensuring that their project is successful—even when they are monitored; and if banks cannot improve monitoring intensity, the financial system may become more vulnerable to adverse shocks. This view is consistent with the evidence relating episodes of financial instability to excessive private borrowing and unsustainable credit growth (see chapter 1).

Formally, this view can be captured by relating π^H inversely to the leverage ratio that prevails in a symmetric equilibrium, l_t/b_t. To fix ideas, suppose that

$$\pi^H = 1 - \pi_0^H \left(\frac{l_t}{b_t}\right), \tag{11.22}$$

where $\pi_0^H > 0$ can be interpreted as measuring the strength of the externality associated with excessive leverage. From (11.17), the equilibrium leverage ratio is simply

$$\frac{l_t}{b_t} = \Phi - 1. \tag{11.23}$$

Suppose now that the initial leverage ratio (and thus the probability of bank failure) is considered too high by the financial regulator. From proposition 11.1 it can readily be established that, at the initial value of π^H, an increase in μ lowers the leverage ratio and consequently raises π^H, to an extent that depends on the magnitude of π_0^H. Thus, the probability of bank failure, $1 - \pi^H$, falls, mitigating financial vulnerability as expected.

However, the increase in π^H also affects incentives to lend. Indeed, when the likelihood of a good project succeeding goes up, a lender's expected return also increases; all else equal, maintaining the incentive to monitor requires a lower gross return for banks, as can be inferred from (11.10). This leads also to a higher gross return to savers, as implied by (11.14), which compounds the incentive effect (alluded to earlier) of a higher required reserve ratio on deposits, thereby increasing further the supply of funds to domestic banks. The net impact on investment depends on the total effect on Φ, which is given by, using (11.22) and (11.23),

$$\frac{d\Phi}{d\mu} = \frac{\partial \Phi}{\partial \mu} + \left(\frac{\partial \Phi}{\partial \pi^H}\right)\left(\frac{\partial \pi^H}{\partial \mu}\right) = \frac{\partial \Phi}{\partial \mu}\left[1 - \pi_0^H \left(\frac{\partial \Phi}{\partial \pi^H}\right)\right].$$

As shown earlier, $\partial \Phi/\partial \mu < 0$. It can also be established from the definition of Φ in (11.16) that $\partial \Phi/\partial \pi^H > 0$. Thus, the net effect on investment is positive if $\pi_0^H(\partial \Phi/\partial \pi^H) > 1$ and negative otherwise—the latter case prevailing if π_0^H is not too large.[12]

These results can be summarized in the following proposition.

Proposition 11.4 *An increase in the required reserve ratio, μ, with constant monitoring intensity and with a systemic externality that relates the probability of successful projects to the borrowers' leverage ratio, may lower investment and the steady-state growth rate, despite improving incentives to save through partial deposit insurance and reducing the probability of bank failure.*

The thrust of the foregoing discussion is thus that, even in the presence of an externality that may enhance the benefits of prudential regulation, an increase in the required reserve ratio motivated solely by financial stability considerations may create a trade-off with economic growth. The issue that is addressed next is whether the financial regulator can internalize this trade-off by setting the required reserve ratio optimally.

11.7 Optimal Policy

In the foregoing analysis, both the intensity of monitoring and the required reserve ratio were taken as given. In the first part of this section the intensity of monitoring is endogenized and solved for optimally by the representative bank. In the second part, the growth- and welfare-maximizing values of the required reserve ratio, taking into account its impact on the optimal degree of monitoring intensity, are derived. For tractability, the focus is on the case where π^H is constant so that the macroprudential rationale for adjusting the required reserve ratio relates solely to improved incentives for depositors. This also makes it easier to convey the intuition behind the results.[13]

12. Note also that from (11.20), π^H has a direct impact on growth, independently on its effect on Φ. This complicates further the calculation of the net effect on the steady-state growth rate.

13. Endogenizing π^H as proposed in (11.22), for instance, would complicate significantly the calculation of the optimal policy.

11.7.1 Optimal Monitoring Intensity

The optimal choice of γ, with $\upsilon = \upsilon(\gamma)$, must also maximize the entrepreneur's expected payoff, $\pi^H R^E_{t+1} I^j_t$, at the equilibrium level of investment. Using (11.13) and (11.16) for R^E_{t+1} and I^j_t yields

$$\pi^H R^E_{t+1} I^j_t = \frac{\pi^H \upsilon(\gamma)}{\Delta\pi} \Phi b^j_t. \tag{11.24}$$

To derive a tractable analytical solution to the problem, suppose, as in Haavio et al. (2015) and Silvo (2019), for instance, that $\upsilon(\gamma)$ takes the following functional form:

$$\upsilon(\gamma) = \begin{cases} \Gamma\gamma^{-\varepsilon/(1-\varepsilon)} & \text{if } \gamma > \gamma_m \\ \upsilon_m & \text{if } \gamma \leq \gamma_m \end{cases}, \tag{11.25}$$

where $\Gamma > 0$, $\upsilon_m > 0$, $\varepsilon \in (0, 1)$, and $\gamma_m \geq 0$. The first row of equation (11.25) shows that $\upsilon(\gamma)$ is differentiable and strictly convex for $\gamma > \gamma_m$. Thus, as before, the private benefit is decreasing in the intensity of monitoring. In addition, the larger Γ is, or the smaller ε is, the more efficient will the monitoring technology be. The second row implies that there is a minimum efficient scale for monitoring investment projects, or equivalently an upper bound for the private benefit. This upper bound ensures that the net rate of return on a bad project is negative even for low levels of γ.

Substituting equation (11.25) in (11.24) with b^j_t given, the first-order condition for this problem is

$$\frac{-\varepsilon}{(1-\varepsilon)\gamma\Phi} - \left\{1 + \frac{(1-\mu)\pi^H}{[R^D - (1-\pi^H)\mu]\Delta\pi}\left[\frac{-\varepsilon}{1-\varepsilon}\frac{\upsilon(\gamma)}{\gamma} + R^D\right]\right\} = 0,$$

which can be solved to give

$$\gamma^* = \varepsilon\left\{1 + \frac{(1-\mu)\pi^H R^D}{[R^D - (1-\pi^H)\mu]\Delta\pi}\right\}^{-1}\left[\frac{(1-\mu)\pi^H}{R^D - (1-\pi^H)\mu}\alpha A - 1\right]. \tag{11.26}$$

Intuitively, a change in γ has conflicting effects on the entrepreneur's expected income. A higher γ reduces directly the private benefit $\upsilon(\gamma)$, which tends to lower the entrepreneur's expected income for Φ given. In addition, there are two indirect effects operating through Φ. On the one hand, the increase in γ raises monitoring costs, which requires from (11.13) an increase in the bank's expected income in order to maintain its incentive to monitor; on the other, savers' expected income may also increase—depending on the sign of $\upsilon + \gamma R^D$ in (11.14)—which may in turn, as can be inferred from (11.15), raise the level of deposits for a given level of investment. The first effect tends to lower Φ and the second to increase it. Consequently, the overall effect on the entrepreneur's expected income is ambiguous. The optimal solution balances out these different effects.[14]

Assuming that an interior solution exists (so that $\gamma > \gamma_m$), equation (11.26) yields directly the following proposition.

Proposition 11.5 *When the private benefit of the low-moral hazard project is decreasing and convex in γ, the optimal level of monitoring intensity is increasing in the elasticity of the monitoring technology, ε, and decreasing in the required reserve ratio, μ.*

Intuitively, a more efficient monitoring technology magnifies the benefit of monitoring and raises the optimal intensity of monitoring. This lowers the private benefit of the low-moral hazard project. However, as implied by proposition 11.2, this does not necessarily promote investment and growth. From proposition 11.1, a higher μ tends to lower Φ, and thus the equilibrium level of investment, which tends to reduce the entrepreneur's expected income. This must be offset by reducing the intensity of monitoring in order to increase the private benefit and keep the entrepreneur's expected income constant. Thus, prudential regulation alters the incentives of banks to monitor and lend.

From equations (11.16), (11.20), and (11.26) the following result can also be established.

Proposition 11.6 *An increase in the required reserve ratio, μ, with monitoring intensity set optimally and with $\upsilon' < 0$, has ambiguous effects on investment and the steady-state growth rate.*

Thus, in contrast to the results reported in proposition 11.3, when monitoring intensity is endogenous and set optimally, it is possible for an increase in the required reserve ratio to have a *positive* effect on investment and growth. The reason is that now, as noted earlier, a higher required reserve ratio tends to reduce the bank's incentive to monitor, which in turn lowers monitoring costs and may increase the effective supply of loanable funds—above and beyond the direct incentive effect on savers—and the ability to lend. As a result the equilibrium level of investment (through a higher Φ) may increase. As discussed next, these results are important to study the determination of the optimal regulatory policy.

14. For γ to be positive in (11.26) it must be that $(1-\mu)\pi^H\alpha A > R^D - (1-\pi^H)\mu$. This condition is imposed numerically in the simulations reported later on.

11.7.2 Optimal Required Reserve Ratio

A natural benchmark for the optimal required reserve ratio set by the financial regulator is the solution that maximizes either growth or welfare. In the first case, it is obvious that, given proposition 11.3, the growth-maximizing value of μ, given by $d\ln(1+g)/d\mu = 0$, is 0 if υ is constant and regardless of whether γ is set optimally or not. Indeed, given that reserve requirements unambiguously lower investment and growth, it is optimal not to impose them in the first place if the goal is to maximize growth.

By contrast, when $\upsilon' < 0$ and γ is set optimally, a nontrivial solution may exist. From (11.20), this solution is obtained by solving the condition

$$\frac{d\ln(1+g)}{d\mu} = \frac{d\ln\upsilon(\gamma^*)}{d\mu} + \frac{d\ln\Phi(\mu,\gamma^*)}{d\mu} = 0, \tag{11.27}$$

where $\upsilon(\gamma^*)$ and γ^* are given by (11.25) and (11.26), and with

$$\ln\Phi(\mu,\gamma^*) = -\ln\left\{1+\gamma^* - \frac{(1-\mu)\pi^H}{R^D-(1-\pi^H)\mu}\left[\alpha A - \frac{\upsilon(\gamma^*)+\gamma^* R^D}{\Delta\pi}\right]\right\}.$$

However, the resulting expression is too complex to be solved analytically and will be solved numerically later on.

Consider next the welfare-maximizing solution. Suppose that the financial regulator is farsighted and benevolent, in the sense that the regulator takes into account the welfare of all future generations of entrepreneurs and workers. To calculate the welfare of each generation, recall that there is no consumption in adulthood and that given (11.1), the indirect utility function of entrepreneurs in old age is linear in income, so that $U^E_{t+1} = \beta^\beta(1-\beta)^{1-\beta}z_{t+1}$. Similarly, for workers, the indirect utility function takes the linear form $c^W_{t+1} = R^D w_t$, given that income (including interest payments) is consumed only in old age. Recall also that each group represents half of the population. Thus, the welfare criterion is the equally weighted within each generation but discounted sum of log-utilities across an infinite sequence of generations (De la Croix and Michel 2002, p. 91):

$$\mathcal{W}_t = \sum_{h=0}^{\infty} \Lambda^h \left\{0.5\ln\beta^\beta(1-\beta)^{1-\beta}z_{t+h+1} + 0.5\ln R^D w_{t+h}\right\}, \tag{11.28}$$

where $\Lambda \in (0,1)$ is the regulator's discount factor. From (11.6) and (11.18), along the balanced growth path,

$$\mathcal{W}_t = \sum_{h=0}^{\infty} \Lambda^h \left\{0.5\ln\left[\frac{\beta^\beta(1-\beta)^{1-\beta}\upsilon\Phi\tilde{b}_{t+h}}{\Delta\pi}\right] + 0.5\ln R^D(1-\alpha)A\tilde{k}_{t+h}\right\}. \tag{11.29}$$

From (11.19) and (11.21), b_t and k_t grow at the same rate along the balanced growth path. Thus, along the steady-state equilibrium path, $\tilde{x}_{t+h} = (1+g)^{t+h}x_0$, where $x = b, k$. Substituting these results in (11.29) and ignoring constant terms yields

$$\mathcal{W}_t = \sum_{h=0}^{\infty} \Lambda^h \left\{0.5[\ln \upsilon(\gamma^*) + \ln \Phi(\mu, \gamma^*)] + (t+h)\ln(1+g)\right\}. \quad (11.30)$$

Given that $\Lambda < 1$, $\mathcal{W}_t$ is strictly concave and bounded and the choice set is convex and compact. Thus, the optimization problem $\max_\mu \mathcal{W}_t$ has a single solution. Approximating (11.30) gives[15]

$$\mathcal{W} \simeq 0.5\frac{\ln \upsilon(\gamma^*)}{1-\Lambda} + \frac{\Lambda}{(\Lambda-1)^2}\ln(1+g) \quad (11.31)$$
$$-\frac{0.5}{1-\Lambda}\ln\left\{1+\gamma^* - \frac{(1-\mu)\pi^H}{R^D - (1-\pi^H)\mu}\left[\alpha A - \frac{\upsilon(\gamma^*)+\gamma^* R^D}{\Delta\pi}\right]\right\},$$

with $1+g$, $\upsilon(\gamma^*)$ and γ^* solved for the solution of (11.20), (11.25) with $\gamma^* > \gamma_m$, and (11.26), respectively. The optimal value of μ is the one for which $d\mathcal{W}/d\mu = 0$ is obtained. However, once again the resulting expression is too complex to allow an explicit analytical solution.

Accordingly, a numerical evaluation is performed. The recursive system of equations (11.20), (11.25) with $\gamma > \gamma_m$, and (11.26) is solved, subject to assumptions 11.1 to 11.3, for values of $\mu \in (0, 1)$. The optimal value of μ is thus the one that maximizes either growth, as in equation (11.27), or welfare, by setting $d\mathcal{W}/d\mu = 0$ in equation (11.31).

To perform the simulations, the following benchmark values are used: $\alpha = 0.3$, $A = 5$, $\beta = 0.55$, $\pi^H = 0.95$, $\pi^L = 0.2$, $\varepsilon = 0.05$, $R^D = 1.02$, and $\Gamma = 0.1$. Assuming an annual discount factor of 0.04 and interpreting a period as 30 years yields an intergenerational discount factor $\Lambda = 0.308$. These values are either fairly standard (α and Λ, for instance) or reasonable for a developing economy. In particular, the base scenario assumes that the elasticity of the monitoring technology is fairly low. In this benchmark case it can be verified that $\mu^* = 0.189$, $\gamma^* = 0.0035$, and $\upsilon(\gamma^*) = 0.135$. For this set of values, and as long as $0.135 < V < 0.7$, the restriction $A > 1/\alpha$ and assumptions 11.1 to 11.3 are all satisfied. Thus, the optimal required reserve ratio in the benchmark case is fairly high, close to the value of 0.2 used in previous chapters.

15. This derivation uses the standard result $\sum_{h=0}^{\infty} hx^h = x/(x-1)^2$ when $|x| < 1$, together with $x = \Lambda$ and $t = 0$.

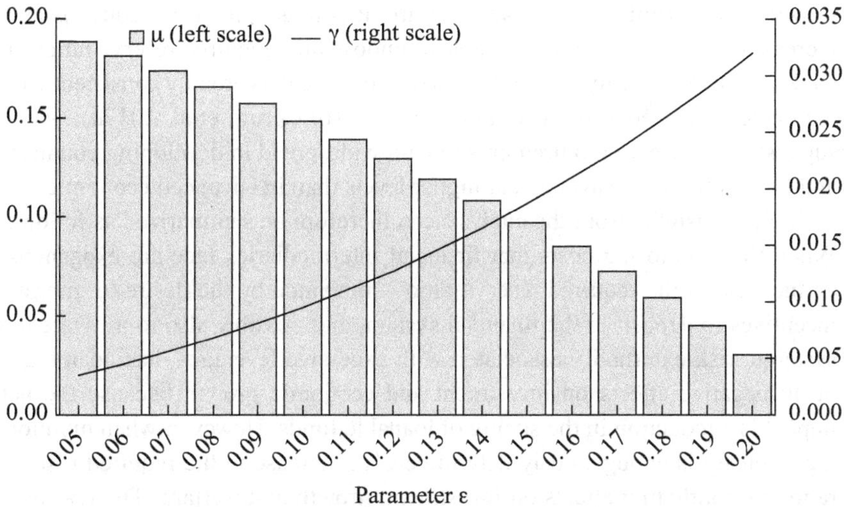

Figure 11.2
Optimal monitoring intensity and reserve requirement rate, monitoring parameter ε varying between 0.05 and 0.2
Source: Agénor (2019).

It is also worth assessing how the optimal required reserve ratio changes when structural parameters vary—especially, given the focus of this book, with respect to the monitoring technology parameter, ε. Specifically, figure 11.2 shows the results for ε varying over the interval (0.05, 0.2); for values higher than 0.22, one (or several) of the assumptions 11.1 to 11.3 is (are) not satisfied. Regardless of the value of ε, the growth- and welfare-maximizing solutions are practically identical, because in explaining changes in welfare, growth effects tend to dominate in the present setting.[16] Thus, only the growth-maximizing solutions are shown in the figure. The key result that the figure illustrates is a positive relationship between γ and ε, and an inverse relationship between the optimal value of μ and ε. For $\varepsilon = 0.1$ and 0.15, for instance, the optimal values of μ are 0.148 and 0.097, respectively. Intuitively, a higher elasticity of the monitoring technology raises the optimal monitoring intensity, as implied by proposition 11.5 and as shown in figure 11.2. In turn, the increase in γ reduces the private benefit of the low-moral hazard project, $\upsilon(\gamma)$, which helps to promote investment and growth. At the same time, however, higher monitoring costs reduce the bank's capacity to lend, which tends to lower investment and

16. The reason is the magnitude of the coefficient of $\ln(1+g)$ in (11.31), compared to the coefficients of the other two terms in that expression.

growth. To maximize growth and welfare, it is thus optimal to reduce μ as ε increases. The idea that it is desirable to impose high required reserve ratios on banks when their ability to monitor borrowers is weak is broadly consistent with the evidence (Agénor and Pereira da Silva 2016; Cerutti et al. 2017*a*), which suggests that reserve requirements remain widespread in developing countries and tend to be set, on average, at higher levels than in advanced economies.

The key insights from the analysis can therefore be summarized as follows. When the monitoring costs that financial intermediaries face are exogenous, an increase in the required reserve ratio—motivated by the desire to improve incentives to deposit in the financial system, and possibly also to mitigate the systemic risk externality associated with excessive leverage—has unambiguously negative effects on investment and economic growth because the net impact is a reduction in the supply of loanable funds. However, when monitoring intensity is endogenously determined, an increase in the required reserve ratio has conflicting effects on investment, growth and welfare. The reason is that, when monitoring intensity is endogenous, the adverse effect on lending may be offset by the fact that tighter regulation also mitigates banks' incentives to monitor. In turn, this is because a higher required reserve ratio tends not only to lower investment (as noted earlier) and thus borrowers' expected income, but it also calls for a reduction in the intensity of monitoring in order to increase the borrowers' nonverifiable private benefits and keep the entrepreneur's expected income constant. This reduction in monitoring intensity translates into lower monitoring costs, which frees up resources to increase loans and mitigates the adverse direct effect of a higher required reserve ratio on lending. The trade-off between promoting financial stability and fostering economic growth can be internalized by choosing optimally the required reserve ratio.

Nevertheless, if the optimal policy calls for reserve requirements to be set at relatively high levels, it may foster disintermediation away from the banking sector and toward less regulated channels, which in turn may distort markets, create risks to financial stability, and reduce investment and growth. The risk of disintermediation—which could be explicitly accounted for in an extension of the model presented earlier—means therefore that in practice financial supervision may also need to be strengthened, and the perimeter of regulation broadened, when there is greater reliance on macroprudential policy.

11.8 Notes on the Literature

As noted earlier, the longer-run effects of regulation on growth have received only scant attention in the research and policy debates that have followed the global financial crisis. Yet, understanding these effects is essential because a potential trade-off may arise: Although regulatory policies can help to promote activity in the short term by mitigating the procyclicality of the financial system and reducing the risk of financial distress, they could also be detrimental to economic growth in the longer term, through their effect on incentives, risk-taking, and lending decisions.

In line with previous chapters, the foregoing analysis has focused on one particular channel through which prudential regulation can affect long-run growth—noncontingent monitoring costs.[17] However, as discussed by Agénor et al. (2018*b*), there are other channels that may matter: an effect on relative prices, an effect on state-contingent verification costs (of the type discussed in chapter 4), an effect on the size of the financial sector, and a broader effect through the distribution of income and wealth. For instance, if reduced volatility (or, more generally, a more stable economic environment) makes it easier for entrepreneurs to perceive and respond more accurately to relative price signals, as well as assess risks and returns associated with their decisions, investment may increase—either directly or indirectly, through a reduction in the risk of failure—thereby promoting growth. However, an increase in capital requirements may also raise the cost of credit (due to banks passing on to borrowers the higher cost of issuing and holding equity, as discussed in chapter 6), which may dampen the demand for investment loans. The design of an optimal bank capital structure in a growth context may need to account for a fairly large range of considerations, beyond the need to mitigate risk-taking.

Prudential regulation can also affect growth, indirectly, through its impact on income and wealth distribution. Most prudential instruments operate through their effect on credit provision to the economy, either directly through quantity constraints (as is the case, for instance, with debt-to-income and loan-to-value ratios on mortgages) or indirectly, by raising the cost of credit (as discussed at length in previous chapters). While this may be important, from a systemic perspective, to safeguard financial stability, it could also affect durably the ability of some groups to access the credit market—either because of the cost effect or because constraints on the ability to acquire real estate may limit the scope for small entrepreneurs to pledge housing as collateral for business loans—with potentially significant distributional consequences among savers and borrowers.[18] If, following an increase in capital requirements, for

17. Note that the analysis did not account for the possibility that banks could make costly investments in monitoring technologies, which in turn may alter the benefits derived from monitoring. See Boot and Marinc (2006) for an analysis of this issue in a model with heterogeneous banks and capital requirements.

18. See, for instance, Iacoviello et al. (2016) for a formal analysis of the distributional effects of loan-to-value ratios and taxes on assets in an economy where heterogeneous agents are subject to collateral constraints. Frost and van Stralen (2018) provided some empirical evidence on the impact of macroprudential policies on income inequality.

instance, banks respond by permanently cutting loans to small and medium-size firms—in effect rationing them out of the credit market—there may be adverse consequences on their ability to generate income and accumulate assets over the long term. In turn, the lack of collateralizable assets may permanently affect their capacity to access the credit market. Whether distributional shifts associated with prudential regulation have a negative impact on growth cannot be ascertained a priori; the relationship between income or wealth inequality and growth is theoretically ambiguous and depends, in particular, on the degree of heterogeneity in the propensity to save across agents and the composition of assets among households. Nevertheless, the recent evidence suggests that this relationship tends to be negative (Cingano 2014; Gründler and Scheuermeyer 2018). Thus, prudential policies may also have a significant impact on growth if their distributional effects are large and persistent. Further exploration of these interactions is essential for optimal policy design.

Epilogue

Since the global financial crisis there has been a renewed effort by macroeconomists to make financial frictions front and center in designing closed- and open-economy macroeconomic models for monetary and macroprudential policy analysis. Among the major issues that have motivated this agenda have been the need to understand better how the financial system amplifies and propagates shocks originating elsewhere in the economy and how it can be itself a source of aggregate fluctuations. Also important have been the extent to which central banks should account for financial stability considerations in the conduct of monetary policy, and whether central banks and regulators should coordinate their policies to achieve and maintain macroeconomic and financial stability. From that perspective, this book has attempted to provide a unified set of theoretical and quantitative macroeconomic models with financial frictions—ranging from static, simple models to more elaborate dynamic stochastic general equilibrium (DSGE) models of closed and open economies—that capture some of the key channels identified in the vast literature of the past decade. All these models are essentially *analytical platforms*, built to gain intuition with respect to specific conceptual and policy issues. These issues include interactions between the monetary transmission mechanism and the regulatory regime and how these interactions affect the performance of monetary and macroprudential policies—both individually and jointly.

As stated at the outset, the focus of this book was squarely on models that are appropriate for middle-income countries (MICs). A key reason is the existence of significant structural differences between these countries and advanced economies—the predominant role of banks, a direct link between credit and the supply side, a weak legal environment, a limited capacity to regulate and supervise financial institutions (which itself militates in favor of implementing relatively simple prudential policy rules), impediments to capital mobility, and a high degree of vulnerability to external shocks. In addition, even though advanced economies and MICs have faced a number of common policy challenges since the global financial crisis in achieving macroeconomic and financial stability (how much should central banks *lean against the wind* and mitigate the amplitude of the financial cycle, for instance), there are also significant and long-standing differences between the two groups of countries in the nature of these challenges and their ability to address them. These differences include coping with volatile capital flows, terms-of-trade shocks, and the fear of floating. As discussed in the introduction, differences in structural features and policy objectives do matter for the design of macroeconomic models and for their use to guide macroeconomic and macroprudential policy formulation. Yet I also believe that much of the analytics and some of the broad policy lessons that can be drawn from the quantitative experiments are likely to be equally relevant for advanced economies—although I will leave it to the informed reader to be the ultimate judge of that claim.

At the same time, there remain a number of issues, both conceptual and empirical, that are not fully understood with respect to the goals mentioned earlier. Many of these issues have been mentioned in the preceding chapters; they relate (in no particular order) to the possibility of borrower and lender default in equilibrium, the links between capital requirements, systemic risk and bank risk-taking, the impact of financial regulation on shadow banking, the constraints imposed by dollarization, the design of institutional arrangements for coordination between central banks and regulators, interactions between macroprudential instruments, managing shocks to world commodity prices in resource-dependent economies, coping with leakages associated with capital controls and their cross-border effects, the scope for international macroprudential policy coordination, and the effects of prudential regulation (possibly through income and asset distribution) on long-run growth. In particular, a more systematic comparison between the gains from combining multiple macroprudential instruments and those resulting from combining monetary policy and alternative individual macroprudential tools would help to better assess whether a financial stability mandate should also be assigned to central banks. Similarly, accounting for a natural resource sector and a link between that sector and the fiscal accounts in a DSGE-FF model of a resource-dependent economy would help to evaluate the macroeconomic and financial effects of fluctuations in world commodity prices and to better evaluate alternative policy responses—including the combination of monetary, macroprudential, and fiscal policies. Finally, even though it was shown that international macroprudential policy coordination can generate gains for the world economy, this is not necessarily the case for individual countries or regions. Moreover, even if all parties may benefit, maintaining coordinated policies may prove difficult in practice: Once an agreement is in place, the incentive to cheat almost invariably emerges.

Moreover, this incentive is stronger the smaller the perceived *ex post* cost of reneging on a cooperative agreement. Thus, a key issue to address is what kind of institutional arrangements—involving, for instance, a reputable international institution playing the role of an *honest broker*, as discussed in Agénor and Pereira da Silva 2018*a*)—or what types of sanctions can mitigate the temptation to renege.

But there are other, equally challenging issues that need to be highlighted. They relate, in particular, to the role of expectations, the role of estimation to discriminate among alternative sources of frictions, the solution of DSGE-FF models and the statistical evaluation of their performance (whether they are fully estimated or not), and the treatment of labor markets and unemployment.

Regarding expectations, the assumption used in most of this book (except for the simple static models presented in chapters 2 and 7) is that of rational expectations. One argument for doing so, as suggested by Woodford (2013), is that it is a useful benchmark from which alternatives can be contrasted. Moreover, under some specific circumstances, a *robustly optimal* policy—a policy, as defined by Woodford (2010), that does not depart too much from the optimal policy under rational expectations—may have many of the qualitative features of the latter policy. However, it is now well established that alternative assumptions about expectations formation, such as adaptive learning or rational inattention theory, can affect significantly the effects of policy and exogenous shocks. With adaptive learning, for instance, in response to news private agents may form either overoptimistic or overpessimistic expectations of the state of the economy due to their partial knowledge of the world they live in. In turn, overoptimism can lead to excessive accumulation of housing assets and create a housing boom that is not based on fundamentals (see Kanik and Xiao 2014). Interactions between learning and financial frictions may further amplify financial accelerator effects because misperceptions about future asset prices and returns may affect collateral-loan values, risk premia, current investment, and loan demand. Under learning, the strong interaction between financial frictions and forecast errors can generate larger responses of the economy to exogenous shocks, whatever the nature of the shock (see Rychalovska 2016; Eusepi and Preston 2018; Pintus and Suda 2019).[1] There is also evidence to suggest that the empirical fit of estimated DSGE models is better with adaptive learning (see Milani 2012; Gaus and Gibbs 2017), and that introducing survey expectations in DSGE models may make them better able to

1. In an inflation-targeting regime, learning can take the form of a relationship between agents' inflation expectations and deviations of actual inflation from the central bank's inflation target. See Neuenkirch and Tillmann (2014), for instance.

account for the high degree of persistence that is typically observed in aggregate macroeconomic time series (see Fuhrer 2017). Some studies, however, found conflicting results. Gabaix (2018), for instance, found that with bounded rationality, monetary policy can exert conflicting effects on inflation in the short and in the long run. For their part, Farhi and Werning (2017) found that bounded rationality, combined with agent heterogeneity, incomplete markets, uninsurable idiosyncratic risk, and occasionally binding borrowing constraints, can weaken significantly the effects of monetary policy compared to what standard New Keynesian models would predict.

Another important set of issues relates to the estimation of DSGE-FF models, their solution, and their empirical evaluation. Given the explicit focus on understanding analytical and policy issues at a fairly abstract level, the DSGE models presented in this book were parameterized, dwelling for the most part on the existing literature on MICs. It was also noted that the impulse response functions associated with some basic financial shocks (a temporary change in the policy rate or in the world risk-free interest rate, for instance) were broadly consistent, *qualitatively*, with the main stylized facts. However, if models of the type developed in this book have to be used to provide practical advice in MICs, and not only as analytical platforms, estimation is an essential step to discriminate among alternative sources of frictions, identify which shocks matter the most, and provide a reliable quantitative evaluation of their impact on macroeconomic and financial stability. Doing so raises a number of practical challenges, due to data limitations. But the use of Bayesian techniques is becoming progressively more widespread in MICs as well. Moreover, in practice it is likely that several types of frictions are present at the same time, so models combining different frictions may be better at matching the data—as the recent literature on advanced economies (discussed in chapter 1) appears to suggest. From that perspective, the issue is therefore to determine what additional frictions should be added to the present framework in order to improve its ability to explain the data in a particular setting.

Understanding how the economy responds in normal times when assessing the effects of various policies is an important benchmark. Equally important, though, are solution methods that involve higher-order approximations, which should be used to better capture the nonlinearities present in periods of financial stress. This matters to account, for instance, for sudden and cumulative shifts in borrowers' credit risk perceptions and the possibility of banks' default, and to ensure that timely policy responses prevent periods of large financial imbalances from turning into full-blown crises. Yet, how best to evaluate the empirical performance of fully estimated or partially calibrated DSGE-FF models remains also a matter of debate, as discussed by Le et al. (2016) and Meenagh et al. (2019). Current thinking is to view all of these models as simplifications of a complex reality; they should therefore be evaluated on the basis of their ability to explain the data that they were designed to account for—by measuring the probability that the data could be generated by the model. In that sense, the performance of a model should be assessed by using formal misspecifications tests. An important issue in this context is the extent to which this procedure can be extended to a subset of the variables of a model, rather than all variables, in order to isolate which features of the data the model is best able to replicate.

Finally, the role of labor market rigidities, and their implications for open or disguised unemployment, needs to be further explored in both simple and more elaborate models. In most of this book, it was assumed that wages are fully flexible and that unemployment cannot emerge. This assumption is adequate for a number of MICs, where a large informal sector tends to act as a shock absorber in response to employment fluctuations in the formal economy. However, this is not the case for all of them; in some countries, open unemployment is high. The DSGE literature on advanced economies has considered a number of channels through which wage rigidities can generate unemployment (see Mattesini and Rossi 2009 and Christiano et al. 2011, for instance, and the references therein). However, there are a number of issues that need to be discussed further, most notably with respect to labor market institutions and regulations. For instance, there is evidence that stronger employment protection strengthens linkages between the macroeconomy and the financial system (see Leroy and Pop 2019). In addition, in MICs these institutions and regulations (such as minimum wage legislation and firing costs) are a critical source of segmentation of labor markets. In some countries, trade unions remain also an important source of labor market duality and unemployment.

This brief appraisal of the analytical and empirical challenges that might be useful to address suggests that the area of research covered in this book, whether it focuses on high- or middle-income countries, is likely to continue to thrive in the coming years. The array of pressing issues that policymakers are confronted with—ranging from practical institutional arrangements for coordinating in the most effective way the decisions of central banks and regulators, to improving the implementation of Basel III's principle of jurisdictional reciprocity—will also help to drive this agenda forward. Indeed, if the pace at which the literature has advanced in the past decade is any guide, it is entirely possible that in a relatively short time, some (or much) of what is described as cutting-edge research in this book is viewed as either too rudimentary or, in retrospect, misguided. Should that occur, however, rather than being a matter of concern it should instead be celebrated as a sign of the vitality of macroeconomics.

References

Abbate, Angela, and Dominik Thaler. 2019. "Monetary Policy and the Asset Risk-Taking Channel." *Journal of Money, Credit, and Banking* 51 (December), 2115–2144.

Abhakorn, Pongrapeeporn, and Nongnuch Tantisantiwong. 2012. "A Reexamination of Capital Controls' Effectiveness: Recent Experience of Thailand." *Journal of Asian Economics* 23 (February), 26–38.

Abo-Zaid, Salem. 2015. "Optimal Monetary Policy with the Cost Channel and Monopolistically Competitive Banks." *Journal of Macroeconomics* 45 (September), 284–299.

Acosta Smith, Jonathan, Michael Grill, and Jan Hannes Lang. 2017. "The Leverage Ratio, Risk-taking, and Bank Stability." Working Paper No. 2079. European Central Bank (June).

Adjemian, Stéphane, Matthieu Darracq Pariès, and Stéphane Moyen. 2008. "Optimal Monetary Policy in an Estimated DSGE Model of the Euro Area." Unpublished, European Central Bank (January).

Adolfson, Malin. 2007. "Incomplete Exchange Rate Pass-through and Simple Monetary Policy Rules." *Journal of International Money and Finance* 26 (April), 468–494.

Adolfson, Malin, Stefan Laséen, Jesper Lindé, and Lars E. O. Svensson. 2011. "Optimal Monetary Policy in an Operational Medium-Sized DSGE Model." *Journal of Money, Credit, and Banking* 43 (October), 1287–1331.

Adolfson, Malin, Stefan Laséen, Jesper Lindé, and Lars E. O. Svensson. 2014. "Monetary Policy Trade-Offs in an Estimated Open-Economy DSGE Model." *Journal of Economic Dynamics and Control* 42 (May), 33–49.

Adolfson, Malin, Stefan Laséen, Jesper Lindé, and Mattias Villani. 2008. "Evaluating an Estimated New Keynesian Small Open Economy Model." *Journal of Economic Dynamics and Control* 32 (August), 2690–2721.

Adrian, Tobias, and Nina Boyarchenko. 2015. "Intermediary Leverage Cycles and Financial Stability." Staff Report No. 567, Federal Reserve Bank of New York (revised, February).

Adrian, Tobias, and J. Nellie Liang. 2018. "Monetary Policy, Financial Conditions, and Financial Stability." *International Journal of Central Banking* 14 (January), 73–131.

Afanasyeva, Elena, and Jochen Güntner. 2018. "Bank Market Power and the Risk Channel of Monetary Policy." Finance and Economics Discussion Paper No. 2018-6. Federal Reserve Board (January).

Agénor, Pierre-Richard. 1997. "Capital-Market Imperfections and the Macroeconomic Dynamics of Small Indebted Economies." Princeton Study in International Finance No. 82 (June).

Agénor, Pierre-Richard. 2002. "Monetary Policy under Flexible Exchange Rates: An Introduction to Inflation Targeting." In *Inflation Targeting: Design, Performance, Challenges*, ed. Norman Loayza and Raimundo Soto. Santiago: Central Bank of Chile.

Agénor, Pierre-Richard. 2006*a*. "Market Sentiment and Macroeconomic Fluctuations under Pegged Exchange Rates." *Economica* 73 (November), 579–604.

Agénor, Pierre-Richard. 2006*b*. "The Analytics of Segmented Labor Markets." In *Adjustment Policies, Poverty and Unemployment: The IMMPA Framework*, ed. Pierre-Richard Agénor, Alejandro Izquierdo, and Henning Tarp Jensen. Oxford: Blackwell Publishing.

Agénor, Pierre-Richard. 2012. "International Financial Integration: Benefits, Costs, and Policy Challenges." In *Survey of International Finance*, ed. H. Kent Baker and Leigh A. Riddick. Oxford: Oxford University Press.

Agénor, Pierre-Richard. 2016. "Optimal Fiscal Management of Commodity Price Shocks." *Journal of Development Economics* 122 (September 2016), 183–196.

Agénor, Pierre-Richard. 2019. "Growth and Welfare Effects of Macroprudential Regulation." *Macroeconomic Dynamics* 23 (December 2019), 3140–3162.

Agénor, Pierre-Richard, and Joshua Aizenman. 1998. "Contagion and Volatility with Imperfect Credit Markets." *IMF Staff Papers* 45 (June), 207–235.

Agénor, Pierre-Richard, and Joshua Aizenman. 2004. "Savings and the Terms of Trade under Borrowing Constraints." *Journal of International Economics* 63 (July), 324–345.

Agénor, Pierre-Richard, and Koray Alper. 2012. "Monetary Shocks and Central Bank Liquidity with Credit Market Imperfections." *Oxford Economic Papers* 64 (July), 563–591.

Agénor, Pierre-Richard, Koray Alper, and Luiz Pereira da Silva. 2012. "Capital Requirements and Business Cycles with Credit Market Imperfections." *Journal of Macroeconomics* 34 (September), 687–705.

Agénor, Pierre-Richard, Koray Alper, and Luiz Pereira da Silva. 2013. "Capital Regulation, Monetary Policy, and Financial Stability." *International Journal of Central Banking* 9 (September), 193–238.

Agénor, Pierre-Richard, Koray Alper, and Luiz Pereira da Silva. 2014*a*. "Sudden Floods, Macroprudential Regulation, and Stability in an Open Economy." *Journal of International Money and Finance* 48 (November), 68–100.

Agénor, Pierre-Richard, Koray Alper, and Luiz Pereira da Silva. 2018*a*. "External Shocks, Financial Volatility, and Reserve Requirements in an Open Economy." *Journal of International Money and Finance* 83 (May), 23–43.

Agénor, Pierre-Richard, and Nihal Bayraktar. 2010. "Contracting Models of the Phillips Curve." *Journal of Macroeconomics* 32 (June), 555–570.

Agénor, Pierre-Richard, George Bratsiotis, and Damjan Pfajfar. 2014*b*. "Credit Frictions, Collateral, and the Cyclical Behavior of the Finance Premium." *Macroeconomic Dynamics* 18 (July), 985–997.

Agénor, Pierre-Richard, and Karim El Aynaoui. 2010. "Excess Liquidity, Bank Pricing Rules and Monetary Policy." *Journal of Banking and Finance* 34 (May), 923–945.

Agénor, Pierre-Richard, and Alessandro Flamini. 2019. "Institutional Mandates for Macroeconomic and Financial Stability." Unpublished, University of Manchester (October).

Agénor, Pierre-Richard, and Robert P. Flood. 1994. "Macroeconomic Policy, Speculative Attacks, and Balance of Payments Crises." In *Handbook of International Macroeconomics*, ed. Frederick van der Ploeg. Oxford: Basil Blackwell.

Agénor, Pierre-Richard, Leonardo Gambacorta, Enisse Kharroubi, and Luiz A. Pereira da Silva. 2018*b*. "The Effects of Prudential Regulation, Financial Development, and Financial Openness on Economic Growth." Working Paper No. 752. Bank for International Settlements (October).

Agénor, Pierre-Richard, and Timothy Jackson. 2019. "Monetary and Macroprudential Policy Coordination with Asymmetric Preferences." Unpublished, University of Manchester (January).

Agénor, Pierre-Richard, Timothy Jackson, Leonardo Gambacorta, Enisse Kharroubi, Giovanni Lombardo, and Luiz A. Pereira da Silva. 2018*c*. "Assessing the Gains from International Macroprudential Policy Cooperation." Unpublished, Bank for International Settlements (March). Forthcoming, *Journal of Money, Credit, and Banking*.

Agénor, Pierre-Richard, Timothy Jackson, and Pengfei Jia. 2018*d*. "Macroprudential Policy Coordination in a Currency Union." Unpublished, University of Manchester (July).

Agénor, Pierre-Richard, Timothy Jackson, and Luiz Pereira da Silva. 2020. "Foreign Exchange Intervention and Financial Stability." Unpublished, University of Manchester (January).

Agénor, Pierre-Richard, and Pengfei Jia. 2020. "Capital Controls and Welfare with Cross-Border Bank Capital Flows." Unpublished, University of Manchester (February). Forthcoming, *Journal of Macroeconomics*.

Agénor, Pierre-Richard, and Peter J. Montiel. 2006. "Credit Market Imperfections and the Monetary Transmission Mechanism. Part I: Fixed Exchange Rates." Working Paper No. 76. Centre for Growth and Business Cycle Research, University of Manchester (October).

Agénor, Pierre-Richard, and Peter J. Montiel. 2007. "Credit Market Imperfections and the Monetary Transmission Mechanism. Part II: Flexible Exchange Rates." Working Paper No. 86. Centre for Growth and Business Cycle Research, University of Manchester (January).

Agénor, Pierre-Richard, and Peter J. Montiel. 2008. "Monetary Policy Analysis in a Small Open Credit-Based Economy." *Open Economies Review* 19 (September), 423–455.

Agénor, Pierre-Richard, and Peter J. Montiel. 2015. *Development Macroeconomics*, 4th ed. Princeton, NJ: Princeton University Press.

Agénor, Pierre-Richard, and Luiz Pereira da Silva. 2010. "Reforming International Standards for Bank Capital Requirements: A Perspective from the Developing World." In *International Banking in the New Era: Post-Crisis Challenges and Opportunities*, ed. S. Kim and M. D. McKenzie, IFR Vol. No 11. Bingley, UK: Emerald.

Agénor, Pierre-Richard, and Luiz Pereira da Silva. 2012. "Cyclical Effects of Bank Capital Requirements with Imperfect Credit Markets." *Journal of Financial Stability* 8 (January), 43–56.

Agénor, Pierre-Richard, and Luiz Pereira da Silva. 2014. "Macroprudential Regulation and the Monetary Transmission Mechanism." *Journal of Financial Stability* 13 (August), 44–63.

Agénor, Pierre-Richard, and Luiz Pereira da Silva. 2016. "Reserve Requirements and Loan Loss Provisions as Countercyclical Macroprudential Instruments." Policy Brief No. IDB-PB-250, Inter-American Development Bank (February).

Agénor, Pierre-Richard, and Luiz Pereira da Silva. 2017. "Cyclically Adjusted Provisions and Financial Stability." *Journal of Financial Stability* 28 (February), 143–162.

Agénor, Pierre-Richard, and Luiz Pereira da Silva. 2018*a*. "Financial Spillovers, Spillbacks, and the Scope for International Macroprudential Policy Coordination." Policy Paper No. 97. Bank for International Settlements (April).

Agénor, Pierre-Richard, and Luiz Pereira da Silva. 2018*b*. "Global Banking, Financial Spillovers, and Macroprudential Policy Coordination." Unpublished, Bank for International Settlements (October).

Agénor, Pierre-Richard, and Luiz Pereira da Silva. 2018*c*. "Capital Requirements, Risk-Taking, and Welfare in a Growing Economy." Unpublished, University of Manchester (November).

Agénor, Pierre-Richard, and Luiz Pereira da Silva. 2019. *Integrated Inflation Targeting*. Basel: BIS Publications, Bank for International Settlements.

Agénor, Pierre-Richard, and Roy Zilberman. 2015. "Loan Loss Provisioning Rules, Procyclicality, and Financial Volatility." *Journal of Banking and Finance* 61 (December), 301–315.

Aghion, Philippe, Philippe Bacchetta, and Abhijit Banerjee. 2004. "A Corporate Balance-Sheet Approach to Currency Crises." *Journal of Economic Theory* 119 (November), 6–30.

Agosin, Manuel R., and Franklin Huaita. 2012. "Overreaction in Capital Flows to Emerging Markets: Booms and Sudden Stops." *Journal of International Money and Finance* 31 (September), 1140–1155.

Aguiar, Alvaro, and Ines Drumond. 2007. "Business Cycle and Bank Capital: Monetary Policy Transmission under the Basel Accords." FEP Working Paper No. 242, Universidade do Porto, (June).

Ahmed, Shaghil, and Andrei Zlate. 2014. "Capital Flows to Emerging Market Economies: A Brave New World?" *Journal of International Money and Finance* 48 (November), 221–248.

Ahmed, Swarnali, Maximiliano Appendino, and Michele Ruta. 2015. "Depreciations without Exports? Global Value Chains and the Exchange Rate Elasticity of Exports." Policy Research Working Paper No. 7390, World Bank (August).

Aikman, David, Andrew G. Haldane, and Benjamin D. Nelson. 2015*a*. "Curbing the Credit Cycle." *Economic Journal* 125 (June), 1072–1109.

Aikman, David, Andreas Lehnert, J. Nellie Liang, and Michele Modugno. 2016. "Financial Vulnerabilities, Macroeconomic Dynamics, and Monetary Policy." Discussion Paper No. 2016-55, Federal Reserve Board (July).

Aikman, David, Benjamin Nelson, and Misa Tanaka. 2015*b*. "Reputation, Risk-taking, and Macroprudential Policy." *Journal of Banking and Finance* 50 (January), 428–439.

Aikman, David, and Matthias Paustian. 2006. "Bank Capital, Asset Prices and Monetary Policy." Working Paper No. 305, Bank of England (August).

Airaudo, Marco, and María Pía Olivero. 2019. "Optimal Monetary Policy with Countercyclical Credit Spreads." *Journal of Money, Credit, and Banking* 51 (June), 787–829.

Aizenman, Joshua, and Reuven Glick. 2009. "Sterilization, Monetary Policy, and Global Financial Integration." *Review of International Economics* 17 (September), 777–801.

Aizenman, Joshua, Michael Hutchison, and Ilan Noy. 2011. "Inflation Targeting and Real Exchange Rates in Emerging Markets." *World Development* 39 (May), 712–724.

Ajello, Andrea. 2016. "Financial Intermediation, Investment Dynamics, and Business Cycle Fluctuations." *American Economic Review* 106 (August), 2256–2303.

Ajello, Andrea, Thomas Laubach, J. David López-Salido, and Taisuke Nakata. 2019. "Financial Stability and Optimal Interest Rate Policy." *International Journal of Central Banking* 15 (March), 279–326.

Akinci, Ozge. 2013. "Global Financial Conditions, Country Spreads, and Macroeconomic Fluctuations in Emerging Countries." *Journal of International Economics* 91 (November), 358–371.

Akinci, Ozge, and Jane Olmstead-Rumsey. 2018. "How Effective Are Macroprudential Policies? An Empirical Investigation." *Journal of Financial Intermediation* 33 (January), 33–57.

Aldasoro, Iñaki, Claudio Borio, and Mathias Drehmann. 2018. "Early Warning Indicators of Banking Crises: Expanding the Family." *Bank for International Settlements Quarterly Review* (March), 29–45.

Alencar, Leonardo S. 2012. "Revisiting Bank Pricing Rules in Brazil: Evidence from Loan and Deposit Rates." *Ensayos Económicos* 1 (March), 35–71.

Aliaga-Díaz, Roger, and María Pía Olivero. 2010*a*. "Is There a Financial Accelerator in US Banking? Evidence from the Cyclicality of Banks' Price-Cost Margins." *Economics Letters* 108 (August), 167–171.

Aliaga-Díaz, Roger, and María Pía Olivero. 2010*b*. "Macroeconomic Implications of 'Deep Habits' in Banking." *Journal of Money, Credit, and Banking* 43 (December), 1495–1521.

Aliaga-Díaz, Roger, and María Pía Olivero. 2019. "Optimal Monetary Policy with Countercyclical Credit Spreads." *Journal of Money, Credit, and Banking* 51 (June), 787–829.

Allen, Franklin, Elena Carletti, and Robert Marquez. 2011. "Credit Market Competition and Capital Regulation." *Review of Financial Studies* 24 (April), 983–1018.

Alpanda, Sami, and Uluc Aysun. 2014. "International Transmission of Financial Shocks in an Estimated DSGE Model." *Journal of International Money and Finance* 47 (October), 21–55.

Alpanda, Sami, and Sarah Zubairy. 2017. "Addressing Household Indebtedness: Monetary, Fiscal or Macroprudential Policy?" *European Economic Review* 92 (February), 47–73.

Alper, Koray. 2007. "Monetary Policy and External Shocks in a Dollarized Economy with Credit Market Imperfections." Working Paper No. 93, Centre for Growth and Business Cycle Research, University of Manchester (December).

Alper, Koray, Mahir Binici, Selva Demiralp, Hakan Kara, and Pınar Özlü. 2018. "Reserve Requirements, Liquidity Risk, and Credit Growth." *Journal of Money, Credit, and Banking* 50 (June), 817–827.

Altunbas, Yener, Mahir Binici, and Leonardo Gambacorta. 2018. "Macroprudential Policy and Bank Risk." *Journal of International Money and Finance* 81 (March), 203–220.

Altunbas, Yener, Leonardo Gambacorta, and David Marques-Ibanez. 2014. "Does Monetary Policy Affect Bank Risk?" *International Journal of Central Banking* 10 (March), 95–135.

Amador, Juan S., Celina Gaitán-Maldonado, José E. Gómez-González, Mauricio Villamizar-Villegas, and Héctor M. Zárate. 2014. "Credit and Business Cycles: An Empirical Analysis in the Frequency Domain." Working Paper No. 843, Central Bank of Colombia (June).

Anand, Rahul, Vic Delloro, and Shanaka J. Peiris. 2015. "A Credit and Banking Model for Emerging Markets and an Application to the Philippines." In *The Evolving Role and Limits of Monetary Policy: New Perspectives for Emerging Market Economies*. Manila: Bangko Sentral ng Pilipinas.

Andreasen, Martin M., Marcelo Ferman, and Pawel Zabczyk. 2012. "The Business Cycle Implications of Banks' Maturity Transformation." *Review of Economic Dynamics* 16 (October), 581–600.

Andrés, Javier, and Oscar Arce. 2012. "Banking Competition, Housing Prices, and Macroeconomic Stability." *Economic Journal* 122 (December), 1346–1372.

Andrés, Javier, Oscar Arce, and Carlos Thomas. 2013. "Banking Competition, Collateral Constraints, and Optimal Monetary Policy." *Journal of Money, Credit, and Banking* 45 (December), 87–125.

Andrés, Javier, J. David López-Salido, and Edward Nelson. 2004. "Tobin's Imperfect Substitution in Optimizing General Equilibrium." *Journal of Money, Credit, and Banking* 36 (August), 665–690.

Angelini, Paolo, Stefano Neri, and Fabio Panetta. 2014. "The Interaction between Capital Requirements and Monetary Policy." *Journal of Money, Credit, and Banking* 46 (September), 1073–1112.

Angeloni, Ignazio, and Ester Faia. 2013. "Capital Regulation and Monetary Policy with Fragile Banks." *Journal of Monetary Economics* 60 (April), 311–324.

Anundsen, André K., Frank Hansen, Karsten Gerdrup, and Kasper Kragh-Sørensen. 2014. "The Role of Credit, House Prices, Non-Core Liabilities, and Exuberance Measures for Predicting Financial Crises." Working Paper No. 14/14, Norges Bank (November).

Aoki, Kosuke, Gianluca Benigno, and Nobuhiro Kiyotaki. 2018. "Monetary and Financial Policies in Emerging Markets." Unpublished, London School of Economics (October).

Aoki, Kosuke, James Proudman, and Gertjan Vlieghe. 2004. "House Prices, Consumption, and Monetary Policy: A Financial Accelerator Approach." *Journal of Financial Intermediation* 13 (October), 414–435.

Apergis, Nicholas. 2017. "Monetary Policy and Macroprudential Policy: New Evidence from a World Panel of Countries." *Oxford Bulletin of Economics and Statistics* 79 (June), 395–410.

Araujo, Aloisio, and Bruno Funchal. 2005. "Bankruptcy Law in Latin America: Past and Future." *Economia* 6 (September), 149–216.

Ariss, Rima Turk. 2010. "On the Implications of Market Power in Banking: Evidence from Developing Countries." *Journal of Banking and Finance* 34 (April), 765–775.

Armantier, Olivier, Eric Ghysels, Asani Sarkar, and Jeffrey Shrader. 2015. "Discount Window Stigma during the 2007–2008 Financial Crisis." Staff Report No. 483, Federal Reserve Bank of New York (revised, August).

Armas, Adrián, Paul Castillo, and Marco Vega. 2014. "Inflation Targeting and Quantitative Tightening: Effects of Reserve Requirements in Peru." Working Paper No. 499, Inter-American Development Bank (April).

Aruoba, S. Boragan, Jésus Fernández-Villaverde, and Juan F. Rubio-Ramírez. 2006. "Comparing Solution Methods for Dynamic Equilibrium Economies." *Journal of Economic Dynamics and Control* 30 (December), 2477–2508.

Ascari, Guido, and Lorenza Rossi. 2011. "Real Wage Rigidities and Disinflation Dynamics: Calvo vs. Rotemberg Pricing." *Economics Letters* 110 (February), 126–131.

Ascari, Guido, and Argia M. Sbordone. 2014. "The Macroeconomics of Trend Inflation." *Journal of Economic Literature* 52 (September), 679–739.

Aslam, Aqib, and Emiliano Santoro. 2009. "Bank Lending, Durable Goods, and Spreads." Unpublished, University of Copenhagen (October).

Aspachs-Bracons, Oriol, and Pau Rabanal. 2011. "The Effects of Housing Prices and Monetary Policy in a Currency Union." *International Journal of Central Banking* 7 (March), 225–274.

Athanasoglou, Panayiotis P., Ioannis Daniilidis, and Manthos D. Delis. 2014. "Bank Procyclicality and Output: Issues and Policies." *Journal of Economics and Business* 72 (March), 58–83.

Atta-Mensah, Joseph, and Ali Dib. 2008. "Bank Lending, Credit Shocks, and the Transmission of Canadian Monetary Policy." *International Review of Economics and Finance* 17 (March), 159–176.

Avdjiev, Stefan, Catherine Koch, Patrick McGuire, and Goetz von Peter. 2018. "Transmission of Monetary Policy through Global Banks: Whose Policy Matters?." *Journal of International Money and Finance* 89 (December), 67–82.

Aysun, Uluc, and Adam Honig. 2011. "Bankruptcy Costs, Liability Dollarization, and Vulnerability to Sudden Stops." *Journal of Development Economics* 95 (July), 201–211.

Ayyagari, Meghana, Asli Demirguc-Kunt, and Vojislav Maksimovic. 2012. "Financing of Firms in Developing Countries Lessons from Research." Policy Research Working Paper No. 6036, World Bank (April).

Bacchetta, Philippe, and Ramon Caminal. 2000. "Do Capital Market Imperfections Exacerbate Output Fluctuations?." *European Economic Review* 44 (March), 449–468.

Bahadir, Berrak, and Inci Gumus. 2016. "Credit Decomposition and Business Cycles in Emerging Market Economies." *Journal of International Economics* 103 (November), 250–262.

Bailliu, Jeannine, Cesaire Meh, and Yahong Zhang. 2015. "Macroprudential Rules and Monetary Policy When Financial Frictions Matter." *Economic Modelling* 50 (November), 148–161.

Banerjee, Ryan, Michael B. Devereux, and Giovanni Lombardo. 2016. "Self-Oriented Monetary Policy, Global Financial Markets and Excess Volatility of International Capital Flows." *Journal of International Money and Finance* 68 (November), 275–297.

Bank for International Settlements. 2018. *Annual Economic Report*. Basel: BIS Publications.

Bank for International Settlements. 2019. *Annual Economic Report*. Basel: BIS Publications.

Bank of England. 2011. "Instruments of Macroprudential Policy." Discussion Paper (December).

Barajas, Adolfo, Roberto Steiner, Leonardo Villar, and César Pabón. 2014. "Inflation Targeting in Latin America." Working Paper No. 473, Inter-American Development Bank (January).

Barth, James, Gerard Caprio Jr., and Ross Levine. 2013. *Measure It, Improve It: Bank Regulation and Supervision in 180 Countries 1999–2011*. Santa Monica, CA: Milken Institute.

Basel Committee on Banking Supervision. 2006. "International Convergence of Capital Measurement and Capital Standards: A Revised Framework." Unpublished, Bank for International Settlements (revised, June).

Basel Committee on Banking Supervision. 2011. "Basel III: A Global Regulatory Framework for More Resilient Banks and Banking Systems." Report No. 189, Bank for International Settlements (revised, June).

Basel Committee on Banking Supervision. 2013. "Basel III: The Liquidity Coverage Ratio and Liquidity Risk Monitoring Tools." Report No. 238 (January).

Basel Committee on Banking Supervision. 2017. "Basel III: Finalising Post-Crisis Reforms." Unpublished, Bank for International Settlements (December).

Bean, Charles, Jens Larsen, and Kalin Nikolov. 2002. "Financial Frictions and the Monetary Transmission Mechanism: Theory, Evidence, and Policy Implications." Working Paper No. 113, European Central Bank (January).

Beavis, Brian, and Ian Dobbs. 1990. *Optimization and Stability Theory for Economic Analysis*. Cambridge: Cambridge University Press.

Bech, Morten, and Todd Keister. 2017. "Liquidity Regulation and the Implementation of Monetary Policy." *Journal of Monetary Economics* 92 (December), 64–77.

Beck, Thorsten, and Asli Demirguc-Kunt. 2006. "Small and Medium-Size Enterprises: Access to Finance as a Growth Constraint." *Journal of Banking and Finance* 30 (November), 2931–2943.

Beck, Thorsten, Asli Demirguc-Kunt, and Vojislav Maksimovic. 2008. "Financing Patterns around the World: Are Small Firms Different?" *Journal of Financial Economics* 89 (September), 467–487.

Begenau, Juliane. 2015. "Capital Requirements, Risk Choice, and Liquidity Provision in a Business Cycle Model." Working Paper No. 15-072, Harvard Business School (March).

Begenau, Juliane, and Tim Landvoigt. 2016. "Financial Regulation in a Quantitative Model of the Modern Banking System." Working Paper No. 16-140, Harvard Business School (July).

Beirne, John, and Christian Friedrich. 2017. "Macroprudential Policies, Capital Flows, and the Structure of the Banking Sector." *Journal of International Money and Finance* 75 (July), 47–68.

Bekiros, Stelios, Rachatar Nilavongse, Gazi Salah Uddin. 2018. "Bank Capital Shocks and Countercyclical Requirements: Implications for Banking Stability and Welfare." *Journal of Economic Dynamics and Control* 93 (August), 315–331.

Benes, Jaromir, and Michael Kumhof. 2015. "Risky Bank Lending and Countercyclical Capital Buffers." *Journal of Economic Dynamics and Control* 58 (September), 58–80.

Benes, Jaromir, and Kirdan Lees. 2010. "Multi-Period Fixed-Rate Loans, Housing, and Monetary Policy in Small Open Economies." Discussion Paper No. 2010/03, Reserve Bank of New Zealand (March).

Bengui, Julien. 2014. "Macroprudential Policy Coordination." Unpublished, University of Montréal (April).

Bengui, Julien, and Javier Bianchi. 2018. "Macroprudential Policy with Leakages." Working Paper No. 25048, National Bureau of Economic Research (September).

Benigno, Gianluca, Huigang Chen, Christopher Otrok, Alessandro Rebucci, and Eric R. Young. 2013. "Financial Crises and Macro-prudential Policies." *Journal of International Economics* 89 (March), 453–470.

Benigno, Gianluca, Huigang Chen, Christopher Otrok, Alessandro Rebucci, and Eric R. Young. 2016. "Optimal Capital Controls and Real Exchange Rate Policies: A Pecuniary Externality Perspective." *Journal of Monetary Economics* 84 (December), 147–165.

Benigno, Pierpaolo. 2009. "Price Stability with Imperfect Financial Integration." *Journal of Money, Credit, and Banking* 41 (February), 121–149.

Benigno, Pierpaolo, and Gianluca Benigno. 2008. "Implementing International Monetary Cooperation through Inflation Targeting." *Macroeconomic Dynamics* 12 (March), 45–49.

Benigno, Pierpaolo, and Michael Woodford. 2005. "Inflation Stabilization and Welfare: The Case of a Distorted Steady State." *Journal of the European Economic Association* 3 (December), 1185–1236.

Benigno, Pierpaolo, and Michael Woodford. 2012. "Linear-Quadratic Approximation of Optimal Policy Problems." *Journal of Economic Theory* 147 (January), 1–42.

Ben Zeev, Nadav. 2017. "Capital Controls as Shock Absorbers." *Journal of International Economics* 109 (November), 43–67.

Berger, Allen N., Marco A. Espinosa-Vega, W. Scott Frame, and Nathan H. Miller. 2011. "Why Do Borrowers Pledge Collateral? New Empirical Evidence on the Role of Asymmetric Information." *Journal of Financial Intermediation* 20 (January), 55–70.

Berger, Wolfram. 2008. "Monetary Policy Rules and the Exchange Rate." *Journal of Macroeconomics* 30 (September), 1064–1084.

Bergin, Paul R., Hyung-Cheol Shin, and Ivan Tchakarov. 2007. "Does Exchange Rate Variability Matter for Welfare? A Quantitative Investigation of Stabilization Policies." *European Economic Review* 51 (May), 1041–1058.

Bernanke, Ben S., and Mark Gertler. 1989. "Agency Costs, Net Worth, and Business Fluctuations." *American: Economic Review* 79 (March), 14–31.

Bernanke, Ben S., Mark Gertler, and Simon Gilchrist. 1999. "The Financial Accelerator in a Quantitative Business Cycle Framework." In *Handbook of Macroeconomics*, ed. John B. Taylor and Michael Woodford. Amsterdam: North Holland.

Berstein, Solange, and J. Rodrigo Fuentes. 2005. "Concentration and Price Rigidity: Evidence for the Deposit Market in Chile." Working Paper No. 311, Central Bank of Chile (March).

Bester, Helmut. 1994. "The Role of Collateral in a Model of Debt Renegotiation." *Journal of Money, Credit, and Banking* 26 (February), 72–86.

Bertay, Ata C. 2014. "The Transmission of Real Estate Shocks through Multinational Banks." Discussion Paper No. 2014-011, Center for Economic Research, Tilburg University (February).

Bhandari, Jagdeep S., Nadeem Ul Haque, and Stephen J. Turnovsky. 1990. "Growth, External Debt, and Sovereign Risk in a Small Open Economy." *IMF Staff Papers* 37 (June), 388–417.

Bhattacharya, Sudipto, Arnoud W. Boot, and Anjan V. Thakor. 1998. "The Economics of Bank Regulation." *Journal of Money, Credit, and Banking* 30 (November), 745–770.

Bianchi, Javier. 2011. "Overborrowing and Systemic Externalities in the Business Cycle." *American Economic Review* 101 (December), 3400–3426.

Billi, Roberto M. 2011. "Output Gaps and Monetary Policy at Low Interest Rates." Federal Reserve Bank of Kansas City, *Economic Review* 96 (March), 5–29.

Binder, Michael, Philipp Lieberknecht, Jorge Quintana, and Volker Wieland. 2018. "Coordinating Monetary and Macroprudential Policy under Model Uncertainty." Unpublished, Goethe University Frankfurt (June).

Binici, Mahir, Michael Hutchison, and Martin Schindler. 2010. "Controlling Capital? Legal Restrictions and the Asset Composition of International Financial Flows." *Journal of International Money and Finance* 29 (June), 666–684.

Birchwood, Anthony, Michael Brei, and Dorian M. Noel. 2017. "Interest Margins and Bank Regulation in Central America and the Caribbean." *Journal of Banking and Finance* 85 (December), 56–68.

Black, Bernard S., Antonio G. de Carvalho, and Érica Gorga. 2010. "Corporate Governance in Brazil." *Emerging Markets Review* 11 (March), 21–38.

Blanchard, Olivier J. 2017. "The Need for Different Classes of Macroeconomic Models." Unpublished, Peterson Institute for International Economics (January).

Blanchard, Olivier J., and Jordi Galí. 2010. "Labor Market Frictions and Monetary Policy: A New Keynesian Model with Unemployment." *American Economic Journal: Macroeconomics* 2 (April), 1–30.

Blum, Jurg. 1999. "Do Capital Adequacy Requirements Reduce Risks in Banking?" *Journal of Banking and Finance* 23 (May), 755–771.

Blum, Jurg, and Martin Hellwig. 1995. "The Macroeconomic Implications of Capital Adequacy Requirements for Banks." *European Economic Review* 39 (April), 739–749.

Bodenstein, Martin, Luca Guerrieri, and Joe LaBriola. 2019. "Macroeconomic Policy Games." *Journal of Monetary Economics* 101 (January), 64–81.

Boissay, Frédéric, and Fabrice Collard. 2016. "Macroeconomics of Bank Capital and Liquidity Regulations." Working Paper No. 596, Bank for International Settlements (December).

Boissay, Frédéric, Fabrice Collard, and Frank Smets. 2016. "Booms and Banking Crises." *Journal of Political Economy* 124 (April), 489–538.

Boot, Arnoud W. A., and Matej Marinc. 2006. "Competition and Entry in Banking: Implications for Stability and Capital Regulation." Discussion Paper No. 5518, Centre for Economic Policy Research (June).

Boot, Arnoud W. A., Anjan V. Thakor, and Gregory F. Udell. 1991. "Secured Lending and Default Risk: Equilibrium Analysis, Policy Implications, and Empirical Results." *Economic Journal* 101 (May), 458–472.

Borio, Claudio, and Haibin Zhu. 2012. "Capital Regulation, Risk-Taking, and Monetary Policy: A Missing Link in the Transmission Mechanism?" *Journal of Financial Stability* 8 (December), 236–251.

Bouvatier, Vincent, and Laetitia Lepetit. 2012. "Provisioning Rules and Bank Lending: A Theoretical Model." *Journal of Financial Stability* 8 (January), 25–31.

Boz, Emine, C. Borda Durdu, and Nan Li. 2015. "Emerging Market Business Cycles: The Role of Labor Market Frictions." *Journal of Money, Credit, and Banking* 47 (February), 31–72.

Braun, R. Anton, and Tomoyuki Nakajima. 2012. "Making the Case for a Low Intertemporal Elasticity of Substitution." Working Paper No. 2012-1, Federal Reserve Bank of Atlanta (January).

Broner, Fernando, Tatiana Didier, Aitor Erce, and Sergio L. Schmukler. 2013. "Gross Capital Flows: Dynamics and Crises." *Journal of Monetary Economics* 60 (January), 113–133.

Brunnermeier, Markus, Andrew Crockett, Charles Goodhart, Avinash D. Persaud, and Hyun S. Shin. 2009. *The Fundamental Principles of Financial Regulation*. Geneva: International Center for Monetary and Banking Studies.

Brunnermeier, Markus K., Thomas M. Eisenbach, and Yuliy Sannikov. 2013. "Macroeconomics with Financial Frictions: A Survey." In *Advances in Economics and Econometrics*, Tenth World Congress of the Econometric Society, ed. Daron Acemoglu, Manuel Arellano, and Eddie Dekel. Vol. 2. Cambridge: Cambridge University Press.

Brunnermeier, Markus K., and Yuliy Sannikov. 2014. "A Macroeconomic Model with a Financial Sector." *American Economic Review* 104 (June), 379–421.

Brunnermeier, Markus K., and Yuliy Sannikov. 2015. "International Credit Flows and Pecuniary Externalities." *American Economic Journal: Macroeconomics* 7 (January), 297–338.

Bruno, Valentina, Ilhyock Shim, and Hyun S. Shin. 2017. "Comparative Assessment of Macroprudential Policies." *Journal of Financial Stability* 28 (February), 183–202.

Bruno, Valentina, and Hyun S. Shin. 2014. "Assessing Macroprudential Policies: The Case of South Korea." *Scandinavian Journal of Economics* 116 (January), 128–157.

Brzoza-Brzezina, Michal, Paolo Gelain, and Marcin Kolasa. 2014. "Monetary and Macroprudential Policy with Multi-Period Loans." Working Paper No. 192, National Bank of Poland (June).

Brzoza-Brzezina, Michal, Marcin Kolasa, and Krzysztof Makarski. 2013. "The Anatomy of Standard DSGE Models with Financial Frictions." *Journal of Economic Dynamics and Control* 37 (January), 32–51.

Brzoza-Brzezina, Michal, Marcin Kolasa, and Krzysztof Makarski. 2017. "Monetary and Macroprudential Policy with Foreign Currency Loans." *Journal of Macroeconomics* 54 (December), 352–372.

Brzoza-Brzezina, Michał, and Jacek Kotłowski. 2019. "The Nonlinear Nature of Country Risk and Its Implications for DSGE Models." forthcoming, *Macroeconomic Dynamics* (December).

Buch, Claudia M., and Linda Goldberg. 2017. "Cross-Border Regulatory Spillovers: How Much? How Important?" *International Journal of Central Banking* 13 (March), 505–558.

Buffie, Edward F. 1984. "Financial Repression, the New Structuralists, and Stabilization Policy in Semi-Industrialized Economies." *Journal of Development Economics* 14 (April), 305–322.

Buiter, Willem H. 1980. "Walras' Law and All That: Budget Constraints and Balance Sheet Constraints in Period Models and Continuous Time Models." *International Economic Review* 21 (February), 1–16.

Buiter, Willem H. 2007. "Seigniorage." Working Paper No. 12919, National Bureau of Economic Research (February).

Burroni, Marco, Mario Quagliariello, Emiliano Sabatini, and Vincenzo Tola. 2009. *Dynamic Provisioning: Rationale, Functioning, and Prudential Treatment*. Rome: Banca d'Italia.

Burstein, A., Neves, J., and Sergio Rebelo. 2003. "Distribution Costs and Real Exchange Rate Dynamics during Exchange-Rate-Based Stabilizations." *Journal of Monetary Economics* 50 (September), 1189–1214.

Bussière, Matthieu, Simona Delle Chiaie, and Tuomas A. Peltonen. 2014. "Exchange Rate Pass-Through in the Global Economy." *IMF Economic Review* 62 (April), 146–178.

Byrne, Joseph P., and Norbert Fiess. 2016. "International Capital Flows to Emerging Markets: National and Global Determinants." *Journal of International Money and Finance* 61 (March), 82–100.

Caballero, Julián A. 2016. "Do Surges in International Capital Inflows Influence the Likelihood of Banking Crises?." *Economic Journal* 126 (March), 281–316.

Caballero, Ricardo J. 2010. "Macroeconomics after the Crisis: Time to Deal with the Pretense-of-Knowledge Syndrome." *Journal of Economic Perspectives* 24 (September), 85–102.

Caballero, Ricardo J., and Arvind Krishnamurthy. 2001. "International and Domestic Collateral Constraints in a Model of Emerging Market Crises." *Journal of Monetary Economics* 48 (December), 513–548.

Cabezon, Ezequiel. 2014. "Working Capital, Financial Frictions and Monetary Policy in Brazil." Unpublished, University of North Carolina at Chapel Hill (November).

Cakici, S. Meral. 2011. "Financial Integration and Business Cycles in a Small Open Economy." *Journal of International Money and Finance* 30 (November), 1280–1302.

Calderón, Cesar, and J. Rodrigo Fuentes. 2014. "Have Business Cycles Changed over the Last Two Decades? An Empirical Investigation." *Journal of Development Economics* 109 (July), 98–123.

Calomiris, Charles W. 2009. "The Subprime Turmoil: What's Old, What's New and What's Next." *Journal of Structured Finance* 15 (March), 6–52.

Calomiris, Charles W., Mauricio Larrain, José Liberti, and Jason Sturgess. 2017. "How Collateral Laws Shape Lending and Sectoral Activity." *Journal of Financial Economics* 123 (January), 163–188.

Calvo, Daniel, Juan Carlos Crisanto, Stefan Hohl, and Oscar P. Gutiérrez. 2018. "Financial Supervisory Architecture: What Has Changed after the Crisis?" FSI Insights on Policy Implementation, No 8., Financial Stability Institute (April).

Calvo, Guillermo A. 1983. "Staggered Prices in a Utility-Maximizing Framework." *Journal of Monetary Economics* 12 (June), 383–398.

Calvo, Guillermo A. 1998. "Capital Flows and Capital-Market Crises: The Simple Economics of Sudden Stops." *Journal of Applied Economics* 1 (November), 35–54.

Calvo, Guillermo A., Oya Celsasun, and Michael Kumhof. 2007. "Inflation Inertia and Credible Disinflation—The Open Economy Case." *Journal of International Economics* 73 (September), 48–68.

Calvo, Guillermo A., and Carlos A. Végh. 1995. "Fighting Inflation with High Interest Rates: The Small Open Economy Case under Flexible Prices." *Journal of Money, Credit, and Banking* 27 (February), 49–66.

Camors, Cecilia D., José-Luis Peydró, and Francesc Rodriguez-Tous. 2019. "Macroprudential and Monetary Policy: Loan-Level Evidence from Reserve Requirements." Working Paper No. 1650, Universitat Pompeu Fabra (March).

Canova, Fabio. 2007. *Methods for Applied Macroeconomic Research*. Princeton, NJ: Princeton University Press.

Cantore, Cristiano, Vasco Gabriel, and Paul Levine. 2011. "The Science and Art of DSGE Modelling: Construction and Bayesian Estimation." Unpublished, University of Surrey (December).

Caprio, Gerard, Jr. 2010. "Safe and Sound Banking: A Role for Countercyclical Regulatory Requirements?" Policy Research Working Paper No. 5198, World Bank (February).

Caputo, Rodrigo, Felipe Liendo, and Juan Pablo Medina. 2007. "New Keynesian Models for Chile in the Inflation-Targeting Period: A Structural Investigation." In *Monetary Policy under Inflation Targeting*, ed. Frederic Mishkin and Klaus Schmidt-Hebbel. Santiago: Central Bank of Chile.

Carlstrom, Charles T., and Timothy S. Fuerst. 1997. "Agency Costs, Net Worth, and Business Cycle Fluctuations: A Computable General Equilibrium Analysis." *American Economic Review* 87 (December), 893–910.

Carlstrom, Charles T., and Timothy S. Fuerst. 2016. "Macro Credit Policy and the Financial Accelerator." *Journal of Money, Credit, and Banking* 48 (December), 1725–1751.

Carney, Mark. 2017. "Lambda." Speech at the London School of Economics (January 16), https://www.bankofengland.co.uk/speech/2017/lambda.

Carrière-Swallow, Yan, Bertrand Gruss, Fabian Valencia, and Nicolas E. Magud. 2016. "Monetary Policy Credibility and Exchange Rate Pass-through." Working Paper No. 16/240, International Monetary Fund (December).

Carrillo, Julio A., Enrique Mendoza, Victoria Nuguer, and Jessica Roldán-Peña. 2017. "Tight Money-Tight Credit: Coordination Failure in the Conduct of Monetary and Financial Policies." Discussion Paper No. IDB-DP-516, Inter-American Development Bank (May).

Carroll, Christopher D. 2018. "Theoretical Foundations of Buffer Stock Saving." Unpublished, Johns Hopkins University (October).

Carvalho, Fabia A. de, and Marcos R. de Castro. 2016. "Macroprudential Policy Transmission and Interaction with Fiscal and Monetary Policy in an Emerging Economy: A DSGE Model for Brazil." Working Paper No. 453, Central Bank of Brazil (December).

Carvallo, Oscar, and Adnan Kasman. 2005. "Cost efficiency in the Latin American and Caribbean Banking Systems." *Journal of International Financial Markets, Institutions and Money* 15 (January), 55–72.

Castillo, Paul, Cesar Carrera, Marco Ortiz, and Hugo Vega. 2015. "Spillovers: The Role of Prudential Regulation and Monetary Policy in Small Open Economies." Unpublished, Central Bank of Peru (January).

Cavalcanti, Marco Antonio F. H. 2010. "Credit Market Imperfections and the Power of the Financial Accelerator: A Theoretical and Empirical Investigation." *Journal of Macroeconomics* 32 (March), 118–144.

Cavallino, Paolo. 2019. "Capital Flows and Foreign Exchange Intervention." *American Economic Journal: Macroeconomics* 11 (April), 127–170.

Cavoli, Tony, and Ramkishen S. Rajan. 2006. "Monetary Policy Rules for Small and Open Developing Economies: A Counterfactual Policy Analysis." *Journal of Economic Development* 31 (June), 89–111.

Cecchetti, Stephen G., Hans Genberg, John Lipsky, and Sushil Wadhwani. 2000. *Asset Prices and Central Bank Policy*. London: Centre for Economic Policy Research.

Cecchetti, Stephen G., and Lianfi Li. 2008. "Do Capital Adequacy Requirements Matter for Monetary Policy?" *Economic Inquiry* 46 (October), 643–659.

Cerutti, Eugenio, Stijn Claessens, and Luc Laeven. 2017*a*. "The Use and Effectiveness of Macroprudential Policies: New Evidence." *Journal of Financial Stability* 28 (February), 203–224.

Cerutti, Eugenio, Stijn Claessens, and Lev Ratnovski. 2014. "Global Liquidity and Drivers of Cross-border Bank Flows." Working Paper No. 14/69, International Monetary Fund (June).

Cerutti, Eugenio, Stijn Claessens, and Andrew K. Rose. 2019. "How Important is the Global Financial Cycle? Evidence from Capital Flows." *IMF Economic Review* 67 (March), 24–60.

Cerutti, Eugenio, Ricardo Correa, Elisabetta Fiorentino, and Esther Segalla. 2017*b*. "Changes in Prudential Policy Instruments—A New Cross-Country Database." *International Journal of Central Banking* 13 (March), 477–503.

Cesa-Bianchi, Ambrogio. 2013. "Housing Cycles and Macroeconomic Fluctuations: A Global Perspective." *Journal of International Money and Finance* 37 (October), 215–238.

Cesa-Bianchi, Ambrogio, and Alessandro Rebucci. 2017. "Does Easing Monetary Policy Increase Financial Instability?." *Journal of Financial Stability* 30 (June), 111–125.

Céspedes, Luis F., Roberto Chang, and Andrés Velasco. 2003. "IS-LM-BP in the Pampas." *IMF Staff Papers* 50 (March), 143–156.

Céspedes, Luis F., Roberto Chang, and Andrés Velasco. 2004. "Balance Sheets and Exchange Rate Policy." *American Economic Review* 94 (September), 1183–1193.

Chadha, Jagjit S., and Young-Kwan Kang. 2016. "Finance and Credit in a Model of Monetary Policy." In *Monetary Policy in India*, ed. C. Ghate and Kenneth Kletzer. New Delhi: Springer.

Chadha, Jagjit S., Lucio Sarno, and Giorgio Valente. 2004. "Monetary Policy Rules, Asset Prices, and Exchange Rates." *IMF Staff Papers* 51 (November), 529–552.

Chakraborty, Shankha, and Tridip Ray. 2006. "Bank-Based versus Market-Based Financial Systems: A Growth-Theoretic Analysis." *Journal of Monetary Economics* 53 (March), 329–350.

Chamon, Marcos, and Márcio Garcia. 2016. "Capital Controls in Brazil: Effective?." *Journal of International Money and Finance* 61 (March), 163–187.

Chaney, Thomas, David Sraer, and David Thesmar. 2012. "The Collateral Channel: How Real Estate Shocks Affect Corporate Investment." *American Economic Review* 102 (October), 2381–2409.

Chang, Roberto. 2008. "Inflation Targeting, Reserves Accumulation, and Exchange Rate Management in Latin America." Working Paper No. 487, Central Bank of Colombia (March).

Chen, Jiaqian, and Francesco Columba. 2016. "Macroprudential and Monetary Policy Interactions in a DSGE Model for Sweden." Working Paper No. 16/74, International Monetary Fund (March).

Chen, Nan-Kuang. 2001. "Bank Net Worth, Asset Prices, and Economic Activity." *Journal of Monetary Economics* 48 (October), 415–436.

Chetty, Raj, Adam Guren, Day Manoli, and Andrea Weber. 2011. "Are Micro and Macro Labor Supply Elasticities Consistent? A Review of Evidence on the Intensive and Extensive Margins." *American Economic Review* 101 (May), 471–475.

Chiang, Alpha C. 1992. *Elements of Dynamic Optimization*. New York: McGraw-Hill.

Choi, Woon G., and David Cook. 2004. "Liability Dollarization and the Bank Balance Sheet Channel." *Journal of International Economics* 64 (December) 247–275.

Choi, Woon G., and David Cook. 2012. "Fire Sales and the Financial Accelerator." *Journal of Monetary Economics* 59 (May), 336–351.

Chowdhury, Ibrahim, Mathias Hoffmann, and Andreas Schabert. 2006. "Inflation Dynamics and the Cost Channel of Monetary Transmission." *European Economic Review* 50 (May), 995–1016.

Christensen, Ian, and Ali Dib. 2008. "The Financial Accelerator in an Estimated New Keynesian Model." *Review of Economic Dynamics* 11 (April), 155–178.

Christensen, Ian, Césaire Meh, and Kevin Moran. 2011. "Bank Leverage Regulation and Macroeconomic Dynamics." Working Paper No. 2011-32, Bank of Canada (December).

Christiano, Lawrence J., Martin S. Eichenbaum, and Charles L. Evans. 2005. "Nominal Rigidities and the Dynamic Effects of a Shock to Monetary Policy." *Journal of Political Economy* 113 (February), 1–45.

Christiano, Lawrence J., Martin S. Eichenbaum, and Mathias Trabandt. 2015. "Understanding the Great Recession." *American Economic Journal: Macroeconomics* 7 (March), 110–167.

Christiano, Lawrence J., Martin S. Eichenbaum, and Mathias Trabandt. 2018. "On DSGE Models." *Journal of Economic Perspectives* 32 (June), 113–140.

Christiano, Lawrence J., Christopher Gust, and Jorge Roldós. 2004. "Monetary Policy in a Financial Crisis." *Journal of Economic Theory* 119 (November), 64–103.

Christiano, Lawrence J., and Daisuke Ikeda. 2014. "Leverage Restrictions in a Business Cycle Model." In *Macroeconomic and Financial Stability: Challenges for Monetary Policy*, ed. Sofía Bauducco, Lawrence J. Christiano, and Claudio Raddatz. Santiago: Central Bank of Chile.

Christiano, Lawrence J., Roberto Motto, and Massimo Rostagno. 2007*a*. "Notes on Ramsey-Optimal Monetary Policy." Unpublished, Northwestern University (January).

Christiano, Lawrence J., Roberto Motto, and Massimo Rostagno. 2007*b*. "Two Reasons Why Money and Credit May Be Useful in Monetary Policy." Working Paper No. 13502, National Bureau of Economic Research (October).

Christiano, Lawrence J., Roberto Motto, and Massimo Rostagno. 2010*a*. "Financial Factors in Economic Fluctuations." Working Paper No. 1192, European Central Bank (May).

Christiano, Lawrence J., Mathias Trabandt, and Karl Walentin. 2010*b*. "DSGE Models for Monetary Policy Analysis." In *Handbook of Monetary Economics*, ed. Benjamin M. Friedman and Michael Woodford. Vol. 3A. Amsterdam: Elsevier.

Christiano, Lawrence J., Mathias Trabandt, and Karl Walentin. 2011. "Introducing Financial Frictions and Unemployment into a Small Open Economy Model." *Journal of Economic Dynamics and Control* 35 (December), 1999–2041.

Christoffel, Kai, and Andreas Schabert. 2015. "Interest Rates, Money, and Banks in an Estimated Euro Area Model." Working Paper No. 1791, European Central Bank (May).

Chugh, Sanjay K. 2013. "Costly External Finance and Labor Market Dynamics." *Journal of Economic Dynamics and Control* 37 (December), 2882–2912.

Chung, Keunsuk, and Stephen J. Turnovsky. 2010. "Foreign Debt Supply in an Imperfect International Capital Market: Theory and Evidence." *Journal of International Money and Finance* 29 (March), 201–223.

Cingano, Federico. 2014. "Trends in Income Inequality and Its Impact on Economic Growth." Working Paper, No. 163, OECD (September).

Cizel, Janko, Jon Frost, Aerdt Houben, and Peter Wierts. 2016. "Effective Macroprudential Policy: Cross-Sector Substitution from Price and Quantity Measures." Working Paper No. 16/94, International Monetary Fund (April).

Claessens, Stijn. 2015. "An Overview of Macroprudential Policy Tools." *Annual Review of Financial Economics* 7 (June), 397–422.

Claessens, Stijn. 2017. "Global Banking: Recent Developments and Insights from Research." *Review of Finance* 21 (July), 1513–1555.

Claessens, Stijn, Swati R. Ghosh, and Roxana Mihet. 2013. "Macro-Prudential Policies to Mitigate Financial System Vulnerabilities." *Journal of International Money and Finance* 39 (December), 153–185.

Claessens, Stijn, and M. Ayhan Kose. 2014. "Financial Crises: Explanations, Types, and Implications." In *Financial Crises: Causes, Consequences, and Policy Responses*, ed. Stijn Claessens, M. Ayhan Kose, Luc Laeven, and Fabián Valencia. Washington, DC: International Monetary Fund.

Claessens, Stijn, M. Ayhan Kose, and Marco E. Terrones. 2011. "Recessions and Financial Disruptions in Emerging Markets: A Bird's Eye View." In *Monetary Policy under Financial Turbulence*, ed. Luis F. Céspedes, Roberto Chang, and Diego Saravia. Santiago: Central Bank of Chile.

Claessens, Stijn, M. Ayhan Kose, and Marco E. Terrones. 2012. "How Do Business and Financial Cycles Interact?" *Journal of International Economics* 87 (May), 178–190.

Clancy, Daragh, and Rossana Merola. 2017. "Countercyclical Capital Rules for Small Open Economies." *Journal of Macroeconomics* 54 (December), 332–351.

Clarida, Richard, Jordi Galí, and Mark Gertler. 1999. "The Science of Monetary Policy: A New Keynesian Perspective." *Journal of Economic Literature* 37 (December), 1661–1707.

Claus, Iris. 2007. "The Effects of Bank Lending in an Open Economy." *Journal of Money, Credit, and Banking* 39 (August), 1213–1243.

Clerc, Laurent, Alexis Derviz, Caterina Mendicino, Stephane Moyen, Kalin Nikolov, Livio Stracca, Javier Suarez, and Alexandros P. Vardoulakis. 2015. "Capital Regulation in a Macroeconomic Model with Three Layers of Default." *International Journal of Central Banking* 11 (June), 9–63.

Cociuba, Simona E., Malik Shukayev, and Alexander Ueberfeldt. 2016. "Collateralized Borrowing and Risk Taking at Low Interest Rates." *European Economic Review* 85 (June), 62–83.

Coco, Giuseppe. 2000. "On the Use of Collateral." *Journal of Economic Surveys* 14 (June), 191–214.

Coenen, Günter, Giovanni Lombardo, Frank Smets, and Roland Straub. 2009. "International Transmission and Monetary Policy Cooperation." In *International Dimensions of Monetary Policy*, ed. Jordi Galí and Mark Gertler. Chicago: University of Chicago Press.

Coenen, Günter, and Roland Straub. 2005. "Does Government Spending Crowd in Private Consumption? Theory and Empirical Evidence for the Euro Area." *International Finance* 8 (December), 435–470.

Cole, Harold. 2011. "Discussion of Gertler and Karadi: A Model of Unconventional Monetary Policy." *Journal of Monetary Economics* 58 (January), 35–38.

Coleman, Anthony D. F., Neil Esho, and Ian G. Sharpe. 2002. "Do Bank Characteristics Influence Loan Contract Terms?" Working Paper No. 2002-01, Australian Prudential Regulation Authority (February).

Collard, Fabrice, Harris Dellas, Behzad Diba, and Olivier Loisel. 2017. "Optimal Monetary and Prudential Policies." *American Economic Journal: Macroeconomics* 9 (January), 40–87.

Committee on the Global Financial System. 2016. "Objective-Setting and Communication of Macroprudential Policies." CGFS Paper No. 57 (November).

Constantinides, George M. 1982. "Intertemporal Asset Pricing with Heterogeneous Consumers and without Demand Aggregation." *Journal of Business* 55 (April), 253–267.

Cook, David. 2004. "Monetary Policy in Emerging Markets: Can Liability Dollarization Explain Contractionary Devaluation?" *Journal of Monetary Economics* 51 (September), 1155–1181.

Cook, David, and Michael B. Devereux. 2006. "Accounting for the East Asian Crisis: A Quantitative Model of Capital Outflows in Small Open Economies." *Journal of Money, Credit, and Banking* 38 (April), 721–749.

Cordella, Tito, Giovanni Dell'Ariccia, and Robert Marquez. 2018. "Government Guarantees, Transparency, and Bank Risk Taking." *IMF Economic Review* 66 (March), 116–114.

Cordella, Tito, Pablo Federico, Carlos Végh, and Guillermo Vuletin. 2014. "Reserve Requirements in the Brave New Macroprudential World." Policy Research Working 6793, World Bank (February).

Cordoba, Juan-Carlos, and Marla Ripoll. 2004. "Credit Cycles Redux." *International Economic Review* 45 (November), 1011–1046.

Correa, Arnildo da Silva, Myrian B. S. Petrassi, and Rafael Santos. 2016. "Price-Setting Behavior in Brazil: Survey Evidence." Working Paper No. 422, Central Bank of Brazil (March).

Correia, Isabel, Fiorella De Fiore, Pedro Teles, and Oreste Tristani. 2016. "Credit Subsidies." Working Paper No. 1877, European Central Bank (January).

Costinot, Arnaud, Guido Lorenzoni, and Iván Werning. 2014. "A Theory of Capital Controls as Dynamic Terms-of-Trade Manipulation." *Journal of Political Economy* 122 (February), 77–128.

Covas, Francisco, and Shigeru Fujita. 2010. "Procyclicality of Capital Requirements in a General Equilibrium Model of Liquidity Dependence." *International Journal of Central Banking* 6 (December), 137–173.

Croushore, Dean. 1993. "Money in the Utility Function: Functional Equivalence to a Shopping-Time Model." *Journal of Macroeconomics* 15 (December), 175–182.

Crowe, Christopher, Giovanni Dell'Ariccia, Deniz Igan, and Pau Rabanal. 2013. "How to Deal with Real Estate Booms: Lessons from Country Experiences." *Journal of Financial Stability* 9 (September), 300–319.

Cuadra, Gabriel, and Victoria Nuguer. 2018. "Risky Banks and Macroprudential Policy for Emerging Economies." *Review of Economic Dynamics* 30 (October), 125–144.

Cúrdia, Vasco. 2009. "Optimal Monetary Policy under Sudden Stops." Staff Report No. 323, Federal Reserve Bank of New York (revised, April).

Cúrdia, Vasco, and Michael Woodford. 2010. "Credit Spreads and Monetary Policy." *Journal of Money, Credit, and Banking* 42 (September), 3–35.

Cúrdia, Vasco, and Michael Woodford. 2011. "The Central-Bank Balance Sheet as an Instrument of Monetary Policy." *Journal of Monetary Economics* 58 (January), 54–79.

Cúrdia, Vasco, and Michael Woodford. 2016. "Credit Frictions and Optimal Monetary Policy." *Journal of Monetary Economics* 84 (December), 30–65.

Darracq Pariès, Matthieu, Christoffer Kok Sørensen, and Diego Rodriguez-Palenzuela. 2011. "Macroeconomic Propagation under Different Regulatory Regimes: Evidence from an Estimated DSGE Model for the Euro Area." *International Journal of Central Banking* 7 (December), 49–113.

Daude, Christian, Eduardo Levy Yeyati, and Arne J. Nagengast. 2016. "On the Effectiveness of Exchange Rate Interventions in Emerging Markets." *Journal of International Money and Finance* 64 (June), 239–261.

Davis, J. Scott, and Kevin X. D. Huang. 2013. "Credit Risks and Monetary Policy Trade-Offs." Unpublished, Federal Reserve Bank of Dallas (February).

Davis, J. Scott, and Ignacio Presno. 2017. "Capital Controls and Monetary Policy Autonomy in a Small Open Economy." *Journal of Monetary Economics* 85 (January), 114–130.

Debortoli, Davide, Jinill Kim, Jesper Lindé, and Ricardo Nunes. 2019. "Designing a Simple Loss Function for Central Banks: Does a Dual Mandate Make Sense?" *Economic Journal* 129 (July), 2010–2038.

De Fiore, Fiorella, and Oreste Tristani. 2013. "Optimal Monetary Policy in a Model of the Credit Channel." *Economic Journal* 123 (September), 906–931.

De Graeve, Ferre. 2008. "The External Finance Premium and the Macroeconomy: US Post-WWII Evidence." *Journal of Economic Dynamics and Control* 32 (November), 3415–3440.

De la Croix, David, and Philippe Michel. 2002. *A Theory of Economic Growth: Dynamics and Policy in Overlapping Generations*. Cambridge: Cambridge University Press.

Deléchat, Corinne, Camila H. Arbelaez, Priscilla S. Muthoora, and Svetlana Vtyurina. 2012. "The Determinants of Banks' Liquidity Buffers in Central America." Working Paper No. 12/301, International Monetary Fund (December).

Dell'Ariccia, Giovanni, Luc Laeven, and Robert Marquez. 2014. "Real Interest Rates, Leverage, and Bank Risk-Taking." *Journal of Economic Theory* 149 (January), 65–99.

Dell'Ariccia, Giovanni, and Robert Marquez. 2006. "Lending Booms and Lending Standards." *Journal of Finance* 61 (October), 2511–2546.

Dell'Ariccia, Giovanni, Pau Rabanal, and Damiano Sandri. 2018. "Unconventional Monetary Policies in the Euro Area, Japan, and the United Kingdom." *Journal of Economic Perspectives* 32 (September), 147–172.

Del Negro, Marco, Marc P. Giannoni, and Frank Schorfheide. 2015. "Inflation in the Great Recession and New Keynesian Models." *American Economic Journal: Macroeconomics* 7 (January), 168–196.

Demirel, Ufuk D. 2010. "Macroeconomic Stabilization in Developing Economies: Are Optimal Policies Procyclical?" *European Economic Review* 54 (April), 409–428.

Demirguc-Kunt, Asli, and Enrica Detragiache. 2005. "Cross-Country Empirical Studies of Systemic Bank Distress: A Survey." *National Institute Economic Review* 192 (April), 68–83.

Demirguc-Kunt, Asli, Enrica Detragiache, and Thierry Tressel. 2008. "Banking on the Principles: Compliance with Basel Core Principles and Bank Soundness." *Journal of Financial Intermediation* 17 (October), 511–542.

De Nicolò, Gianni, Giovanni Favara, and Lev Ratnovski. 2012. "Externalities and Macroprudential Policy." Staff Discussion Note No. 12/05, International Monetary Fund (June).

De Nicolò, Gianni, and Marcella Lucchetta. 2012. "Bank Competition and Financial Stability: A General Equilibrium Exposition." Unpublished, International Monetary Fund (August).

De Paoli, Bianca. 2009. "Monetary Policy and Welfare in a Small Open Economy." *Journal of International Economics*77 (February), 11–22.

De Paoli, Bianca, and Anna Lipinska. 2013. "Capital Controls: A Normative Analysis." Staff Report No. 600, Federal Reserve Bank of New York (February).

De Paoli, Bianca, and Matthias Paustian. 2017. "Coordinating Monetary and Macroprudential Policies." *Journal of Money, Credit, and Banking* 49 (March), 319–349.

Devereux, Michael B., Philip R. Lane, and Juanyi Xu. 2006. "Exchange Rates and Monetary Policy in Emerging Market Economies." *Economic Journal* 116 (April), 478–506.

Devereux, Michael B., and James Yetman. 2014*a*. "Capital Controls, Global Liquidity Traps, and the International Policy Dilemma." *Scandinavian Journal of Economics* 116 (January), 158–189.

Devereux, Michael B., and James Yetman. 2014*b*. "Globalisation, Pass-through and the Optimal Policy Response to Exchange Rates." *Journal of International Money and Finance* 49 (December), 104–128.

Devereux, Michael B., and Changhua Yu. 2019. "Evaluating the Role of Capital Controls and Monetary Policy in Emerging Market Crises." *Journal of International Money and Finance* 95 (July), 189–211.

De Walque, Gregory, Olivier Pierrard, and Abdelaziz Rouabah. 2010. "Financial (In)Stability, Supervision, and Liquidity Injections: A Dynamic General Equilibrium Approach." *Economic Journal* 120 (December), 1234–1261.

Dewatripont, Mathias, and Jean Tirole. 2012. "Macroeconomic Shocks and Banking Regulation." *Journal of Money, Credit, and Banking* 44 (December), 237–254.

Diamond, Douglas W. 1984. "Financial Intermediation and Delegated Monitoring." *Review of Economic Studies* 51 (July), 393–414.

Diamond, Douglas W., and Raghuram G. Rajan. 2012. "Illiquid Banks, Financial Stability, and Interest Rate Policy." *Journal of Political Economy* 120 (June), 552–591.

Díaz, Sergio Ocampo. 2013. "Rule-of-Thumb Consumers, Nominal Rigidities, and the Design of Interest Rate Rules." Working Paper No. IDB-WP-400, Inter-American Development Bank (May).

Dib, Ali. 2010*a*. "Banks, Credit Market Frictions, and Business Cycles." Working Paper No. 2010-24, Bank of Canada (October).

Dib, Ali. 2010*b*. "Capital Requirements and Financial Frictions in Banking: Macroeconomic Implications." Working Paper No. 2010-26, Bank of Canada (October).

Dib, Ali. 2011. "Monetary Policy in Estimated Models of Small Open and Closed Economies." *Open Economies Review* 22 (November), 769–796.

Di Bartolomeo, Giovanni, Marco Di Pietro, and Bianca Giannini. 2016. "Optimal Monetary Policy in a New Keynesian Model with Heterogeneous Expectations." *Journal of Economic Dynamics and Control* 73 (December), 373–387.

Dietrich, Andreas, and Gabrielle Wanzenried. 2014. "The Determinants of Commercial Banking Profitability in Low-, Middle-, and High-Income Countries." *Quarterly Review of Economics and Finance* 54 (August), 337–354.

Dijkstra, Mark A. 2013. "Economies of Scale and Scope in the European Banking Sector 2002–2011." Unpublished, University of Amsterdam (June).

Disyatat, Piti. 2004. "Currency Crises and the Real Economy: The Role of Banks." *European Economic Review* 48 (February), 75–90.

Dixit, Avinash, and Jospeh E. Stiglitz. 1977. "Monopolistic Competition and Optimum Product Diversity." *American Economic Review* 67 (June), 297–308.

Djankov, Simeon, Oliver Hart, Caralee McLiesh, and Andrei Shleifer. 2008. "Debt Enforcement around the World." *Journal of Political Economy* 116 (December), 1105–1149.

Dooley, Michael. 1996. "A Survey of Literature on Controls over International Capital Transactions." *IMF Staff Papers* 43 (December), 639–687.

Dotsey, Michael, Robert G. King, and Alexander L. Wolman. 1999. "State-Dependent Pricing and the General Equilibrium Dynamics of Money and Output." *Quarterly Journal of Economics* 114 (May), 655–690.

Dou, Winston W., Andrew W. Lo, Ameya Muley, and Harald Uhlig. 2017. "Macroeconomic Models for Monetary Policy: A Critical Review from a Finance Perspective." Unpublished, University of Pennsylvania (January).

Dräger, Lena, and Christian R. Proaño. 2019. "Cross-Border Banking and Macroprudential Policies in Asymmetric Monetary Unions." forthcoming, *Macroeconomic Dynamics* (December).

Drehmann, Mathias, Claudio Borio, Leonardo Gambacorta, Gabriel Jimenez, and Carlos Trucharte. 2010. "Countercyclical Capital Buffers: Exploring Options." Working Paper No. 317, Bank for International Settlements (July).

Drehmann, Mathias, and Kostas Tsatsaronis. 2014. "The Credit-to-GDP Gap and Counter-cyclical Capital Buffers: Questions and Answers." *Bank for International Settlements Quarterly Review* (March), 55–73.

Dressler, Scott J., and Erasmus K. Kersting. 2015. "Excess Reserves and Economic Activity." *Journal of Economic Dynamics and Control* 52 (March), 17–31.

Drumond, Ines. 2009. "Bank Capital Requirements, Business Cycle Fluctuations, and the Basel Accords: A Synthesis." *Journal of Economic Surveys* 23 (December), 798–830.

Edwards, Sebastian. 2010. "The International Transmission of Interest Rate Shocks: The Federal Reserve and Emerging Markets in Latin America and Asia." *Journal of International Money and Finance* 29 (June), 685–703.

Edwards, Sebastian. 2012. "The Federal Reserve, the Emerging Markets, and Capital Controls: A High-Frequency Empirical Investigation." *Journal of Money, Credit, and Banking* 44 (December), 151–184.

Edwards, Sebastian, and Carlos A. Végh. 1997. "Banks and Macroeconomic Disturbances under Predetermined Exchange Rates." *Journal of Monetary Economics* 40 (November), 239–278.

Eichengreen, Barry, and Poonam Gupta. 2016. "Managing Sudden Stops." Policy Research Working Paper No. 7639, World Bank (April).

Eichengreen, Barry, and Andrew Rose. 2014. "Capital Controls in the 21st Century." Policy Insight No. 72, Centre for Economic Policy Research (June).

Elekdag, Selim, Alejandro Justiniano, and Ivan Tchakarov. 2006. "An Estimated Small Open Economy Model of the Financial Accelerator." *IMF Staff Papers* 53 (June), 219–241.

Engel, Charles. 2016. "Macroprudential Policy in a World of High Capital Mobility: Policy Implications from an Academic Perspective." *Journal of the Japanese and International Economies* 42 (December), 162–172.

Ennis, Huberto M., and John A.Weinberg. 2013. "Over-the-counter Loans, Adverse Selection, and Stigma in the Interbank Market." *Review of Economic Dynamics* 16 (October), 601–616.

Erceg, Christopher J., Dale W. Henderson, and Andrew T. Levin. 2000. "Optimal Monetary Policy with Staggered Wage and Price Contracts." *Journal of Monetary Economics* 46 (October), 281–313.

Erceg, Christopher J., and Andrew T. Levin. 2003. "Imperfect Credibility and Inflation Persistence." *Journal of Monetary Economics* 50 (May), 915–944.

Escudé, Guillermo J. 2014. "The Possible Trinity: Optimal Interest Rate, Exchange Rate, and Taxes on Capital Flows in a DSGE Model for a Small Open Economy." Working Paper No. 2014-13, Kiel Institute for the World Economy (March).

Escudero, Matias, Martin Gonzalez-Rozada, and Martin Sola. 2014. "Towards a 'New' Inflation Targeting Framework: The Case of Uruguay." Unpublished, Northwestern University (January).

Estrella, Arturo. 2015. "The Price Puzzle and VAR Identification." *Macroeconomic Dynamics* 19 (December), 1880–1887.

Eusepi, Stefano, and Bruce Preston. 2018. "The Science of Monetary Policy: An Imperfect Knowledge Perspective." *Journal of Economic Literature* 56 (March), 3–59.

Evandro, Paulo, and Tony Takeda. 2013. "Reserve Requirements as a Macroprudential Instrument: Empirical Evidence from Brazil." Unpublished, Central Bank of Brazil (October).

Faia, Ester. 2011. "Credit Risk Transfers and the Macroeconomy." Working Paper No. 1677, Kiel Institute for the World Economy (January).

Faia, Ester, and Eleni Iliopulos. 2011. "Financial Openness, Financial Frictions, and Optimal Monetary Policy." *Journal of Economic Dynamics and Control* 35 (November), 1976–1996.

Falagiarda, Matteo, and Alessandro Saia. 2017. "Credit, Endogenous Collateral, and Risky Assets: A DSGE Model." *International Review of Economics and Finance* 49 (May), 125–148.

Farhi, Emmanuel, Gita Gopinath, and Oleg Itskhoki. 2014. "Fiscal Devaluations." *Review of Economic Studies* 81 (April), 725–760.

Farhi, Emmanuel, and Iván Werning. 2012. "Dealing with the Trilemma: Optimal Capital Controls with Fixed Exchange Rates." Working Paper No. 18280, National Bureau of Economic Research (June).

Farhi, Emmanuel, and Iván Werning. 2016. "A Theory of Macroprudential Policies in the Presence of Nominal Rigidities." *Econometrica* 84 (September), 1645–1704.

Farhi, Emmanuel, and Iván Werning. 2017. "Monetary Policy, Bounded Rationality, and Incomplete Markets." Working Paper No. 23281, National Bureau of Economic Research (September).

Federico, Pablo, Carlos A. Végh, and Guillermo Vuletin. 2014. "Reserve Requirement Policy over the Business Cycle." Working Paper No. 20612, National Bureau of Economic Research (October).

Feenstra, Robert C. 1986. "Functional Equivalence between Liquidity Costs and the Utility of Money." *Journal of Monetary Economics* 17 (March), 271–291.

Fendoglu, Salih. 2017. "Credit Cycles and Capital Flows: Effectiveness of the Macroprudential Policy Framework in Emerging Market Economies." *Journal of Banking and Finance* 79 (June), 110–128.

Fernández, Andrés, and Adam Gulan. 2015. "Interest Rates and Business Cycles in Emerging Economies: The Role of Financial Frictions." *American Economic Journal: Macroeconomics* 7 (July), 153–188.

Fernández, Andrés, Alessandro Rebucci, and Martín Uribe. 2015. "Are Capital Controls Countercyclical?" *Journal of Monetary Economics* 76 (November), 1–14.

Fernandez-Corugedo, Emilio, Michael McMahon, Stephen Millard, and Lukasz Rachel. 2011. "Understanding the Macroeconomic Effects of Working Capital in the United Kingdom." Working Paper No. 422, Bank of England (April).

Fernández-Villaverde, Jesús, Juan Rubio-Ramirez, and Frank Schorfheide. 2016. "Solution and Estimation Methods for DSGE Models." In *Handbook of Macroeconomics*, ed. John B. Taylor and Harald Uhlig. Vol. 2. Amsterdam: Elsevier.

Ferrucci, Gianluigi. 2003. "Empirical Determinants of Emerging Market Economies' Sovereign Bond Spreads." Working Paper No. 205, Bank of England (November).

Fève, Patrick, and Jean-Guillaume Sahuc. 2017. "In Search of the Transmission Mechanism of Fiscal Policy in the Euro Area." *Journal of Applied Econometrics* 32 (April), 704–718.

Filardo, Andrew, and Phurichai Rungcharoenkitkul. 2016. "A Quantitative Case for Leaning against the Wind." Working Paper No. 594, Bank for International Settlements (December).

Financial Stability Board. 2018. *Global Shadow Banking Monitoring Report 2017*. London: FSB Publications.

Finocchiaro, Daria, Magnus Jonsson, Christian Nilsson, and Ingvar Strid. 2016. "Macroeconomic Effects of Reducing Household Debt." *Sveriges Riksbank Economic Review* 2 (June), 57–88.

Fisher, Irving. 1933. "The Debt-Deflation Theory of Great Depressions." *Econometrica* 1 (October), 337–357.

Fleming, J. Marcus. 1962. "Domestic Financial Policies under Fixed and under Floating Exchange Rates." *IMF Staff Papers* 9 (March), 369–380.

Fonseca, Ana R., Francisco González, and Luiz A. Pereira da Silva. 2010. "Cyclical Effects of Bank Capital Buffers with Imperfect Credit Markets: International Evidence." Working Paper No. 216, Central Bank of Brazil (October).

Forbes, Kristin, Marcel Fratzscher, Thomas Kostka, and Roland Straub. 2016. "Bubble Thy Neighbour: Portfolio Effects and Externalities from Capital Controls." *Journal of International Economics* 99 (March), 85–104.

Forbes, Kristin, Marcel Fratzscher, and Roland Straub. 2015. "Capital-Flow Management Measures: What Are They Good For?" *Journal of International Economics* 96 (July), s76–s97.

Forbes, Kristin, Dennis Reinhardt, and Tomasz Wieladek. 2017. "The Spillovers, Interactions, and (Un)Intended Consequences of Monetary and Regulatory Policies." *Journal of Monetary Economics* 85 (January), 1–22.

Forbes, Kristin J., and Francis E. Warnock. 2012. "Capital Flow Waves: Surges, Stops, Flight, and Retrenchment." *Journal of International Economics* 88 (November), 235–251.

Fornaro, Luca. 2015. "Financial Crises and Exchange Rate Policy." *Journal of International Economics* 95 (March), 202–215.

Frache, Serafín, Javier García-Cicco, and Jorge Ponce. 2018. "Countercyclical Prudential Tools in an Estimated DSGE Model." Unpublished, Central Bank of Uruguay (February).

Frankel, Jeffrey A., and Katharine Rockett. 1988. "International Macroeconomic Policy Coordination When Policymakers Do Not Agree on the Model." *American Economic Review* 78 (June), 318–340.

Fratzscher, Marcel, Oliver Gloede, Lukas Menkhoff, Lucio Sarno, and Tobias Stöhr. 2019. "When Is Foreign Exchange Intervention Effective? Evidence from 33 Countries." *American Economic Journal: Macroeconomics* (January), 132–156.

Freixas, Xavier, Luc Laeven and José-Luis Peydró. 2015. *Systemic Risk, Crises, and Macroprudential Regulation*. Cambridge, MA: MIT Press.

Freixas, Xavier, and Jean-Charles Rochet. 2008. *Microeconomics of Banking*, 2nd ed. Cambridge, MA: MIT Press.

Friedrich, Christian, Kristina Hess, and Rose Cunningham. 2019. "Monetary Policy and Financial Stability: Cross-Country Evidence." *Journal of Money, Credit, and Banking* 51 (March), 403–443.

Frost, Jon, and René van Stralen. 2018. "Macroprudential Policy and Income Inequality." *Journal of International Money and Finance* 85 (July), 278–290.

Fuhrer, Jeffrey C. 2017. "Expectations as a Source of Macroeconomic Persistence: Evidence from Survey Expectations in a Dynamic Macro Model." *Journal of Monetary Economics* 86 (April), 22–35.

Fuhrer, Jeffrey C., and Geoffrey R. Moore. 1995. "Inflation Persistence." *Quarterly Journal of Economics* 110 (February), 127–159.

Fujiwara, Ippei, and Yuki Teranishi. 2011. "Real Exchange Rate Dynamics Revisited: A Case with Financial Market Imperfections." *Journal of International Money and Finance* 30 (November), 1562–1589.

Fujiwara, Ippei, and Yuki Teranishi. 2017. "Financial Frictions and Policy Cooperation: A Case with Monopolistic Banking and Staggered Loan Contracts." *Journal of International Economics* 104 (January), 19–43.

Funke, Michael, Robert Kirkby, and Petar Mihaylovski. 2018. "House Prices and Macroprudential Policy in an Estimated DSGE Model of New Zealand." *Journal of Macroeconomics* 56 (June), 152–171.

Furceri, Davide, Stéphanie Guichard, and Elena Rusticelli. 2011. "Episodes of Large Capital Inflows and the Likelihood of Banking and Currency Crises and Sudden Stops." Working Paper No. 865, OECD (May).

Gabaix, Xavier. 2018. "A Behavioral New Keynesian Model." Unpublished, Harvard University (March).

Gabaix, Xavier, and Matteo Maggiori. 2015. "International Liquidity and Exchange Rate Dynamics." *Quarterly Journal of Economics* 130 (August), 1369–1420.

Gabriel, Vasco, Paul Levine, and Bo Yang. 2016. "An Estimated DSGE Open-Economy Model of the Indian Economy with Financial Frictions," Discussion Paper No. 03/16, University of Surrey (February).

Gaggl, Paul, and Maria T. Valderrama. 2019. "Do Banks Take Unusual Risks When Interest Rates Are Expected to Stay Low for a Long Time." *Macroeconomic Dynamics* 23 (September), 2409–2433.

Gagnon, Edith, and Hashmat Khan. 2005. "New Phillips Curve under Alternative Production Technologies for Canada, the United States, and the Euro Area." *European Economic Review* 49 (August), 1571–1602.

Gaiotti, Eugenio, and Alessandro Secchi. 2006. "Is There a Cost Channel of Monetary Policy Transmission? An Investigation into the Pricing Behavior of 2,000 Firms." *Journal of Money, Credit, and Banking* 38 (December), 2013–2037.

Galati, Gabriele, and Richhild Moessner. 2013. "Macroprudential Policy—A Literature Review." *Journal of Economic Surveys* 27 (December), 846–878.

Galati, Gabriele, and Richhild Moessner. 2018. "What Do We Know about the Effects of Macroprudential Policy?" *Economica* 85 (October), 735–770.

Gale, Douglas. 2004. "Notes on Optimal Capital Regulation." In *The Evolving Financial System and Public Policy*, ed. Pierre St-Amant and Carolyn Wilkins. Ottawa: Bank of Canada.

Gale, Douglas, and Martin Hellwig. 1985. "Incentive-Compatible Debt Contracts: The One-Period Problem." *Review of Economic Studies* 52 (October), 647–663.

Galí, Jordi. 2015. *Monetary Policy, Inflation, and the Business Cycle: An Introduction to the New Keynesian Framework*, 2nd ed. Princeton, NJ: Princeton University Press.

Galí, Jordi. 2018. "The State of New Keynesian Economics: A Partial Assessment." Working Paper No. 24845, National Bureau of Economic Research (July).

Galí, Jordi, and Mark Gertler. 1999. "Inflation Dynamics: A Structural Econometric Analysis." *Journal of Monetary Economics* 44 (October), 195–222.

Galí, Jordi, and Mark Gertler. 2007. "Macroeconomic Modeling for Monetary Policy Evaluation." *Journal of Economic Perspectives* 21 (September), 25–45.

Galí, Jordi, Mark Gertler, and J. David López-Salido. 2001. "European Inflation Dynamics." *European Economic Review* 45 (May), 1237–1270.

Galí, Jordi, Mark Gertler, and J. David López-Salido. 2003. "Erratum to 'European Inflation Dynamics.' " *European Economic Review* 47 (August), 759–760.

Galí, Jordi, J. David López-Salido, and Javier Valls. 2004. "Rule-of-Thumb Consumers and the Design of Interest Rate Rules." *Journal of Money, Credit, and Banking* 36 (August), 739–763.

Gallego, Francisco, Leonardo Hernández, and Klaus Schmidt-Hebbel. 2002. "Capital Controls in Chile: Were They Effective?" In *Banking, Financial Integration, and International Crises*, ed. Leonardo Hernández and Klaus Schmidt-Hebbe. Santiago: Central Bank of Chile.

Gambacorta, Leonardo, and Sudipto Karmakar. 2018. "Leverage and Risk Weighted Capital Requirements." *International Journal of Central Banking* 14 (December), 153–191.

Gambacorta, Leonardo, and Federico M. Signoretti. 2014. "Should Monetary Policy Lean against the Wind? An Analysis Based on a DSGE Model with Banking." *Journal of Economic Dynamics and Control* 43 (June), 146–174.

Garcia, Carlos J., Jorge E. Restrepo, and Scott Roger. 2011. "How Much Should Inflation Targeters Care about the Exchange Rate?" *Journal of International Money and Finance* 30 (November), 1590–1617.

García-Cicco, Javier, and Markus Kirchner. 2015. "Macroeconomic and Financial Interactions in Chile: An Estimated DSGE Approach." Unpublished, Central Bank of Chile (January).

García-Cicco, Javier, Markus Kirchner, Julio Carrillo, Diego Rodríguez, Fernando Perez, Rocio Gondo, Carlos Montoro, and Roberto Chang. 2017. "Financial and Real Shocks and the Effectiveness of Monetary and Macroprudential Policies in Latin American Countries." Working Paper No. 668, Bank for International Settlements (October).

Garín, Julio. 2015. "Borrowing Constraints, Collateral Fluctuations, and the Labor Market." *Journal of Economic Dynamics and Control* 57 (August), 112–130.

Gaus, Eric, and Christopher G. Gibbs. 2017. "Expectations and the Empirical Fit of DSGE Models." Unpublished, Haverford College (September).

Geanakoplos, John. 2011. "What's Missing from Macroeconomics: Endogenous Leverage and Default." In *Approaches to Monetary Policy Revisited: Lesson from the Crisis*, ed. Marek Jarocinski, Frank Smets, and Christian Thimann. Frankfurt: ECB Publications.

Gelain, Paolo, and Pelin Ilbas. 2017. "Monetary and Macroprudential Policies in an Estimated Model with Financial Intermediation." *Journal of Economic Dynamics and Control* 78 (May), 164–189.

Gelain, Paolo, Kevin J. Lansing, and Caterina Mendicino. 2013. "House Prices, Credit Growth, and Excess Volatility: Implications for Monetary and Macroprudential Policy." *International Journal of Central Banking* 9 (June), 219–276.

Gelain, Paolo, Kevin J. Lansing, and Gisle J. Natvik. 2018. "Leaning against the Credit Cycle." *Journal of the European Economic Association* 16 (October), 1350–1393.

Gelos, R. Gaston. 2009. "Banking Spreads in Latin America." *Economic Inquiry* 47 (October), 796–814.

Gerali, Andrea, Stefano Neri, Luca Sessa, and Federico M. Signoretti. 2010. "Credit and Banking in a DSGE Model of the Euro Area." *Journal of Money, Credit, and Banking* 42 (September), 107–141.

Gersbach, Hans, Volker Hahn, and Yulin Liu. 2017. "Macroprudential Policy in the New Keynesian World." Unpublished, ETH Zurich (May).

Gersbach, Hans, and Jean-Charles Rochet. 2012. "Aggregate Investment Externalities and Macroprudential Regulation." *Journal of Money, Credit, and Banking* 44 (December), 73–109.

Gersbach, Hans, and Jean-Charles Rochet. 2017. "Capital Regulation and Credit Fluctuations." *Journal of Monetary Economics* 90 (October), 113–124.

Gertler, Mark, and Simon Gilchrist. 2018. "What Happened: Financial Factors in the Great Recession." *Journal of Economic Perspectives* 32 (June), 3–30.

Gertler, Mark, Simon Gilchrist, and Fabio M. Natalucci. 2007. "External Constraints on Monetary Policy and the Financial Accelerator." *Journal of Money, Credit, and Banking* 39 (March), 295–330.

Gertler, Mark, and Peter Karadi. 2011. "A Model of Unconventional Monetary Policy." *Journal of monetary Economics* 58 (January), 17–34.

Gertler, Mark, and Nobuhiro Kiyotaki. 2010. "Financial Intermediation and Credit Policy in Business Cycle Analysis." In *Handbook of Monetary Economics*, ed. Benjamin M. Friedman and Michael Woodford. Vol. 3. Amsterdam: Elsevier.

Gertler, Mark, Nobuhiro Kiyotaki, and Andrea Prestipino. 2016. "Wholesale Banking and Bank Runs in Macroeconomic Modelling of Financial Crises." In *Handbook of Macroeconomics*, ed. John B. Taylor and Michael Woodford. Vol. 2. Amsterdam: Elsevier.

Gertler, Mark, Nobuhiro Kiyotaki, and Albert Queralto. 2012. "Financial Crises, Bank Risk Exposure, and Government Financial Policy." *Journal of Monetary Economics* 59 (December), 17–34.

Gertler, Pavel, and Boris Hofmann. 2016. "Monetary Facts Revisited." Working Paper No. 566, Bank for International Settlements (June).

Ghosh, Atish R., Jun Kim, Mahvash S. Qureshi, and Juan Zalduendo. 2012. "Surges." Working Paper No. 12/22, International Monetary Fund (January).

Ghosh, Atish R., Jonathan D. Ostry, and Mahvash S. Qureshi. 2017. "Managing the Tide: How Do Emerging Markets Respond to Capital Flows?" Working Paper No. 17/69, International Monetary Fund (March).

Ghosh, Atish R., Mahvash S. Qureshi, and Naotaka Sugawara. 2014. "Regulating Capital Flows at Both Ends: Does It Work?." Working Paper No. 4/188, International Monetary Fund (October).

Giese, Julia, Benjamin Nelson, Misa Tanaka, and Nikola Tarashev. 2013. "How Could Macroprudential Policy Affect Financial System Resilience and Credit? Lessons from the Literature." Financial Stability Paper No. 21, Bank of England (May).

Giordani, Paolo E., Michele Ruta, Hans Weisfeld, and Ling Zhu. 2017. "Capital Flow Deflection." *Journal of International Economics* 105 (March), 102–118.

Givens, Gregory E. 2012. "Estimating Central Bank Preferences under Commitment and Discretion." *Journal of Money, Credit, and Banking* 44 (September), 1033–1061.

Glocker, Christian, and Pascal Towbin. 2012. "Reserve Requirements for Price and Financial Stability: When Are They Effective?" *International Journal of Central Banking* 8 (March), 65–114.

Glocker, Christian, and Pascal Towbin. 2015. "Reserve Requirements as a Macroprudential Instrument: Empirical Evidence from Brazil." *Journal of Macroeconomics* 44 (June), 158–176.

Gómez, Esteban, Angélica Lizarazo, Juan C. Mendoza, and Andrés M. Pabón. 2017. "Evaluating the Impact of Macroprudential Policies on Credit Growth in Colombia." Working Paper No. 634, Bank for International Settlements (May).

Gong, Liutang, Chan Wang, and Heng-fu Zou. 2016. "Optimal Monetary Policy with International Trade in Intermediate Inputs." *Journal of International Money and Finance* 65 (July), 140–165.

Gonzalez, Rodrigo B., Joaquim Lima, and Leonardo Marinho. 2015. "Business and Financial Cycles: An Estimation of Cycles' Length Focusing on Macroprudential Policy." Working Paper No. 385, Central Bank of Brazil (April).

Goodfriend, Marvin, and Bennett T. McCallum. 2007. "Banking and Interest Rates in Monetary Policy Analysis: A Quantitative Exploration." *Journal of Monetary Economics* 54 (July), 1480–1507.

Goodhart, Charles, Anil K Kashyap, Dimitrios P. Tsomocos, and Alexandros P. Vardoulakis. 2013. "An Integrated Framework for Analyzing Multiple Financial Regulations." *International Journal of Central Banking* 11 (January), 109–143.

Goodhart, Charles, Nikolas Romanidis, Dimitrios P. Tsomocos, and Martin Shubik. 2016. "Macro-Modelling, Default and Money." Discussion Paper No. 755, London School of Economics (June).

Gordy, Michael B. 2003. "A Risk-Factor Model Foundation for Ratings-Based Bank Capital Rules." *Journal of Financial Intermediation* 12 (July), 199–232.

Gordy, Michael B., and Bradley Howells. 2006. "Procyclicality in Basel II: Can We Treat the Disease without Killing the Patient?" *Journal of Financial Intermediation* 15 (July), 395–417.

Gourio, François, Anil K. Kashyap, and Jae Sim. 2018. "The Tradeoffs in Leaning against the Wind." *IMF Economic Review* 66 (March), 70–115.

Gray, Simon. 2011. "Central Bank Balances and Reserve Requirements." Working Paper No. 11/36, International Monetary Fund (February).

Greenwald, Daniel L. 2016. "The Mortgage Credit Channel of Macroeconomic Transmission." Unpublished, Sloan School of Management (November).

Greenwood, Jeremy, Zvi Hercowitz, and Gregory W. Huffman. 1988. "Investment, Capacity Utilization, and the Real Business Cycle." *American Economic Review* 78 (June), 402–417.

Gründler, Klaus, and Philipp Scheuermeyer. 2018. "Growth Effects of Inequality and Redistribution: What Are the Transmission Channels?" *Journal of Macroeconomics* 55, (March), 293–313.

Guerron-Quintana, Pablo, Atsushi Inoue, and Lutz Kilian. 2017. "Impulse Response Matching Estimators for DSGE Models." *Journal of Econometrics* 196 (January), 144–155.

Güntner, Jochen H. 2011. "Competition among Banks and the Pass-through of Monetary Policy." *Economic Modelling* 28 (July), 1891–1901.

Gupta, Ranjan, and Xiaojin Sun. 2016. "Housing Market Spillovers in South Africa: Evidence from an Estimated Small Open Economy DSGE Model." Working Paper No. 2016-41, University of Pretoria (May).

Ha, Jongrim, Marc Stocker, and Hakan Yilmazkuday. 2019. "Inflation and Exchange Rate Pass-through." In *Inflation in Emerging and Developing Economies*, ed. Jongrim Ha, M. Ayhan Kose, and Franziska Ohnsorge. Washington, DC: World Bank Publications.

Haavio, Markus, Antti Ripatti, and Tuomas Takalo. 2015. "Macroeconomic Effects of Bank Recapitalizations." Unpublished, Bank of Finland (December).

Habib, Maurizio M., and Fabrizio Venditti. 2019. "The Global Capital Flows Cycle: Structural Drivers and Transmission Channels." Working Paper No. 2280, European Central Bank (May).

Hansen, James. 2018. "Optimal Monetary Policy with Capital and a Financial Accelerator." *Journal of Economic Dynamics and Control* 92 (July), 84–102.

Havranek, Tomas, Marek Rusnak, and Anna Sokolova. 2017. "Habit Formation in Consumption: A Meta-Analysis." *European Economic Review* 95 (June), 142–167.

He, Zhigu, and Arvind Krishnamurthy. 2012. "A Model of Capital and Crises." *Review of Economic Studies* 79 (April), 735–777.

Heathcote, Jonathan, and Fabrizio Perri. 2016. "On the Desirability of Capital Controls." *IMF Economic Review* 64 (March), 75–102.

Heer, Burkhard, and Stefan F. Schubert. 2012. "Unemployment and Debt Dynamics in a Highly Indebted Small Open Economy." *Journal of International Money and Finance* 31 (October), 1392–1413.

Heid, Frank. 2007. "The Cyclical Effects of the Basel II Capital Requirements." *Journal of Banking and Finance* 31 (December), 3885–3900.

Hellmann, Thomas F., Kevin C. Murdock, and Joseph E. Stiglitz. 2000. "Liberalization, Moral Hazard in Banking, and Prudential Regulation: Are Capital Requirements Enough?" *American Economic Review* 90 (March), 147–165.

Henzel, Steffen, Oliver Hülsewig, Eric Mayer, and Timo Wollmershäuser. 2009. "The Price Puzzle Revisited: Can the Cost Channel Explain a Rise in Inflation after a Monetary Policy Shock?" *Journal of Macroeconomics* 31 (June), 268–289.

Herbst, Edward P., and Frank Schorfheide. 2016. *Bayesian Estimation of DSGE Models*. Princeton, NJ: Princeton University Press.

Hirakata, Naohisa, Nao Sudoy, and Kozo Ueda. 2013. "Capital Injection, Monetary Policy, and Financial Accelerators." *International Journal of Central Banking* 9 (June), 101–145.

Hirata, Hideaki, M. Ayhan Kose, Christopher Otrok, and Marco Terrones. 2013. "Global House Price Fluctuations: Synchronization and Determinants." Working Paper No. 13/38, International Monetary Fund (February).

Hnatkovska, Viktoria V., and Friederike Koehler-Geib. 2018. "Characterizing Business Cycles in Small Economies." Policy Research Working Paper No. 8527, World Bank (July).

Hoffmann, Andreas, and Axel Löffler. 2014. "Low Interest Rate Policy and the Use of Reserve Requirements in Emerging Markets." *Quarterly Review of Economics and Finance* 54 (August), 307–314.

Hoggarth, Glenn, Lavan Mahadeva, and Jeremy Martin. 2010. "Understanding International Bank Capital Flows during the Recent Financial Crisis." Financial Stability Paper No. 8, Bank of England (September).

Holmström, Bengt, and Jean Tirole. 1997. "Financial Intermediation, Loanable Funds, and the Real Sector." *Quarterly Journal of Economics* 112 (September), 663–691.

Horvath, Jaroslav. 2018. "Business Cycles, Informal Economy, and Interest Rates in Emerging Countries." *Journal of Macroeconomics* 55 (March), 96–116.

Hoyle, David F., Chris Limnios, and Carl E. Walsh. 2018. "Monetary Policy Operating Procedures, Lending Frictions, and Employment." Working Paper No. 118, Peruvian Economic Association (February).

Hristov, Nikola, and Oliver Hülsewig. 2017. "Unexpected Loan Losses and Bank Capital in an Estimated DSGE Model of the Euro Area." *Journal of Macroeconomics* 54 (December), 161–186.

Huang, Kevin X., and Zheng Liu. 2007. "Business Cycles with Staggered Prices and International Trade in Intermediate Inputs." *Journal of Monetary Economics* 54 (May), 1271–1289.

Hubbard, R. Glenn, Kenneth N. Kuttner, and Darius N. Palia. 2002. "Are There Bank Effects in Borrowers' Costs of Funds?: Evidence from a Matched Sample of Borrowers and Banks." *Journal of Business* 75 (October), 559–581.

Hülsewig, Oliver, Eric Mayer, and Timo Wollmershauser. 2009. "Bank Behavior, Incomplete Interest Rate Pass-through, and the Cost Channel of Monetary Policy Transmission." *Economic Modelling* 26 (November), 1310–1327.

Hurtado, Samuel. 2014. "DSGE Models and the Lucas Critique." *Economic Modelling* 44 (Suppl.), s12–s19.

Hwang, Yu-Ning. 2012. "Financial Friction in an Emerging Economy." *Journal of International Money and Finance* 31 (March), 212–227.

Iacoviello, Matteo. 2005. "House Prices, Borrowing Constraints, and Monetary Policy in the Business Cycle." *American Economic Review* 95 (June), 739–764.

Iacoviello, Matteo. 2015. "Financial Business Cycles." *Review of Economic Dynamics* 18 (January), 140–163.

Iacoviello, Matteo, and Stefano Neri. 2010. "Housing Market Spillovers: Evidence from an Estimated DSGE Model." *American Economic Journal: Macroeconomics* 2 (April), 125–164.

Iacoviello, Matteo, Ricardo Nunes, and Andrea Prestipino. 2016. "Optimal Macroprudential Policy: Frictions, Redistribution, and Politics." Unpublished, Federal Reserve Board (February).

Ilzetzki, Ethan, Carmen Reinhart, and Kenneth Rogoff. 2019. "Exchange Arrangements Entering the 21st Century: Which Anchor Will Hold?" *Quarterly Journal of Economics* 134 (May), 599–646.

Imbs, Jean, and Isabelle Méjean. 2017. "Trade Elasticities." *Review of International Economics* (May), 383–402.

IMF-FSB-BIS. 2016. "Elements of Effective Macroprudential Policies: Lessons from International Experience." Unpublished, Bank for International Settlements (August).

Inter-American Development Bank. 2005. *Unlocking Credit*. Baltimore: Johns Hopkins University Press.

International Monetary Fund. 2009. "Lessons for Monetary Policy from Asset Price Fluctuations." In *World Economic Outlook, October 2009*, chap. 3. Washington, DC: International Monetary Fund.

International Monetary Fund. 2010. *Global Financial Stability Report: Meeting New Challenges to Stability and Building a Safer System*. Washington, DC: IMF Publications.

International Monetary Fund. 2012. *The Liberalization and Management of Capital Flows: An Institutional View*. Washington, DC: IMF Publications.

International Monetary Fund. 2015. "Monetary Policy and Financial Stability." Unpublished Staff Report (August).

International Monetary Fund. 2016. "Capital Flows: Review of Experience with the Institutional View." Unpublished Staff Report (November).

International Monetary Fund. 2018. *Global Financial Stability Report: A Bumpy Road Ahead*. Washington, DC: IMF Publications.

Ireland, Peter N. 2001. "Sticky-Price Models of the Business Cycle: Specification and Stability." *Journal of Monetary Economics* 47 (February), 3–18.

Ireland, Peter N. 2003. "Endogenous Money or Sticky Prices?" *Journal of Monetary Economics* 50 (November), 1623–1648.

Izquierdo, Alejandro, Rudy Loo-Kung, and Liliana Rojas-Suarez. 2013. "Macroprudential Regulations in Central America." Working Paper No. 318, Center for Global Development (March).

Jacob, Punnoose, and Anella Munro. 2018. "A Prudential Stable Funding Requirement and Monetary Policy in a Small Open Economy." *Journal of Banking and Finance* 94 (September), 89–106.

Jeanne, Olivier. 2014. "Macroprudential Policies in a Global Perspective." Working Paper No. 19967, National Bureau of Economic Research (March).

Jeanne, Olivier, and Anton Korinek. 2019. "Managing Credit Booms and Busts: A Pigouvian Taxation Approach." *Journal of Monetary Economics* 107 (November), 2–17.

Jermann, Urban, and Vincenzo Quadrini. 2012. "Macroeconomic Effects of Financial Shocks." *American Economic Review* 102 (February), 238–271.

Jiménez, Gabriel, Vicente Salas, and Jesús Saurina. 2006. "Determinants of Collateral." *Journal of Financial Economics* 81 (August), 255–281.

Jin, He-hui, and Kenneth L. Judd. 2002. "Perturbation Methods for General Dynamic Stochastic Models." Unpublished, Hoover Institution (April).

Jones, Barry E., and Livio Stracca. 2006. "Are Money and Consumption Additively Separable in the Euro Area? A Non-Parametric Approach." Working Paper No. 704, European Central Bank (December).

Jones, Barry E., and Livio Stracca. 2008. "Does Money Matter in the IS Curve? The Case of the UK." Working Paper No. 904, European Central Bank (June).

Jordá, Óscar, Moritz Schularick, Alan M. Taylor, and Felix Ward. 2018. "Global Financial Cycles and Risk Premiums." Working Paper No. 24677, National Bureau of Economic Research (June).

Kamber, Gunes, Konstantinos Theodoridis, and Christoph Thoenissen. 2017. "News-driven Business Cycles in Small Open Economies." *Journal of International Economics* 105 (March), 77–89.

Kanik, Birol, and Wei Xiao. 2014. "News, Housing Boom-Bust Cycles, and Monetary Policy." *International Journal of Central Banking* 10 (December), 249–298.

Kannan, Prakash, Pau Rabanal, and Alasdair M. Scott. 2012. "Monetary and Macroprudential Policy Rules in a Model with House Price Booms." *The B.E. Journal of Macroeconomics* 12 (issue 1), Article 16.

Kaplan, Greg, Benjamin Moll, and Giovanni I. Violante. 2018. "Monetary Policy According to HANK." *American Economic Review* 108 (March), 697–743.

Kara, Gazi I. 2016*a*. "Systemic Risk, International Regulation, and the Limits of Coordination." *Journal of International Economics* 99 (March), 192–222.

Kara, Gazi I. 2016*b*. "Bank Capital Regulations around the World: What Explains the Differences?" Discussion Paper No. 2016-057, Federal Reserve Board (July).

Kashyap, Anil, Dimitrios Tsomocos, and Alexandros Vardoulakis. 2014. "How Does Macroprudential Regulation Change Bank Credit Supply?" Working Paper No. 20165, National Bureau of Economic Research (May).

Kashyap, Anil K., Raghuram G. Rajan, and Jeremy C. Stein. 2008. "Rethinking Capital Regulation."

Kashyap, Anil K., and Jeremy C. Stein. 2004. "Cyclical Implications of the Basel II Capital Standards." Federal Reserve Bank of Chicago, Economics Perspectives 1 (March), 18–31.

Kashyap, Anil K., and Jeremy C. Stein. 2012. "The Optimal Conduct of Monetary Policy with Interest on Reserves." *American Economic Journal: Macroeconomics* 4 (January), 266–282.

Kato, Ryo. 2006. "Liquidity, Infinite Horizons, and Macroeconomic Fluctuations." *European Economic Review* 50 (July), 1105–1130.

Kaufmann, Sylvia, and Johann Scharler. 2009. "Financial Systems and the Cost Channel Transmission of Monetary Policy Shocks." *Economic Modelling* 26 (January), 40–46.

Kawamura, Enrique, and Lucas Ronconi. 2015. "Firms' Investment and Savings in Latin America: Stylized Facts from the Enterprise Survey." Working Paper No. IDB-WP-638, Inter-American Development Bank (December).

Keen, Benjamin D. 2009. "Output, Inflation, and Interest Rates in an Estimated Optimizing Model of Monetary Policy." *Review of Economic Dynamics* 12 (April), 327–343.

Keen, Benjamin D., and Yongsheng Wang. 2007. "What Is a Realistic Value for Price Adjustment Costs in New Keynesian Models?" *Applied Economics Letters* 14 (September), 789–793.

Khan, Aubhik, and Julia K. Thomas. 2013. "Credit Shocks and Aggregate Fluctuations in an Economy with Production Heterogeneity." *Journal of Political Economy* 121 (December), 1055–1107.

Kiley, Michael T. 2000. "Endogenous Price Stickiness and Business Cycle Persistence." *Journal of Money, Credit, and Banking* 32 (March), 28–53.

Kiley, Michael T. 2013. "Output Gaps." *Journal of Macroeconomics* 37 (September), 1–18.

Kiley, Michael T., and Jae Sim. 2014. "Bank Capital and the Macroeconomy: Policy Considerations." *Journal of Economic Dynamics and Control* 43 (June), 175–198.

Kiley, Michael T., and Jae Sim. 2017. "Optimal Monetary and Macroprudential Policies: Gains and Pitfalls in a Model of Financial Intermediation." *Journal of Macroeconomics* 54 (December), 232–259.

Kim, Jinill, and Sunghyun H. Kim. 2003. "Spurious Welfare Reversals in International Business Cycle Models." *Journal of International Economics* 60 (August), 471–500.

Kim, Jinill, and Sunghyun H. Kim. 2007. "Two Pitfalls of Linearization Methods." *Journal of Money, Credit, and Banking* 39 (June), 995–1001.

Kim, Jinill, and Sunghyun H. Kim. 2018. "Conditional versus Unconditional Utility as Welfare Criterion: Two Examples." *Computational Economics* 51 (March), 719–730.

Kim, Jinill, Sunghyun Kim, Ernst Schaumburg, and Christopher A. Sims. 2008. "Calculating and Using Second Order Accurate Solutions of Discrete Time Dynamic Equilibrium Models." *Journal of Economic Dynamics and Control* 32 (November), 3397–3414.

Kimbrough, Kent P. 1992. "Speculative Attacks: The Roles of Intertemporal Substitution and the Interest Elasticity of the Demand for Money." *Journal of Macroeconomics* 14 (September), 689–710.

Kirman, Alan P. 1992. "Whom or What Does the Representative Individual Represent?" *Journal of Economic Perspectives* 6 (Spring), 117–136.

Kitano, Shigeto, and Kenya Takaku. 2018. "Capital Controls, Monetary Policy, and Balance Sheets in a Small Open Economy." *Economic Inquiry* 56 (April), 859–874.

Kiyotaki, Nobuhiro. 1998. "Credit and Business Cycles." *Japanese Economic Review* 49 (March), 18–35.

Kiyotaki, Nobuhiro, and John Moore. 1997. "Credit Cycles." *Journal of Political Economy* 105 (April), 211–248.

Klenow, Peter J., and Benjamin A. Malin. 2011. "Microeconomic Evidence on Price-Setting." In *Handbook of Monetary Economics*, ed. Benjamin Friedman and Michael Woodford. Vol. 3A. New York: Elsevier.

Kletzer, Kenneth, and Mark M. Spiegel. 2004. "Sterilization Costs and Exchange Rate Targeting." *Journal of International Money and Finance* 23 (October), 897–915.

Klomp, Jeroen, and Jakob de Haan. 2014. "Bank Regulation, the Quality of Institutions, and Banking Risk in Emerging and Developing Countries: An Empirical Analysis." *Emerging Markets Finance and Trade* 50 (November), 19–40.

Kocherlakota, Narayana. 2000. "Creating Business Cycles through Credit Constraints." *Quarterly Review* (Federal Reserve Bank of Minneapolis) 24 (March), 2–10.

Kockerols, Thore, and Christoffer Kok. 2019. "Leaning against the Wind: Macroprudential Policy and the Financial Cycle." Working Paper No. 2223, European Central Bank (January).

Kolasa, Marcin, and Giovanni Lombardo. 2014. "Financial Frictions and Optimal Monetary Policy in an Open Economy." *International Journal of Central Banking* 10 (March), 43–94.

Kollintzas, Tryphon, and Venghelis Vassilatos. 2000. "A Small Open Economy with Transaction Costs in Foreign Capital." *European Economic Review* 44 (August), 1515–1541.

Kopecky, Kenneth J., and David VanHoose. 2004*a*. "A Model of the Monetary Sector with and without Binding Capital Requirements." *Journal of Banking and Finance* 28 (March), 633–646.

Kopecky, Kenneth J., and David VanHoose. 2004*b*. "Bank Capital Requirements and the Monetary Transmission Mechanism." *Journal of Macroeconomics* 26 (September), 443–464.

Kopecky, Kenneth J., and David VanHoose. 2006. "Capital Regulation, Heterogeneous Monitoring Costs, and Aggregate Loan Quality." *Journal of Banking and Finance* 30 (August), 2235–2255.

Kopecky, Kenneth J., and David VanHoose. 2012. "Imperfect Competition in Bank Retail Markets, Deposit and Loan Rate Dynamics, and Incomplete Pass-through." *Journal of Money, Credit, and Banking* 44 (September), 1185–1205.

Kollmann, Robert. 2001. "The Exchange Rate in a Dynamic-Optimizing Business Cycle Model with Nominal Rigidities: A Quantitative Investigation." *Journal of International Economics* 55 (December), 243–262.

Kollmann, Robert. 2002. "Monetary Policy Rules in the Open Economy: Effects on Welfare and Business Cycles." *Journal of Monetary Economics* 49 (July) 989–1015.

Kollmann, Robert. 2004. "Welfare Effects of a Monetary Union: The Role of Trade Openness." *Journal of the European Economic Association* 2 (April), 289–301.

Korinek, Anton. 2011. "Systemic Risk-Taking: Amplification Effects, Externalities, and Regulatory Responses." Working Paper No. 1345, European Central Bank (June).

Korinek, Anton. 2014. "International Spillovers and Guidelines for Policy." Unpublished, Johns Hopkins University (October).

Korinek, Anton. 2017. "Currency Wars or Efficient Spillovers? A General Theory of International Policy Cooperation." Working Paper No. 17/25, International Monetary Fund (February).

Korinek, Anton. 2018. "Regulating Capital Flows to Emerging Markets: An Externality View." *Journal of International Economics* 111 (March), 61–80.

Korinek, Anton, and Enrique G. Mendoza. 2014. "From Sudden Stops to Fisherian Deflation: Quantitative Theory and Policy." *Annual Review of Economics* 6 (August), 299–332.

Korinek, Anton, and Damiano Sandri. 2016. "Capital Controls or Macroprudential Regulation?" *Journal of International Economics* 99 (March), s27–s42.

Kozicki, Sharon, and Peter A. Tinsley. 2002. "Dynamic Specifications in Optimising Trend-Deviation Macromodels." *Journal of Economic Dynamics and Control* 26 (August), 1585–1611.

Krishnamurthy, Arvind. 2003. "Collateral Constraints and the Amplification Mechanism." *Journal of Economic Theory* 111 (August), 277–292.

Krueger, Steffen, Daniel Roesch, and Harald Scheule. 2018. "The Impact of Loan Loss Provisioning on Bank Capital Requirements." *Journal of Financial Stability* 36 (June), 114–129.

Krugman, Paul R. 2000. "How Complicated Does the Model Have to Be?" *Oxford Review of Economic Policy* 16 (December), 33–42.

Krugman, Paul R. 2008. "The International Finance Multiplier." Unpublished, Princeton University (October).

Krugman, Paul R., Maurice Obstfeld, and Marc Melitz. 2018. *International Finance: Theory and Policy, Global Edition*, 11th ed. London: Pearson.

Krznar, Ivo, and Troy D. Matheson. 2017. "Financial and Business Cycles in Brazil." Working Paper No. 17/12, International Monetary Fund (January).

Kwapil, Claudia, and Johann Scharler. 2010. "Interest Rate Pass-through, Monetary Policy Rules, and Macroeconomic Stability." *Journal of International Money and Finance* 29 (March), 236–251.

Kwon, Hyosung, and Jianjun Miao. 2019. "Woodford's Approach to Robust Policy Analysis in a Linear-Quadratic Framework." *Macroeconomic Dynamics* 23 (July), 1895–1920.

Lagoa, Sérgio. 2014. "Inflation Dynamics in Open Economies: Empirical Evidence for G7 Countries on the Role of Import Prices and the Cost Channel." *Research in Economics* 68 (December), 354–371.

Lambert, Frederic, Julio Ramos-Tallada, and Cyril Rebilard. 2011. "Capital Controls and Spillover Effects: Evidence from Latin American Countries." Working Paper No. 357, Banque de France (December).

Lambertini, Luisa, Caterina Mendicino, and Maria T. Punzi. 2013. "Leaning against Boom-Bust Cycles in Credit and Housing Prices." *Journal of Economic Dynamics and Control* 37 (August), 1500–1522.

Lartey, Emmanuel K. 2008. "Capital Inflows, Dutch Disease Effects, and Monetary Policy in a Small Open Economy." *Review of International Economics* 16 (October), 971–989.

Lartey, Emmanuel K. 2012. "Financial Openness, Nontradable Inflation, and Optimal Monetary Policy." *Economics Letters* 17 (December), 782–785.

Laséen, Stefan, Andrea Pescatori, and Jarkko Turunen. 2017. "Systemic Risk: A New Trade-off for Monetary Policy?" *Journal of Financial Stability* 32 (October), 70–85.

Laureys, Lien, Roland Meeks, and Boromeus Wanengkirtyo. 2017. "Should Banks Be Central to Central Banking? Optimal Monetary Policy in the Euro Area." Unpublished, Bank of England (February).

Lawless, Martina, and Karl T. Whelan. 2011. "Understanding the Dynamics of Labor Shares and Inflation." *Journal of Macroeconomics* 33 (June), 121–136.

Lazopoulos, Ioannis, and Vasco Gabriel. 2019. "Policy Mandates and Institutional Architecture." *Journal of Banking and Finance* 100 (March), 122–134.

Le, Vo P., David Meenagh, Patrick Minford, Michael Wickens, and Yongdeng Xu. 2016. "Testing Macro Models by Indirect Inference: A Survery for Users." *Open Economies Review* 27 (March), 1–38.

Leblebicioglu, Asli. 2009. "Financial Integration, Credit Market Imperfections, and Consumption Smoothing." *Journal of Economic Dynamics and Control* 33 (February), 377–393.

Leduc, Sylvain, and Jean-Marc Natal. 2018. "Monetary and Macroprudential Policies in a Leveraged Economy." *Economic Journal* 128 (March), 797–826.

Lee, Junhee, and Wooheon Rhee. 2013. "Financial Factors in the Business Cycle of a Small Open Economy: The Case of Korea." *Open Economies Review* 24 (November), 881–900.

Leith, Campbell, and Ding Liu. 2016. "The Inflation Bias under Calvo and Rotemberg Pricing." *Journal of Economic Dynamics and Control* 73 (December), 283–297.

Leroy, Aurélien, and Adrian Pop. 2019. "Macro-Financial Linkages: The Role of the Institutional Framework." *Journal of International Money and Finance* 92 (April), 75–97.

Levin, Andrew T., and J. David López-Salido. 2004. "Optimal Monetary Policy with Endogenous Capital Accumulation." Unpublished, Federal Reserve Board (June).

Levin, Andrew T., Alexei Onatski, John Williams, and Noah M. Williams. 2006. "Monetary Policy under Uncertainty in Micro-Founded Macroeconometric Models." In *NBER Macroeconomics Annual 2005*, ed. Mark Gertler and Kenneth S. Rogoff. Vol. 20. Cambridge, MA: MIT Press.

Levin, Gabriel, Calixto López, and Fabrizio Lopez-Gallo. 2016. "The Impact of Expected Losses Provisioning on Credit Growth: The Case of Mexico." Unpublished, Banco de México (May).

Levine, Paul, and Diana Lima. 2015. "Policy Mandates for Macro-Prudential and Monetary Policies in a New Keynesian Framework." Working Paper No. 1784, European Central Bank (April).

Levine, Paul, Peter McAdam, and Joseph Pearlman. 2012. "Probability Models and Robust Policy Rules." *European Economic Review* 56 (February), 246–262.

Li, Jie, and Ramkishen S. Rajan. 2015. "Do Capital Controls Make Gross Equity Flows to Emerging Markets Less Volatile?" *Journal of International Money and Finance* 59 (December), 220–244.

Li, Victor E. 2000. "Household Credit and the Monetary Transmission Mechanism." *Journal of Money, Credit, and Banking* 32 (August), 335–356.

Li, Victor E. 2018. "Search, Financial Market Frictions, and Monetary Transmission." *Journal of Money, Credit, and Banking* 50 (December), 1935–1968.

Liberti, Jose M., and Jason Sturgess. 2013. "Uncovering Collateral Constraints." In *Understanding Banks in Emerging Markets*, ed. Thorsten Beck, T., Ralph De Haas, and Steven Ongena. VoxEU Book.

Lindé, Jesper. 2018. "DSGE Models: Still Useful in Policy Analysis?" *Oxford Review of Economic Policy* 34 (January), 269–286.

Lindé, Jesper, Marianne Nessén, and Ulf Söderström. 2009. "Monetary Policy in an Estimated Open-Economy Model with Imperfect Pass-through." *International Journal of Finance and Economics* 14 (October), 301–333.

Lindé, Jesper, Frank Smets, and Raf Wouters. 2016. "Challenges for Central Banks' Macro Models." Working Paper No. 323, Sveriges Riksbank (May).

Liu, Guangling, and Nkhahle E. Seeiso. 2012. "Basel II Procyclicality: The Case of South Africa." *Economic Modelling* 29 (May), 848–857.

Liu, Philip. 2006. "A Small New Keynesian Model of the New Zealand Economy." Discussion Paper No. 2006/03, Reserve Bank of New Zealand (May).

Liu, Zheng, and Mark M. Spiegel. 2015. "Optimal Monetary Policy and Capital Account Restrictions in a Small Open Economy." *IMF Economic Review* 63 (September), 298–324.

Liu, Zheng, Pengfei Wang, and Tao Zha. 2013. "Land-Price Dynamics and Macroeconomic Fluctuations." *Econometrica* 81 (May), 1147–1184.

Loayza, Norman, and Romain Rancière. 2006. "Financial Development, Financial Fragility, and Growth." *Journal of Money, Credit, and Banking* 38 (June), 1051–1076.

Lodge, David, and Ana-Simona Manu. 2019. "EME Financial Conditions: Which Global Shocks Matter?" Working Paper No. 2282, European Central Bank (May).

Lombardo, Giovanni, and Federico Ravenna. 2014. "Openness and Optimal Monetary Policy." *Journal of International Economics* 93 (May), 153–172.

Lombardo, Giovanni, and David Vestin. 2008. "Welfare Implications of Calvo vs. Rotemberg-Pricing Assumptions." *Economics Letters* 100 (August), 275–279.

López, Martha, Fernando Tenjo, and Hector Zárate. 2014. "Credit Cycles, Credit Risk, and Countercyclical Loan Provisions." *Ensayos sobre Política Económica* 32 (June), 9–17.

Lorenzoni, Guido. 2008. "Inefficient Credit Booms." *Review of Economic Studies* 75 (July), 809–833.

Lozej, Matija, Luca Onorante, and Ansgar Rannenberg. 2016. "Countercyclical Capital Regulation in a Small Open Economy DSGE Model." Unpublished, Central Bank of Ireland (February).

Lucas, Robert E. 1976. "Econometric Policy Evaluation: A Critique." In *The Phillips Curve and Labor Markets*. Carnegie-Rochester Conference Series on Public Policy 1, ed. Karl Brunner and Allan H. Meltzer. Amsterdam: North Holland.

Lucas, Robert E. 1987. *Models of Business Cycles*. Oxford: Basil Blackwell.

Lucas, Robert E. 1990. "Supply-Side Economics: An Analytical Review." *Oxford Economic Papers* 42 (April), 293–316.

Lusardi, Annamaria. 2019. "Financial Literacy and the Need for Financial Education: Evidence and Implications." *Swiss Journal of Economics and Statistics* 155 (March), 1–8.

Ma, Guonan, Yan Xiandong, and Liu Xi. 2013. "China's Evolving Reserve Requirements." *Journal of Chinese Economic and Business Studies* 11 (June), 117–137.

Magud, Nicolas E., Carmen M. Reinhart, and Kenneth S. Rogoff. 2011. "Capital Controls: Myth and Reality—A Portfolio Balance Approach." Working Paper No. 16805, National Bureau of Economic Research (February).

Maliar, Serguei, Lilia Maliar, and Kenneth Judd. 2011. "Solving the Multi-Country Real Business Cycle Model Using Ergodic Set Methods." *Journal of Economic Dynamics and Control* 35 (February), 207–228.

Mandelman, Federico S. 2010. "Business Cycles and Monetary Regimes in Emerging Economies: A Role for a Monopolistic Banking Sector." *Journal of International Economics* 81 (May), 122–138.

Mankart, Jochen, Alexander Michaelides, and Spyros Pagratis. 2018. "Bank Capital Buffers in a Dynamic Model." Unpublished, Imperial College London (August)

Mankiw, N. Gregory, and Ricardo Reis. 2002. "Sticky Information versus Sticky Prices: A Proposal to Replace the New Keynesian Phillips Curve." *Quarterly Journal of Economics* 117 (November), 1295–1328.

Manove, Michael, A. Jorge Padilla, and Marco Pagano. 2001. "Collateral versus Project Screening: A Model of Lazy Banks." *RAND Journal of Economics* 32 (December), 726–744.

Marins, Jaqueline T., and Myrian B. Eiras das Neves. 2013. "Credit Default and Business Cycles: An investigation of This relationship in the Brazilian Corporate Credit Market." Working Paper No. 304, Central Bank of Brazil (March).

Markovic, Bojan. 2006. "Bank Capital Channels in the Monetary Transmission Mechanism." Working Paper No. 313, Bank of England (November).

Martinez-Miera, David, and Rafael Repullo. 2019. "Monetary Policy, Macroprudential Policy, and Financial Stability." Working Paper No. 1901, CEMFI (February).

Martinez-Miera, David, and Javier Suarez. 2014. "Banks' Endogenous Systemic Risk Taking." Unpublished, Universidad Carlos III (September).

Mattesini, Fabrizio, and Lorenza Rossi. 2009. "Optimal Monetary Policy in Economies with Dual Labor Markets." *Journal of Economic Dynamics and Control* 33 (July), 1469–1489.

McCallum, Bennett T., and Edward Nelson. 2000. "Monetary Policy for an Open Economy: An Alternative Framework with Optimizing Agents and Sticky Prices." *Oxford Review of Economic Policy* 16 (December), 74–91.

Medina, Juan Pablo, and Jorge Roldós. 2018. "Monetary and Macroprudential Policies to Manage Capital Flows." *International Journal of Central Banking* 14 (January), 201–257.

Medina, Juan Pablo, and Claudio Soto. 2005. "Oil Shocks and Monetary Policy in an Estimated DSGE Model for a Small Open Economy." Working Paper No. 353, Central Bank of Chile.

Medina, Juan Pablo, and Claudio Soto. 2007. "The Chilean Business Cycles through the Lens of a Stochastic General Equilibrium Model." Working Paper No. 457, Central Bank of Chile (December).

Medina, Leandro, and Friedrich Schneider. 2018. "Shadow Economies around the World: What Did We Learn over the Last 20 Years?" Working Paper No. 18/17, International Monetary Fund (January).

Meeks, Roland, Benjamin Nelson, and Piergiorgio Alessandri. 2017. "Shadow Banks and Macroeconomic Instability." *Journal of Money, Credit, and Banking* 49 (October), 1483–1516.

Meenagh, David, Patrick Minford, Michael Wickens, and Yongdeng Xu. 2019. "Testing DSGE Models by Indirect Inference: A Survey of Recent Findings." *Open Economies Review* 30 (July), 593–620.

Meh, Césaire, and Kevin Moran. 2010. "The Role of Bank Capital in the Propagation of Shocks." *Journal of Economic Dynamics and Control* 34 (March), 555–576.

Mehran, Hamid, and Anjan Thakor. 2011. "Bank Capital and Value in the Cross Section." *Review of Financial Studies* 24 (April), 1019–1067.

Meier, André, and Gernot J. Müller. 2006. "Fleshing Out the Monetary Transmission Mechanism: Output Composition and the Role of Financial Frictions." *Journal of Money, Credit, and Banking* 38 (December), 2099–2133.

Mendicino, Caterina. 2012. "On the Amplification Role of Collateral Constraints." *Economics Letters* 117 (November), 429–435.

Mendicino, Caterina. 2016. "Literature Review on Integration of Regulatory Capital and Liquidity Instruments." Working Paper No. 30, Basel Committee on Banking Supervision 30 (March).

Mendicino, Caterina, Kalin Nikolov, Javier Suarez, and Dominik Supera. 2018. "Optimal Dynamic Capital Requirements." *Journal of Money, Credit, and Banking* 50 (September), 1271–1297.

Mendicino, Caterina, Kalin Nikolov, Javier Suarez, and Dominik Supera. 2019. "Bank Capital in the Short and in the Long Run." Working Paper No. 2286, European Central Bank (May).

Mendicino, Caterina, and Maria T. Punzi. 2014. "House Prices, Capital Inflows and Macroprudential Policy." *Journal of Banking and Finance* 49 (December), 337–355.

Mendoza, Enrique G. 2010. "Sudden Stops, Financial Crises, and Leverage." *American Economic Review* 100 (December), 1941–1966.

Mendoza, Enrique G. 2016. "Macroprudential Policy: Promise and Challenges." Working Paper No. 22868, National Bureau of Economic Research (November).

Menkhoff, Lukas, Doris Neuberger, and Chodechai Suwanaporn. 2006. "Collateral-based Lending in Emerging Markets: Evidence from Thailand." *Journal of Banking and Finance* 30 (January), 1–21.

Merola, Rossana. 2015. "The Role of Financial Frictions during the Crisis: An Estimated DSGE Model." *Economic Modelling* 48 (August), 70–82.

Milani, Fabio. 2012. "The Modeling of Expectations in Empirical DSGE Models: A Survey." In *DSGE Models in Macroeconomics: Estimation, Evaluation, and New Developments*, ed. Nathan Balke, Fabio Canova, Fabio Milani, and Mark A. Wynne. Bingley, UK: Emerald.

Milcheva, Stanimira, and Bing Zhu. 2016. "Bank Integration and Co-Movements across Housing Markets." *Journal of Banking and Finance* 72 (November), 148–171.

Mimir, Yasin, and Enes Sunel. 2019. "External Shocks, Banks, and Optimal Monetary Policy in an Open Economy." *International Journal of Central Banking* 15 (June), 235–299.

Mimir, Yasin, Enes Sunel, and Temel Taskin. 2013. "Required Reserves as a Credit Policy Tool." *B.E. Journal of Macroeconomics* 13 (January), 823–880.

Minaya, Elias, José Lupú, and Miguel Cabello. 2017. "Macroprudential Policies in Peru: The Effects of Dynamic Provisioning and Conditional Reserve Requirements." Working Paper No. 675, Bank for International Settlements (November).

Modigliani, Franco, and Merton H. Miller. 1958. "The Cost of Capital, Corporation Finance, and the Theory of Investment." *American Economic Review* 48 (June), 261–297.

Molnar, Margit, Yusuke Tateno, and Amornrut Supornsinchai. 2013. "Capital Flows in Asia-Pacific: Controls, Bonanzas, and Sudden Stops." Working Paper No. 320, OECD Development Centre (September).

Monacelli, Tommaso. 2007. "Optimal Monetary Policy with Collateralized Household Debt and Borrowing Constraints." In *Asset Prices and Monetary Policy*, ed. John Campbell. Chicago: University of Chicago Press.

Morón, Eduardo, and Diego Winkelried. 2005. "Monetary Policy Rules for Financially Vulnerable Economies." *Journal of Development Economics* 76 (February), 23–51.

Montoro, Carlos. 2011. "Assessing the Role of Reserve Requirements under Financial Frictions." Unpublished, Bank for International Settlements (March).

Montoro, Carlos, and Ramon Moreno. 2011. "The Use of Reserve Requirements as a Policy Instrument in Latin America." *Bank for International Settlements Quarterly Review* (March), 53–65.

Mora, Nada. 2014. "Reason for Reserve? Reserve Requirements and Credit." *Journal of Money, Credit, and Banking* 46 (March), 469–501.

Morandé, Felipe G. 1992. "Dynamics of Real Asset Prices, the Real Exchange Rate, and Foreign Capital Inflows: Chile, 1976–1989." *Journal of Development Economics* 39 (July), 111–139.

Moura, Marcelo L., and Alexandre de Carvalho. 2010. "What Can Taylor Rules Say about Monetary Policy in Latin America?" *Journal of Macroeconomics* 32 (March), 392–404.

Muellbauer, John. 2010. "Household Decisions, Credit Markets, and the Macroeconomy: Implications for the Design of Central Bank Models." Working Paper No. 306, Bank for International Settlements (March).

Muellbauer, John. 2016. "Macroeconomics and Consumption." Working Paper No. 811, Oxford University (November).

Mumtaz, Haroon, and Francesco Zanetti. 2016. "The Effect of Labor and Financial Frictions on Aggregate Fluctuations." *Macroeconomic Dynamics* 20 (January), 313–341.

Munakata, Ko, Koji Nakamura, and Yuki Teranishi. 2013. "Optimal Macroprudential Policy." Working Paper No. 51/2013, Centre for Applied Macroeconomic Analysis (August).

Mundell, Robert A. 1963. "Capital Mobility and Stabilization Policy under Fixed and Flexible Exchange Rates." *Canadian Journal of Economics and Political Science* 29 (November), 475–485.

Murcia, Andrés, and Emanuel Kohlscheen. 2016. "Moving in Tandem: Bank Provisioning in Emerging Market Economies." Working Paper No. 548, Bank for International Settlements (March).

Nakamura, Emi, and Jón Steinsson. 2013. "Price Rigidity: Microeconomic Evidence and Macroeconomic Implications." *Annual Review of Economics* 5 (March), 133–163.

Neuenkirch, Matthias, and Matthias Nöckel. 2018. "The Risk-Taking Channel of Monetary Policy Transmission in the Euro Area." *Journal of Banking and Finance* 93 (August), 71–91.

Neuenkirch, Matthias, and Peter Tillmann. 2014. "Inflation Targeting, Credibility, and Non-linear Taylor Rules." *Journal of International Money and Finance* 41 (March), 30–45.

Neumeyer, Pablo A., and Fabrizio Perri. 2005. "Business Cycles in Emerging Economies: The Role of Interest Rates." *Journal of Monetary Economics* 52 (March), 345–380.

Nguyen, Ha, and Rong Qian. 2012. "The Cross-Country Magnitude and Determinants of Collateral Borrowing." Policy Research Working Paper No. 6001, World Bank (March).

Nguyen, Thien. 2015. "Bank Capital Requirements: A Quantitative Analysis." Fisher College of Business Working Paper 2015-03-14, Ohio State University (March).

Niepelt, Dirk. 2019. *Macroeconomic Analysis*. Cambridge, MA: The MIT Press.

Nolan, Charles, and Christoph Thoenissen. 2009. "Financial Shocks and the US Business Cycle." *Journal of Monetary Economics* 56 (May), 596–604.

Norden, Lars, and Stefan van Kampen. 2013. "Corporate Leverage and the Collateral Channel." *Journal of Banking and Finance* 37 (December), 5062–5072.

Notarpietro, Alessandro, and Stefano Siviero. 2015. "Optimal Monetary Policy Rules and House Prices: The Role of Financial Frictions." *Journal of Money, Credit, and Banking* 47 (March), 383–410.

Obstfeld, Maurice. 1985. "The Capital Inflows Problem Revisited: A Stylized Model of Southern Cone Disinflation." *Review of Economic Studies* 52 (October), 605–625.

Obstfeld, Maurice. 2015. "Trilemmas and Tradeoffs: Living with Financial Globalisation." In *Spillovers to Emerging Markets and Policy Responses*, ed. Claudio Raddatz, Diego Saravia, and Jaime Ventura. Santiago: Central Bank of Chile.

Obstfeld, Maurice, and Kenneth S. Rogoff. 1996. *Foundations of International Macroeconomics*. Cambridge, MA: MIT Press.

Ogaki, Masao, Jonathan Ostry, and Carmen M. Reinhart. 1996. "Saving Behavior in Low- and Middle-Income Developing Countries: A Comparison." *IMF Staff Papers* 43 (March), 38–71.

Orland, Andreas, and Michael W. Roos. 2013. "The New Keynesian Phillips Curve with Myopic Agents." *Journal of Economic Dynamics and Control* 37 (November), 2270–2286.

Ostry, Jonathan, Atish Ghosh, Marcos Chamon, and Mahvash Qureshi. 2012. "Tools for Managing Financial-Stability Risks from Capital Inflows." *Journal of International Economics* 88 (November), 407–421.

Ouyang, Alice Y., and Shen Guo. 2019. "Macro-prudential Policies, the Global Financial Cycle, and the Real Exchange Rate." *Journal of International Money and Finance* 96 (September), 147–167.

Özbilgin, H. Murat. 2017. "Welfare Implications When Closing Small Open Economy Models." *Journal of International Money and Finance* 70 (February), 471–493.

Özmen, M. Utku, and Orhun Sevinç. 2016. "Price Rigidity in Turkey: Evidence from Micro Data." Working Paper No. 11/25, Central Bank of Turkey (November).

Packer, Frank, Jimmy Shek, and Haibin Zhu. 2014. "Countercyclical Loan Loss Provisions in Asia." *SEACEN Financial Stability Journal* 3 (March), 25–58.

Paez-Farrell, Juan. 2015. "Taylor Rules, Central Bank Preferences, and Inflation Targeting." Working Paper No. 2015-23, University of Sheffield (November).

Palek, Jakob, and Benjamin Schwanebeck. 2019. "Optimal Monetary and Macroprudential Policy in a Currency Union." *Journal of International Money and Finance* 93 (May), 167–186.

Palma, Andreza A., and Marcelo S. Portugal. 2014. "Preferences of the Central Bank of Brazil under the Inflation Targeting Regime: Estimation Using a DSGE Model for a Small Open Economy." *Journal of Policy Modeling* 36 (September), 824–839.

Panetta, Fabio, and Paolo Angelini, ed. 2009. *Financial Sector Pro-Cyclicality: Lessons from the Crisis*, Occasional Paper No. 44, Bank of Italy (April).

Pasricha, Gurnain K., Matteo Falagiarda, Martin Bijsterbosch, and Joshua Aizenman. 2018. "Domestic and Multilateral Effects of Capital Controls in Emerging Markets." *Journal of International Economics* 115 (November), 48–58.

Peltonen, Tuomas A., Ricardo M. Sousa, and Isabel Vansteenkiste. 2012. "Wealth Effects in Emerging Market Economies." *International Review of Economics and Finance* 24 (October), 155–166.

Pesaran, M. Hashem, Til Schuermann, Bjorn-Jakob Treutler, and Scott M. Weiner. 2006. "Macroeconomic Dynamics and Credit Risk: A Global Perspective." *Journal of Money, Credit, and Banking* 38 (August), 1211–1261.

Pesaran, M. Hashem, and TengTeng Xu. 2016. "Business Cycle Effects of Credit Shocks in a DSGE Model with Firm Defaults." Unpublished, Cambridge University (April).

Pfajfar, Damjan, and Emiliano Santoro. 2014. "Credit Market Distortions, Asset Prices, and Monetary Policy." *Macroeconomic Dynamics* 18 (April), 631–650.

Pintus, Patrick A., and Jacek Suda. 2019. "Learning Financial Shocks and the Great Recession." *Review of Economic Dynamics* 31 (January), 123–146.

Pirovano, Mara. 2013. "Household and Firm Leverage, Capital Flows, and Monetary Policy in a Small Open Economy." Working Paper No. 2013-14, University of Antwerp (August).

Ponticelli, Jacopo, and Leonardo S. Alencar. 2016. "Court Enforcement, Bank Loans, and Firm Investment: Evidence from a Bankruptcy Reform in Brazil." *Quarterly Journal of Economics* 131 (August), 1365–1413.

Pool, Sebastiaan, Leo de Haan, and Jan P. Jacobs. 2015. "Loan Loss Provisioning, Bank Credit, and the Real Economy." *Journal of Macroeconomics* 45 (September), 124–136.

Pozsar, Zoltan, Tobias Adrian, Adam Ashcraft, and Hayley Boesky. 2013. "Shadow Banking." Federal Reserve Bank of New York, *Economic Policy Review* 19 (December), 1–16.

Prada, Juan D. 2008. "Financial Intermediation and Monetary Policy in a Small Open Economy." Working Paper No. 531, Banco de la República de Colombia (September).

Prasad, Nalini. 2018. "Sterilized Interventions and Capital Controls." *Journal of International Money and Finance* 88 (November), 101–121.

Primus, Keyra. 2017. "Excess Reserves, Monetary Policy, and Financial Volatility,' *Journal of Banking and Finance* 74 (January), 153–168.

Quadrini, Vincenzo. 2011. "Financial Frictions in Macroeconomic Fluctuations." Federal Reserve Bank of Richmond, *Economic Quarterly* 97 (September), 209–254.

Quint, Dominic, and Pau Rabanal. 2014. "Monetary and Macroprudential Policy in an Estimated DSGE Model of the Euro Area." *International Journal of Central Banking* 10 (June), 169–236.

Quirk, James P., and R. Saposnik. 1968. *Introduction to General Equilibrium Theory and Welfare Economics*. New York: McGraw-Hill.

Rabanal, Pau. 2007. "Does Inflation Increase after a Monetary Policy Tightening? Answers Based on an Estimated DSGE Model." *Journal of Economic Dynamics and Control* 31 (March), 906–937.

Ranasinghe, Ashantha, and Diego Restuccia. 2018. "Financial Frictions and the Rule of Law." *Journal of Development Economics* 134 (September), 248–271.

Rannenberg, Ansgar. 2016. "Bank Leverage Cycles and the External Finance Premium." *Journal of Money, Credit, and Banking* 48 (December), 1569–1612.

Ravenna, Federico, and Carl E. Walsh. 2006. "Optimal Monetary Policy with the Cost Channel." *Journal of Monetary Economics* 53 (March), 199–216.

Reinhardt, Dennis, and Steven J. Riddiough. 2014. "The Two Faces of Cross-Border Banking Flows: An Investigation into the Links between Global Risk, Arms-Length Funding, and Internal Capital Markets." Working Paper No. 498, Bank of England (April).

Reinhart, Carmen M., and Vincent R. Reinhart. 1999. "On the Use of Reserve Requirements in Dealing with Capital Flow Problems." *International Journal of Finance and Economics* 4 (January), 27–54.

Reis, Ricardo. 2018. "Is Something Really Wrong with Macroeconomics?" *Oxford Review of Economic Policy* 34 (January), 132–155.

Repullo, Rafael, and Javier Suarez. 2013. "The Procyclical Effects of Bank Capital Regulation." *Review of Financial Studies* 26 (June), 452–490.

Rhee, Hyuk-jae, and Nurlan Turdaliev. 2012. "Optimal Monetary Policy in a Small Open Economy with Inflation and Output Persistence." *Economic Modelling* 29 (November), 2533–2542.

Richter, Alexander W., and Nathaniel A. Throckmorton. 2016. "Is Rotemberg Pricing Justified by Macro Data?" *Economics Letters* 149 (December), 44–88.

Riggi, Marianna. 2010. "Nominal and Real Wage Rigidities in New Keynesian Models: A Critical Survey." *Journal of Economic Surveys* 24 (July), 539–572.

Roberts, John M. 1995. "New Keynesian Economics and the Phillips Curve." *Journal of Money, Credit, and Banking* 27 (November), 975–984.

Robitaille, Patrice. 2011. "Liquidity and Reserve Requirements in Brazil." International Finance Discussion Paper No. 1021, Federal Reserve Board (June).

Rochet, Jean-Charles. 2004. "Macroeconomic Shocks and Banking Supervision." *Journal of Financial Stability* 1 (September), 93–110.

Rochet, Jean-Charles. 2008. "Procyclicality of Financial Systems: Is There a Need to Modify Current Accounting and Regulatory Rules?" *Financial Stability Review* 12 (October), 101–114.

Roger, Scott, Jorge Restrepo, and Carlos Garcia. 2009. "Hybrid Inflation Targeting Regimes." Working Paper No. 9/234, International Monetary Fund (October).

Rotemberg, Julio J. 1982. "Monopolistic Price Adjustment and Aggregate Output." *Review of Economic Studies* 49 (October), 517–531.

Rotemberg, Julio J., and Mark Woodford. 1997. "An Optimization-based Econometric Framework for the Evaluation of Monetary Policy." In *NBER Macroeconomics Annual 1996*, ed. Ben Bernanke and Julio J. Rotemberg. Cambridge, MA: MIT Press.

Rubio, Margarita. 2019. "Monetary and Macroprudential Policies under Fixed and Variable Interest Rates." *Macroeconomic Dynamics* 23 (April), 1024–1061.

Rubio, Margarita, and José A. Carrasco-Gallego. 2014. "Macroprudential and Monetary Policies: Implications for Financial Stability and Welfare." *Journal of Banking and Finance* 49 (December), 326–336.

Rubio, Margarita, and José A. Carrasco-Gallego. 2016. "The New Financial Regulation in Basel III and Monetary Policy: A Macroprudential Approach." *Journal of Financial Stability* 26 (October), 294–305.

Rychalovska, Yuliya. 2016. "The Implications of Financial Frictions and Imperfect Knowledge in the Estimated DSGE Model of the US Economy." *Journal of Economic Dynamics and Control* 73 (December), 259–282.

Samuelson, Paul A. 1941. "The Stability of Equilibrium: Comparative Statics and Dynamics." *Econometrica* 9 (March), 97–120.

Sarno, Lucio, Ilias Tsiakas, and Barbara Ulloa. 2016. "What Drives International Portfolio Flows?" *Journal of International Money and Finance* 60 (February), 53–72.

Sbordone, Argia M. 2002. "Prices and Unit Labor Costs: A New Test of Price Stickiness." *Journal of Monetary Economics* 49 (March), 265–292.

Schabert, Andreas. 2014. "Optimal Monetary Policy, Asset Purchases, and Credit Market Frictions." Working Paper No. 1738, European Central Bank (October).

Schargrodsky, Ernesto, and Federico Sturzenegger. 2000. "Banking Regulation and Competition with Product Differentiation." *Journal of Development Economics* 63 (October), 85–111.

Scharler, Johann. 2008. "Do Bank-based Financial Systems Reduce Macroeconomic Volatility by Smoothing Interest Rates?" *Journal of Macroeconomics* 30 (September), 1207–1221.

Schmitt-Grohé, Stephanie, and Martín Uribe. 2004. "Solving Dynamic General Equilibrium Models Using a Second-Order Approximation to the Policy Function." *Journal of Economic Dynamics and Control* 28 (January), 755–775.

Schmitt-Grohé, Stephanie, and Martín Uribe. 2007. "Optimal Simple and Implementable Monetary and Fiscal Rules." *Journal of Monetary Economics* 54 (September), 1702–1725.

Schoenmaker, Dirk. 2011. "The Financial Trilemma." *Economics Letters* 111 (April), 57–59.

Schularick, Moritz, and Alan M. Taylor. 2012. "Credit Booms Gone Bust: Monetary Policy, Leverage Cycles, and Financial Crises, 1870–2008." *American Economic Review* 102 (June), 1029–1061.

Sheedy, Kevin D. 2010. "Intrinsic Inflation Persistence." *Journal of Monetary Economics* 57 (November), 1049–1061.

Shi, Kang, and Juanyi Xu. 2010. "Intermediate Goods Trade and Exchange Rate Pass-through." *Journal of Macroeconomics* 32 (June), 571–583.

Silos, Pedro. 2007. "Housing, Portfolio Choice, and the Macroeconomy." *Journal of Economic Dynamics and Control* 31 (August), 2774–2801.

Silvo, Aino. 2019. "The Interaction of Monetary and Macroprudential Policies." *Journal of Money, Credit, and Banking* 51 (July), 859–894.

Smets, Frank, and Raf Wouters. 2002. "Openness, Imperfect Exchange Rate Pass-through, and Monetary Policy." *Journal of Monetary Economics* 49 (July), 947–981.

Smets, Frank, and Raf Wouters. 2003. "An Estimated Stochastic General Equilibrium Model of the Euro Area." *Journal of the European Economic Association* 1 (September), 1123–1175.

Soderlind, Paul. 1999. "Solution and Estimation of RE Macromodels with Optimal Policy." *European Economic Review* 43 (April), 813–823.

Södersten, Bo, and Geoffrey Reed. 1999. *International Economics*, 3rd ed. London: Palgrave.

Söderström, Ulf, Paul Söderlind, and Anders Vredin. 2005. "New-Keynesian Models and Monetary Policy: A Re-examination of the Stylized Facts." *Scandinavian Journal of Economics* 107 (September), 521–546.

Steijvers, Tensie, and Wim Voordeckers. 2009. "Collateral and Credit Rationing." *Journal of Economic Surveys* 23 (December), 924–946.

Stein, Jeremy. 2012. "Monetary Policy as Financial-Stability Regulation." *Quarterly Journal of Economics* 127 (March), 57–95.

Stein, Jeremy. 2013. "Overheating in Credit Markets: Origins, Measurement, and Policy Responses." Speech at a Research Symposium Sponsored by the Federal Reserve Bank of St. Louis (February 7).

Steinsson, Jon. 2003. "Optimal Monetary Policy in an Economy with Inflation Persistence." *Journal of Monetary Economics* 50 (October), 1425–1456.

Stiglitz, Joseph E. 2017. "Monopolistic Competition, the Dixit-Stiglitz Model, and Economic Analysis." *Research in Economics* 71 (December), 798–802.

Stiglitz, Joseph E., and Andrew Weiss. 1981. "Credit Rationing in Markets with Imperfect Information." *American Economic Review* 53 (June), 393–410.

Stiglitz, Joseph E., and Andrew Weiss. 1992. "Asymmetric Information in Credit Markets and Its Implications for Macroeconomics." *Oxford Economic Papers* 44 (October), 694–724.

Stockman, Alan C. 1989. "The Cash-in-Advance Constraint in International Economics." In *Finance Constraints and the Theory of Money*, edited by S. C. Tsiang and Meier Kohn. Orlando, FL: Academic Press.

Straub, Roland, and Ivan Tchakarov. 2004. "Non-Fundamental Exchange Rate Volatility and Welfare." Working Paper No. 328, European Central Bank (April).

Suh, Hyunduk. 2017. "Optimal Simple Rule for Monetary Policy and Macroprudential Policy in a Financial Accelerator Model." Working Paper No. 2017-9, Institute of Business and Economic Research (August).

Suh, Hyunduk, and Todd B. Walker. 2016. "Taking Financial Frictions to the Data." *Journal of Economic Dynamics and Control* 64 (March), 39–65.

Sveen, Tommy, and Lutz Weinke. 2013. "The Taylor Principle in a Medium-scale Macroeconomic Model." *Journal of Economic Dynamics and Control* 37 (December), 3034–3043.

Svensson, Lars E. O. 2010. "Inflation Targeting." In *Handbook of Monetary Economics*, ed. Benjamin M. Friedman and Michael Woodford. Vol. 3. Amsterdam: North Holland.

Svensson, Lars E. O. 2017. "Cost-Benefit Analysis of Leaning against the Wind." *Journal of Monetary Economics* 90 (October), 113–124.

Tabak, Benjamin M., Marcela T. Laiz, and Daniel O. Cajueiro. 2010. "Financial Stability and Monetary Policy: The Case of Brazil." Working Paper No. 217, Central Bank of Brazil (October).

Takamura, Tamon. 2013. "A General Equilibrium Model with Banks and Default on Loans." Working Paper No. 2013-3, Bank of Canada (January).

Tan, Tatum B. 2012. "Determinants of Credit Growth and Interest Margins in the Philippines and Asia." Working Paper No. 12/123, International Monetary Fund (May).

Tanaka, Misa. 2002. "How Do Bank Capital and Capital Adequacy Regulation Affect the Monetary Transmission Mechanism?" CESIFO Working Paper No. 799 (October).

Tayler, William, and Roy Zilberman. 2016. "Macroprudential Regulation, Credit Spreads, and the Role of Monetary Policy." *Journal of Financial Stability* 26 (October), 144–158.

Taylor, Alan M. 2015. "Credit, Financial Stability, and the Macroeconomy." *Annual Review of Economics* 7 (August), 309–39.

Taylor, John B. 2013. "International Monetary Policy Coordination: Past, Present, and Future." Working Paper No. 437, Bank for International Settlements (December).

Taylor, John B., and John C. Williams. 2010. "Simple and Robust Rules for Monetary Policy." In *Handbook of Monetary Economics*, ed. Benjamin M. Friedman and Michael Woodford, Vol. 3. Amsterdam: North Holland.

Taylor, Lance. 1983. *Structuralist Macroeconomics*. New York: Basic Books.

Teranishi, Yuki. 2015. "Smoothed Interest Rate Setting by Central Banks and Staggered Loan Contracts." *Economic Journal* 125 (February), 162–183.

Tesfatsion, Leigh. 2006. "Agent-Based Computational Economics: A Constructive Approach to Economic Theory." In *Handbook of Computational Economics* Amsterdam: North Holland.

Thimme, Julian. 2017. "Intertemporal Substitution in Consumption: A Literature Review." *Journal of Economic Surveys* 31 (February), 226–257.

Tillmann, Peter. 2008. "Do Interest Rates Drive Inflation Dynamics? An Analysis of the Cost Channel of Monetary Transmission." *Journal of Economic Dynamics and Control* 32 (September), 2723–2744.

Tomura, Hajime. 2010. "International Capital Flows and Expectation-Driven Boom-Bust Cycles in the Housing Market." *Journal of Economic Dynamics and Control* 34 (October), 1993–2009.

Tornell, Aaron, and Frank Westermann. 2004. "Credit Market Imperfections in Middle-Income Countries." In *Financial Market Development in Latin America*, ed. Vittorio Corbo, José A. Gonzalez, and Aaron Tornell. Stanford, CA: Stanford University Press.

Tovar, Camilo E. 2005. "The Mechanics of Devaluations and the Output Response in a DSGE Model: How Relevant Is the Balance Sheet Effect?" Working Paper No. 192, Bank for International Settlements (November).

Tovar, Camilo E., Mercedes Garcia-Escribano, and Mercedes Vera Martin. 2012. "Credit Growth and the Effectiveness of Reserve Requirements and Other Macroprudential Instruments in Latin America." Working Paper No. 12/143, International Monetary Fund (June).

Townsend, Robert M. 1979. "Optimal Contracts and Competitive Markets with Costly State Verification." *Journal of Economic Theory* 21 (October), 265–293.

Turnovsky, Stephen J. 1997. "Equilibrium Growth in a Small Open Economy Facing an Imperfect World Capital Market." *Review of Economic Dynamics* 1 (March), 1–22.

Turnovsky, Stephen J. 2011. "On the Role of Small Models in Macrodynamics." *Journal of Economic Dynamics and Control* 35 (September), 1605–1613.

Valencia, Oscar C., and Alberto O. Bolaños. 2018. "Bank Capital Buffers around the World: Cyclical Patterns and the Effect of Market Power." *Journal of Financial Stability* 38 (October), 119–131.

Valencia, Oscar C., Daniel Osorio, and Pablo Garay. 2017. "The Role of Capital Requirements and Credit Composition in the Transmission of Macroeconomic and Financial Shocks." *Ensayos sobre Política Económica* 35 (December), 203–221.

Van den Heuvel, Skander J. 2007. "The Bank Capital Channel of Monetary Policy." Unpublished, Wharton School, University of Pennsylvania (July).

Van den Heuvel, Skander J. 2008. "The Welfare Cost of Bank Capital Requirements." *Journal of Monetary Economics* 55 (March), 298–320.

VanHoose, David. 2007. "Theories of Bank Behavior under Capital Regulation." *Journal of Banking and Finance* 31 (December), 3680–3697.

Van Wijnbergen, Sweder. 1982. "Stagflationary Effects of Monetary Stabilization Policies." *Journal of Development Economics* 10 (April), 133–169.

Vargas, Hernando, Andrés González, and Diego Rodríguez. 2013. "Foreign Exchange Intervention in Colombia." Working Paper No. 757, Central Bank of Colombia (March).

Vargas, Hernando, Carlos Varela, Yanneth R. Betancourt, and Norberto Rodríguez. 2010. "Effects of Reserve Requirements in an Inflation Targeting Regime: The Case of Colombia." Working Paper No. 587, Central Bank of Colombia (February).

Verona, Fabio, Manuel M. Martins, and Inês Drumond. 2017. "Financial Shocks, Financial Stability, and Optimal Taylor Rules." *Journal of Macroeconomics* 54 (December), 187–207.

Villa, Stefania, and Jing Yang. 2012. "Financial Intermediaries in an Estimated DSGE Model for the United Kingdom." Working Paper No. 431, Bank of England (March).

Villamil, Anne P. 2008. "Modigliani-Miller Theorem." In *The New Palgrave Dictionary of Economics*, ed. Steven N. Durlauf and Lawrence E. Blume. London: Palgrave Macmillan.

Villamizar-Villegas, Mauricio, and David Perez-Reyna. 2017. "A Theoretical Approach to Sterilized Foreign Exchange Intervention." *Journal of Economic Surveys* 31 (February), 343–365.

Vitola, Kristine, and Viktors Ajevskis. 2011. "Housing and Banking in a Small Open Economy." Working Paper No. 3/2011, Bank of Latvia (February).

Vlieghe, Gertjan W. 2010. "Imperfect Credit Markets: Implications for Monetary Policy." Working Paper No. 385, Bank of England (March).

Vujanovic, Petar. 2011. "Understanding the Recent Surge in the Accumulation of International Reserves." Working Paper No. 866, OECD Economics Department (May).

Wadhwani, Sushil. 2008. "Should Monetary Policy Respond to Asset Price Bubbles? Revisiting the Debate." *National Institute Economic Review* 206 (March), 25–34.

Walentin, Karl. 2014. "Housing Collateral and the Monetary Transmission Mechanism." *Scandinavian Journal of Economics* 116 (July), 635–668.

Walsh, Carl. 2005. "Labor Market Search, Sticky Prices, and Interest Rate Policies." *Review of Economic Dynamics* 8 (October), 829–849.

Walsh, Carl. 2010. *Monetary Theory and Policy*, 3rd ed. Cambridge, MA: The MIT Press.

Walther, Ansgar. 2016. "Jointly Optimal Regulation of Bank Capital and Liquidity." *Journal of Money, Credit, and Banking* 48 (March), 415–448.

Wasmer, Etienne, and Philippe Weil. 2004. "The Macroeconomics of Labor and Credit Market Imperfections." *American Economic Review* 94 (September), 944–963.

Wen, Yi. 2009. "An Analytical Approach to Buffer-Stock Saving under Borrowing Constraints." Working Paper No. 2009-026, Federal Reserve Bank of St. Louis (July).

Wezel, Torsten, Jorge A. Chan-Lau, and Francesco Columba. 2012. "Dynamic Loan Loss Provisioning: Simulations on Effectiveness and Guide to Implementation." Working Paper No. 12/110, International Monetary Fund (May).

Wickens, Michael. 2012. *Macroeconomic Theory*, 2nd ed. Princeton, NJ: Princeton University Press.

Wickens, Michael. 2017. "A DSGE Model of Banks and Financial Intermediation with Default Risk." *Research in Economics* 71 (September), 636–642.

Wieland, Volker, Elena Afanasyeva, Meguy Kuete, and Jinhyuk Yoo. 2016. "New Methods for Macro-Financial Model Comparison and Policy Analysis." In *Handbook of Macroeconomics*, ed. John B. Taylor and Harald Uhlig. Vol. 2. Amsterdam: North Holland.

Williamson, Stephen D. 1986. "Costly Monitoring, Financial Intermediation, and Equilibrium Credit Rationing." *Journal of Monetary Economics* 18 (September), 159–179.

Woodford, Michael. 2003. *Interest and Prices: Foundations of a Theory of Monetary Policy*. Princeton, NJ: Princeton University Press.

Woodford, Michael. 2010. "Optimal Monetary Stabilization Policy." In *Handbook of Monetary Economics*, ed. B. Friedman and Michael Woodford. Vol. 3. Amsterdam: North Holland.

Woodford, Michael. 2013. "Macroeconomic Analysis without the Rational Expectations Hypothesis." *Annual Review of Economics* 5 (March), 303–346.

Woodford, Michael. 2016. "Quantitative Easing and Financial Stability." Working Paper No. 22285, National Bureau of Economic Research (May).

World Bank. 2018. *Global Financial Development Report: Bankers without Borders*. Washington, DC: World Bank.

World Bank. 2019. *Global Economic Prospects*. Washington, DC: World Bank Publications.

World Trade Organization. 2019. *Global Value Chain Development Report: Technological Innovation, Supply Chain Trade, and Workers in a Globalized World*. Geneva: WTO Publications.

Yépez, Carlos A. 2017. "Financial Intermediation, Consumption Dynamics, and Business Cycles." *Economic Modelling* 60 (January), 231–243.

You, Yu, Yoonbai Kim, and Xiaomei Ren. 2014. "Do Capital Controls Enhance Monetary Independence?" *Review of Development Economics* 18 (August), 475–489.

Yun, Tack. 1996. "Nominal Price Rigidity, Money Supply Endogeneity, and Business Cycles." *Journal of Monetary Economics* 37 (April), 345–370.

Zhang, Longmei. 2009. "Bank Capital Regulation, the Lending Channel and Business Cycles." Discussion Paper No. 33, Deutsche Bundesbank (November).

Zhang, Yahong. 2019. "Household Debt, Financial Intermediation, and Monetary Policy." *Journal of Macroeconomics* 59 (March), 230–257.

Zhu, Haibin. 2008. "Capital Regulation and Banks' Financial Decisions." *International Journal of Central Banking* 4 (March), 165–211.

Zicchino, Lea. 2006. "A Model of Bank Capital, Lending, and the Macroeconomy: Basel I versus Basel II." *Manchester School* 74 (August), 50–77.

Zietz, Joachim. 2008. "A Clarifying Note on Converting to Log-Deviations from the Steady State." *Economics Bulletin* 3 (March), 1–15.

Zilberman, Roy. 2012. "Supply Shocks and the Cyclical Behaviour of Bank Lending Rates under the Basel Accords." Working Paper No. 161, Centre for Growth and Business Cycle Research (January).

Name Index

Note: Footnote information is indicated with n and note number following the page number.

Subject Index

Note: Footnote information is indicated with n and note number following the page number.